International Conflict Resolution Processes

International Conflict Resolution Processes

Carrie Menkel-Meadow
Distinguished and Chancellor's Professor of Law
(and Political Science)
University of California Irvine

Andrea Kupfer Schneider
Professor of Law & Director
Kukin Program for Conflict Resolution
Benjamin N. Cardozo School of Law

CAROLINA ACADEMIC PRESS
Durham, North Carolina

Library of Congress Cataloging-in-Publication Data

Names: Menkel-Meadow, Carrie, author. | Schneider, Andrea Kupfer, author.
Title: International conflict resolution processes / Carrie Menkel-Meadow, Andrea Kupfer Schneider.
Description: Durham, North Carolina : Carolina Academic Press, 2025. | Includes bibliographical references and index.
Identifiers: LCCN 2024052531 | ISBN 9781531012205 (paperback) | ISBN 9781531012212 (ebook)
Subjects: LCSH: Pacific settlement of international disputes. | Dispute resolution (Law) | Conflict management.
Classification: LCC KZ6010 .M46 2025 | DDC 341.5--dc23/eng/20241106
LC record available at https://lccn.loc.gov/2024052531

Carolina Academic Press
700 Kent Street
Durham, North Carolina 27701
(919) 489-7486
www.cap-press.com

Printed in the United States of America

Contents

Preface

The issue of whether international law is really law has long dominated both scholarly and practical conversations about the efficacy of law and international legal institutions. This book was written to explore how international conflicts and disputes are actually handled, managed, and sometimes resolved with combinations of law and legal principles, but also political, diplomatic, and economic factors, used with a number of different processes that involve law, as well as human, social, political, and other sources of actions. The materials here take a socio-legal approach to international, cross-border conflicts and disputes so that law students, lawyers, diplomats, and public officials can learn how to utilize a wide variety of potential avenues for dispute resolution. We call this concept of multiple possible choices process pluralism. We examine different bodies of international law, but also look at international relations, political theory, political economy, and geopolitical approaches to understanding human conflicts. We look at conflicts over materiel and resources, as well as identity, ethnicity ,and economic investment and the newer forms of aspirations for human rights recognition. In short, as we study conflict and war, we search for more effective ways to achieve and sustain peace for all of humankind.

In our legal field it is common to think of legal issues as "disputes" to be handled in courts (adjudication) or as "cases" to be managed through negotiation or mediation, resulting in decisions, treaties, or awards (arbitration). In the broader field of conflict resolution, disputes are situated within contexts, often spanning many years, many borders, different cultures, different kinds of parties (private and public), and even different legal systems (civil, common law, mixed systems). Moreover, they operate at many different layers of legal action—international diplomacy, international public legal institutions, private international institutions and processes, hybrid processes (e.g., state-private investors, individual vs. state human rights), and regional as well as international and local or "municipal" (domestic) processes and institutions. Without a real "World Court" at the top of a vertical hierarchy of legal institutions, international disputes are actually conducted through many different kinds of processes—negotiation, mediation, arbitration, adjudication, hybrids of these, and newer forms of reckoning and restitution, e.g., transitional justice and truth and reconciliation commissions, among others.

Modern dispute resolution can occur in person or online or electronically, both facilitating or hindering human understanding and recognition. New ideas for both human cooperation, but sadly also human competition and harm (see our chapter on "wicked problems" in international relations), are explored here as we seek both systematic and one-off solutions to seemingly intractable problems (e.g., the environment, the Middle East, resource allocations, poverty, health, cyberattacks, etc.).

The materials here have been developed over fifteen years of teaching in over twenty-five different countries as we have sought to flesh out how international law and diplomacy is actually practiced in the world. Both of us have been negotiation, mediation, and arbitration scholars and practitioners for decades. We have worked in many countries and taught students and professionals on virtually every continent. We wrote this book to provide both theory and practical instruction in how international conflict resolution is practiced in both public law and private commercial settings. We provide excerpts of theory, practice, illustrative examples of international disputes and conflicts, actual decisions, opinions, treaties, awards, and problems for students to reflect on. Notes and questions follow each section for students to engage actively with the material. A prior course in public international law might be desirable but is not necessary, as would a prior course in general dispute resolution or procedure. Students no longer need documentary supplements—they can follow along on their laptops with appropriate websites and documents of relevant legal materials.

The teacher's manual, available with this text, provides ideas for instruction, including role-plays and simulations, and suggestions for how to respond to the questions asked. We also provide many references to relevant films, videos, and other supplementary material. We have successfully used this material both in the United States and in many other countries where the study of law is both undergraduate (as a first degree) and graduate or professional education.

Our goal in writing this book is to share a belief that "one size will not fit all"—be that litigation, diplomacy, or war. Different kinds of matters (dyadic private international commercial disputes and multi-lateral cooperation agreements on the environment, cross border family disputes, migration, trade and economic development, and individual and group violence and harm) require different kinds of processes for management, handling, and resolution. New forms of conflict are developing every day (cybercrime), and new forms of cooperation are also developing (dispute system design, online dispute resolution, artificial intelligence, crowdsourcing).

We are peacemakers in our work and personal lives, and we hope this book will inspire a new generation to think creatively about how to solve problems and contribute to the education of more international (and domestic) peacemakers.

Let us know what you think.

In peace,

Carrie Menkel-Meadow
Andrea Kupfer Schneider

Acknowledgments

This book began when one of us was the Faculty Director and Professor at the Centre for Transnational Legal Studies in London (a joint program of Georgetown Law School and fifteen other law faculties, with students from all over the world). Most law students were busy studying legal texts, doctrines, treaties, codes, treatises, books, and articles and had little to no idea about how international law was actually practiced. The CTLS program introduced, through a Global Practice Exercise (written by one of the co-authors here), engagement of students in international practice (using private commercial arbitration, public law legal argument, human rights proceedings, environmental and anti-proliferation of weapons treaty negotiations, and international criminal matters). In subsequent years, both Georgetown Law Center (through the initiative of then Dean Alex Aleinikoff) and the University of California, Irvine, founded as a new law school in 2008, required some form of international law instruction in the first year of law school, for which one of the co-authors here wrote several experiential teaching exercises.

Since that time these materials were further developed and honed in courses taught in the United States, Singapore, Italy, France, Germany, Israel, the United Kingdom, Argentina, Chile, Paraguay, Costa Rica, Nicaragua, Belgium, China, Hong Kong, Canada, Mexico, Australia, and Switzerland, among others. Students utilizing these materials have competed in international competitions in negotiation, mediation, arbitration, and international adjudication (e.g., Jessup). Faculty at a number of law schools have used these materials to develop more participatory and experiential methods of instruction in their otherwise more conventional courses, so we hope we have contributed to the growing diversification of legal pedagogy throughout the world.

We are indebted to and grateful for Carol McGeehan who brought us to Carolina Academic Press where we have been well edited by Ryland Bowman and TJ Smithers, among others.

Carrie thanks her research assistants on this project, Celine Gruaz and Alexandra Cadena, who were wonderful students in the International Dispute Resolution course which first tested these materials; her faculty assistant who solved many problems along the way, Maria Gonzalez De Toro; and UCI librarians extraordinaire Dianna Sahhar and Jeff Latta. She especially thanks her many international colleagues who have worked with her on many courses, conferences, and legal matters in different countries and invited her to teach in many of the world's greatest law schools—Silvia Faerman, Orna Rabinovitz-Einy, Moti Moroni, Oran Gayzal, Katherine Lynch, Alain Verbeke, Hugo Rojas, Ana Silva, Carlos Silva, Carlos Ruffinelli, Loukas Mistelis, Maxi Scherer, Rutger Metsch, Remy Gerbay, Victor Ramraj, Naomi Creutzfeldt, Horst Eindmuller, Linda Mulcahy, Jeff Waincymer, Franz Werro, Ulrike Schultz, Avrom Scher, Eleanor Myers, Joel Lee, Pierre Tercier, Michael Freeman (deceased), Michael Palmer, Maria Moscati, Marion Roberts, Chiara Besso, Leticia Coppo, Chris Honeyman, Amy Cohen, and others. Merci, gracias, toda raba, obrigada, danke, grazie, and more. Much of the final work and editing on this book was completed when Carrie was resident at Oxford's Centre for Socio-legal Studies, and she thanks Linda Mulcahy and Florian Grisel for great hospitality, and the graduate students at the Centre for brilliant conversations and tea in troubled times—keeping me internationally and peace focused with large dollops of political theory argumentation! The University of California's generous sabbatical and leave policies has allowed sufficient time for both the production of this book and residencies in other places to test it out. Her ten years of teaching our first year required course (no longer required) in International Legal Analysis, with its curious first year students, inspired much of the instructional focus of this book. At UC Irvine, the Center for Global Peace and Conflict Resolution Studies has provided a helpful venue for presentation of some of the chapters, case studies, and ideas developed here.

Finally, without Robert Meadow, linguist and political scientist extraordinaire, none of this would have been possible. Traveling the physical world and the world of ideas for over fifty years has been Carrie's great joy.

Andrea is grateful for years of support at Marquette University Law School to first teach international conflict resolution in general and then make it a "traveling" course that, over the years, visited European courts, Israel, Cuba, and Ireland. Each year and each course brought new challenges and insights into how these many processes worked—and did not work—in creating peace around the world. She looks forward to more trips in the future with Cardozo law students. The many students who have traveled with her were inspirational in motivating research, writing, and yet more teaching in this field. To April Kutz, Morgan Henson, and Margaret Spring from Marquette Law School and Emily Glazier and Samantha Harberg from Cardozo School of Law—she is grateful for all of their help in pulling together these materials.

Andrea also thanks her extended family for being "dragged" on trips to conflict zones—to Belfast, to Sarajevo, all over Israel—to do field research and advance planning for her student trips. Mixing education and tourism has always been a joy for her.

We both thank Scott Goodman for tireless and detailed work on our permissions and making sure we are set to publish!

We want to especially thank each other for a collaboration that is now over twenty years old on many textbooks, conferences, and joint activities that has united us in friendship and in seeking a more peaceful world, together. Collaboration is a beautiful thing—proving that two heads are better than one, and that we always learn something when working with someone else.

We hope you, readers, will also learn well with others, and make the world a better, more peaceful place.

CMM
AKS

Los Angeles and New York

November 2024

International
Conflict Resolution Processes

Chapter 1

Introduction to International Conflict Resolution: Disputing across Borders

A child is injured in California by a product manufactured in Germany.

A multi-national corporation discharges a high-level employee, who is based in three countries, when he holds a press conference to denounce his company's environmental and labor law violations.

An American commits a murder and flees to a European country which prohibits extradition to any nation with the death penalty.

A movie star and noted political activist brings a libel claim in the United Kingdom, seeking damages and an injunction to prevent publication of an article, written in the United States, which describes her childhood in less than flattering terms.

A foreign government announces it will turn off internet access to a particular browser, owned and managed by an American company.

Three major corporations from different countries agree on a joint venture to construct a major public works project in a developing nation (with financing supported by private investment and a grant from the World Bank) and then have several disputes about the payment schedules and quality of goods in the contract.

The United States incarcerates and mistreats (tortures) detainees captured during the post-September 11th period in various offshore locations and claims neither American law or international law (the Geneva Conventions) applies to either procedural rights or substantive claims about their treatment.

An American member of a political group posts a racist and hateful comment on his blog, which is blocked by the French government.

A Swiss pharmaceutical company perfects a pill to prevent implantation of a fertilized egg which is legally sold in Canada and made available to Americans through mail or internet ordering, though it is not available for sale in the United States.

A ballet company from one country travels to another and is told by representatives of the host country that its female dancers may not wear their sheer costumes at the scheduled performance.

> *American and Mexican fishermen dispute tuna fishing rights off the coast of San Diego and Tijuana, as the American and Mexican governments seek to cooperate by building water and waste treatment plants on both sides of the border that will serve the larger bi-national—metropolitan area.*
>
> —Carrie Menkel-Meadow, *Why and How to Study Transnational Law*, 1 U.C. IRVINE L. REV. 97 (2011)

International conflict occurs in many forms and with many parties. It can involve two or more nation states, two or more private parties or entities (corporations or non-governmental organizations), private parties in conflict with states, and states in conflict with private individuals or entities. Conflict can be "official" (litigation, war, treaty negotiations), "virtual" (online), or informal and unregulated (terrorism, migration, familial and informal relations across borders). International conflict can involve criminal acts, aggressive acts (war or physical or other harms), and civil acts (breaches of contract, breaches of treaties, tortious injury, economic harm, personal hurt).

This book examines the public and private, formal and informal processes that public and private parties in cross-border conflicts use to try to resolve their conflicts. Formal international law involves treaties, public tribunals, courts, arbitration panels, negotiation and diplomacy, conciliation, intervention by international organizations like the United Nations or by regional courts like the European Court of Human Rights, customary law, codes, and global administrative regulations, as well as "soft" law (consented-to agreements), court decisions, compacts, and private contract enforcement. Unlike in our own domestic legal system, there is no "final" Supreme Court serving as the ultimate arbiter of legal rights, duties, and responsibilities in international disputes. As you will learn, the International Court of Justice (established in 1945 by the Statute of the International Court of Justice in the United Nations Charter) has limited jurisdiction over disputes between and among nations, a part of public international law; as a court of limited jurisdiction, it does not deal with most international disputes and conflicts. Most international disputes and conflicts are dealt with either by informal processes (negotiation, diplomacy, mediation) or by specialized tribunals, which can be public (regional international courts), private (arbitration panels), or hybrid (state-investor arbitration). In this book, we cover leading examples of these processes and also focus on newer processes (online dispute resolution) and institutions (treaty-monitoring organizations) that are developing and evolving now.

We begin by touching on basic principles of conflict (its varieties and the many ways it may be managed, dealt with, exacerbated, or "resolved"). Then we look at specific processes that may be used to deal with such conflicts so that you may begin to see which might be appropriate or best for a given situation. Each chapter provides descriptions and examples of different processes which are then followed by problem sets that allow you to work through how each process (or a mix of processes in hybrid forms) might be or has been used in particular international conflict situations. We address the basic processes of negotiation; diplomacy; mediation; conciliation; fact-finding; arbitration; hybrid processes such as mediation-arbitration; formal adjudication (courts and other tribunals); newer forms of online dispute resolution; innovative and changing hybrid processes such as restorative and transitional justice; and ombuds services. We then turn our attention to the field itself and discuss dispute-system design, a process that seeks to conceptualize, operationalize, and implement appropriate dispute resolution processes for particular kinds of conflicts. We conclude the text by illustrating how modern conflict resolution processes might be applied to current and future international "wicked" problems.

I. Introduction to International Dispute Processes: The *Rainbow Warrior*

Case Study: *The Rainbow Warrior*

As you consider the complicated facts below, see if you can list and describe all of the different processes that were employed.

On July 10, 1985, the Rainbow Warrior, a ship owned by Greenpeace (a non-governmental organization that opposes nuclear weapons and supports environmental causes), was blown up as it prepared to move from Auckland Harbor in New Zealand to the French-controlled Moruroa Atoll to protest French nuclear testing that was to be conducted there. The explosives were placed in the ship by agents of the French Directorate General of the External Security (DGSE). The explosion caused the death of a Dutch national who was aboard (Fernando Pereira) and resulted in the ship's total destruction. Most of the French team fled New Zealand, but two French agents, Major Alain Mafart and Captain Dominque Prieur, were arrested and charged with murder and arson under New Zealand law. At first, France denied involvement. But after the head of the DGSE was fired and the French Minister of Defense resigned, France acknowledged its role and, indeed, pleaded for the release of Mafart and Prieur, claiming that they had acted under the orders of superiors and that France itself would take responsibility if the individuals were released. (Much later it was revealed that the president of France, François Mitterrand, had been aware of the French agents' plans.)

Mafart and Prieur pleaded guilty in New Zealand to charges of manslaughter and willful damage to a ship and were sentenced to ten years' imprisonment. New Zealand refused to release the agents to France, claiming that nothing in New Zealand or international law excused criminal acts on the ground that they were carried out pursuant to official orders and that France would not likely imprison the defendants because of its own laws protecting such actions taken under orders. Negotiations between representatives of the two countries were unsuccessful.

France then began to restrict certain New Zealand exports to France and French territories and also to threaten New Zealand's exports of butter to the

European Union. New Zealand filed a complaint with the Organization for Economic Cooperation and Development (OECD) and also initiated a complaint under the General Agreement on Tariffs and Trade (GATT), which would now be cognizable under the procedures of the World Trade Organization, a multilateral international organization based in Geneva and now under some distress as the United States and other countries have modified their commitment to the various trade agreements and their dispute resolution procedures (such as the Dispute Settlement Body, an appellate international arbitral body established by treaty).

With these various disputes in play, the parties continued to engage in bilateral negotiations and then agreed to have the issues arbitrated by then UN Secretary General Javier Perez de Cueller. Perez de Cuellar's ruling was issued on July 6, 1986, and the GATT and OECD complaints were withdrawn.

Official Document: *Case Concerning the Differences between New Zealand and France arising from the* Rainbow Warrior *Affair*

19 U.N. Rep. Int'l Arb. Awards 199, 213–15 (1986)
(ruling of 6 July 1986 by the Secretary-General of the United Nations)

1. Apology

New Zealand seeks an apology. France is prepared to give one. My ruling is that the Prime Minister of France should convey to the Prime Minister of New Zealand a formal and unqualified apology for the attack, contrary to international law, on the "Rainbow Warrior" by French service agents which took place on 10 July 1985.

2. Compensation

New Zealand seeks compensation for the wrong done to it and France is ready to pay some compensation. The two sides, however, are some distance apart on quantum. New Zealand has said that the figure should not be less than US Dollars 9 million, France that it should not be more than US Dollars 4 million. My ruling is that the French Government should pay the sum of US Dollars 7 million to the Government of New Zealand as compensation for all the damage it has suffered.

3. The Two French Service Agents

It is on this issue that the two Governments plainly had the greatest difficulty in their attempts to negotiate a solution to the whole issue on a bilateral basis before they took the decision to refer the matter to me.

The French Government seeks the immediate return of the two officers. It underlines that their imprisonment in New Zealand is not justified, taking into account in particular the fact that they acted under military orders and that France is ready to give an apology and to pay compensation to New Zealand for the damage suffered.

Figure 1. The bombing of the *Rainbow Warrior*

The New Zealand position is that the sinking of the "Rainbow Warrior" involved not only a breach of international law, but also the commission of a serious crime in New Zealand for which the two officers received a lengthy sentence from a New Zealand court. The New Zealand side states that their release to freedom would undermine the integrity of the New Zealand judicial system. In the course of bilateral negotiations with France, New Zealand was ready to explore possibilities for the prisoners serving their sentences outside New Zealand.

But it has been, and remains, essential to the New Zealand position that there should be no release to freedom, that any transfer should be to custody, and that there should be a means of verifying that.

The French response to that is that there is no basis either in international law or in French law on which the two could serve out any portion of their New Zealand sentence in France, and that they could not be subjected to new criminal proceedings after a transfer into French hands.

On this point, if I am to fulfil my mandate adequately, I must find a solution in respect of the two officers which both respects and reconciles these conflicting positions.

My ruling is as follows:

(a) The Government of New Zealand should transfer Major Alain Mafart and Captain Dominique Prieur to the French military authorities. Immediately thereafter, Major Mafart and Captain Prieur should be transferred to a French military facility on an isolated island outside of Europe for a period of three years.

(b) They should be prohibited from leaving the island for any reason, except with the mutual consent of the two Governments. They should be isolated during their assignment on the island from persons other than military or associated personnel and immediate family and friends. They should be prohibited from any contact with the press or other media whether in person or in writing or in any other manner. These conditions should be strictly compiled with and appropriate action should be taken under the rules governing military discipline to enforce them.

(c) The French Government should every three months convey to the New Zealand Government and to the Secretary-General of the United Nations, through diplomatic channels, full reports on the situation of Major Mafart and Captain Prieur in terms of the two preceding paragraphs in order to allow the New Zealand Government to be sure that they are being implemented.

(d) If the New Zealand Government so requests, a visit to the French military facility in question may be made, by mutual agreement by the two Governments, by an agreed third party.

(e) I have sought information on French military facilities outside Europe. On the basis of that information, I believe that the transfer of Major Mafart and Captain Prieur to the French military facility on the isolated island of Hao in French Polynesia would best facilitate the enforcement of the conditions which I have laid down in paragraphs (a) to (d) above. My ruling is that that should be their destination immediately after their transfer.

4. Trade Issues

The New Zealand Government has taken the position that trade issues have been imported into the affair as a result of French action, either taken or in prospect. The French Government denies that, but it has indicated that it is willing to give some undertakings relating to trade, as sought by the New Zealand Government. I therefore rule that France should:

(a) Not oppose continuing imports of New Zealand butter into the United Kingdom in 1987 and 1988 at levels proposed by the Commission of the European Communities in so far as these do not exceed those mentioned in document COM(83)574 of 6 October 1983 that is to say, 77,000 tonnes in 1987 and 75,000 tonnes in 1988; and

(b) Not take measures that might impair the implementation of the agreement between New Zealand and the European Economic Community on Trade in Mutton, Lamb and Goatmeat which entered into force on 20 October 1980 (as complemented by the exchange of letters of 12 July 1984).

5. Arbitration

The New Zealand Government has argued that a mechanism should exist to ensure that any differences that may arise about the implementation of the agreements concluded as a result of my ruling can be referred for binding decision to an arbitral tribunal. The Government of France is not averse to that. My ruling is that an agreement to that effect should be concluded and provide that any dispute concerning the interpretation or application of the other agreements, which it has not been possible to resolve through the diplomatic channel, shall, at the request of either of the two Governments, be submitted to an arbitral tribunal under the following conditions:

(a) Each Government shall designate a member of the tribunal within 30 days of the date of the delivery by either Government to the other of a written request for arbitration of the dispute, and the two Governments shall, within 60 days of that date, appoint a third member of the tribunal who shall be its chairman;

(b) If, within the times prescribed, either Government fails to designate a member of the tribunal or the third member is not agreed, the Secretary General of the United Nations shall be requested to make the necessary appointment after consultations with the two Governments by choosing the member or members of the tribunal;

(c) A majority of the members of the tribunal shall constitute a quorum and all decisions shall be made by a majority vote;

(d) The decisions of the tribunal, including all rulings concerning its constitution, procedure and jurisdiction, shall be binding on the two Governments.

6. The two Governments should conclude and bring into force as soon as possible binding agreements incorporating all of the above rulings. These agreements should provide that the undertaking relating to an apology, the payment of compensation and the transfer of Major Mafart and Captain Prieur should be implemented at the latest on 25 July 1986.

7. On one matter I find no need to make a ruling. New Zealand, in its written statement of position, has expressed concern regarding compensation for the family of the individual whose life was lost in the incident and for Greenpeace. The French statement of position contains an account of the compensation arrangements that have been made; I understand that those assurances constitute the response that New Zealand was seeking.

Although this was issued as a formal "ruling," the parties had essentially negotiated these terms on their own. Why do you think they sought this ruling from the UN Secretary-General? This did not end the matter. Mafart and Prieur were, by agreement, transferred to a "French military facility on the island of Hao for a period of not less than three years." They were prohibited from leaving without the consent of both governments. France issued an apology for the death of the Dutch crew member and paid the family of Pereira 2.3 million francs. In a separate dispute, Greenpeace threatened to sue France for damage to its ship. This matter was submitted to another arbitration panel consisting of a former New Zealand judge and two law professors, which awarded Greenpeace $5 million for the loss of the ship and another $1.2 million for legal fees, costs, and "aggravated damages."

However, in late 1987, the French government, upon being advised of Mafart's health problems, asked New Zealand for permission to remove him for treatment. After some dispute about medical examinations, France, without New Zealand's permission, moved Mafart to France, where later a doctor found his condition did not require emergency aid. Mafart was never returned to the island of Hao, and New Zealand protested that this was a violation of the Perez de Cueller ruling. Then, in 1988, France announced that Prieur was pregnant and needed special medical care which was unavailable on Hao. Although France had given assurances that it would return Prier to New Zealand after providing her with necessary medical care in France, within a few days it announced that Prieur's father was dying in France, and so, without New Zealand's permission, it flew Prieur back to France, never to return to Hao. The question of "France's sovereignty" over its own citizens then became an issue in the French electoral process. After New Zealand's protest that all of this violated the UN arbitration ruling, a third, separate arbitration panel was convened, chaired by the former president of the International Court of Justice. The panel ruled in New Zealand's favor, stating that France's actions were in breach of the original award and treaty obligations; however, it failed to send Mafart or Prieur back to Hao because, by the time of the ruling, the "three-year" period of confinement was due to be concluded. The panel condemned France's breaches of treaty obligations to New Zealand. Although New Zealand had not asked for monetary compensation, this last panel "recommended" that France pay $2 million to a fund devoted to promoting good relations between the two countries, which it did.

Ten years later, after protests by many countries and bodies, France announced that it would conduct more nuclear tests in the South Pacific, despite such tests being banned by the South Pacific Nuclear Free Zone Treaty, which was signed in 1985 by 15 South Pacific nations. France was not a party to this treaty, and, indeed, it had been signed particularly in protest of France's nuclear-testing program. Following strong condemnations and resolutions by the European Union, the UN, and various NGOs to boycott various French products and activities, France finally succumbed to the political pressure. In 1996, it agreed to the anti-nuclear protocols of the South Pacific Nuclear Free Zone treaty and ceased nuclear testing in the South Pacific.

Notes & Questions

1. How many different conflict resolution processes do you see being used in this dispute?
2. What were the issues in these conflicts? What principles or laws seemed to have governed these conflicts?
3. Who were the decision makers and primary actors at each stage of the conflicts? Were the parties to this dispute all "public" parties?

4. What does this matter say about the efficacy of international law?
5. Is this a public international-law conflict or a hybrid (public and private) conflict? What difference does this make?
6. Why would the parties want the UN Secretary-General to "confirm" an agreement they had actually negotiated in private?
7. Were the processes used here successful in "resolving" the disputes? How are you defining "success"? How was power used in resolving these disputes? Who "won" in your view? Is there a winner?
8. What other processes might have been used to deal with these conflicts?

II. Introduction to Conflict Theory

Carrie Menkel-Meadow, *Roots and Inspirations: A Brief History of the Foundations of Dispute Resolution*

in The Handbook of Dispute Resolution 13, 14–15
(Michael L. Moffitt & Robert C. Bordone eds., 2005)

Early History: Descriptions of the Field and Foundational Theories

The social sciences now include a field called "conflict resolution," whereas modern legal studies more often describe the field as "dispute resolution." The different terms signal an important distinction between the two approaches.

Nineteenth-century founders of the field of sociology, including Emile Durkheim, Georg Simmel, and Karl Marx, looked at widespread social and political conflicts and sought to understand their origins, trajectories, and impacts on the larger society. Early on, tensions developed about whether conflict was beneficial for social change, whether it should be managed for social stability, or whether it was simply a normal part of human existence. These intellectual tensions remain with us today. Seen as a social phenomenon, conflict exists at many different levels—individual, familial, group, or nation-state. Indeed, as social psychologists have noted, conflict can also be intrapersonal or intrapsychic. Within a single human being one can find conflicts linked to diverging perceptions, values, attitudes, or behavioral choices.

In law and legal studies, the unit of analysis has been the dispute, or "case"—an activated conflict in which someone has experienced a wrong and "named it, blamed someone or [some] entity and claimed against them" in a formal way. This activation process often plays out in a binary or polarized format of plaintiff and defendant, or complainant and respondent. Seeing a dispute as a separate, self-contained unit of social interaction, requiring some form of formal or legal intervention, is different from seeing a dispute as located in a more socially enmeshed world of multiple parties, interconnected issues, and social and relational history.

Thus, the very nomenclature or definition of the relevant unit of analysis tells us something about how a conflict or dispute might be handled, treated, or resolved. For the most part, social scientists have focused on the embeddedness of disputes in larger fields or patterns of conflict and social relations, while lawyers and other dispute resolution professionals have focused on the concrete nature of particular disputes, suggesting use of particular techniques for dispute settlement or other resolution.

Socio-legal scholars who are both lawyers and anthropologists have bridged these disciplines by studying disputes in a broader social context, looking at how cases are socially constructed, labeled, and enacted. Scholars and practitioners of the school of "legal realism" were similarly attracted to looking at how disputes were formed and dealt with in particular settings, and so created a "jurisprudence of dispute resolution" and its institutions.

Together, the insights of these different approaches to studying conflict resolution have given us some basic propositions about the field, what some call a canon of dispute resolution. Within these approaches, some have aimed to provide a taxonomy for analyzing conflict. Others have sought to link description and prescription. Some have focused on the "constructive" and "destructive" aspects of conflicts. Still others have aimed to describe the institutionalized processes best suited to deal with particular kinds of disputes.

Carrie Menkel-Meadow, *Conflict Theory*

in Encyclopedia of Community: From the Village to the Virtual World 323–26 (Karen Christensen & David Levinson eds., 2003)

There are many reasons for conflicts to develop, at both the individual and at the group level. Some conflicts are based on belief systems or principles, some are based on personality differences, and others on conflicts about material goods or personal or group status or reputation. Because there are so many different reasons conflicts develop and because much conflict is dangerous and unproductive, the theory of conflict attempts to understand the different sources of conflict, the dynamics of how conflict develops, escalates or declines and how conflict can be managed, reduced or resolved.

At the same time, it must be recognized that conflict can have social utility as well. Many important changes in human society, many for the betterment of human life, have come from hard-fought conflicts that resulted in the change of human institutions, relationships or ideas. The United States Civil War, for example, was a bloody and painful war in which over a million Americans died, but this war eliminated slavery in the United States and ushered in a long period of change in race relations in the United States (which is not yet over and still marked by many different kinds of conflicts, such as whether there should be reparations paid to the descendants of slaves or whether there should be affirmative action in education and employment to compensate for past wrongs of the society). Even small interpersonal conflicts (like between a husband and wife or parent and child) can lead to important changes, not only in relationships between the people in conflict, but in larger social movements, such as the women's rights or feminist movement and the children's rights movement. Conflicts with outsiders often clarify and reinforce commitments and norms of one's own group. And internal conflict within the individual can lead to changed views and intellectual and emotional growth.

Conflict theory tries to explain the types of conflicts that exist and whether they are productive or destructive and then goes on to attempt to explain the ways in which conflict proceeds or is structured (both by internal and external forces) and how it can be managed or resolved.

A conflict can be experienced as a simple disagreement, a feeling of discomfort or opposition, and a perception of difference from others, or a competition or incompatibility with others. Conflicts, then, can be perceptual, emotional or behavioral. When a conflict is actually acted on it becomes a dispute with someone or a group of others. In order for a conflict to fully develop into a dispute we have to experience some sense of wrong to ourselves, someone else to "blame" for that wrong and some way to take action against those we think caused our difficulty—what one set of scholars have called, "naming, blaming and claiming."[1] How the conflict turns into a dispute and how it is labeled ("framing") then may affect how it progresses and how it may either escalate and get worse, leading in extreme cases to war, or how it can be handled, managed or resolved ("reclaiming").

Types of Conflicts

Conflict can exist on many different levels, including the intrapersonal, interpersonal, intragroup, intergroup, and international. Conflicts can exist about different subject matters—ideational or beliefs, values, materiel and resources, emotions, roles and responsibilities. Conflicts vary in terms of the social contexts in which they are located (two old friends, family members, neighbors, strangers, consumers and merchants, distant nation-states) and in the time span in which they are located ("one-off" or "one-shot" encounters and conflicts, long-standing or "embedded" conflicts, temporary or "repeated" conflicts in ongoing relationships like families and employment settings). Conflicts vary, even within the same social environment or subject matter by how the disputants treat the conflict, in the strategies, tactics and behaviors they employ (avoidance, self-help, peaceful negotiation, argument, escalation, physical violence, peace seeking, mediation or settlement) and how the strategies chosen interact with each other. And conflicts are often classified by how they affect the parties in the conflict (the consequences of the conflict) and those outside of the conflict (the "externalities" of the conflict, like children in a marital argument or divorce and neighbors of warring states who accept refugees).

1. William L.F. Felstiner, Richard Abel & Austin Sarat, *The Emergence and Transformation of Disputes: Naming, Blaming and Claiming ...*, 15 L. & Socy. Rev. 631–654 (1980–1981).

In an effort to describe and diagnose conflicts so that we can understand and manage them better, social theorist and psychologist Morton Deutsch[2] has developed a useful typology of conflicts which contrasts "objective conditions" with "perceived" concerns of the parties:

Veridical Conflict—"true" conflict with matched perceptions and realities, such as when two or more parties want to use the same scarce resource for different purposes (a piece of land, a room in a house, a finite number of dollars, water).

Contingent Conflict—perceptions here do not match objective reality, such that a change in resources or perceptions of the conflict could readily resolve it. If more land, water or dollars were available or could be created, for example, multiple or shared uses might be possible. Another room or space could be built or found somewhere else. Such conflicts are "resolvable" if the parties can change their perceptions or cognitions or use creativity to expand resources or seek resolution from outside their "limited resources" frame of thinking.

Displaced Conflict—here parties in conflict have manifest or express conflicts about one thing when they are really arguing or caring about something different—the underlying conflict. Parents and children may argue about the use of a car, but the "real" conflict is about separation, responsibility and growing up. Countries will have disputes about borders and land when the "real" dispute is about power, sovereignty, control and economic well-being or identity.

Misattributed Conflict—parties here have conflicts with the wrong "others" or about the wrong issues. Siblings might fight with each other when they are really angry at the control of their parents. Disempowered groups might fight with each other (former colonized groups, racial minorities) rather than take on the powerful party that has dominated both groups. Individuals or groups may feel they are being treated differently (and less well) when the real issue might be unavailable resources for all.

Latent Conflict—this is conflict that may be just beneath the surface but is not yet expressed, but perhaps should be. In relationships people may not want to start a fight so they will suppress things that make them angry, or an employee may be afraid to express dissatisfaction with a working condition or assignment. If the "latent" conflict is not expressed, things may actually get worse if the parties are not honest and cannot work out their differences.

False Conflict—parties may create conflicts or disputes where there is no objective reason for them, especially if there are generally bad relations between the parties or if someone prefers "conflictual" states of unrest or activity to relative peace. In situations of opposition (employer-employee, parent-child, academic or sports competition) disputes or conflicts may develop over minor or even major issues when there is no real reason to be in a dispute.

---

2. THE RESOLUTION OF CONFLICT: CONSTRUCTIVE AND DESTRUCTIVE PROCESSES 12 (1973).

Conflicts have also been classified by various social scientists and conflict theorists by virtue of what is at stake in the conflict such as:

Resources (land, power, property, natural resources like water, oil, minerals, money);

Values or Beliefs (class, religious, nationality, political aspirations and codes that create systemic belief systems for groups or individual members);

Preferences or Interests (incompatible desires, wants or objectives of action);

Relationship (differences in desires or objectives about relationships);

Identity (concerns about recognition of and respect for group memberships).

The theory of such classifications is that if we can analyze different kinds of conflict, we can determine how they might unfold and whether a particular conflict is amenable to a positive outcome (whether harnessing the conflict to constructive solutions or processes) or whether it is likely to become destructive (for the parties or others affected by the parties)....

Conflicts often take somewhat predictable turns ranging from precipitating event, response or reaction, development of in-group-out-group loyalties and the development of both offensive and defensive strategies, followed by escalation, impasse or stalemate and then, motivation for resolution, settlement and solution seeking (or, in highly competitive or violent conflicts, victory or "annihilation" of the other). But while many think of conflicts as necessarily competitive and antagonistic, there really are a wider range of behaviors that occur in most conflict situations, many of them dependent on the situation and social and political environment of the conflict, as well as the parties in using multiple strategies. Many of those who study conflict see a greater variety of possible conflict modes or strategies in handling conflict that can occur at individual, group, organizational, and even nation-state levels of actions. There are those who *compete* (or seek to maximize their own self-interest, even at the expense of others), those who *cooperate* (seeking to work with the other side(s) to find some middle or compromise grounds), those who *accommodate* (who may simply give in to the other party), those who *avoid* (by exiting or absenting themselves from the conflict) and those who *collaborate* (by seeking to work for joint and mutual gains for all parties, without unnecessary harm to others or needless compromise or giving in).[3]

What makes conflict processes so complex are the strategic interactions that occur when more than one party must interact to start, maintain, interrupt or resolve the conflict. These different conflict management strategies interact with each other and can produce reactive and unproductive responses, such as when competing leads to more competing and escalation of competitive behavior causes more violence, less information sharing and an inability to seek mutual gain possibilities. This "mirroring" effect, when each party merely returns the behavior that is offered to it, often leads to

3. Kenneth Thomas, *Conflict and Conflict Management*, in HANDBOOK OF INDUSTRIAL ORGANIZATIONAL PSYCHOLOGY (Marvin V. Dunnette ed., 1976).

stalemates or the impossibility of achieving some resolution because the parties cannot even see or hear beyond the one strategy they have chosen.

Thus, much recent empirical work in conflict processes has been to study the conditions under which parties in conflict can alter their behavioral or strategy choices and open themselves up to new ways of communicating or testing the possibilities with other parties. Conflicts have been studied at the level of community relations, ethnic-racial conflicts, economic and resource competition, environmental disputes, lawsuits (both individual and class actions) and international conflicts. Parties in conflict are now asked to explore their underlying interests (apart from their conflict-producing "positions"), to consider the needs and interests of other parties ("role-reversals" and other communication technologies) and to develop strategies of collaborative and creative problem solving (by expanding and creating resources and alternatives, by trading non-mutually exclusive preferences or goods, by using contingent or "trial" agreements, rather than permanent solutions, by developing processes and rules for respectful co-existence, such as in Truth and Reconciliation Commissions in politically divided nations).

Notes & Questions

1. *Look Around!* Read a newspaper or magazine and find a conflict that is described. Do you think the conflict you identified has positive or negative aspects, or both? What are they? What are the issues in dispute?
2. How might the disputants (private parties, national leaders) have avoided such a conflict in advance? Can you start to recognize different processes being used in these disputes?

Conflicts will always exist. While we may prevent and avoid some, clearly we will never succeed in eliminating all of them.

In focusing on conflict, it is critically important to examine what it means to "win" in one. While many people assume that someone must lose when another person wins, this either-or mentality is often fallacious.

III. Mapping Conflicts

Michael Klare, *The New Geography of Conflict*

80 Foreign Aff. 49, 52–54 (2001)

Although obtaining sufficient supplies of energy is becoming the foremost resource priority for some states, the pursuit of adequate water will be the central focus for others. Water supplies are already insufficient in many parts of the Middle East and Southwest Asia; continued population growth and the increased likelihood of drought from global warming will likely create similar scarcities elsewhere. To further complicate the problem, water supplies do not obey political boundaries, and so many of the countries in these regions must share a limited number of major water sources. With all the states that touch these waters seeking to increase their allotted supplies, the danger of conflict over competition for these shared supplies will inevitably grow.

In other parts of the world, localized conflicts have broken out for control of valuable timber and minerals....

All of these phenomena—increased competition over access to major sources of oil and gas, growing friction over the allocation of shared water supplies, and internal warfare over valuable export commodities—have produced a new geography of conflict, a reconfigured cartography in which resource flows rather than political and ideological divisions constitute the major fault lines. Just as a map showing the world's tectonic faults is a useful guide to likely earthquake zones, viewing the international system in terms of unsettled resource deposits—contested oil and gas fields, shared water systems, embattled diamond mines—provides a guide to likely conflict zones in the twenty-first century...

In the early 1990s, violence in the former Yugoslavia, Kashmir, and Central Africa made the world community concentrate on preventing ethnic and intercommunal conflict, but this focus on ethnicity could not predict or address the violence in Africa over control of diamond fields, copper mines, and farmlands. Economic globalization is turning some poor areas into centers of prosperity and growth but leaving others behind in abject poverty, sparking conflicts that have more to do with resources than with nationalism. In short, contemporary world affairs defy exclusively political, security-related, and economic definitions.

A better analysis of stresses in the new international system, and a better predictor of conflict, would view international relations through the lens of the world's contested resources and focus on those areas where conflict is likely to erupt over access to or the possession of vital materials. The analysis would begin with a map showing all major deposits of oil and natural gas lying in contested or unstable areas. These zones of potential trouble include the Persian Gulf, the Caspian Sea basin, and the South China Sea, along with Algeria, Angola, Chad, Colombia, Indonesia, Nigeria, Sudan, and Venezuela—areas and states that together house about four-fifths of the world's known petroleum reserves. The map would also trace the pipelines and tanker routes used to carry oil and natural gas from their points of supply to markets in the West; many of these routes pass through areas that are themselves subject to periodic violence...

A map of contested resource zones would also show all major water systems shared by two or more countries in arid or semi-arid areas. These would include large river systems such as the Nile (shared by Egypt, Ethiopia, and Sudan, among others), the Jordan (shared by Israel, Jordan, Lebanon, and Syria), the Tigris and Euphrates (shared by Iran, Iraq, Syria, and Turkey), the Indus (shared by Afghanistan, India, and Pakistan), and the Amu Darya (shared by Tajikistan, Turkmenistan, and Uzbekistan).

Also included would be underground aquifers that similarly cross borders, such as the Mountain Aquifer lying beneath the West Bank and Israel.

Such a map, if properly designed, would truly delineate the places where armed combat is most likely to erupt in the years ahead. The mere presence of valuable resources in a particular area does not, of course, mean that conflict is likely to break out there. Other factors including the relative stability of the countries or regions involved, the history of relations between them, and the local military balance must also be considered.

Identifying areas of potential conflict over natural resources is also becoming increasingly important as the pressure on these fault lines grows. The pressure derives from a number of sources, beginning with the basic mechanics of supply and demand. As populations increase and economic activity expands in many parts of the world, the appetite for vital materials will swell more quickly than nature (and the world's resource firms) can accommodate. The result will be recurring shortages of key materials, becoming chronic in some cases. Technologies that introduce alternative materials and production techniques will help overcome some of these scarcities but can also present problems of their own—as shown, for example, by the soaring demand for electricity in Silicon Valley and other centers of digital technology. As shortages of critical materials rise in frequency and severity, the competition for access to the remaining supplies of these commodities will grow more intense.

Notes & Questions

1. See if you can draw a map of the world, as suggested above, to indicate the likely trouble spots or "flash points" of conflict described in the excerpt. (Hint: *see* Klare, *The New Geography of Conflict*, at 55.) See also Chapter 11, *infra*, where we will revisit some of these issues.
2. Consider how some conflicts seem to reoccur, while others seem to be "resolved." What might be some of the differences between these conflicts?

I. William Zartman & Siniša Vuković, Rethinking Conflict Resolution and Management

1 (2023)

The most striking element of the tectonic change that impels the need for new conflict management thinking is the collapse of the very basis of conflict management and resolution: World Order. The World System has eroded down to World Disorder on both its international level and its equivalent on the national level, removing the moral, institutional and practical conditions on which conflict control operates. Conflict management is the essence of World Order, since it is the mechanism of peaceful social and political change and institutionalized life, while at home, governance is the management of conflict. Managing conflict without a basis of order is fly-by-night and ad hoc, and that is our challenge.... Rethinking conflict management has to be relevant to the world going into the second quarter century, both with improvements around the current edges as well as with initiatives for a new design.... Now the big challenge looms before the world, alongside the "smaller" needs of handling state collapse or ripe moments of natural disasters. Now the need is to think big, because the coming decade will be faced with major order-reconstructing, while thinking small as we muddle through.

In their book, Zartman and Vuković suggest that many of the key concepts in conflict resolution—hurting stalemates, "ripeness" (for conflict resolution interventions), mutually enticing opportunities, escalation, mediation, hybridization, prevention of conflict, inclusion and participation in governance and representation, and the role of protest—are in need of rethinking and revision as we seem to have shifted away from a more optimistic time marked by peace-seeking and conflict resolution toward one characterized by war (e.g., Russia-Ukraine, Israel-Gaza) and ongoing conflict. Although we have learned a great deal from the ongoing efforts to create processes and institutions to prevent or manage conflict since World War II, it seems that we still have much more to learn.

As you read, ask yourself what generalities can be made about conflict resolution processes—for example, key or core concepts that might apply to all or most conflicts or what processes must be specifically tailored to different kinds of disputes. After studying the different processes covered in this book, you will be asked to apply your learning to a variety of "wicked" or intractable conflicts the world now faces, which require what Zartman and Vuković call a "tectonic change" in conflict management. Do you think our "system" of conflict management has, as they say, "collapsed," or do you think we are still building on older forms of conflict resolution as we attempt to create new ones (*see* Chapters 7, 8, 9 and 10)?

Mary Parker Follett, an important early theorist in the field of conflict resolution (who worked in the first decades of the 20th century), focused on different approaches to handling, but not necessarily "resolving," all conflicts.

Mary Parker Follett, *Constructive Conflict*

in Mary Parker Follett—Prophet of Management: A Celebration of Writings from the 1920s 67–69, 75, 77, 79, 82, 84–86 (Pauline Graham ed., 1995)

As conflict—difference—is here in the world, as we cannot avoid it, we should, I think, use it. Instead of condemning it, we should set it to work for us. Why not? What does the mechanical engineer do with friction? Of course, his chief job is to eliminate friction, but it is true that he also capitalizes friction. The transmission of power by belts depends on friction between the belt and the pulley.... The music of the violin we get by friction. We talk of the friction of the mind on mind as a good thing. So in business too, we have to know when to try to eliminate friction and when to try to capitalize it, when to see what work we can make it do. That is what I wish to consider here, whether we can set conflict to work and make it *do* something for us.

Methods of Dealing with Conflict

There are three main ways of dealing with conflict: domination, compromise and integration. Domination, obviously, is a victory of one side over the other. This is the easiest way of dealing with conflict, the easiest for the moment but not usually successful in the long run....

The second way of dealing with conflict, that of compromise, we understand well, for it is the way we settle most of our controversies; each side gives up a little in order to have peace, or, to speak more accurately in order that the activity which has been interrupted by the conflict can go on. Compromise is the basis of trade union tactics. In collective bargaining, the trade unionist asks for more than he expects to get, allows for what is going to be lopped off in the conference. Thus, we often do not know what he really thinks he should have, and this ignorance is a great barrier to dealing with conflict fruitfully....

Yet no one really wants to compromise, because that means a giving up of something. Is there any other method of ending conflict? There is a way now beginning to be recognized at least, and even occasionally followed: when two desires are *integrated*, that means that a solution has been found in which both desires have found a place, that neither side has to sacrifice anything. Let us take some very simple illustration. In the Harvard Library one day, in one of the smaller rooms, someone wanted the window open, I wanted it shut. We opened the window in the next room, where no one was sitting. This was not a compromise because there was no curtailing of desire; we both got what we really wanted. For I did not want a closed room, I simply did not want the north wind to blow directly on me; likewise the other occupant did not want that particular window open, he merely wanted more air in the room....

One advantage of integration over compromise I have not yet mentioned. If we get only compromise, the conflict will come up again and again in some other form, for in compromise we give up part of our desire, and because we shall not be content to rest there, sometimes we shall try to get the whole of our desire....

[T]he revaluing of interests on both sides may lead the interests to fit into each other, so that all find some place in the final solution. If the first step is to uncover the real conflict, the next is to take the demands of both sides and break them up into their constituent parts. On the other hand, one often has to do just the opposite; find the whole demand, the real demand, which is being obscured by miscellaneous minor claims or by ineffective presentation....

Finally, let us consider the chief *obstacles to integration.* It requires a high order of intelligence, keen perception and discrimination, more than that, a brilliant *inventiveness.* Another obstacle to integration is that our way of life has habituated many of us to enjoy domination. Integration seems a tamer affair, it leaves no "thrills" of conquest. Finally, perhaps the greatest of all obstacles to integration is our lack of training for it. In our college debates we try always to beat the other side....

I should like to emphasize our responsibility for integration.... One test of business administration should be: is the organization such that both employers and employees, or co-managers, co-directors, are stimulated to a reciprocal activity which will give more than mere adjustment, more than in equilibrium? Our outlook is narrowed, our activity restricted, our chances of business success largely diminished when our thinking is constrained within the limits of what has been called an "either-or" situation. We should never allow ourselves to be bullied by an "either-or." There is always the possibility of something better than either of two given alternatives.

Notes & Questions

How do we "think big" for new design of international conflict resolution while, at the same time, "muddling through" so-called smaller or more local conflicts? Do you share Follett's conception of "constructive conflict" to deal with some of the difficult or potentially intractable conflicts identified by Klare and Zartman and Vuković?

This text and your course focus primarily on legal forms of conflict resolution, but an important backdrop to legal institutional and process design (*see* Chapter 9) is the field of international relations, which provides some of the important conceptualization for diplomatic negotiation (*see* Chapter 2), treaty formation, and enforcement and implementation of both private (*see* Chapter 3) and public international agreements and dispute resolution (*see* Chapters 6, 7, and 8).

IV. International Conflicts— Public, Private, Hybrid: What Remedies?

As the *Rainbow Warrior* matter illustrates, conflicts involving parties from different countries often permit a choice of process. Nation states can sue each other in the International Court of Justice if treaties or *customary law principles* (a type of informal law that is accepted based on the belief that near-universally accepted norms evidenced by national practices (*opinio juris*—an opinion of law or necessity will be adhered to) are violated. They can negotiate publicly and diplomatically or in private. Or they can ask a third party to intervene (as Perez de Cueller did above) as a fact-finder, conciliator, mediator, or decision-maker (arbitrator). Private parties (e.g., businesses from different countries) can negotiate, litigate (in their own national courts with jurisdiction over foreign nationals), mediate, or, most commonly, arbitrate. The arbitration process (see Chapter 4) is a system where private organizations (e.g., the International Chamber of Commerce or the London Court of International Arbitration) provide both procedural rules and private decision makers (arbitrators) who are contractually agreed-to, and where awards are enforceable in any country (170 as of the time of this writing) which has signed on to a treaty (New York Convention on the Recognition and Enforcement of Foreign Arbitral Awards, 21 U.S.T. 2517, 330 U.N.T.S. 38 (1958)). Similarly, if a private company invests in another country (supported by either a bilateral or multilateral trade agreement) and there is a dispute with the host country, a hybrid arbitration process is usually employed. This is arbitration by private arbitrators, usually using rules of the sponsoring body, the International Center for Settlement of Investment Disputes (ICSID), supported by enforcement through international treaty (the Washington Convention, Convention on the Settlement of Investment Disputes Between States and Nationals of Other States (17 U.S.T. 1270; 575 U.N.T.S 159 (1965)) which authorizes enforcement in national courts of those who have signed the treaty. Until recently, countries in dispute over trading practices (subsidies, export-import discrimination, tariffs, etc.) have committed to a more public arbitration and appellate system managed by the World Trade Organization (for example, the type of dispute between France and New Zealand regarding France's efforts to retaliate for the Greenpeace bombing prosecutions by limiting imports of New Zealand butter to France).

More recently, the international community has, through the Rome Statute (adopted in 1998, in force in 2002), created the International Criminal Court (ICC). Comprising 108 member nations as of the time of this writing (note that the United States, China, and Russia are not members, and some current member nations are threatening withdrawal), the ICC has jurisdiction over a limited set of particularly heinous crimes (e.g., genocide, war crimes, torture, rape), which likely would not include a single-explosion incident as the one that occurred on the *Rainbow Warrior*. Also newer to the international stage is the development of various quasi-legal processes designed to create different forms of remedies—apologies, amnesties, restitution, reparations, and local criminal prosecutions—for transitions out of civil wars, for unjust regimes (e.g., apartheid in South Africa, Khmer Rouge in Cambodia), and for the commission of atrocities. These new remedies represent different types of restorative justice that aim to create a more direct "reckoning" for parties that have engaged in horrible crimes against humanity, or even, in some cases, to allow for reconciliation. There are also now three separate regional courts of human rights: the European Court of Human Rights, the Inter-American Court of Human Rights, and the African Court of Human Rights. These courts adjudicate and settle claims based on regional treaties and charters (such as the UN Charter of Human Rights and customary law) that involve the protection of particular human rights (e.g., freedom of expression, bodily integrity, and due process), and in doing so, make complex determinations with respect to cultural variations (using the margin of appreciation doctrine for national differences within a proposed system of "universal" human rights, which is itself a contested concept (*see* Chapter 13)).

Other kinds of international conflicts include more "local" matters, such as domestic relations (child custody, family support, and recognition of same-sex marriages); issues involving multinational families (a few international treaties deal with such issues as child abduction, *see, e.g.*, Convention on the Rights of the Child, 1577 U.N.T.S 3 (1989); Hague Convention of the Civil Aspects of Child Abduction (1980)); extradition of the criminally accused who flee from one country to another; and issues of migration from one country to another (another hybrid of national rules of immigration and citizenship) in light of international treaties governing refugees and asylum law (Protocol Relating to the Status of Refugees, 606 U.N.T.S. 267, 6 I.L.M.78 (1967)).

In recent decades, an increase in treaty-making for "global" problems that know no boundaries, such as environmental conditions (climate change), cybercrime, and terrorism, has led to the development of many treaty-monitoring organizations. These organizations constitute a form of global administrative governance (e.g., the UN Whaling Commission) and publish reports on various commitments and conditions (such as the Rio, Kyoto, Copenhagen, and Paris Climate Accords), with some having the authority to charge fines or impose other sanctions.

This book introduces you to variations of these processes and institutions. Major questions to consider in any international conflict or dispute are the following:

a. What bodies have legal jurisdiction over this process?
b. What are the interests of the parties?
c. What process might be most appropriate for handling this conflict (private, public, diplomatic, principled, practical compromise, need for a ruling, or precedent)?
d. What compliance or enforcement mechanisms are possible with respect to each process choice?
e. What are the likely legal, political, or moral consequences of using a particular conflict resolution process?

At the larger policy or macro level, it will be useful for you to consider whether the ability to choose from among so many processes and the involvement of various institutions (thickly layered international dispute resolution) is beneficial, or whether having so many different processes and bodies leads to fragmentation and a virtual tower of Babel with limited enforcement mechanisms. For years, international law scholars have debated whether international law is really law, as it does not have the support of a single supreme court or an army to back up orders and decisions. We invite you to consider, as we review here, what has been accomplished so far in the international order, whether there is more to international conflict resolution than "law" as it is so narrowly defined. Conflict processes and international reputations, legitimacy and ongoing relationships, and global interdependence on so many matters, in our view, requires us to consider international dispute resolution as varied, complex, and hybridized, and as consisting of more than "law on the books," including the numerous forms of more peaceful and party-tailored methods to handle or manage, if not totally resolve, conflicts that cross borders.

Before we move on to the specific processes in great detail, we provide a taxonomy of different kinds of international dispute resolution processes and the issues they raise.

Carrie Menkel-Meadow, *Alternative Dispute Resolution*

in Max Planck Encyclopedias of International Law (2018)

This entry defines and describes the non-adjudicatory or non-court processes used in international dispute resolution and outlines the basic issues and controversies that have developed with respect to their use. The term *alternative dispute resolution* (ADR) has come to connote all dispute resolution processes other than formal court adjudicatory processes (Menkel-Meadow, Love, Schneider, Moffitt, and Blankley 2024), but the term *appropriate dispute resolution* may now more accurately reflect the fact that other forms of dispute resolution are more commonly used than courts, especially in international dispute resolution. The more interesting issue is what process is most appropriate for the particular issue, dispute or conflict in question, taking account of: the parties involved; the context of the dispute; the level of jurisdiction, e.g. nation-states, regions, individuals, international organizations, non-governmental organizations (NGOs); and the desired outcome, e.g. public award, peace agreement, private settlement. In this entry the term "ADR" will be used generically to connote all non-court processes, but it is more accurate to think of it as "appropriate" (or "access to") dispute resolution, rather than "alternative" in the international context.

In an era of "process pluralism" and proliferation of international bodies to deal with a great variety of international issues, "appropriate" dispute resolution expresses the idea that no one process, including full court adjudication, may be best suited to resolve, manage or handle particular kinds of disputes. Some disputes will require an authoritative, precedent producing resolution, (e.g. border disputes); others, such as environmental standards, may require more contingent, revisable agreements, which include monitoring, reporting, fines and sanctions, which may change as conditions and knowledge bases change. Some dispute resolution processes like cross border dealings are primarily for the parties themselves (cross border business dealings) and others like standard setting, use of force, peace agreements, and foreign investment have implications for the larger polity or global governance (standard setting, use of force, peace agreements, and foreign investment).

The modern recognition and development of processes other than formal court adjudication is attributable to at least three sources: historical accuracy; efficiency of enforcement, speed and cost; and qualitative, flexible, tailored, party-driven solutions to complex disputes and conflicts. An increasing number of formal international agreements and treaties now provide for either a choice of process, e.g. *Law of the Sea, Settlement of Disputes* or a tiered ordering of movement from more consensual processes such as mediation and conciliation, to more decisional processes such as arbitration and adjudication. Some forms of less formal dispute resolution such as commercial and investment arbitration still ultimately rely on public bodies and courts for legitimacy and enforcement, e.g. through the New York Convention on the Recognition and Enforcement of Foreign Arbitral Awards and the Washington Convention on the Settlement of Investment Disputes Between States and Nationals of Other States. Thus, ADR in the international context may be both public and private at the same time.

The development of ADR, as a contrast to formal court or tribunal adjudication, is due to the recognition that many disputes are better handled with party participation, party development of both procedural rules and substantive solutions, tailored and flexible outcomes, and in some cases, the desire for some confidentiality, privacy, and lack of "precedential" force in particular cases.

ADR offers the potential of greater compliance with outcomes being negotiated directly and consensually by the parties and more "creative," less brittle outcomes without the winners and losers in bipolar courts. Some forms of ADR promise more contingent solutions, allowing for continuing engagement in dealing with a variety of international issues as conditions change from the time of the initial dispute. Examples include environmental, economic, national security and technological regulations. Historically, processes such as negotiation, and both formal and informal diplomacy, have long supported international dispute resolution with both public agreements and treaties, and also more private agreements between and among both public, predominantly state entities, and private, predominantly corporate, businesses and NGO entities. Modern dispute resolution theory and practice recognizes a continuum of dispute processes ranging from party chosen or consensual processes to more command or adjudicative processes.

Historically, disputes have been handled for thousands of years between states or state-like entities informally through negotiation and diplomacy and formally through early peace treaties and covenants and of course, by force. War is also a form of dispute "resolution" and, some would argue, not only one of the oldest, but one of the most common forms of international dispute resolution (Sun Tzu, *The Art of War*, 5th C B.C.). In the late 19th century through a series of meetings in the Hague, nations convened to try to limit the recourse to war and to encourage more peaceful means of conflict resolution, culminating in the *Hague Peace Convention of 1899* and the formation of the *Permanent Court of Arbitration.* Despite many efforts to promote peaceful conflict resolution through the League of Nations and its new international tribunals and the 1928 Kellogg-Briand Pact, World War II resulted in an unprecedented conflagration, leaving millions dead on many continents. With the formation of the *United Nations* (1945) and its sections on seeking "pacific" solutions to problems of international conflict (UN Charter, Art. 1, 33), the post-World War II quest for processes and institutions to maintain and preserve world peace and security continued. The UN Charter created the *International Court of Justice* as a judicial body to deal with formal disputes between nations. But, in the modern world disputes exist as international disputes among and between nation-states, international organizations, private parties, non-governmental international organizations, multi-national corporations and now even individuals have "standing" to raise legal claims in some international tribunals.

Key Issues in Usages of Non-Adjudicatory Processes: Type of Process and Process Integrity

Because different dispute processes can have different purposes—e.g. settlement of a boundary dispute, peace agreement after conflict, compensation for a private investment after state regulation or expropriation, resolution of a private commercial cross-border contract dispute, punishment of a criminal or civil wrong, restitution for a human rights violation—someone involved in the dispute will have the responsibility for choosing or "allocating" the dispute to a particular process. Parties can make such choices ex ante in contracts and treaties, or ex post after a dispute has arisen, if it is not already assigned to a particular process. It has been suggested by procedural scholars and practitioners (Fuller, 1981) that each process has its own "integrity" or "morality," and particular characteristics, and so disputants and their representatives should choose processes appropriately. When a public decision and possibly a precedential ruling is required, adjudication before a formal tribunal is best used; when there is contested evidence to present and rules are either clear or needing interpretation by an authoritative body, fact-finding may be necessary to resolve the dispute. In situations of ongoing relations between the parties who may want to design their own rules of relations for the future separately from "resolving" issues of what happened in the past, mediation, (facilitated negotiation, see below) is most appropriate. When a particular already existing agreement between the parties, e.g. a commercial contract or an investment treaty, needs interpretation or application and "expert" decision-making is desired, arbitration, being decision-making by party chosen third parties, may be most appropriate. In many cases, such as some peace negotiations and some commercial settlements, some form of confidentiality may make resolution more likely. As more fully indicated in Chart I below *Characteristics of Different Dispute Resolution Processes*, disputants need to know what qualities of dispute resolution they require for their dispute management. *Primary* processes such as negotiation, mediation and arbitration are now often combined to form more *hybrid* processes such as med-arb, arb-med, and ombuds and use new forms of evidence, technology or even "artificial intelligence" and algorithms for decisions such as online dispute resolution. Whether each type of process has its own special qualities, rules, formations, type of outcomes and "integrities" are important theoretical and practical questions explored more fully in Section D below. Whether each different form of process should have its own procedural and ethical rules is explored in both the scholarly and practical literature.

Different processes are characterized by whether they are *voluntary or optional* in that they are chosen by the parties, as in trans-border contracts, or *compelled or mandatory* in that they exist by formal treaty language or other law; whether they are *public* in that the venues are accessible by other than the immediate parties and their representatives or *private* like commercial international arbitration; how *formal or informal* they are according to procedural rules; the *different roles of the "third parties"*,

Process	Rule of Law	Open/Closed	Consent	Role of Third Party	Formality/Review	Outcome
Negotiation	No	Both	Yes	No	None	Agreement
Mediation	Maybe	Usually closed	Yes	Facilitative	None	Agreement
Arbitration (ICA)	Maybe	Closed	Consent to arbitrate but not to outcome	Decisional (award)	Rules of procedure, no appeal, some 'review' allowed by NY Convention	Award (enforceable in national courts)
Arbitration (ISA)	Yes	Closed with publication afterward	By treaty	Decisional	Rules of procedure; some review; ICSID annulment	Award (enforceable in national courts)
Conciliation	No	Closed	Yes	Suggested outcome	None	Agreement of order
Fact-Finding/Inquiry	No	Either	Usually	Investigative and conclude 'facts'	No	Report (binding or not at parties choice)
Adjudication	Yes	Open	No—not needed, except some cases, ICJ	Decisional on law and facts	Formal rules of procedure and may apply formal law (Art. 38, Statute of ICJ); appeal depends	Judgment, Decision, Opinion
Arb-med	No	Closed	Yes	Facilitative instead of decide	No	Decision or Agreement
Med-arb	Depends	Closed	Yes	Facilitative, then decide	No	
Ombuds	Depends	Usually closed	Yes	Investigative, recommend, counsel	No	Report of Agreement
Public Policy Facilitation (negotiated rule making)	Yes	Open (usually)	Yes	Facilitate agenda and process	Depends on legal rules	Agreement and new regulation
Transitional Justice (e.g. TRCs)	Not usually	Both	Mixed	Record, preside, some rulings	No	Apologies, amnesties, new relationships

e.g. arbitrator or judge as decision-maker or mediator as facilitator without decision authority, and whether *"neutral"* or *"expert" or "interested"* as in "muscle mediation"; whether there are *written or formal awards* or decisions or informal or oral commitments; whether they utilize *formal public law* be that treaty or customary international law or other "general law principles" *Art. 38 UN Statute of International Court of Justice, lex mercatoria*) or only *contractual* or situation specific *rules or norms*; whether they appeal to *rights* or *interests or needs* of the parties; whether they can be denominated *legal* or *political* resolutions; whether any *appeal* to another layer of process is possible; whether the process is agreed to before the dispute *ex ante* in a contract or treaty or agreed to after the dispute ripens *ex post,* and whether the process concludes with a more or less *final outcome* or is more open-ended or *contingent* for renegotiation, revisiting and variations based on changing conditions or premises of dispute agreement.

1. Role of Law and Rule of Law

One major issue in the use and structure of particular forms of dispute resolution is whether decision making and dispute settlement are, on the one hand, based on a set of formal rules of law such as treaty, Security Council resolutions, customary international law, general principles of law and even non-precedential case law or, on the other hand, political or situation specific norms or reasons for settlement. At the most formal level, the Statute of the International Court of Justice (Art. 38) provides the authoritative sources to be considered as "law" for its decisions. At the other end of the dispute settlement spectrum are the many peace agreements which are ad hoc negotiated to end conflict and fighting for situation specific reasons and do not rely on any formal legal source, but simply on political and military pragmatics. In between these two extremes are treaties and formal agreements, contracts, rules of arbitral institutions and compromise that specify both procedural rules and choice of law provisions for what kind of rules and principles of decisions may be applied to particular situations. On an array or continuum, mediation and negotiation are considered the least affected by formal law, and arbitration and adjudication most associated with application of formal rules to particular situations, with varying degrees of reasoned decisions in written awards or opinions. Related to issues of privacy and transparency, discussed in the next section, commercial international arbitration now often applies a form of customary international law, through principles of lex mercatoria, although still remaining mostly inaccessible to non-parties, while international investment arbitration under the ICSID-Washington Convention has now a relatively well-developed and slightly more transparent, with ICSID publishing most investment awards, customary international law of particular doctrines. In international trade disputes through the GATT and WTO, the Dispute Settlement Understanding, creating panels and an Appellate Body (1994) which reviews panel decisions, was until recently considered a very successful and legalized, being "rule-based", system of state-to-state dispute resolution for disputes over trade and tariff actions. The WTO is now facing a crisis of appointments and legitimacy and changes in trade policy which will not leave the system untouched.

2. Transparency, Privacy and Confidentiality

Formal dispute resolution in courts is characterized by public hearings, in most cases with public filings of documents, and in some cases, e.g. the International Criminal tribunals, with public witness presentations and testimony. In contrast, some forms of ADR are conducted in private, such as international commercial arbitration, where the parties choose the decision makers or arbitrators, the rules of procedure to be applied and the venue or "seat" where the arbitration will be held, usually in a law office or conference room. Commercial arbitration cases involve trans-border contracts where one party alleges a breach or violation of an agreement and usually seeks compensation. Involving mostly, but not always, private parties, these dispute processes are designed to affect only those with the actual disputes. Sometimes they involve confidential and proprietary information such as trade secrets and so because this form of dispute resolution originated in private commercial dealings, the default position for arbitration has been to have private settings. One important argument for confidentiality, even in public state to state disputes, is the claim that parties may be freer to state actual preferences in more private settings and may be able to craft on-going relations and new arrangements in private settings. Consider how many peace agreements were achieved in private, not public, settings, e.g. the "conclusion" of the Viet Nam war, when more formal diplomacy in Paris was less successful, and the privately mediated "end" to the US-Iranian hostage crisis, e.g. the Algiers Accord. Also, by design, this dispute resolution process results in an award or decision that affects only those parties in the dispute, given that it may interpret only a particular contract or agreement. There has been much criticism of all forms of dispute resolution that remain private, as theoretically any dispute may have "public" consequences or effects on others, e.g. employees of corporate parties, competitors in the same industry, environmental, economic and health effects on the community generally, etc. As a result, newer forms of ADR have provided for some disclosure of some aspects of dispute resolution, e.g. ICSID investment arbitration awards are now generally published and might arguably have generated a form of more public customary international law in doctrines developed in both treaty and contract interpretation which are visible to the parties and lawyers who work in that field. A few of the newer trade agreements require some transparency and uses of court-like institutions, sometimes after more private mediation efforts fail (Euler, Gehring & Scherer, 2015).

3. Voluntariness (Consent)/Compulsion or Mandate

How parties arrive at a particular dispute resolution process depends on whether they have provided for a particular process in a contract or treaty ex ante before the dispute arises; whether a particular treaty or law assigns a particular process or institution to a particular dispute, i.e. the jurisdictional remit of a court, treaty or agreement; or whether after a dispute ripens the parties choose a particular process. Most of these forms of choice are considered "consensual" or "voluntary" in that the parties have chosen the forum for dealing with their dispute. Increasingly, some treaties and contracts provide for either a "menu" of choice, allowing the parties to select one of many forms of dispute resolution, e.g. Law of the Sea Convention, Art. 280 (1982), or what is known as a "tiered" clause requiring the parties to begin with consensual processes, such as negotiation and mediation, and then moving to more involvement by third parties, most likely arbitrators or adjudicators. In contrast, or in addition to a tiered clause, many treaties and contracts mandate that the parties use a particular process, such as arbitration or conciliation. For example, the Law of the Sea Convention provides that if the parties have not reached a settlement of a covered issue on their own, either party may submit a claim to a court or tribunal having jurisdiction of the issue, including the Convention-created Tribunal of the Law of the Sea, a specialized international court. There is little actual compulsion or command jurisdiction in international law, as even the International Court of Justice jurisdiction depends on consent and voluntary submissions for full adjudication of a state-to-state dispute. And, given the larger issues of enforcement in international law, there is little compulsion in international dispute resolution at the formal level, though both private commercial and investment arbitration, with their treaty provisions for enforcement in national courts, and international criminal law, which still often requires nation-state cooperation for arrest and evidence production, have some compulsory process and enforcement means.

4. Role of Third Parties

When parties cannot resolve their dispute on their own through negotiation and diplomacy they may turn to "third parties" to help them. A third party who acts as a mediator helps the party with their own negotiations, hoping to facilitate an amicable settlement or agreement, usually by managing communication patterns, providing an agenda, and helping the parties review particular solutions to their problem. This is facilitative mediation. Sometimes the mediator is asked to provide an evaluation of the strengths and weaknesses of cases or matter or helps in the provision of specific ideas for resolution. This is known as "evaluative" mediation, usually provided only by agreement of the parties. Another form of third-party intervention is conciliation, which is similar to mediation in that the third party seeks to help the parties resolve their dispute through communication management, often in separate sessions or caucuses. In many legal systems, however, particularly in labor relations, conciliation processes also include the power of the conciliator to actually provide a binding solution to the dispute. This is closer to arbitration, in which the third party does make a decision and usually issues an award and often a reasoned opinion. Thus, the third-party role may be one of assistance to the negotiating principal parties or ultimately can also be more like an adjudicator as decision-maker and, if provided by law or agreement, arbitral awards may be binding. An agreement reached in a mediation has the effect, in most cases, of being an agreement or contract. In a few national jurisdictions, e.g. Israel and Singapore, a mediation agreement meeting certain legal requirements such as registration and notarization may be enforced as a judgment. [The new Singapore Convention (2018) (which so far has very few signatories), allows for enforcement of commercial mediation settlements in all countries which have signed the treaty (attempting to do the same things for mediation agreement enforceability as arbitral awards).]

One of the major issues in choosing third party dispute professionals is whether the mediator should be "neutral" with no relationship to the parties, no bias and a confirmed impartiality to the parties and the matter. In other settings, both state and private parties may prefer a third party who is an expert or knowledgeable in the particular subject matter and thus might have particular relations to the parties. In state-to-state conflicts another state may serve as a mediator employing what is known as muscle mediation, such as efforts to control nuclear proliferation in North Korea or peace in the Middle East, e.g. with the United States "mediating" while threatening loss of economic and other aid. Thus, the role of the "third party" can be variously defined and used and nomenclature should be made clear.

5. Formality, Informality and Semi-formality

Conventional dispute resolution in courts is formal, with formal rules of procedure, argumentation by lawyers and representatives, commitment to the enforcement of particular laws which the court has jurisdiction over, and almost always in public proceedings, open to both disputants and others, followed by formal court judgments and usually reasoned opinions. Informal proceedings, like much mediation and some arbitration, include more direct communication between the parties, without procedural or evidentiary rules, sometimes without lawyers or representatives, and often conducted in private settings with commitments to confidentiality, as well as a "nonbinding" commitment to participate. In negotiation and mediation, for example, the parties may exit the process at any time. A variety of ADR processes are now also "semi-formal" or hybridized in that they combine features of formality with informality. Good examples of formality would be arbitration tribunal rules which can be as complex as formal rules of procedure, and increasingly reasoned written awards and opinions while informality occurs through confidentiality, more direct communication, etc.

International Uses of Alternative Dispute Resolution and Sources of Law

1. Public International Law

Provisions for the use of various forms of dispute resolution are located in many different sources in international law. *Treaties* now routinely provide for some kind of consensual or pacific dispute resolution process either alone or in conjunction with other more adjudicative processes (*UN Charter, Law of the Sea Convention, European Convention for the Protection of Human Rights and Fundamental Freedoms, Art 39 "friendly settlements"; NY Convention on the Recognition and Enforcement of Foreign Arbitral Awards (1958); Convention on the Settlement of Investment Disputes Between States and National of Other States (ICSID Convention, 1965); North American Free Trade Agreement (1993); World Trade Organization and Settlement of Disputes (Uruguay Round 1994); American Convention on Human Rights, Art 49 "friendly settlements (1970)*). Most of the modern environmental treaties provide for processes other than formal adjudication including reporting requirements, cooperation agreements, use of negotiation, mediation, conciliation and arbitration usually over non-compliance and standards before any litigation can be filed (see, e.g. the *Vienna Convention for the Protection of the Ozone Layer, Art. 11 (1987)). International courts* may also suggest, encourage or participate in efforts to negotiate settlements through their own *procedural rules*, as in the "friendly settlement" processes in the human rights conventions of Europe, Latin America and Africa.

In state-to-state disputes ADR may also be used *ad hoc* as the parties negotiate conflicts confidentially, so called "two track diplomacy", and publicly at summits, meetings of world leaders, such as the G-20 or G-7 or specifically arranged meetings. See, for example, the *Rainbow Warrior Dispute (1978–1988)* between France and New Zealand, which utilized diplomatic negotiations, UN ad hoc arbitration, complaints before international organizations (GATT, OECD) and other forms of informal dispute resolution. Such complex cases, involving many issues, affecting states, international organizations, NGOs such as Greenpeace in the Rainbow Warrior Dispute, and individuals exemplify the modern "process pluralism" that may be used to deal with disputes at many levels simultaneously or seriatim. Historically, monarchs, Popes and other international leaders have been called on to arbitrate, on an ad hoc basis, border disputes like Chile-Argentina, and US-Canada, hostage crises (*UN-Iran Claims Tribunal*) and interstate conflicts such as Lebanon-Israel. The United Nations and other international or regional bodies may also be called on to examine disputes in fact-finding inquiries, with or without the power to make recommendations for resolution (see, e.g. *UN Inquiry re Gaza-Turkey*).

Within major *international and regional organizations*, such as the UN, World Bank and others, committees with particular expertise, such as the *United Nations Commission on International Trade Law (UNCITRAL)* or the *International Law Commission* propose *model rules, treaties and other documents* that provide legal sources for the development of both transnational and domestic forms of dispute resolution. For example, *UNCITRAL's Model Rules of Arbitration and Model Arbitration Law* are used as procedural rules in a variety of international settings and also provide legal guidance for domestic legislation supporting the use of arbitration.

2. Private International Law

When two private parties from different nation states contract with each other for commercial or other purposes it is now common to provide for private commercial international arbitration using private decision makers and rules of procedure in the *contract* itself. As a result of the NY Convention for Recognition and Enforcement of Foreign Arbitral awards, now signed by more than 170 countries, such provisions ensure finality ad enforcement in the municipal courts of all signatories. There are many private arbitral institutions (see, e.g. *International Chamber of Commerce (Paris), London Court of International Arbitration, CIETAC, Singapore International Arbitration Center, Hong Kong International Arbitration Centre, Stockholm Chamber of Commerce, Cairo Regional Centre for International Arbitration, Center for International Dispute Resolution (American Arbitration Association)* which administer such private international arbitrations, as well as promulgate their own rules of procedure, evidence and ethics, all of which is private "transnational" law. If such a provision for arbitration does not exist in a contract, parties may proceed with litigation in the municipal courts where they may obtain jurisdiction. National courts must then determine what substantive rules of law to apply, often called conflicts of law, choice of law and private international law. There are some international efforts seeking to afford the same enforcement in municipal courts of foreign judgments with negotiations ongoing in the Hague for recognition and enforcement of foreign judgments treaties.

Recently, a treaty for the enforcement of trans-border mediation agreements has been drafted, the *Singapore Convention* now awaiting ratification, but so far, no international treaty has provided for the full enforcement of judgments or mediation as arbitration. (*UNCITRAL Proposed Treaty for the Recognition of Mediated Settlement Agreements in Trans-border Commercial Disputes—Singapore Convention* (2018).

3. Hybrids

In modern international law, there are now many venues for non-state actors to engage in activities and therefore have disputes with each other. Investors, mainly private corporations engaging in foreign direct investment (FDI) in a country other than their home of incorporation, are now "protected" against certain forms of state expropriation or overly restrictive and discriminatory regulation by *bi-lateral or multi-lateral investment and/or trade agreements (BIT or MLITs).* These are treaties between states which provide for some form of dispute resolution for the private investor to challenge host-state actions which are in violation of such treaties or, indeed, the contracts which form the investment, usually called investor-state arbitration (ISA), the most common being *ICSID arbitration.* This form of arbitration is now regarded as "hybrid" because parties are both state and private parties, and the process of international investment arbitration borrows heavily from private commercial arbitration but is often more public and transparent due to published awards and the development also of an iterative body of customary law. Like the private arbitral institutions discussed above, the International Centre for the Settlement of Investment Disputes, *ICSID,* within the framework of the World Bank, administers most of these arbitrations including providing procedural rules, appointment of arbitrators, an annulment process for a limited review process and other services. In some circumstances, administration of these arbitrations is ad hoc, provided by one of the existing arbitration institutions such as the Stockholm Chamber of Commerce or the Permanent Court of Arbitration.

Notes & Questions

1. See if you can create a map of what kinds of remedies are available in each of the processes described above.
2. Now that you have some exposure to various processes that are available in international conflicts, do you think some forms of process are best used for certain kinds

of disputes? Can you, as is commonly said in the dispute resolution field, "fit the forum to the fuss"?

3. What kind of process would you have suggested for the *Rainbow Warrior* dispute(s)?

In the next chapter(s), we examine these conflict resolution processes in international disputes in greater depth, through case studies and examples.

Further Reading

Robert B. Ahdieh, *Between Dialogue and Decree: International Review of National Courts*, 79 N.Y.U. L. Rev. 2029–63 (2004).

Karen J. Alter, Lawrence R. Helfer, & M.R. Madsen, International Court Authority (2017).

Paul S. Berman, *Global Legal Pluralism*, 80 S. Cal. L. Rev. 1155–1238 (2007).

Christopher Blattman, Why We Fight: The Roots of War and the Paths to Peace (2022).

Jeffrey Dunoff, Monica Hakimi, Steven Ratner, & David Wippman, International Law: Norms, Actors, Process (5th ed. 2020)

Lon Fuller, The Principles of Social Order: Selected Essays of Lon L Fuller (K.I. Winston ed., 1981).

Oona A. Hathaway & S. Shapiro, The Internationalists: How a Radical Plan to Outlaw War Remade the World (2017).

Gleider Hernandez, International Law (2019).

Carrie Menkel-Meadow, *Hybrid and Mixed Dispute Resolution Processes: Integrities of Process Pluralism, in* Comparative Dispute Resolution Research Handbook (M. Palmer, M. Roberts, & M Moscati eds., 2020).

Carrie Menkel-Meadow, *International Dispute Resolution, Vol. III, in* Complex Dispute Resolution (2012).

Carrie Menkel-Meadow, *Why and How to Study Transnational Law*, 1 U.C. Irvine L. Rev. 97–129 (2011).

Carrie Menkel-Meadow, Lela P. Love, Andrea Kupfer Schneider, Michael Moffitt & Kristen Blankley, Dispute Resolution: Beyond the Adversarial Model (4th ed. 2025).

J.G. Merrills, International Dispute Settlement (6th ed. 2017).

Frank E.A. Sander & Stephen B. Goldberg, *Fitting the Forum to the Fuss: A User-Friendly Guide to Selecting and ADR Process*, 10 Negot. J. 49–68 (1994).

Anne Marie Slaughter, A New World Order (2004).

Ramesh Thakur, *A Dispute of Many Colours: France, New Zealand and the Rainbow Warrior Affair*, The World Today, Oct. 1986, 209–14.

Jodi Wexler, Note: *The Rainbow Warrior Affair: State and Agent Responsibility for Authorized Violations of International Law*, 5 B.U. Int'l L.J. 389–412 (1987).

I. William Zartman & Siniša Vuković, Rethinking Conflict Resolution and Management (2023).

Chapter 2

Negotiation

Having outlined general theories of conflict in the previous chapter, we now turn to international negotiations in particular. In this chapter, we try to answer a few larger questions about international negotiation. These answers may differ from those you would receive regarding domestic negotiation and the traditional negotiation theories taught in a dispute resolution or negotiation course. International negotiations can challenge us with their broader contextual and cultural issues and their global implications, and so we begin this chapter by seeking to understand when to negotiate at all. Are there times when negotiation may grant recognition to parties or issues that should not be given a global stage? Will negotiation be effective when a vast power imbalance exists? We use the problem of the *Maersk Alabama* hijacking (made famous in the 2013 film *Captain Phillips*, starring Tom Hanks) to address issues raised by piracy but also by the prospect of negotiating with terrorists, hijackers, cybercriminals, and despots throughout the world. Is it even moral to acknowledge them?

This chapter also asks you to consider how to approach particular negotiations from different orienting frameworks, taking into consideration what is at stake in a given negotiation, the negotiation's context, who the parties and their representatives are, and the inevitable complexity of having multiple parties, as commonly occurs in international negotiations such as treaty development. The respective parties' histories and future plans may also contribute to the complexity, as in, for example, international contract negotiations, and therefore should be considered as well. International diplomacy, or international negotiation, has been written about since there were advisors to political leaders and is its own subject of study, not only in negotiation but in international relations, politics, history, etc. We include in Part II a short selection from *The Prince*, famous for its advice on ruling, to consider what Machiavelli tells us about what makes an effective negotiator.

Often we learn about personalities in negotiation and the importance of trust among the parties. In international negotiation, there are times when this personal connection can make all the difference, while in others, the parties are incapable of trusting each other and yet figure out how to get a deal done. Similarly, culture is an issue that can divide or link together the parties in an international negotiation. Figuring out how to manage these layers of complexity is the challenge, and so we include case studies of excellent negotiators who worked on behalf of the United States in order to illustrate what qualities make for an effective negotiator.

I. When Do We Negotiate? When Do We Not?

Case Study: *Maersk Alabama* Hijacking

The Academy Award-winning film *Captain Phillips* is based on the true story of a U.S.-flagged cargo ship, the *Maersk Alabama*, that was held hostage by four Somali pirates. For five days, the world was glued to their television screens as negotiations over the release of the hostages, including Richard Phillips, the captain of the U.S. ship, ensued.

As you read about the *Maersk Alabama* hijacking below, consider the issue of whether one should negotiate with terrorists at all, and, if so, what negotiation approach should you take?

The *Maersk Alabama* was sailing from Şalālah, Oman, to Mombasa, Kenya, with a crew of 20 Americans on board. Despite warnings to stay at least 600 miles out from the Somalian coast, the ship sailed within about 250 miles of a notorious pirate den in Somalia. On April 7, 2009, several pirate boats pursued the ship, but the pirates ultimately turned back without confrontation. However, the pirates were successful on their second attempt, made on April 8, marking the first hijacking of a U.S. ship in about 200 years. When the emergency alarm sounded, 14 crew members took shelter in a fortified engine room. The armed pirates seized the ship, capturing Captain Phillips and several others on the bridge. Abduwali Muse, the pirates' leader, explained to the captain that no one would get hurt, that they were only interested in money, and that this was "business, just business." Captain Phillips offered the pirates $30,000, a concession that he hoped would persuade them to leave the ship without harming the crew, but the pirates found the offer insulting and rejected it. Attempting to regain control, the U.S. chief engineer tackled the pirate Muse and took him captive at knifepoint. This shifted the balance of power. The crew tried to exchange Muse, the $30,000, and a covered lifeboat for Captain Phillips, but once the pirates settled into the lifeboat, the exchange went awry. The crew released Muse, but then the pirates reneged on the agreement and fled toward Somalia in the lifeboat, taking Captain Phillips as a hostage and demanding $2 million in ransom (the rest of the crew was now safe). The U.S. Navy arrived on the scene on April 9, and a stand-off began. The two ships established radio communication, enabling the pirates to communicate their increased demands to the naval ship captain and FBI hostage negotiators. The FBI hostage negotiators now ran the negotiations. It turns out that a covered lifeboat can be sweltering, and the extreme heat in the lifeboat raised tensions between the lifeboat's occupants. At one point, the captain noticed one of his captors suffering from an injury to his foot. He offered to clean and bandage the pirate's foot, perhaps to build positive rapport with the injured captor. On April 10, the captain took advantage of his rapport with the injured captor and attempted to escape the lifeboat, but he failed. Negotiations broke down on April 11, after the Americans refused a deal proposed by a group of Somali elders in which the pirates would release the captain without receiving ransom in exchange for allowing the pirates to escape. Tensions rose among the pirates, so the negotiators calmed them and persuaded them to be towed by the naval ship. One of the pirates effectively surrendered. The stand-off continued until April 12, when Navy SEAL snipers saw one of the pirates aim his gun at the captain's back. The SEALs killed the three pirates remaining on the lifeboat and rescued Captain Phillips.

Notes & Questions

1. Consider your readings about the *Maersk Alabama* hijacking (or any other hostage negotiation). Does negotiation convey legitimacy to the pirates?
2. The United States has a policy of not paying ransom or making other concessions to secure the release of Americans held by terrorists. How should one decide whether it makes sense to explore the possibility of resolving conflict through negotiation? Do you know whether the United States has ever modified this policy? What is accomplished by announcing such policies in advance (i.e., "We don't negotiate with hostage-takers.")?
3. The *Maersk Alabama* hijacking involved a variety of negotiation techniques. Can you identify when the parties were negotiating? From a negotiator's standpoint, were the negotiations working? What might have happened if negotiations continued?
4. Many piracy situations have been peacefully resolved through the payment of ransoms. One report estimates that Somali pirates were paid between $339 and $413 million over seven years.[1] At the time Captain Phillips was taken hostage, about 250 other hostages were being held by Somali pirates. When should one refuse to negotiate? Are there costs associated with negotiating? What about benefits?

As you read the following materials on whether to negotiate, you will begin to appreciate the challenges involved in making this key decision. Consider the *Maersk Alabama* hijacking and how the facts might fit into the respective frameworks set forth by authors Robert Mnookin and Carrie Menkel-Meadow.

1. Christopher Harress, *Secret Flow of Somali Piracy Ransoms: 179 Hijacked Ships Generated Some $400M in Payments Since 2005. So Where Has it All Gone?*, INT'L BUS. TIMES (Nov. 4, 2013), http://www.ibtimes.com/secret-flow-somali-piracy-ransoms-179-hijacked-ships-generated-some-400m-payments-2005-so-where-has.

In the first excerpt, Professor Robert Mnookin reflects upon September 11th in considering what factors should be addressed when deciding whether to negotiate. As a self-proclaimed "negotiation imperialist" generally in favor of negotiation, his perspective on why and when negotiation is *not* the answer can help us to reflect on the limits of this process.

Robert Mnookin, *When Not to Negotiate: A Negotiation Imperialist Reflects on Appropriate Limits*

74 U. Colo. L. Rev. 1077, 1077–1108 (2003)

In this [article] I would like to share my thinking on some interrelated questions that came to my mind in light of the September 11, 2001, terrorist attacks on the U.S.: What are the limits of negotiation? How should one decide whether it makes sense to explore the possibility of resolving conflict through negotiation? And when should one refuse to negotiate? There is surprisingly little scholarship addressing these questions.

In the present discussion, I narrow my interest to the strategic decision of not entering into the negotiation. The implicit assumption of many negotiation imperialists—that everything is or should be negotiable—certainly doesn't describe the world. In the family, at the workplace, and in the market, many matters are said to be "non-negotiable." A department store won't haggle over the price of its ties and a restaurant won't negotiate the price of an entrée. A political leader may refuse to negotiate with a terrorist kidnapper. Sometimes the refusal to negotiate may be unwise. But sometimes it is better not to negotiate. What considerations are and should be taken into account in deciding whether to negotiate at all? In various contexts, where a party refuses to negotiate, what reasons are typically used to justify that decision? How should a party think about and decide whether to enter into or begin a negotiation at all?

My framework poses six questions that should be addressed, four of which draw from negotiation analysis. Negotiation imperialists—myself included—suggest that in preparing for a negotiation a party should identify its own interests and those of the other parties; think about each side's BATNA (best alternative to negotiated agreement); try to imagine options that might better serve the negotiators' interests than their BATNAs; and ensure that commitments made in any negotiated deal have a reasonable prospect of actually being implemented. These same considerations are equally valid in informing an individual's decision whether one should enter into a negotiation. In addition, one must also consider the expected costs—both direct and indirect—of engaging in the negotiation process, as well as issues of legitimacy and morality.

What considerations of legitimacy and morality should be taken into account? In considering the benefits and costs of the decision whether to negotiate, there is no avoiding questions of legitimacy and morality. One aspect was mentioned earlier: when thinking about alternatives to negotiation, one must consider the legitimacy of those alternatives. A bigger child may have the power to grab the toy of a younger and smaller sibling, but most parents would prefer that the child not exercise that alternative but instead ask to use the toy. A self-help alternative to negotiation may not be considered legitimate, at least without some institutional approval. Few doubted the capacity of the U.S. to bring about a regime change in Iraq [in 1990], but many have questioned the legitimacy of the American resort to force in the absence of U.N. Security Council authorization.

The mere process of negotiation with a counterpart is perceived as conferring some recognition and legitimacy on them. Providing a counterpart with "a place at the table" acknowledges their existence, actions, (and to some degree) the validity of their interests. To avoid validation of interests or claims, countries have often refused to negotiate with rebels or insurgent groups, denying them any recognition or legitimacy. Thus, for decades, Israel refused to negotiate with the Palestinian Liberation Organization, Britain denied any status from the Irish Revolutionary Army, the Spanish would not negotiate with the Basque separatist rebels, Peru would not engage in a dialogue with the Tupac Amaru, and Russia announced an absolute policy of not negotiating with the Chechen rebels.

The policy of refusing to negotiate with terrorists derives not only from the fear of conferring legitimacy or recognition, but also from aversion to rewarding past bad behavior. When previous interactions have failed to satisfy the claims of a party, satisfying its claims under the pressure of violence implies that violence was indeed worthwhile. This consideration, of course, is problematic. Although most of the national liberation movements around the world have employed violence in their struggle to gain independence or self-determination (among very few Gandhi-like exceptions), once violence is employed it usually entrenches political rivals, at least in the short term following violence.

Perhaps the most renowned example of a refusal to negotiate for moral considerations is Sir Winston Churchill's refusal to negotiate directly or indirectly with Adolf Hitler in May of 1940. For Churchill, the refusal derived not only from the questionable effectiveness of such negotiations, given the dismal history of Hitler's negotiations with [British Prime Minister] Chamberlain, or the potential effects of failed negotiations on his fellow citizens, but also from a strong moral aversion to "doing business with the devil." Churchill truly believed that Britain had a deep moral obligation, on behalf of itself as well as the rest of the world, to fight Nazi Germany. In relation to British advocates of appeasement, he said: "An appeaser is one who feeds a crocodile—hoping it will eat him last."

The members of the Taliban were not innocent bystanders. They had been given advance warning by the U.S. government: according to a State Department official who had testified before Congress in the summer of 2000, the U.S. had let the Taliban "know, in no uncertain terms, that we will hold [the Taliban] responsible for any terrorist acts undertaken by bin Laden." There could be little doubt that the Taliban harbored thousands of Islamic terrorists from around the world and allowed its territory to serve as a training ground for armed secret agents capable of terrorist acts in the U.S. and elsewhere. Under these circumstances, there would be moral costs associated with negotiating with the Taliban. Negotiating a deal that would save the Taliban regime would be tantamount to rewarding it for its flagrant defiance of the U.S. and the international community regarding its responsibility for al Qaeda's operations in Afghanistan. Moreover, it would have required the U.S. to negotiate with an intolerant and repressive regime that the U.S. had been unwilling officially to recognize heretofore and which the U.S. had already declared it would hold directly responsible for any future al Qaeda attack. Finally, although negotiation with the Taliban did take place after the 1998 bombing of the U.S. embassies, the nature, magnitude, and horror of the September 11th attacks brought many to feel that there would be something repulsive in negotiating the fate of the chief perpetrator of the attacks with the regime that was complicit.

To conclude, analyzed through the framework offered here, and specifically, by weighing the interests, the probability of a good, negotiated outcome, the available BATNAs, and the costs associated with negotiating, I believe President Bush's decision not to negotiate with the Taliban, and instead, to use force to achieve U.S. goals, was correct. To negotiate with the Taliban would have imposed substantial costs: 1. In deterring future terrorists and those who might harbor them; 2. In maintaining credibility and self-respect; 3. In legitimizing a regime that the U.S. had not previously recognized; 4. In building and sustaining a broad international coalition and maintaining domestic political support. 5. In allowing heinous acts to be the occasion for dialogue with a party that the U.S. believes is at least partially responsible for such acts.

Because of the combined weight of these costs, the lack of Taliban credibility, and the improbability of a negotiated outcome that would serve American interests, the U.S. refusal to negotiate with the Taliban was justified. However, taken individually these costs should not be considered determinative of the decision whether to negotiate. For example, there may be cases where the costs of negotiating with a regime that the U.S. has not previously recognized would be outweighed by substantial benefits....

My basic preference in favor of negotiation remains. For any number of reasons, disputants may tend to exaggerate the potential costs of entering into negotiations and may underestimate the possible benefits in comparison with more coercive alternatives. Indeed, it would be useful to explore both theoretically and empirically this possibility, which if true, might go some distance in justifying the preference of negotiation imperialists. But even if true this would do no more than justify a presumption in favor of using negotiation to resolve conflict. This presumption must be rebuttable.

For too long, negotiation imperialists have implicitly assumed that negotiation always makes sense. This is, of course, nonsense. Such a conclusion would require that the expected net benefits of negotiation are always greater than the expected net benefits of any alternative form of dispute resolution. Negotiation is not without costs, and my primary purpose in writing this article is to suggest a framework for the analysis of not only the expected benefits but also the expected costs of entering into negotiation."

In the subsequent excerpt, Professor Carrie Menkel-Meadow uses the approach of philosopher and professor Avishai Margalit to examine when compromise (and therefore negotiation) is moral. By outlining key questions on context and content, she asks us to consider whether proceeding with negotiation is wise or beneficial. Does your perspective change depending on who the prospective negotiating parties are? Consider also the issues and risks that arise in negotiating with parties or regimes representing inhumane or illegitimate orders. When can we negotiate ethically and morally?

Carrie Menkel-Meadow, *Compromise, Negotiation, and Morality*

26 Negot. J. 483, 496–97 (2010)

If on the nation-state or political level, a rotten compromise is one which "agrees to the establishment or support of an inhumane regime" we can easily apply this analysis to more everyday negotiations. Throughout his book [Avishai] Margalit suggests criteria that should guide all who are concerned about negotiating ethically (with friends and kin) and morally (with the rest of humanity). Here are some of his criteria applied to virtually all of our negotiations and compromises:

- Consider whether the other party (regime) is establishing or supporting an inhumane (or illegitimate) order. When should we not negotiate at all? (With Hitler, Al-Qaeda? A fraudulent business? A non-trustworthy spouse?) Remember that for Margalit, not all compromises with rotten regimes are themselves rotten. Sometimes, because of necessity, we must negotiate with "rotten" parties. How we negotiate and what we negotiate with them are separate questions.
- What is the content of our agreement or compromise? Compromises or deals, even with non-rotten parties, can result in rotten outcomes (agreements that knowingly subjugate others or agree to "unconscionable" terms).
- Who is affected by the compromises or deals we make? Does a deal cause harm directly to the parties to the negotiation or indirectly to third parties who might be affected? (Were the Allies justified in agreeing to Soviet domination of Eastern Europe? How are children affected by bad divorce settlements? Are future generations affected by environmental treaties?)
- Is the agreement coerced and if so, by whom? Margalit draws a distinction between parties coercing each other directly in negotiations from those in which third parties coerce compromises (e.g., those offering aid, security, or threatening worse harms). If "ordinary" negotiations are justified by the concept of consent, how can we know if consent is real?
- What are the alternatives to the compromise or deal on offer? We may think a deal or compromise or negotiation looks bad, or unfortunate (shady, shabby, or shoddy in Margalit's terms) but then again, other outcomes may be worse (war, death, serious economic loss, suffering). The moral assessment of compromise and negotiation is necessarily a comparative and not ideal metric.

- What are the conditions under which we are negotiating? Is there a necessity to negotiate or is it only expedient or efficient to negotiate? The concepts of necessity and coercion are very closely linked here and must be critically examined in assessing when we feel we have to negotiate or when we feel coerced and have literally no or little choice (such as for self-preservation, survival or other moral equivalents).
- How stable is the compromise/agreement likely to be? The concepts of irredentism and revanchism can usefully be applied to all negotiated agreements. Will the parties comply with the terms of the agreement or seek to regain lost value, face or "territory"? Will they want revenge and thus seek to overturn or undermine the deal? No negotiated agreement or compromise is secure if too much is given away or asked for—a stable negotiated agreement must approximate some form of rough or actual justice between the parties to be more than a simple "truce."
- What is the relationship of the intent or words of our agreement (what Margalit calls the expressive part of negotiation) to its actuality? Is it a rotten (or immoral) compromise to knowingly sign an agreement with words the parties know are not likely to be fulfilled? (E.g., Stalin's promise of self-determination for post-war central and eastern Europe at Yalta.)

Notes & Questions

1. Returning to the *Maersk* case study, how you would answer the above questions from Professor Menkel-Meadow? Should the United States have negotiated at all? How should this be determined?
2. The argument is often given that negotiating will encourage more piracy. Yet leaders often face domestic pressure to take action when the hostage has a name and face. Consider the widespread criticism that US leaders faced when the United States would not negotiate with ISIS or the North Koreans for the return of US citizens held as hostages. How should negotiations with the Taliban to effectuate a withdrawal of US troops be considered in this calculus? Does the passage of time help governments (the United States, the Taliban, or both) become more realistic and less positional in terms of negotiation?
3. For another scenario in which even deciding whether to negotiate had moral implications, consider the Joint Comprehensive Plan of Action, informally known as the Iran nuclear deal, signed in 2015 by then President Barack Obama. The terms of the deal required Iran to dismantle its nuclear power program and most of its facilities in exchange for billions of dollars in sanctions relief. Iran, China, France, Russia, Germany, the European Union, the United Kingdom, and the United States all participated in the negotiations, while nations in the region, such as Saudi Arabia and Israel, were left out. Many in the United States were highly critical of the deal. What

factors may have led the United States to negotiate with Iran, a country that it had not previously recognized?

4. Some countries *not* at the table (e.g., Israel and Saudi Arabia) were strongly opposed to this deal. What considerations should be given to other nation's views of whether to negotiate? Does the fact that these nations are Iran's neighbors matter?
5. The United States withdrew from this agreement under former president Trump in 2018. What might this say about views regarding when and with whom to negotiate? How should changing politics and morality or ideas about when to negotiate impact our foreign policy? Would you advise President Biden (or future presidents) to rejoin this agreement? Why or why not? What do regime changes, whether by election, coup, or other type of leadership transition, do to international negotiations?
6. Consider a hostage exchange with Iran in 2023: the US released 5 Iranian nationals from US prisons and $6 billion in frozen Iranian funds to secure the release of 5 Americans held in Iran. Was this a good deal?

II. Negotiation Strategies: To Compete or Collaborate?

In this section, we turn to the decision of *how* to engage in international negotiations. The choice has long been viewed as a binary one—whether to compete or to collaborate—and much advice has been given about choosing between them. Machiavelli famously presented this as a choice between being feared or being loved. The prisoner's dilemma—to compete or to cooperate—also presents this choice starkly. We argue that this binary choice is actually a bit limiting—and also false. Most effective negotiators will have both of these (and other) approaches in their repertoire. As the following excerpt demonstrates, even Machiavelli promoted a flexible approach to negotiation. The second excerpt illustrates how different models of negotiation will depend on what is at stake (the "*res*" of negotiation) and how outcomes can depend on what orienting frameworks are chosen, which in turn affect the behavioral choices made. In the third excerpt, political scientist Robert Axelrod, author of *The Evolution of Cooperation* and someone who is well-known for his analysis of the prisoner's dilemma, exhorts those engaged in international negotiation to compete only as a second choice, forgive often, and choose to collaborate when possible in order to achieve the best possible agreements.

Machiavelli, *The Prince*

61, 68–70, 98–100 (Harvey Mansfield trans., 2d ed. 1998)

In What Mode Faith Should Be Kept by Prayers

How praiseworthy it is for a prince to keep his faith, and to live with honesty and not by astuteness, everyone understands. Nonetheless one sees by experience in our times that the princes who have done great things are those who have taken little account of faith and have known how to get around men's brains with their astuteness; and in the end they have overcome those who have founded themselves on loyalty.

Thus, you must know that there are two kinds of combat: one with laws, the other with force. The first is proper to man, the second to beasts; but because the first is often not enough, one must have recourse to the second. Therefore it is necessary for a prince to know well how to use the beast and the man....

Thus, it is not necessary for a prince to have all the above-mentioned qualities in fact, but it is indeed necessary to appear to have them. Nay, I dare say this, that by having them and always observing them, they are harmful; and by appearing to have them, they are useful, as it is to appear merciful, faithful, humane, honest, and religious, and to be so; but to remain with a spirit built so that, if you need not to be those things, you are able and know how to change to the contrary. This has to be understood: that a prince, and especially a new prince, cannot observe all those things for which men are held good, since he is often under a necessity, to maintain his state, of acting against faith, against charity, against humanity, against religion. And so he needs to have a spirit disposed to change as the winds of fortune and variations of things command him, and as I said above, not depart from good, when possible, but know how to enter into evil, when forced by necessity....

How Much Fortune Can Do in Human Affairs, and in What Mode It May Be Opposed

I believe further, that he is happy who adapts his mode of proceeding to the qualities of the times; and similarly, he is unhappy whose procedure is in disaccord with the times. For one sees that in the things that lead men to the end that each has before him, that is, glories and riches, they proceed variously: one with caution, the other with impetuosity; one by violence, the other with art; one with patience, the other with its contrary—and with these different modes each can attain it. One also sees two cautious persons, one attaining his plan, the other not; and similarly two persons are equally happy with two different methods, one being cautious, the other impetuous. This arises from nothing other than from the quality of the times that they conform to or not in their procedure. From this follows what I said, that two persons working differently come out with the same effect; and of two persons working identically, one is led to his end, the other not. On this also depends the variability of the good: for if one governs himself with caution and patience, and the times and affairs turn in such a way that his government is good, he comes out happy; but if the times and affairs change, he is ruined because he does not change his mode of proceeding. Nor may a man be found so prudent as to know how to accommodate himself to this, whether because he cannot deviate from what nature inclines him to or also because, when one has always flourished by walking on one path, he cannot be persuaded to depart from it. And so the cautious man, when it is time to come to impetuosity, does not know how to do it, hence comes to ruin: for if he would change his nature with the times and with affairs, his fortune would not change.

Notes & Questions

1. Consider how Machiavelli was writing about governing as much as he was writing about diplomacy. How would your advice change in those different contexts? When considering whether to negotiate either the release of hostages or the Iran nuclear agreement, how might negotiators who have to deal with domestic constituencies follow (or not follow) Machiavelli's advice?
2. Does Machiavelli suggest that all statesmen or international negotiators must be guarded adversaries or competitive negotiators? Or that they must be flexible, with multiple repertoires of behaviors? Is problem-solving or principled negotiation possible in international negotiation? Remember that Roger Fisher's ideas for *Getting to YES* came out of his experience as an international negotiator. *See* ROGER FISHER, INTERNATIONAL CONFLICT FOR BEGINNERS (1969); *see also* ROGER FISHER, ELIZABETH KOPELMAN, & ANDREA KUPFER SCHNEIDER, BEYOND MACHIAVELLI: TOOLS FOR COPING WITH CONFLICT (1994); ROGER FISHER, ANDREA KUPFER SCHNEIDER, ELIZABETH BORGWARDT & BRIAN GANSON, COPING WITH INTERNATIONAL CONFLICT: A SYSTEMATIC APPROACH TO INFLUENCE IN INTERNATIONAL NEGOTIATION (1997); F.C. IKLÉ, HOW NATIONS NEGOTIATE (1964).
3. Do models of prescription for negotiation change in different times (e.g., Machiavelli's notion of fortune)? Did we think differently about what was possible in international negotiation models after the Dayton Accords (which ended the violence in Bosnia in 1995), the Good Friday Accords (which ended the violence in Northern Ireland in 1998), and the Oslo Accords (which laid out a peace plan for Israel and Palestine in 1993) than we did after September 11? How about in light of the ongoing violence between Israelis and Palestinians? What makes the times or fortunes change? Events, circumstances, or negotiation models themselves? *See* DENNIS ROSS, THE MISSING PEACE: THE INSIDE STORY OF THE FIGHT FOR MIDDLE EAST PEACE (2004).

The next excerpt describes the analytic framework for considering what is at stake in negotiations and some of the factors that go into choosing negotiation behaviors.

CARRIE MENKEL-MEADOW, NEGOTIATION: A VERY SHORT INTRODUCTION

5–6, 12–13 (2022)

What's in a Negotiation?

Negotiations begin with a mindset or perspective on what is to be accomplished, which in turn affects the choices we make about how to behave, so we must consider different models and conceptual frameworks (note I did not say "styles") of negotiation. This is the "science" of negotiation. We always ask first: what is at *stake* in the negotiation? *What* is the *res* (thing) about which we are negotiating? Is it a scarce resource, or something that can be shared? Can something new emerge from the negotiation (think the American Constitution of 1787)? *How many* issues are there to be negotiated? *Who* are the parties? How many parties are there? *When* do we need an agreement (Now? Can it wait for new information?) *Where* are we negotiating (different legal rules in different jurisdictions? A bucolic retreat or a hostile courtroom?). Most importantly, *Why* are we negotiating? Are we buying or selling, creating a law or new entity, ending a war, beginning, or ending a business or personal relationship? Can we *solve a problem by negotiating?* This is the analysis of any negotiation that must occur before we can decide how to act. There are more choices than just *competing* or *cooperating*—there are "mixed" or hybrid models of negotiation and sometimes sequential choices will have to be made.

Negotiations are not all the same. Beware of those books that tell you "Winning at All Costs," "You Can Negotiate Anything!," "Splitting the Difference," "Negotiating with the Russians/Chinese/French/Americans," "How to Negotiate Anything With Anyone Anywhere in the World," etc. Negotiations come in different types, sizes, situations, and industries. *Contexts* matter in negotiations—how do the subject matter, industry, setting, materiel, routineness, history of the parties and their relationships to each other (and to others outside the negotiation) affect what is possible or desirable to achieve? Do we need a precedent or publicity? Do we want to keep negotiations private (trade secrets, personal privacy, nondisclosure agreements)? How many parties are involved? Are the parties trying to create, preserve, change, or leave a relationship? Does the status, gender, race, class, age, or profession of the negotiators matter in what they think and do? Are the parties negotiating in person, by phone, via text, instant message, email, or on Zoom? Is the negotiation synchronous or asynchronous?

After the analysis, we come to the negotiating "table" (physical or virtual). What shall we say or do? What are the differences between competing, compromising, cooperating, or collaborating (the 4 C's of behavioral negotiation)? So we look at the classic dilemmas of negotiation strategy (overall game plan) and tactics (particular behavioral moves). How should we set goals and objectives, who should make the first offers or proposals, should we use an agenda, what research do we need to do, how do we assess what others tell us (how to trust and verify), how do we develop creative solutions to seemingly intractable problems, when do we concede anything and how do we deal with the competitive "tricks" or bullying tactics our counterparts may use? All of these behavioral choices should be made for a purpose, consistent with planning and goals for the particular negotiation. Behavioral choices cannot be made uniformly or in a vacuum—they are necessarily tied to the contexts and analysis that have preceded any actual engagement with the "other" side(s). Of course, once a negotiator acts and does something, the other side will respond and we will have to consider our next actions. Consider a chess game with potentially infinite moves and countermoves, with the need to react and rethink, but with a clear goal in mind. We consider productive responses, countermoves, and interventions, which include not only the "science" of negotiation, but also its "art."

Analysis (Framework) → Contexts → Behavior = Process → Outcome

Then: Assessment – Evaluation

Frameworks of Negotiation

	Goal	Model	Behavior	Outcomes
I.	Win (Maximizing individual gain)	*Adversarial Distributive/ Competitive*	• Competitive or Positional debate • Arguments/Persuasion • Hiding information • Demands • Threats • Deceit • Few concessions	• Win/Lose • Impasse • Split the difference
II.	Problem Solve (Maximizing joint gain)	*Integrative Problem-solving Principled Interest and needs-based*	• Collaborative • Ask questions • Propose suggestions/offers • Listen • Explore needs/interests • Create new solutions/ideas • Brainstorm • Find trades of complementary interests and needs • Use objective criteria, reasons, principles • Have curiosity	• Creative solutions • Expanded issues and opportunities • Contingent agreements
III.	Compromise-Cooperation (Relationship preserving	*Accommodative Sharing*	• Cooperate • Give In • Make Concessions	• Compromise • Split the difference
IV.	Allocate created resources/ solutions	*Mixed*	• Create, then claim • Trades • Revisit	• Pareto optimal sharing gain • Contingent agreements • Solved problems

Notes & Questions

1. Can you think of particular international negotiations that might fall into one of these frameworks? For example, environmental treaty negotiations, post-conflict peace negotiations, or multilateral trade negotiations?
2. Should all diplomats who engage in negotiation receive negotiation training?
3. What might Machiavelli make of this taxonomy?

Another way of thinking about the challenges in choosing a negotiation approach comes from the Prisoner's Dilemma, explained below in the first excerpt. The second excerpt, from Robert Axelrod, applies the Dilemma to international relations examining the incentives to cooperate or compete.

Douglas R. Hofstadter, Metamagical Themas: Questing for the Essence of Mind and Pattern

716 (1985)

In case you're wondering why it is called "Prisoner's Dilemma," here's the reason. Imagine that you and an accomplice (someone you have no feelings for one way or the other) committed a crime, and now you've both been apprehended and thrown in jail, and are fearfully awaiting trials. You are being held in separate cells with no way to communicate. The prosecutor offers each of you the following deal (and informs you both that the identical deal is being offered to each of you—and that you both know *that* as well!): "We have a lot of circumstantial evidence on you both. So if you both claim innocence, we will convict you anyway and you'll both get two years in jail. But if you will help us out by admitting your guilt and making it easier for us to convict your accomplice—or, pardon me, your *alleged* accomplice—why, then, we'll let you free. And don't worry about revenge—your accomplice will be in for five years! How about it?" Warily you ask, "but what if we *both* say we're guilty?" "Ah, well, my friend—I'm afraid you'll both get four-year sentences, then."

Now you're in a pickle! Clearly, you don't want to claim innocence if your partner has sung, for then you're in for five long years. Better you should both have sung—then you'll only get four. On the other hand, if your partner claims innocence, then the best possible thing for you to do is sing, since then you're out scot-free! So at first sight, it seems obvious what you should do: Sing! But what is obvious to you is equally obvious to your opposite number, so now it looks like you both ought to sing, which means—Sing Sing for four years! At least that's what *logic* tells you to do. Funny, since if both of you had just been *illogical* and maintained innocence, you'd both be in in for only half as long!

Robert Axelrod, The Evolution of Cooperation

7, 30–31, 40–42, 54, 73–74, 110–113, 117–23 (1984)

A good example of the fundamental problem of cooperation is the case where two industrial nations have erected trade barriers to each other's exports. Because of the mutual advantages of free trade, both countries would be better off if these barriers were eliminated. But if either country were to unilaterally eliminate its barriers, it would find itself facing terms of trade that hurt its own economy. In fact, whatever one country does, the other country is better off retaining its own trade barriers. Therefore, the problem is that each country has an incentive to retain trade barriers, leading to a worse outcome than would have been possible had both countries cooperated with each other.

This basic problem occurs when the pursuit of self-interest by each leads to a poor outcome for all. To make headway in understanding the vast array of specific situations that have this property, a way is needed to represent what is common to these situations without becoming bogged down in the details unique to each. Fortunately, there is such a representation available: the famous *Prisoner's Dilemma* game.

Wanting to find out what would happen [in an iterated game], I invited professional game theorists to send in entries to just such a computer tournament. It was structured as a round robin, meaning that each entry was paired with each other entry. As announced in the rules of the tournament, each entry was also paired with its own twin and with RANDOM, a program that randomly cooperates and defects with equal probability....

TIT FOR TAT ... won the tournament. This was the simplest of all submitted programs and it turned out to be the best! TIT FOR TAT, of course, starts with a cooperative choice, and thereafter does what the other player did on the previous move....

The analysis of the tournament results indicate[s] that there is a lot to be learned about coping in an environment of mutual power. Even expert strategists from political science, sociology, economics, psychology, and mathematics made the systematic errors of being too competitive for their own good, not being forgiving enough, and being too pessimistic about the responsiveness of the other side.

The results of [a] second round provide substantially better grounds for insight into the nature of effective choice in the Prisoner's Dilemma. The reason is that the entrants to the second round were all given the detailed analysis of the first round, including a discussion of the supplemental rules that would have done very well in the environment of the first round....

TIT FOR TAT was the simplest program submitted in the first round, and it won the first round. It was the simplest submission in the second round, and it won the second round. Even though all the entrants to the second round knew that TIT FOR TAT had won the first round, no one was able to design an entry that did any better....

TIT FOR TAT won the tournament because it did well in its interactions with a wide variety of other strategies. On average, it did better than any other rule with the other strategies in the tournament. Yet TIT FOR TAT never once scored better in a game than the other player! In fact, it can't. It lets the other player defect first, and it never defects more times than the other player has defected. Therefore, TIT FOR TAT achieves either the same score as the other player, or a little less. TIT FOR TAT won the tournament, not by beating the other player, but by eliciting behavior from the other player which allowed both to do well.

Sometimes cooperation emerges where it is least expected. During World War I, the Western Front was the scene of horrible battles for a few yards of territory. But between these battles, and even during them at other places along the five-hundred-mile line in France and Belgium, the enemy soldiers often exercised considerable restraint. A British staff officer on a tour of the trenches remarked that he was "astonished to observe German soldiers walking about within rifle range behind their own line. Our men appeared to take no notice.... These people evidently did not know there was a war on. Both sides apparently believed in the policy of 'live and let live.'"

This is not an isolated example. The live-and-let-live system was endemic in trench warfare. It flourished despite the best efforts of senior officers to stop it, despite the passions aroused by combat, despite the military logic of kill or be killed, and despite the ease with which the high command was able to repress any local efforts to arrange a direct truce....

The advice takes the form of four simple suggestions for how to do well in a durable iterated Prisoner's Dilemma:

1. Don't be envious.
2. Don't be the first to defect.
3. Reciprocate both cooperation and defection.
4. Don't be too clever.

1. Don't Be Envious ...

People tend to resort to the standard of comparison that they have available—and this standard is often the success of the other player relative to their own success. This standard leads to envy. And envy leads to attempts to rectify any advantage the other player has attained. In this form of Prisoner's Dilemma, rectification of the other's advantage can only be done by defection. But defection leads to more defection and to mutual punishment. So envy is self-destructive.

2. Don't Be the First to Defect

Both the tournament and the theoretical results show that it pays to cooperate as long as the other player is cooperating.... The single best predictor of how well a rule performed was whether or not it was nice, which is to say, whether or not it would ever be the first to defect. In the first round, each of the top eight rules were nice, and not one of the bottom seven were nice. In the second round, all but one of the top fifteen rules were nice (and that one ranked eighth). Of the bottom fifteen rules, all but one were not nice....

When the future of the interaction is not important enough relative to immediate gains from defection, then simply waiting for the other to defect is not such a good idea.... [I]f the other player is not likely to be seen again, defecting right away is better than being nice.... Short interactions are not the only condition which would make it pay to be the first to defect. The other possibility is that cooperation will simply not be reciprocated. If everyone else is using a strategy of always defecting, then a single individual can do no better than to use this same strategy....

Of course, one could try to "play it safe" by defecting until the other player cooperates, and only then starting to cooperate. The tournament results show, however, that this is actually a very risky strategy. The reason is that your own initial defection is likely to set off a retaliation by the other player. This will put the two of you in the difficult position of trying to extricate yourselves from an initial pattern of exploitation or mutual defection. If you punish the other's retaliation, the problem can echo into the future. And if you forgive the other, you risk appearing to be exploitable. Even if you can avoid these long-term problems, a prompt retaliation against your initial defection can make you wish that you had been nice from the start....

The lesson is that not being nice may look promising at first, but in the long run it can destroy the very environment it needs for its own success.

3. Reciprocate Both Cooperation and Defection

The extraordinary success of TIT FOR TAT leads to some simple, but powerful advice: practice reciprocity. After cooperating on the first move, TIT FOR TAT simply reciprocates whatever the other player did on the previous move....

In responding to a defection from the other player, TIT FOR TAT represents a balance between punishing and being forgiving. TIT FOR TAT always defects exactly once after each defection by the other.... What is clear is that extracting more than one defection for each defection of the other side risks escalation. On the other hand, extracting less than one-for-one risks exploitation....

The moral of the story is that the precise level of forgiveness that is optimal depends upon the environment. In particular, if the main danger is unending mutual recriminations, then a generous level of forgiveness is appropriate. But, if the main danger is from strategies that are good at exploiting easygoing rules, then an excess of forgiveness is costly. While the exact balance will be hard to determine in a given environment, the evidence of the tournament suggests that something approaching a one-for-one response to defection is likely to be quite effective in a wide range of settings. Therefore it is good advice to a player to reciprocate defection as well as cooperation.

4. Don't Be Too Clever

The tournament results show that in a Prisoner's Dilemma situation it is easy to be *too* clever. The very sophisticated rules did not do better than the simple ones. In fact, the so-called maximizing rules often did poorly because they got into a rut of mutual defection. A common problem with these rules is that they used complex methods of making inferences about the other player—and these inferences were wrong....

In deciding whether to carry an umbrella, we do not have to worry that the clouds will take our behavior into account.... Likewise in a zero-sum game, such as chess, we can safely use the assumption that the other player will pick the most dangerous move that can be found, and we can act accordingly....

Non-zero-sum games, such as the Prisoner's Dilemma, are not like this. Unlike the clouds, the other player can respond to your own choices. And unlike the chess opponent, the other player in a Prisoner's Dilemma should not be regarded as someone who is out to defeat you. The other player will be watching your behavior for signs of whether you will reciprocate cooperation or not, and therefore your own behavior is likely to be echoed back to you.

Rules that try to maximize their own score while treating the other player as a fixed part of the environment ignore this aspect of the interaction, no matter how clever they are in calculating under their limiting assumptions. Therefore, it does not pay to be clever in modeling the other player if you leave out the reverberating process in which the other player is adapting to you, you are adapting to the other, and then the other player is adapting to your adaptation and so on....

In other words, too much complexity can appear to be total chaos. If you are using a strategy which appears random, then you also appear unresponsive to the other player. If you are unresponsive, then the other player has no incentive to cooperate with you. So being so complex as to be incomprehensible is very dangerous.... Keeping one's intentions hidden is useful in a zero-sum setting where any inefficiency in the other player's behavior will be to your benefit. But in a non-zero-sum setting it does not always pay to be so clever. In the iterated Prisoner's Dilemma, you benefit from the other player's cooperation. The trick is to encourage that cooperation. A good way to do it is to make it clear that you will reciprocate. Words can help here, but as everyone knows, actions speak louder than words. That is why the easily understood actions of TIT FOR TAT are so effective. What accounts for TIT FOR TAT's robust success is its combination of being nice, retaliatory, forgiving, and clear. Its niceness prevents it from getting into unnecessary trouble. Its retaliation discourages the other side from persisting whenever defection is tried. Its forgiveness helps restore mutual cooperation. And its clarity makes it intelligible to the other player, thereby eliciting long-term cooperation.

Notes & Questions

1. How do the structures outlined by Axelrod play out in international diplomacy? Some have analogized trade negotiations to a prisoner's dilemma game. In what other contexts might the Prisoner's Dilemma's strategies fit?
2. What about the lessons of tit for tat? Was part of the negotiation challenge with the Somali pirates their envy of other deals made? Was it the United States' attempt to be clever?
3. Note the story about how British and German troops "cooperated" by not shooting across the trenches in World War I. Have you seen other areas of surprising cooperation between enemies in an effort to mitigate the prisoner's dilemma?

A Note on Two-Level Diplomacy

Any conversation on international negotiation needs to recognize that diplomats are often negotiating with their counterpart from another country, on the one hand, and with their domestic constituency, which may or may not have an opinion (or a voice) in what is happening on the international level, on the other. The cooperation between soldiers across the trenches broke down not because of "negotiations" between them but rather because new domestic constituencies (new generals) came into power. As outlined by Professor Robert Putnam in his article *Diplomacy and Domestic Politics: The Logic of Two-Level Games*, the two levels refer to the interests at the national and the international levels that intersect in a negotiation. On the national level, domestic groups seek to promote their interests by pressuring their government to establish favorable policies while the government seeks to build its power by gaining the trust of these domestic groups.[2] On the international level, individual governments pursue ways to advance their domestic interests while reducing adverse consequences internationally.[3] Negotiators cannot ignore either level, and so each greatly influences a negotiator's decisions.[4] If we consider the pressure that domestic politics brings to bear in international negotiations, we can understand the constraints that leaders may face. Even when leaders might have ideas about best policies, these can be overrun by domestic considerations; for example, domestic politics have played a (perhaps outsized) role in both the Iran nuclear deal (and the United States' subsequent withdrawal and possible reentry) and US policy toward Cuba. As we turn to the next section on establishing trust, the distinctions between personal and professional trust and individual and national trust can also come into play.

III. Trust

Negotiation texts in law and business often promote trust-building measures between the parties in order to promote settlement. Particularly if the relationship is ongoing (as in a joint venture or parenting after divorce), trust is seen as necessary to ensure future compliance. How does this play out in international relations, where personal connections might be made but official relations can vary or even be non-existent?

In this first excerpt, political scientists I. William Zartman and Maureen Berman outline how to promote trust based on years of interviews with diplomats. They show how diplomats can use trust to advance negotiations even when their countries might be at odds (note the similarities between their advice and Axelrod's). In the second excerpt, negotiator Moty Cristal argues that negotiation between adversaries might involve no trust at all and advises how negotiations should proceed in this context.

---

2. Robert D. Putnam, *Diplomacy and Domestic Politics: The Logic of Two-Level Games*, 42 Int'l Org. 427, 434 (2021).

3. *Id.*

4. *Id.*

I. William Zartman & Maureen R. Berman, The Practical Negotiator

28–41 (1984)

Some of the concern about personality and attitude traits comes down to the matter of trust, one of the cardinal underlying characteristics of a fruitful negotiation.... [Here are some guidelines]:

> Trust is enhanced if a negotiator demonstrates a capacity to understand the problems of the other side and help solve them, and brings his own problems as well....
>
> Trust is enhanced if a negotiator can demonstrate a genuine interest in trying to help the other side reach its objective while retaining his own objective and making the two appear compatible....
>
> Trust is enhanced by not threatening or promising wildly....
>
> Trust is enhanced by step-by-step agreements with "accounting points" along the way....
>
> Trust is enhanced by "free offers" to trust....
>
> Trust is enhanced when a party would be taking a proffered action anyhow....
>
> Trust is enhanced when a party can show or be shown that the action is in its interest....
>
> Trust is enhanced when there are no (other) preferred alternatives....
>
> Trust is enhanced by a party agrees to punish violators....
>
> Trust is enhanced when interdependence is increased....
>
> Trust is enhanced when there is an early return on the agreement....

There are many instances when the element of trust between negotiators—even those coming from countries that are not allies—has made a difference. Lord Caradon, formerly British Permanent Representative to the United Nations, recalls such an incident:

> In 1967 when we put forward a British resolution, 242, on the Middle East, we worked of course not only in the corridors and offices of New York, but in all the capitals of the world, the telegrams were going, and we worked over a period of weeks. I thought we had the nine votes in the [Security] Council and we had worked for it and we thought we had got it. We were going in to take the votes on the Monday, when on the Sunday night they called up from my delegation and said, "It's no use." I said, "What's happened?' they said, "At this last moment there is a Russian revolution put down, clearly a wrecking resolution, and extreme resolution."
>
> You go down the next day, in the evening, for the vote. People wait for you to try and get you to make the last minute amendments. No, you can't wait any longer. I still think I have the nine votes.

Then Deputy Foreign Minister Kuznetsov wants to see me. I greatly respect him. Could he see me alone? Certainly. So we go into a little room by the Security Council, and he says at once, "I want you to give me two days." And I say, "Look, ask me anything else, but don't ask me that. We haven't been to bed for several nights and I don't suppose you have either. We've got the nine votes, I think."

I wasn't quite sure, actually, since we hadn't heard from the Latin Americans—we needed the two Latin American votes for the nine. You speak very frankly together on such occasions. And then he said, "I am not sure you understand what I am saying to you. I am personally asking you for two days."

So I wonder what my delegation will think or what my Government will think about it, but I go back into the Council and say that at this last moment a request has been made for a postponement of this all-important vote, and I ask for an adjournment till Wednesday evening.

On the Wednesday you go down—there can't be any postponements now. The first question you ask is, "Who is down to speak?" Syria is down to speak. Then as the long Syrian speech comes toward an end you realize that no one is going to speak. They are all bit confused by the Russian resolution that had been put down the previous Sunday night.

You proceed to the vote, and you vote by raising your hand as you know. You raise your right hand in support of the British resolution because it was down first. Then there is a sort of ragged cheer from the back of the press gallery, and then you realize that it's a unanimous vote. The Russians too voted for the British resolution; that's why he was asking me for the two days. He couldn't have asked me in those terms unless he was going to work with the rest of the delegates; actually, I didn't expect him to do more than to abstain. But when he said, "I am personally asking you for two days," he meant that he was not out to wreck my own initiative; he wanted time to refer back to his government to get support for our resolution. What he was saying to me was a question of trust; it all depended on working together (Caradon interview).

Note this personal connection between diplomats is often highlighted in popular US television shows: consider *The Americans*, *Madam Secretary*, and the *Diplomat*, each of which illustrated over several episodes how connections, even with "enemies," can reap rewards. The next excerpt is based on Moty Cristal's own experiences in the Israeli-Palestinian conflict, an intractable, "wicked" conflict that will be discussed in greater depth in Chapter 11. For now, simply consider his advice on negotiating where trust is a challenge.

Moty Cristal, *Negotiation in a Low-to-No-Trust Environment*

in 1 The Negotiator's Desk Reference 231–42
(Chris Honeyman & Andrea Kupfer Schneider eds., 2017)

We all want trust. We all need trust. We would all like to be trusted. In negotiation, in particular, we all want a trustworthy partner.... [H]owever ... trust ... can and should be considered as neither a pre-requisite for a successful outcome nor as a foundation for negotiation processes conducted in a low-to-no-trust environment.

Low-To-No-Trust Environment: A Definition

In his book "Bargaining with the Devil" Robert Mnookin [excerpted earlier in this chapter—Eds.] presents a comprehensive analysis, as well as prescriptive steps, on when to negotiate and when to fight your devil's counterpart. In domestic affairs, in politics or in business, negotiating in a low-to-no trust state goes a step beyond this, and offers a conceptual framework for negotiations with the devil when you do not have the choice of fighting and you can't establish trust with the other side.

"Low-to-no trust" represents a reality where a party has no alternate counterpart to negotiate with rather than the one whom he or she does not trust. It represents a reality when the other side is someone you know well and with whom you have shared past adverse experiences. Negotiating in a low-to-no trust state means negotiating with someone who hurt you, damaged you, or with whom you already declared war.

A low-to-no trust environment represents a reality which is not just the absence of trust, but rather the existence of a strong, solid and deep-rooted distrust. A low-to-no trust environment, be it in the domestic, business, public, or international arena, is a reality where two or more parties are negotiating in order to come to an agreement, either because they were forced to by a third party (court decision or political power) or because they face a Mutually Hurting Stalemate and both sides see no other alternative that satisfies their interests rather than negotiating an agreement.

Building on this description, negotiating in a low-to-no trust environment would be defined as a negotiation system ("Negosystem") which exhibits a complex interaction of three dimensions (past, present, and future)—across different levels of the conflict (personal, structural, and procedural) that brings it to an extreme state of untrustworthiness.

Past is represented by grievances, mutual damages caused by the negotiating counter-parties, and their constant need to articulate these, refer to them, seek compensation, and most important—allow these past events to dictate not only their current behavior, but also their individual or collective identity.

Present is represented by a series of behaviors which "stir the negosystem", primarily through impasse, reluctance to come to the table, inflammatory statements, coalition-building with third parties in order to elevate one's bargaining power, long ventilation sessions once sitting at the negotiation table, and adopting all-or-nothing negotiation strategies.

Future is represented by the simple fact that the well-being of the parties is tied together. A family court judge once said to me, "One can always divorce his wife, but can never divorce his ex-wife." Their future lives or quality of life, and often those of other individuals, organizations or societies, depends on the negotiated outcome—i.e. the outcome that they will achieve with someone they do not trust.

Therefore, negotiating in a low-to-no trust state means negotiating in a human dynamic system that resides in a permanent state of mutual untrustworthiness. It has its roots in past hurting conflicts, it is manifested in belligerent behaviors across the negotiation table; and yet, both parties need to reach an agreement due to the fact that the cost-of-no-deal is higher for both parties....

The 2009 mini-deal between Hamas and Israel involved release of 20 female terrorists in exchange for a two-minute proof-of-life video of the kidnapped Israeli corporal Gilad Shalit. Waiting impatiently for the deal's implementation, one of Israel's security officers whispered: "I doubt that they [Hamas] will implement the deal. I never trusted them. We are enemies, therefore bound to fight. Not to implement mediated deals." I smiled and said: "Today, they are not only our enemies; they are mainly our negotiating partners". Needless to say, not only was that mini-deal implemented in full, but in turn, a comprehensive prisoner exchange deal was concluded. (For those unfamiliar with this chain of events, the plot of the well-known historical movie *Bridge of Spies (2015, dir. Stephen Spielberg)* follows essentially the same arc.)

You *can* negotiate, and you *can* reach an agreement with people whom you consider to be your enemies or adversaries. That could be a frustrated employee who was fired last week; or a cyber-criminal who tries to extort money for not releasing embarrassing data; or an angry husband in a painful divorce; or a political rival or a violent union leader. Unlike the common thesis in the world of negotiation that calls for establishing trust, and research the importance of being trustworthy, I argue that trust is overrated in the operation and practice of high-tension negotiation processes.

Relying on trust, at least in the setting I describe, could and should be replaced by three other elements:

1. legitimizing the bad feelings, or even hatred, toward your negotiating partner;
2. respecting him or her despite this, as a human being, and
3. building a carefully designed *process* which both sides will own—and hence, trust.

This concept, which I believe is shared and supported by scholars as well as numerous practitioners, can and should be further developed in research and operational processes.

Notes & Questions

1. Consider the extent to which US negotiations with Iran are an example of a low-to-no-trust environment. What would Cristal advise for the United States moving forward? What would he advise for the actual diplomats? In following Zartman's advice, could you imagine developing personal trust?
2. How would this advice apply to negotiations with Russia (formerly the Soviet Union) over Ukraine or China over trade?
3. How would this advice apply to eventual Israeli-Palestinian negotiations?

Cristal uses *Bridge of Spies* as an example of negotiating in a low-trust environment while building personal trust. Yet again, actor Tom Hanks is teaching us how to negotiate!

Case Study: *Bridge of Spies*

(Spoilers ahead. If you have not seen the movie, place your book aside and rent it. Seriously, it is worth it!)

Based on true events, *Bridge of Spies* is a historical drama that depicts the story of an insurance attorney turned defense lawyer for a KGB spy in the midst of the Cold War. The film begins in 1957, when Rudolf Abel is arrested and charged with spying for the Soviet Union in New York City. In an effort to demonstrate that the United States provides due process to all, James Donovan, an American insurance attorney, is appointed as Abel's defense counsel. Donovan, dedicated to the principle that every defendant deserves a proper legal defense, agrees to take on the case.

Throughout the case, Donovan repeatedly visits Abel in jail. Donovan treats Abel with respect by referring to him as "sir" and only agreeing to be Abel's defense counsel if Abel agrees to hire him. In these meetings, Donovan brings Abel a radio so that he can listen to music, pen and paper so that he can draw, and cigarettes so that he can smoke. Donovan learns that Abel has a wife who lives in Moscow and plays the harp. In their last meeting before the sentencing (after Abel's conviction for spying), Abel tells Donovan that he sees Donovan as a "standing man," a man who never gives up no matter the circumstances.

In fact, while Abel is awaiting sentencing, Donovan visits the presiding judge in his home to try to persuade the judge not to give Abel the death penalty. Donovan argues the death penalty is too harsh because Abel was actually acting honorably in terms of his own duty to his country. Donovan also urged the judge to consider the situation in the context of the Cold War: Abel may prove to be useful to the United States for a prisoner exchange. The judge dismisses Donovan's argument at the end of their brief meeting, yet, at the sentencing hearing, the judge shocks those in the courtroom when he sentences Abel to 30 years in prison rather than the death penalty.

And, of course, Donovan turns out to be correct in his prediction that Abel might be useful. Just three years later, in 1960, an Air Force pilot employed by the CIA, Francis Gary Powers, is shot down while flying over the Soviet Union on a reconnaissance mission. He is immediately captured and sentenced to ten years of confinement, with the first three years to be served in prison. At the same time, an American graduate student, Frederick Pryor, is arrested and (falsely) accused of spying in East Germany. Donovan is now tasked with negotiating an exchange of Abel for both Powers and Pryor without the official support of the American government, which refused to negotiate with East Germany or the Soviet Union out of concern that doing so would give them legitimacy.

Donovan arrives in Berlin for the negotiations just as the Berlin Wall is being built and tensions are escalating. After being greeted by people staged as Abel's family (which did not trick Donovan because of his relationship with Abel), Donovan meets with a KGB officer. Donovan opens by requesting an exchange of Abel for both Powers and Pryor; however, the KGB officer pushes back, hoping to limit the exchange to just Abel and Powers. The KGB officer's efforts make it clear that the Soviet government aims to save face with the Americans and give the impression of doing the United States a favor. The officer ends the meeting by offering to relay the exchange deal to Moscow, leaving Donovan unsure and apprehensive.

Donovan then meets with Wolfgang Vogel, a representative of the attorney general for the German Democratic Republic (GDR) which is holding Pryor. The objective of this second negotiation is slightly different from the first. Vogel wants an exchange of Abel for Pryor, while Donovan remains committed to the retrieval of both Powers and Pryor. Again, Donovan leaves the negotiation feeling uncertain.

Donovan and the KGB officer later agree to exchange Abel for both Powers and Pryor. However, this upsets Vogel, who is angered by Donovan's dealing with the Soviets without consulting him as well. Vogel's underlying goal is to gain legitimate recognition of the GDR by the United States, something Donovan cannot officially offer. Donovan realizes then that rather than orchestrating one deal, he is instead negotiating with two parties who each want Abel for themselves.

Donovan's risk taking in the two simultaneous negotiations pays off. The exchange is set. Powers is to be released by the KGB to Abel at the Glienicke Bridge in Berlin (the actual Bridge of Spies), and Pryor is to be simultaneously released by the GDR to American officials at Checkpoint Charlie. Abel is brought to the bridge where he sees Donovan for the first time since before the negotiations. They happily greet each other, and Abel is visibly moved by the fact that Donovan arranged the whole exchange so that he could return home.

But once everything is in place for the exchanges, the East Germans, in an effort to call Donovan's bluff, delay in bringing Pryor. Understanding that Donovan wants both Powers and Pryor, Abel refuses to move until it is certain that Pryor is handed over to the Americans. *Abel is loyal to his American lawyer.* Once Pryor is in American custody, Abel walks across the bridge to KGB officers. Before leaving, Abel turns to Donovan, whom he now refers to as his friend, and tells him that he has left him a gift because Donovan gave him the gift of going home to Moscow. The gift is a portrait of Donovan that Abel painted while he was in prison.

To note, the Abel-Powers-Pryor exchange was not James Donovan's only successful negotiation. In 1962, Donovan negotiated the release of 1,113 prisoners held in Cuba after the Bay of Pigs invasion in exchange for $53 million. Later, he secured the release of an additional 8,500 political prisoners who were held in Cuba.

Notes & Questions

1. What were the elements of trust demonstrated in this case? By whom? To whom?
2. What about elements of no or low trust? Between whom? How does this impact the outcome?
3. As you watch the movie, note the different negotiation styles the respective parties utilize. One could argue that Donovan was well-versed in tit-for-tat as outlined by Axelrod. He started out by cooperating, forgiving violations, and not trying to be clever—he was clear with everyone at all times about his goals.

IV. Culture

This section focuses on cultural differences in negotiations. These next three excerpts discuss the important role culture plays in the negotiation process. Consider what assumptions we might have about negotiating with different cultures and even how those cultural differences may impact a given negotiation. Whether it is Sebenius's warning not to stereotype or Rubin and Sanders's advice to be aware of our own biases, these readings are unified in their warnings against making overly simplistic cultural assumptions.

James K. Sebenius, *Caveats for Cross-Border Negotiations*

18 Negot. J. 121, 122–28 (2002)

1. The John Wayne v. Charlie Chan Fallacy: Stereotyping National Cultures

Start with the obvious: All American negotiators are not like John Wayne and all Chinese negotiators are not like Charlie Chan. Or Bill Gates and Mao Zedong. Or Michael Jordan and Zhu Chen, the phenomenal women's world chess champion who recently also defeated the world's men champion. We also know that some negotiators in southeastern France may bear more resemblance to northern Italian negotiators than

Figure One
Cooperative and Competitive Negotiators of Country X

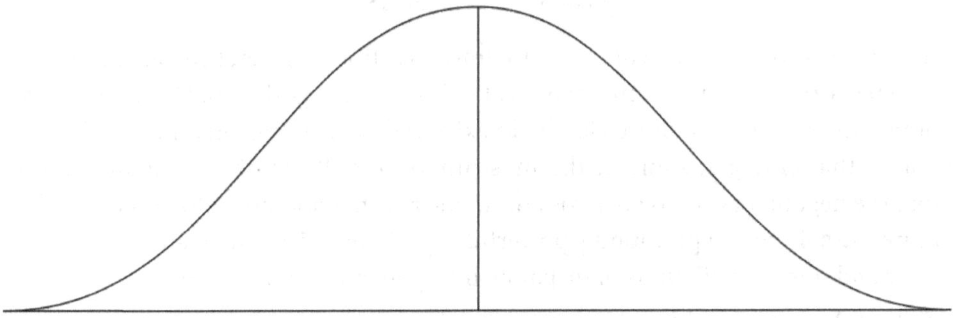

to their Parisian compatriots. Likewise, the culture of Western Chinese Uyghurs is far more akin to neighbors in Pakistan than comrades in Beijing. On another front, what is distinctively "Canadian" when its citizens vary from francophone Quebecois to traditional anglophone Torontonians and to transplanted Hong Kong tycoons now living in Vancouver? In the fact of such internal variation, we wisely caution ourselves against mindless stereotyping by nationality (as well as by gender, religion, race, profession, or age). Even so, in many situations, it remains all-too-common to hear offhand remarks such as "all Chinese negotiators ..." (as well as generalizations about "women ..." or "engineers"). To combat this, a strong version of the anti-stereotyping prescription calls for ignoring nationality altogether in preparing for negotiation.

That advice by itself is too strong. Nationality often does have a great deal to do with cultural characteristics, particularly in relatively homogeneous countries like Japan. The careful work of many researchers confirms significant associations between nationality and a range of traits and outcomes [see, e.g., Brett 2001 and Salacuse 1998—Eds.]. It would be foolish to throw away potentially valuable information. But what does information of a particular group's behavioral expectations or deeper cultural characteristics really convey? Typically, cultural descriptions are about central tendencies of populations that also exhibit "within-group" variation. Suppose that a trait like "cooperativeness" (versus "competitiveness") is carefully measured by a psychological testing instrument for the citizens of County X. The results will be a distribution with a few citizens rating highly cooperative, a few rating highly uncooperative, and the majority clustered around a more middle range.

Suppose that this distribution was a normal or bell-shaped curve with the most likely value equal to the mean of the distribution (see Figure One). Extremely homogenous cultures would be characterized by a "tight" distribution around the mean: the greater the heterogeneity on the cooperative-competitive dimension, the more "spread out" the distribution would be.

Jeffrey Z. Ruben & Frank E.A. Sanders, *Culture, Negotiation, and the Eye of the Beholder*

7 Negot. J. 121, 249 (1991)

The purpose of this brief column is to draw attention to several considerations that should be borne in mind in any analysis of culture and negotiation. Our thesis is that, although differences in culture clearly do exist and have a bearing on the style of negotiation that emerges, some of the most important effects of culture are felt even before the negotiators sit down across from one another and begin to exchange offers. Culture, we believe, is a profoundly powerful organizing prism, through which we tend to view and integrate all kinds of disparate interpersonal information....

Robert Rosenthal and his colleagues have demonstrated the power of expectations and labels in an important series of experimental studies. In one of these experiments, teachers were told that some of the children in their elementary school classes had been identified as "intellectual bloomers," children who were likely to grow and develop substantially in the coming year. About other children (who had been privately matched with the "bloomers" in terms of measured aptitude) nothing was said. When an achievement test was administered at the end of the academic year, a shocking and important discovery was made: those children who had been labeled as intellectual bloomers scored significantly higher than those with whom they had been matched. In explanation, the researchers hypothesized that children who were expected to do very, very well were given more attention by their teachers; this increased attention, organized by hypothesis that the child in question was a talented individual, created a self-fulfilling prophecy.

The label of culture may have an effect very similar to that of gender or intellectual aptitude; it is a "hook" that makes it easy for one negotiator (the perceiver) to organize what he or she sees emanating from that "different person" seated at the other side of the table. To understand how culture may function as a label, consider the following teaching exercise, used during a two week session on negotiation.... During one class session, the fifty or so participants were formed into rough national groups, and were asked to characterize their national negotiating style—as seen by others. That is, the task was not to describe true differences that may be attributable to culture or nationality, but to characterize the stereotypic perceptions that others typically carry around in their heads.

This exercise yielded a set of very powerful, albeit contradictory, stereotypic descriptions of different nationalities. To give a couple of examples, British participants characterized others' stereotypic characterization of the British as "reserved, arrogant, old-fashioned, eccentric, fair, and self-deprecating."... And a cluster of Central Americans listed others' stereotypes of them as negotiators as "idealistic, impractical, disorganized, unprepared, stubborn in arguments, and flowery in style."

Now imagine that you have begun to negotiate with someone from another culture, who at some point in the proceedings simply insists that he or she can go no further, and is prepared to conclude without an agreement if necessary; in effect, says this individual, his BATNA has been reached, and he can do just as well by walking away from the table. How should you interpret such an assertion? If you share the general cluster of stereotypes described by the students, your interpretation will probably depend on the other person's culture or nationality. Thus, if the other negotiator is British, and (among other things) you regard the British as "fair," you may interpret this person's refusal to concede further as an honest statement of principle. The same behavior issuing from a Central American, however (someone you suspect of being "stubborn in arguments"), may lead you to suspect your counterpart of being stubborn and perhaps deceitful. Wouldn't you therefore be more likely to strike an agreement with a British than a Central American negotiator—despite the fact that each has behaved in the identical way?

If there is any truth to our surmise, you can see how powerful the effects of culture may prove to be, leading us (even before we have had a chance to gather information about our counterpart) to hold a set of expectations that guide and inform our judgments. Moreover, once our "hypotheses" about others are in place, it becomes very difficult to disprove them. We tend to gather interpersonal information in such a way that we pay attention only to the "facts" that support our preconceived ideas, ignoring or dismissing disconfirming data....

[P]robably the wisest thing any of us can do to prepare for such negotiations is to: be aware of our biases and predispositions; acquire as much information as possible about our counterpart as an individual; and learn as much as we can about the norms and customs (of all kinds) that are to be found in our counterpart's home country.

Notes & Questions

1. Consider how Americans negotiate. What traits would you say are typical? How is US culture characterized? Is there a homogenous American negotiation culture? How about in diplomacy, legal negotiations, and business negotiations? How does US diversity affect possible negotiation approaches?
2. What biases or predispositions might you have about other cultures? And what biases or predispositions might others have about US negotiators?
3. Anthropologist Jayne Seminare Docherty writes,

    > One commonly used heuristic device for thinking about culture is the iceberg. This model begins with the empirical observation that cultures differ in terms of normative behaviors and other traits, but assumes that these are like the tip of an iceberg. There is much more to culture under the surface of what we can readily observe. Above the surface we find behaviors, artifacts, and institutions. Just below the surface we find norms, beliefs, values, and attitudes. A sensitive observer can "uncover" these and become more knowledgeable about a culture. The deepest level is all but invisible even to members of a cultural group. It contains the deepest assumptions about the

> world, the sense-making and meaning-making schemas and symbols, the beliefs about what is real in the world, and beliefs about how individuals experience the world. This is a useful model, but it is also misleading. It does not reflect the dynamic quality of cultures, which are far from frozen. It also implies that all of the individuals in a given iceberg (culture) share that culture evenly; this is never the case.

Jayne Seminare Docherty, *Culture: Culture and Negotiation: Symmetrical Anthropology for Negotiators*, 87 MARQ. L. REV. 711 (2004). Can you think of some examples (from the United States or another culture) of behaviors or assumptions that fall below the tip of the iceberg?

4. In the two case studies we have examined in this chapter so far, how do you think cultural differences may have played into the negotiations? What kinds of cultural differences should we consider (e.g., national, professional, or ethnic)? In the *Maersk Alabama* case study, do you think it's significant that everyone involved (Captain Phillips, the pirate captain, and the US Navy) was a sailor, or do you think that national differences were stronger than any professional similarities? In the *Bridge of Spies* case study, do you think that the US intelligence officers might have been more similar to their counterparts in the Soviet Union than to the American lawyer (Donovan)?
5. Consider how cultural differences and trust building might also play out in an international negotiation such as the 2015 Iran nuclear deal. A story from US Ambassador Wendy Sherman illustrates how similar cultural constructs can help build trust. Much like British diplomat Lord Caradon, who was on the Russians' "opposing side," Sherman was on the Iranian diplomats' opposing side. Nonetheless, she was able to find common personal ground, which helped to smooth substantive differences:

> Conservative Muslims in many cultures are forbidden by custom from physical contact with members of the opposite sex, however incidental.... These rules don't evaporate when Iranians cross the border, not even when they enter worlds where a handshake can mean a great deal.... In a negotiation as consequential, difficult, and long as this one promised to be, you need to lower the barriers between you and your adversary. Establishing a common sense of mission and shared success is crucial. Unexpectedly, this make-do gesture provided me with a great opening to address the cultural differences between me and the Iranians. One day ..., I turned the conversation with Araghchi and Ravanchi toward our inability to shake hands. I explained that I had grown up in a Jewish neighborhood outside Baltimore, and that many of my neighbors were strictly observant Orthodox Jewish families. Just as in conservative Islam, the Orthodox are not permitted to touch anyone of the opposite sex besides their spouse, child, or parent. Araghchi and Ravanchi were at first slightly mortified to have their behavior become a point of discussion, but as I told my story they were fascinated. They'd never known that they shared this custom with Judaism—understandably perhaps, since fewer than ten thousand

> Jews are thought to still live in Iran.... Talking about the awkwardness of our greeting transformed its significance. These two Iranians knew more about my background. They could see me a little better, not just as a representative of the United States, or as an untouchable member of the opposite sex, but as a human being with a history and an appreciation for their cultural norms. After this, we still bowed instead of shaking hands, but the fact that we could not shake hands became not an obstacle but a point of commonality. Establishing common ground with the Iranians was especially important precisely because our cultures were so different.

WENDY R. SHERMAN, NOT FOR THE FAINT OF HEART: LESSONS IN COURAGE, POWER & PERSISTENCE 38–39 (2018).

V. Skills

In this final section of the chapter, we step back and bring together some of the key skills illustrated so far. The next excerpt reflects on famed diplomat Henry Kissinger's lessons from his career, followed by a case study involving US Trade Representative Charlene Barshefsky.

Carrie Menkel-Meadow, *Deconstructing Henry: Negotiation Lessons from Kissinger's Career*

35 NEGOT. J. 348, 356–58 (2019)

These lessons [from an analysis of Kissinger's career], paraphrased below are:

1. Zoom out to overall strategy; zoom in to counterpart and keep both views in constant alignment;
2. Evaluate and revaluate fundamental premises;
3. Develop deep familiarity with the subject of your negotiation;
4. Take the long view;
5. Adopt a wide-angle perspective (Bigger picture? More parties?);
6. Be realistic and assess the deal/no deal balance (what is attainable?);
7. Don't assume elements of negotiation are fixed; look for "game-changing moves";
8. Evaluate the potential of a "multi-front negotiation campaign";
9. Develop multi-party dexterity, including coalition dynamics, sequencing, and information;
10. Think strategically; act opportunistically;
11. Understand counterpart's perspective, demonstrate understanding with rapport and a relationship, while still asserting own needs and interests;
12. Reconsider the conventional "start high, concede slowly strategy" (in other words, use a well justified moderate, "sustainable" first proposal);

13. Cultivate the art of "constructive ambiguity" and creative wordsmithing and use "tacit agreement" when you need to;
14. Secrecy is a double-edged sword; use it carefully;
15. Be relentlessly persistent (and use as much stamina as you can!)....

This study of Henry Kissinger's major negotiations is important for some of the organizing frames and different metaphors it gives us to try to make sense of an often complex and messy process. So, I conclude here with some observations about what important lessons are, in fact, takeaways, from reading these case analyses of academic (and practitioner) negotiation experts, but also what we cannot or should not learn from the sui generis negotiation practices of a very unusual negotiator.

First, the important takeaways:

1. Negotiation is almost never dyadic. Even when it seems there are only two parties (US-China, US-Soviet Union, Israel-Egypt, plaintiff-defendant, buyer-seller) there are always other parties surrounding the negotiation to be analyzed and "used" (for coalitions, for additional resources, for additional ideas, for motivations, incentives, disincentives and likely for "enforcement" and compliance monitoring). So, "multi-party dexterity" is a must, always.
2. Similarly, almost no negotiations (and certainly no international negotiations) are "one-shot deals." Negotiation (or the need to work with others to get what you want) almost always involves some form of repeat or iterative interaction. Thus, it is foolhardy to not think about what comes "after" the agreement (if there is one). Who will be satisfied with an agreement? Who will want revenge?
3. ALL negotiations require planning and strategic thinking before they begin. Whether or not one requires extensive staff and briefing books for all negotiations, every negotiation has a "before," as well as a "during," and an "after." Preparation and much work away from the table is essential to any negotiation (in my view, regardless of the context and subject matter—this is one of my few "blackletter rules" of negotiation).
4. Planning is substantive, processual (think George Mitchell's elaborate negotiations over the procedure in Northern Ireland), and personal ("zoom in" on your counterparts—know whom you are dealing with).
5. "Zooming out" is also important for almost every negotiation—how is this negotiation situated in any longer-term plan for what needs to be accomplished? What is the sought-after "long-game" or goal? What needs to be done here (and elsewhere), and how many times, and with what other people or parties to accomplish particular goals? Note that Kissinger said if you want something done, go to James Baker (more short-term), but he also said, don't stand between Baker and an objective. Good negotiators think strategically beyond the moment and beyond any particular move or tactic. (Here I heed the advice of Roger Fisher—think of some negotiations like marriage—if you want, need, or

are in a relationship, you need to think of the long term, not "winning" every issue. The same is true for faculty, governmental, as well as organizational relationships and accomplishments.)

6. What are all the "deal/no deal" options? Whatever we call this analysis, BATNA, WATNA, ATNA, or MLATNA ("most likely alternative to a negotiated agreement"), it always is useful to do schematic decision trees or analyses of whatever we can try to analyze or foresee, while realizing that:
7. All negotiations are dynamic. All the planning in the world did not anticipate 9/11 (Pearl Harbor, perhaps a different story). So, [it] is always good advice [to]: think strategically, but be prepared to act "opportunistically" as events, facts and situations change, sometimes gradually (economic conditions); sometimes abruptly. Think about what changes are possible and in what directions, with what needs for likely adjustments to plans.
8. Be hardworking, patient, persistent and, if you can, either be very smart (as Henry Kissinger [was]) or surround yourself with very smart advisors (as John Kennedy did). Listen to your smart advisors (unlike some other unnamed presidents have done and are doing).
9. Think a lot about what the other side wants and says. As so many negotiation teachers and wise people have said: "you never learn much by talking"—listening, both empathetically and substantively, is one of the most important aspects of negotiation. This helps a lot with other important lessons; constantly test assumptions and consider what changes need to be made to both processes and your own goals in light of what you see and hear (and feel).

Now, the caveats or limits of learning too much from one "great"? negotiator:

1. Beware the teachings of "charismatic" singly important, charming, skillful negotiators (or mediators). Personality is yes, extremely important in negotiations (and mediation) and I have seen it have terrible effects, as people agree to things because of the force of personality (or "muscle" resource-based mediation) that later they regretted and tried to get out of. What is the relationship between personality and learning? It is dangerous, in my view, to "mimic" the personality traits of those we think are good negotiators if they do not fit who we are or our own values.
2. International, high-stakes negotiations are their own thing. There is a limit to the applicability of what one (either charismatic negotiators or the hardworking members of the State Department, foreign service, or civil service) does in such settings, compared to the more normal or mundane, iterative, and time-consuming aspects of everyday negotiation, which means that:
3. Context is really important. The lessons derived ... from Henry Kissinger, or with most efforts to generalize precepts useful in negotiation, are often made at relatively high (or bland) levels of abstraction. The sociologist/realist/lawyer in me

always asks—when and under what conditions is that an appropriate precept? Should I always make "moderate/sustainable" first offers? Should I never be secretive? Should I always be transparent? My experience as a law professor and practicing lawyer (OK, so perhaps I am a lawyer-trained negotiator like President Obama or Secretary of State William Rogers) tells me that situations differ from each other (we are trained to "distinguish" one case from another), so that different negotiation precepts will apply in different situations. I have always had some trouble with one of the commandments of Getting to YES—use "objective criteria." Lawyers find "objective" criteria on all sides of "the law" as they argue for different interpretations of the law or try to "characterize" facts. So, using the Lessons to prepare well, know one's own "case" and that of any counterpart, still suggests that every Lesson suggested here still needs to be filtered through a variety of contextual factors in every negotiation.

4. Finally, what are the limits of what this one man accomplished in an ethical (means) and moral (ends) sense? I worry that the characterization of particular negotiators as "great" or "weak" (Chamberlain) after the fact in historical analysis can elide judgments made at the time in the moment. International negotiators, in particular, have to act with the information they have to do what they think is best and then we evaluate (later or contemporaneously) with different information, and with potentially very different individual and collective ethical codes and values

---

It is noteworthy that, for many of you, the primary negotiators representing the United States in high-profile negotiations (secretaries of state, ambassadors to the UN, trade representatives, etc.) during your lifetime have been equally likely to be women as men.

Each of our female secretaries of state has written books reflecting on her tenure and lessons from her experiences. *See* Madeline Korbel Albright, *Madam Secretary* (2003); Condoleezza Rice, *No Higher Honor: A Memoir of My Years in Washington* (2011); and Hillary Rodham Clinton, *Hard Choices: A Memoir* (2015). While reflecting specifically on what was different about serving as a female secretary of state, each noted that strong diplomatic skills are required for the role, regardless of gender. The debate over what skills are needed in negotiation, and whether they are masculine or feminine traits, dates back at least to Machiavelli, who noted that excellent leaders needed both *virtú* (virtue) and *fortuna* (fortune), which were considered masculine and feminine traits, respectively.

We now turn to a story from US Trade Representative Charlene Barshefsky, who served from 1997 to 2001 and was well known for having excellent negotiation skills and being persistent, particularly in dealing with Chinese representatives, over the course of her tenure. In 2020, the *Negotiation Journal* devoted significant space comprising multiple essays that all reflected on an incident involving Barshefsky, the Chinese, and the negotiation of intellectual property rights. As you read Barshefsky's account, consider the skills outlined by Carrie Menkel-Meadow above.[5]

Case Study: U.S.-China Trade Talks

Charlene Barshefsky was engaging in intellectual property rights trade talks with China regarding China's entry to the World Trade Organization when the negotiations reached a tense and critical point. At about 2 am, Barshefsky's Chinese counterpart became very angry and physically lunged toward her. He pounded on the table and demanded, "That's it, take it or leave it!" (Before we continue with the story, take a moment to think about how you might have responded to this behavior and consider the choices you think Barshefsky could have made. Should she have matched his anger and pounded the table back, stormed out, or taken the proposal in order to make the deal?)

Barshefsky's reaction to her counterpart's outburst surprises most people. She sat still and remained silent. She recalls that she waited until her heart stopped pounding because she was afraid that if she spoke too soon, she would reveal her vulnerability through her wavering voice. The 30 or 40 seconds of silence allowed Barshefsky to evaluate her next move. She decided to reframe her counterpart's words and replied,

> Well, if you're saying take it or leave it, well, obviously I have to leave it. But I don't think that's what you meant. I don't really think you mean take it or leave it in the sense that we should no longer be talking about this issue.... I think what you're conveying to me, and I appreciate fully, is that we probably ... that I need to give your proposal very serious thought. And that if I can't give it serious thought well then maybe we shouldn't be talking anymore. And I think you're right. I think any proposal you make to me I should give serious thought. I don't think this is gonna work but I don't want to say that here because you've made it clear you want me to think about this and I intend to do that. Why don't we break and meet again in the morning.

Barshefsky realized that her counterpart knew he had made a mistake, and she perceived that he felt relief after she gave her response. Following this impasse, the two parties were able to move forward and reach an agreement.

Commentators have noted Barshefsky's wisdom in not escalating the situation while providing grace for her counterpart who had made a strategic mistake. Kenneth Sharpe called this "a lesson in practical wisdom for negotiations."[6] She exem-

5. Kenneth Sharpe, *Learning the Wisdom to Seize the Moment: How Negotiators Encourage the Learning of Practical Wisdom for Themselves and Others*, 36 NEGOT. J. 169, 171 (2020).

6. *Id.* at 170.

plified patience, empathy, and self-control in the face of a thoughtless, threatening incident.[7] She gave herself the time to reflect and deliberate on how to respond, and she acted on those choices with composure.[8] Barshefsky remembered what was at stake and committed to reaching an agreement even though she could have easily let the negotiations fail.

Other commentators have noted that Barshefsky's story illustrates more than just wisdom. They believe it reveals a skill and perspective that is deeply gendered. Barshefsky's non-combative response to her male counterpart's violent action is all too familiar to many American women who have learned to deflect and evade male aggression or to act as if no aggression has even occurred.[9] They understand that the best response in certain situations is to act and speak in ways that will soothe the ego and allow the other to maintain some dignity. These commentators argue that in the male-dominated field of negotiation, this inherently gendered, feminine characteristic is also a crucial skill for successful negotiators. What do you think? Have society's expectations of women changed since the 1990s when this story occurred? If so, what advice would you give to Barshefsky now?

Further Reading

Christine Bell, The Law of Peace: Peace Agreements and the *Lex Pacificatoria* (2008).

Jeanne M. Brett, Negotiating Globally: How to Negotiate Deals, Resolve Disputes, and Make Decisions across Cultural Boundaries (1st ed. 2001, 3d ed. 2014).

Complex Dispute Resolution: International Dispute Resolution (Carrie Menkel-Meadow ed., 2011).

Stuart Eisenstadt, The Art of Diplomacy: How American Negotiators Reached Historic Agreements that Changed the World (2024).

Roger Fisher, William Ury, & Bill Patton, Getting to YES: Negotiating Agreement without Giving In (3d ed. 2011).

Victor Kremenyuk, International Negotiation: Analysis, Approaches, Issues (2002).

Avishai Margalit, On Compromises and Rotten Compromises (2010).

Paul Meerts, Diplomatic Negotiations: Essence and Evolution (2019).

Carrie Menkel-Meadow, Very Short Introduction to Negotiation (2022).

Carrie Menkel-Meadow, Andrea Kupfer Schneider, & Lela P. Love, Negotiation: Processes for Problem Solving (3d ed. 2020).

7. *Id.* at 171.
8. *Id.*
9. *Id.*

Robert Mnookin, Bargaining with the Devil: When to Negotiate, When to Fight (2010).

Gary Noesner, Stalling for Time: My Life as an FBI Hostage Negotiator (2018).

Roland Pennock & John Chapman, NOMOS: Compromise in Ethics Law and Politics (1979).

Public International Law & Policy Group, The International Negotiations Handbook: Success through Preparation, Strategy and Planning (2007).

Jeswald Salacuse, The Global Negotiator: Making, Managing and Mending Deals Around the World in the Twenty-First Century (1998).

Joseph Siracusa, Diplomacy: A Very Short Introduction (2010).

Frederick Stanton, Great Negotiators: Agreements that Changed the Modern World (2010).

Emmanuel Vivet, Landmark Negotiations from Around the World: Lessons for Modern Diplomacy (2019).

Elsa Walsh, *The Negotiator*, The New Yorker, Mar. 18, 1996, at 86–97.

Chapter 3

Mediation and Conciliation

When parties in conflict, be they nations, organizations, or individuals, cannot resolve their differences with negotiations, they often turn to a third party for assistance in resolving their dispute(s). Third-party assistance can take many forms. In other chapters, we explore formal adjudication (where formal judges or tribunals "decide" on who is right and owes something to other parties), arbitration (where private parties or appointed officials decide issues of conflict between parties, which are usually binding decisions), and hybrid combinations of these forms of dispute resolution (such as use of public-private arbitration panels, Ombuds, treaty-based monitoring commissions, and new forms of restorative justice that seek to provide reconciliation, and not adjudication, between parties).

In this chapter, we focus on two more or less voluntary processes: in the first one, the third party facilitates negotiation and problem-solving among the parties in conflict (*mediation*) or becomes involved in encouraging particular resolutions (*evaluative* or *muscle mediation*), and in the second one, the third party has some authority to command or strongly suggest particular outcomes, as in some forms of international *conciliation* processes. In many countries, conciliation is a process where employers and trade unions are convened, usually along with government agencies, to negotiate wages, hours, and other terms and conditions of employment (it is a process often used in labor-management relations). If the parties fail to reach an agreement, the conciliators may be empowered (usually by statute) to impose terms. Some international disputes may be governed by similar rules, or the parties may agree to use such processes (see *Tesoro* case below) which may also be called *med-arb* (mediation-arbitration) or *binding evaluative mediation*. The key to this process is that the choice of some form of mediation be *voluntary*; in its purest form, *facilitative mediation*, the parties decide on their own (i.e., without the command of the third party) whether or not to make an agreement.

The mediation process is used in both *private international disputes* (e.g., commercial disputes) and *public disputes* (disputes involving states, such as violent conflicts, environmental issues, and investment and trade disputes). One of the many important issues in the use of mediation is deciding what kind of a mediator will be acceptable to the parties (as usually the parties choose their own mediators). Many mediators are chosen for their "neutrality," which is why mediators are often called "third-party neutrals." Increasingly, however, parties (individuals, companies, and states) may decide that they want a mediator who has expertise in the matter in question and who may be well-known to the parties. It is also possible in many complex disputes for there to be a panel or group of mediators (as in the mediation efforts employed to reach the Good Friday Accords in Northern Ireland). Questions may arise about who is qualified to mediate a dispute (e.g., a United Nations official, or a former head of state, such as when then president Bill Clinton asked former president Jimmy Carter to engage in nuclear talks with North Korea), who has some "authority" in the eyes of the parties to "encourage" enforcement of any agreement, and whether it is better to utilize a mediator who has no prior relationship with the parties in order to avoid bias or the appearance of bias. These ideas about appropriate mediators (their level of expertise, authority to enforce or monitor agreements, and prior relations with the parties) vary from situation to situation and also may be culturally based. Some cultures have used mediative conflict resolution processes for centuries ("it takes a village" in Africa, or Confucian harmony-preserving dispute resolution processes in China); for others, these forms of consensual conflict resolution may be relatively new. However, the expectation in almost all mediation, whatever its form, is that the parties have agreed to enlist the services of someone else to help them negotiate a resolution to their conflict(s).

This chapter introduces you to some of the ways mediation has been used in international conflicts and exposes you to some of the issues that may arise when dispute resolution processes are supposed to be voluntary, consensual, and based on notions of self-determination of the parties. Different mediators may use very different skills, techniques, and processes (elaborated below). Some examples are Henry Kissinger's shuttle diplomacy (use of separate meetings or caucuses) in the Middle East; Jimmy Carter's use of a "one-text" negotiating procedure at the 1978 Camp David Egypt-Israel peace talks; George Mitchell's participatory, consensus-based processes in Northern Ireland; Richard Holbrooke's more coercive processes in the Dayton Accords; and the mediative processes suggested by multiparty participation in environmental-resources disputes (e.g., law-of-the-sea processes) or in facilitated-treaty formation and multinational agreements. As was noted in Chapter 2, some disputes are more distributive (as when there are scarce resources), while some are more likely to allow trades, contingent agreements, or resource-expanding solutions; therefore, analysis of what is at stake is an important element in deciding what kind of mediation process and what kind of mediator to choose. All mediation processes raise important questions about consent, compliance, and enforcement. Mediated agreements are often kept confidential (by agreement of the parties), and there is always a question about whether a dispute can or should be resolved only by the parties involved or whether public or third-party interests might militate in favor of using more public or transparent processes. Thus, policy and ethical issues are implicated in the decision to choose mediation as a conflict resolution process. Though mediation is often thought of as an "informal" dispute resolution process, when international organizations, such as the United Nations, the International Chamber of Commerce (ICC), or the Centre for the Settlement of Investment Disputes (ICSID), sponsor mediative processes, they may also provide rules, guidelines, or standards for their use.

I. What Type of Mediation? What Kind of Mediator?

As mentioned above, various types of mediation formats and mediators are available to facilitate an appropriate mediation for the conflict at hand. Because each comes with its own set of advantages and disadvantages, it is important to identify the interests and needs of the parties when trying to decide which format and type of mediator is most suitable.

Mediation acknowledges that conflicts are complex and varied. At the end of the day, it is the willingness between the parties that determines the success of a resolution. The following excerpt identifies several fundamentals that contribute to the success of a mediation.

United Nations Guidance for Effective Mediation

3, 23–24 (2012), https://peacemaker.un.org/guidance-effective-mediation

The Guidance identifies a number of key fundamentals that should be considered in a mediation effort: preparedness, consent, impartiality, inclusivity, national ownership, international law and normative frameworks; coherence, coordination, and complementarity of the mediation effort; and quality peace agreements.... Throughout, the Guidance recognizes the complexity of the environment within which mediators work and that in many instances mediators confront problems and difficulties they may not be able to resolve. Each situation must be approached differently and ultimately the political will of the conflict parties is the determining factor for success....

The Guidance identifies some key fundamentals for effective mediation and provides some suggestions as to how they may be applied in practice. It makes the case for mediators to have expertise and professional support and recognizes the need for careful assessment, proper planning and regular monitoring and evaluation in order to enhance the chances for success and minimize mediator error. The importance of a supportive external environment for the mediation process is underscored, with emphasis placed on the need for cooperation among entities involved in mediation. While all these factors are important, the success or failure of a mediation process ultimately depends on whether the conflict parties accept mediation and are committed to reaching an agreement. If the parties are genuinely willing to explore a negotiated solution, [a] mediator can play an invaluable role.

[The fundamentals are]:

- Preparedness
- Consent
- Impartiality [which is not necessarily neutrality]
- Inclusivity
- National ownership

- International law and normative frameworks
- Coherence, coordination and complementarity of the mediation effort
- Quality peace agreements

The United Nations Department of Political Affairs has recently issued a series of initiatives for enhancing the use of mediation in peace-seeking and peacekeeping settings, including a special Mediation Support Unit and specific mediation guidance and guidelines on particular issues. *See, e.g.*, UN Dep't Pol. Affairs, *Guidance for Mediators: Addressing Conflict-Related Sexual Violence in Ceasefire and Peace Agreements* (2012), https://peacemaker.un.org/node/1447.

Notes & Questions

1. What do you think of these concepts for guiding mediation sponsored by the United Nations?
2. Can you think of other fundamental principles that have been left out?
3. Do you think it is more or less effective to have formal international organizations, rather than particular individuals, conduct mediations?
4. What different contexts might call for different forms of mediation or different kinds of mediators? See some of the case studies below.

Case Study: Chagos Archipelago

Consider the complex, multi-party dispute over the Chagos Archipelago (described below), which has been the subject of several different processes, including bilateral negotiations; domestic litigation under the U.S. Alien Tort Statute; appeals to the European Court of Human Rights; arbitration; and, most recently, a 2019 advisory opinion from the International Court of Justice, *Advisory Opinion on the Legal Consequences of the Separation of the Chagos Archipelago from Mauritius* (Feb. 25, 2019).

The Chagos Archipelago consists of 65 islands located approximately 1,200 miles from Mauritius. Between 1965 and 1968, the government of Mauritius negotiated for its independence from British colonial rule, in what is now known as the Lancaster House Agreement. Unbeknownst to the Mauritians at the time, the United States had entered into secret talks with the British government to detach the Chagos islands from Mauritius so that it could build a military base there. The U.K. government guaranteed the Chagos islands to the United States (without inhabitants) and transformed the Lancaster House Agreement into a *fait accompli*: the Mauritians would receive independence from colonial rule in exchange for the Chagos islands. On November 8, 1965, Mauritius received

$3 million in compensation for signing away the islands. The United Kingdom then merged the Chagos islands into a quasi-colonial territory known as the British Indian Ocean Territory. Between 1965 and 1973, the Chagossians were forcibly relocated to make way for the U.S. military base.

Today, the United Kingdom claims it had a legal right to detach the Chagos Archipelago from Mauritius without the latter's consent. The Mauritians claim the deal was in contravention of international norms governing decolonization and the right to self-determination; thus, sovereignty over the islands belongs to them. The Chagossians argue that their forcible removal from the islands was contrary to international law. Additionally, the Mauritian government contends that the Lancaster House Agreement should be void based on coercion and fraud, especially since the British government made no mention that the islands' inhabitants would never be able to return after being relocated. The U.K. government has taken the position that Mauritius's acceptance of money waived its claims to the islands, and even if it didn't, the United Kingdom has had sovereignty since 1814, when it assumed power over Mauritius from France.

This dispute is far from over. In February 2022, nearly 50 years after Chagossians were forced to abandon the islands, five original inhabitants, without prior authorization from the U.K. government, set foot on the sandy beaches of the place they call home. For further discussion of this international dispute, see Philippe Sands, *The Last Colony—A Tale of Exile Justice and Britain's Colonial Legacy* (2023).

Could this dispute be mediated? If so, by whom (persons, countries, institutions)? With what possible outcomes? Who has an interest in the resolution of this dispute?

II. Mediation Processes, Tools, and Techniques

A. State-to-State or Diplomatic Mediation

A key feature of mediation, especially in the international context, is the inclusion of an unbiased third-party facilitator. Countries, non-profits, and international figures are some of the many third-party facilitators that can be utilized to encourage problem-solving. The following article highlights how facilitators can be used and notes a common strategy employed by mediators.

Roger Fisher, Elizabeth Kopelman, & Andrea Kupfer Schneider, Beyond Machiavelli: Tools for Coping with Conflict

123–31 (1994)

Players who are not principals in a conflict can play a wide range of constructive roles. Third-party interventions can contribute to problem-solving by making sure that disputants attack the problem rather than each other, and by keeping the focus on interests rather than on positions. Some roles are purely administrative, such as the functions associated with hosting a Devising Session or a conference. Other roles engage the third party in the substance of the dispute.

In a world filled with ready-made dispute resolution procedures, it is important to look beyond the labels of "alternative dispute resolution," "negotiation," "mediation," and "arbitration" when considering useful roles for third parties. [The chart below] ... illustrates a variety of roles that third parties can play, ranging from primarily process-oriented ones, such as hosting a diplomatic conference, to primarily substance-oriented ones, such as monitoring compliance after an agreement. In any action plan involving the participation of a third party, what is most important is to design a role for the third party that addresses the particular diagnosis of why a given conflict has not been settled....

Some Third-Party Roles for Coping with a Conflict

Range of roles	Examples	Who might play them
Primarily process-oriented roles	Hosting a diplomatic conference	Another government
	Developing tools for the parties to use in diagnosing their conflict	Academic institutions
	Facilitating a brainstorming session	A trained facilitator
Mixed process and substantive roles	Holding a devising session to develop a range of options for the parties' consideration	A nonprofit foundation
	Facilitating a one-text procedure	A prominent international figure
	Providing peace-keeping forces to maintain a ceasefire while negotiations continue	The U.N. or a regional group such as the OAS
Primarily substance-oriented roles	Providing neutral evaluation of the merits of parties' claims	A professional association or specialized arbitration organization
	Providing a binding decision for outstanding issues in a dispute	The World Court

One way in which third parties often try to assist the parties is in mediating between them. The mediation technique perhaps most commonly used by third parties—concession hunting—often fails because it does not address the underlying interests of the disputants that have impeded a settlement. Focusing on positions rather than interests, this strategy tries to persuade the parties to give up bits of their opposing positions piece by piece. The goal is to edge the parties' positions toward each other until they eventually converge....

Most players, in anticipation of this common strategy, adopt extreme positions from which they will later be able to make concessions without giving up anything important. Unfortunately, the "fat" that was originally included in order to pad a position is likely, through the process of public debate and commitment to one's constituents, to harden into "bone" that is now difficult to cut away....

It is easy to see how this process encourages foot-dragging and haggling. This concession-hunting process tends to foreclose the possibility of generating creative options—the possibility that the pie can be enlarged through joint problem-solving.

A better process can change the choice. Rather than talking about two plans that reflect extreme partisan perceptions, it is usually better to talk about one plan that reflects some third party's judgment of what options might be acceptable to both sides. [The intervenor can] listen to the two parties discuss their individual and joint interests, and then ... produce a rough draft of points that might be included in a partnership agreement. This draft would be an open draft for all to discuss.... Over the ensuing days and weeks, the mediator refines the draft by circulating among the parties, learning of concerns they may still have, and drafting new language designed to meet them as best he can. When the mediator feels that they cannot improve the draft any further—that it is fair, workable, and reconciles their conflicting interests as well as possible—he polishes the text and presents a final document to the parties for their approval....

The One-Text Process was used by President Carter and Secretary of State Cyrus Vance at the 1978 Camp David negotiations between President Anwar Sadat of Egypt and Prime Minister Menachem Begin of Israel. The U.S. negotiating team prepared some twenty-three consecutive drafts or redrafts of parts of a text over ten days, each responding to some point raised by a party. On the last day, President Carter decided that this was the best he could do and asked each party to agree. A few hours later, the Camp David Accords were signed.

Some differences between the widely used strategy of hunting for concessions and the One-Text procedure are summarized below.

Two Ways of Generating a Draft Proposal

Concession-hunting	One-text
Ask the parties for their positions and proposals.	Ask the parties about their interests and concerns.
Focus discussion on each party's position.	Focus discussion on a single text aimed at reconciling conflicting interests and developing joint gains.
In turn, ask each party for a concession.	Ask each party to criticize the text wherever it fails to meet a legitimate interest.
Communicate the concessions obtained.	Prepare a revised single text in light of criticism and suggestions.
Repeat the process of pressing the first one and then the other party for more concessions.	Repeat the process of revision until [you] have the best draft you can prepare.
Press one party or the other for a final concession to produce an agreement between the original positions of the parties.	Ask each party to accept the final draft if the other will. The final agreement may bear no relationship to the parties' original positions.

In some cases, a mediator might want to employ a variation on the One-Text Process by producing two alternative drafts. These would not reflect partisan positions but, starting from different assumptions, would seek to meet as well as possible the interests of both parties. An architect, for example, might develop in parallel two alternative plans for his client, one a single-story house, the other a two-story house. Or, a mediator working on a long-term settlement of the Palestinian-Israeli conflict might similarly develop parallel drafts of two possible treaties. One would seek to meet Palestinian interests in acceptance, equality, self-government, and so forth without establishing a wholly independent sovereign Palestinian state. The other might start with such a state and then consider how best to meet Israeli interests, particularly in security, through provisions about neutrality, mutual inspection, restrictions on weapons, and so on. If the parties become unable to choose between the two texts, they might go to the Security Council for its recommendation or decision....

The article below exemplifies how two seemingly similar third-party facilitators can diverge on their methods of mediation yet still be successful. Both George Mitchell and Richard Holbrooke achieved success in facilitating peace in the context of two different European ethnic and religious conflicts; however, the strategies, roles, and means each used to achieve that peace directly conflicted with one other.

Daniel Curran, James K. Sebenius, & Michael Watkins, *Case Analysis: Two Paths to Peace: Contrasting George Mitchell in Northern Ireland with Richard Holbrooke in Bosnia-Herzegovina*

20 Negot. J. 513–31 (Oct. 2004)

In August 1995, Richard Holbrooke stepped in to lead a new, aggressive attempt to negotiate peace [in Bosnia-Herzegovina], ultimately backed up by North Atlantic Treaty Organization (NATO) air assaults and economic sanctions. After three months of frenetic shuttle diplomacy, Holbrooke and his team were able to negotiate a series of agreements on basic principles and a cease-fire that ultimately led to the Dayton Accords, ending the bloodiest European conflict since World War II; in total, the Balkan wars caused more than 100,000 deaths.

At roughly the same time, George Mitchell was agreeing to chair a British-Irish effort to break the deadlock on the issue, which had become the most significant roadblock to peace in Northern Ireland—the decommissioning of weapons by both sides in the conflict. In 1995, Mitchell was about to step into a three-hundred-year-old feud between a largely Catholic nationalist minority, which wanted the province to become part of Ireland, and the mainly Protestant unionist majority, which wanted the province to remain part of the United Kingdom. Paramilitary groups on both sides had been conducting terrorist attacks since the late 1960s in this slow-burning conflict that had cost more than three thousand Catholic and Protestant lives. Ten parties and two governments were involved in the peace process. Many of these parties refused to talk with each other, in some cases, those on the same side attacked each other, and a virtual chasm yawned between the negotiating positions on major issues.... An excruciating two-year process to define the rules and agenda for the talks ensued while the participants slowly disentangled the contentious issues. Finally, the parties made a two-week sprint to a final agreement by the self-imposed deadline of Easter 1998.

At least superficially, the efforts of George Mitchell in Northern Ireland and Richard Holbrooke in Bosnia offer strong similarities. Two white, male, Democratic, U.S. citizens assumed third-party roles in ethnic and religious conflicts in Europe in the latter half of the 1990s. Each man took actions leading to what most observers would regard as a provisional success—at least over the short to medium term, and certainly relative to violent alternatives. Yet, the personalities of these two men could hardly be more different nor could they have taken more divergent approaches to their roles....

Theoretical Approach

... Third parties face three fundamental and early decisions: First, they have to determine their *basic objectives*. At first blush, seeking to foster an agreement among the warring parties might appear to be the obvious basic objective, but more subtle goals are possible: transforming relationships, modeling a more constructive process, delaying the conflict, and others. Second, they have to choose their *fundamental role* (e.g., neutral, advocate for one party or outside player, etc.). Third, they have to consider their best *means of influence* on the situation (e.g., forceful, persuasive, facilitative, and so forth). Along with these three key choices, the third party must, at least implicitly, formulate a strategy to form a "winning coalition" on behalf of the chosen objective. Supporting this *coalition strategy* are three concurrent and overlapping strands: (1) An *issues strategy* with respect to the substantive aspects of the agreements sought, (2) a *process strategy* with respect to the choices of process for the mediation, and (3) a *timing strategy* with respect to the timing of their efforts. These are neither independent from each other nor always equal in their influence on the negotiations. While many other formulations are possible, these dimensions at least capture major elements of the choices made by third parties. We will use this framework to compare the approaches of Mitchell and Holbrooke....

Comparisons of Fundamental Choices

Basic Objectives

Richard Holbrooke's evident objective was to stop the violent and bloody war in Bosnia—and he needed to do it quickly. He wanted an immediate and comprehensive deal that would end the killing and create a new Bosnia. His approach was deal-oriented, focused on the substantive issues at stake, and transactional.... Holbrooke was less focused on its long-term sustainability, and more interested in "getting the deal done." It took a scant three months from the time he became centrally involved in the conflict until the signing of the Dayton Accords.

George Mitchell's objective in Northern Ireland was also to end the conflict. He found party leaders from both sides who were articulate in their understanding that unemployment and violence were inextricably linked and that a durable peace rested on a foundation of trust and prosperity. Yet, their hatred for one another remained and they were unable to act to realize shared interests. Mitchell was amazed to find that, although the party leaders had lived together in the same community all of their lives, many of them literally did not talk with each other.

By contrast with Holbrooke, Mitchell's approach had the apparent objective of helping the political leadership of the warring factions of Northern Ireland to begin to cooperate in a rudimentary way in creating an institutional and constitutional framework in which the parties could govern Northern Ireland for the future. From the start of the all-party talks, he took almost two years in a highly process-oriented, relationship-focused effort at transforming the working and political relationships among key players.

Fundamental Role

The roles of Mitchell and Holbrooke were well aligned with their objectives. Holbrooke assumed the role of an advocate with substantial potential clout from both the U.S. and NATO. He had an unambiguous mandate and could claim strong powers to punish and reward. He and his team became "active engineers" in the process to meet a clear national interest of the U.S. to stop the violence as expeditiously as possible. The U.S. was already practicing maneuvers for a possible UN withdrawal from Bosnia involving 25,000 U.S. troops.... [T]hey ... faced a high cost of failure. Their plan for reaching a comprehensive settlement based on assertive diplomacy put U.S. credibility on the line.

Thus, their actions could be interpreted both as "solving" problems and tactical "manipulation." Throughout Holbrooke's shuttle diplomacy, for example, Serbian President Slobodan Milosevic would press Holbrooke for economic sanctions relief. But Holbrooke planned to save that incentive for an eventual peace conference. "I would tell him that it wasn't in my authority, that's Washington's. But I was always playing a game," Holbrooke recalled. Likewise, Holbrooke viewed the Balkan leaders as the most difficult he had ever dealt with. "They're thugs, they're murderers, they're entrenched," he declared....

By contrast, George Mitchell assumed the role of a neutral mediator on behalf of an agreement among the parties. The situation in Northern Ireland was of relatively peripheral concern to U.S. policy makers, although it had entangled a key ally (Britain) and served as something of a test bed for U.S. influence on post-Cold War ethnic conflicts. Mitchell first became involved in Northern Ireland in early 1995 when President Clinton announced his intention to sponsor a White House Conference on Trade and Investment in Northern Ireland and asked Mitchell to help organize the conference....

Although the British government had long been reluctant to involve outsiders in what it saw as a domestic political matter, its leaders came to the conclusion that a peace settlement in Northern Ireland could benefit from a detached third-party role. Mitchell arrived without a strong interest in the final substance of the negotiated deal but with a desire that the needs of parties be met. He had an unclear mandate and no powers to tangibly reward or punish. Over time, he blamed the problems of the province on the situation rather than the people. Mitchell viewed the leaders of Northern Ireland differently than Holbrooke viewed the Balkan leaders. "I was impressed by the energy and intelligence of the people. They are productive, literate, and articulate," he said....

Means of Influence

In Bosnia, Holbrooke arguably adopted an approach of "whatever it takes to force a deal." In the language of negotiation, it was a best alternative to a negotiated agreement (BATNA)-focused approach of lowering the value of no-agreement alternatives and influencing the dynamics to impose ever higher costs on the various parties who refused to play. Holbrooke had the might of the U.S. and NATO to back up his mediation. He could greatly shape and manipulate the situation through bombing and promised aid and sanctions....

By contrast to this BATNA-lowering approach, George Mitchell followed a strategy that focused on joint gains, continually alluding to the political and economic value of a deal. Mitchell had no formal power and only had a few carrots and sticks with which to influence negotiators and their constituents. "I felt, throughout the discussion, that ultimately my ability to be effective would depend more upon gaining the participants' trust and confidence than on the formal description of my authority," Mitchell said....

Mitchell sought to model constructive future dealings among the parties to show that, in living together in the future, they would be more productive and secure. Arguably, by analogy, Holbrooke was affecting a workable divorce while Mitchell was engaged in relationship therapy.

Comparisons of Strategies: Coalitional, Process, Issue, and Timing

Coalition Strategy: Minimum Necessary versus Maximum Feasible

Holbrooke's strategy in Bosnia, with respect to the various parties, consisted of four basic steps. First, he sought to simplify the overall decision-making within the U.S., NATO, and the European Union (EU). He took steps to disentangle the U.S.-NATO-EU process from that of the UN with his efforts to do away with the infamous "dual key" arrangement requiring the approval of both UN and NATO officials to authorize air strikes.

Second, Holbrooke acted to take advantage of, and foster, the simplification of the hitherto fragmented Balkan parties. This was accomplished, in part, through exploiting the fortuitous actions of Milosevic in obtaining the "Patriarch Paper," which ensured that, in all negotiations, the interests of the Bosnian Serbs would be represented by Milosevic himself. Holbrooke's support of the strengthened Muslim-Croat Federation furthered the simplification process.

Third, he sought to apply considerable pressure on the Serbs to weaken their thus-far dominant position.... Finally, when Bosnian Muslims began to press their newfound advantage on the battlefield, Holbrooke took steps to isolate the Bosnian Muslims, to block further battlefield progress by this group, and to effectively force a settlement.

In seeking an agreement, Holbrooke wanted the narrow participation of the minimum necessary number of parties, hardly a broad-based stakeholder effort (as was the case, for example, with the ten political parties who played roles in the all-party Northern Irish talks). His tightly defined mediation team then discouraged direct communication between the parties in favor of themselves acting as the conduit of information. Holbrooke had co-opted potential spoilers to the agreement, such as Serbian President Slobodan Milosevic, through enticements and later pushed them to make concessions....

When Holbrooke finally got the leaders together in Dayton, they were edgy, angry, and distrustful. But, drawing on his carefully nurtured reputation as a wielder of great power, he kept them there by threatening that the alternative to agreement would be dire, and convincing them that he and his team provided the best opportunity for success.

By contrast with Holbrooke's sequential, divide-conquer-and-force approach and desire to limit participation, George Mitchell carefully built an outwardly rippling, relatively inclusive, coalition of the center against the extremes.... Mitchell fostered the creation of a center and helped to give it voice in a manner that significantly displaced the prior political influence of the extremes.

He sought wide participation of parties by first recommending the election to a negotiating forum and later allowing all parties to remain involved as long as they adhered to the "Mitchell Principles" of democracy and nonviolence. Throughout the negotiations, Mitchell and his loosely organized team encouraged the parties to communicate among themselves.... Mitchell effectively reduced the influence of potential spoilers to the agreement by allowing extremists from both sides to leave of their own accord....

Process Strategy: Control versus Consensus

Holbrooke essentially imposed a negotiation process by fiat. He engineered and manipulated representation in the talks and undertook his shuttles and summits to meet what he saw as the requirements of rapid closure. He apparently worried very little about explicitly defining a clear strategy for the negotiation process and disliked sharing his thoughts with others outside of his team....

Holbrooke was a master at artfully concealing and revealing information in his actions. He frequently kept the international Contact Group in the dark, claiming that it was necessary to exclude the Europeans until the last moment due to their internal divisions. Having to accommodate extraneous demands was something Holbrooke was anxious to avoid. He paid close attention, however, to the details of the process by dictating the precise dimensions of negotiation tables at the summits and carefully arranging the accommodations at Dayton....

As part of the process, Holbrooke used the press to further the idea of an "abyss" in the event of no-deal and he consistently sought to lower expectations for the results he sought at each stage.... Yet, when progress was made, Holbrooke trumpeted the publicity to lock in gains.... Holbrooke also used the press and the process as tools to build perceptions in the minds of the players of his personal credibility and power.

By contrast, Mitchell acted as the steward of a deliberate process of principled inclusion. The delegates were formally elected to a comprehensive forum and had to endorse the "Mitchell Principles" of democracy and nonviolence in order to enter the talks and continue participating. At first, Mitchell's chairmanship was not even accepted by the unionist parties.... To gain acceptance, Mitchell agreed to dispense with the process and agenda created in advance by the Irish and British governments. Instead, he agreed to negotiate his role, the rules, the agenda, and the procedures of the talks; including the principle of "sufficient consensus," which gave veto power to all of the largest players and ensured the reality of power sharing. For months, he and his team sought proposals from parties, provided comparative tables to guide discussion, and used bilateral meetings to ease things forward.... Throughout the talks, Mitchell kept the process going at all costs—however threadbare it seemed at any given time. He and the other chairmen were routinely called upon to speak to the press. Mitchell used the press to hold out a "pot of gold" waiting at the end of a negotiated settlement. He felt a need to optimistically assess the state of the talks. But it grew difficult....

Mitchell's process was highly transparent and, even in despairing moments, he found positive ways to interpret the talks' future potential to the parties and the press.

Unlike Holbrooke, whose process actions built perceptions of personal credibility and power, which could be deployed to force a deal, Mitchell used the process to build perceptions of fairness, respect, dedication, and credibility.

When Mitchell decided to set a deadline for the talks, he negotiated it with the two governments and met with representatives of each of the parties several times, refining his proposal at each meeting. The proposal included a process for the preparation of two drafts that would allow all parties to object and make proposals for the final version so that there would be no last-minute surprises. He effectively modeled the means of debate and governance that would be required by the institutions established under the Good Friday Agreement.

Issue Strategy: Substance versus Procedure

Richard Holbrooke placed more emphasis on substance than procedure in the Bosnian negotiations. His agenda for discussion changed frequently and always revolved around substantive issues. It was highly sequential, using shuttles and late-night diplomatic pressure to explore concessions and then hold summits to lock in gains and build momentum toward a larger package. At these summits, Holbrooke consistently sought a series of agreed-upon principles followed by specifics on the issues. His seven-member team artfully concealed and revealed information in order to benefit the process.

The first summit was "a tense affair with hostile officials clustered tightly around the custom-built table," but Holbrooke emerged with a list of agreed basic principles that recognized Bosnia's existing borders, created two entities within Bosnia, and allowed each entity the right to establish ties with neighboring countries. The second summit, three weeks later, resulted in another contentious list of principles defining the structures of government such as a parliament, a presidency, a constitutional court, and a commitment to elections.

Holbrooke deferred for a later time toxic issues such as the map with boundaries and delimitations of the post-conflict country, which he deemed to be "too hard." … Still, Holbrooke sought to leave no issues that could be negotiated untouched. By the time the leaders arrived in Dayton, the U.S. State Department presented them with a comprehensive Framework Peace Agreement complete with annexes covering military issues, elections, the constitution, human rights, and an international police task force. The idea was to present them with a complete package and ram it through by way of an intensive negotiation process to be completed as rapidly as humanly possible.

By contrast, George Mitchell deferred the difficult substantive issues until the very end of his involvement in favor of focusing on negotiations over the procedures and agendas themselves. His early discussions slogged through arcane debates about rules. He not only negotiated the process and procedures for the all-party talks, but he negotiated a preliminary agenda, and then a more detailed agenda with the parties—all of which took more than a year. This extreme procedural focus was a mirror image of Holbrooke's extreme substantive focus.

When Mitchell did deal with substantive issues, he methodically separated them into three strands for the parties to discuss the nuances of each issue. His team shared information widely in an effort to avoid surprises or misunderstandings. The parties canvassed their various proposals, concepts, and models but, more importantly, they explored each other's ideas, seeking further explanations or offering explanations for their own reservations or objections....

Mitchell later repackaged the issues in the final agreement for mutual gain. Mitchell progressively isolated and deferred the hardest issue, the decommissioning of IRA weapons, in the hope that enough of a relationship would be built up among the parties to tackle it later in a more productive way.

Timing Strategy: Forcing versus Fostering

Holbrooke's timing strategy called for building momentum by gaining early wins through agreements on principles. He then accelerated the pace with a series of partial agreements and forcible actions to prevent backsliding on promises. He used several imposed deadlines—backed by the threat of bombing—to forge agreements. He also made well-timed persuasive arguments—backed by intelligence data—to force parties to back down....

By contrast, Mitchell's patient strategy used time, not only to begin to foster a more constructive relationship among the parties, but to increase their sense of respect, obligation, liking, and credibility toward him. Mitchell, in turn, used his credibility—and only his credibility—to create a culminating event in December 1997 when he felt further interaction was pointless.

"Much has been said about my patience. I have a lot of it, but I felt I had just about used it up. Rarely in my life have I felt as frustrated and angry. We had been meeting for a year and a half. For hundreds and hundreds of hours I had listened to the same arguments. Very little had been accomplished. It had taken two months to get an understanding on the rules to be followed once the negotiations began. Then it took another two months to get agreement on a preliminary agenda. Then we had tried for fourteen more months to get an accord on a detailed final agenda. We couldn't even get that, and we were about to adjourn for the Christmas break. Our failure ... would be crushing ... I began to think about a deadline." (Mitchell, Making Peace, 1999: 126)

Mitchell deployed his hard-earned credibility on the final deadline, which he carefully negotiated with the parties and governments at the talks. To emphasize that this would be the parties' last clear chance for agreement, and that his participation was at an end, he stated at the outset of the final talks, "I am Humpty Dumpty. I can only jump once."

The remarkable differences between Holbrooke and Mitchell are summarized in Table One, which outlines their fundamental choices, and Table Two, which compares the strategies they each chose to employ. While suggestive, these categories of choice are neither mutually exclusive nor collectively exhaustive. In many respects, these two superficially similar third-party episodes could scarcely be more different, once critically examined.

Table One

Differences between Holbrooke and Mitchell Approaches

	Holbrooke Bosnia-Herzegovina	Mitchell Northern Ireland
Fundamental objectives	Deal-oriented Substantive Transactional	Process-oriented Relationship Transformational
Fundamental interest/role	Mediator/advocate (with clout)	Mediator/neutral
Fundamental influence strategy	BATNA-focused "Whatever it takes"	Joint Gains-focused Model-future dealings

Table Two

Strategies Employed by Holbrooke and Mitchell

Strategic Element	Holbrooke Bosnia-Herzegovina	Mitchell Northern Ireland
Coalition strategy	Simplify structure Equalize core parties Sequence	Coalition of center against extremes
Issue strategy	Process by fiat	Process an issue for negotiation
	Principles, then specifics	Procedure, then substance
	Sequential, then lock in gains	Separate into three strands, then package
	Defer deal-breakers	Decouple decommissioning
Process strategy	Engineer/manipulate representation	Principled inclusion (Mitchell Principles, "sufficient consensus")
	Sequence shuttles and summits	Keep going at all costs ("variable geometry")
	Conceal/reveal information Use press to paint abyss/lower expectations, yet lock in gains	Highly transparent Relentlessly positive press spin
	Use process to build perceptions of personal credibility and power	Use process to build perceptions of fairness, dedication, and respect
Timing strategy	As fast as possible Build "momentum" by early wins, accelerating series of partial agreements, forcible actions, and process choices	As long as it takes; use time to bootstrap a sense of respect, obligation, liking, and credibility; expend personal credibility on the final deadline

The Men and Their Mission: Were Their Personalities, Experience, and Approaches a "Fit"?

The relatively bloodless comparisons of strategies and approaches in Tables One and Two largely sidestep the question of the specific individuals involved along with the "fit" between the person and the situation. Indeed, arguably as a function of the actors themselves, these twin cases—at least in their central tendencies—contrast force with tact, acting with listening, and manipulation with process stewardship. While Holbrooke turned to coercive means to forge peace, Mitchell first created and then presided over a "Senate" in Northern Ireland.

Richard Holbrooke possessed one of the most assertive personalities in Washington. He could be bombastic and brash. Some considered him a "showman" and he had a reputation for being unpredictable and often difficult. He had served on the U.S. delegation to the Paris peace talks with the Vietcong in 1968 and, as Assistant Secretary of State for East Asian and Pacific Affairs, he had conducted difficult negotiations with the Chinese and with former Filipino President Ferdinand Marcos.... Holbrooke was not only blunt and impatient, but he also used all the means at his disposal to force agreements....

George Mitchell, on the other hand, had a reputation for being diligent, cautious, and levelheaded. He had served for fourteen years in the U.S. Senate, seven of those years as Democratic Majority Leader. Throughout his political career, he displayed a fairness and calm temperament that made him a natural intermediary between senators, administration officials, and staff. As a legislator, Mitchell was quiet and judicious. He massaged details and soothed tempers, always seeking consensus over mundane issues.... Mitchell developed a sense of patience and timing in the U.S. Senate where passion was more effective in opposition than when in the majority. Yet a restrained style did not imply an unwillingness to exert power; indeed, Mitchell could be fiercely partisan. In his early career, he learned when to use this passion.... He frequently allowed room for events to unfold....

It would be too easy to caricature and exaggerate the extent of the personality differences between Holbrooke and Mitchell, when in fact, observers have also remarked on Mitchell's toughness and Holbrooke's empathy and charm. Yet the contrasting central personality attributes and prior experiences of the two men were strongly consistent with the nature of the approaches they chose to the two conflicts. Perhaps ironically, the character of the two negotiated outcomes also seemed to differ along similar lines.

Representatives of the Republic of Bosnia and Herzegovina, the Republic of Croatia, and the Federal Republic of Yugoslavia hastily initialed Holbrooke's General Framework Agreement for Peace in Bosnia and Herzegovina. Even at the signing ceremony, however, Izetbegovic and the rest of his delegation described it as "a bitter and unjust peace" and called it a "brutal process." Maintenance of the peace hinged on the ongoing presence of outside military forces with many participants asserting that "if they were removed, the parties would be back killing each other the next day."

By contrast, the representatives of eight political parties, including the largest Catholic party, SDLP; and the largest Protestant party, UUP; and representatives of the Irish and British governments, signed Mitchell's Belfast Agreement. At the signing ceremony, UUP leader David Trimble and John Hume of SDLP called it a "principled compromise" forged in "learning and understanding." ...

Concluding Thoughts

To sharpen the contrasts between these two men and the episodes in which they played central roles, consider the following thought experiment: Imagine the likely process and outcome in each case if Holbrooke had been assigned to Northern Ireland and Mitchell to Bosnia. While each man might have flexibly adapted to radically different situations, it is clear that simply juxtaposing the two approaches would sharply lower the chances of success in each case....

Perhaps the most important contribution of this comparison of the sharply divergent approaches taken in Northern Ireland and Bosnia is the challenge it poses to easy generalizations about effective mediation. Holbrooke's results may confound those who see the essence of successful mediation as scrupulous neutrality buttressed by patient, interest-based, empathetic joint problem solving to find mutually beneficial solutions. For others who may see the coercive diplomacy of Holbrooke as the essential ingredient to cutting through intractable and violent situations, the success of Mitchell's low-key, even-handed, endlessly persistent style may seem almost magical. Yet, in the course of their respective efforts, both men helped forge peace agreements in two immensely challenging situations that had defeated many prior attempts. While two data points do not a theory make, these twin cases highlight the range of tactical and strategic dimensions required of any candidate theory of third-party action.

Notes & Questions

1. What are the key differences between the mediation approaches taken in Bosnia and Northern Ireland?
2. How might these approaches be translated into other contexts?

III. Mediation in Commercial, Trade, and Investment Settings

A. Investment Conciliation

The Tesoro Petroleum Corporation subjected itself to a conciliation agreement if conflict were to arise. This example of mediation on a smaller scale demonstrates how the use of an international figure chosen by both parties fits the needs of the corporation and benefits both parties involved.

Lester Nurick & Stephen J. Schnably, *The First ICSID Conciliation: Tesoro Petroleum Corporation v. Trinidad and Tobago*

ICSID Rev.: Foreign Inv. L.J., Sept. 1986, at 340–47

Tesoro and the Government of Trinidad and Tobago entered into a joint venture in 1968 to purchase and develop oil fields in Trinidad that were then owned by the British Petroleum Company Limited. Tesoro and the Government each took a 50 percent ownership in the stock of the joint venture, which was named the Trinidad-Tesoro Petroleum Company Limited. The board of directors consisted of a chairman appointed by the Government and approved by Tesoro, with the Government and Tesoro each appointing half of the other members. In connection with the joint venture, the parties signed a number of documents. One was a "Heads of Agreement," a comprehensive document setting out the terms of the joint venture. The Heads of Agreement contained a provision that no dividends would be declared by Trinidad-Tesoro for the first five years of its existence. After that, the Heads of Agreement provided:

> Dividends may be declared or recommended to the shareholders by a majority of the Board of Directors of the Joint Company, following a policy of reinvestment of a substantial portion of current earnings each year in viable and attractive projects, primarily in oil and gas development [and] exploratory and processing projects [in Trinidad.] The parties also signed ten "side letters" of the same date as the Heads of Agreement, touching on a number of matters also covered in the Heads of Agreement. The fourth side letter provided that "[after the first five years of the operations of the Joint Company, there shall be declared and paid as dividends at the request of either the Government or Tesoro, and to the extent that cash is available, 50% of the net earnings after tax as certified by the auditors of the Joint Company." The Heads of Agreement also provided for Tesoro or a wholly owned subsidiary to be Trinidad-Tesoro's Manager. Pursuant to that clause the Government and Tesoro entered into a Management Contract approximately two years later. In the Management Contract Tesoro, as the Manager, agreed among other things to recommend petroleum-related projects in Trinidad for the reinvestment of the Joint Company's earnings, for the purpose of the "creation of new business ventures within the State of Trinidad and Tobago, the employment of additional Trinidad Nationals and the general stimulation of the economy of Trinidad and Tobago."

Finally, the parties included in the Heads of Agreement the following provisions regarding ICSID jurisdiction:

> The Government and Tesoro hereby consent to submit to the jurisdiction of the International Centre for Settlement of Investment Disputes all disputes arising out of these Heads of Agreement, or relating to any investment made hereunder, for settlement by conciliation followed, if the dispute remains unresolved after six months following the communication of the report of the

> Conciliation Commission to the parties, by arbitration, both pursuant to the Convention on the Settlement of Investment Disputes between States and Nationals of Other States (hereinafter called the "SID Convention"), which has been signed and ratified by the Government of Trinidad and Tobago and by the United States Government. It is hereby stipulated by the parties that Tesoro is a National of the United States of America. The Government hereby waives its rights to require, pursuant to Article 26 of the SID Convention, the exhaustion of local administrative or judicial remedies as a condition of its consent to arbitration under the SID Convention....

The Government hereby waives any right of sovereign immunity as to it and its property in respect of these Heads of Agreement, both during any conciliation or arbitration proceedings and in respect of the enforcement and execution of any award resulting therefrom.

For the first five years of Trinidad-Tesoro's operations, no dividends were declared, as was provided in the Heads of Agreement. After that, dividends were paid each year through fiscal year 1980. In one year during that period, dividends equal to one-third of Trinidad-Tesoro's net after-tax earnings were declared; in the other years, the dividends were approximately half the net after-tax earnings. From 1981 on, relations between the Government and Tesoro became strained for a number of reasons. In response to the second round of OPEC price increases in 1979, the Government made clear in 1980 that it was planning to impose a new petroleum tax and in 1981 it did so, effective as of January 1980. Tesoro denounced the new tax in strong terms. Around the same time, significant exploration expenditures that the Government wished to see Trinidad-Tesoro make were blocked by the Tesoro-appointed members of the board of directors under a provision of the Joint Company's Articles that required a two-thirds majority of the directors to approve large investment expenditures. Also during the same period, the Government refused—first informally, and then at shareholders' meetings in 1982 and 1983—to give its approval to the declaration of dividends for 1981and 1982. In August 1982, Tesoro announced its intention to sell its shares in Trinidad Tesoro. Under the Heads of Agreement, Tesoro was obligated to offer them to the Government first, and the two parties entered into negotiations over the Government's possible purchase of the shares....

Tesoro filed a Request for the Initiation of Conciliation Proceedings with the Secretary-General of ICSID on August 22, 1983. The request contained a brief description of the dispute and the parties; attached to it was a copy of the Heads of Agreement and the side letters. In essence, Tesoro asserted that it was entitled under the Heads of Agreement and side letters to dividends equal to 50 percent of net earnings, and that the Government had breached the agreement by failing to instruct its appointees on the Trinidad-Tesoro board to vote to recommend dividends.

In this case, the parties agreed to have a single conciliator, and to negotiate directly between themselves in choosing the conciliator. By mid-December 1983, the parties had decided upon Lord Wilberforce, and notified the Secretary-General of their appointment. Lord Wilberforce is a highly distinguished and experienced British judge, who retired as Lord of Appeal in Ordinary in 1982, after having served as a Law Lord for eighteen years. Pursuant to Conciliation Rule 5,30 the Secretary-General notified Lord Wilberforce. On January 6, 1984, the Secretary-General notified the parties that Lord Wilberforce had accepted the appointment as sole conciliator.... With that, the commission was deemed to have been constituted, and the conciliation proceedings begun. The decision to have one conciliator, rather than a commission consisting of three or more members, significantly expedited the commencement of the proceedings. In ICSID arbitration, where panels of three members are routinely used, it typically has taken from five to thirteen months to constitute the tribunal. Here, in contrast, a conciliator was agreed upon in approximately four months, and the commission constituted within a month after that....

On February 5, 1985, Lord Wilberforce issued his recommendation. After reviewing the procedural history of the case, he stated that he conceived] that his task in these proceedings is to examine the contentions raised by the parties, to clarify the issues, and to endeavor to evaluate their respective merits and the likelihood of their being accepted, or rejected, in Arbitration or Court proceedings, in the hope that such evaluation may assist the parties in reaching an agreed settlement. Lord Wilberforce then went on to find that ICSID had jurisdiction over the dispute, on the ground that the fourth side letter and the Heads of Agreement constituted one agreement, and the Heads of Agreement clearly contained an ICSID clause. He also analyzed in detail the merits of the arguments-both factual and legal-presented by the parties, and finally concluded with a proposed settlement (involving a suggested percentage of the amount sought by Tesoro) based on "[h]is estimate of the parties' chances of success on the issue in the dispute." In addition, he made recommendations concerning other issues in dispute....

Over the next eight months, the parties negotiated between themselves concerning the terms of a possible settlement. They also communicated with Lord Wilberforce regarding their views on his recommendation. In response to the Government's comments on one aspect of that recommendation, Lord Wilberforce modified the recommendation.

On October 15, 1985, Trinidad-Tesoro issued a press release announcing settlement of the dispute:

> For the period 1981–1985 Trinidad-Tesoro Petroleum Company Limited had not paid dividends to its shareholders instead preserving annual earnings in those years for reinvestment. This however led to a disagreement as a result of which one shareholder referred the matter of dividend payment to The International Centre for the Settlement of Investment Disputes. Following conciliation proceedings and in light of the recommendation of the Conciliator, Lord Wilberforce, it was agreed by way of final settlement to pay dividends to the A & B shareholders (Government and Tesoro) amounting to U.S. $143 million payable in cash and petroleum products to cover all outstanding dividends up

> to and including 1985. In November 1985, the parties submitted notices to Lord Wilberforce indicating the settlement of the dispute. On November 27, 1985, Lord Wilberforce issued his report pursuant to Conciliation Rules 30–32, in which he formally closed the proceedings.

The main advantage of conciliation over arbitration lies in its relative informality and inexpensiveness. The Conciliation Rules are designed to permit even greater flexibility than do the Arbitration Rules. Further, precisely because no binding award is rendered, the parties' presentations to the conciliator may be less extensive than would be the case if they were before an arbitral tribunal. For example, the parties might agree simply to summarize relevant facts they believe they could prove, together with supporting evidence, rather than call witnesses to testify to those facts. The conciliator, moreover, may be able to reach a decision more readily if he or she [or they] is [are] required only to gauge the relative strength of the parties' positions rather than render an award that will bind the parties and constitute an arbitral precedent. And inasmuch as a conciliation is aimed from the start toward settlement, the parties may be more likely to reach an agreement than they would if they were participating in a full-scale adversary proceeding. Finally, for all these reasons, conciliation is likely to be less costly than arbitration, in terms both of expenses and attorneys' fees incurred.

These advantages must be considered in light of the central difference between conciliation and arbitration: a conciliation proceeding does not result in a binding award, and if the parties are unable to reach a settlement, arbitration proceedings must begin de novo. In such a circumstance, the conciliation proceedings may appear to the parties to be little more than a needless (and time-consuming) exercise. Where a settlement does not appear likely at the outset, arbitration may well be preferable. The parties, after all, can always reach a settlement agreement during the arbitral proceedings, and have done so in a significant number of ICSID arbitrations. Indeed, in certain cases the prospect of a binding award may be necessary to motivate one party or the other to bargain seriously. Obviously, it is difficult to predict in any given case whether conciliation proceedings would be helpful. At their best-as in the Tesoro/Trinidad conciliation, conciliation proceedings may help the parties reach a settlement of their differences at relatively small cost of time and money; at worst, conciliation proceedings might simply delay ultimate resolution of the dispute. It is clear, however, that the use of ICSID's conciliation facilities deserves serious consideration in every case, whether at the time the ICSID clause is written into an investment agreement, or when a dispute has arisen and the parties are seeking an alternative to arbitration.

Notes & Questions

1. Consider how the conciliator here, Lord Wilberforce, made recommendations to the parties. Does this process still "count" as a mediation? What concerns would you have about the neutral's making recommendations?
2. How would you describe the differences between conciliation and mediation? Why might you recommend these to states and parties?

B. State-Investor Mediation

The traditional reconciliation method for states and foreign investors is rights-based arbitration; however, both parties, the states and the investors, have recently denounced this method because its focus on legal rights ignores forward-looking interests. Mediation has provided an answer to their outcries.

Nancy Welsh & Andrea Kupfer Schneider, *Becoming "Investor-State Mediation"*

1 Penn. St. J. L. & Int'l Aff. 86 (2012)

Within the last decade, there has been a noticeable surge in the number of investors accessing investment treaty arbitration. Perhaps as a result of this phenomenon, coupled with the heavy costs of investment treaty arbitration and the size of some arbitral awards, both states and investors are now raising multiple concerns. The parties decry the expense, delays, and political challenges associated with relying exclusively on a rights-based arbitral process. Most seriously, the current investment arbitration system is viable only if states voluntarily comply with, and enforce, the arbitral awards produced by the system—and such compliance cannot be presumed when the awards are adverse to nations' interests. Indeed, some states have begun to threaten to refuse to abide by arbitral awards. Such threats are not new, or even unique to international arbitration. In the U.S., the famous case of *Marbury v. Madison* involved a freshly minted Supreme Court similarly struggling to establish its legal and political authority while also acknowledging its dependence on the enforcement power wielded by the executive branch of government. Despite the familiarity of the dynamic, however, the seriousness of states' threats to refuse to comply with awards is very real. If unchecked, such threats have the potential to introduce a level of uncertainty that could cause serious retraction in international investment and trade.

The current investor-state arbitration process tends to focus the parties on their legal rights—and the need to resolve ambiguities regarding such legal rights—when the parties' extra-legal interests may be even more important and helpful in fashioning a resolution. Indeed, some commentators fear that arbitration may marginalize the parties' helpful socio-cultural characteristics and mutual interests that have the potential to sustain a concurrently troubled business relationship. As Jeswald Salacuse notes, "[n]either the aim nor the consequence of arbitration is to repair a broken business relationship." Particularly noteworthy have been the comments made by Grant Kesler, the Chief Executive Officer of Metalclad, after his company won a 17 million dollar arbitral award against Mexico. In retrospect, and despite being victorious, Kesler said that arbitration had been so dissatisfying that he wished his company had relied upon its "political options" to resolve the dispute. These comments suggest that losing parties, and some of those who have won, may seek a process with fewer transaction costs that allows them to focus a greater percentage of their resources on problem-solving and the development of satisfactory solutions rather than formalized, principled fighting. Responding to these concerns, Professors Jack Coe, Jeswald Salacuse, and Susan Franck have urged consideration of procedures and systems that could reduce the likelihood that investor-state disputes will arise, or once they have arisen, could channel such disputes into forums that encourage communication and the development of consensual solutions. Such forums include mandatory negotiation, conciliation, early neutral evaluation, ombudspersons, and mediation. Some states have begun to put such procedures into place, generally focusing on those that require communication before the submission of a dispute to arbitration and thus fostering early information exchange and negotiation. Investors, states, and interested international bodies and scholars have also begun to develop rules to encourage the use of mediation. Some stakeholders have even proposed that mediation should not just be encouraged but made mandatory, at least to some degree.

... [M]ediation in common law countries is a much less-obviously structured affair. The process often, but not always, begins with pre-mediation submissions and telephonic conferences with the mediator. On the day of the mediation, the parties meet in a conference room; the process generally begins with an orientation by the mediator and opening statements by each side. The mediators and parties may then stay together throughout the process or separate into different rooms, with the mediator "shuttling" among them. If the parties have separated and reach resolution, they may reconvene for a joint meeting to confirm the terms of the settlement. The process is structured to ensure that the parties have the information they need to allow them to reach a decision that they can accept and will implement.

There are also mediation models that are described as "evaluative," "directive," and focused on facilitating distributive outcomes. Again, mediators are likely to engage in substantial pre-mediation work. In this second set of models, though, the mediators and lawyers play the central roles, and the focus is usually on law-related issues. The understanding of who should be involved in the mediation is likely to be limited by the lawyers' perceptual map, thus tending to exclude stakeholders who do not have legally-cognizable interests or legal standing. Initial presentations by the lawyers are likely to focus on legal issues, followed by legal and litigation-oriented analysis and the mediator's provision of indirect or direct advice to the parties and their lawyers to help them be realistic regarding their options in civil litigation or administrative adjudication and to guide them toward a resolution generally consistent with those options. Notice that the focus of, and remedy produced by, this set of models of mediation begins to sound much like what is applicable to conciliation or even non-binding arbitration.

Interestingly, though, there are indications that sophisticated mediation users prefer mediators and mediation sessions that can uncover and use the parties' extralegal interests as well as engage the lawyers and parties in a discussion of the relevant law and litigation realities. Mediation has the capacity to house both functions, without one dominating or marginalizing the other. Available research in the U.S. generally suggests that the most effective court-connected mediators are those who can combine elements of all of the mediation models described supra, with mediators thoroughly preparing themselves and facilitating the preparation of the disputants and their lawyers, seeking to understand important interests and develop trust, listening carefully and effectively, asking parties to explore or justify their assumptions and predictions regarding legal outcomes, carefully challenging unrealistic assumptions and helping parties to be more realistic, offering face-saving strategies, and assisting disputants and lawyers to develop responsive, realistic solutions. In other words, the presumptively interest-based process of mediation is most likely to be helpful when it includes both legal analysis and probing for interests. Note, however, that the process still presumes that no agreement will occur without the parties' voluntary assent. Note further that this inclusive model of mediation requires both clear differentiation from other available processes, and legal and procedural protection of the time commitment required for its operation.

In the investment treaty context, it will presumably be important for the parties to maintain or improve ongoing relationships, collaborate on the implementation of any agreement, and acknowledge volatile political situations to enable representatives (and their constituencies) to embrace effective solutions, even if they are not the preferred solutions. All of these factors suggest the value of the last model of mediation described supra, one that is presumptively facilitative and preceded by careful preparation, but supplemented as necessary with more evaluative interventions, and involving the consideration of both legal issues and extra-legal interests. Such a process might facilitate the parties' "mutual consideration" of each other's perspectives and underlying needs as well as their legal analysis. In other words, it will be important for the mediator to offer a procedurally just process and to facilitate the parties' ability to engage in a procedurally just process with each other. Investors and states will need sufficient opportunity to speak and be heard, but also to listen to each other, reflect upon what was said, demonstrate that they have listened to each other—and also make meaningful movement toward resolution.

A few states, however, have expanded the usual list of options available in the investor-state context by establishing new structures and procedures designed to encourage early communication and information-sharing between states and investors, thus identifying difficulties before they escalate into disputes or resolving such disputes very early on. Examples include Peru's coordination and response system, including its Special Commission; China's domestic administrative review process; and Colombia's establishment of a lead agency model. Interestingly, the state officials leading these efforts have the potential to serve a "quasi-mediator" function, meeting many of the needs that would otherwise fall to third party mediators using the model of mediation described supra. Trust, however, is the key. If investors perceive these quasi-mediators as biased against them—as insufficiently benevolent, insufficiently even-handed, or insufficiently open-minded—then investors are unlikely to perceive their procedures as fair. Mediation involving an outside mediator is likely to be perceived as more procedurally just—or fairer—and thus preferable. At the very least, then, the easy availability of a corps of outside, independent and trusted mediators, as an alternative to the state's judicial or administrative officials, has the potential to incentivize the state to make its own processes equally even-handed, in order to attract foreign investors.

A procedure called "mediation" is likely to be useful in the investor-state context, but mediation's value will depend upon the particular model that is integrated, and whether it responds to the parties' needs and complements the other available processes in this dispute resolution system. Thus, key actors must devote some time and attention to identifying the key goals and essential practices that should characterize the process that "becomes investor-state mediation." Once the desired goals and essential practices are identified, much more work remains to be done—e.g., developing relevant rules and supportive organizational structures, identifying an appropriate pool of mediators, etc. Being clear regarding the goal, however, is the first step.

C. International Commercial Mediation

The Singapore Convention, a treaty promulgated in August 2019 by the UN Convention on International Settlement Agreements Resulting from Mediation (UNCITRAL), attempts to make international commercial mediation agreements for transborder trade and commercial disputes enforceable in any signatory country. As of the time of this writing, it has been signed by 46 countries but has not yet been ratified by most.

UN Convention on International Settlement Agreements Resulting from Mediation (Singapore Convention)

Article 1. Scope of application 1. This Convention applies to an agreement resulting from mediation and concluded in writing by parties to resolve a commercial dispute ("settlement agreement") which, at the time of its conclusion, is international in that: (a) At least two parties to the settlement agreement have their places of business in different States; or (b) The State in which the parties to the settlement agreement have their places of business is different from either: (i) The State in which a substantial part of the obligations under the settlement agreement is performed; or (ii) The State with which the subject matter of the settlement agreement is most closely connected. 2. This Convention does not apply to settlement agreements: (a) Concluded to resolve a dispute arising from transactions engaged in by one of the parties (a consumer) for personal, family or household purposes; (b) Relating to family, inheritance or employment law. 3. This Convention does not apply to: (a) Settlement agreements: (i) That have been approved by a court or concluded in the course of proceedings before a court; and (ii) That are enforceable as a judgment in the State of that court; (b) Settlement agreements that have been recorded and are enforceable as an arbitral award.

Article 2. Definitions 1. For the purposes of article 1, paragraph 1: (a) If a party has more than one place of business, the relevant place of business is that which has the closest relationship to the dispute resolved by the settlement agreement, having regard to the circumstances known to, or contemplated by, the parties at the time of the conclusion of the settlement agreement; (b) If a party does not have a place of business, reference is to be made to the party's habitual residence. 2. A settlement agreement is "in writing" if its content is recorded in any form. The requirement that a settlement agreement be in writing is met by an electronic communication if the information contained therein is accessible so as to be useable for subsequent reference. 3. "Mediation" means a process, irrespective of the expression used or the basis upon which the process is carried out, whereby parties attempt to reach an amicable settlement of their dispute with the assistance of a third person or persons ("the mediator") lacking the authority to impose a solution upon the parties to the dispute.

Article 3. General principles 1. Each Party to the Convention shall enforce a settlement agreement in accordance with its rules of procedure and under the conditions laid down in this Convention. 2. If a dispute arises concerning a matter that a party claims was already resolved by a settlement agreement, a Party to the Convention shall allow the party to invoke the settlement agreement in accordance with its rules of procedure and under the conditions laid down in this Convention, in order to prove that the matter has already been resolved.

Article 4. Requirements for reliance on settlement agreements 1. A party relying on a settlement agreement under this Convention shall supply to the competent authority of the Party to the Convention where relief is sought: (a) The settlement agreement signed by the parties; (b) Evidence that the settlement agreement resulted from mediation, such as: (i) The mediator's signature on the settlement agreement; (ii) A document signed by the mediator indicating that the mediation was carried out; (iii) An attestation by the institution that administered the mediation; or (iv) In the absence of (i), (ii) or (iii), any other evidence acceptable to the competent authority. 2. The requirement that a settlement agreement shall be signed by the parties or, where applicable, the mediator is met in relation to an electronic communication if: (a) A method is used to identify the parties or the mediator and to indicate the parties' or mediator's intention in respect of the information contained in the electronic communication; and (b) The method used is either: (i) As reliable as appropriate for the purpose for which the electronic communication was generated or communicated, in the light of all the circumstances, including any relevant agreement; or (ii) Proven in fact to have fulfilled the functions described in subparagraph (a) above, by itself or together with further evidence. 3. If the settlement agreement is not in an official language of the Party to the Convention where relief is sought, the competent authority may request a translation thereof into such language. 4. The competent authority may require any necessary document in order to verify that the requirements of the Convention have been complied with. 5. When considering the request for relief, the competent authority shall act expeditiously.

Article 5. Grounds for refusing to grant relief 1. The competent authority of the Party to the Convention where relief is sought under article 4 may refuse to grant relief at the request of the party against whom the relief is sought only if that party furnishes to the competent authority proof that: (a) A party to the settlement agreement was under some incapacity; (b) The settlement agreement sought to be relied upon: (i) Is null and void, inoperative or incapable of being performed under the law to which the parties have validly subjected it or, failing any indication thereon, under the law deemed applicable by the competent authority of the Party to the Convention where relief is sought under article 4; (ii) Is not binding, or is not final, according to its terms; or (iii) Has been subsequently modified; (c) The obligations in the settlement agreement: (i) Have been performed; or (ii) Are not clear or comprehensible; (d) Granting relief would be contrary to the terms of the settlement agreement; (e) There was a serious breach by the mediator of standards applicable to the mediator or the mediation without which breach that party would not have entered into the settlement agreement; or (f) There was a failure by the mediator to disclose to the parties circumstances that raise justifiable doubts as to the mediator's impartiality or independence and such failure to disclose had a material impact or undue influence on a party without which failure that party would not have entered into the settlement agreement. 2. The competent authority of the Party to the Convention where relief is sought under article 4 may also refuse to grant relief if it finds that: (a) Granting relief would be contrary to the public policy of that Party; or (b) The subject matter of the dispute is not capable of settlement by mediation under the law of that Party.

IV. When and How to Mediate

A. When Can a Matter Be Mediated? Is Timing Everything?

The following two excerpts, the first by I. William Zartman and the second by John Paul Lederach, illustrate a point-counterpoint debate on the importance of timing and "ripeness" in helping parties to settle a dispute. Some suggest that there are special opportunities for settling cases; these arise, in the international context, from the threat of a "hurting stalemate" (in Zartman's terms), or from the danger of violent conflict. Such conditions create a necessary "ripe moment" for mediation. John Paul Lederach, on the other hand, emphasizes the long-term nature of peace-building. See which argument seems more persuasive to you.

I. William Zartman, *The Timing of Peace Initiatives: Hurting Stalemates and Ripe Moments*

in Contemporary Peacemaking: Conflict, Violence, and Peace Processes 19–20, 24, 26 (John Darby & Roger MacGinty eds., 2003)

Parties resolve their conflict only when they are ready to do so—when alternative, usually unilateral, means of achieving a satisfactory result are blocked and the parties feel that they are in an uncomfortable and costly predicament. At that ripe moment, they grab onto proposals that usually have been in the air for a long time and that only now appear attractive....

The concept of a ripe moment centers on the parties' perception of a mutually hurting stalemate (MHS), optimally associated with an impending, past or recently avoided catastrophe. The concept is based on the notion that when the parties find themselves locked in a conflict from which they cannot escalate to victory and this deadlock is painful to both of them (although not necessarily in equal degree or for the same reasons), they seek an alternative policy or way out. The catastrophe provides a deadline or a lesson indicating that pain can be sharply increased if something is not done about it now; catastrophe is a useful extension of MHS but is not necessary either to its definition or to its existence.

Ripeness is necessarily a perceptual event, and as with any subjective perception, there are likely to be objective referents to be perceived. These can be highlighted by a mediator or an opposing party when they are not immediately recognized by the party itself, and resisted so long as the conflicting party refuses or is otherwise able to block out their perception.... If the parties do not recognize "clear evidence" (in someone else's view) that they are in an impasse, an MHS has not (yet) occurred, and if they do perceive themselves to be in such a situation, no matter how flimsy the "evidence," the MHS is present.

The other element necessary for a ripe moment is [the perception of] ... a way out. Parties do not have to be able to identify a specific solution, only a sense that a negotiated solution is possible and that the other party shares that sense and the willingness to search too. Without a sense of a way out, the push associated with the MHS would leave the parties with nowhere to go....

Implications

In itself, the concept explains the difficulty of achieving pre-emptive conflict resolution and preventive diplomacy, even though nothing in the definition of the MHS requires it to take place at the height of the conflict or at a high level of violence. The internal (and unmediated) negotiations in South Africa between 1990 and 1994 stand out as a striking case of negotiations opened (and pursued) on the basis of an MHS perceived by both sides on the basis of impending catastrophe, not of present casualties. However, the greater the objective evidence, the greater the subjective perception of the stalemate and its pain is likely to be, and this evidence is more likely to come late, when all other courses of action and possibilities of escalation have been exhausted. In notable cases, a long period of conflict is required before the MHS sinks in. Yet given the infinite number of potential conflicts which have not reached "the heights," evidence would suggest that perception of an MHS occurs either (and optimally) at a low level of conflict, where it is relatively easy to begin problem-solving in most cases, or, in salient cases, at rather high levels of conflict....

Unripeness should not constitute an excuse for second or third parties' inaction, even if one or both of the conflicting parties are mired in their hopes of escalation and victory. Crocker states very forcefully (in boldface in the original) that "the absence of 'ripeness' does not tell us to walk away and do nothing. Rather, it helps us to identify obstacles and suggests ways of handling them and managing the problem until resolution becomes possible."

John Paul Lederach, *Cultivating Peace: A Practitioner's View of Deadly Conflict and Negotiation*

in Contemporary Peacemaking: Conflict, Violence, and Peace Processes 33–35, 37 (John Darby & Roger MacGinty eds., 2003)

Ripeness Sees Mediator Action as Cherry Picking

When I played basketball many years ago our coach had a phrase with which he provoked us whenever we missed an easy shot, "I can't believe you missed that cherry picker." Essentially it meant that a lot of work had gone into place and then just when everything was right and a giveaway opportunity was presented, the basket was missed.

There are times when I have the impression that the metaphor of ripeness leads towards an emphasis on mediator action as if it were "cherry picking." The impression emerges from two understandings about mediation that I believe have significant limitations and implications....

What the ripeness metaphor does not provide is a sense of the long-term nature of the process, the building and sustaining of the relationships, nor the multiplicity of roles, activities and functions that may be necessary to make a sustained dialogue and change in the relationships possible.

It is not a metaphor that provides a vision of cultivating the soil, planting the seeds or nourishing the seedling in the face of winds, burning sun or icy storms, all of which speak to process, relationship, and sustainability rather than a momentary action....

Cultivation: The Building of Long-Term Authentic Relationships

The cultivation metaphor suggests that a deep respect for, and connection to, the context is critical for sustaining a change process that is moving from deadly expressions of conflict to increased justice and peace in relationships. The context of protracted deadly conflict, like soil, is the people, commonly shared geographies but often sharply differing views of history, rights, and responsibilities, and the formation of perception and understandings based on cultural meaning structures. Cultivation is recognizing that ultimately the change process must be taken up, embraced, and sustained by people in these contexts. The cultivator, as a connected but outside element in the system, approaches this soil with a great deal of respect, the suspension of quick judgment in favor of the wisdom of adaptation, and an orientation towards supporting the change process through highs and lows, ebbs and flows of violence and thawing of tensions, whether or not the situation appears ripe. The cultivator gives attention to the well-being of the ecosystem, not just the quick production of a given fruit....

So, what do I say when the journalist asks, "And do you really believe it is possible to talk about negotiation and peace when war is raging?" I say hope is not negotiated. It is kept alive by people who understand the depth of suffering and know the cost of keeping a horizon of change as a possibility for their children and grandchildren. Quick fixes to long-standing violent conflict are like growing a garden with no understanding of seeds, soils and sweat. This conflict traces back across decades, even generations. It will take that long to sort out.

Journalists generally do not quote me in their papers. Sound bites about ripeness, people coming to their senses, and the need for realism and pressure seem to find their way into print more often. But I believe in cultivation. Cultivation as a metaphor suggests that the core of the peacebuilding work—fostering and sustaining committed, authentic relationships across the lines of conflict over time—does not rise and fall with the temporal ups and downs of the conflict cycles. It answers the question—is it possible to pursue peace when things are bad—with a resounding "Yes!" just as it also suggests that when things are suddenly headed towards an agreement the work is hardly over. It has only begun.

Notes & Questions

1. Are these two visions of ripeness at odds with one another? Can they be reconciled?
2. Can you think of examples that fit under each of these theories?
3. How does the idea of ripeness work (or not work) in domestic mediation or negotiation?

B. Mediating Cross-Culturally

Mediation of any international dispute, whether public or private, involves parties from different countries which likely have different cultural and legal traditions. How should mediators (who themselves come from a particular legal system and culture) manage the possibly different approaches and strategies for conflict resolution?

Carrie Menkel-Meadow, *Cross-Cultural Disputes and Mediator Strategies*

in ROUTLEDGE HANDBOOK OF INTERCULTURAL MEDIATION (Dominic Busch ed., 2022)

Does mediation have a culture all its own? Mediation is derived historically from the Bible (it was Solomon who was going to cut the baby in half to resolve a dispute between two mothers mediating or arbitrating when the 'real' mother said "give it her, rather than cut it in half"?), Confucian 'harmony' culture, sulha (peace or 'resolution') in Islamic and Middle Eastern cultures, and various forms of African community dispute resolution processes ("it takes a village"; Ubuntu, gacaca)....

Is mediation a new 'lingua franca' or Esperanto language of common or more 'universal' customs or practices of dispute resolution to be used in cross-border international disputes, where both different languages and different legal systems may make traditional court-based dispute resolution more difficult. Does mediation require compromise, the seeking of 'joint gain,' and creative tailored solutions of substance while focusing on mutual understanding, empathy, party participation, self-determination, dialogue, and consent in process, to distinguish it from more rule and command-based processes of adjudication and arbitration?

Yet modern mediation and the standard form of mediation training occurring in courts and private organizations today is likely to use a relatively common format and template for behaviors—one that I and others (Gunning 1995; Press and Deason 2021) have called an overly "westernized" (and White) assumption of a "neutral" third party (mediator) presiding over or facilitating an individualized "talking cure" with protocols of story/claim narration, agenda creation and managed into "re-framed" solvable issues, facilitated brainstormed negotiated agreements and a pragmatic sense of problem solving and future oriented solutions. This ideology and practice of mediation can be both highly effective, but also culturally very specific, all while generating a variety of critiques for "privatizing" justice (removing disputes from the transparency of public court settings for accountability) or ignoring past injustices (Gunning 1995, Izumi 2010, Menkel-Meadow 2004).

What Strategies, Techniques, Tools for Mediation in Intercultural Settings?

There is no shortage of scholarship, training manuals, and advice from professionals on how to conduct intercultural mediations, both in obviously international contexts, but also in domestic inter or multi-cultural settings (e.g., Barkai 2008, Gunning 1995; Press and Deason 2021, Izumi 2010; LeBaron and Pillay 2006, International Mediation Institute 2022a; 2022b). This section highlights some of the strategies, interventions, techniques, tools, skills, and interpersonal accountability devices presented in the literature, followed by a brief review of some of the current critiques of standard mediation practices and schemas.

To begin, every mediation which has an intercultural element (isn't that all mediations where parties have some dispute and see the world and their particular situation differently?) needs to begin with a serious intercultural *analysis*. Who are the parties? *How many* of them are there? From *where* do they come? *What is the dispute* about (it's 'res')? How might each of the parties *see or interpret the dispute differently*? How might *context and type of dispute* matter? Commercial, employment, family, identity, education, health, housing, injury, personal or community? What is the *desired outcome* of the parties? Peace treaty, contract, settlement of a lawsuit or dispute, making a new relationship, forging a new country, family, setting borders and boundaries? All of these are variations on what kinds of disputes might require different sets of interventions or choices of behaviors. Then, in multi-cultural settings the preparation must also include as much learning as possible about both the particular 'cultures' involved (which may include not only nationality, ethnicity, race, gender, political, but profession, class, education and other 'cross-cutting' statuses and identities) and the subject matter of the dispute. Mediators of intercultural disputes must develop 'meta' preparation as well,—standing outside of the dispute, what processes, techniques, tools, and interventions may be more appropriate for particular problems. Thus, there are at least three layers to prepare for—process, substantive matter and the intermediation of 'differences' however they are perceived, constructed and enacted at individual, organizational and even national levels.

Self-Assessment

Any mediator beginning a multi or intercultural mediation session of any kind, should ask, "am I the right person for this job"? What competence do I have to offer the parties? Language, familiarity with the culture, substantive expertise? Should I get a co-mediator to add diversity, knowledge, assistance, ability to do several caucuses or separate meetings at the same time, aid with process management? How was I invited into this process? By the parties themselves, by some authority or mandated scheme (e.g., court mandated mediation), by the request of another third party or institution? Should there be 'matching' of mediator(s) to nationalities, race, ethnicity or gender of the parties? What is my stance with respect to the parties—can I really be 'neutral' (can anyone?) or 'unbiased' or 'without bias or prejudice'? As human beings we are all likely to have predispositions and our own cultural identities in any dispute. How should these be described, disclosed and monitored? Are there any conflicts of interest—personal, professional? Am I aware of my own implicit/unconscious biases and any cultural (White, Western, Northern, male?) characteristics that assume I (or the methods I use) am the 'norm' by which the mediation will be conducted?

Case Assessment

How might case type affect the kind of mediation which is offered: International crisis diplomats (see the different approaches and styles of George Mitchell in Northern Ireland, contrasted to Richard Holbrooke in Bosnia, back-channel mediators, complex business deals, family disputes, employment disputes, educational disputes. How many parties are involved? Are all the stakeholders at the table—should others be invited? Consider such issues as future generations in environmental disputes or children in divorce disputes, or insurers in construction disputes. Are there serious power imbalances between or among the parties? How might that affect who should be invited, how mediation is conducted (separate sessions, joint sessions) and how decisions will be made about what is agreed to. Are the parties pro se (alone) or represented by lawyers or other helpers? Are the parties from the same spoken language or will they need translators? Do the parties share culture(s) (religion, workplace, nationality, ethnicity, race, gender) or are the parties demographically or culturally from 'different' situations or understandings? Are the parties of close to equal statuses-titles, educational achievement, economic class, business partners—or will the 'power' or class or race or ethnicity or gender or economic differences manifest in power and communication differentials? Will the parties identify their own 'differences' or will mediators be sensitive or oblivious to more subtle racial, class, gender, ethnic issues, and ways of communicating?

Preparation and Ground Rules

Before any meeting of the parties, it is always advisable to consider what the parties' expectations are likely to be—is this a first encounter, with other parties, with mediation itself? Many suggest the use of pre-meetings (done separately, either in person or on phone or video chat) to learn about parties and their expectations, to develop trust, to answer questions and to begin to understand what is important to the parties. Many mediators use pre-mediation written submissions but note this too could be a cultural issue—is writing a favored form of communication, does a written document of any sort make positions in a mediation more rigid, less flexible, advantage those with sophisticated professional helpers? How should the physical space be structured (e.g., sitting on the floor or chairs, with a table or not, in a circle or rectangular conference table)? How much physical/social distance between parties and with the mediator(s)? How shall the parties be addressed (formally, or first names?) What food or drink should be served? What ground rules of engagement should be set in advance—is confidentiality a need, can it be guaranteed, who will parties share information with? Complex international business disputes will have to provide for some mediation of shared procedural rules (as international arbitrations do in *Terms of Reference* meetings—whose evidence rules will prevail (discovery of documents, expert witnesses, privilege, all of which vary by legal (common law, civil law, or mixed system) culture. Do ground rules of no interruptions, 'tone control' and etiquette policing 'privilege' certain cultural communication practices?

Mediator Role(s)

Mediators have different approaches—facilitative, evaluative, narrative, transformative, and hybrid combinations of all these. In situations where parties may not all share understandings of what mediators do, it is especially important for mediators to describe what they do and where appropriate to negotiate particular roles with the parties. While the American conception of a 'third party neutral' became an expected norm in many kinds of mediations, many parties now choose 'expert' mediators (as in intellectual property or high-tech disputes) who may know the parties and operate more like the 'wise elders' (in suggesting possible solutions and outcomes) that looks more like traditional mediation in Asian or African practices. Community mediation and various forms of indigenous and religious mediation have panels of 'elders' or facilitators (often too patriarchal in some contexts) or more 'inclusive' participation by whole communities in facilitating dispute processes.

Communication/Facilitation

In intercultural disputes mediators are likely best advised to use more elicitive, (asking questions and drawing out from the parties) approaches than more directive statements to encourage parties to express what is important to them on their own terms. It is especially important to consider the order of talk—who goes first often sets the terms and terrain (primacy) and controlling the narrative. A skilled mediator should be able to sensitively 'reframe' issues and create agendas that do not privilege or give primacy to particular parties. Active listening, restating, and confirming what is being said is always important, but is especially important in settings where the parties may need not only language translations, but conceptual and interest translations. For some parties, decision making will be 'rational' and 'principled,' for others' emotions, religious or ethical commitments will be most salient, and others may simply want to accomplish what is most 'practical' (what I call the *head, heart and stomach discourses of dispute resolution*, Menkel-Meadow 2018). Caucuses are likely to be needed, especially in situations of different expectations of privacy, decision making, and information sharing. One of the great ironies of intercultural mediation is often that where mediators might prefer 'face to face' dialogues and empathic communication to encourage mutual understanding, the need for 'face-saving' is often best achieved through the use of caucus meetings where the parties are not face to face and mediators can more 'neutrally' present proposals and reduce the reactive devaluation that occurs when parties devalue what is offered by their adversaries. When communication patterns (direct vs indirect modes of communication) are not 'matched' by the parties, mediators can literally either 'sit in the middle' of communications, help to interpret meanings, or offer proposals, whether in separate rooms or in joint sessions. Consider how many international crises and peace agreements have been accomplished by shuttle diplomacy and 'go-betweens' without the principal parties being in the same room at the same time (e.g., Viet Nam Paris Agreement, US-Iranian hostage crisis 'resolution', Oslo Accords, Dayton Accords).

Bargaining/Problem Solving

Modern (western) approaches to mediation prefer to facilitate party agency and autonomy by using such specific techniques as brainstorming, storyboarding, nominal voting procedures, and exercises to create joint gain and shared solutions to problems. In some settings, this pressure to 'create' and openly share is just the opposite of what some parties will want (closer to an evaluative, command idea coming from a wise elder). Some parties in mediation (whether from individual preferences or cultural expectations) will be collaborative, active, and keen to resolve problems—others will be adversarial, seeking to 'win' even in what is supposed to be a consensual setting. A culturally sensitive mediator has to be able to navigate different negotiation styles, again often by using questions—"what would happen if [...]", "if you don't like X, what would you propose instead?" "who else do you need to consult to see if Y will be acceptable?" Where the parties come from different negotiation traditions and practices, interventions (e.g., power balancing) and mediator suggestions or proposals are tools that can move things forward. Modern critiques of the mediator's 'neutral' stance (see below) suggest mediators may need to take responsibility for and 'call out' improper behavior or unfair proposals (Menkel-Meadow and Wheeler 2004). For many mediators, the challenge is to 'mediate' the different discourses of reason/principle, political, ethical, and religious commitments, as well as practical deal-making and necessary compromise for mediation to function as a process that produces some improved conditions for the parties.

Reaching Agreements

There are often different understandings of the appropriate time for reaching agreements. In complex international settings, time for relationship building, socializing, gift-giving, rituals and ceremonies, or banquets may be expected. Task oriented Americans often want to conclude deals quickly and see the transaction as more important than the relationship. A culturally skilled mediator needs to conduct, orchestrate, and manage the timing of negotiations and deal-making, and to confirm in many different ways that agreements (and the procedures for their realization and execution are clear—'reality testing') are understood by all parties (and committed to writing, if culturally or legally mandated) and approved by those with authority to do so. 'The devil is often in the details' as we say and the mediator of a dispute with parties who don't always share world views will have to work doubly hard to be sure there actually is a mediated outcome that will be complied with. Good agreements may have contingent provisions for adaptation to new conditions, new evidence or data (consider environmental and economic disputes) or re-evaluation of terms (consider agreements made in restorative justice or transitional justice settings.) Good mediators plan ahead with the parties to craft dispute resolution provisions for any issues that may arise from a mediation agreement.

Evaluation, Feedback, Assessment

No mediation is complete until the parties and mediators assess what they have done and engage in any mutually agreed-upon feedback process. The best mediators are self-reflecting (and reflexive) and seek to de-brief, not only particular interventions (with co-mediators and participants where possible) they have engaged in, but consideration of "what went well," "what might have been done differently" and what other possible options were available for substantive solutions. Where parties agree, mediators might meet again after the mediation is concluded to learn about implementation and reactions to the process. A learning model would allow the parties to consult with others to assess what they have accomplished. Perhaps a mediator will learn they need some further training in diversity, equity, and cultural inclusion sensitivity and methods or to be updated on substantive matters, law, or uses of technology. A spirited debate in the largely unregulated field of mediation is the extent to which mediators should be 'accountable' for the agreements they facilitate. For many mediators, the accountability is in the parties' consent and agreement to whatever outcome is reached as a core value of 'self-determination.' For others, mediators have a responsibility to ensure that agreements reached with their assistance should not be unjust, unfair, unenforceable, or unlawful. In many jurisdictions around the world, some case law and court decisions now adjudicate some claims of unfair influence, coercion, or defective contracting as some check on mediation processes.

Critiques of the 'Standard' Mediation Templates

In recent years much of the 'standard' template of mediation has been criticized from a number of quarters. As mediation began to gain currency in both court and legal settings, as well as private commercial settings, it moved out from its initial sources in community and indigenous models and practices of dispute resolution. Some were concerned about the privatization of justice, with processes and agreements occurring in secret without transparency or the application of the rule of law, often used in settings where the parties in dispute were of unequal 'arms' (economic status, access to lawyers and legal advice, race, gender, ethnicity, immigration status, etc.,). From the beginning, there was criticism of specific tools, techniques, and strategies that were considered derived only from Western-Northern cultures (e.g., the notion of a 'neutral' third party, the requirement to talk directly in narrative form, to search for future-oriented pragmatic solutions and relinquish the 'past' and claims of hurt, harm or anger "for the good of the [...] future" (children, company, country, community"). There have been specific charges of some mediation as being manipulative as mediators use 'selective facilitation' techniques to move parties toward the mediator's desired outcomes. More recently some have claimed that mediation is not only Western or 'Northern' but White (Press and Deason 2021), not permitting a voice for subordinate groups, particularly Blacks in cultures (like the US) with systemic racism. Others see the potential promise of mediation for interpersonal communication and understanding and practical business agreements, as well as international law disputes between countries in some cases, but express concerns that mediative approaches to highly polarized societies cannot be so easily 'scaled up' to whole societies, even with many groups organizing town halls, living room conversations and other deliberative democracy events that use mediative tools for facilitating dialogue in search of mutual understanding.

At an institutional level, Truth and Reconciliation processes have used mediative techniques of narrative, apologies, requests for forgiveness and amnesty even when reparations and restitution (as in smaller scale criminal restorative justice Victim-Offender settings have worked) are rare.

Most mediators of cross-cultural disputes are optimists (and realists!). Where some see intractable differences between and among people of different faiths, political systems, races, genders, and ethnicities, most of us see hope in the curiosity that we feel about different approaches to the problems that humans must confront. A well conducted intercultural mediation is one committed to learning, curiosity, empathy, some creativity, and some forms of human communication. Intercultural mediation is talk in service to human understanding and peaceful co-existence and hopefully, human flourishing. Mediation is a sensibility to approach others with whom one is in conflict to understand them (and ourselves) better and to seek a better situation than one was in before the mediation (and with solutions that may be specifically tailored to parties' needs and interests). We try to make lemonade or lemon pie out of lemons. (Or think of all the uses of lemons in different cultures!!) It is not simple or easy in many cases, but without it we may be doomed. As one who grew up in the shadows of the United Nations, I still harbor a belief that we have more similarities as humans than differences—at least enough to try to resolve our many disputes without unnecessary harm or violence.

Notes & Questions

1. Looking back to some of the examples presented in this chapter, how might cross-cultural differences explain some of the issues? Note the examples of "Western" mediators in Northern Ireland, Bosnia, and Trinidad.
2. How might conceptions of conciliation versus mediation, issues of timing and ripeness, and mediation styles be impacted by culture?

Further Reading

NADIA ALEXANDER, INTERNATIONAL AND COMPARATIVE MEDIATION: LEGAL PERSPECTIVES (2009).

John Barkai, *What's a Cross-Cultural Mediator to Do? A Low-Context Solution for a High-Context Problem*, 10 CARDOZO J. CONFLICT RESOL. 43 (2008).

JACOB BERCOVITCH, STUDIES IN INTERNATIONAL MEDIATION (2003).

GABRIELLA BLUM, ISLANDS OF AGREEMENT: MANAGING ENDURING ARMED RIVALRIES (2007).

COMPLEX DISPUTE RESOLUTION: INTERNATIONAL DISPUTE RESOLUTION (Carrie Menkel-Meadow ed., 2012).

COMPLEX DISPUTE RESOLUTION: MULTI-PARTY DISPUTE RESOLUTION, DEMOCRACY, AND DECISION-MAKING (Carrie Menkel-Meadow ed., 2012).

Isabelle Gunning, *Diversity Issues in Mediation: Controlling Negative Cultural Myths*, 1995 J. DISP. RESOL., 1995, at 55.

INTERNATIONAL NEGOTIATION: ANALYSIS, APPROACHES, ISSUES (Victor Kremenyuk ed., 2002).

Carol Izumi, *Implicit Bias and the Illusion of Mediator Neutrality,* 54 Wash, U. J. L. & Policy 71.

SVEN G. KOOPMANS, NEGOTIATING PEACE: A GUIDE TO THE PRACTICE, POLITICS, AND LAW OF INTERNATIONAL MEDIATION (2018).

Joel Lee, *Culture and Its Importance in Mediation*, 16 PEPP. DISP. RESOL. J. 317 (2016).

MEDIATION: PRINCIPLES AND REGULATION IN COMPARATIVE PERSPECTIVE (Klaus J. Hopt & Felix Steffek, eds. 2013).

Carrie Menkel-Meadow, *Correspondences and Contradictions in International and Domestic Conflict Resolution*, 2003 J. DISP. RESOL., 2003, at 319.

Carrie Menkel-Meadow, *Mediation 3.0: Merging the Old and the New*, 2018 ASIAN J. ON MED., Jan. 2019, at 1–20.

Carrie Menkel-Meadow, *Variations in the Uptake and Resistance to Mediation Outside of the United States, in* CONTEMPORARY ISSUES IN INTERNATIONAL MEDIATION AND ARBITRATION: THE FORDHAM PAPERS 1914 (Arthur Rovine ed., 2015).

CARRIE MENKEL-MEADOW, LELA P. LOVE, & ANDREA KUPFER SCHNEIDER, MEDIATION: PRACTICE, POLICY, AND ETHICS (3d ed. 2020).

J.G. MERRILLS, INTERNATIONAL DISPUTE SETTLEMENT (6th ed. 2017).

JACQUELINE NOLAN-HALEY, ELLEN DEASON, & MARIANA HERNANDEZ-CRESPO GONSTEAD, GLOBAL ISSUES IN MEDIATION (2019).

Sarah M. H. Nouwen, *Exporting Peace? The E.U.'s Mediator's Backpack, 1 European Law Open 26–59; doi:10.1017/e/0/2022.9.*

Sharon Press & Ellen Deason, *Mediation: Embedded Assumptions of Whiteness?*, 22 Cardozo J. Conflict Resol. 453 (2021).

Jeswald Salacuse, *Is There a Better Way? Alternative Methods of Treaty-Based, Investor–State Dispute Resolution*, 31 Fordham Int'l L.J. 128 (2007).

Andrea Kupfer Schneider, *Public and Private International Dispute Resolution*, *in* The Handbook of Dispute Resolution (M.L. Moffitt & Robert C. Bordone eds., 2005).

Jean Sternlight, *Is Alternative Dispute Resolution Consistent with the Rule of Law?*, 56 DePaul L. Rev. 569 (2007).

Chapter 4

Arbitration

Recall from Chapter 1 that France and New Zealand were in a dispute over the bombing of the *Rainbow Warrior*. France claimed its sovereign rights to test nuclear weapons freely within its own territory and sent agents to prevent the *Rainbow Warrior* from sailing into the testing location. In turn, New Zealand claimed criminal jurisdiction over the French agents whose actions resulted in the death of a person aboard the *Rainbow Warrior*, which had been docked in the Port of Auckland in New Zealand. After the agents responsible for the bombing were convicted in New Zealand and France subsequently threatened an embargo against New Zealand exports to the European Economic Community, the two countries agreed to arbitration.

Arbitration between two sovereign nations is a type of dispute resolution method that has a long history. Litigation in court has only become available to nations through the International Court of Justice (or perhaps through regional courts) in the last century, and these courts still have limited jurisdiction and capacity, as we will discuss in Chapter 6. A peaceful and relatively speedy process like arbitration avoids further violence or economic damage. The first part of this chapter focuses on "public law" arbitrations—that is, arbitrations between countries.

Yet arbitration also has a long history of being used between merchants from different countries who, for many of the same reasons as nations, do not want to rely on domestic courts for redress (fearing either their bias or their inability to enforce judgments from one country in another country where assets might be located to satisfy judgments, for example) and prefer a speedy and peaceful method of resolution. The second part of this chapter examines how these "private law" disputes are resolved through international commercial arbitration.

In the last 50 years, supported by both sets of actors, a hybrid form of arbitration has been created at the intersection of nations and those companies from other nations which invest in them. This investor-state arbitration has provided a unique avenue for resolving disputes. The third part of this chapter discusses the evolution of arbitration as the favored method for such mixed disputes.

Finally, the chapter examines some of the issues raised by these cross-cultural methods of dispute resolution in terms of who serves as the arbitrators and how different domestic laws and legal processes are applied under these international structures. It concludes by providing materials for a simulation so that you may see how arbitrators are chosen in multi-jural systems and the procedural issues that are often dealt with in public, private, and hybrid international arbitrations.

I. Introduction to International Arbitration

The following excerpt provides an overview of how arbitration has been used in the public and private arenas.

Andrea Kupfer Schneider, *Public and Private International Dispute Resolution*

in The Handbook of Dispute Resolution 438, 446–48 (Michael Moffitt & Robert Bordone eds., 2004)

International Arbitration & Hybrid Processes

Private International Arbitration

Arbitration has its roots in international commercial dispute resolution. Merchant guilds in Europe developed arbitration as a swift and fair method for dealing with commercial disputes across borders when domestic laws were varying and unclear. The popularity and ease of international commercial arbitration persist today. Much like domestic arbitration, international arbitration can offer the advantages of speed, cost-efficiency, finality, and subject-matter expertise of the arbitrator. In addition, avoiding litigation in foreign courts remains a significant advantage.

Countries have encouraged the use of arbitration to resolve commercial disputes by committing to enforce arbitration awards. As of this writing, 134 countries [now 172] have signed the *New York Convention on the Recognition and Enforcement of Foreign Arbitral Awards* (1958). This treaty provides that enforcement of arbitral awards among the signatory countries shall be virtually automatic—much faster than the process required to enforce a foreign court judgment. Under the New York Convention, there are very few reasons that a court can set aside an arbitration award. These limited grounds for setting aside or refusing recognition of an award include procedural defects like improper notice of hearings, inappropriate composition of the arbitral panel under various rules and doctrines, or failure of the arbitration award to be within contemplated agreement of parties. An award can also be set aside in some limited cases where recognition or enforcement of the award would be contrary to public policy of the enforcing country.

Responding to the proliferation of international arbitration, international arbitration centers worldwide have developed arbitral rules and procedures based on legal and cultural differences. These centers offer disputants a choice in location, rules, and underlying law, making international arbitration even more popular. Some of these arbitration centers include the London Court of International Arbitration, the American Arbitration Association, the Center for Public Resources in New York, the International Chamber of Commerce in Paris, as well as centers in Stockholm, Hong Kong, and the Middle East. Centers like these start by providing a basic set of procedures and can also help choose and appoint the arbitrators, organize the logistics of the arbitration, and coordinate the exchange of documents, reports, and experts.

Public International Arbitration & Mixed Processes

Arbitration between countries was rare historically. Countries usually want to resolve disputes among themselves and not have a third party impose a decision on them. For example, the Permanent Court of Arbitration, created in 1899 to voluntarily resolve disputes between countries, has heard only 47 cases. One famous arbitration in U.S. history was the *Alabama* arbitration cases between the U.S. and Great Britain growing out of the U.S. Civil War. The U.S. accused Great Britain of helping the South in violation of its obligation as a neutral under international law; rather than negotiate the claims or resort to force, both countries agreed to arbitration. An arbitration panel agreed with the U.S. and awarded the U.S. over $15 million in damages.

In the late twentieth century, more countries started to turn to arbitration for a number of reasons. First, the International Court of Justice (ICJ), created in 1945, has had great success in acting as an arbiter between countries over issues such as boundaries, territorial disputes, and fishing rights. Using the ICJ is most attractive for countries in contexts in which the dispute is law-based, the issue is politically sensitive enough that compromise would be difficult, and the stakes are low enough that the use of force would be absurd. For example, the U.S. and Canada could not reach a negotiated agreement over fishing rights in the Gulf of Maine. Compromising for either country would have been politically difficult with important domestic constituencies involved. The countries submitted the case to the ICJ and used a panel process by which the parties agreed to five judges with maritime expertise. This process, which looked much like arbitration, successfully resolved the case between the two neighbors.

The second reason for the expansion of arbitration between countries is the creation of new forums to handle disputes. For example, the [World Trade Organization] was created in 1994 with a separate dispute settlement body to arbitrate trade cases between countries. The disputes are heard by rotating panels of arbitrators with expertise in trade law. More recently, a tribunal was established to hear disputes arising under the Law of the Sea Convention.

A third reason that arbitration has expanded internationally is that countries are often involved in disputes with private parties rather than another country. Neither the ICJ nor the WTO process is available to private parties to pursue their investment disputes with countries. Domestic courts are also not available because countries often have sovereign immunity both at home and in foreign courts. Therefore, the International Centre for the Settlement of Investment Disputes (ICSID), established under the World Bank, was created to handle disputes between countries and private parties in order to facilitate investment and development. Most of the U.S.'s bilateral investment treaties around the world, as well as NAFTA, refer any disputes arising under the treaty to ICSID or ad hoc arbitration rules created by the United Nations Commission on International Trade Law (UNCITRAL). An example of this type of dispute would be one well-known case under NAFTA involving a Canadian company arbitrating against the U.S. for an unfair state jury trial outcome. These public-private disputes have been growing dramatically as foreign investment grows.

The expansion of arbitration has also led to the development of mixed processes in order to deal with different types of disputes and parties. The development of international hybrid processes responds to the varying needs of the states for control over the outcome, level of enforcement desired, different parties involved, and underlying international law. For example, as discussed above, Chapter 11 of NAFTA deals with disputes between private investors and the host country, using and enforcing arbitration under the New York Convention rules. Other provisions of NAFTA permit arbitration only between the member countries rather than arbitration with private companies. Another variation is found at the WTO where the panel process between states alone is supplemented by the right of appeal. WTO member countries wanted to ensure that the international trade law is applied consistently and narrowly across cases. Enforcement under the WTO, however, remains with each country's executive branch rather than its court system. [We return to hybrid arbitration in Chapter 7.—Eds.]

Now we dive further into the arbitrations between the United States and Great Britain to help us understand why states choose to use this process. As you read about the relationship between the two countries, consider why the process of arbitration was chosen. Should the countries have negotiated a settlement? Or, if they wanted to mediate, who could have served as a mediator? The challenges in answering those questions likely explain the process chosen.

Case Study: United States-Great Britain Arbitrations in the 19th Century

The United States has used arbitration to resolve disputes, particularly with our former sovereign. During the American Civil War, Confederate agents contracted with British boatyards for warships even though Britain had declared that it would stay neutral. Because this arrangement violated British neutrality laws, the warships were disguised as merchant vessels although their true purpose was to serve as commerce raiders. The most successful of the warships, the CSS *Alabama*, captured 58 Union merchant ships. Moreover, the *Alabama*, with the other British-built Confederate warships, sank more than 150 Union ships. It wasn't until after Union spies gathered enough evidence to expose Britain's lack of neutrality and President Lincoln's minister in London had applied immense pressure to the British government that Britain seized the remaining warships before they were able to be transferred to the Confederacy.

After the war, the U.S. government demanded compensation from Great Britain for the damage, arguing that these actions were a violation of Britain's neutrality laws. The cost to the United States was estimated to be in the hundreds of millions (in 2023 dollars). Initially, some U.S. officials proposed that Great Britain offer Canada to the United States for compensation. Years of unsuccessful negotiations ensued until 1871, when the two nations signed the Washington Treaty.

The Washington Treaty established an arbitration commission to review the validity of the U.S. financial claims against Great Britain and addressed various other American-British disputes, such as boundaries and fishing rights. The United States and Great Britain agreed that the tribunal would comprise five arbitrators, one each from the United States, Great Britain, Italy, Switzerland, and Brazil. In addition, the treaty outlined the specific rules and procedures for arbitration, which would be held in Geneva. While the commission eventually rejected the U.S. government's claims for indirect damages, Great Britain was ordered to pay the United States $15.5 million as compensation for the damage caused by the *Alabama*.

Less than a decade later, the United States and Great Britain were back in arbitration over fishing rights in the Bering Sea. After purchasing Alaska from Russia, the United States claimed total control over the Bering Sea, which included all seal hunting in the Bering Sea waters.

The U.S. Revenue Cutter Service, known today as the U.S. Coast Guard, captured several Canadian ships killing seals near the Pribilof Islands, located within the Bering Sea. The United States had two main arguments against this activity. First, the area of the Bering Sea was under exclusive U.S. jurisdiction following the purchase of Alaska from Russia in 1867. Second, the United States had outlawed the killing of seals in this area, which it had the right to police due to its alleged exclusive jurisdiction. Britain argued against the United States' jurisdiction over the concerned area, and the tribunal ultimately sided with the former. The final amount awarded to the British sealers was almost $500,000.

Notes & Questions

1. How did arbitration meet the interests of the United States and Great Britain in these two cases? What were the factors that drove the two countries to arbitration?
2. Would other interests have been served in litigation in either of their domestic courts? What about in an international court, had there been one in existence at the time?

II. International Commercial Arbitration

This section begins with an excerpt by Carrie Menkel-Meadow that explains how arbitration was historically used among merchants to efficiently and effectively resolve disputes in order to facilitate trade and mobility. The next reading, an article by Professor Edward Brunet, reviews the evolution of arbitration from these historic and trade-based venues into the professional cadre and process that is utilized today. Finally, an article by Professor Matthew Erie describes the creation of international legal hubs built around an arbitration process and legal services that now dot the global landscape and make up the modern international commercial arbitration map.

Carrie Menkel-Meadow, *Are Cross-Cultural Ethics Standards Possible or Desirable in International Arbitration?*

in Melangés en l'honneur de Pierre Tercier 5–7 (Peter Gauch, Franz Werro, Pascal Pichonnaz eds., 2008)

A Brief History

Arbitration of disputes is as old as commercial markets. There is evidence that the Sumerian, Egyptian, Persian, Greek, Roman and Chinese ancient civilizations all had some form of third party "arbitration" of trading disputes. Whenever two merchants or a buyer and seller of goods or services have a dispute (about quantity, quality, price, delivery or other common commercial terms) there has been a need for a timely and efficient (and legitimate) resolution. Most commonly, through human commercial history, such disputes were settled, where possible, on the spot, with some knowledgeable expert or by some trusted "wise elder." As commerce developed and became both more specialized, (guilds of medieval Europe) and international, more and more disputes were resolved "after the fact." With the development of formal legal systems in the thirteenth to nineteenth centuries some commercial disputants began to rely on more formal courts and "public" judges (who served the kind and often depended for their fees on a percentage of the amount in controversy). Commercial disputants often still preferred the more informal system of arbitration, where they might choose both the decision maker and the substantive and procedural rules, but increasingly (at least in common law systems) courts would not enforce arbitral awards (under the doctrine of "ouster"—that arbitrators could not "oust" courts of their rightful jurisdiction, in what many commentators see as "competition" for control (and economic gain) of dispute resolution mechanisms.

Thus, early in the history of commercial dispute resolution the tension of competition for control of the dispute resolution mechanisms emerged and, with it, a tension between perhaps competing values of the commercial system—the need for privacy (and protection of trade secrets and practices), internal industry or guild control, efficiency (speed and low cost), but also predictability (knowledge about applicable rules of practice and decision) and legitimacy (which governs whether a decision will be complied with or can be enforced through some official mechanism, like a domestic or national court). Most histories of arbitration and dispute resolution conclude that for most of arbitration's history trust was the glue that held the system together. Either merchants or decision makers lived in the same community and knew each other or decision makers were chosen because they knew about the industry or the disputants and were trusted to arrive at roughly "fair" solutions.

As international trade grew exponentially in the late 19th century and especially with the advent of modern technologies' dependence, for resources (oil, fuel and raw materials), on nations other than those producing or consuming the final products, the need for a truly international dispute resolution mechanism became apparent. In what is one of those historical moments of convergence, business lawyers active in both Europe and the North American continents, were able to develop an effective private international arbitration system and, at roughly the same time, they were able to achieve some formal legal recognition of this private justice system.

The precursor of the London Court of Arbitration dates from 1883, functioning with various institutional name changes continuously since 1903, until its 1981 incarnation as the LCIA (which is not really a court, but an international arbitration administrative tribunal, to manage arbitration).

The ICC International Court of Arbitration was founded in 1923, following the founding, in 1919, in Paris, of the International Chamber of Commerce "to serve the interests of world business, by promoting trade and investment, open markets for goods and services, and the free flow of capital." While the ICC initially represented the business sectors of Britain, Belgium, France, Italy, and the United States, it eventually expanded to include representation of the private business sector in over 130 countries. The Secretariat is based in Paris and since 1923, at the time of the founding of the ICC Arbitration process, the ICC has received over 14,000 cases for dispute resolution.

In 1925 an active committee of the American Bar Association was able to successfully lobby the United States Congress for a federal act, the Federal Arbitration Act, which formally recognized (and required court enforcement of) private contractual arbitral agreements in domestic contexts. The US ratified the United Nations (New York) Convention on the Recognition and Enforcement of Foreign Arbitral Awards of 1958 much later (1970), and it then became part of the Federal Arbitration Act (9 U.S.C. sect. 201 et seq.)

In time, other international institutions of arbitration (e.g., the Arbitration Institute of the Stockholm Chamber of Commerce, the Cairo Regional Center for International Commercial Arbitration (since 1979), the China International and Economic Trade Arbitration Commission (CIETAC), and others, were created to serve as administrators and managers of the growing international dispute resolution process, some with regional (Asia, Russia, Northern Europe, Middle-east) or industry (oil, transport, energy, construction) specializations.

International arbitration truly "bloomed" when, in 1958, the United Nations Convention on Recognition and Enforcement of Foreign Arbitral Awards (known as "the New York Convention") was approved by the United Nations Commission on International Trade Laws (UNCITRAL) and subsequently ratified by over 130 [now 172] countries. This treaty requires signatories to recognize and enforce arbitration awards granted in one jurisdiction but enforced in another, with relatively few legal requirements (the written agreement to arbitrate, a written arbitration award with appropriate translation) and only a few grounds for refusal to enforce such awards (gross procedural irregularities, and some recognition of local or domestic public and legal policy issues). This treaty, designed to avoid the complexities of enforcement of legal judgments rendered in foreign courts (with many grounds for non-recognition, given different legal cultures and quite different rules of jurisdiction and procedure) has been enormously successful in supplanting "public" international litigation by substituting "private" international arbitration. Where parties in dispute with another party in another legal jurisdiction fear "home court" bias and domestic party and law preferences, international arbitration permits the parties to choose neutral decision makers, and the substantive and procedural law of their choice (through contract, and through adoption of either ad hoc procedural rules or acceptance of one of the arbitral institutions' rule systems).

In the next excerpt, Brunet outlines how the myth of folklore arbitration—magically fast, cheap, and fair—is not accurate.

Edward Brunet, *Replacing Folklore Arbitration with a Contract Model of Arbitration*

74 TULANE L. REV. 39, 42–47 (1999)

Unlike the competing models of arbitration, folklore arbitration is both a mythical perception and a reality. The oversimplified perception is that folklore arbitration is the only type of arbitration that exists. It is speedy, cheap, informal, and equitable. In arbitration orthodoxy, the results of folklore arbitration leave no room for the courts because arbitration awards are final. The partners to an arbitration contract have intentionally opted out of the court system. The expert arbitrator fashions a result by applying Solomon-like principles of equity and eschewing the rigidity of doctrinal formalism. Folklore arbitrators decide disputes based upon factual context and avoid application of substantive legal rules.

The historical roots of folklore arbitration lie in the use of arbitration to resolve intra-industry disputes in the late nineteenth and early twentieth centuries. Garment or textile industry arbitration, one of the earliest industry-wide examples of arbitration use, is illustrative. Under this procedure, two textile merchants, each of whom had previously contracted with the other, agreed to a supply contract containing an arbitration clause. While each party was pleased to employ a simple, informal process that would probably be a less expensive way to resolve a dispute than conventional litigation, it is likely that the popularity of folklore arbitration grew because of the selection of the arbitrator. Rather than allowing a judge, a stranger who knew little or nothing about the matter, to resolve their dispute, the parties selected one of their own fellow textile merchants to be their arbitrator. This selection of a trusted and expert decision maker dominated the arbitration process. The choice of an intra-industry arbitrator guaranteed a knowledgeable decision maker who was likely to rule on the equities of the factual context in an informal manner. The selection of a knowledgeable expert with credentials within the same group also satisfied a strong need for industry self-governance.

In early twentieth-century textile arbitration, the facts were likely to matter much more than the law to the nonlawyer expert experienced in the textile business of each of the parties. Law played a truly subordinate role. While it is possible that the arbitrator could use the law as a basis for decision, the reality was that the parties selected the arbitrator hoping and even knowing that this particular arbitrator was prone to make equitable, fact-based decisions. Compromise results, fair to each party, were the order of the day and played a major role in the ability of arbitrators to obtain repeat business and the parties' selection of the arbitration process....

[T]he results of a conventional jury verdict and an arbitration award are not dissimilar. Both share the use of informal community values and local culture. The nature of the industry used by the arbitrator to fashion an equitable award resembles the community values used by a civil jury to reach a verdict. Both jury verdicts and folklore arbitration awards are typically conclusory and lack reasoned opinions.

Privacy is also a prime characteristic of folklore arbitration. The textile businesses that opted for arbitration desired as little publicity as possible regarding any future controversies. Just as their contract was a private matter, any disputes between the textile merchants were conducted in private. The disputants had no wish to conduct their disputes in public where negative publicity might occur. The public nature of courts and juries was incompatible with a strong desire for privacy.

In the historic folklore arbitrations, informal procedures dominated. There was little or no discovery. Evidence rules were inapplicable, in part because the expert arbitrator selected by the partners was not a lawyer. The fact that these lay arbitrators were untrained in the law helps explain why there were no written opinions. In addition, the need for private dispute resolution made formal written opinions (which would generate publicity) seem imprudent....

Today, many arbitrations resemble litigation. The characteristics of what some may label a "judicialized model of arbitration" include (1) routine discovery, (2) motion practice, (3) application of substantive legal rules, (4) written, discursive awards with findings of fact and conclusions of law or reasons, and (5) enhanced judicial review pursuant to arbitration clauses that require courts to evaluate awards for legal error. Such procedures are a far cry from the historical, hypothetical textile arbitration.

The evolution of modern arbitration to include judicialized features has been accomplished through contract. In a sense, a "contract model" of arbitration has emerged in which the parties craft their own private dispute procedures. The parties now exercise party autonomy by writing their own style of arbitration into the agreement. They select the procedure they think appropriate and need not follow the template of prior arbitration adversaries.

This is not to suggest that the contract model of arbitration bears no resemblance to folklore arbitration. Contract model arbitration continues to draw on selected elements of folklore arbitration. Arbitrators in a contract model arbitration are still likely to temper their awards with the rough justice of equity. Similarly, contract model arbitration and folklore arbitration share the use of the expert arbitrator who is knowledgeable in the subject matter of the dispute and avoids the potential arbitrariness of a jury. Contract model arbitration is not totally differentiated from folklore arbitration. These models share a place in the continuum of arbitration and are not always polar opposites.

Folklore arbitration, an agreement to arbitrate on the assumption that the arbitration procedures will be settled and definite without any particular contract language setting forth specific arbitration features, can still be found. Its existence may be due to the contracting parties' lack of experience or knowledge regarding arbitration.... Experienced parties with a background in arbitration are more likely to carefully constrain the ambiguity inherent in a loose agreement to "arbitrate."

Even parties who dislike the expense of a judicialized type of arbitration may employ the contract model. For example, contracting parties who want the features of folklore arbitration can agree to prohibit discovery, set a quick hearing date, and forbid the arbitrator from holding a preliminary hearing or issuing a written decision containing reasons. By specifying their procedural desires, the parties constrain the discretion of the arbitrator and the arbitration-sponsoring organization.

Of course, if courts held to a static folklore model of arbitration, arbitration parties could not contract for procedures that differ from folklore arbitration.... [T]he Supreme Court has interpreted the Federal Arbitration Act to make parties the masters of their own disputes and to create a framework in which the courts enforce the procedures selected in the disputants' arbitration clause.

Notes & Questions

1. Historically, many arbitrators have not been lawyers but rather subject experts. What are the advantages and disadvantages of this practice?
2. One industry in which arbitration has been studied is the diamond industry, which is governed by its own unique rules for contract formation. *See* Lisa Bernstein, *Opting Out of the Legal System: Extralegal Contractual Relations in the Diamond Industry*, 21 J. LEGAL STUD. 115 (1992). Rather than making written agreements regarding the purchase and sale of valuable diamonds, dealers often seal their agreements simply by shaking hands and uttering the words "mazel and broche" (luck and blessing in Yiddish). Alternatively, an offer is sometimes made by placing a diamond in an envelope that is folded and sealed in a precise way. When breaches of these unique contractual rules are alleged, the diamond industry uses its own specialized, private, secret arbitration to resolve disputes. Although the arbitrators' rulings are not written, they are powerful. Dealers who do not comply with an industry arbitral ruling are likely to find it difficult if not impossible to continue as a diamond merchant. For another

discussion of the diamond industry, see Barak D. Richman, *Community Enforcement of Informal Contracts: Jewish Diamond Merchants in New York*, 31 L. & Soc. Inquiry, no. 2, Spring 2006, http://papers.ssrn.com/sol3/papers.cfm?abstract_id=349040. You may also watch the Netflix series *Rough Diamonds* for more on this unique world.

The next article excerpt provides an analysis of the business of arbitration—and how creating a center for arbitration can lead to a focus on the lawyers, experts, and financial support around arbitration. Such "new legal hubs" are emerging in countries that are not otherwise necessarily tied to the rule of law. Some argue that there now exists an economic competition in establishing local, regional, national, and international centers or tribunals of arbitration, which are used to attract both general business and the "business of dispute resolution," which generates hefty fees, creating income for both state-run and private arbitral bodies.

Matthew S. Erie, *The New Legal Hubs: The Emergent Landscape of International Commercial Dispute Resolution*

60 Va. J. Int'l L. 225, 228–30, 234–39, 248–50, 262–63, 265–66 (2020)

I define a NLH [New Legal Hub] as a "one-stop shop" for cross-border commercial dispute resolution, often located in financial centers, and promoted as an official policy by nondemocratic or hybrid states. First, the idea of the one-stop shop derives from late legal scholar Frank Sander's concept of the "multi-door courthouse." Sander thought that the courts of the future would provide parties with a menu of dispute resolution mechanisms and offer not just litigation, but also mediation, arbitration, and ombudsmen, with an intake office to triage disputes. NLHs are modern-day versions of the multi-door courthouse for sophisticated parties whose lawyers choose which mechanism to use. Second, NLHs overlap with other sectoral hubs: mainly financial but also infrastructural, telecom, and insurance. As centers of finance, hubs require clear rules for creating capital markets. Third, NLHs are located mainly in nondemocratic or hybrid states which I define as nonwestern states wherein power is concentrated in the hands of a few (or one) with the result that the system lacks true political pluralism, representation, and an electoral process. Examples of these forms of government include autocracies, kleptocracies, authoritarian systems, single-party states, and hybrid regimes. Nondemocratic and hybrid states have different and overlapping goals, including political legitimacy (foremost in the eyes of international business parties and secondarily for domestic audiences) and economic development. Legitimacy as a legal service provider can be a precondition for economic growth. Depending on the relative socio-economic development of the host state, NLHs can either attract FDI [foreign direct investment] or export legal services, thus serving as a multi-purpose growth strategy....

Dispute Resolution Mechanisms

The core of the "one-stop shop" idea is that both at the predispute and dispute stages, a NLH provides all relevant legal services, including dispute resolution. The benefit of the concept of the "one-stop shop" is that it combines both litigation and non-litigation mechanisms (i.e., arbitration and mediation), overcoming some of the "either/or" logic that has characterized the ADR literature. Sander's "multi-door courthouse" was not necessarily meant for nondemocratic regimes, but it is such postcolonial Inter-Asian contexts where the idea may find most traction. One consequence of hubs being jurisdictional carve-outs that apply transnational law is that by having procedural rules that can potentially be independent from the host state's legislature, NLHs are able to develop cross-institutional mechanisms that are responsive to parties' needs and market preferences. For example, NLHs can create links between in-house arbitral tribunals and commercial courts. However, as I will show, some of these innovations are not practical given that they may require enforcement outside the forum.

In analyzing the foregoing elements, it becomes apparent that much of the legal work that NLHs do touches on matters of conflict of laws: jurisdiction, choice of law, and enforcement. Thus, in considering NLHs' functions, hubs develop institutions and rules that promote flexibility for international parties to choose transnational law to resolve problems. From a managerial perspective, the NLH seeks not only to generate profits, but also to maximize its own utility to the host state as stakeholder. NLHs have both functional and symbolic purposes as they are equal parts capital requirements, on the one hand, and intrastate and public relations, on the other hand.

Beginning with the former, NLHs are designed to hook capital by attracting cross-border commercial disputes through a number of business models. I use London as a reference since many NLHs emulate London. First, there are the arbitration fees (i.e., arbitrators' fees, institution fees, court reporters, cost of the hearing facilities, etc.), which, for purposes of analysis, I distinguish from lawyers' fees. According to a study conducted by the London-based Chartered Institute of Arbitrators in 2011, the average international commercial arbitration case cost 1,348,000 GBP (US $1,773,341) in common law jurisdictions and 1,521,000 GBP (US $2,000,928) in civil law countries.

Arbitration houses vary in their costs, but a common complaint is that, since two-thirds of the *total* costs (i.e., arbitration fees plus lawyers' fees) can be lawyers' fees and lawyers drive the process, arbitration has become excessively costly. Hence, a second business model is that of the law firm, including U.K. firms, U.S. firms, internationalizing Chinese firms, and local law firms, that generate revenue through billable hours in handling matters for clients who are either incorporated at the hub or who have elected to use that forum for their dispute resolution. Lawyers' fees include not just transactional matters but also litigation, arbitration, and mediation. To give one data point, the top fifty law firms in London earned a total of 20 billion GBP (US $26.3 billion) in 2017. So, while proponents of hubs have some incentive to push the application of their own substantive law, as it benefits the local bar who are experts in that specific jurisdiction, most hubs feature international law firms that are proficient in transnational law. As opposed to arbitration and lawyers' fees, court fees and mediation fees are relatively insignificant. For instance, for the DIFC Courts [Dubai International Financial Centre], fees are $135,000 for a claim over $50 million, and upon early settlement, fees are returned to the parties. Business mediation centers charge similar nominal numbers. In addition to the core mechanisms for dispute resolution, there are also auxiliary services, such as law clerks, paralegals, notaries, and instructors at legal academies who are affiliated with hubs. In total, the revenues generated by the legal industry and its dispute resolution services can be substantial means of capturing capital for the host state.

Notes & Questions

1. As international commercial arbitration evolves, it is becoming more law-based than business-practices based. How would you advise a client in light of the changes in international arbitration? If you were designing a commercial arbitration center, would you require that the arbitrators be lawyers?
2. Consider how the burgeoning practice of arbitration leads to business growth in related industries. As we turn to the blending of private and public law in international investment law, we can consider how state support of the new legal hubs might already be blurring these lines.

III. International Investment Arbitration— State and Private Interests

We now turn to what happens when public and private law—and disputes—collide. These disputes occur between private companies and the states in which they invest. Typically, most states are protected by sovereign immunity from lawsuits in their domestic courts and are additionally protected in foreign courts through laws such as the US Foreign Sovereign Immunities Act. Historically, this meant that it was up to each country to protect its own citizens from the acts of a foreign government. Sometimes this resulted in diplomatic negotiations (to free citizens or to repatriate their assets), but other times, it resulted in more violent forms of enforcement. Much of US "gunboat diplomacy," through which the United States threatened Latin American countries in one way or another, came from these governments in disputes with US citizens. Hoping to create a more peaceful dispute resolution alternative and to build upon the success of arbitration in both private and public venues, bilateral trade agreements, which provided rights to foreign investors, also started to include arbitration clauses under the UN auspices (through the UN Commission on International Trade Law (UNCITRAL)) or through the World Bank (under the International Convention for the Settlement of International Disputes (ICSID). As we review the processes created under these structures, consider the case below:

Case Study: *Chromalloy Aeroservices v. Arab Republic*

In June 1988, Chromalloy, an American corporation, contracted with the Air Force of the Arab Republic of Egypt to provide it with parts, maintenance, and repair for the Air Force's helicopters. After three years, Egypt terminated the contract with Chromalloy, citing extensive delays in the performance of services. However, Chromalloy rejected the cancellation of the contract and began arbitration proceedings based on the arbitration clause included in the contract. The arbitration proceedings took place in Cairo under Egyptian law and were governed by UNCITRAL arbitration rules. The panel concluded that under Egyptian law, Egypt was not permitted to terminate the contract because the formal notice period outlined in the contract had not been fulfilled nor had the conditions for termination been satisfied. Following the proceedings, an arbitral panel ordered Egypt to compensate Chromalloy the sums of $272,900 with 5 percent interest and $16,940,958 with 5 percent interest. Chromalloy was ordered to pay Egypt 606,920 pounds sterling with 5 percent interest.

However, Egypt refused to pay. Accordingly, Chromalloy filed a petition to enforce this arbitral award with the U.S. District Court for the District of Columbia. Egypt countered by filing an appeal with the Egyptian Court of Appeals to nullify the award and by filing a motion to dismiss Chromalloy's petition with the U.S. district court. In 1995, the Egyptian Court of Appeals nullified the award, finding that the arbitration panel incorrectly applied Egyptian administrative law. In particular, the court held that the misuse of administrative law resulted in a failure to apply the choice of law of the parties at issue, and thus the award was invalid.

The district court had to decide whether the arbitral award should be valid despite its nullification in Egypt, thus allowing for its confirmation under the New York Convention, and whether the rules relating to foreign judgments under the New York Convention overrode similar rules in the United States. In a controversial opinion, the district court chose to recognize the arbitral award as valid. For the first time, the district court applied the more favorable U.S. domestic law contained in the Federal Arbitration Act (FAA) on international arbitration. Specifically, the court concluded that the provisions in the New York Convention allowed Chromalloy to invoke the FAA for the recognition and enforcement of the award. The court held that because the Egyptian court's nullification of the award did not constitute a reason for nonenforcement under the FAA, the district court had to validate the award. Even though the New York Convention acknowledges the disregard of an award by an international court as grounds for nonenforcement, Egypt could not rely on this provision because Chromalloy's right to invoke the FAA superseded the New York Convention. Furthermore, the court also reasoned that the Egyptian court's decision constituted open hostility toward the institution of arbitration and that upholding its judgment would go against the United States' stance in favor of arbitration.

Notes & Questions

1. How would you apply the standards for non-recognition of an arbitral award in a case like this under Art. V of the New York Convention, excerpted below?

   1. Recognition and enforcement of the award may be refused, at the request of the party against whom it is invoked, only if that party furnishes to the competent authority where the recognition and enforcement is sought, proof that:

      (a) The parties to the agreement referred to in article II were, under the law applicable to them, under some incapacity, or the said agreement is not valid under the law to which the parties have subjected it or, failing any indication thereon, under the law of the country where the award was made; or

      (b) The party against whom the award is invoked was not given proper notice of the appointment of the arbitrator or of the arbitration proceedings or was otherwise unable to present his case; or

      (c) The award deals with a difference not contemplated by or not falling within the terms of the submission to arbitration, or it contains decisions on matters beyond the scope of the submission to arbitration, provided that, if the decisions on matters submitted to arbitration can be separated from those not so submitted, that part of the award which contains decisions on matters submitted to arbitration may be recognized and enforced; or

      (d) The composition of the arbitral authority or the arbitral procedure was not in accordance with the agreement of the parties, or, failing such agreement, was not in accordance with the law of the country where the arbitration took place; or

      (e) The award has not yet become binding on the parties or has been set aside or suspended by a competent authority of the country in which, or under the law of which, that award was made.

   2. Recognition and enforcement of an arbitral award may also be refused if the competent authority in the country where recognition and enforcement is sought finds that:

      (a) The subject matter of the difference is not capable of settlement by arbitration under the law of that country; or

      (b) The recognition or enforcement of the award would be contrary to the public policy of that country.

2. How do these standards for enforcement of arbitral awards compare to the standards for enforcement of an international mediated agreement in the Singapore Convention (excerpted in Chapter 3)?

The next two excerpts further explain the history of investor-state arbitration and discuss its evolution. Over the last 30 years, it has not always been easy to strike a balance between the fair and equal treatment that is guaranteed to foreign investors and the sovereign rights of national governments to security, environmental protection, and independent financial policy.

Jeswald W. Salacuse, *The Emerging Global Regime for Investment*

51 Harv. Int'l L.J. 427, 428–35, 437–41, 451 (2010)

Since the end of World War II, in what is certainly one of the more active efforts at international lawmaking in the last half-century the nations of the world have negotiated and signed approximately 3000 investment treaties. During that time, three basic types of investment agreements have evolved: (1) bilateral investment treaties, commonly known as "BITs," of which 2608 were in effect at the end of 2008, with 179 countries as parties to at least one such BIT, (2) some 254 bilateral economic agreements containing investment chapters, such as the free trade agreements pursued by the United States, and economic partnership and cooperation treaties advanced by Japan, which replicate many, if not most, of the provisions in bilateral investment treaties, and (3) other investment related agreements involving more than two states, such as the North American Free Trade Agreement ("NAFTA"), a treaty among the United States, Canada, and Mexico, in which Chapter Eleven, itself an investment treaty, and the Energy Charter Treaty, a multilateral convention among fifty-one countries, set down rules for trade and investment in the energy sector.

The six decades since the end of World War II have thus witnessed a widespread *treatification* of international investment law. Today, unlike the situation that prevailed before World War II, "foreign investors in many parts of the world are protected primarily by international treaties. . . ." For all practical purposes, treaties have become the fundamental source of international law in the area of foreign investment. Indeed, in 2003, an arbitral tribunal that included a former president of the International Court of Justice suggested that the 2000 BITs then in existence had shaped the customary international law with respect to the rights of investors. . . .

I. A Regime for International Investment

An international regime is essentially a system of governance in a particular area of international relations. Focusing on the elements of a regime, a leading scholar of international relations has advanced a more particularized and widely accepted definition of an international regime as ". . . principles, norms, rules, and decision-making procedures around which actors' expectations converge to a given area of international relations." International regimes, according to two other scholars, ". . . constrain and regularize the behavior of participants, affect which issues among protagonists are on and off the agenda, determine which activities are legitimized or condemned, and influence where, when, and how conflicts are resolved." Thus, one may argue that international investment treaties as a group represent a convergence of expectations by states as to how host governments will behave toward investments from other regime members. The norms and rules embodied in investment treaties are intended to constrain and regularize such behavior in order to fulfill those expectations.

One of the ways in which international law becomes a reality, in the sense of actually affecting the behavior of both states and private parties, is through the creation of international regimes. For nearly three decades, international relations scholars have worked to develop a theory of regimes to explain the phenomenon of cooperation among states in an otherwise anarchic world. Although regime theory as a body of scholarly endeavor has been the almost exclusive province of political scientists rather than international lawyers, some of its insights and frameworks may be useful in explaining how and why international investment law works the way it does.

Although each of the 3000 investment treaties is legally separate and distinct, thus binding only the states that have concluded it, investment treaties as a group are remarkably similar with respect to structure, purpose, and principles. For example, nearly all international investment agreements cover the following nine topics: (1) definitions and scope of application; (2) investment promotion and conditions for the entry of foreign investments and investors; (3) general standards for the treatment of foreign investors and investments; (4) monetary transfers; (5) expropriation and dispossession; (6) operational and other conditions; (7) losses from armed conflict or internal disorder; (8) treaty exceptions, modifications, and terminations; and (9) dispute settlement. In addition, the language used in expressing these principles is often identical, so that it is not uncommon, for example, to find that both counsel and arbitrators will refer to arbitral decisions in cases interpreting one type of investment treaty, such as the investment chapter of NAFTA, to interpret a similar provision in a totally separate and unrelated treaty, like a BIT between Chile and Malaysia. It is for this reason that one may view these agreements, despite individual differences in text, as constituting a single international regime for investment....

Nations create and join regimes out of a desire to reduce the relative costs of desired transactions. Thus, capital-importing states have been led to sign investment treaties in the belief that the treaty commitments they make to protect foreign investment will reduce the perceived risks associated with investing in their territories and thereby lower their costs of obtaining needed foreign capital and technology. Capital-exporting countries, for their part, have joined the regime in hopes of reducing the foreign investment transaction costs associated with adverse actions by host country governments, such as expropriation without compensation and negative governmental interference with enterprises owned by their nationals. In a similar vein, international regimes, while lowering the costs of transactions that are considered legitimate, also raise the costs of those that are deemed illegitimate. Thus, the investment regime, through its dispute resolution mechanisms and particularly investor-state arbitration, secures compliance with regime norms and rules by imposing costly payments in the form of damage awards on regime members who engage in actions that violate regime norms and rules....

B. The Interests of Capital-Exporting States

Capital-exporting states have been the primary force driving the negotiation of investment treaties and the resulting creation of an international investment regime. They undertook this effort to build an international regime for investment because they believed that the existing international law at the end of World War II—what one might call the "*ancient regime*"—failed to adequately protect the foreign investments of their nationals from. Injurious actions by host country governments, such as the expropriation of investor property rights of the cancellation of investor contractual rights. The need for such protection was heightened by the prospect of post-War economic expansion and the decolonization of territories that had previously been under the control of capital-exporting states. At that time, foreign investors and their home governments seeking "the protection of international investment law encountered an ephemeral structure consisting largely of scattered treaty provisions, a few questionable customs, and [some] contested general principles of law." …

In sum, as global economic expansion began to accelerate in the years following World War II, the existing international law on foreign investment was, for most foreign investors, incomplete, vague, contested, and without an effective enforcement mechanism. Indeed, one may say that the *ancient régime* for investments under international law was not an international regime at all.… Because of these defects, investors and their home governments needed to find another means to protect foreign investments from the injurious actions of host country governments. To protect the interests of their companies and investors, capital-exporting countries sought to build an international regime for investment that, to the furthest extent possible, would be complete, clear, specific, uncontestable, and enforceable. The means to achieve that end would lie in negotiating investment treaties. Beginning in the late 1950s, individual capital-exporting countries prepared bilateral investment models or prototypes, often after significant consultation with domestic interest groups, and then embarked on a program of negotiating individual BITs with those countries in which their nationals had actual or potential investments. These models, from which they were not usually willing to depart significantly, gave capital-exporting countries distinct advantages in their treaty negotiations, and can therefore be viewed as an important foundation of the regime-building effort. The process of regime building through bilateral treaties continues unabated today.…

One can identify five possible motivations to explain this treatification puzzle: (1) encouraging foreign investment in capital-importing countries; (2) relationship building; (3) economic liberalization; (4) encouraging domestic investment; and (5) improving governance and strengthening rule of law.…

Thus one may summarize the structure of the principles underlying the investment treaty regime as follows:

(1) Increased international investment fosters economic development and prosperity.

(2) Favorable conditions in host countries lead to increased investment.

(3) Appropriate host country laws and institutions create favorable conditions for investment by increasing the predictability of economic transactions.

(4) Increasing the predictability ("calculability" in Weber's terms) of transactions has the effect of reducing perceived risk and therefore promoting investment.

Enforceable international rules that restrain host country governmental actions protect and therefore promote investment.

Susan D. Franck, *The Legitimacy Crisis in Investment Treaty Arbitration: Privatizing Public International Law through Inconsistent Decisions*

73 Fordham L. Rev. 1521, 1525–35, 1577–80 (2005)

A. The Evolution of Investment Treaties

In order to avoid the historical difficulties associated with "gunboat diplomacy," countries have promulgated treaties to promote foreign investment and instill confidence in the stability of the investment environment. This movement began with Treaties of Friendship, Commerce and Navigation, but soon moved beyond this as these treaties were limited commitments that did not have a forum for resolving disputes. There were soon efforts to enact multilateral investment treaties, which would grant investors and sovereigns a series of rights and obligations in the hopes of fostering foreign direct investment. Given the difficulties in promulgating sweeping reforms on a multilateral basis, these initiatives were largely unsuccessful.

Thereafter, various countries turned to bilateral treaties to secure rights for international investors and encourage efforts to promote stable investment climates. Sovereigns quickly learned that investment treaties can be a major tool for "enhance[ing] the type of asset protection that facilitates wealth-creating cross-border capital flows, bringing net gains for both host state and foreign investor[s]. The existence and negotiation of BITs has had a great influence on the formulation of international public policy, and these treaties are now a touchstone of international relations. While many of these investment treaties were initially between capital exporting and capital importing countries, at present, many investment treaties have been concluded between developed countries, and developing nations have also signed investment treaties among themselves. As investments continue to flow between developed and developing countries, investment treaties can no longer be seen purely from the point of view of industrialized nations.

The number of BITs has exploded in recent years. In the 1990s alone, investment treaties were negotiated at a rate of one every other day. Several multilateral investment treaties were also enacted. At the same time as the number of bilateral investment treaties quintupled, foreign direct investment has also experienced a fivefold increase. Unsurprisingly, given the success of bilateral treaties, even broader regional investment agreements, such as the Free Trade Agreement of the Americas, are now under consideration.

B. What Makes Investment Treaties So Special?

The proliferation of investment treaties is due in part to the rights in the treaties themselves. Investment treaties have two fundamental innovations, which represent a departure from previous international agreements. First, they grant investors a series of specific substantive rights, which help contribute to the stable investment climate of an investment. Second, they offer investors direct remedies to address violations of those substantive rights. The first of these will be addressed in this part....

The provisions of investment treaties are remarkably similar. While there are variations in the specific substantive rights and obligations that result from treaty-specific negotiations, there are several trends in the rights that Sovereigns choose to provide. In general, Sovereigns agree to protect the investments of investors from the other Sovereign in their own territory. They do this by delineating the specific substantive standards that govern the host state's treatment of an investment. In essence, the treaties indicate what rights are granted to investments, the types of investments that are covered, and when the coverage begins and ends.

There are different permutations of the substantive rights granted to investors. A typical investment treaty generally provides investors with a combination of up to seven different substantive rights. First, investors are often guaranteed the payment of adequate compensation in the event an investment is expropriated. Second, Sovereigns are prohibited from enacting currency controls so as to promote the free flow of capital. Third, Sovereigns are required not to discriminate on the basis of nationality; this typically means investors cannot be treated worse than the Sovereign's own citizens or other foreigners. Fourth, Sovereigns promise to treat investments fairly and equitably. Fifth, Sovereigns promise to provide full protection and security to an investment. Sixth, sovereigns guarantee that investments will not be treated less favorably than the minimum standard required by customary international law. Finally, Sovereigns sometimes agree to honor commitments they have made regarding an investment. While some of these rights are a confirmation of obligations Sovereigns owe under customary international law, others are new.

Most treaties delineate which investors and investments are entitled to receive substantive protections. Establishing entitlement to protection is an important threshold issue as it permits investors to obtain protection and bargaining leverage of investment treaties. The standards that must be met are typically broad, and to secure the benefits of an investment treaty, there must be a qualifying person or entity (the *ratione personae* requirement), a qualifying subject matter (the *ratione materiae* requirement) and a dispute within a qualifying time frame (the *ratione temporis* requirement). The impact of these three "standing" requirements is that—depending entirely upon how the investment is structured and the rules of the relevant investment treaty—investments that relate to more than one country might permit investors to benefit from more than one investment treaty simultaneously. For example, a U.S. citizen making an investment in the Czech Republic through a Dutch company may receive rights under both the U.S.-Czech Republic BIT and the Netherlands-Czech Republic BIT. This possibility creates an incentive for investors to structure investments that provide them with legitimate expectations of benefitting from rights under at least one investment treaty, if not multiple treaties. When the same set of facts permits arbitrations under different treaties, this enhances the potential for inconsistent decisions....

Notes & Questions

1. If investment treaties are entered into by states to encourage private investment, how do you think disputes should be resolved: in state or national courts or, as has become the common practice, a more private or "hybrid" form of decision-making in investment arbitration? Why should investment disputes be treated differently from other kinds of disputes?
2. How important do you think it is to have a reliable form of dispute resolution for continuity of trade and investment?
3. What power imbalances can you see in the global investment regime, and what consequences might that have for dispute resolution processes?

The next article, also by Professor Franck and published ten years after the article you just read, discusses the challenges that arise when states feel that investors have the upper hand or that tribunals are not sufficiently respectful of sovereign prerogatives to manage their countries' economies.

Susan D. Franck, *Predicting Outcomes in Investment Treaty Arbitration*

65 Duke L.J. 459, 470–80, 489–90, 520–26 (2015)

A. The Doctrine and Policy of ITA [International Treaty Arbitration]

The net objective of an IIA [International Investment Agreement] is to entice inbound foreign investment and to protect a state's own investors abroad while minimizing the risk of state liability. IIAs grant reciprocal investment rights—of a procedural and substantive nature—to foreign investors from the signatory countries. Procedurally, IIAs offer clear dispute resolution rights, including the right to arbitrate treaty disputes. After complying with certain prerequisites, including submitting dispute notices and attempting amicable settlement, IIAs permit investors to initiate arbitration directly against a state. Substantively, IIAs involve state promises that foreign investors will receive certain basic treatment, including the right to freedom from expropriation without proper compensation, the right to freedom from discrimination, and guarantees of fair and equitable treatment. These rights are similar to some, but not all constitutional rights. Some ITA disputes involve public law elements, like Zimbabwe's expropriation of land belonging to certain white farmers or the imposition of an environmental regulation that has a de facto disparate impact on foreign companies. Other disputes have a more commercial flavor, like revocation of a banking license, breach of contract, or failure to pay a dividend. Irrespective of whether they are representative, some ITA disputes have become iconic. For example, investors sued Argentina for its 2001 currency crisis that led to damages deriving from the devaluation of the Argentine peso and Argentina's imposition of other emergency measures to stabilize its economy; and Philip Morris sued Australia and Uruguay for plain-packaging cigarette regulations claiming state administrative regulation of cigarette packages constituted unlawful expropriation of intellectual property.

Historically, there were few options for investors to redress state activity that adversely affected their foreign investments. Investors' informal options entailed ignoring the conflict, absorbing the cost, and pricing the investment accordingly. Other options included securing political risk insurance coverage or otherwise asking the investor's home state to provide diplomatic support. More formal options for resolving international investment disputes included declarations of war, exercises of "gunboat diplomacy," lobbying the investor's home state to invoke formal diplomatic relief, or soliciting an investor's home state to espouse its claim at the International Court of Justice (ICJ). These options were largely unsatisfactory as they generate large fiscal costs, politicized dispute resolution by situating it within the sphere of international relations, prohibited direct access to neutral dispute resolution, or otherwise failed to provide a remedy to a damaged investor.

Against this backdrop, states signed IIAs to clarify substantive rights and grant investors the capacity to pursue direct dispute resolution for international investment law violations. ITA provided investors with a direct forum for depoliticized adjudication that is conducted by arbitrators who are required to be independent and impartial and generates an enforceable award. The objective was for states to avoid deciding whether to espouse an investor's claim and instead let investors choose, in light of net costs and benefits, whether pursuing a claim was appropriate. ITA used a tried and tested process—namely international arbitration—whose historical pedigree offered an opportunity for adjudicative neutrality and an established enforcement regime. In theory, ITA generated a balanced and efficient form of dispute resolution that minimized commercial risk and maximized rule of law.

B. The Mechanics of ITA

As a matter of mechanics, when an investor asserts that a host state's conduct violated a treaty's substantive protections and damaged the investment, IIAs generally permit the affected investor to begin a formal dispute resolution. If the dispute is not otherwise resolved through negotiation or mediation, the investor requires the state to arbitrate in one of the predesignated forums to resolve the dispute. Thereafter, each party can select one arbitrator; then either an arbitral institution or the two co-arbitrators appoint a presiding arbitrator. After signing statements of independence and impartiality, arbitrators resolve investment disputes in accordance with the applicable law, which generally includes the substantive provisions of the IIA and other international law principles. Parties then gather facts and generate legal arguments for different phases of the dispute, namely jurisdiction, merits, quantum, and costs. If investors fail to establish jurisdictional prerequisites, the case terminates and the state is not liable. Otherwise, the dispute continues to the merits where the tribunal assesses if the state violated the treaty's substantive protections by failing to provide the promised protection. If there is no breach, the case terminates and the state is not liable. Should there be jurisdiction and a breach on the merits, the parties establish the value of the treaty breach at the quantum phase. Cost awards, which allocate fiscal responsibility for lawyer and arbitrator fees, can be made at any point in the proceedings but typically occur at the end. Irrespective of whether tribunals issue multiple awards in a single case, the tribunal ultimately renders a final award that is enforceable worldwide under an international arbitration convention....

Recent commentary expresses discontent with ITA. The Asian-Pacific Economic Cooperation refers to problematic "unpredictable" ITA outcomes. UNCTAD's World Investment Report echoed these fears and highlighted concerns about "inconsistent readings of key provisions in IIAs and poor treaty interpretation, improving the impartiality and quality of arbitrators" and "assisting developing countries in handling [ITA] cases." Other state cases "can reach into the billions" of dollars, citing one case that is a statistical outlier without providing a holistic context. Meanwhile commentators suggest ITA is a "legal monster" that involves "[p]rofiting from [i]njustice" since "agreeing to arbitration [means] states have accepted to be sued by the devil in hell." Against this backdrop, debates about ITA in South Korea, a country with over seventy IIAs and no adverse ITA awards at the time, spawned physical fights by parliamentarians in 2011. Academics issued a Public Statement claiming ITA is not a "fair, independent, and balanced method for the resolution of investment disputes and therefore should not be relied on for this purpose." Others have stated that ITA should be abandoned to "reassert the integrity of our domestic legal processes." In an effort to critique ITA, protestors have even performed a self-styled "exorcism" of lawyers practicing ITA.

Beyond concerns about unpredictable outcomes or inconsistency, some complain that ITA reflects a reliable pro-investor bias. Under this critique, while ITA outcomes may be predictable, they are influenced by spurious adjudication variables like arbitrator identity or arbitration venue. For example, some commentators suggest that arbitrators themselves are biased in favor of investors and otherwise posit that arbitrator identity is a critical component of outcomes. Likewise, commentators suggest the arbitration venue determines outcomes, and awards rendered at ICSID are biased. Rather than focusing on adjudicative variables, other commentators critique ITA by suggesting that outcomes may depend upon case-specific variables, such as the identity of the investor, the respondent, or their counsel.

Some states have voted with their feet. Russia has withdrawn from the Energy Charter Treaty after an investor established jurisdiction over disputes related to the dissolution of Yukos Oil, and a July 2014 award subjected Russia to over fifty billion in damages. Venezuela, Ecuador, and Bolivia have withdrawn from the ICSID Convention.

The President of Ecuador has rejected ICSID, claiming ICSID "signifies colonialism, slavery with respect to transnationals, with respect to Washington, with respect to the World Bank." In October 2012, Ecuador's Minister of Foreign Affairs, Trade and Integration similarly called an ICSID award "unjust, illegal, illegitimate and absurd." Other states have encouraged the "reemergence of the 'toothless' investment treaty" which, like older treaties of Friendship Navigation and Commerce, provides substantive rights but no forum. Australia stated its intention to reject ITA in future IIAs because of efficiency concerns related to costs, fractious disputes, and treaties' net value.

Not all states agree and instead have retained ITA. In April 2012, after a contentious consultation process, the United States crafted a model IIA that provided for ITA. China also changed its approach to ITA by broadening the scope of arbitration to permit tribunals to assess both merits and damages. Canada, which has had its investors bring claims, and paid awards after losing cases as a respondent, changed its model IIA while retaining ITA. A trilateral investment treaty among China, Japan, and Korea likewise preserved ITA as a means of dispute settlement. Even Australia, after a national election leading to a change in government, included ITA in a treaty recently negotiated with South Korea. Meanwhile, although recent commentary in the media reflects varying perspectives on ITA's value, states continue to renegotiate investment treaties, and ITA appears to be a viable option in TPP and TTIP.

Ultimately, the policy debate about ITA is a live issue with critical international political and economic ramifications. The normative and institutional design of dispute settlement will benefit from information that scientifically identifies variables contributing to ITA outcomes....

C. Binary Win Rates

Potential risk, however, is not realized risk. One of the most basic questions in arbitration, particularly ITA, is who wins. Earlier research, limited to pre-2007 data analyzing fifty final awards (excluding settlements and discontinuances), indicated that investors won 40% of the cases and respondents won 60%. Jose Alvarez wrote, these "numbers pour cold water on unexamined assertions by many critics of the [ITA] regime" that ITA exhibits a pro-investor bias. The original historical snapshot analyzed fewer than sixty final awards, and the results could have changed over time.

Backed by a nearly 300% increase in cases analyzed, the current research replicated the proportions identified in earlier research. For the 144 awards finally resolving treaty disputes, fifty-seven cases (39.6%) were investor wins. By contrast, there were eighty-seven cases (60.4%) where respondents won with no state liability.... The rough pattern was that, for every two cases where investors won, states won three cases....

VII. Discussion

[T]he data call into question conventional characterizations that ITA outcomes exhibit pro-investor bias. Although nontrivial amounts were involved in investor claims, the descriptive data either reflected a state-favorable or rough balance in outcomes. For the subset of cases where investors won, investors generally only obtained roughly one-third of their claimed compensation. These results were akin to limited plaintiff success in whistleblower, qui tam, Bivens, or medical-malpractice litigation, which experienced respondent-favorable outcomes. Other empirical research on U.S. domestic litigation suggests that success rates in ITA were similar to respondent-favorable or state-favorable outcomes.

Finally, despite concerns about the lack of consistency and predictability in ITA, case-related and hybrid models demonstrated that ITA outcomes exhibited a degree of predictability, and the results were not completely random. The variables most likely to predict outcomes were arguably case selection effects, including investor identity and the presence of experienced counsel....

Although ITA is not perfect, the data cast doubt on the assumption that eradication of ITA is the only solution to perceived problems. Likewise, the data cast doubt on a triumphalist narrative about the value of ITA. Rather, the data suggested ITA outcomes are complex. Strategic adaptations to a complex problem are more normatively appropriate. We propose that, where states choose to provide investors with substantive rights, the question should be how best to provide dispute resolution. Recognizing that resolution in national courts might, fairly or unfairly, generate concerns related to perceived bias and any national-court judgment will face substantial doctrinal enforcement challenges, the objective should be to improve dispute settlement by making it as efficacious and fair as possible. We therefore recommend three structural safeguards.

First, stakeholders may wish to explore creating an appellate body to articulate clear rules, to harmonize inconsistent applications of law, and to redress substantive inconsistency. Post-award clarity could generate prospective predictability allowing investors and states to organize their conduct in accordance with those determinations. The enhanced predictability, determinacy and consistency of outcomes could enhance ITA legitimacy. Moreover, having clear interpretative rules from an appellate body facilitates future quantitative modeling that reliably controls for a claim's legal merits. The creation of a reliable legal baseline for analyzing investment disputes also promotes complimentary dispute settlement mechanisms such as negotiation and mediation that depend upon clear rules and adjudicative integrity to "bargain in the shadow of the law."

Second, should stakeholders be dissatisfied by the degree of predictability from the models or otherwise discontent with their ability to effectively influence predictors, they may wish to pursue other forms of dispute settlement. Negotiation or mediation, for example, could complement, support, or replace ITA. Predispute conflict management, negotiation or mediation could eliminate formal disputes. Likewise, even after a dispute has crystallized, mediation may minimize the scope of the dispute or address conflicts that arise during arbitration. Use of these forms of dispute settlement could save time and costs. For investors interested in ongoing investments within a state, these processes could preserve relationships. Mediation also means states need not outsource dispute settlement to arbitrators, and parties can retain control over the outcome by generating solutions that need not purely involve fiscal remuneration. Several treaties recommend "amicable settlement" of investment disputes. Yet, the broad and undefined reference generates confusion, particularly within states, about how settlement discussions occur, the procedural ground rules for the discussions, who will serve as a mediator (if any), and a myriad of other procedural concerns. When negotiating treaties, states may therefore wish to provide clear guidelines about how, when, and where to use alternative forms of dispute settlement. States may wish to consider incorporation of the recent Rules for Investor-State Mediation or create a separate annex providing details on mediation protocols.

Third, given the value of providing access to justice for smaller entities and people, stakeholders may wish to explore the possibility of creating a small-claims facility or other body to provide redress to investors that may lack economic and political advantages. For human beings who might wish to access dispute settlement, a small claims facility could provide immediate, efficient, and cost-effective access to justice. The solution reflects the success that people experienced, but captures states' risk by creating a single facility for streamlined dispute settlement of small-value claims.

Ultimately, these recommendations will require assessment and adaptation based upon data and the experience of stakeholders. Although the results demonstrated ITA was not completely unpredictable, states should pursue normative solutions designed to improve ITA and dispute settlement. Should states choose to grant substantive rights but fail to provide an effective forum for dispute settlement, there may be negative externalities that will minimize the potential joint gains derived from treaties promoting economic integration. In any event, the results of the data necessitate that debates about the future of ITA remain both robust and professional. Nevertheless, the debate will benefit from evidence-based insights, relying on data, and minimizing the influence of nonreplicable intuition that may create normative solutions that—while emotively satisfying—are suboptimal.

Conclusion

Without a careful analysis of ITA outcomes, it is not possible to generate proper normative reforms. The analyses in this Article neither suggested that ITA exhibited a pro-investor bias nor otherwise demonstrated that ITA was wholly unpredictable. While concern is understandable given the stakes for the international political economy, care must be taken to avoid generating dispute resolution systems that could generate suboptimal outcomes or normative solutions that either redress the wrong problem or fail to address a subsisting harm.

ITA outcomes were a complicated, multivariate phenomenon, and proposals for reform must be tested against data, lest a hasty transition harms the economic and political interests of international trade and investment agreements. Ultimately, international investment law may be best served by designing dispute resolution systems tailored to generate meaningful solutions to demonstrable problems. By focusing on variables reliably linked to ITA outcomes, rather than variables with an intuitive appeal that do not withstand empirical scrutiny, stakeholders can properly assess ITA's value in a time of international economic transition.

In the face of much criticism of the investor-state regime, the following article examined in more empirical detail what was actually happening with awards through these processes. See if you are surprised by the study results reported here.

Alec Stone Sweet, Michael Yunsuck Chung & Adam Saltzman, *Arbitral Lawmaking and State Power: An Empirical Analysis of Investor-State Arbitration*

8 J. Int'l Disp. Settlement 608–09 (2017)

To what extent have tribunals failed to take seriously the public interest when pleaded by the state? Have they, in effect, placed a thumb on the scales in favour of investors? Of course, even the most informed observers may disagree on the proper response to these questions, which we sought to address as systematically as possible.

In the vast majority of awards, tribunals made explicit, good faith efforts to take seriously the respondent state's 'right to regulate'. We found no support for the view that arbitral doctrine biases tribunals against states in any structural sense. Claimants win more often under the FET heading, but the success rate for FET claims is 50%: a coin toss. The outcome conforms to certain well-known theories of adjudication, including Priest-Klein,[1] which predicts a 'tendency toward 50 percent plaintiff victories among litigated cases' under conditions of uncertainty. In FET cases (and balancing situations, more generally), it is the factual matrix, not the law, that varies across cases, a strong condition of uncertainty.

Moreover, the evidence provides no support for the view that the regime has generated 'backlash' in any systemic sense. We fully recognize the importance of state officials, as treaty-makers, who may seek to override arbitral lawmaking, or try to block unwanted future development. To date, they have not done so in any sustained or significant way. We are aware of another empirical study that examines these issues relatively systematically, and it arrived at similar conclusions.[2] We do not wish to be misunderstood on this point. This article directs empirical attention to the question of how states, *as treaty-makers*, have responded to the most important lines of arbitral lawmaking, across time. We do not claim that this focus exhausts other important

1. George Priest and Benjamin Klein, *The Selection of Disputes for Litigation*, 13 J. of Legal Studies 1 (1984).

2. Tomer Broude, Yoram Z. Haftel, and Alexander Thompson, *Who Cares About Regulatory Space in BITs? A Comparative International Approach*, *in* Comparative International Law (A. Roberts et al. eds., 2018.).

issues involving the nature of state interests, or the content and intensity of state preferences when it comes to the design of the regime's institutions. Nonetheless, when states make new investment treaties, they act authoritatively, in ways that reveal underlying preferences.

Why have states not pursued a more radical reform agenda? We would highlight four main factors. First, the generic problems of inter-state contracting and coordination are acute in international economic law. Officials have found it difficult to write more complete contracts when it comes to the most highly arbitrated protections, InEx and FET illustrating the point. Most of the relevant provisions of new BITs, revised models and draft treaties in these areas have consolidated, not repudiated, approaches that had already been mapped in major strains of arbitral jurisprudence. The delegation theorist would assume that states (as contracting Principals) are choosing from a menu of options that Tribunals (their Agents) produce, on an ongoing basis. In the foreign investment regime, cooperative interactions between states and arbitrators are far more prevalent than conflict. Secondly, and relatedly, the decision-rule governing treaty-revision (consensus) favours inertia, not radical regime change. Thirdly, even when states have contemplated proposals to restrict treaty protections for foreign investment, domestic investors and the national bar have pushed back. India has become a major capital exporter, and Indian investors want the same protections that their counterparts from other countries enjoy. Fourthly, it has proven difficult, even for the most skeptical and disgruntled states (and critical scholars), to demonstrate that the regime is biased in favour of investors in a systemic sense, or against developing states. While some 27% of all filings are settled, states prevail in nearly 60% of the cases at the merits stage.

These points add up to a rather banal conclusion: most states, even those that are reform-minded, find the basics of what tribunals have done to be in their interest.

Notes & Questions

1. What do you think about Stone Sweet et al.'s conclusion that the investor-state regime operates in the interest of states, even as they have lost some big cases?
2. We will return to investor-state arbitration in Chapter 7 as an example of a hybrid dispute process that has evolved to meet the specific needs of the parties. But for now, consider how, in terms of the reasons why countries choose it, investor-state arbitration differs from commercial or state arbitration. And, given the criticisms of investor-state arbitration, consider how other processes we have studied could be integrated into that process, for example, negotiation and mediation.

IV. Ethics of Cross-Cultural Arbitration

This next set of articles addresses the specific issues facing individual arbitrators as they apply arbitration standards across different countries, nationalities, legal systems, and cultures. Moreover, in the ongoing effort to diversify arbitration panels, the challenges of standardizing and promoting predictable results can be at odds with the support of varying arbitration backgrounds and expertise.

Carrie Menkel-Meadow, *Are Cross-Cultural Ethics Standards Possible or Desirable in International Arbitration?*

in MELANGÉS EN L'HONNEUR DE PIERRE TERCIER 890–891;893–895; 897–898; 902–903 (Peter Gauch, Franz Werro, Pascal Pichonnaz eds., 2008)

Core Ethical Issues:
Consent, Choice, Confidentiality, Conflicts of Interest

The core concepts of international arbitration are the *consent* of the parties in their substantive contracts to this process of dispute resolution, *party choice* of substantive governing law, as well as the procedural rules by which the dispute will be determined, and with a signatory nation to the New York Convention, ease of *enforcement* of the arbitral award in any other signatory nation's courts. Most importantly, parties may *choose their decision makers* (and the place, language, and governing law) of their dispute. Arbitration awards are typically confidential (unless the award is challenged in a court proceeding or it is published in one of the new arenas of arbitration transparency, as in investment disputes, some labor disputes, and by some of the international tribunals).

For decades this system of "private" justice has been recognized as a consensual, private, efficient, expertise-based system of dispute resolution. For decades its primary participants were a relatively closed group of European academic and practitioner "notables" as arbitrators and a slightly wider group of European (and then American) litigators as representatives in the arbitration process. Disputing Parties interviewed potential arbitrators and checked references with other known customers. The bigger international tribunals (like the ICC, the LCIA, and now the international arm of the AAA—the International Center for Dispute Resolution) assisted in the selection of arbitrators by making lists of experienced experts available and even, where the parties requested it, or deadlocked on their own choices, chose the arbitrators.

Most of the established international tribunals have developed rules of procedure and practice that recognize a core concept of arbitration—that of *impartiality* of the decision maker—but have differed in how that standard is defined and enforced, varying in their disclosure requirements of past or present relationships to parties, experts, counsel and substance, and what constitutes an acceptance of a "conflict of interest" or a waiver by the parties (whether explicit or implicit by failing to contest appointment within the requisite number of days)....

Ethical Issues: Content of Standards

What kinds of conduct should be addressed, with what particularity or generality? While some, like this author, have attempted to identify a "core set of ethical values" in international arbitration (truthfulness, fairness, independence, loyalty and confidentiality), what we have discovered in practice and reality is that even the seeming "core" concepts have cultural and national legal differences (more fully explored below). In international arbitration the following issues of conduct and standards of practice for the arbitrator, and lawyers or other representatives in the arbitration, are potentially ethically significant, and possibly culturally variable:

- Impartiality/Neutrality (lack of bias)
- Independence (relation to parties and other sources of influence)
- Conflicts of interest (degrees of knowledge, relationships (economic and personal) with parties, counsel, experts, witnesses, other potential clients, law firm partners, company structures (parents and subsidiaries)
- Disclosure of potential conflicts of interests/grounds for "justifiable doubts" about impartiality
- Competence (taking/representing in cases competent in; jurisdictional issue too, such as *Kompetenz/Kompetenz*)
- Truthfulness or candor (to the tribunal, to other parties)
- Loyalty (to clients, degrees of zeal in representation)
- Preparation of witnesses and evidence (contact rules with parties, witnesses, "coaching")
- Disclosure/discovery of evidence, information
- Presentation of evidence
- Attorney-client (and other) evidentiary privileges (what can be inquired into in an arbitration proceeding and what is protected information)
- Communication (ex parte communication with parties, other arbitrators, parties, witnesses, experts)
- Fees/Compensation/Expenses
- Availability/Diligence (in person, scheduled sessions, completion of awards, incapacity)
- Fairness (in conduct of proceedings)
- Justness (responsibility for "just" decisions; adherence to legal mandatory standards or other principles (parties' contract, common business usage, *lex mercatoria*); reasoned awards, not arbitrary or corrupt
- Confidentiality (of proceedings, to parties, to others; conflicting mandatory disclosure rules, as in reporting of crimes or other malfeasance)
- Advertising/Promotion of Business, etc.

- Special duties/obligations of party-appointed arbitrators
- Transparency (clarity of conduct of arbitration and rules of publicity of awards)
- Duties to institutional tribunal (reporting misconduct of other arbitrators, parties, etc.; diligence, honesty, participation, governance, grievances, etc.)
- Institutional liability/responsibility for ethical infractions or other irregularities in arbitral process (selection, conduct of proceedings and awards)

The specific content of rules governing these issues can vary in domestic legal systems, based on different background or foundational values or approaches of different legal systems, thus making agreement or consensus on what the ethical regulations should be potentially quite difficult....

This "divergence" in background legal systems has led many practitioners and commentators to focus on practice differences that emerge in the conduct of international arbitration proceedings where lawyers and arbitrators from different legal cultures meet. The key claimed practice and process differences are those of witness contact and preparation (where, for example, it is a violation of ethics to either contact and coach witnesses, or not to, depending on the domestic legal system), retention and use of experts, creativity and zealousness of legal arguments, discovery and information exchange, the vigor and conduct of both direct and cross-examinations, evidentiary rule differences on such matters as lawyer-client privilege and protected communications, duties of loyalty and independence, the role of non-neutral or "partisan" arbitrators, and as more fully explored below, required disclosures and standards of potential conflicts of interests among lawyers, parties, witnesses and arbitrators.

Beyond these obvious differences of formal legal and ethical obligations, there is also an undercurrent of informal cultural practices. While in many European countries lawyers and arbitrators might share a meal, social event, or even a longer term social relationship (even during the pendency of a case), such close fraternization is considered informally unethical in the "arms-length" distance prescribed in American legal culture and may also be grounds for more formal disciplinary complaints or motions to set aside an arbitral award. Outside the scope of this essay is discussion of whether legal cultural differences also account for different interpretations of substantive law and different outcomes and awards in international arbitration....

To ensure that choices about what process to use and which institution to pick as the administering tribunal are well informed, standards of ethics should be as clearly delineated, in my view, as rules of procedures currently are. Yes, there are legal cultural variations in the presentation and preparation of cases, but those differences have not prevented each of the major tribunals from crafting rules of procedure which serve as the default (or selected) rules when parties specify a particular institution. These days, as sophisticated representatives and litigators may look for ways to challenge an award after the fact if they are not happy with a final award, specifying and enforcing clear standards of practice and ethical behavior (with assumed waivers if institutional standards have been met) should increase the likelihood of enforcement of an award. In my view, to the extent that arbitral institutions (like the ICC) do not specify standards of some kind (as required disclosures and conflicts of interests) and the grounds for decision of challenges to their arbitrators, they are inviting "second guesses" of further litigation in efforts to challenge the enforcement of an award.

More importantly, to the extent that the major tribunals are largely responsible for the core procedural rules (with a great deal of convergence and just a bit of divergence and choice among institutions) that have come to characterize international commercial arbitration, drafting, approving, and publicizing good practices and core ethics would serve both a practical and symbolic function of demonstrating public commitment to fairness and quality control of the process. Like all the procedural rules of these tribunals, rules of conduct, ethics, and conflicts of interest are "default" rules—they can be changed, modified, or rejected by parties electing arbitration in their initial agreement to arbitrate or even in consensual agreements during the negotiation of Terms of Reference. Furthermore, looking at standards like the IBA Guidelines for Conflicts of Interest in International Arbitration or the CPR-Georgetown Commission's Model Rule for Third Party Neutrals, the norm for many ethical issues in arbitration is "disclose" and then "consent" (or not) in a consensual process. Choice of "wise elders" (with both arbitral experience and industry expertise) with many interconnecting relationships to the parties can continue (as long as all parties know about those connections and consent to the use of such wise elders). And, if more disclosure, while adding burdens (and possibly confidentiality issues) of increased work, leads to more contests about who is a neutral or unbiased arbitrator, then we will at least expose some of the conflicts of interests that have existed in the system for so long. Finally, it would seem to any scholar and practitioner (and even to out innocent students) that making clear standards of ethics and disclosure clear, transparent, and dealt with early in the process (during arbitrator selection and screening) would tend to eliminate later challenges (in court enforcement proceedings) which are more costly to the parties and more dangerous to the legitimacy of the entire system.

Carrie Menkel-Meadow, *Ethical Ordering in Transnational Legal Practice? A Review of Catherine A. Rogers's Ethics in International Arbitration*

29 Geo. J. Legal Ethics 207, 209, 216–20, 233–38 (2016)

Although issues of ethics in international arbitration began with a focus on international (private) commercial arbitration, which continues to constitute an overwhelming majority of international arbitrations, recent attention to the controversial aspects of investment (investor-state dispute settlement ("ISDS")) arbitration and increasing demands for transparency and accountability in such public policy affecting rulings has resulted in increased attention to ethics and standards in all forms of arbitral decision-making. Further complicating the question of specifying ethical standards in international arbitration are the variety of roles within the arbitral process that might be affected by such efforts. This includes the practices and behaviors of representatives-advocates, arbitrators (including party-appointed, neutrals, chairs of panels), experts, witnesses, parties (including both private and public entities and individuals), and now, third-party funders and investors in the litigation.

As discussed more fully below, arbitration is governed by its own form of *legal pluralism*—the *contract* (supported by international treaty) and then party chosen *procedural rules*. By specifying the use of arbitration in a transborder contract, dispute resolution is removed from formal court or other institutional adjudication (until, perhaps, if a challenge is later leveled, at the enforcement of the award stage). The conduct of any arbitration hearing is therefore governed by any rules or procedures specified in contractual terms, between the parties, and/or by procedural rules provided by the chosen arbitration institution (such as the ICC, the London Court of International Arbitration ("LCIA"), the Centre for International Dispute Resolution ("CIDR," the American Arbitration Association's international arm), or any other chosen rules (e.g. *United Nations Committee on International Trade Law ("UNCITRAL") Model Rules of Arbitration*) or any ad hoc agreed to procedural rules. All of these rules, which may provide explicit or implicit "ethical" practice standards, unfortunately have little provision for enforcement by either arbitral administering institutions or particular arbitral panels or tribunals. The line dividing procedural and practice rules from so-called "ethical" rules is fuzzy and murky in arbitration, as it can also be in formal adjudication. Challenges to arbitrators might be made at the beginning of a case to the arbitral administering institution, or to a court in the "seat" of the arbitration. Challenges also are made at the end (challenging enforcement of an arbitral award under several grounds of the New York Convention on Recognition and Enforcement of Foreign Arbitral Awards). However, there is little to no place for ethical complaint or challenge in the middle of a case (except to the arbitration panel, which may or may not think it has the authority to rule on ethical issues during the conduct of a substantive case).

In the last few decades, several organizations have drafted non-compulsory (because there is no formal enforcement mechanism) ethical standards for international arbitration, particularly, but not exclusively, in relation to issues of possible conflicts of interest of arbitrators and more recently for "attorney misconduct" in international practice. Professor Rogers's earlier work as a scholar in this area has been highly influential in the discussion and drafting of such standards. In addition to the International Bar Association's *Guidelines on Conflicts of Interests for International Arbitrators*, several of the international arbitral institutions that have now promulgated their own rules or ethical guidelines (e.g. International Institute for Conflict Prevention and Resolution ("CPR"). LCIA, the ICC and the International Centre for the Settlement of Investment Disputes ("ICSID")), have been urged to promulgate such standards. Even the ICC, the institution that most resisted development of ethical guidelines because of objections reviewed here, has now contemplated its own process of ethical guideline development. This may be a reaction to the claims that the arbitral institutions are engaged in a competition over the delivery of dispute resolution services and ethical standards are one of the distinguishing features of the competition.

Finally, when and if parties seek enforcement, non-recognition, vacatur, or annulment of an arbitral award under the New York Convention, national courts may rule on challenges to the award, implicating ethical issues, such as "evident" partiality," or "corruption or bias" of the arbitrator or other grounds for non-recognition under the treaty and its applicable case law. Thus, those who may be asked to rule or opine on ethical issues include arbitration institutions, panels of or individual arbitrators, national courts, some international tribunals (ICSID), the World Trade Organization (WTO), formal governmental disciplinary bodies (national or state in the case of federal countries), non-governmental professional associations (e.g. International Bar Association) and other international or transnational bodies, or domestic bar associations and disciplinary bodies, and even private law firms or other practice units.

Thus, any regime of international arbitration ethics is likely to be "plural," both in substantive content (different legal regimes and different subject matter disputes) and in the bodies or institutions that may ultimately rule on whether some ethical standard, rule or guideline has been transgressed. Despite the likely pluralism of content, interpretation and enforcement, Professor Rogers still proposes that we can and should have "ethics in international arbitration." ...

But, even at the most general level there are potentially conflicting values of "ethics." Consider as examples of these potentially conflicting duties: loyalty to clients and duties to tribunals; keeping client information confidential and being honest and transparent to tribunals; treating others with integrity and respect and American-style "zealous" representation in the form of rigorous cross-examination; duty to protect clients (think corporate clients with many different individuals) and their information (documents, trade secrets etc.) and varying duties of disclosure to opposing parties or to the tribunal; duties to present, past and possible future clients; conflicts presented by role changes, from lawyer to arbitrator, from lawyer to judge, and movement from one law firm to another or movement from private law work to engagement by the state' movement from one "side" or argument on an issue to the "other" (known as issue conflicts). These tensions exist in any legal ethics regime but may be even more intensely experienced in international arbitration as lawyers serve as both representatives and arbitrators or work in different kinds of practice unites (barrister chambers and multi-national law firms)....

In what long has plagued international arbitral practice, American ethical and professional malpractice rules of witness preparation (and likely testimonial rehearsal and coaching) have openly collided with several legal traditions of explicitly prohibiting this practice. To varying degrees, France, Belgium, Germany and the United Kingdom, have placed restrictions on how much pre-testimonial contact a lawyer may have with witnesses....

Similar ethical cultural divides are explored in the book with respect to conflicts of interests. The United States has the most detailed and particularized rules about what constitutes a conflict (prior clients, former government service, law firm imputation conflict if one member has a conflict, business dealings with clients, acceptance of gifts or payments for legal services by third parties, organizational conflicts). Other nations have either a different conception of "conflicts of interest" (France's notion of avoidance of "indelicacy") or an absence of formal regulation and sanction. Different configurations of practice in different countries, including Asia, South America, and Europe with smaller units of practice or shared office arrangements without stringent conflicts rules have led in recent years to more complicated challenges to international arbitrators coming from the same legal "chambers" or offices as some of the advocating lawyers. At the level of award enforcement and challenges, some national systems discipline such conflicts (as does the U.S. in some contexts) only when actual harm has been shown (e.g., revelation of confidential information, disloyal conduct, rulings in favor of former clients, actual financial interests in outcomes). As Professor Rogers suggests, some arbitral bodies are reluctant to rule on such challenges, claiming lack of authority or lack of standards in international settings. I would suggest they are also reluctant to rule on this issue because they are often implicitly ruling on their own potential conflicts of interest (of either the past, or the future, as they contemplate further work in the field, as either arbitrators or representatives, known as "upstream" conflicts).

Another area of different understandings of basic principles occurs with client confidentiality and attorney-client privilege, especially as it affects representatives of corporate or organizational bodies. In many civil law countries confidentiality is both broader and narrower than in the United States. Corporate or trade secrets communicated from client to lawyer are often protected from disclosure by the lawyer, but the advice from the lawyer to the client is not. Also contrary to American rules and practices, in some jurisdictions, lawyers may have to keep their own communications with each other across adversary lines confidential from their own clients! And, not unlike the variations among states in the United States, different national systems require different responses from lawyers who learn about client wrongdoing. Issues of what can be argued or treated as evidence in international arbitrations may turn on different ethical rules and practices in different national systems which require international arbitrators to make evidentiary rulings that may, in fact, implicate ethical requirements, with potential for discipline or other penalty within a lawyer's (or witness's) home country.

Perhaps the trickiest and most common ethical differences have over time been the rules and practices of *ex parte communication.* American parties and lawyers have moved into international arbitration with their domestic customs of choosing partisan arbitrators with whom they continued to have private and advocacy conversations during the arbitration proceedings. The tradition of international arbitration most often requires "impartiality" or "neutrality" at least after all the arbitrators are chosen. Over time even the American arbitration institutions, such as the American Arbitration Association and its international arm, International Center for Dispute Resolution, have moved to a notion of "impartiality" and prohibition of most ex parte communication between representatives and arbitrators. Ironically, ex parte communications continue to be a cultural issue as tradition and practice has not generally prohibited meals and social contacts among arbitrators, lawyers and parties in Continental practice. Now, in some cases involving China and other Asian countries, blurring of roles from mediator to arbitrator or other function has blurred some of the lines of communication, both prohibited and permitted. Just as in American med-arb (mediation-arbitration hybrids) dispute resolution practice, there can be issues with separate meetings (caucuses) with mediators who try to settle cases and then later serve as arbitrators deciding matters on the basis of secret or non-shared or responded to information. These issues, described with several case examples, demonstrate the great variety of practices and confusion that may occur when different nationals, subject to different, or no rules at all, participate in an international hearing. Particular arbitral tribunals can set their own single case "rules" for their proceedings. Increasingly, the rules of each of the arbitration institutions may provide for default rules on the issue of ex parte communications and expectations of impartiality. However, if the lawyers have different cultural expectations about what is appropriate (conversations, sharing a meal, staying in the same hotel), there may be different behaviors with respect to communications that can have an effect on outcomes, and can lead to post-award challenges. Professor Rogers does not offer a specific solution to these issues, but she demonstrates how cultural practices may differ, but also may be converging, in practice, if not in formal rules or decisions....

The arbitration institutions have now all had to focus on new rules, at the intersection of ethical and procedural rules, for allowing third party participation, both from a financial and interest basis in order to structure systems with integrity and to satisfy demands for due process and public participation, important values from the "macro-ethical" perspective. To the extent that international arbitration has become more "judicialized," Americanized" or "complexified" (all critiques leveled at current administration and conduct of both investment and commercial arbitration), the leading international arbitration institutions (ICC, LCIA, ICSID, ICDR AAA) have all had to confront making new rules for the participation (either financially or on an amicus-interest basis) by those beyond the actual parties....

Some Concluding Observations

Legal ethics jurisprudence in international arbitration appears to be developing at both inductive (from particular cases) and deductive (general rules laid down in advance) levels at the same time, with the enactment of generalized ethics codes by arbitral institutions and the decisions and cases of arbitrators and national court rulings. At a philosophical level these developments could be analyzed from a deontological (specific duties) or ontological (essentialism or natural law, e.g. are arbitrators ducks or rabbits?) rationale, or both. At a practical level, the field of ethics in international arbitration must confront the important question of whether to draft and regulate in aspirational, general and transsystemic language or whether to aim, with greater specificity, to provide behavioral guidance through clear guidelines. The danger of the first is to be so vague as to provide no guidance; the danger of the latter is that significant ethical issues cannot be dealt with by specific, brittle, binary rules, when nuance, wisdom and judgment may be called for.

For further development of a jurisprudence of legal ethics, Professor Rogers has well outlined the leading ethical issues that international arbitration presents from her conceptualization of a "Functional" (role-defined) approach, often exploring the conflation or complication of ethics and procedural matters. These include:

- *Role of arbitrator*—impartiality, integrity, non-bias and independence, conflicts of interest, disqualifications, fees, confidentiality (privacy), competence, diligence, and liability, selection procedures, decisional powers (written awards, interim measures), dealing with corruption and other illegal activities (e.g. bribes);
- *Role of attorney* in international arbitration—conflicts of interest, duty to client, tribunal, others (state, organization), privilege, competence, diligence and experience, practice duties (e.g., witness preparation, disclosure and information exchange, ex parte communications), litigation "manners" (e.g. cross-examination), fees;
- *Role of experts*—competence, neutrality, loyalty, selection, duty to tribunal or party, fees;
- *Role of Third Party Funders*—disclosure, relation to parties, attorneys and arbitrators, conflicts of interests, manipulation of cases and issues, fee-splitting, confidences.

Beyond this "micro" role-based functional approach, Professor Rogers also adduces the "macro" or systemic ethical issues raised by international arbitration, even as these are less susceptible of rule or standard drafting:

- *System Legitimacy*—procedural justice, participation, fairness, transparency, rule of law or other decisional justification, outcomes, different measurements of "justice"—to parties, others affected, public, reviews and appeals;
- *Licensing, certification of arbitrators/attorneys*;
- *Enforcement*—venues, locations and levels of enforcement of ethical, procedural and other standards; finality, appeal; self-regulation (proposed by Professor Rogers), arbitral institutions, courts, international bodies or other/sanctions/ external regulation-national courts?

Professor Rogers's "functional" and "self-regulating" approaches provide a useful framework for assessing the specific role-based ethics issues of the participants inside arbitral processes and provide a useful resource for considering alternative issues and formulations of rules and policies for those roles. This functional approach, however, provides less guidance for consideration of the systemic and public issues implicated in the use of international arbitration. Thus, issues of accountability or transparency, including publication of awards, creation of appeals bodies and participation of outsiders to the immediate dispute, get less attention here, but are the subjects of much of the current debate about the use of arbitration in international trade treaties. Professor Rogers book is *Ethics in International Arbitration*; not "ethics *of* international arbitration."

In the next excerpt, the authors review the history of *who* actually has served as arbitrators. Consider the previous reading on ethics and cross-cultural differences—how should arbitrators be selected to match the needs and goals of state actors as well as private parties?

Yves Dezalay & Bryant Garth, *Merchants of Law as Moral Entrepreneurs: Constructing International Justice Out of the Competition for Transnational Business Disputes*

in Dealing in Virtue: International Commercial Arbitration and the Construction of a Transnational Legal Order 34–36 (1996)

Grand Old Men and Technocrats

The starting point of the generational warfare is diverging ideas of arbitral competence—the characteristics that qualify one to be an arbitrator. For the pioneers of arbitration, exemplified especially, but not only, by very senior European professors imbued with the traditional values of the European legal elites, the dominant opinion has been that arbitration should not be a profession: "Arbitration is a duty, not a career". For true independence of judgment, in the words of another senior insider, "The person who goes into this business as an arbitrator to make a living should not be encouraged". Arbitrators, they insist, should render an occasional service, provided on the basis of long experience and wisdom acquired in law, business, or public service. Those who hold this opinion are, indeed, individuals who have risen to the top of their national legal professions and gained financial independence before being asked to serve as arbitrators.

The specific criteria for these "grand notable" arbitrators allow for numerous variations. Different countries and legal systems have different hierarchies in their legal professions. The great professors and a few high judges have for a long time controlled the arbitration terrain of Continental Europe, while the comparable role is assumed in the Anglo-American system by the most respected of the practitioners, senior barristers or Queen's Counsel (QCs), or senior partners in firms of solicitors or U.S. law firms. Retired judges such as Lord Wilberforce have been important as well to England. The arbitration market has selected those at the top of their domestic professions to become senior arbitrators: "high profile, high visibility ... national aura behind them".

These relatively few grand old men, as they are often referred to (there were no women), have played a central role in the emergence and the recognition of arbitration, and they continue to have a quasi-monopoly for very large matters. As a U.S. litigator stated, "There are some categories of disputes where you're going to need the grand old men who are known to each other". Stated another longtime observer of the field, "In these big, big cases, you go for people who have already years of experience". But these "divas"—sometimes defined also as dinosaurs—are increasingly criticized by a new generation of practitioners who came to arbitration because of the rapid growth of this market in the 1980s.

To the aura or the charisma of their elders, these new arrivals oppose their specialization and technical competence. In the words of a Swiss member of the new generation, "Arbitration was characterized by a limited, small group of impeccable, outstanding professionals—characters known around the world.... Today I have difficulty in seeing the outstanding personality [among] a big crowd of people". Put in more aggressive terms by a member of the same cohort, an arbitrator cannot now just step in "with all ... [the] glorious past" and provide the "great old man's opinion". Indeed, charisma is said even to be a source of error. In the words of an ICC insider, "Some of the biggest problems that we see are probably with some of the big names". Why? "They're probably just more full of themselves than other people". Furthermore, "Sometimes an eminent arbitrator feels he doesn't have to explain things". A leading figure of the younger generation thus describes his generation as "technically better equipped in procedure and substance".

They present themselves in this new generation as international arbitration professionals, and also as entrepreneurs selling their services to business practitioners, contrasting their qualities to the "amateurism" or "idealism" of their predecessors....

Indeed, now that arbitration has become accepted in commercial international mores, they assert, even citing Max Weber in one instance, that the time has come for the "routinization of charisma" essential to the transition from the stage of artisans to that of mass production. This transition requires the "rationalization" of arbitration know-how.

These technocrats play key roles now in institutions like the International Chamber of Commerce, which they not only have come to direct but also have used for their education in arbitration. The quick route to arbitration expertise is through the major institutions, which hire young lawyers to administer the arbitrations. These organizations, which the pioneers used for evangelical purposes to promote arbitration, now have added a more technical involvement in the administration of the arbitrations themselves.

The large Anglo-American law firms, which dominate the international market of business law, are also central to this conflict between grand old men and technocrats. With the growth of trade and the success of the pioneers in building international arbitration, they now consider it important to include this specialty in the gamut of services that they put at the disposition of their multinational clients. The attitude of the large law firms has been to favor overtly this "banalization" and rationalization of arbitration, which permits them to introduce themselves into the closed "club" and to introduce the legal techniques that are at the basis of their preeminence. As a U.S. lawyer stated about the Swiss, "It's the younger generation that I like, because all of them have gone to school in the United States. They all speak fluent English. They know how to deal with Americans and English, and they move cases along"....

This opposition between grand old men and young technocrats—supported by Anglo-American firms—is one of the keys that permits decoding a great number of the debates and the fights—in scholarship as well as in institutions—that affect this field of practice. One controversy, discussed further below, is whether the major institutions, the ICC notably, are now too involved in the actual work of the arbitrators. A second is whether arbitration is becoming too much like litigation. The perspective of the senior generation is highly critical of both of these trends. A leading senior arbitrator thus reported that procedural infighting was "suicidal" to arbitration and that he was likewise "absolutely opposed to drowning arbitration in paperwork". With respect to the ICC, the same individual noted that the weakness of the ICC was that its arbitration was "overly regulated" by the secretariat who had "never seen arbitration from the inside"....

Between the Club and the Market

The secretariat of the Court of Arbitration of the ICC makes no secret of its desire to open the market of arbitration beyond the narrow circle of the grand old men. Certainly these efforts can be justified by the growth in the number of cases submitted to the ICC, as well as by their great geographical diversity. The arrival into arbitration of the third world and of the Anglo-Americans rendered necessary the recruitment of new arbitrators who did not fit the profile of the Continental academic or the other pioneers. Many new users are bound to nominate arbitrators—and a fortiori lawyers—from their own legal settings. According to Stephen Bond, then the secretary-general of the ICC, "In such instances, given the importance of party autonomy and consensus as basic principles of international commercial arbitration, the ICC has not refused confirmation of such persons, even when they are unknown to the Court itself".

These newcomers, however, are by definition not the progeny of the club. Their entry into the practices and norms of the club cannot be ensured by a long apprenticeship or by an informal process controlled by a small group of senior men. The institutionalization of these tasks of enlisting new arbitrators and observing their performance, in fact, justifies the growth and transformation of the ICC bureaucracy (the secretariat) and also the Court of Arbitration. This "bureaucratization" of the ICC, and also the retention of two of the most controversial aspects of the ICC procedure—the terms of reference and the review of the arbitrators' opinions by the court—can therefore be seen as part of the effort to bring in newcomers, accommodate their situation, and preserve the universality of the ICC and arbitration....

The ICC and the Recentering of the Field of International Commercial Arbitration: The Arrival and Role of the Anglo-American Law Firms

The tensions implicated by these transformations are not explained only by a crisis of growth. They are also the corollary of displacement from the center of gravity of arbitration. The recentering favors the world of Anglo-American law firms, who have used their power in the international business world to impose their conception of arbitration and more largely of the practice of law. It is thus no accident that, within the ICC itself, the politics of rationalization has been conducted since the beginning of the eighties by young Anglo-American lawyers recruited from outside of the club, and whose key words have been transparency, rationalization, and competition. The Anglo-Americans, including the two most recent secretaries-general of the ICC (from the United States), have clashed with leading members of the senior arbitration club over a number of issues, including the necessity of bureaucratization. A recent example, which provides a good illustration of the conflict and the trend in management, has been the effort of the ICC to expand the requirements of ICC arbitrators to disclose relationships with counsel and other arbitrators.

In response to the "grand old man" identity of many arbitrators, institutions around the globe have tried to diversify the set of neutrals in use. The next article addresses some of the challenges in meeting the goal of more diversity in international arbitration.

Susan D. Franck et al., *The Diversity Challenge: Exploring the "Invisible College" of International Arbitration*

53 Colum. J. Transnat'l L. 429, 451–53, 495–99, 502–05 (2015)

Gender, Age, Legal Training, Native Language, and Nationality of International Arbitrators and Counsel

Existing literature on arbitrators has provided some information on arbitrator background, usually from information released from individual institutions or specific subject matter. While difficult to prove a negative, we are unaware of any existing research that systematically explores the gender, age, and nationality of international arbitrators across institutions and subject matter. Likewise, we are unaware of any research on demographic information about the background of counsel in international arbitration. This research offers a baseline for future inquiries. Although it provides quantitative information on counsel, the discussion in this section primarily focuses on international arbitrators.

There have been suggestions in the popular press that international arbitrators tend to be "pale, male, and stale." Presuming the phrase reflects public concerns about diversity in international arbitration, the question is whether inclusiveness (or lack thereof) is empirically verifiable. We acknowledge that it is difficult, if not impossible, to generate a unitary definition of diversity and inclusiveness in international arbitration. We therefore focus on several aspects to create a pluralistic assessment. First, we explored the gender composition of ICCA subjects, as gender is generally a stable characteristic. Second, we explored the age distribution of ICCA participants. Third, we identified variations in legal training, linguistic capacity, nationality, and development status.

Given the existing literature reflecting questions about gender disparity in international arbitration, the descriptive data on gender is vital.... For all ICCA subjects and the subset of counsel, roughly three-quarters were men, and one quarter were women. The distribution shifted when evaluating those serving as arbitrators—with men becoming more dominant. Namely, 82.4% of arbitrators were men and 17.6% were women.

The results also suggest a degree of a "grey hair factor" where, although all subjects were typically in their late forties, those individuals serving as arbitrators were somewhat older. Table 3 indicates that the mean age of all subjects was 48 (median=47); and mean counsel age (48) was similar (median=46). In contrast, the mean age of responding arbitrators was 54 (median=53). These results may not be unusual. Other research suggests the average age of an active member of the bar in California was 48, whereas the average age of California judges was 60; but the age of median judges has been decreasing in several jurisdictions....

Discussion

The results of the data indicate that there were non-trivial issues related to diversity in international arbitration related to age, gender, and nationality. The international arbitration community should explore what factors contribute to the backgrounds of the current arbitration bench and bar. Focusing on these aspects, and the factors contributing to those demographics, provides an opportunity to explore what inhibits the full utilization of untapped talent to permit broader systemic value and avoid waste of human capital. There are several systemic benefits to such an undertaking.

First, taking diversity issues seriously offers an opportunity to strengthen and create infrastructure for international arbitration's future. As the core group of international arbitrators (and counsel) continues to age, it is worthwhile investing in a new generation of arbitrators and counsel to ensure that know-how and capacity is not lost over time. Efforts and mentoring programs, such as Young ICCA and other groups focused on developing the next generation of the arbitration community, offer constructive solutions to address this gap. Bringing younger individuals into the fold increases diversity and the breadth of ideas and experiences, and could benefit the community as a whole.

The benefits of diversity go beyond age. The parties involved in dispute settlement, who control the appointment of lawyers and often exercise choice in the appointment of arbitrators, may benefit from the diversity. Shareholders and boards focusing on diversity, for example, may wish to use their choice of counsel and arbitrators to showcase their commitment to diversity. Similarly, state parties involved in international arbitration might have transparency requirements requiring them to comply with equal opportunity or diversity obligations. Moreover, parties may not always identify with, feel fully heard by, or be able to communicate in a manner that is fully forthright with lawyers within the international arbitration community; this, in turn, suggests arbitration services might be enhanced through expanded market competition.

Second, exploring diversity levels and identifying methods for enhancing diversity could serve to enhance legitimacy, public trust, and procedural justice. When considering long-term efficacy, the international arbitration community could benefit from exploring how to maintain and develop reservoirs of goodwill during a time of global economic transition. One strategic way of enhancing legitimacy is to have appropriate and balanced representation before courts and tribunals, international or domestic.

Where adjudication is "representative of the people, [it] will be considered more legitimate, and can count on greater trust and confidence from the public at large. Conversely, lack of diversity in [adjudication] could undermine public confident...." The former Chief Judge of the United States Court of Appeals for the Eleventh Circuit, Deanell Tacha, notes that, "diversity is about bringing together collective knowledge, born from an array of experiences, in order to ensure the judiciary and its decisions are respected and followed. These concerns translate to the international context, whether international courts and tribunals or international arbitration. As Chiara Giorgetti explains, an "important measure that can be taken to strengthen the international arbitration system is to enlarge the pool of arbitrators. More arbitrators from outside Europe and North America, and more women, are needed. Observing that it "is widely accepted both at domestic and international levels that 'a diverse judiciary is an indispensable requirement of any democracy,'" Giorgetti argues that in a transnational setting with global economic implications like international arbitration, broad representation is even more important. International arbitration could therefore benefit from enhanced legitimacy and procedural justice by having adjudicators who reflect the society to whom they are responsible. Particularly for ITA, which involves policy matter, it is critical to both do and be seen to do justice. Given the value of symbolic legitimacy, there is untapped value in having an inclusive group of international adjudicators that provides expressive, representational and modeling functions.

Third, although more speculative, it is possible that greater diversity could facilitate distributive justice and higher quality outcomes. Having greater representation of different perspectives during deliberation could aid a more comprehensive appreciation of parties' positions and underlying evidence. This, in turn, could generate higher quality awards. There is, however, difficulty in demonstrating that appointing non-median arbitrators creates different outcomes—or that different types of diversity will generate specific effects of the process or the outcome.

Generating diversity, however, could prove challenging as international arbitration permits parties to directly control two arbitrator appointments (and potentially the appointment of the chair, as well). Parties have incentives to select arbitrators that either maximize the likelihood of their preferred result in a given case or minimize the possibility of a negative result. Likewise, parties may wish to appoint known-qualities in their arbitration counsel and arbitrators and thereby decrease the risks outcomes generated by untested arbitrators. These incentives place new international arbitrators at a disadvantage, which minority status may exacerbate. Nevertheless, boards of directors or other entities could create pressure to foster diversity in their use of lawyers and arbitrators, or there may be natural incentives to appoint more broadly. Where such incentives do not exist, arbitral institutions such as ICSID, the LCIA, the ICC, or the Permanent Court of Arbitration at The Hague can generate increased diversity by strategically utilizing those appointments they control. Initial analyses exploring ITA cases reflected that chair appointments by institutions like ICSID exhibited greater diversity (in terms of development status) as compared to appointments made by co-arbitrators. This suggests that stakeholders may wish to follow institutions' lead in promoting greater diversity in international arbitration....

Conclusion

The data reflect that the modern "invisible college" of international arbitration is complex and not subject to a flat, unitary narrative. An appreciation of the nuance and complexity creates a powerful opportunity. The data can aid the international arbitration community's exploration of evidence-based solutions to identifiable challenges rather than reliance on unrepresentative anecdotes.

The demographics of key actors in international arbitration reflected bright spots but likewise reflected areas for improvement. International arbitration has moved past historic Cold War divides. The data demonstrated that arbitrators and counsel comprised a broad spectrum of nationalities, continents, and languages. Nevertheless, the data reflected disproportionate levels of representation by men from states in North American and Europe, which have high levels of economic development. Only 24% of counsel and 17.6% of arbitrators were women. Meanwhile 68.6% of counsel and 76% of arbitrators were from Europe and North America; 75.2% of counsel and 82.4% of arbitrators were from OECD states, and 76.5% of counsel and 84.8% of arbitrators were from high-income countries. The data supported claims that international arbitration is a "white male game."

Diversity challenges within international arbitration are some of the most challenging, but also the most rewarding, as they generate an opportunity for arbitration to take a leadership role within the broader community of international courts and tribunals. More than 75% of ICCA subjects identified that they agreed (either somewhat or strongly) with the proposition that international experiences diversity challenges. Yet, the data reflected heterogeneities in perceived challenges. Women and younger subjects were *more* likely to identify diversity challenges than men or older subjects. Subjects from developing countries (no matter how defined) were *less* likely than their developed world counterparts to identify diversity challenges. These perceived experiences, however, were juxtaposed with actual experiences related to gender and development status.

The data also reflected that becoming an international arbitrator can be challenging, and the proportion of women arbitrators was only 17.6%. Once women broke the "glass ceiling," statistical tests could not identify a meaningful difference in the number of appointments that women obtained as compared to men. Yet, roughly one-third of arbitrators had never sat on a tribunal with a woman, and more than 75% of counsel reported they had never had a tribunal with multiple female arbitrators.

Analyzing the development status of international arbitration specialists also reflected diversity was complex. Recognizing that developing world arbitrators were *less* likely to identify diversity problems in international arbitration, two aspects were noteworthy. The first was the demographic data reflecting that OECD and/or high-income arbitrators made up more than 75% of the arbitrators in our sample. The second was, irrespective of how development status was defined, developing world arbitrators experienced statistically lower numbers of appointments than their developed world colleagues. Even counting developing world arbitrators' own appointments, approximately 40% of arbitrators reported never having sat on a tribunal with a developing world arbitrator; and 59.4% of counsel reported never having worked with a tribunal containing multiple arbitrators from developing countries. Those findings must be contextualized against tests demonstrating that counsel from developing countries were much more likely to experience tribunals comprised of developing world arbitrators.

There is an important normative question about what is the appropriate baseline against which diversity in international arbitration should be evaluated. On the one hand, one might look to baselines established by national legislatures and judiciaries. On the other hand, given the transnational nature of international arbitration, perhaps the baseline offered by public international law is most appropriate. Using either baseline, the small size of the pool of women and developing world arbitrators was noteworthy. As suggested by Sundaresh Menon and Salim Moollan, discussions about diversity are worthwhile and may enhance arbitration's long-term legitimacy and sustainability. In a time when there is a broad pool of talent in international arbitration, and that talent extends across national borders and encompasses both genders, there is untapped value in diversifying the pool of arbitrators.

There may also be pragmatic reasons to consider how best to diversify the "invisible college" of arbitrators. First, as international business activity becomes more complex and international arbitration expands, it is critical to have a pool of arbitrators who are available to resolve disputes and appreciate the unique context from which the dispute arises. This minimizes risk of delay, decreases costs and increases stakeholder satisfaction. Second, as the existing pool of international arbitrators continues to age, it is necessary to ensure institutional and historical knowledge is transferred to the next generation. The objective should be to prevent an over-concentration of arbitration experience, so that a broad pool of arbitrators can continue to offer quality adjudicative services in the future. Third, to the extent that conflicts of interests within law firms or subject-matter conflicts of interest limit the services that arbitrators can provide, it is necessary to have both breadth and depth in the pool of potential appointees. Finally, as more countries' economies grow, the demand for international legal services may increase and generate new opportunities for individuals in developing world legal systems.

Notes & Questions

1. Considering all the cross-cultural elements of an arbitration (e.g., civil versus common law; substantive legal expertise; ethnicity; national background; gender; age), how should arbitrators be selected?
2. What part of the responsibility of diversification should fall to the providers: ICSID, UNCITRAL, AAA? What about the parties themselves? And should this calculus differ in private commercial arbitrations versus investor-state arbitrations?

V. Skills and Practice Issues in International Arbitration

Case Study: Starlight Coffee

Starlight Coffee, a U.S. company headquartered in Seattle, Washington, signed a contract with LARAZZA, an Italian company headquartered in Rome, Italy, for the purchase of 25,000 cappuccino makers at a cost of $2,000 each, for a total of $50,000,000. The cappuccino makers were supposed to be delivered on December 23, 2022, but they were not delivered on time. As a result, Starlight had to "cover" by purchasing inferior products from a U.S. company at a cost of $20,000,000, an amount that covered only half the number of cappuccino makers ordered and which included rush delivery charges. Since that time, one half of the LARAZZA shipment has arrived, but one-third of the machines are damaged and not usable. The contract reads "any and all disputes arising out of this contract will be subject to international arbitration under the Rules of the International Chamber of Commerce for Arbitration. The law of Washington state will govern this contract unless an issue must be determined by European law in order to enforce any arbitration award."

Starlight has filed a claim with the International Chamber of Commerce. LARAZZA has responded, claiming that COVID and supply-chain delays in Italy as well as shipping delays are to blame and that it has a defense under the doctrine of *force majeure and impossibility of performance under U.C.C. (U.S.) law.* It seeks to be released from any liability under the contract.

The parties have agreed to have an in-person terms-of-reference conference (pursuant to Rules 23 and 24 of the ICC arbitration rules) in New York to create a document with all the procedural issues to be considered and dates to be scheduled for the arbitration, including the place of arbitration; manner of choice and number of arbitrators; language of the arbitration; document exchange and discovery schedule; proposed claims and defenses, lists of experts, and time schedule for hearings, briefings, and submissions; whether the award will have a written opinion; and any other issues that need to be specified for the arbitration to proceed and be enforceable under the New York Convention.

Below you will find the ICC's Rules of Procedure, which provide that the parties to an international commercial dispute who have chosen ICC rules must participate in a terms-of-reference conference. They must prepare certain documents pertaining to agreements to procedures, choice of arbitrators, conflicts of laws (if the governing contract has not specified the substantive law to be applied), whether the arbitrators have *ex aqueo* powers (equity powers), the site of the arbitration (*lex arbitri*), the language of the arbitration, and other matters. Read the simple rules below and then be prepared to represent (as assigned in class) one of the roles suggested in the fact pattern immediately following the rules. What kinds of issues come up when parties, lawyers, and arbitrators from different legal systems try to specify in advance the procedures that will govern their proceedings?

International Chamber of Commerce, Rules for Arbitration (2021)

Rule 23 Terms of Reference

1) As soon as it has received the file from the Secretariat, the arbitral tribunal shall draw up, on the basis of documents or in the presence of the parties and in the light of their most recent submissions, a document defining its Terms of Reference. This document shall include the following particulars:
   a) the names in full, description, address and other contact details of each of the parties and of any person(s) representing a party in the arbitration;
   b) the addresses to which notifications and communications arising in the course of the arbitration may be made;
   c) a summary of the parties' respective claims and of the relief sought by each party, together with the amounts of any quantified claims and, to the extent possible, an estimate of the monetary value of any other claims;
   d) unless the arbitral tribunal considers it inappropriate, a list of issues to be determined;
   e) the names in full, address and other contact details of each of the arbitrators;
   f) the place of the arbitration; and
   g) particulars of the applicable procedural rules and, if such is the case, reference to the power conferred upon the arbitral tribunal to act as amiable compositeur or to decide ex aequo et bono.
2) The Terms of Reference shall be signed by the parties and the arbitral tribunal. Within 30 days from the date on which the file has been transmitted to it, the arbitral tribunal shall transmit to the Court the Terms of Reference signed by it and by the parties. The Court may extend this time limit pursuant to a reasoned request from the arbitral tribunal or on its own initiative if it decides it is necessary to do so.
3) If any of the parties refuses to take part in the drawing up of the Terms of Reference or to sign the same, they shall be submitted to the Court for approval. When the Terms of Reference have been signed in accordance with Article 23(2) or approved by the Court, the arbitration shall proceed.
4) After the Terms of Reference have been signed or approved by the Court, no party shall make new claims which fall outside the limits of the Terms of Reference unless it has been authorized to do so by the arbitral tribunal, which shall consider the nature of such new claims, the stage of the arbitration and other relevant circumstances.

Rule 24 Case Management and Procedural Timetable

1) When drawing up the Terms of Reference or as soon as possible thereafter, the arbitral tribunal shall hold a case management conference to consult the parties on procedural measures that may be adopted pursuant to Article 22(2).

2) During such conference, or as soon as possible thereafter, the arbitral tribunal shall establish the procedural timetable that it intends to follow for the efficient conduct of the arbitration. The procedural timetable and any modifications thereto shall be communicated to the Court and the parties.

3) To ensure continued effective case management, the arbitral tribunal, after consulting the parties by means of a further case management conference or otherwise, may adopt further procedural measures or modify the procedural timetable.

4) Case management conferences may be conducted through a meeting in person, by video conference, telephone or similar means of communication. In the absence of an agreement of the parties, the arbitral tribunal shall determine the means by which the conference will be conducted. The arbitral tribunal may request the parties to submit case management proposals in advance of a case management conference and may request the attendance at any case management conference of the parties in person or through an internal representative.

Notes & Questions

1. Prepare to conduct a terms-of-reference (TOR) conference in class for the following roles: (a) ICC case manager (to facilitate the TOR meeting and take notes for the final TOR document), (b) counsel for Starlight, (c) business manager for Starlight, (d) counsel for LARAZZA, (e) business manager for LARAZZA.
2. What have you learned about international arbitration procedures from this exercise? How does this differ from a Rule 16 pre-trial conference in American civil procedure practice?
3. What are the advantages and disadvantages of this kind of process? Consider issues such as privacy, law generation (or lack thereof), party control of dispute resolution, etc.

Further Reading

Paul Schiff Berman, *Global Legal Pluralism*, 80 S. Cal. L. Rev. 1155 (2007).

Gary Born, International Arbitration: Cases and Materials (2021).

Tony Cole & Pietro Ortolani, Understanding International Arbitration (2020).

Contemporary Issues in International Arbitration and Mediation—The Fordham Papers (Arthur Rovine ed., 2014).

YVES DEZALAY & BRYANT GARTH, DEALING IN VIRTUE: INTERNATIONAL COMMERCIAL ARBITRATION AND THE CONSTRUCTION OF A TRANSNATIONAL LEGAL ORDER (1996).

Christopher Drahozal, Donald Earl Childress III, Jack Coe, & Catherine Rogers, *Challenging and Enforcing International Arbitral Awards in U.S. Federal Courts: An Empirical Study*, 65 VA. J. INT'L L. (2023).

Ji Li & Carrie Menkel-Meadow, *Dispute Process Choices among Chinese Companies in the United States: Some Preliminary Data and Analysis*, 27 HARV. NEGOT. L. REV. 295–335 (2022).

Luke Nottage, *The Vicissitudes of Transnational Commercial Arbitration and the* Lex Mercatoria: *A View from the Periphery*, 16 ARB. INT'L 53 (2000).

JAN PAULSSON, THE IDEA OF ARBITRATION (2014).

CATHERINE ROGERS, ETHICS IN INTERNATIONAL ARBITRATION (2014).

THOMAS SCHULTZ & THOMAS GRANT, A VERY SHORT INTRODUCTION TO ARBITRATION (2021).

ALEC STONE-SWEET & FLORIAN GRISEL, THE EVOLUTION OF INTERNATIONAL ARBITRATION: JUDICIALIZATION, GOVERNANCE, LEGITIMACY (2017).

White & Case LLP & Queen Mary University of London, *2021 International Arbitration Survey: Adapting Arbitration to a Changing World.*

Chapter 5

Multiparty and Multi-Issue International Conflicts

By definition, all international disputes and conflicts involve at least two parties; however, most involve more than two parties. Boundary disputes; environmental issues; migration; crime; terrorism; and commercial, economic, and trade issues may be the subject of bilateral, multilateral, regional, or global conflicts. And of course, there are general national and political conflicts that result in wars. As recent political conflicts (e.g., Russia-Ukraine, Syria, North Korea, the Middle East, Sudan), economic crises (e.g., the Great Recession, oil crises), and health emergencies (e.g., the COVID-19 pandemic) have revealed, no nation-state is entirely alone and sovereign in all of its decisions, actions, and policies. As we highlight in this book, there are many processes for dealing with international and transnational issues, problems, and disputes. In this chapter, we study how managing, handling, and resolving conflicts involving more than two parties may differ from two-party disputes in negotiation, mediation, arbitration, and other hybrid processes that we will examine in the next few chapters.

While significant issues of system-level dynamics in conflict studies over time are debated and observed, international conflicts occur over matters involving the environment, trade, commerce, resources, ideologies, and so on, while nation-states, multinational corporations, and non-governmental organizations continue to seek negotiated, mediated or adjudicated resolutions to many issues. The overarching question in this chapter is "Are more than two heads better than just two?" In other words, although more parties may be more challenging to manage in resolving conflicts, may more parties also present opportunities for more "solutions," for example, greater contributions ("deeper and more pockets") and more ideas? This chapter considers the appropriate processes for analyzing dispute management when there are more than two parties. Chapters 6 through 9 dive deeper into these issues, focusing on classic adjudication of disputes, hybrid processes of dispute resolution, and guidance for dispute-system design—and how to put all these processes together in the varied contexts in which conflicts arise.

In fact, you have already reviewed multiparty negotiations in previous chapters. The Singapore Convention on Mediation was mediated among a large group of nations. The NAFTA Convention creating the arbitration process for trade and investment disputes was negotiated among three countries—the United States, Canada, and Mexico. But in this chapter we turn our attention to environmental disputes, an area which provides classic examples of countries' attempting to mitigate negative impacts of human activity, with various levels of success. We begin our exploration of this topic by considering how shifts in the global political system also impact these types of negotiations.

I. Introduction: When Are More Than Two Heads Better than Just Two?

Political scientists, game theorists, and historians now study and debate whether the world is "safer" today than it was during the Cold War, when the threat of nuclear war between the Soviet Union and the West provided a sort of bipolar global deterrence. Following the fall of the Berlin Wall and the end of the Soviet regime in 1989, there began an increase in "small wars"[1] and civil wars, and today we see more significant wars and threats coming from decentralized, post-colonial, and more nationalistic "hubs" of conflicting power.[2] In the area of conflicts studies, scholars debate whether the demise of the Soviet Union telegraphed an "end to history" with the ascendance of capitalism and democracy,[3] or whether it telegraphed a more complex "clash of civilizations" involving more than two oppositional political orders, an idea explored in the excerpt below.

Samuel P. Huntington, *The Clash of Civilizations?*

FOREIGN AFF., Summer 1993, at 22, 23–26

The Nature of Civilizations

What do we mean when we talk of a civilization? A civilization is a cultural entity. Villages, regions, ethnic groups, nationalities, and religious groups all have distinct cultures at different levels of cultural heterogeneity. The culture of a village in southern Italy may differ from that of a village in northern Italy; however, both share a common Italian culture, distinguishing them from German villages. European communities, in turn, will share cultural features which distinguish them from Arab or Chinese communities. Arabs, Chinese, and Westerners are not part of any broader cultural entity. They constitute civilizations. A civilization, thus, is the highest cultural grouping of people and the broadest level of cultural identity people have, short of that which distinguishes humans from other species.

Civilizations may involve a significant amount of people, as in the case of China, or a minimal number of people, such as, the Anglophone Caribbean. A civilization may include several nation-states, as is the case with European, Latin American, and Arab civilizations, or only one, as is the case with Japanese civilization. Civilizations blend

---

1. *See* BENJAMIN MILLER, WHEN OPPONENTS COOPERATE: GREAT POWER CONFLICT AND COLLABORATION IN WORLD POLITICS (2002).

2. *See* STEPHEN PINKER, THE BETTER ANGELS OF OUR NATURE: WHY VIOLENCE HAS DECLINED (2011); MICHAEL IGNATIEFF, BLOOD AND BELONGING: JOURNEYS INTO THE NEW NATIONALISM (1994).

3. FRANCIS FUKUYAMA, THE END OF HISTORY AND THE LAST MAN (1992).

and overlap, and at least one civilization, the West, has two major variants: European and North American. Civilizations are nonetheless meaningful entities, and while the lines between them are seldom sharp, they are real. Civilizations are also dynamic; they rise and fall; they merge and divide; and, as any student of history knows, they also disappear and can be buried in the sands of time.

Why Civilizations Will Clash

Civilization identity will be increasingly important in the future, and the world will be shaped in considerable measure by the interactions among eight or nine major civilizations. These include the two variants of Western civilization, the Confucian, Japanese, Islamic, Hindu, Slavic-Orthodox, Latin American, and possibly African civilizations. The most important future conflicts will occur along the cultural fault lines separating these civilizations from one another.

Why May This Be the Case?

First, differences among civilizations are not only existent; they are fundamental. Civilizations are differentiated by history, language, culture, tradition, and, most importantly, religion. The people of different civilizations have different views on the relations between God and man, the individual and the group, the citizen and the state, parents and children, husband and wife, as well as differing views of the relative importance of rights and responsibilities, liberty and authority, equality and hierarchy. These differences are the product of centuries. They will not soon disappear. They are far more fundamental than differences among political ideologies and political regimes....

Second, the world is becoming a smaller place: the interactions between peoples of different civilizations are increasing; these increasing interactions intensify civilization consciousness and awareness of differences between civilizations and commonalities within civilizations.... Americans react far more negatively to Japanese investment than to larger investments from Canada and European countries. Similarly, as Donald Horowitz has pointed out, "An Ibo may be an Owerri Ibo or an Onitsha Ibo in what was the Eastern region of Nigeria. In Lagos, he is simply an Ibo. In London, he is a Nigerian. In New York, he is an African." The interactions among peoples of different civilizations enhance the civilization-consciousness of people, which, in turn, reinvigorates traditional differences and animosities stretching deep into history.

Third, the processes of economic modernization and social change throughout the world are separating people from traditional local identities. They also weaken the nation-state as a source of identity. In almost every part of the world, religion has moved in to fill this gap, often by movements labeled "fundamentalist." Such movements are found in Western Christianity, Judaism, Orthodox Christianity, Hinduism, and Islam. In most countries, the leaders of and people most active in fundamentalist movements are young, college-educated, middle-class technicians, professionals, and businesspersons.... The revival of religion, "la revanche de Dieu," as Gilles Kepel labeled it, provides a basis for identity and commitment that transcends national boundaries and unites civilizations.

Fourth, the growth of civilization consciousness is enhanced by the dual role of the West. On the one hand, the West is at the peak of its power. However, at the same time, and perhaps as a result, a return to the roots phenomenon is occurring among non-Western civilizations. Increasingly one hears references to trends towards a turning inward and "Asianization" in Japan, the end of the Nehru legacy and the "Hinduization" of India, the failure of Western ideas of socialism and nationalism and hence "re-Islamization" of the Middle East, and now a debate over Westernization versus Russianization in Mr. Yeltsin's country. A West at the peak of its power confronts non-Wests that increasingly have the desire, the will, and the resources to shape the world in non-Western ways....

Fifth, cultural characteristics and differences are less mutable and, hence, less easily compromised and resolved than political and economic ones. In the former Soviet Union, communists can become democrats, the rich can become poor, and the poor rich, but Russians cannot become Estonians and Azeris cannot become Armenians. In class and ideological conflicts, the key question was "Which side are you on?" and people could and did choose sides as well as change sides. In conflicts between civilizations, the question is "What are you?" That is a given that cannot be changed. And as we know, from Bosnia to the Caucasus to the Sudan, the wrong answer to that question can mean a bullet in the head. Even more than ethnicity, religion discriminates sharply and exclusively among people. A person can be half-French and half-Arab and simultaneously a citizen of two countries. It is more difficult to be half-Catholic and half-Muslim.

Finally, economic regionalism is increasing. The proportions of total trade that were intraregional rose between 1980 and 1989 from 50.6% to 58.9% in Europe, 32.8% to 37.4% in East Asia, and 32.3% to 36.3% in North America. The importance of regional economic blocs is likely to continue to increase in the future. On the one hand, successful economic regionalism will reinforce civilization-consciousness. On the other hand, economic regionalism may succeed only when it is rooted in a common civilization. The European Community rests on the shared foundation of European culture and Western Christianity. The North American Free Trade Area is developing a comparable common cultural basis. Japan, in contrast, faces difficulties in creating a comparable economic entity in East Asia because Japan is a society and civilization unique to itself....

Common culture, in contrast, is clearly facilitating the rapid expansion of the economic relations between the People's Republic of China and Hong Kong, Taiwan, Singapore, and the overseas Chinese communities in other Asian countries. If cultural commonality is a prerequisite for economic integration, the main East Asian economic bloc of the future is likely to be centered on China. Culture and religion also form the basis of the Economic Cooperation Organization, which brings together ten non-Arab Muslim countries: Iran, Pakistan, Turkey, Azerbaijan, Kazakhstan, Kyrgyzstan, Turkmenistan, Tajikistan, Uzbekistan, and Afghanistan. One impetus to the revival and expansion of this organization, founded originally in the 1960s by Turkey, Pakistan, and Iran, is the realization by the leaders of several of these countries that they had no chance of entering the European Community.

As people define their identity in ethnic and religious terms, they will likely see an "us" versus "them" relation between themselves and people of different ethnicity or religion. The end of ideologically defined states in Eastern Europe and the former Soviet Union permits traditional ethnic identities and animosities to come to emerge. Differences in culture and religion create differences over policy issues, ranging from human rights to immigration to trade and commerce to the environment. Geographical propinquity gives rise to conflicting territorial claims from Bosnia to Kashmir. Most importantly, the efforts of the West to promote its values of democracy and liberalism as universal values, to maintain its military predominance, and to advance its economic interests, engender countering responses from groups in other civilizations. Decreasingly able to mobilize support and form coalitions based on ideology, governments and groups will increasingly attempt to mobilize support by appealing to common religion and civilization identity.

The clash of civilizations thus occurs at two levels. At the micro-level, adjacent groups along the fault lines between civilizations struggle, often violently, over the control of territory and each other. At the macro-level, states from different civilizations [that] compete for relative military and economic power struggle over the control of international institutions and third parties and competitively promote their particular political and religious values.

Case Study: Climate Change

The international negotiations on climate change and clear air have been going on for decades. They are perhaps the master challenge for multiparty, multi-issue negotiations for several reasons. First, an ideological debate about the sources and seriousness of the problem persists for some outside of the scientific community. Second, developing nations, such as China, India, and Brazil, among others, note that the developed nations are responsible for generating most of the CO2 in the atmosphere, having used fossil fuels and other harmful products for centuries, in furtherance of their own development. So these developing nations make an equity argument: Why should they now bear the burden of decreasing their fossil-fuel usage when it is disadvantageous to their own development? Third, there are conflicts about the best means of ameliorating the causes of "global warming," which include not only fossil-fuel usage but also the methane gas produced by cattle raised for beef production, the destruction/exploitation of the rain forest, and other known and still unknown causes. As a result of these issues, various "holdout" or "blocking" coalitions comprising developing nations have formed. Internal-external issues such as climate-change denialism in the United States and the Trump administration's withdrawal from the Paris Climate Accords, or Paris Agreement, has introduced issues such as inconsistent negotiation behavior and compliance. The Paris Agreement, which the United States rejoined in 2021 under President Joseph Biden Jr., provides for agreements on reduced emissions, research commitments, monitoring provisions, and financing agreements. While we will return to the language of the agreement at the end of this chapter, for now, simply consider how the theories and strategies outlined in this chapter could be applied to the incredibly complex negotiations that were conducted.

Notes & Questions

1. What issues can you identify in trying to negotiate treaties and agreements with negotiators from "different civilizations"?
2. Before the air-quality negotiations were conducted in Kyoto in the mid-1990s, all key negotiators were invited to "negotiation training" with the hope that such training would create a common language and equalize some of the power or knowledge disparities among national negotiators. Do you think it is possible to create a "negotiation culture" outside of national and political cultures?
3. How do treaties and other international agreements come into being if there are such "civilizational" differences?

II. Multiparty Dispute Resolution Theory: Numbers and Processes

In dispute resolution theory and practice, multiple parties are not just a problem of numbers. How do we negotiate with more than one other party? When do we know if we have an agreement or not? When should we/do we form alliances with others to accomplish our goals? What processes (informal, diplomatic, backchannel, or formal (treaty negotiations, tribunals, adjudication)) should we use in multiparty, multi-issue conflicts? Who are our allies in war and conflicts, and with whom can we create joint efforts in conflict prevention and resolution? Who might be appropriate arbiters or mediators of conflicts and disputes? What enforcement mechanisms do we have?

Carrie Menkel-Meadow, Introduction

in Multi-Party Dispute Resolution, Democracy, and Decision Making xiii–xv (Carrie Menkel-Meadow ed., 2012)

The Problem of Numbers: New Theory

[T]he outpouring of both intellectual and practical work in this new field of negotiation and conflict resolution produced a canon of new concepts to be explored and tested in both laboratories and real-world situations. It was not long before Howard Raiffa, a mathematician turned decision scientist and negotiation theorist, and others, began to notice that *numbers matter.* And numbers matter in important and different ways. The *number of parties* quickly challenged some of the basic canonical concepts in conflict resolution theory and practice:

- What happens to *BATNAs* (best alternatives to negotiated agreements) or WATNAs (worst alternatives to negotiated agreements) when there are more than two parties and there may be many more possible alternative arrangements (with some, but not all, of the parties involved)?
- How can ZOPAs (*zone of possible agreements*) be mapped on a two-dimensional playing field (or piece of paper) when adding parties to the mix makes many multi-dimensional zones possible?
- What happens when those *ZOPAs* do not overlap with all of the parties, but only with some?
- While two-party negotiations can be successfully accounted for by the concept of "*consent*" or agreement when there is, by definition, no agreement if one party refuses to agree, what happens in a multi-party setting when some, but not all, consent? By what measure (or voting or *decision rule*) do we determine if there is "an" agreement in a multi-party setting? (*Consensus*, all, most, majority, plurality?)
- What are the dangers to any agreement reached by only a few of the parties when others seek to sabotage the agreement (vetoes, "*holdouts*," saboteurs, defectors)?
- How is *enforcement* of or *compliance* with a multi-party agreement to be achieved? How might this be different from a two-party agreement?
- What happens when parties form *coalitions* or *alliances* to engage in group action and what happens when, after agreements to cooperate in such alliances are defected on, there is *betrayal* or *defection*? How are coalitions and alliances disciplined? How do we measure *trust* in multi-party situations? How *stable* are alliances and coalitions in multi-party settings?
- How are *information sharing* strategies complexified when there are more than two parties asking for or giving information? What if information is distributed differentially to the parties?
- Power imbalances are difficult enough to manage in two-party settings, what happens when there are *power differentials* among numbers of parties? (Consider, in international negotiations, the developed and developing nations, the oil-rich and resource-poor, coastal versus inland nations, etc. And within nations consider indigenous groups vs. settlers or colonizers or multi-ethnic/religious or other "cultural" differences.
- Does it matter if the parties have *iterative* (on-going, repeat) *relationships* with each other or are simply dealing with a one-shot issue?
- What are different groups and parties like *internally*? Who makes decisions for each party? A single leader? A constituency with or without clear voting procedures?

- Who is the "*representative*" or *agent* of each party and what are they authorized to do? How do we know when a party or group has "agreed" to something? What happens when a party or group has *internal dissension*? How can even single parties become multiple parties with negotiations that are both "across the table" and "behind the table" (with constituents)?
- Who talks when? How are complex multi-party or group negotiations structured? What *processes* are possible? Helpful, destructive?

Howard Raiffa, along with his colleagues at Harvard's innovative Program on Negotiation, including Nobel laureate Thomas Schelling, began (but never quite finished) an evocative questioning of how numbers of parties in negotiation might help us develop a fully elaborated theory (and practice) related to how many participants exist in a negotiation. Beginning with the *intrapersonal* negotiations we all have with ourselves (should I do *x* or not? What happens when I want to do *x*, but instead do *y*?) ("cognitive dissonance"), we can look at different conditions of negotiation when there is an *n of 2* (conventional two-party negotiation), *n of 3* (two negotiators with a mediator or other third party assistant), *n of 5* (parties, lawyers or other representatives and a third party), *more than 5*, and ultimately *more than 100* (most international negotiations, like most treaty negotiations now, may include as many as 200 negotiators; and more if one considers the negotiations of a full polity in democratic deliberation or even larger, "global" negotiations). Raiffa (and almost all of us who labor practically in these fields) has concluded that there are some sharp breaking points in the conduct and process of conflict resolution with different numbers of negotiators. Beyond about 100 people in a room, people do not really listen to each other without clear process management and amplification of attention, and any group over about 30 suffers a reduction in individual participation (ask any teacher!). The number of participants in a group affects consensus building, dissent, and disciplining of both individual and group behavior....

The *number of issues* may further complicate the questions above. In some situations, the *more issues the merrier* (more issues means that *trades* are more likely to forge more integrative agreements); in other cases, if there are too many issues it might be more difficult to trade, especially if valuation is different about those issues for different parties. Though some have suggested complex metrics for quantifying preferences in complex negotiations, the number of issues tends to increase (not always) with the number of parties and makes negotiation structure and management of both process and outcome more difficult:

- Should one start with the easiest issues or the most difficult?
- Should all parties be present for all discussions of all issues? When are private *caucuses* appropriate/dangerous? Is *transparency* in negotiation always advantageous? When not?
- Should one go to parties in agreement first (those who are "with us?) Or should we try to win over our most difficult "enemies" first? What are more optimal ways of *sequencing* multi-party negotiations (see Sebenius, later in this chapter)?

- Is trading or "*log-rolling*" with some, but not all, of the parties permissible?
- Can issues not formally on the "*agenda*" be used privately or with just a few parties, without involving everyone? How *public or transparent* should the agenda for multi-party negotiations be?
- Must there be *agreement on all contested issues* for there to be an agreement at all?
- Are all issues equally important? How should *priorities* be established with differential utilities or valuations by different parties in "mixed" "*coopetition*" situations?
- How can parties assure "*fair divisions*" among many parties when allocating values (especially when the parties may have differential endowments and/or needs)? Are all issues for division *quantifiable*? *Divisible*? *Commensurable*? What do we do with "*non-material*" issues?
- How are *monetary and material issues* to be compared to (traded with) *non-material* desiderata (e.g., identity, respect, dignity, needs and values)? (the problem of *incommensurability*).

All of these issues (and more) suggest that much of the theory developed with two-party negotiation, even with the assistance of third-party facilitators (like mediators), may have to be re-examined in the different contexts of more than two or three parties.

Carrie Menkel-Meadow, Negotiation: A Very Short Introduction

93 (2022)

Numbers in Negotiation: From One to Many

How do the numbers participating in a negotiation affect both how we conceptualize the negotiation issues (the "science" of negotiation) and how we should behave (the "art" of negotiation)? Consider the different issues that arise with different numbers of participants:

Number	Issues of process or outcome
N=1	Internal negotiation with self
N=2	"Classic" negotiation choices—distributive, integrative, Compete or collaborate, outcome is two-party agreement
N=3	Coalition, alliance formation, what is agreement? Consent of all or some? Commitments, Blocking
N=4	Two-party negotiations with agents, lawyers, or four-way negotiation, what are the decision rules for agreement?
N=3 or 5	Negotiators, with or without agents and a third-party Mediator/facilitator, decision rules, information sharing issues

N>5	Need for formal agenda, information sharing, decision rules, need for facilitator or leader rules, need for facilitator or leader
N>25	Organizations, groups, communities—process rules, agenda, leader-facilitator, formal or informal, voting rules
N> 100	Large groups, political entities, agenda, information, process rules, decision rules, public or private, representativeness, agency issues
N>200	International treaty negotiations, large group deliberation, meeting management, leadership, process, and decision rules (voting methods), plenary or caucus (committee); transparency of deliberations, records
N>beyond 200	Polity, governments, very large organizations, agents, and representatives, speaking and deliberation rules open or closed processes, decision rules, facilitators, processes, decision rules, facilitators, leaders, voting, consent? legitimacy? transparency or private deals, coalitions?

Notes & Questions

1. Can you think of examples of international negotiations and agreements with different numbers of parties? What are some examples of bilateral agreements and multilateral agreements?
2. How do large groups of negotiators interact? Consider process and voting rules in the US Congress, the United Nations, and the European Parliament. Also consider how different numbers of participants should affect how choices are made about voting or other forms of decision-making (such as consensus).
3. How do we know if there is consent to an agreement with many parties?

III. Organizing Multiparty Conflict Resolution Processes

As we saw in Chapter 1, there are many different kinds of conflicts in international interactions: veridical/true conflicts (e.g., those over water, land, or other resources); identity/recognition conflicts (e.g., most post-colonial conflicts); economic/trade conflicts (e.g., United States-China); security conflicts; and cultural/ideological conflicts (e.g., the Cold War or the "Axis of Evil"). Some kinds lend themselves to peaceful trades (e.g., economic agreements), while others may be harder to deal with when there are real value differences. The latter type are often called intractable-values conflicts (e.g., religious conflicts). They contrast with interest- or preference-based conflicts, where different issues can be traded, compromised on, or altered to meet the needs and interests of various parties (as in interest-based logrolling in congressional budget allocations). Thus, as discussed in Chapter 2, being able to analyze what is at stake, that is, the "res" of any conflict, is an important step in deciding what conflict resolution process will be most appropriate.

Researchers in international relations have studied not only actual international negotiations but also, through the use of simulations, the kinds of processes and outcomes that may occur in different types of conflicts. It is also significant to look at *who* is doing the conflict resolution activity (for example, the neutrality or expertise of third-party mediators/arbitrators, representatives/principals in negotiation, or individuals/teams of conflict resolution personnel—consider the panel of mediators involved in the Northern Ireland Good Friday Agreement versus single-person shuttle diplomacy).

Social scientist Daniel Druckman has spent his career empirically studying how different configurations of dispute types and actors may affect outcomes in conflict resolution. Among other significant findings, Druckman and his colleagues have found that where there is some dissent within a group (think potential conflicts between the Department of Defense and the Department of State in particular disarmament proposals), there may be less rigidity and more possibility for agreements and compromises with other parties. Druckman's findings from research conducted in different conditions, namely, conflicts of interests/preferences versus ideological differences, suggest that "cross-cutting" interests can prevent some of the polarization that may occur when there is too much "in-group" convergence on particular issues. Irving Janis and Cass Sunstein have suggested that one advantage of having more parties in the room where some dissent exists can produce more ideas and less rigidity in devising solutions for complex matters.[4] Thus, having a greater number of parties (so long as the number is not unwieldy) and issues can lead to more trades, some mediational effects of reduced polarization, and different approaches to intractable problems. Consider how the involvement of more parties (e.g., insurance companies, signatories to a treaty, members of the World Bank, or an alliance) can enhance the resources available.

Designing appropriate dispute processes for different kinds of international disputes requires an analysis of what kind of dispute is involved; who the parties are; what rules of decision will be made in determining if there is an agreement; whether an agreement is ad hoc, permanent, or contingent; and, most importantly, whether the process will be managed, facilitated, or designed by the parties themselves, their representatives, experts in process facilitation, or particular institutions. (Chapter 9 covers the topic of dispute-system design in greater depth.)

Carrie Menkel-Meadow, Negotiation: A Very Short Introduction

98–103, 107–12 (2022)

Process and Ground Rules

When there are many parties and many issues in a negotiation it is often useful for an official agenda and a set of ground rules for deliberation to be separately negotiated. In the negotiation of the Northern Ireland Easter Peace Accords, close to one and a half

4. *See* Irving Janis, Groupthink: Psychological Studies of Policy Decisions and Fiascoes (2d ed. 1982); Cass Sunstein, *Deliberative Trouble: Why Groups Go to Extremes*, 110 Yale L. J. 71 (2000).

years were spent developing rules of engagement including de-commissioning of arms, speaking, and talking rules, permitted participants (prohibiting violent individuals), representation rules and some rules and customs about separate meetings (caucuses) and sanctions for process rule violations. Two full days were spent on process rules in the three-month deliberations which formed the United States Constitution in 1787. These rules included: total confidentiality of the deliberations, attendance rules (voting only when all were present in the plenary sessions) and speaking rules (only two comments per delegate per issue and could not speak a second time until all who wanted to speak on the issue could). In addition, the delegates developed task groups and committees to work on specific issues (rather than full plenary deliberations on each issue), assignment of roles of a recorder (James Madison), a "neutral" leader of the meeting (George Washington, who spoke only once on a matter of substance), and a process commentator (Benjamin Franklin who often appealed to prayer to calm heated negotiations and an attempt to keep the focus on the desired end of the negotiation). The delegates also used voting rules that included no attribution to particular individuals (now known as *Chatham House* rules), votes to allow reconsideration of previously agreed to items (in order to encourage *linkage, trades, contingent agreements,* and *compromise*), and finally, an agreement that the final document would be voted on *in toto* (preparing the way for seeking the legitimacy of the finished agreement for a contested ratification process). As is common in so many large number negotiations, it was assumed that a majority vote of states (12 in attendance out of 13) and delegates (55 present) would control decision making.

In modern complex negotiations it is often useful to have a combination of George Mitchell, George Washington and Benjamin Franklin—what we call *process experts* (facilitators, mediators, and consensus builders) to help frame and manage the process of difficult negotiations seeking to accomplish a particular outcome, such as in urban planning, environmental regulations, community relations, budget allocations, legislation, and international treaties. Professional process experts can help groups negotiate their own ground rules in an effort to help legitimacy and enforcement of those self-imposed ground rules. They may use a template of ground rules which have been used with other groups (e.g., no interruptions, use of a "talking stick" to rotate turns of speaking, contingency or revision rules, and prohibitions on violence, insults, threats, or other counter-productive actions in the deliberations).

Decision Rules and Voting

When negotiating with multiple parties, how do we know an agreement has been reached? In complex settings, it is useful to agree on *decision rules for the substantive terms* of any agreement. This is a complicated issue and is affected by mathematics, game theory and strategic voting theory. How we vote has enormous consequences for what agreements can be reached. All negotiators should understand the implications of each possible method of voting.

Consider that in Western democracies the default voting rules for most decisions is *majority* rule (50% + 1 of all voters). This assumes all voters are equal, which sometimes they are not. The European Union, the World Bank, and many other organizations allocate percentage of voting powers by financial contributions, size of population, GNP, or some other "weighted" expression of a particular member's power within the group so that some members have a greater "share" of votes. The majority voting rule is often effective and efficient for reaching a decision which has some strong support (but not total consensus), but it also means that a very large minority (49.99%) might not be happy with final decisions. All voting rules are also subject to "rules within the rules" that affect outcomes. Is it a majority of votes cast (including abstentions)? Of those eligible to vote? Those present at the meeting? Some groups and organizations use more demanding voting rules for greater legitimacy of the decision—some form of *super-majority* voting rule such as a 2/3 or 3/4 or even total *unanimity* of those voting. Where a single entity can veto the will of the majority (such as in the United Nations Security Council) even a super-majority rule will not authorize an agreement.

Consider the different effects of different voting rules. Simple majority of votes cast are easier to obtain but also potentially unstable with a strong dissenting minority. Larger super majority votes may be harder to obtain (taking more time to bring more people along) but once achieved may have greater acceptance. Seeking total *consensus* or close to it can motivate the parties to seek more creative solutions to meet more of the needs and preferences of all parties (constantly seeking "improvement" of what is being voted on). Or more problematically, searching for unanimous agreement or total consensus can lead to "satisficing" (not optimal) compromises or the "lowest common denominator."

An example can illustrate what difference voting rules make. Hiring appointments to university faculties can use any of these rules. A majority vote means most, but not all, agree on a candidate. But not requiring everyone to agree may yield greater diversity of successful candidates. For many years at least one university department required unanimity—total consensus for appointment, assuming that was a high standard for the quality of candidate. Alas, it resulted in a faculty of people with very similar views about conflictual issues in the field and not much diversity. The 2/3 and 3/4 rules provide a middle point, where most, but not all, agree on an appointment so some dissent is permitted, but a greater degree of acceptability to "most" is also assured. In the university setting, this has consequences for a possible second vote (later in time) for tenure or promotion. With a strong dissent at appointment (minority within majority rule) there may be a greater chance of a later negative vote. Stronger numbers of initial vote (2/3 or 3/4) may signal greater consensus and a greater likelihood of a positive vote at the second stage. Note that these voting rules and their consequences are true in any situation of groups of people voting on decisions and are especially important when groups of people vote on many things, so that there may be *linkages* or *history of voting patterns* that affect each vote (whether on each issue, each candidate, or even total "packages" of agreements). Another form of voting issue here is *logrolling* or trading of votes to affect particular outcomes—if you vote for my candidate now, I will vote for yours next time (without others knowing such "side deals" have been made). Some political systems now use ranked choice or sequential preference voting with several rounds to determine intensity of support and to create several elimination rounds.

Voting on preferences for a negotiation (especially when deciding among and between possible options) is complicated by a variety of mathematical paradoxes. The *Condorcet paradox* tells us that how people will vote may turn on the order in which options are presented. Consider that there are three parties and three options from which to choose. When preferences differ among the parties' rankings 1, 2, and 3, the parties may decide to vote on each sequentially. When this is done, option *A* defeats B, and B ranked against C might be first, but what happens when C defeats A? In sequential voting those options that come later will tend to do better than those that come first (seeming to be a better comparison!) Compare this to anchor effects with a single proposal or offer. Clever negotiators in multi-party and multi-issue settings will know how to manipulate presentations of proposals to affect the vote they desire. When individuals vote (and have equal votes) in group settings, with different preferences, ranked when there are multiple issue options, it might be impossible (the *impossibility theorem)* to ever determine a single *stable preference of the whole group for all the issues.* In these settings, votes may be taken on single issues to determine preferences, but when multiple issues are combined to create a "package," proposal preferences may differ, and aggregation of different issues will provide what is called an intransitive (unstable) preference. This may be exacerbated when new proposals (linked or seriatim) are presented by the other parties to the negotiation and parties have different preferences with respect to different elements of the proposal.

A serious problem in any voting situation is *strategic voting*, which is the misrepresentation of true preferences in order to block other proposals or manipulation of the voting rules. Returning to the example of faculty voting, if we have a limited number of jobs to offer and we have to have a ranking of candidates for a preference vote, people can put last those candidates whom they think others will favor in order to move them to the bottom of aggregate voting.

Some of these (and other) voting problems have no simple or mathematical solutions but they can be managed by having the parties fully understand how voting rules may affect the substance of what they are deciding. Professional mediators and facilitators can help manage such processes by explaining both process rules and decision rules before any substantive negotiations occur. In the international negotiations for what became the Kyoto Environmental Clean Air Accords, professionals were engaged to provide negotiation instructions to the diplomatic negotiators present so that power imbalances in negotiation expertise might be reduced and everyone could be subject to the same process and decision rules. Part of such pre-negotiation training can also help advise parties that are representatives of larger groups to develop protocols for assessing client preferences and communication rules for sharing (public transparency and press relations) or keeping confidential interim proposals. Remember that although transparency often sounds like a good value, making public commitments can hinder more creative solutions and constrict what negotiators may be authorized to do....

Facilitation/Mediation/Consensus Building

All these issues and others, including power imbalances, representativeness and accountability of agents or spokespeople for groups in negotiation, suggest that complex multi-party negotiation settings may benefit from more formal structures, with facilitators, mediators and consensus building professionals. These professionals are knowledgeable in managing meetings, agenda development, process rules and design, voting, and other decision-making choices. They can assist negotiators in different contexts to deal with issues of interest and needs specification, emotional, political, and other differences to create the process which is appropriate for particular negotiations. Good negotiators, trying to achieve agreements in many different spheres, must learn to work with *process pluralism* or *appropriate dispute resolution (ADR)*. Different modes of negotiation are necessary for different kinds of issues and require different kinds of leaders and facilitators.

Facilitators are process managers, expected to be neutral and unconnected to the parties, and can help design and enforce, ground rules, process rules, voting, and decision rules.

Mediators are facilitators of negotiation, third party "neutrals" (though sometimes known to the parties or chosen for their substantive expertise or official position) who both manage negotiation processes, but also help the parties substantively by facilitating substantive and creative solutions and coaching parties during a negotiation (in caucus or joint sessions) or evaluating possible proposals and sometimes suggesting proposals themselves. In international relations, some mediators are known as "muscle mediators" by making promises to the parties to provide aid or other incentives if the parties themselves come to an agreement. Mediators do not decide anything substantive—that would be a different process of arbitration or adjudication. But mediators can be especially effective at asking questions and encouraging parties to explore their doubts, curiosity about the other party, need for more information about facts or values, and they can encourage a more empathic interpersonal process to enhance communication and mutual understanding.

Consensus Builders are a newer form of professional negotiation assistance. These negotiation experts do case analyses, stakeholder review, agenda drafting, and problem mapping (with detailed interviews of interested parties and interest groups) to facilitate more formal negotiations in public policy, community, regulatory and international settings and, increasingly in crisis or highly conflictual situations as in social protests.

Modes of Complex Negotiation

Complex negotiations involve many different kinds of issues, including constitutive (Constitutional, organization formation, partnerships), more temporary or *ad hoc* agreements or single issue, task-based negotiation with many parties. Some negotiations are intended to result in primarily permanent agreements (ante-nuptial agreements, Constitutions, treaties, corporate Articles of Incorporation), others are more contingent and will be revisable (By-laws, employment contracts), and other negotiations may be one-shot deals for sales. Some negotiations will involve claims about values in arguments; other negotiations may involve strong emotions or political commitments. In our current world, some negotiations may involve more than one kind of discourse (reason, passion, morals, political) requiring the "middle" path of bargaining and negotiation to provide options for reconciling differing interests. The chart below illustrates some different kinds of negotiation which might be assisted by different models of party direct or facilitated negotiation.

Modes of Conflict Resolution[5]

Mode of Discourse	Principled (Reasons)	Bargaining (Interests)	Passions (Needs/ Emotions/Religion)
Forms of Process:			
Closed	Some court proceedings; arbitration	Negotiation-U.S. Constitution; diplomacy	Mediation (e.g., divorce)
Open	French Constitution; courts; arbitration	Public negotiations; Some labor	Dialogue movement
Plenary	French Constitution	Reg-Neg	Town meetings
Committees	Faculty committees; task groups	U.S. Constitution/U.S. Congress	Caucuses-interest groups
Expert/ Facilitator	Consensus building	Mini-trial	Public conversations
Naturalistic (Leaderless)			Grassroots organizing/ WTO protests
Permanent	Government, institutions	Business organizations, unions	Religious organizations, Alcoholics Anonymous, Weight Watchers
Constitutive	UN, national constitutions	National constitutions/ Professional associations	Civil justice movements, peace
Temporary/ Ad Hoc	Issue organizations/ social justice	Interest groups	Yippies, New Age, vigilantes

Principles = reasons, appeals to universalism, law
Bargaining = interests, preferences, trading, compromises

Open = public or transparent meetings or proceedings
Closed = confidential, secret process or outcomes (settlements)

Plenary = full group participation, joint meetings
Committees = task groups, caucuses, parts of the whole

Expert-facilitator = led by expertise (process or substantive or both)
Naturalistic = leaderless, grassroots, ad hoc

Permanent = (Organizational, institutional),
Constitutive = constitutional

5. Carrie Menkel-Meadow, *Introduction*, *in* From Legal Disputes to Conflict Resolution and Human Problem Solving (Carrie Menkel-Meadow ed., 2003).

Thus, in the chart above, we can separate processes with expert facilitators and those without. Many commentators, for example, suggest that the lack of success of the Occupy Wall Street political movement was that it never had "leaders" to articulate demands and practical proposals to both the larger public and the government for concrete reforms. The Occupy movement deliberately attempted to create a more natural, leaderless movement but failed to sustain itself or its demands for more economic equality. One of the ironies and challenges for democratic deliberation negotiations is the potential need for expertise in process facilitation to organize agendas, consider voting rules, and to help guide negotiations for productive outcomes. Majority votes are not necessarily "best" practices.

As this chart illustrates, when a negotiation involves different discourses of reason (principles, laws), as well as emotions, strongly held political commitments, morals, appeals to ethics, and religious or other values (e.g., abortion rights, animal rights, gun use), the "middle" column of "bargaining" or trading for interests and needs which is problem solving negotiation may be the only way to bridge such differences to reach any kind of solution.

International Complex Negotiation (Diplomacy)

International negotiations (even if they are bilateral, but more often, multi-lateral) are a special case of complex negotiations. In addition to all of the issues discussed above, there are issues of language, cultural assumptions, history, and virtually always, linkage of different issues (trade, military, cultural exchanges, currency, etc.). Though many books offer advice about negotiating with "other cultures," these are often simplistic, and more often, inaccurate, making assumptions that a culture is homogeneous or monolithic with no individual variations. As in any business, legal or domestic negotiation, doing research about particular parties and issues and where needed, engaging a third-party facilitator, mediator (or, where needed, an interpreter) to manage cross-national negotiations is a better approach than making assumptions about so called cultural differences. The cultural differences literature (whether backed up by empirical anthropological and sociological work or more popular treatments) makes claims about differences in timing (exact or relaxed), direct or non-direct communication styles, "high context or low context" cultures, hierarchical or egalitarian cultures, gender differences, class differences and chains of accountability. Such negotiation advice manuals tell negotiators how to speak, what body language to use, what gifts to bring, how to say yes or no (head nodding means different things in different cultures), and even what to wear.

Experienced international negotiators, whether public diplomats or private business or legal professionals, now often constitute its own "class" of cosmopolitan negotiators. Cultural differences are more likely to be observed in approaches to negotiation (collaboration or competition) depending on the issues involved. As US Secretary of State Anthony Blinken said about US-China relations, "we will be competitive when we should be, collaborative where we can be, and adversarial when we must," noting that approaches to negotiation will vary by issues, stakes, subject, timing, and parties.

Like any negotiation with agents and principals (lawyers, brokers, and diplomats), international negotiations are always engaged on many fronts and layers simultaneously, with allies, with constituencies, with political parties and presidents/premiers, and of course, opponents.

Notes & Questions

1. Can you think of different kinds of voting rules that have been employed in different kinds of large group settings? With what effects?
2. Do you think it is possible and/or desirable to lay down voting rules at the beginning of a negotiation or wait until the end to see what might be most effective? What did the framers of the US Constitution do? The drafters of the UN Charter? How is voting different in the World Bank and the European Union (hint: not simple majority by single country vote)?
3. How can negotiation and decision-making be multicultural? Are there any "universal" principles for good negotiated agreements in international settings?
4. How are complex multiparty agreements enforced in the international arena? With what variations in different subject matters?

IV. Strategies for Multiparty Dispute Resolution: Sequencing and Coalition Building

Perhaps the key issue in multiparty international dispute resolution is the formation, maintenance, and even dissolution of coalitions for joint actions. Negotiation scholars and practitioners have both theorized about and studied the trajectories of nations and others using joint action to accomplish their goals. Consider that most wars in modern times have involved multiple actors whether in bi-polar alliances (e.g., the "Allies" or the "Axis" in World War II; the Soviet Bloc (Warsaw Pact) and NATO or "the West" in the Cold War) or more multiparty looser alignments (e.g., the wars in Afghanistan and Iraq). In the 20th century, many regional alliances formed in order to create legal and diplomatic entities of cooperation (e.g., the European Union and its several courts, NATO) or economic alliances (MERCOSUR in South America, ASEAN in Asia). Membership in such entities may be formal, through negotiated treaty processes, or informal, through carrot-and-stick diplomacy involving promises of military, economic, and cultural aid. These coalitions and alliances are often fragile, as nations may withdraw from treaties (e.g., the UK's withdrawal from the European Union (Brexit) or Bolivia's, Venezuela's, and Ecuador's withdrawal from the 1965 Washington Convention on investor-state dispute resolution) or otherwise weaken such international agreements (e.g., the more recent US policy of blocking appointments to the World Trade Organization's dispute resolution body). The materials below explore some of the issues involved in forming coalitions, sequencing actions in multiparty settings, and organizing processes in complex multiparty international dispute resolution.

Leigh L. Thompson, The Mind and Heart of the Negotiator

229, 235, 240 (7th ed. 2022)

Key Challenges of Multiparty Negotiations

There are several challenges at both the cognitive (mind) and the emotional (heart) level that crop up in multiparty negotiations.

Coalitions

A key difference between two-party and group negotiations is the potential for two or more parties within a group to form a coalition to pool their resources and have a greater influence on outcomes. A coalition is a (sub) group of two or more individuals who use their joint resources to affect the outcome of a decision in a mixed-motive situation involving at least three parties. For example, parties may seek to maximize control over other members, maximize their status in the group, maximize similarity of attitudes and values, or minimize conflict among members. Coalition formation is one way that otherwise weak group members may marshal a greater share of resources. Coalitions involve both cooperation and competition: Members of coalitions cooperate with one another in competition against other coalitions but compete against one another regarding the allocation of rewards the coalition obtains....

Coalitions

Coalitions face three sets of challenges: (1) the formation of the coalition, (2) coalition maintenance, and (3) the distribution of resources among coalition members. Next, we take up these challenges and provide strategies for maximizing coalition effectiveness.

Key Challenges of Coalitions

Optimal Coalition Size

What is the ideal size for a winning coalition? Ideally, coalitions should contain the minimum number of people sufficient to achieve a desired goal. Coalitions are difficult to maintain because members are tempted by other members to join other coalitions, and agreements are not enforceable.

Trust and Temptation in Coalitions

Coalitional integrity is a function of the costs and rewards of coalitional membership; when coalitions are no longer rewarding, people will leave them. Nevertheless, there is a strong pull for members of coalitions to remain intact even when it is not rational to do so. According to the status quo bias, even when a new coalition structure that offers greater gain is possible, members are influenced by a norm of coalitional integrity, such that they stick with their current coalition. The implication is that negotiators should form coalitions early so as to not be left without coalitional partners.

Dividing the Pie

The distribution of resources among members of coalitions is complex because a normative method of fair allocation does not exist....

Tips for Low-Power Players.... It is easy to be a high-power player in coalition situations. However, the real trick is to know how to be an effective low-power player. Weakness can be power if you can recognize and disrupt unstable coalitions.

Power is intimately involved in the formation of coalitions and the allocation of resources among coalition members. Power imbalance among coalition members can be detrimental for the group. Compared to egalitarian power relationships, unbalanced power relationships produce more coalitions defecting from the larger group, fewer integrative agreements, greater likelihood of bargaining impasse, and more competitive behavior. Power imbalance makes power issues salient to group members, whose primary concern is to protect their own interests. What is best for the coalition is often not what is best for the organization.

Is there an optimal way for multiple parties to allocate resources so that group members are not tempted to form coalitions that may hinder group welfare? Usually not. Whereas there are several defensible ways to allocate resources among coalition members, there is no single best way.

Strategies for Maximizing Coalitional Effectiveness

Make Your Contacts Early

Because of the commitment process, people tend to feel obligated to others with whom they have made explicit or implicit agreements. For this reason, it is important to make contact with key parties early in the process of multiparty negotiation before they become psychologically committed to others.

Verbal Commitments

One of the most effective strategies for enhancing coalitional effectiveness is to obtain verbal commitments from people with whom you want to develop trust and follow-through. Most people feel obligated to follow through with promises they make to others, even when verbal commitments are not legally binding in any sense.

Unbiased-Appearing Rationale to Divide the Pie

If one or more coalition members regard the proposed allocation of resources to be unfair, the coalition will be less stable, and they will be likely to renege. To the extent to which coalitional members feel that the distribution of the coalition pie is fair, they are more likely to resist persuasion from others to break away from the coalition.

International negotiations in diplomatic, treaty-formation, peace-seeking, and trade and commercial settings may involve engaging with multiple parties at the same time or in sequential gatherings (compare the complexity of climate change negotiations in Rio,

Kyoto, Copenhagen, and Paris, which involved delegations from most countries meeting in one place over a limited period of time, with the shuttle diplomacy engaged in by Secretary of State Henry Kissinger in seeking peace agreements in the Middle East, or consider the backchannels used to resolve the Iran hostage crisis, in which Algeria served as a mediator). Major international peace negotiations have focused on *who* gets to participate (e.g., the controversial decision to recognize the National Liberation Front of South Vietnam (Viet Cong) in the Paris Peace Accords which ended the Viet Nam War, the ultimate recognition of the Palestinian Liberation Organization (PLO) and Yasser Arafat in the Oslo Peace Accords, and the role of Sinn Fein and the IRA in the Northern Ireland peace talks). World leaders, their ministers, and their representatives employ different levels of strategic planning in developing the processes they engage in to accomplish national and international goals. Some, like Henry Kissinger (whom you read about in Chapter 2), utilize a "world order" or global plan. Others respond case by case to accomplish incremental goals, such as peace/ceasefire or specific tariff reductions. Over the last century, as world leaders dealt with major wars and crises like WWI, WWII, Korean War, the invasion of Kuwait, and post-September 11 wars and counterterrorism efforts, they had to consider how to develop alliances and multinational responses to world crises. In most democracies, having the support of one's own constituencies (legislators, voters, political parties) is another aspect of the multiparty structure of international conflict resolution.

In the following excerpt, James Sebenius discusses the process of "backward mapping," an organizing framework for building different kinds of alliances for joint action, whether within one's own constituency or with other allies or joint actors.

James K. Sebenius, *Mapping Backward: Negotiating in the Right Sequence?*

NEGOT., no. 6, June 2004, at 7 (reprinted as *A Better Way to Negotiate: Backward*, WORKING KNOWLEDGE (July 26, 2004))

How often have you heard that, when entering a negotiation, you should get your allies onboard first? Conventional wisdom, but not always the best advice. When the United States sought to build a global anti-Iraq coalition following Iraq's 1990 invasion of Kuwait, for instance, Israel appeared to be its strongest regional ally. Yet because Israel's formal membership might have kept numerous Arab states from joining the coalition, the U.S. government pointedly excluded the Israelis, starting negotiations elsewhere. Careful sequencing plus tacit Israeli membership avoided a potential setback.

Here's another bit of conventional wisdom on proper sequencing: "Get your own house in order first." Yet this was not the path that President George H. W. Bush followed in preparing for the first Gulf War. Instead of approaching Congress first, Bush committed U.S. troops to the region, built international political and military coalitions, and negotiated a U.N. Security Council Resolution authorizing "all necessary means" to eject Iraq from Kuwait. Only after these steps were taken did the Bush administration begin negotiating in earnest for congressional approval to use force in the Gulf.

Had Bush first approached a deeply skeptical Congress, agreement on the use of force would have been unlikely. A negative vote would have stymied any subsequent American efforts to build an international coalition. Getting the right players involved at the right moment opened the door to success. Getting the sequence wrong could have led to failure.

Though often overlooked, sequencing matters greatly in negotiation. Whether you're trying to get the "right" people to attend a charity event, invest in a new venture, or sign onto a complex deal, you'll face elaborate sequencing choices. With whom should you speak first? Whom next? Rules of thumb such as "allies first" or "negotiate internally, then externally" are unreliable guides. Yet a more effective approach, the logic of backward mapping, can help you choose your partners wisely—and negotiate in the right order.

Sorting Out the Possibilities

When Steve Perlman was preparing to launch WebTV in 1996, he faced a critical sequencing dilemma. He had obtained seed funding, developed the technology to bring the Internet to ordinary television sets, created a prototype, and hired core technical and management team members. Now running desperately low on cash, Perlman had to contend with many potential deal partners, including VCs, angels, and industrial partners (as potential sources of cash); consumer electronics firms, Internet service providers (ISPs), and content providers (for possible alliances and partnerships); manufacturers (for manufacturing set-top boxes); non-U.S. licensees; and wholesale and retail distributors (for sales). With his promising venture running on fumes, Perlman's next obvious negotiation might have been with venture capital firms for funding. Yet Perlman knew that, while VCs might have been willing to make small investments in his new firm, they were, at the time, quite wary of making major financial commitments to consumer electronics plays such as WebTV.

Instead, Perlman mapped backward from his VC target, reasoning that WebTV's appeal and value to the VCs would be greatly enhanced by partnership with a prominent consumer electronics firm. Perlman started by pitching his product to Sony, his first choice, which initially turned him down. But he then negotiated successfully with Philips and used the agreement to forge a complementary deal with Sony. With Sony and Philips onboard, Perlman was able to negotiate for VC money—at a far higher valuation. With this additional funding, Perlman had little difficulty threading a path of supporting agreements through manufacturers, wholesale and retail distribution channels, content providers, ISPs, and alliance partners abroad—and ultimately sold his young but thriving business to Microsoft for $425 million.

The Logic of Backward Mapping

When you map a negotiation backward, you envision your preferred outcome and think in reverse about how to get there. Here are the basic steps:

1. Draw a "map" of the parties who are currently involved and those who might potentially get on board, along with their interests and their no-deal options.
2. Estimate the difficulty and cost of gaining agreement with each party as well as the value of having that person or group onboard.
3. Identify key relationships among the parties: who influences whom, who tends to defer to whom, who owes something to whom, and so on.
4. Focus on the most-difficult-to-persuade player—your ultimate target or someone else who's critical to the deal. Ask these questions: Which *prior* agreement or agreements among which set of the other players—if such agreements were in place—would maximize the chances of the target saying yes on your terms? Whom would you like to have onboard when you initiate negotiations with the target?
5. Ask analogous questions about the player(s) at this next-to-final stage: Whom would you ideally like to have onboard to maximize the chances of the most difficult player at this stage saying "yes"? How can you win that party over? Map backward in this fashion until you have found the most promising path through the cloud of possibilities.

To better understand the logic of backward mapping, consider the logic of project management. When deciding how to undertake a complex project, you focus first on your endpoint, then develop a critical path and a timeline by working backward to the present. A successfully completed project is comparable to a value-creating agreement supported by a sustainable coalition.

Once you begin applying the logic of backward mapping, you'll find yourself facing a number of questions: How can you identify critical players? Should your negotiations be secret or open, separate or collective? How can you avoid being harmed by the sequencing tactics of others?

Here's Some Advice

Study patterns of influence and deference. Would-be coalition builders learn quickly that approaching the most difficult—and perhaps most critical—party first may offer slim chances for a deal. To improve the odds, try to discern who influences the target player and to whom that player defers. In a 1993 *New Yorker* article, Sidney Blumenthal described how Bill Daley, then President Clinton's key strategist for congressional approval of the North American Free Trade Agreement, went about securing a buy-in: "News might arrive that a representative who had been leaning toward yes had come out as a no.... When he heard the bad news, [Daley went into action].... 'Can we find the guy who can deliver the guy? We have to call the guy who calls the guy who calls the guy....'"

Careful sequencing can help manage sensitive information. For a building developer worried about being squeezed on price if her intentions become public, the property acquisition sequence may depend on the likelihoods of different paths. Other factors involve the physical relationship of the parcels acquired to those remaining. Rather than waiting for a later acquisition, can the developer use parcels already obtained to push forward some version of the project?

Beware Sneaky Sequencers

Be cautious: others may try to pull devious sequencing moves on you. Most parents quickly wise up to the household version of this gambit: to get Dad to say "yes," Junior will claim that "Mom said it was OK," then scurry to tell Mom that Dad has given the green light. Some children grow up to use these time-honored tactics in the workplace. For example, when a private equity firm negotiates with a major institutional investor, the investor might informally commit capital, relying on the supposed commitments of another investor known to be savvy. Knowing of this reliance, a less than scrupulous firm may be tempted to keep the two negotiations separate, using Party A's alleged agreement as a reason for Party B to close—and vice versa. Advice: explicitly verify the assertions of anyone who claims to have secured a prior commitment from another negotiator—who may be under the false impression that you've already said "yes."

Opening Up the Process

The secrecy that surrounds some sequenced deals can make them appear manipulative. By contrast, a group of negotiators who know and trust one another and are skilled at joint problem-solving may find that an open, collective process generates better, more creative options than a separated, sequential approach. Open negotiations can also enhance feelings of legitimacy and group ownership of an eventual agreement.

Yet relying on inclusive meetings can be risky. Interests and agendas may surface that are better dealt with privately in careful order. Large, open meetings may help opponents to identify each other, meet, join forces, and thus mount a more powerful combined challenge.

With each negotiation, you should consider whether to create a private or public sequential strategy, launch a group process, or opt for a hybrid. When sequencing appears to have an advantage—in coalition building, managing sensitive information, and dealing with potential opponents—the logic of backward mapping will help guide your path.

Notes & Questions

1. Can you think about of some current alliances in world conflicts? How did they come to be? Consider, for example, how China and Russia have recently developed something of a rapprochement for economic trade, even as other countries have applied sanctions to isolate Russia in its war with Ukraine. Is this an illustration of "the enemy of my enemy is my friend" maxim, or is something else at work?
2. How stable have political alliances and coalitions been in the 20th and 21st centuries? Consider how quickly our WWII enemies, Germany, Italy, and Japan, became our friends in the Cold War.

3. Do strong alliances and coalitions help prevent conflict (e.g., the "stand-off" of Cold War deterrence) or do they exacerbate conflict (e.g., the start of WWI and promises to defend allies)?
4. In your view, would it be good to admit Ukraine to the NATO alliance? Why or why not?

V. Case Studies: Environmental Conflict Resolution with Many Parties and Many Issues = Many Processes with Many "Solutions"

The negotiation of several major environmental treaties and monitoring regimes illustrates the interactions of multiple parties, multiple issues, and coalitional behavior. In a pathbreaking article comparing the different structures of negotiation and treaty-making used in three major environmental issues, James Sebenius compared the long, arduous, and "package-deal" approach adopted in negotiation of the Law of the Sea Convention (a treaty which the United States did not ratify) with the more incremental, step-by-step framework of specific and adaptable provisions in the Montreal Protocol on Substances That Deplete the Ozone Layer to suggest negotiation design elements for the contentious and fractious issue of climate change. Sebenius's analysis of these international negotiation regimes suggests that careful attention needs to be placed on both "winning coalitions" (those which will support an agreement) and "blocking coalitions" (those which will attempt to thwart a larger group agreement). Different issues produce different coalitions, which themselves are subject to change not only as conditions change (e.g., as the science changes) but also as interests change (e.g., economic interests, ideological interests, the interests of maritime states vs. coastal states or developing countries vs. developed countries, etc.).

As outlined above, rules of protocols, procedure, voting, and, in the case of international treaties, ratification, greatly affect what can be accomplished. Below we summarize some of the structural aspects of these different approaches to multiparty environmental disputes and then ask you to consider how you would design a good process for the more complex climate change negotiations which have been taking place since 1980s.

A. Negotiations on the Law of the Sea

When the United Nations' International Law Commission launched its Third Conference on the Law of the Sea in 1970, it initially conceived of four different treaties dealing with issues of territoriality: fishing; boundary demarcation for trade and military and defense purposes; seabed mining and oceanic resources; and even codification of old common law rules of sea piracy. The initial intent was to get agreement seriatim by issue. What emerged during the highly contested negotiations is that nations had different national interests with respect to different issues (e.g., maritime states and coastal states had different ideas concerning military and trade boundaries and about access to potentially profitable seabed mining). Thus, parties might vote to agree on some issues or treaties and not others, leaving the law of the sea as uncodified and confusing as it had been for hundreds of years, with essentially only one institution for adjudication of some, but not all, conflicts—the International Court of Justice.

What emerged from a long and tortuous 12-year process was a "package" Convention on the Law of the Sea (LOS) in which different interests and coalitions came together to form as much "joint gain" as possible (with compromises on particular but universal items, such as the demarcations for certain zones: territorial sea at 12 miles, exclusive economic zone at 200 nautical miles, and the "high seas" beyond that, with rules for determining coastal measurements and passage rules for particular vessels)).

The LOS Convention also established one of the first international dispute resolution system "menus," allowing parties to choose mediation, conciliation, arbitration, or specialized tribunals (LOS Tribunal or ICJ) to deal with various disputes. Although many nations ratified this treaty in 1982, the United States did not, due to the treaty's complex but highly innovative provisions relating to mining the as-yet unexplored deep seabed.

The "packaging" of many elements into a formal ratified legal regime with rules and processes for dispute resolution was consistent with earlier efforts at universal, "global" agreements that all UN nation-state members would endorse. At the many negotiation meetings which produced this agreement, developing nations concerned about the oceanic military activity of the developed world (remember the *Rainbow Warrior* from Chapter 1) wanted to constrict the power of maritime states (i.e., navy and militarily powerful states) in coastal waters. Developing nations negotiated for a conception of the potentially rich seabed as a "global common" (a conception now used in climate change and atmospheric negotiations), which they argued should be shared with all of humanity. This presented not just an economic issue (only the developing nations had the wherewithal to extract and mine such resources) but also an ideological issue, namely, should world resources be "shared" with all of humanity or "owned" and "capitalized" by those who are already "haves" in the global order?

The LOS conferences chose a consensus-based rule for agreement on terms to protect developing and maritime nations which had the most to gain with wider global agreements, ultimately leading to the treaty's adoption (without US ratification). In a dualist international law regime (like ours), ratification requires adherence to constitutional principles (which, in the United States, means that it requires Senate approval). Because all the issues were packaged together into one final treaty, nations could determine whether the document offered "enough gain" to sign.[6] Much like the negotiation process that led to ratification of the US Constitution,[7] which resulted in terms like a

---

6. *See* Miles Kahler, *Multilateralism with Small and Large Numbers*, 46 INT'L ORGS. 681–94 (1992).

7. *See* Carrie Menkel-Meadow, *Negotiating the American Constitution (1787–89): Coalitions, Process Rules, and Compromises*, *in* LANDMARK NEGOTIATIONS FROM AROUND THE WORLD: LESSONS FOR

bicameral legislature comprising a non-democratic Senate and a democratic House as well as compromises on slavery, a package agreement with recognition of "linked" but often unrelated issues made it possible to have an agreement on a "whole" despite there being clear objections to some of its parts. As parties negotiated the rules of territorial limits for fishing rights, passage of ships, and exploitation of mineral rights in different sections of a single treaty, the negotiators developed one highly innovative compromise for resolution of the "economic zone" for exploitation of the mineral seabed:

United Nations Convention on the Law of the Sea

1833 U.N.T.S 3 (1982)

Article 76

Definition of the Continental Shelf

1. The continental shelf of a coastal State comprises the seabed and subsoil of the submarine areas that extend beyond its territorial sea throughout the natural prolongation of its land territory to the outer edge of the continental margin, or to a distance of 200 nautical miles from the baselines from which the breadth of the territorial sea is measured where the outer edge of the continental margin does not extend up to that distance.

2. The continental shelf of a coastal State shall not extend beyond the limits provided for in paragraphs 4 to 6.

3. The continental margin comprises the submerged prolongation of the land mass of the coastal State and consists of the seabed and subsoil of the shelf, the slope, and the rise. It does not include the deep ocean floor with its oceanic ridges or the subsoil thereof.

4. (a) For the purposes of this Convention, the coastal State shall establish the outer edge of the continental margin wherever the margin extends beyond 200 nautical miles from the baselines from which the breadth of the territorial sea is measured, by either:

(i) a line delineated in accordance with paragraph 7 by reference to the outermost fixed points at each of which the thickness of sedimentary rocks is at least 1 per cent of the shortest distance from such point to the foot of the continental slope; or

(ii) a line delineated in accordance with paragraph 7 by reference to fixed points not more than 60 nautical miles from the foot of the continental slope.

(b) In the absence of evidence to the contrary, the foot of the continental slope shall be determined as the point of maximum change in the gradient at its base.

5. The fixed points comprising the line of the outer limits of the continental shelf on the seabed, drawn in accordance with paragraph 4 (a)(i) and (ii), either shall not

---

Modern Diplomacy (E. Vivet ed., 2019).

exceed 350 nautical miles from the baselines from which the breadth of the territorial sea is measured or shall not exceed 100 nautical miles from the 2,500-metre isobath, which is a line connecting the depth of 2,500 metres.

6. Notwithstanding the provisions of paragraph 5, on submarine ridges, the outer limit of the continental shelf shall not exceed 350 nautical miles from the baselines from which the breadth of the territorial sea is measured. This paragraph does not apply to submarine elevations that are natural components of the continental margin, such as its plateaux, rises, caps, banks and spurs.

7. The coastal State shall delineate the outer limits of its continental shelf, where that shelf extends beyond 200 nautical miles from the baselines from which the breadth of the territorial sea is measured, by straight lines not exceeding 60 nautical miles in length, connecting fixed points, defined by coordinates of latitude and longitude.

8. Information on the limits of the continental shelf beyond 200 nautical miles from the baselines from which the breadth of the territorial sea is measured shall be submitted by the coastal State to the Commission on the Limits of the Continental Shelf set up under Annex II on the basis of equitable geographical representation. The Commission shall make recommendations to coastal States on matters related to the establishment of the outer limits of their continental shelf. The limits of the shelf established by a coastal State on the basis of these recommendations shall be final and binding.

9. The coastal State shall deposit with the Secretary-General of the United Nations charts and relevant information, including geodetic data, permanently describing the outer limits of its continental shelf. The Secretary-General shall give due publicity thereto.

10. The provisions of this article are without prejudice to the question of delimitation of the continental shelf between States with opposite or adjacent coasts.

Article 77

Rights of the Coastal State over the Continental Shelf

1. The coastal State exercises over the continental shelf sovereign rights for the purpose of exploring it and exploiting its natural resources.

2. The rights referred to in paragraph 1 are exclusive in the sense that if the coastal State does not explore the continental shelf or exploit its natural resources, no one may undertake these activities without the express consent of the coastal State.

3. The rights of the coastal State over the continental shelf do not depend on occupation, effective or notional, or on any express proclamation.

4. The natural resources referred to in this Part consist of the mineral and other non-living resources of the seabed and subsoil together with living organisms belonging to sedentary species, that is to say, organisms which, at the harvestable stage, either are immobile on or under the seabed or are unable to move except in constant physical contact with the seabed or the subsoil.

Article 78

Legal Status of the Superjacent Waters and Air Space and the Rights and Freedoms of Other States

1. The rights of the coastal State over the continental shelf do not affect the legal status of the superjacent waters or of the air space above those waters.

2. The exercise of the rights of the coastal State over the continental shelf must not infringe or result in any unjustifiable interference with navigation and other rights and freedoms of other States as provided for in this Convention.

Article 82

Payments and Contributions with Respect to the Exploitation of the Continental Shelf Beyond 200 Nautical Miles

1. The coastal State shall make payments or contributions in kind in respect of the exploitation of the non-living resources of the continental shelf beyond 200 nautical miles from the baselines from which the breadth of the territorial sea is measured.

2. The payments and contributions shall be made annually with respect to all production at a site after the first five years of production at that site. For the sixth year, the rate of payment or contribution shall be 1 per cent of the value or volume of production at the site. The rate shall increase by 1 per cent for each subsequent year until the twelfth year and shall remain at 7 per cent thereafter. Production does not include resources used in connection with exploitation.

3. A developing State which is a net importer of a mineral resource produced from its continental shelf is exempt from making such payments or contributions in respect of that mineral resource.

4. The payments or contributions shall be made through the Authority, which shall distribute them to States Parties to this Convention, on the basis of equitable sharing criteria, taking into account the interests and needs of developing States, particularly the least developed and the land-locked among them.

These provisions have not come totally into force as economic downturns have delayed much extraction and exploitation of the seabed. However, the principles developed here for recognition of a *sharing model* for global resources have helped to guide ongoing negotiations on the exploitation of Arctic resources.

B. Negotiation on the Ozone Layer

Recognizing that earth's ozone layer was disintegrating and letting in high amounts of solar radiation harmful to all forms of life on the planet, in 1977 the UN convened a working group to create a "framework" convention whose goal was to protect the ozone layer by reducing chlorofluorocarbons (CFCs). When an actual "hole" in the atmosphere was documented in Antarctica in 1985, a compromise convention was signed by 20 countries and the European Community. As the emerging science on CFCs and their role in creating the hole in the ozone layer became clearer by 1987 many nations of the world entered into the Montreal Protocol to Limit Substances that Deplete the Ozone Layer, which was followed by over 90 countries' signing on in the early 1990s.

The Montreal Protocol was designed using a general "framework" of goals along with a series of separate "protocols" that allowed for adaptations and amendments should conditions change. The protocols also provided for a technology transfer in which the developed nations would subsidize and provide less-toxic (lower CFC) substitutes for goods (such as refrigerants) to developing nations that were otherwise opposed to the strictures of the agreement (such as India, China, and Brazil). Here, the idea was that a relatively simple, single issue could be dealt with by everyone's sharing in some of the burdens and expenses. And there was a recognition that requirements might need to change as the science evolved and more facts came to light. This particular emergency demonstrated that a blocking coalition might be brought into the fold by getting the supporting coalition to subsidize or make side payments to members of the blocking coalition (in less legitimate settings, these would be considered bribes). While these protocols were enacted step by step and gradually, the process was much more efficient than that of the more complex Law of the Sea Convention.

London Amendment to the Montreal Protocol on the Substances that Deplete the Ozone Layer

UNEP/OzL.Pro. 2/3 Annex 11 (1990)

Article 10: Financial Mechanism

Article 10 of the Protocol shall be replaced by the following:

Article 10: Financial Mechanism

1. The Parties shall establish a mechanism for the purposes of providing financial and technical cooperation, including the transfer of technologies, to Parties operating under paragraph 1 of Article 5 of this Protocol to enable their compliance with the control measures set out in Articles 2A to 2E of the Protocol. The mechanism, contributions to which shall be additional to other financial transfers to Parties operating under that paragraph, shall meet all agreed incremental costs of such Parties in order to enable their compliance with the control measures of the Protocol. An indicative list of the categories of incremental costs shall be decided by the meeting of the Parties.

2. The mechanism established under paragraph 1 shall include a Multilateral Fund. It may also include other means of multilateral, regional and bilateral cooperation.

3. The Multilateral Fund shall:

(a) Meet, on a grant or concessional basis as appropriate, and according to criteria to be decided upon by the Parties, the agreed incremental costs;

(b) Finance clearinghouse functions to:

(i) Assist Parties operating under paragraph 1 of Article 5, through country specific studies and other technical cooperation, to identify their needs for cooperation;

(ii) Facilitate technical cooperation to meet these identified needs;

(iii) Distribute, as provided for in Article 9, information and relevant materials, and hold workshops, training sessions, and other related activities, for the benefit of Parties that are developing countries; and

(iv) Facilitate and monitor other multilateral, regional and bilateral cooperation available to Parties that are developing countries;

(c) Finance the secretarial services of the Multilateral Fund and related support costs.

4. The Multilateral Fund shall operate under the authority of the Parties who shall decide on its overall policies.

5. The Parties shall establish an Executive Committee to develop and monitor the implementation of specific operational policies, guidelines and administrative arrangements, including the disbursement of resources, for the purpose of achieving the objectives of the Multilateral Fund. The Executive Committee shall discharge its tasks and responsibilities, specified in its terms of reference as agreed by the Parties, with the cooperation and assistance of the International Bank for Reconstruction and Development (World Bank), the United Nations Environment Programme, the United Nations Development Programme or other appropriate agencies depending on their respective areas of expertise. The members of the Executive Committee, which shall be selected on the basis of a balanced representation of the Parties operating under paragraph 1 of Article 5 and of the Parties not so operating, shall be endorsed by the Parties.

6. The Multilateral Fund shall be financed by contributions from Parties not operating under paragraph 1 of Article 5 in convertible currency or, in certain circumstances, in kind and/or in national currency, on the basis of the United Nations scale of assessments. Contributions by other Parties shall be encouraged. Bilateral and, in particular cases agreed by a decision of the Parties, regional cooperation may, up to a percentage and consistent with any criteria to be specified by decision of the Parties, be considered as a contribution to the Multilateral Fund, provided that such cooperation, as a minimum:

(a) Strictly relates to compliance with the provisions of this Protocol;

(b) Provides additional resources; and

(c) Meets agreed incremental costs.

7. The Parties shall decide upon the programme budget of the Multilateral Fund for each fiscal period and upon the percentage of contributions of the individual Parties thereto.

8. Resources under the Multilateral Fund shall be disbursed with the concurrence of the beneficiary Party.

9. Decisions by the Parties under this Article shall be taken by consensus whenever possible. If all efforts at consensus have been exhausted and no agreement reached, decisions shall be adopted by a two thirds majority vote of the Parties present and voting, representing a majority of the Parties operating under paragraph 1 of Article 5 present and voting and a majority of the Parties not so operating present and voting.

10. The financial mechanism set out in this Article is without prejudice to any future arrangements that may be developed with respect to other environmental issues.

U. Article 10A: Transfer of Technology

The following Article shall be added to the Protocol as Article 10A:

Article 10A: Transfer of Technology

Each Party shall take every practicable step, consistent with the programmes supported by the financial mechanism, to ensure:

(a) That the best available, environmentally safe substitutes and related technologies are expeditiously transferred to Parties operating under paragraph 1 of Article 5; and

(b) That the transfers referred to in subparagraph (a) occur under fair and most favourable conditions.

The London Amendment also provided some permitted "delay" times for compliance for developing countries.

Negotiations for the ozone layer agreements differed from other treaty negotiations in that they were conducted in stages and included variable, rather than uniform, requirements for all countries. In reaching an agreement in complex multiparty negotiations, it may be that not all parties receive equal or equivalent benefits, or achieve the same things. It may be that parties get just enough benefit to make having an agreement a better outcome than having no agreement (recall BATNAs and WATNAs from Chapter 2).

C. Climate Change and Clean Air

We return here to the Case Study at the beginning of the chapter for you to consider, in light of some the negotiated agreements here, what kind of process might be appropriate for climate change treaty negotiations. What kinds of substantive agreements and treaty language might be used?

The international negotiations on climate change and clear air have been going on for decades. They are perhaps the master challenge for multiparty, multi-issue negotiations. First, an ideological debate about the sources and seriousness of the problem persists for some outside of the scientific community. Second, developing nations, such as China, India, and Brazil, among others, note that the developed nations are responsible for generating most of the CO2 in the atmosphere, having used fossil fuels and other harmful products for centuries, in furtherance of their own development. So these developing nations make an equity argument: Why should they now bear the burden of decreasing their fossil-fuel usage when it is disadvantageous to their own development? Third, there are conflicts about the best means of ameliorating the causes of "global warming," which include not only fossil-fuel usage but also the methane gas produced by cattle raised for beef production, the destruction/exploitation of the rain forest, and other known and still unknown causes. As a result of these issues, various "holdout" or "blocking" coalitions comprising developing nations have formed. Internal-external issues such as climate-change denialism in the United States and the Trump administration's withdrawal from the Paris Climate Accords, or Paris Agreement, has introduced issues such as inconsistent negotiation behavior and compliance. The Paris Agreement, which the United States rejoined in 2021 under President Joseph Biden Jr., provides for agreements on reduced emissions, research commitments, monitoring provisions, and also, pursuant to the ozone agreements, financing agreements, and is excerpted below.

United Nations Framework Convention on Climate Change—Paris

(2015)

Article 9

1. Developed country Parties shall provide financial resources to assist developing country Parties with respect to both mitigation and adaptation in continuation of their existing obligations under the Convention.

2. Other Parties are encouraged to provide or continue to provide such support voluntarily.

3. As part of a global effort, developed country Parties should continue to take the lead in mobilizing climate finance from a wide variety of sources, instruments and channels, noting the significant role of public funds, through a variety of actions, including supporting country-driven strategies, and taking into account the needs and priorities of developing country Parties. Such mobilization of climate finance should represent a progression beyond previous efforts.

4. The provision of scaled-up financial resources should aim to achieve a balance between adaptation and mitigation, taking into account country-driven strategies, and the priorities and needs of developing country Parties, especially those that are partic-

ularly vulnerable to the adverse effects of climate change and have significant capacity constraints, such as the least developed countries and small island developing States, considering the need for public and grant-based resources for adaptation.

5. Developed country Parties shall biennially communicate indicative quantitative and qualitative information related to paragraphs 1 and 3 of this Article, as applicable, including, as available, projected levels of public financial resources to be provided to developing country Parties. Other Parties providing resources are encouraged to communicate biennially such information on a voluntary basis.

6. The global stock take referred to in Article 14 shall take into account the relevant information provided by developed country Parties and/or Agreement bodies on efforts related to climate finance.

7. Developed country Parties shall provide transparent and consistent information on support for developing country Parties provided and mobilized through public interventions biennially in accordance with the modalities, procedures and guidelines to be adopted by the Conference of the Parties serving as the meeting of the Parties to this Agreement, at its first session, as stipulated in Article 13, paragraph 13. Other Parties are encouraged to do so.

8. The Financial Mechanism of the Convention, including its operating entities, shall serve as the financial mechanism of this Agreement.

9. The institutions serving this Agreement, including the operating entities of the Financial Mechanism of the Convention, shall aim to ensure efficient access to financial resources through simplified approval procedures and enhanced readiness support for developing country Parties, in particular for the least developed countries and small island developing States, in the context of their national climate strategies and plans.

Though the Paris Agreement sets no particular mobilization goals and mostly contains reports and promises to reduce emissions by set country percentages, over 160 nations have signed it. In 2017, President Trump announced that the United States would no longer participate in the Paris Agreement, claiming that it required the United States to take on too much of an economic burden and did not contain adequate enforcement mechanisms or obligate other countries to make financial payments, and in 2020, the United States formally withdrew. To what extent do you think the Trump administration's position reflected "internal" multiparty issues with certain American industrial forces that did not want international regulation? The United States claimed to have already reduced its emissions beyond what the Paris Climate Accords requires. (Note that United States rejoined the Paris Agreement in 2021 under President Joseph Biden Jr.)

The following are some words of advice from Professor Sebenius (who participated in the Law of the Sea negotiations).

James K. Sebenius, *Dealing with Blocking Coalitions and Related Barriers to Agreement: Lessons from Negations on the Oceans, the Ozone, and the Climate*

in BARRIERS TO CONFLICT RESOLUTION (K. Arrow et al. eds., 1995)

The power of the coalitions that will arise to block greenhouse action not merely for reasons of economic interest, but also for reasons of science, ideology, and/or opportunism must be taken into account in designing an effective negotiating process. Preventing and overcoming these forces could be aided by a sophisticated choice and sequence of protocols, as well as innovative devices such as "ratchet" mechanisms, negotiated "baselines," and voluntary actions short of negotiated targets. Even if these hazards are avoided, the possibility of a North-South impasse looms; a number of actions could mitigate it, including workshops, negotiation process choices, creative linkages, and advancement of new ideological "templates." If these measures are unsuccessful, attention may shift to a smaller scale, expanding convention that could use incentives and penalties to later bring other states into its fold. Good candidates to start this process include those countries that have unilaterally committed to greenhouse targets.

In sum, to an advocate of a new greenhouse control regime, the fundamental negotiating task is to craft and sustain a meaningful winning coalition of countries backing such a regime. Two powerful barriers to this fundamental task are (1) that each member of the coalition fails to see enough gain in the regime relative to the alternatives to adhere, and (2) that potential and actual "blocking" coalitions of interests opposed to the regime are neither prevented from forming, acceptably accommodated, nor otherwise neutralized. The negotiation design recommendations developed in this chapter suggest that over time, as the science and politics warrant, there are many ways to surmount these daunting barriers for the climate, and, one hopes, in other areas.

Many of the issues in multi-party environmental negotiations are also evident in international trade and investment issues (and political and peace issues too) as we will explore in other chapters. The Partial Test Ban Treaty of 1963, among others, used a disaggregation, step-by-step approach to nuclear disarmament when a comprehensive test ban treaty became impossible to negotiate. How can international negotiators, mediators and world leaders transform multi-party problems into issues that are seen as needing "shared" and "common good" solutions.

Notes & Questions

1. Given the complexity of world negotiations on climate change, which involves discussions about sources of emissions, measurement, monitoring, enforcement, conflicts over development, and environmental health, what kind of multiparty, multi-issue treaty negotiation process would you design? A global package agreement or a "framework" agreement with detailed protocols with respect to particular substanc-

es? What voting and ratification rules would you choose, and what enforcement mechanisms?

2. Can climate change be dealt with in a single, global, permanent treaty, or does it require adaptable, contingent agreements to account for changing conditions? How can such agreements be ratified and approved? Should we proceed with voluntary agreements without enforcement or wait until enough parties are on board to have something enforceable? Can there be a "partial" non-unanimous agreement on climate change?
3. What can happen when there are internal coalition changes in governments? What kinds of "cross-cutting" coalitions can you imagine being developed to encourage climate change action (e.g., a coalition of industries that produce alternative sources of energy)?
4. Would it help or hurt to link climate change to other issues such as agricultural aid, technology transfer, or economic trade? What kinds of commitments are required for agreements when there are multiple parties? Is it ever possible to have a stable multiparty, multi-issue agreement?
5. Should meetings be transparent, public, or secret, and who should attend? What voting rules should be employed in such international environmental negotiations?
6. Which do you think are better: incremental and changeable agreements or more comprehensive global statements and standards?
7. How much would you be willing to compromise to get any international agreement on environmental issues?

Further Reading

Daniel Druckman, Negotiation, Identity, and Justice: Paths to Agreement (2023).

Francis Fukuyama, The End of History and the Last Man (1992).

John Graham, AND?: How to Build Relationships through Inventive Negotiation (2013).

Samuel Huntington, The Clash of Civilizations and the Remaking of the World Order (1996).

Michael Ignatieff, Blood and Belonging: Journeys into the New Nationalism (1994).

International Dispute Resolution (Carrie Menkel-Meadow ed., 2012).

Irving Janis, Groupthink: Psychological Studies of Policy Decisions and Fiascos (2d ed. 1982).

Miles Kahler, *Multilateralism with Small and Large Numbers*, 46 Int'l Orgs. 681–94 (1992).

Henry Kissinger, World Order (2015).

Paul Meerts, Diplomatic Negotiation: Essence and Evolution (2015).

Carrie Menkel-Meadow, *Negotiating the American Constitution (1787–89): Coalitions, Process Rules, and Compromises*, *in* Landmark Negotiations from Around the World: Lessons For Modern Diplomacy (E. Vivet ed., 2019).

Benjamin Miller, When Opponents Cooperate: Great Power Conflict and Collaboration in World Politics (2002).

George Mitchell, Making Peace (1999).

Multi-Party Dispute Resolution, Democracy, and Decision Making (Carrie Menkel-Meadow ed., 2012).

Vidya Nadkarni, *Bipolarism and Its End, from the Cold War to the Post-Cold War World*, *in* International Studies (2010), https://doi.org/10.1093/acrefore/9780190846626.013.325.

Stephen Pinker, The Better Angels of Our Nature: Why Violence Has Declined (2011).

David Reynolds, Summits: Six Meetings That Shaped the Twentieth Century (2007).

James K. Sebenius, *Dealing with Blocking Coalitions and Related Barriers to Agreement: Lessons from Negotiations on the Oceans, Ozone, and the Climate*, *in* Barriers to Conflict Resolution (K. Arrow et al., eds. 1995).

James K. Sebenius, Negotiating the Law of the Sea (1984).

The Consensus Building Handbook: A Comprehensive Guide to Reaching Agreement (Lawrence Susskind, Sarah McKearnan, & Jennifer Thomas-Larmer, eds. 1999).

Landmark Negotiations from Around the Word: Lessons for Modern Diplomacy (Emmanuel Vivet ed., 2019).

Chapter 6

Adjudication

When we have a conflict or dispute in domestic settings, we often think of going to court. "I am going to sue you" is a common refrain for legal disputes we have with other people, companies, and even our own government. But when our disputes cross borders, or when countries have disputes with each other, going to court is not so simple. There are a number of reasons for this.

First, until the 20th century, there were not any courts at all for transnational or international conflicts. Most modern international courts (whether general or specific subject-matter courts) were established by treaties, and these courts usually have jurisdiction only over those countries that signed the treaties which created them.

Second, as a general matter, international tribunals only have jurisdiction over countries when they *consent to jurisdiction.* Jurisdiction ("the power to speak the law") resides in most tribunals as a matter of voluntary consent. There are virtually no command international courts (and no international police forces to enforce international court judgments). Judgments, awards, and other sanctions (e.g., fines, compensatory orders) may be issued, but compliance is generally enforced only by reputation, shaming, or other countries' threatening to take some military, economic, or political action. It is also possible to withdraw consent, either from a whole treaty (e.g., some nations have withdrawn from the Inter-American Court of Human Rights in recent years) or from a particular matter (e.g., the United States withdrew its participation in a case brought against it by Nicaragua in the International Court of Justice that involved the United States' improper invasion of Nicaragua (explored in more detail later in this chapter)).

Third, most international and regional (multinational) courts and tribunals have limited jurisdiction over particular kinds of disputes (think of this as subject-matter jurisdiction). As we explore more fully in this chapter, the International Court of Justice can generally only hear disputes *between countries,* and there are currently only three regional human rights courts (the European Court of Human Rights, Inter-American Court of Human Rights, and African Court on Human and People's Rights). Many nations, including the United States and those in Asia, are not subject to tribunal rulings on their human rights violations. As we discuss below, many major nations, including the United States, Russia, and China, have not ratified the Rome Statute, which entered into force in 2002 and created the International Criminal Court. As a result, there is limited jurisdiction over the major powers as they engage in potential war crimes.

Fourth, many new courts have been created over the last few decades, for example: general regional civil courts (e.g., the European Court of Justice), human rights courts, the International Criminal Court, hybrid courts (which combine national and international judges and procedures, such as in Timor Leste), and other tribunals (e.g., the Appellate Body of the World Trade Organization, and monitoring and reporting commissions created by treaties (such as those dealing with environmental issues)).

Fifth, individuals and countries can still sue each other. With that said, they may do so subject to sovereign immunity and extraterritoriality doctrines in each other's national courts, which raises the issue whether judgments issued by one nation's court will be enforced in the other nation. (Which laws have effect in which countries constitutes a separate field of law: conflict of laws. This field is a sub-branch of transnational law, and it is concerned with whose law applies when litigants are from different legal systems.) Additionally, matters involving currency, banking and other financial regulations, labor, measurement standards, policing, anti-terrorism activities, migration, aviation, and space law are all regulated by administrative agencies that have adopted litigation-like procedures (this field, now known as globalized administrative law, is not covered here).

Sixth, new tribunals established by treaty have proliferated and seen their jurisdictional reach extend to nonstate parties. The regional human rights courts permit individuals to sue, and increasingly, organizations such as non-governmental organizations (NGOs) may sue or participate, through amicus briefs and other procedural innovations, in particular proceedings. Similarly, respondents or defendants in many international tribunals can now be individuals (as in prosecutions for war crimes) or governmental organizations or sub-divisions. How to make multinational corporations, which operate transnationally, subject to international law and regulations is an important issue that has yet to be completely resolved.

Given the many possible venues for transnational litigation, an important question has arisen: is it a good thing to have so many tribunals (thick layers of international law and adjudicatory processes), or is having so many layers of tribunals or private adjudicatory bodies (as in commercial and investment arbitration) resulting in too much fragmentation and a virtual "Tower of Babel" of possible awards, orders, and decisions leading to potentially different legal obligations and precedents? There is no clear hierarchy of authority in international adjudication; the International Court of Justice is not an international Supreme Court having authority over all other international or regional tribunals, even though many refer to it as "the World Court."

This chapter introduces you to some examples of how these tribunals and courts rule on international conflict issues and asks you to consider certain questions: Is it good to have so many courts? Should there be more such courts (e.g., an International Court of Human Rights or an International Court for the Environment)? What kind of enforcement exists for different international legal judgments from different tribunals, or for fact-finding proceedings of the UN or other transnational agencies and organizations? Has the existence of international tribunals and courts improved conditions of peace and well-being in the world? There are those who argue that since many international tribunals lack enforcement mechanisms for their judgments, there is no real "international law," and some scholars suggest that nations only comply with international law when it is in their self-interest.[1]

As a way to tackle these questions, we will consider the Russian invasion of Ukraine.

Case Study: Russian Invasion of Ukraine

In March 2022, Russia invaded Ukraine, claiming that it was obligated under the International Convention on the Prevention and Punishment of the Crime of Genocide (1948) to take action against acts of genocide that it claimed Ukraine allegedly committed. Ukraine and many other nations objected that the Russian invasion was a violation of Chapter VII of the UN Charter (an act of aggression against another state). As of the time of this writing, the ongoing war has killed thousands of people, orphaned children, destroyed cities and property, and has allegedly resulted in the torture of soldiers and civilians. Claims abound of violations of the UN Charter, the Geneva Conventions of 1949, the European Convention on Human Rights, the Rome Statute (which created the International Criminal Court), and a variety of international customary (non-treaty) laws and rules.

Once you have read through the chapter, return back to this case study. Then, after consulting the appropriate treaties and jurisdictional rules (*see* The Statute of the International Court of Justice immediately following the United Nations Charter), make a list of all the possible tribunals in which these claims could be heard. Also consider the following questions: *Who can sue whom for what, and where can they sue*? Who are all the possible plaintiffs/petitioners and respondents/defendants? Which tribunals could take jurisdiction of which claims? What relief or remedies might be possible? See the preliminary decision of the International Court of Justice in *Ukraine v. Russian Federation*, ICJ GL No. 182, ICGJ 559 (Mar. 16, 2022), https://www.icj-cij.org/public/files/case-related/182/182-20220316-ORD-01-00-EN.pdf.

I. Establishing International Law and the International Court of Justice

The starting point for international law will vary depending on what the focus is: customary international law (created by repeated state action and having informal but observed rules on piracy and international waters, if not wars and humanitarian rules of conduct), scholarly writings (such as Hugo Grotius's *On the Law of War and Peace*), or the establishment of formal international institutions through treaties. In the wake of devastation caused by various 19th-century European wars, including the Crimean,

1. Jack L. Goldsmith & Eric A. Posner, The Limits of International Law (2011).

Napoleonic, and Franco-Prussian wars, international peace meetings held in 1899 and 1907 (the Hague Conventions) sought to establish the first formal international institutions devoted to resolving disputes and promoting peace, and the Permanent Court of Arbitration was established during the Hague Convention of 1899. Unfortunately, none of this effort prevented World War I. But following WWI, there was again great international interest in establishing processes and institutions to ensure world peace, including the League of Nations (which the United States did not join, despite its being a major project of then President Woodrow Wilson) and its Court of Justice, and the 1928 Kellogg-Briand Pact, a treaty renouncing war, which the United States did sign. Sadly, these efforts also did not prevent a second world war.

We tend to think of modern institutionalized international law with courts and tribunals as dating back to post-World War II efforts, beginning with the Nuremberg and Tokyo tribunals which prosecuted war crimes committed by the Germans and Japanese. While these proceedings are credited with the birth of modern international tribunals for the prosecution of international crimes, they were not without their own controversies. With no formal treaty law then in existence to govern both the substance and procedure of prosecutions, these tribunals relied on customary law (*jus cogens*) for crimes against humanity, which included the new crime of genocide and other war crimes defined in the 1945 London Charter. Germany defended on the ground of *nullem crimen sine leges* (no crimes without (written) law, a principle in our own US Constitution (i.e., no *ex post facto* or retroactive law)). Since the Allies were not prosecuted for their war crimes (e.g., bombings of civilians in Dresden, Hiroshima, and Nagasaki), some consider these tribunals to reflect "victor's justice." You may be surprised to learn that the Nazi architects of the Holocaust cited eugenics, America's institutionalized racism, and the US Supreme Court's upholding of the state's right to carry out compulsory sterilization of the "unfit" (e.g., the mentally disabled) in *Buck v. Bell*[2] as justifications for their actions, arguing that their prosecution was invalid under the defense of *tu quoque* (you did it, too).

Nonetheless, the London Charter, which established both the substantive and procedural rules for prosecutions at Nuremberg, became the model on which much international criminal law is now based (e.g., the International Criminal Tribunal for the former Yugoslavia (ICTY) (1993) and the International Criminal Tribunal for Rwanda (1994), both authorized by the UN Security Council, and the International Criminal Court, authorized by the Rome Statute (adopted in 1998 and entered into force in 2002, without ratification by the United States, Russia, China, and others)). The end of World War II also led to the signing and ratification of several treaties which are now considered part of international humanitarian law, such as the 1948 and 1949 Geneva Conventions on the treatment of civilians, prisoners of war, and injured soldiers. It also led to the creation of conventions and declarations on human rights more generally, which is now considered part of international human rights law (and which is mostly adjudicated in regional and national courts).

---

2. 274 U.S. 200 (1927).

A. The International Court of Justice

The International Court of Justice, which has a very limited jurisdiction, was established in 1945 by the UN Charter. All UN members are automatically parties to the statute.

Statute of the International Court of Justice

59 Stat. 1055, T.S. No 993 (1945)

Article 36

1. The jurisdiction of the Court comprises all cases which the parties refer to it and all matters specially provided for in the Charter of the United Nations or in treaties and conventions in force.

2. The states parties to the present Statute may at any time declare that they recognize as compulsory ipso facto and without special agreement, in relation to any other state accepting the same obligation, the jurisdiction of the Court in all legal disputes concerning:

The Interpretation of a treaty;

any question of international law,

the existence of any fact which, if established, would constitute a breach of an international obligation;

the nature or extent of the reparation to be made for the breach of an international obligation.

3. The declarations referred to above may be made unconditionally or on condition of reciprocity on the part of several or certain states, or for a certain time.

4. Such declarations shall be deposited with the Secretary-General of the United Nations, who shall transmit copies thereof to the parties to the Statute and to the Registrar of the Court.

5. Declarations made under Article 36 of the Statute of the Permanent Court of International Justice, and which are still in force shall be deemed, as between the parties to the present Statute, to be acceptances of the compulsory jurisdiction of the International Court of Justice for the period which they still have to run and in accordance with their terms.

6. In the event of a dispute as to whether the Court has jurisdiction, the matter shall be settled by the decision of the Court.

Article 37

Whenever a treaty or convention in force provides for reference of a matter to a tribunal to have been instituted by the League of Nations, or to the Permanent Court of International Justice, the matter shall, as between the parties to the present Statute, be referred to the International Court of Justice.

Article 38

1. The Court, whose function is to decide in accordance with international law such disputes as are submitted to it, shall apply:

international conventions, whether general or particular, establishing rules expressly recognized by the contesting states;

international custom, as evidence of a general practice accepted as law;

the general principles of law recognized by civilized nations;

subject to the provisions of Article 59, judicial decisions and the teachings of the most highly qualified publicists of the various nations, as subsidiary means for the determination of rules of law.

This provision shall not prejudice the power of the Court to decide a case *ex aequo et bono*, if the parties agree thereto.

Over the course of nearly 80 years of litigation before it, the ICJ has handled a wide variety of disputes, including boundary disputes, fishing and water rights, environmental issues, art appropriation, territorial disputes, and, increasingly, issues of aggression and other violations of international treaties. As we will see below, as more international courts come into being, questions are being raised about whether these courts are using precedents set by other international courts that have decided similar issues but used different procedural rules and fact-finding. The ICJ is not bound by Anglo-American conceptions of *stare decisis*.

The Statute of the International Court of Justice provides the rules for the appointment of judges (art. 2-33). The ICJ has 15 judges, including at least one from each of the permanent members of the Security Council (the United States, Russia, China, England, and France), and each serves for a term of nine years and may be re-elected for subsequent terms. The UN General Assembly elects members of the court from nominations made by the Security Council. There are rules about not serving as an advocate or agent in any matter while serving on the court. When a country that does not have a judge of its own nationality sitting on the bench files a lawsuit in the ICJ, a judge may be appointed to serve on that particular case. The court is authorized to sit in smaller chambers (there are three types of chamber) and has, from time to time, attempted to establish specialty chambers (e.g., the Chamber for Environmental Matters). Many of the more recently constituted international courts, as discussed below, have followed some of the ICJ's criteria for appointments, but some have adopted more specific requirements regarding diverse representation from different parts of the world (specifying that a certain number be from different regions or continents) and representation from different legal systems (common law, civil law, a mixture of common and civil law, or religious law).

To illustrate how the ICJ can work, we use *Nicaragua v. the United States* as an example here as well as later in the chapter. After Nicaragua initiated proceedings against the United States alleging that the latter had interfered in its affairs and funded paramilitary organizations in Nicaragua, the United States tried to limit the ICJ's ability to hear the case. This first excerpt contains arguments about the ICJ's jurisdiction in this matter.

Case Concerning Military and Paramilitary Activities in and against Nicaragua (*Nicaragua v. United States*)

Judgment of 26 November 1984, General List No. 70

Jurisdiction of the Court and
Admissibility of the Application

THE COURT,
composed as above,
delivers the following Judgment:

11. The present case concerns a dispute between the Government of the Republic of Nicaragua and the Government of the United States of America occasioned, Nicaragua contends, by certain military and paramilitary activities conducted in Nicaragua and in the waters off its coasts, responsibility for which is attributed by Nicaragua to the United States. In the present phase the case concerns the jurisdiction of the Court to entertain and pronounce upon this dispute, and the admissibility of the Application by which it was brought before the Court. The issue being thus limited, the Court will avoid not only all expressions of opinion on matters of substance, but also any pronouncement which might prejudge or appear to prejudge any eventual decision on the merits.

12. To found the jurisdiction of the Court in the present proceedings. Nicaragua in its Application relied on Article 36 of the Statute of the Court and the declarations, described below, made by the Parties accepting compulsory jurisdiction pursuant to that Article. In its Memorial, Nicaragua, relying on a reservation contained in its Application (para. 26) of the right to "supplement or to amend this Application", also contended that [p 398] the Court has jurisdiction under Article XXIV, paragraph 2, of a Treaty of Friendship, Commerce and Navigation between the Parties signed at Managua on 21 January 1956.

13. Article 36, paragraph 2, of the Statute of the Court provides that: "The States parties to the present Statute may at any time declare that they recognize as compulsory ipso facto and without special agreement, in relation to any other State accepting the same obligation, the jurisdiction of the Court in all legal disputes concerning:

(a) the interpretation of a treaty;

(b) any question of international law:

(c) the existence of any fact which, if established, would constitute a breach of an international obligation;

(d) the nature or extent of the reparation to be made for the breach of an international obligation."

The United States made a declaration, pursuant to this provision, on 14 August 1946, containing certain reservations, to be examined below, and expressed to "remain in force for a period of five years and thereafter until the expiration of six months after notice may be given to terminate this declaration".

On 6 April 1984 the Government of the United States of America deposited with the Secretary-General of the United Nations a notification, signed by the United States Secretary of State. Mr. George Shultz, referring to the Declaration deposited on 26 August 1946 and stating that; "the aforesaid declaration shall not apply to disputes with any Central American State or arising out of or related to events in Central America, any of which disputes shall be settled in such manner as the parties to them may agree.

Notwithstanding the terms of the aforesaid declaration, this proviso shall take effect immediately and shall remain in force for two years, so as to foster the continuing regional dispute settlement process which seeks a negotiated solution to the interrelated political, economic and security problems of Central America."

This notification will be referred to, for convenience, as the "1984 notification".

14. In order to be able to rely upon the United States Declaration of 1946 to found jurisdiction in the present case. Nicaragua has to show that it is a "State accepting the same obligation" within the meaning of Article 36, paragraph 2, of the Statute. For this purpose. Nicaragua relies on a [p 399] Declaration made by it on 24 September 1929 pursuant to Article 36, paragraph 2, of the Statute of the Permanent Court of International Justice. That Article provided that: "The Members of the League of Nations and the States mentioned in the Annex to the Covenant may, either when signing or ratifying the Protocol to which the present Statute is adjoined, or at a later moment, declare that they recognize as compulsory ipso facto and without special agreement, in relation to any other Member or State accepting the same obligation, the jurisdiction of the Court" in any of the same categories of dispute as listed in paragraph 2 of Article 36 of the Statute of the postwar Court, set out above. Nicaragua relies further on paragraph 5 of Article 36 of the Statute of the present Court, which provides that: "Declarations made under Article 36 of the Statute of the Permanent Court of International Justice and which are still in force shall be deemed, as between the parties to the present Statute, to be acceptances of the compulsory jurisdiction of the International Court of Justice for the period which they still have to run and in accordance with their terms."

109. The Court thus has found that Nicaragua, as authorized by the second paragraph of Article 36 of the Statute of the Permanent Court of International Justice, made, on 24 September 1929, following its signature of the Protocol to which the Statute was adjoined, an unconditional Declaration recognizing the compulsory jurisdiction of the Permanent Court, in particular without conditions as to ratification and without limit of time, though it has not been established that the instrument of ratification of that Protocol ever reached

the Secretariat of the League. Nevertheless, the Court has not been convinced by the arguments addressed to it that the absence of such formality excluded the operation of Article 36, paragraph 5, of the Statute of the present Court, and prevented the transfer to the present Court of the Declaration as a result of the consent thereto given by Nicaragua which, having been represented at the San Francisco Conference, signed and ratified the Charter and thereby accepted the Statute in which Article 36, paragraph 5, appears. It has also found that the constant acquiescence of Nicaragua in affirmations, to be found in United Nations and other publications, of its position as bound by the optional clause constitutes a valid manifestation of its intent to recognize the compulsory jurisdiction of the Court.

110. Consequently, the Court finds that the Nicaraguan Declaration of 24 September 1929 is valid, and that Nicaragua accordingly was, for the purposes of Article 36, paragraph 2, of the Statute of the Court, a "State accepting the same obligation" as the United States of America at the date of filing of the Application, so as to be able to rely on the United States Declaration of 26 August 1946. The Court also finds that despite the United States notification of 6 April 1984, the present Application is not excluded from the scope of the acceptance by the United States of America of the compulsory jurisdiction of the Court. Accordingly the Court finds that the two Declarations do afford a basis for the jurisdiction of the Court.

111. Furthermore, it is quite clear for the Court that, on the basis alone of the Treaty of Friendship, Commerce and Navigation of 1956, Nicaragua and the United States of America are bound to accept the compulsory jurisdiction of this Court over claims presented by the Application of Nicaragua in so far as they imply violations of provisions of this treaty.

112. In its above-mentioned Order of 10 May 1984, the Court indicated provisional measures "pending its final decision in the proceedings instituted on 9 April 1984 by the Republic of Nicaragua against the United States of America". It follows that the Order of 10 May 1984, and the provisional measures indicated therein, remain operative until the delivery of the final judgment in the present case.

113. For these reasons, The Court,

(1) (a) finds, by eleven votes to five, that it has jurisdiction to entertain the Application filed by the Republic of Nicaragua on 9 April 1984, on the basis of Article 36, paragraphs 2 and 5, of the Statute of the Court;

(b) finds, by fourteen votes to two, that it has jurisdiction to entertain the Application filed by the Republic of Nicaragua on 9 April 1984, in so far as that Application relates to a dispute concerning the interpretation or application of the Treaty of Friendship, Commerce and Navigation between the United States of America and the Republic of Nicaragua signed at Managua on 21 January 1956, on the basis of Article XXIV of that Treaty;

(c) finds, by fifteen votes to one, that it has jurisdiction to entertain the case;

(2) finds, unanimously, that the said Application is admissible.

The United States lost on the merits its claims of the ICJ's lack of jurisdiction and the inadmissibility of Nicaragua's claims. Further, the ICJ found that the United States violated international law by "training, arming, equipping, financing and supplying the contra forces or otherwise encouraging, supporting and aiding military and paramilitary activities in and against Nicaragua." The United States gave notice of its termination of its optional clause declaration for jurisdictional purposes and then submitted a letter to the ICJ that it would no longer participate in the proceedings. It then refused to abide by the judgment on the merits and used its veto power on the UN Security Council to block all Security Council resolutions that would have required it to comply. (Interestingly, very distinguished American law professors and international lawyers appeared on both sides of this case, with some arguing for Nicaragua and others for the United States. At the time of the Contras' military actions in Nicaragua, there was a great deal of opposition within the United States to the Reagan administration's policy. Later, when relations between the two countries had been restored, Nicaragua withdrew its lawsuit in the ICJ.)

Notes & Questions

1. What can be said about the authority of a court whose judgments may be ignored or disapproved of by nations with the power to veto sanctions in the Security Council?
2. What precedential effect can such decisions have? Is this international law?
3. Consider how arguments over the jurisdiction of the International Court of Justice could play out in the case of the Russian invasion of Ukraine.

Countries have also used international tribunals for environmental disputes. The United States brought a case in front of the Permanent Court of Arbitration, which predated the International Court of Justice, to arbitrate state responsibility regarding a Canadian company's downstream pollution into the United States. *See* Trail Smelter Case (*United States v. Canada*), 3 R.I.A.A. 1905–82 (1938 and 1941) (with the Tribunal "constituted under, and its powers [] derived from and limited by" the Convention of Ottawa, April 15, 1935). In that case, the arbitrators found that Canada violated international law and was responsible for the pollution created by a private party under its jurisdiction.

The following is an overview of a case concerning a similar issue. In that case, Argentina sued Uruguay for downstream pollution originating from privately owned pulp mills in Uruguay.

Pulp Mills on the River Uruguay (Argentina v. Uruguay): *Overview*

INT'L COURT OF JUSTICE, https://www.icj-cij.org/case/135

On 4 May 2006, Argentina filed an Application instituting proceedings against Uruguay concerning alleged breaches by Uruguay of obligations incumbent upon it under the Statute of the River Uruguay, a treaty signed by the two States on 26 February 1975 (hereinafter "the 1975 Statute") for the purpose of establishing the joint machinery necessary for the optimum and rational utilization of that part of the river which constitutes their joint boundary. In its Application, Argentina charged Uruguay with having unilaterally authorized the construction of two pulp mills on the River Uruguay without complying with the obligatory prior notification and consultation procedures under the 1975 Statute. Argentina claimed that those mills posed a threat to the river and its environment and were likely to impair the quality of the river's waters and to cause significant transboundary damage to Argentina. As a basis for the Court's jurisdiction, Argentina invoked the first paragraph of Article 60 of the 1975 Statute, which provides that any dispute concerning the interpretation or application of that Statute which cannot be settled by direct negotiations may be submitted by either party to the Court.

Argentina's Application was accompanied by a Request for the indication of provisional measures, whereby Argentina asked that Uruguay be ordered to suspend the authorizations for construction of the mills and all building works pending a final decision by the Court; to co-operate with Argentina with a view to protecting and conserving the aquatic environment of the River Uruguay; and to refrain from taking any further unilateral action with respect to the construction of the two mills incompatible with the 1975 Statute, and from any other action which might aggravate the dispute or render its settlement more difficult. Public hearings on the Request for the indication of provisional measures were held on 8 and 9 June 2006. By an Order of 13 July 2006, the Court found that the circumstances, as they then presented themselves to it, were not such as to require the exercise of its power under Article 41 of the Statute to indicate provisional measures.

On 29 November 2006, Uruguay in turn submitted a Request for the indication of provisional measures on the grounds that, from 20 November 2006, organized groups of Argentine citizens had blockaded a "vital international bridge" over the River Uruguay, that that action was causing it considerable economic prejudice and that Argentina had made no effort to end the blockade. At the end of its Request, Uruguay asked the Court to order Argentina to take "all reasonable and appropriate steps ... to prevent or end the interruption of transit between Uruguay and Argentina, including the blockading of bridges or roads between the two States"; to abstain "from any measure that might aggravate, extend or make more difficult the settlement of this dispute"; and to abstain "from any other measure which might prejudice the rights of Uruguay in dispute before the Court". Public hearings on the Request for the indication of provisional measures were held on 18 and 19 December 2006. By an Order of 23 January 2007, the

Court found that the circumstances, as they then presented themselves to it, were not such as to require the exercise of its power under Article 41 of the Statute.

Following public hearings held between 14 September 2009 and 2 October 2009, the Court delivered its Judgment on 20 April 2010. With respect to Argentina's argument that projects had been authorized by Uruguay in violation of the mechanism for prior notification and consultation laid down by Articles 7 to 13 of the 1975 Statute (the procedural violations), the Court noted that Uruguay had not informed the Administrative Commission of the River Uruguay (CARU) of the projects as prescribed in the Statute. The Court concluded that, by not informing CARU of the planned works before the issuing of the initial environmental authorizations for each of the mills and for the port terminal adjacent to the Orion (Botnia) mill, and by failing to notify the plans to Argentina through CARU, Uruguay had violated the 1975 Statute.

With respect to Argentina's contention that the industrial activities authorized by Uruguay had had, or would have, an adverse impact on the quality of the waters of the river and the area affected by it, and had caused significant damage to the quality of the waters of the river and significant transboundary damage to Argentina (the substantive violations), the Court found, based on a detailed examination of the Parties' arguments, that there was "no conclusive evidence in the record to show that Uruguay has not acted with the requisite degree of due diligence or that the discharges of effluent from the Orion (Botnia) mill have had deleterious effects or caused harm to living resources or to the quality of the water or the ecological balance of the river since it started its operations in November 2007".

Consequently, the Court concluded that Uruguay had not breached substantive obligations under the Statute. In addition to this finding, however, the Court emphasized that, under the 1975 Statute, "[t]he Parties have a legal obligation ... to continue their co-operation through CARU and to enable it to devise the necessary means to promote the equitable utilization of the river, while protecting its environment".

Notes & Questions

1. In summer 2023, smoke from large-scale Canadian wildfires blanketed huge swaths of the midwestern and eastern United States, resulting in very poor air quality that lasted up to five days and necessitated that people stay indoors or wear a mask during that time. Many people had difficulty breathing, and some deaths have been directly attributed to the smoke. Additionally, many outdoor events had to be canceled on account of the poor air quality. Should the United States sue Canada in the International Court of Justice for failing to prevent and control these wildfires? What would be the substantive environmental claims? Would it make any difference if the air pollution had been caused by factories rather than "natural" causes?
2. Note that cases of climate and environmental harm are increasing around the world. Consider whether the International Court of Justice is the right venue for these cases. Also note that these cases are only between state parties and provide neither specific remedies for the individuals harmed nor specific punishment for the violators.

II. Criminal Courts: Former Yugoslavia, Rwanda, and the International Criminal Court

After the Nuremberg and Tokyo tribunals completed their work of prosecuting Germany and Japan for the atrocities they committed during World War II, there was much interest within the international legal community to create a more permanent international criminal court. Post-WWII there were also a number of prosecutions being carried out at the national level, giving rise to many fraught legal issues concerning who had jurisdiction over which acts committed on whose soil during the war. The Cold War (1949–89) put a damper on efforts to create international institutions and treaties, though there was progress on anti-nuclear proliferation, leading to the Partial Nuclear Test Ban Treaty in 1963 and other weapons treaties (e.g., Strategic Arms Limitation Talks (SALT)). Recently, Russia, under Vladimir Putin, has pulled out of talks to extend some of these treaties.

When the Berlin Wall came down in 1989, many had hoped that a new era of relative peace would ensue. In the months leading up to its fall, one commentator declared that recent events signaled "the end of history" (and the triumph of capitalism and democracy).[3] Alas, this was not to be. With the post-Communist breakup of Yugoslavia and Czechoslovakia, ethnic wars contesting land, political power, and religious and ethnic differences broke out in several areas in Eastern Europe in the early 1990s. News reports on deaths, destruction of property, and active concentration camps in Bosnia-Herzegovina shocked many, particularly because those fleeing their homes were carrying modern appliances and sporting modern athletic wear. This was not supposed to happen again—*Nunca Mas!* and *Nie Wieder Krieg!* Then in 1994, a massive civil war and genocide broke out in the former Belgian colony of Rwanda, as Hutus massacred hundreds of thousands of Tutsis, an ethnic group also constituted the leading political group in Rwanda at this time. Though there had been minimal efforts by the rest of the world to intervene in these conflicts, the UN Security Council took unusual action (with the agreement of all the permanent members) and established two special international criminal courts, in 1993 and 1994, respectively: the International Criminal Court for the former Yugoslavia (located in The Hague, Netherlands) and the International Criminal Court for Rwanda (located in Arusha, Tanzania). These two courts were authorized by UN Security Council Resolutions under the auspices of Chapter VII of the UN Charter (Action with Respect to Threats to the Peace, Breaches of the Peace, and Acts of Aggression). They shared one common appellate body, though there were some differences in their statutory mandates on procedural and certain substantive matters. They were innovative in recognizing the crimes of rape and violence against women and children in addition to recognizing substantive legal violations of the Geneva Conventions. Prosecutors and judges came from various countries and were selected for some representation

3. Francis Fukuyama, The End of History and the Last Man (2006).

from different countries; one of the International Criminal Court's first prosecutors, Luis Moreno-Ocampo, had worked on prosecuting military commanders in Argentina after the country's dictatorship fell (and many of these prosecutions for atrocities committed during the military junta are ongoing to this day).

These new courts were not without their controversies. They were very expensive (requiring various countries to make contributions to the UN to fund them), took a very long time, and raised many legal issues. Furthermore, it was often difficult, if not impossible, to capture and serve process on those accused of crimes. And some who were finally captured, like Slobodan Milošević, died before their trials were completed (and Milošević contributed to the unruliness of his court proceedings by contesting the court's jurisdiction and insisting on representing himself).[4]

Some of the difficult issues in these cases were who was responsible (i.e., state or private actors), what "crimes" were committed, who had the burden of proof, what was the burden of proof, and what evidence was admissible (and available for presentation). In many cases, witnesses to atrocities were afraid to testify, and some had to be kept in protective custody far away from home. There were also issues regarding the location of the international courts (e.g., whether they should have been situated closer to where the crimes were committed) and their relation to national or indigenous courts (e.g., in Rwanda, an indigenous form of justice, *gacaca*, was used for some "lesser" crimes). These courts raise important issues in legal pluralism: From what sources do applicable laws and procedures come? And what precedential or other effects does each court have on all the others?

We now revisit *Nicaragua v. United States* to help illuminate the problem of state versus nonstate actors, an issue that each of the criminal courts must deal with as it develops it jurisprudence. Here, the ICJ held that the United States was not legally responsible for the actions of the Contras, the paramilitary force that it was funding. (Note, however, that in a part of the opinion not reproduced here, the ICJ did hold the United States responsible for mining Nicaraguan ports, which it found to be a violation of international law.)

Case Concerning Military and Paramilitary Activities in and against Nicaragua (*Nicaragua v. United States*)

1986 I.C.J. 14 (June 27)

109. What the Court has to determine at this point is whether or not the relationship of the contras to the United States Government was so much one of dependence on the one side and control on the other that it would be right to equate the contras, for legal purposes, with an organ of the United States Government, or as acting on behalf

4. Carla del Ponte, Madame Prosecutor: Confrontations with Humanity's Worst Criminals and the Culture of Impunity (2009).

of that Government. Here it is relevant to note that in May 1983 the assessment of the Intelligence Committee, in the Report referred to in paragraph 95 above, was that the contras "constitute[d] an independent force" and that the "only element of control that could be exercised by the United States" was "cessation of aid". Paradoxically this assessment serves to underline, a contrario, the potential for control inherent in the degree of the contras' dependence on aid. Yet despite the heavy subsidies and other support provided to them by the United States, there is no clear evidence of the United States having actually exercised such a degree of control in all fields as to justify treating the contras as acting on its behalf.

110. So far as the potential control constituted by the possibility of cessation of United States military aid is concerned, it may be noted that after 1 October 1984, such aid was no longer authorized, though the sharing of intelligence, and the provision of "humanitarian assistance" as defined in the above-cited legislation (paragraph 97) may continue. Yet, according to Nicaragua's own case, and according to press reports, contra activity has continued. In sum, the evidence available to the Court indicates that the various forms of assistance provided to the contras by the United States have been crucial to the pursuit of their activities, but is insufficient to demonstrate their complete dependence on United States aid. On the other hand, it indicates that in the initial years of United States assistance the contra force was so dependent. However, whether the United States Government at any stage devised the strategy and directed the tactics of the contras depends on the extent to which the United States made use of the potential for control inherent in that dependence. The Court already indicated that it has insufficient evidence to reach a finding on this point. It is a fortiori unable to determine that the contra force may be equated for legal purposes with the forces of the United States. This conclusion, however, does not of course suffice to resolve the entire question of the responsibility incurred by the United States through its assistance to the contras.

...

115. The Court has taken the view (paragraph 110 above) that United States participation, even if preponderant or decisive, in the financing, organizing, training, supplying and equipping of the contras, the selection of its military or paramilitary targets, and the planning of the whole of its operation, is still insufficient in itself, on the basis of the evidence in the possession of the Court, for the purpose of attributing to the United States the acts committed by the contras in the course of their military or paramilitary operations in Nicaragua. All the forms of United States participation mentioned above, and even the general control by the respondent State over a force with a high degree of dependency on it, would not in themselves mean, without further evidence, that the United States directed or enforced the perpetration of the acts contrary to human rights and humanitarian law alleged by the applicant State. Such acts could well be committed by members of the contras without the control of the United States. For this conduct to give rise to legal responsibility of the United States, it would in principle have to be proved that that State had effective control of the military or paramilitary operations in the course of which the alleged violations were committed.

116. The Court does not consider that the assistance given by the United States to the contras warrants the conclusion that these forces are subject to the United States to such an extent that any acts they have committed are imputable to that State. It takes the view that the contras remain responsible for their acts, and that the United States is not responsible for the acts of the contras, but for its own conduct vis-à-vis Nicaragua, including conduct related to the acts of the contras.

Notes & Questions

1. The case above establishes the test of "effective control" for determining state responsibility for paramilitary and nonstate actors which are funded, trained, or otherwise supported by a state actor. In the current Russian-Ukrainian conflict, what are possible ramifications of this distinction for atrocities committed by the Wagner Group (supported by Russia) versus the Russian army?
2. In the criminal context, consider whether it is better for states to resolve this issue among themselves or to give the wrongdoers both individual rights and punishments.

With the next excerpt, we turn to a different conflict: the atrocities, including mass killings, committed by Serbia against Bosnia following the breakup of Yugoslavia. (In 1992, after the fall of the Soviet Union, Yugoslavia was divided up into various independent countries that matched what were once its constituent republics—Slovenia, Croatia, Serbia, and Bosnia and Herzegovina. These countries warred against each other; Slovenia was mostly exempt from civil war, but intense fighting between Croatia, Serbia, and Bosnia continued for several years. The article analyzes how both the International Court of Justice, in a direct case between Bosnia and Serbia, and the International Criminal Tribunal for the former Yugoslavia (ICTY), in an individual prosecution of a Bosnian-Serb member of the paramilitary forces, assessed state responsibility. Note the discussion of the ICJ effective-control test.

Richard J. Goldstone & Rebecca J. Hamilton, Bosnia v. Serbia: *Lessons from the Encounter of the International Court of Justice with the International Criminal Tribunal for the Former Yugoslavia*

21 Leiden J. Int'l L. 95–96; 100–103; 106–107; 111–112 (2008)

The recent judgment of the International Court of Justice (ICJ) in the Case Concerning the Application of the Convention on the Prevention and Punishment of the Crime of Genocide (Bosnia and Herzegovina v. Serbia and Montenegro) was a historic moment for the global community. The question before the ICJ was whether Serbia could be held responsible for genocide on the basis of atrocities committed in Bosnia and Herzegovina following the 1992 break-up of the former Yugoslavia. The case represented the first time that a court had adjudicated whether a sovereign state could be held responsible for genocide in the almost sixty years since the Convention on the Prevention and Punishment of the Crime of Genocide was unanimously approved by the General Assembly of the United Nations. The ICJ's 171-page judgment is likely to generate a plethora of journal articles as legal scholars assess the long-term impact of the judgment on previously uncharted territories of international jurisprudence. In this respect, one of the most interesting issues arising from the case involves the challenges presented when different international courts have to adjudicate on overlapping factual situations.

The general issue of the fragmentation of international law has already been the topic of much legal writing, and the International Law Commission has conducted a working-group study on the potential for the fragmentation of jurisprudence with the proliferation of international adjudicative systems. In the arena of international criminal law this discussion came to prominence following the creation of the first ad hoc criminal tribunal, the International Criminal Tribunal for the former Yugoslavia (ICTY) in 1993, and is likely to remain a topical issue with the advent of the permanent International Criminal Court (ICC)....

2.4. The ICTY Appeals Chamber's ejection of the ICJ's Nicaragua standard

In 1999 the ICTY Appeals Chamber entered the fray, creating an explicit conflict with *Nicaragua*. The Appeals Chamber agreed with the trial chamber that *Nicaragua* was relevant to determining the nature of the armed conflict. Rejecting Judge McDonald's dissenting argument that *Nicaragua* should not be used to assess the nature of the conflict, the Appeals Chamber explained, What is at issue is ... the conditions on which under international law an individual may be held to act as a de facto organ of a State. Logically these conditions must be the same both in the case: (i) where the court's task is to ascertain whether an act performed by an individual may be attributed to a State, thereby generating the international responsibility of that State; and (ii) where the court must instead determine whether individuals are acting as de facto State officials, thereby rendering the conflict international and thus setting the necessary precondition for the 'grave breaches' regime to apply.

The Appeals Chamber also disagreed with Judge McDonald's assertion that the 'effective control' test in *Nicaragua* was a subsidiary test to what she had termed the 'agency' test. However, it also disagreed with the trial chamber majority's acceptance of *Nicaragua*'s 'effective control' test, and in an unexpected move it set itself up in direct conflict with the ICJ, stating that 'the Appeals Chamber, with respect, does not hold the *Nicaragua* [effective control] test to be persuasive'. Its justification for this attack on the jurisprudence of the ICJ was that the 'effective control' test did not comport either with the logic of the law of state responsibility, or with judicial or state practice....

The handling of *Nicaragua* in the Tadić appeal has been criticized, not only for the substance of what the Appeals Chamber said about the 'effective control' test, but also for the fact that the Appeals Chamber even addressed the *Nicaragua* test in the first place. It is not too difficult to see the intuition behind the ICTY's general inclination to look for an attribution test in trying to determine whether an external state exercises so much control over the actions of a group of non-state actors that the conflict is substantively an international one. Nevertheless, the Appeals Chamber violated the basic principle of judicial economy by offering a wholesale criticism of the validity of the *Nicaragua* attribution test for the purposes of state responsibility, when the only issue it needed to decide in the case before it was whether the alleged acts with which Tadić was charged took place within an international or an internal armed conflict. It was therefore not surprising that when presented with a case that required the application of this test of attribution, the ICJ would take the opportunity to explicate its position on *Nicaragua* in the context of comments made by the ICTY in the Tadić appeal....

Accordingly, the final outcome of the interplay between the ICJ and ICTY on this question of attribution suggests that the ICJ will continue to use its *Nicaragua* test in assessing questions of state responsibility that come before it, and that the ICTY will continue to use its 'overall control' test in characterizing whether a conflict is internal or international for the purposes of applying the 'grave breaches' regime of IHL. [International Humanitarian Law]

The ICJ's language of deference towards the ICTY with regard to the issues that come before that Tribunal give the appearance of a court that is being guided by principles of judicial restraint: the ICJ commented as much as was necessary for it to adjudicate the case before it, while reserving judgment on the appropriateness of the ICTY's approach to the questions it faces. However, the Court's approach might also be understood as having been driven by purely pragmatic concerns. One might observe the likely futility had the ICJ attempted to fight the ICTY's judgment on the issue of how to assess the nature of the conflict, given that since the Tadić appeal the ICTY has developed a solid body of jurisprudence that is grounded in the 'overall control' test for determining the nature of the conflict, and to which the Pre-trial Chamber of the ICC has already referred approvingly.

To the extent that this more pragmatic view has any credence, it may just be the by-product of a current legal order in which there have not yet been any formal or enforced guidelines to govern the interrelationship between the ICJ and the ICTY. However, this possibility notwithstanding, the lesson from *Bosnia v. Serbia* may well be that any attempt to guide different international adjudicative bodies towards a principled system in order to avoid the potential for fragmented jurisprudence between the international bodies will need to be flexible enough to accommodate the concerns for consistency within each of the international bodies....

3.1.2. Drawing inferences from the absence of ICTY charges

The Court reaches its conclusion that specific intent was lacking in all situations other than Srebrenica not only by drawing negative inferences from the absence of ICTY genocide convictions; it also gives weight to the absence of ICTY genocide charges. In one of the most questionable portions of the judgment the Court applies this belief in the significance of what is not in an indictment to refute Bosnia and Herzegovina's proposition that the pattern of atrocities, committed across many regions, demonstrated specific intent. In coming to the conclusion that specific intent could not be inferred from the pattern of atrocities, the Court not only relies on the ICTY findings, but also on 'actions of the Prosecutor (of the ICTY) including decisions *not to charge* genocide offenses in *possibly relevant* indictments and to enter into plea agreements ... by which the genocide related charges were withdrawn.

Giving evidentiary weight to the Prosecutor's decision not to include a genocide charge in any given indictment, or to negotiate a plea agreement that involves withdrawing a genocide charge, is troublesome. First, the Prosecutor's decision not to charge genocide in an indictment may have nothing at all to do with the absence of evidence that genocide was committed in any particular situation. The evidence might indeed be conclusive as to the actus reus but wanting with regard to the criminal liability of the particular individual accused person or persons before the Tribunal. Second, crucial evidence may have been obtained from a state intelligence source under the provisions of Rule 70B of the ICTY Rules of Procedure and Evidence. Reference to such evidence in an indictment would thus be precluded. And, with regard to a plea agreement, the acceptance by the Prosecutor of a confession of guilt to a less serious crime than genocide might well be driven by the advantages of avoiding a lengthy trial or the unavailability of essential evidence. There might, indeed, be other weaknesses in the prosecution case that are unrelated to whether or not genocide was actually committed....

Conclusion

In *Bosnia v. Serbia*, the UN's principal adjudicative body held that, as a matter of law, it can find a state responsible for the commission of genocide. As the first case to be adjudicated by the ICJ on this question in the almost sixty years since the Genocide Convention was adopted, this alone makes for a historic moment in international law. However, the ICJ's approach to dealing with legal and factual issues that overlapped with the work of the ICTY will also become a focal point for those interested in the development of international law in the coming years. The ICJ's approach in *Bosnia v. Serbia* to the challenge the ICTY raised against the *Nicaragua* standard for assessing state responsibility can be viewed as being guided by principles of judicial restraint; the ICJ commented as much as was necessary for it to adjudicate the case before it, while reserving judgment on the appropriateness of the ICTY's approach to the questions it faces. However, the Court's approach might also be understood as having been driven by purely pragmatic concerns that steered the Court away from upsetting already decided cases before the ICTY. Those who are interested in establishing a framework through which to mitigate the potential problems arising from the fragmentation of international law are generally concerned with a lack of consistency between different international bodies. However, to the extent that the ICJ's approach to the question of the appropriate legal standard for assessing state responsibility in *Bosnia v. Serbia* was driven by pragmatic concerns, the case draws attention to the issue of jurisprudential consistency within different adjudicative bodies. Any attempt to standardize inter-court relations should be sufficiently flexible as to accommodate the—sometimes competing—need for intra-court jurisprudential consistency.

While the issues arising from the failure of one international court to defer to the previous judgments of another international court have been articulated at length in the academic literature, our critique of the fact-finding approach taken by the ICJ in the *Bosnia v. Serbia* judgment suggests that scholars, judges, and litigants should perhaps be equally concerned about the potential problems arising from an inappropriate reliance on the findings of other courts. Furthermore, this is not a concern unique to the ICJ. The Pre-trial Chamber of the ICC recently relied on the ICJ's factual findings of the presence of Ugandan forces as an occupying power in Ituri in order to decide that, contrary to the charges presented by the prosecution, the nature of the conflict within which the alleged crimes took place was international, not non-international. As the case load of the ICC grows, one can predict the question of the circumstances under which it is appropriate for one international body to adopt the factual findings of another international body will become a significant issue for those interested in international criminal cases.

However, it is in terms of the implications for future applicants trying to establish state responsibility for genocide before the ICJ that the fact-finding approach taken by the Court in this case raises the most concerns. If one is to accept the Court's position that it has the ability and jurisdiction to make a positive finding of state responsibility for genocide, even in the absence of a genocide conviction for any individual perpetrator, then the Court should not use the absence of a genocide conviction to preclude it from finding that genocide was committed. If its factfinding approach in *Bosnia v. Serbia* is to set any precedent for how the ICJ will adjudicate future cases under the Genocide Convention, it is hard to see how the Court will ever make a positive genocide determination in the absence of a criminal court having already convicted individual perpetrators of genocide. On the basis of this case, the Court's approach seems to be that if another judicial body with jurisdiction over the events at issue has not already established genocide, the ICJ will not either. If this is correct, then the *Bosnia v. Serbia* judgment may have taken away with one hand what it has offered with the other—promising an international legal system that can hold states accountable for the commission of genocide, while simultaneously ensuring that in practice that promise will only rarely be fulfilled.

Notes & Questions

1. Compare what the ICJ decided about state responsibility in the *Nicaragua* case to what it decided in *Bosnia v. Serbia*. What legal standards were used in these cases? What facts or evidence did each court rely on?
2. What did the ICTY decide about state responsibility and genocide in its rulings in the Tadić case? What legal standards were used? What facts or evidence did it rely on?

3. What are Goldstone and Hamilton concerned about? Too much inconsistency among international courts or too much deference from one court to another?
4. What are your views on how all international court jurisprudence should be handled from one court to another?

A. The International Criminal Court

In 1989 (after the fall of the Berlin Wall but before the atrocities in Bosnia-Herzegovina and Rwanda), diplomats from various countries began the process of negotiating for the creation of an international criminal court. The result was the Rome Statute,[5] ratified in 1998. Just as he was leaving office, then President Bill Clinton signed the treaty, but his successor, George W. Bush, rescinded his approval in one of his first acts as president. The Rome Statute was never ratified by the US Senate in any case. Other major countries that have not signed on to the Rome Statute include Russia and China. The ICC has been subject to criticism as nearly all of its prosecutions thus far have targeted African actors; because of this, a number of African leaders have either threatened to withdraw or have withdrawn from the ICC. The Rome Statute provides for the prosecution of four crimes: crimes against humanity, genocide, war crimes, and crimes of aggression. The first three became operative at the time of ratification, but the fourth proved to be controversial, with diplomatic negotiations failing to achieve a consensus on its precise definition for decades. Among the ICC's major achievements so far include the 2012 conviction of Thomas Lubanga Dyilo of the Democratic Republic of the Congo (DRC) for his use of child soldiers (the ICC's first conviction of a country's leader) and the recognition of responsibility for new crimes against women (e.g., rape and sexual violence). Note that the ICC is meant to confer "supplemental" jurisdiction over international criminal acts only when such crimes are not pursued by national courts, under the principle of admissibility found in Article 17 of the Rome Statute.

Notes & Questions

1. As noted above, Russia is not a party to the Rome Statute creating the International Criminal Court. When the war in Ukraine ends, should there be a special court to prosecute war crimes and atrocities committed during that war? How should such a court be created, for example, through treaty or the UN Security Council? (And is the latter even possible given Russia's veto power?) How should such a court be structured (think judges, rules of procedures, location, and substantive laws)?
2. In the alternative, should these prosecutions be conducted in each country's national courts? Consider that, in December 2023, the United States charged four Russian soldiers with war crimes under US law for torturing a US citizen during the Ukrainian invasion.

---

5. Rome Statute of the International Criminal Court, http: www.icc-cpi.int (adopted July 17, 1998, by a vote of 120 in favor, 7 against, 21 abstentions, entered into force July 1, 2002, with 114 parties).

3. The relationships between these courts is complicated. Some fear potential inconsistency in rulings and rationales, and others fear that one court might give too much deference to another court's rulings without sufficient independent analysis or evidence production. Should the ICC be bound by the ICJ determinations?

III. Human Rights Courts: European Court of Human Rights, Inter-American Court of Human Rights, and African Court of Human and People's Rights

Some argue that early attention to human rights can be found in the writings of ancient and medieval philosophers, and continuing in the eras of enslavement, colonialism, and conquest of indigenous peoples (e.g., the Spanish philosopher Francisco de Vitoria 1486–1548). However, modern human rights conceptions are generally attributed to the French Revolution in the late 18th century[6] and in modern times to the 1948 UN Universal Declaration of Human Rights, which is *not* a treaty or convention but rather a declaration now considered to constitute customary, but not positive, international law. The framers of the UN Declaration (among them, Eleanor Roosevelt[7]) believed that it would be difficult to get formal ratification for an international treaty that specified less-than-universally accepted and often culturally-based human rights, so they opted for a less "compulsory" international document; thus, when the UN was formed, there was no formal positive law granting litigable rights to individuals at the international level, and this is still true today.

Instead, several separate regions of the world adopted treaties and conventions establishing substantive human rights and commissions and courts to hear human rights claims: the European Convention on Human Rights (signed 1950, in force 1953), which was signed by all 46 members of the Council of Europe (not to be confused with the European Union, a smaller group of countries); the American Convention on Human Rights, also known as the Pact of San Jose (signed 1969, in force 1978), which the United States has not ratified; and the African Charter on Human and People's Rights (in force 1986). These conventions provide definitions of human rights—such as freedom of speech, freedom of religion, due process, and "social" human rights like the right to education or the right to work—that have been used to create regional adjudicative bodies (i.e., the European Court of Human Rights, the Inter-American Court of Human Rights, and the African Court for Human and People's Rights). Each of these courts has relatively complex procedural rules usually requiring some form of exhaustion of remedies in national courts before the regional body will entertain the "admissibility" of a claim. Both the European Court of Human Rights and the

6. *See* Lynn Hunt, Inventing Human Rights: A History (2008).

7. *See* Mary Ann Glendon, A World Made New: Eleanor Roosevelt and the Universal Declaration of Human Rights (2002).

Inter-American Court of Human Rights have a commission that investigates claims before allowing a case to be formally filed, and both also provide for "amiable settlements" (a settlement conference procedure which permits injunctive-like consent agreements) as well as compensatory relief. Both also now have relatively thick bodies of jurisprudence as many cases have been formally adjudicated in a number of areas. Newer conventions, such as the Convention on the Prohibition of Disappearances and the Convention Against Torture, often provide for jurisdiction in these courts. Additionally, although it is not a court, the UN Commission on Human Rights conducts investigations and hearings and issues monitoring reports on the state of human rights in countries, and it also attempts to impose sanctions, where possible. It also has jurisdiction to hear claims from some of the newer international conventions, many of which the United States has not signed (e.g., the Convention on the Rights of Children and the Convention of the Elimination of Discrimination against Women).

Several major issues have arisen in the jurisprudence of all of these courts: What is the relation of the regional court's ruling to the national court or national legislature whose actions are being questioned? Does a ruling against one country have any precedential value for other countries? [Hint: there is differential compliance with the rulings of human rights courts.] What legal value does a human rights court decision have with respect to countries that are not signatories to particular conventions? How can we measure if these courts have been successful in promoting human rights?

The Inter-American Court of Human Rights has been subject to more political critique than the European Court of Human Rights.[8] Some countries have withdrawn their consent to jurisdiction and their ratification of the conventions. How to validly withdraw from the jurisdiction of courts or from substantive-rights guarantees are ongoing issues of international law.

We now turn to a few examples illustrating some of these issues, first in the European Court of Human Rights and then in the Inter-American Court of Human Rights.

A. The European Court of Human Rights

France enacted a law banning face-covering in public places in 2011. The day the law went into effect, a French woman challenged the ban in the European Court of Human Rights. She argued that she wore a face covering for religious reasons and chose to do so herself, not because anyone else, such as her husband, required her to do so, heading off claims of gendered coercion and sex discrimination. She agreed to remove her face covering in security situations. The European Court of Human Rights acknowledged that the French law might be considered a violation of her right under Article 9 of the European Convention on Human Rights to a "private life" and her religious freedom, and it rejected the French government's argument that the law was required for "public safety." But as you will see below, the court accepted other arguments that the French

8. *See* Angel E. Oquendo, Through Thick and Thin: From Human Rights Principles to Politics across the Americas and Beyond (2022).

government made in defense of the law, and it sustained the law. As you read the case, consider what legal standards are being applied here.

Case of *S.A.S. v. France*

Application no. 43835/11, 2014 Eur. Ct. H.R. 695,
Judgment Strasbourg, 1 July 2014

(iv) Whether the measure is necessary in a democratic society

(a) General principles concerning Article 9 of the Convention

123. As the Court has decided to focus on Article 9 of the Convention in examining this part of the application, it finds it appropriate to reiterate the general principles concerning that provision.

124. As enshrined in Article 9, freedom of thought, conscience and religion is one of the foundations of a "democratic society" within the meaning of the Convention. This freedom is, in its religious dimension, one of the most vital elements that go to make up the identity of believers and their conception of life, but it is also a precious asset for atheists, agnostics, sceptics and the unconcerned. The pluralism indissociable from a democratic society, which has been dearly won over the centuries, depends on it. That freedom entails, *inter alia*, freedom to hold or not to hold religious beliefs and to practise or not to practise a religion.

125. While religious freedom is primarily a matter of individual conscience, it also implies freedom to manifest one's religion, alone and in private, or in community with others, in public and within the circle of those whose faith one shares. Article 9 lists the various forms which the manifestation of one's religion or beliefs may take, namely worship, teaching, practice and observance.

Article 9 does not, however, protect every act motivated or inspired by a religion or belief and does not always guarantee the right to behave in the public sphere in a manner which is dictated by one's religion or beliefs.

126. In democratic societies, in which several religions coexist within one and the same population, it may be necessary to place limitations on freedom to manifest one's religion or beliefs in order to reconcile the interests of the various groups and ensure that everyone's beliefs are respected. This follows both from paragraph 2 of Article 9 and from the State's positive obligations under Article 1 of the Convention to secure to everyone within its jurisdiction the rights and freedoms defined therein.

127. The Court has frequently emphasized the State's role as the neutral and impartial organiser of the exercise of various religions, faiths and beliefs, and has stated that this role is conducive to public order, religious harmony and tolerance in a democratic society. As indicated previously, it also considers that the State's duty of neutrality and impartiality is incompatible with any power on the State's part to assess the legitimacy of religious beliefs or the ways in which those beliefs are expressed, and that this duty requires the State to ensure mutual tolerance between opposing

groups. Accordingly, the role of the authorities in such circumstances is not to remove the cause of tension by eliminating pluralism, but to ensure that the competing groups tolerate each other.

128. Pluralism, tolerance and broadmindedness are hallmarks of a "democratic society". Although individual interests must on occasion be subordinated to those of a group, democracy does not simply mean that the views of a majority must always prevail: a balance must be achieved which ensures the fair treatment of people from minorities and avoids any abuse of a dominant position....

129. It is also important to emphasize the fundamentally subsidiary role of the Convention mechanism. The national authorities have direct democratic legitimation and are, as the Court has held on many occasions, in principle better placed than an international court to evaluate local needs and conditions. In matters of general policy, on which opinions within a democratic society may reasonably differ widely, the role of the domestic policy-maker should be given special weight. This is the case, in particular, where questions concerning the relationship between State and religions are at stake. As regards Article 9 of the Convention, the State should thus, in principle, be afforded a wide margin of appreciation in deciding whether and to what extent a limitation of the right to manifest one's religion or beliefs is "necessary". That being said, in delimiting the extent of the margin of appreciation in a given case, the Court must also have regard to what is at stake therein. It may also, if appropriate, have regard to any consensus and common values emerging from the practices of the States Parties to the Convention.

130. In the judgment in *Leyla Şahin*, the Court pointed out that this would notably be the case when it came to regulating the wearing of religious symbols in educational institutions, especially in view of the diversity of the approaches taken by national authorities on the issue. Referring to the judgment in *Otto-Preminger-Institut v. Austria* (20 September 1994, § 50, Series A no. 295-A) and the decision in *Dahlab v. Switzerland* ((dec.), no. 42393/98, ECHR 2001-V), it added that it was thus not possible to discern throughout Europe a uniform conception of the significance of religion in society and that the meaning or impact of the public expression of a religious belief would differ according to time and context. It observed that the rules in this sphere would consequently vary from one country to another according to national traditions and the requirements imposed by the need to protect the rights and freedoms of others and to maintain public order. It concluded from this that the choice of the extent and form of such rules must inevitably be left up to a point to the State concerned, as it would depend on the specific domestic context.

131. This margin of appreciation, however, goes hand in hand with a European supervision embracing both the law and the decisions applying it. The Court's task is to determine whether the measures taken at national level were justified in principle and proportionate....

144. Some of the arguments put forward by the applicant and the intervening non-governmental organisations warrant particular attention.

145. Firstly, it is true that only a small number of women are affected. It can be seen, among other things, from the report "on the wearing of the full-face veil on national territory", prepared by a commission of the National Assembly and deposited on 26 January 2010, that about 1,900 women wore the Islamic full-face veil in France at the end of 2009, of whom about 270 were living in French overseas administrative areas (see paragraph 16 above). This is a small proportion in relation to the French population of about sixty-five million and to the number of Muslims living in France. It may thus seem excessive to respond to such a situation by imposing a blanket ban.

146. In addition, there is no doubt that the ban has a significant negative impact on the situation of women who, like the applicant, have chosen to wear the full-face veil for reasons related to their beliefs. As stated previously, they are thus confronted with a complex dilemma, and the ban may have the effect of isolating them and restricting their autonomy, as well as impairing the exercise of their freedom to manifest their beliefs and their right to respect for their private life. It is also understandable that the women concerned may perceive the ban as a threat to their identity.

147. It should furthermore be observed that a large number of actors, both international and national, in the field of fundamental rights protection have found a blanket ban to be disproportionate. This is the case, for example, of the French National Advisory Commission on Human Rights, non-governmental organisations such as the third-party interveners, the Parliamentary Assembly of the Council of Europe and the Commissioner for Human Rights of the Council of Europe....

153. Furthermore, admittedly, as the applicant pointed out, by prohibiting everyone from wearing clothing designed to conceal the face in public places, the respondent State has to a certain extent restricted the reach of pluralism, since the ban prevents certain women from expressing their personality and their beliefs by wearing the full-face veil in public. However, for their part, the Government indicated that it was a question of responding to a practice that the State deemed incompatible, in French society, with the ground rules of social communication and more broadly the requirements of "living together". From that perspective, the respondent State is seeking to protect a principle of interaction between individuals, which in its view is essential for the expression not only of pluralism, but also of tolerance and broadmindedness without which there is no democratic society. It can thus be said that the question whether or not it should be permitted to wear the full-face veil in public places constitutes a choice of society.

154. In such circumstances, the Court has a duty to exercise a degree of restraint in its review of Convention compliance, since such review will lead it to assess a balance that has been struck by means of a democratic process within the society in question. The Court has, moreover, already had occasion to observe that in matters of general policy, on which opinions within a democratic society may reasonably differ widely, the role of the domestic policy-maker should be given special weight.

155. In other words, France had a wide margin of appreciation in the present case.

156. This is particularly true as there is little common ground among the member States of the Council of Europe as to the question of the wearing of the full-face veil in public. The Court thus observes that, contrary to the submission of one of the third-party interveners, there is no European consensus against a ban. Admittedly, from a strictly normative standpoint, France is very much in a minority position in Europe: except for Belgium, no other member State of the Council of Europe has, to date, opted for such a measure. It must be observed, however, that the question of the wearing of the full-face veil in public is or has been a subject of debate in a number of European States. In some it has been decided not to opt for a blanket ban. In others, such a ban is still being considered. It should be added that, in all likelihood, the question of the wearing of the full-face veil in public is simply not an issue at all in a certain number of member States, where this practice is uncommon. It can thus be said that in Europe there is no consensus as to whether or not there should be a blanket ban on the wearing of the full-face veil in public places.

157. Consequently, having regard in particular to the breadth of the margin of appreciation afforded to the respondent State in the present case, the Court finds that the ban imposed by the Law of 11 October 2010 can be regarded as proportionate to the aim pursued, namely the preservation of the conditions of "living together" as an element of the "protection of the rights and freedoms of others".

158. The impugned limitation can thus be regarded as "necessary in a democratic society". This conclusion holds true with respect both to Article 8 of the Convention and to Article 9.

159. Accordingly, there has been no violation either of Article 8 or of Article 9 of the Convention.

Other European nations have been more tolerant of religious dress. The United Kingdom has seen several challenges to school dress codes, but it usually grants a fair amount of deference to the schools, especially those which have had parental input into policies, see *R. Begum v. Headteacher and Governors of Denbigh High School,* 2006 UKHL 15. After the *S.A.S.* case, the European Court of Human Rights sustained similar laws in Belgium. *S.A.S.* remains controversial for its pitting religious values, cultural values, and gender issues against France's policies of "secularity" and universal "living together." It has also divided feminists who argue for "universal" rules of "equality" and for cultural self-determination. The larger issue here is whether human rights take sufficient account of cultural values. Should there be "cultural relativism" or "universal" human rights? Are some human rights more "universal" than others? We continue this issue discussion in Chapter 13.

Notes & Questions

1. Was the French law "proportional" to the government's stated goal? What is the role of "proportionality" here in the court's judgment? Do you think it is possible to have "universal" human rights?
2. Is international court adjudication of national laws a good thing? What values are expressed in this kind of adjudication? Do you think these issues are for national courts or for international or regional courts? Do you think Europe is more "unified" on human rights principles than the United States? Why or why not?
3. In 2022, the US Supreme Court held in *Dobbs v. Jackson Women's Health*[9] that the US Constitution does not guarantee the right to an abortion, thus overruling the precedent of *Roe v. Wade*. Can you think of any human rights claim or argument an American woman could make if she is denied this medical procedure in a US state? What substantive international claims might she have? Where could she raise such claims? France has enshrined a woman's right to abortion in its Constitution as of March 2024.

Case Study: *Soering v. United Kingdom*, Application no. 14038/88, 161 Eur. Ct. H.R. (ser. A) (1989), Judgment Strasbourg 7 July 1989

Consider whether international human rights law should apply extraterritorially.

In 1985, a Virginia couple, William and Nancy Haysom, were murdered in their home by their daughter, Elizabeth Haysom (age 20), and her boyfriend, Jens Soering (age 18), a German student who was studying at the University of Virginia. The murders were violent and grisly, and eventually Elizabeth Haysom and Jens Soering were found in England. The United States requested extradition of both accused to stand trial for murder. Pursuant to the 1972 extradition treaty, the UK requested assurances that the United States would not pursue the death penalty, as the death penalty was prohibited in the UK and under Article 3 of the European Charter of Human Rights. However, the U.S. prosecutor promised only to represent to any U.S. court that the UK wished that the death penalty should not be imposed. Legal appeals ensued while Mr. Soering was placed in a psychiatric hospital on suicide watch. Eventually, an extradition order was signed, and Mr. Soering received representation in the UK from a human rights lawyer who filed a claim with the European Court of Human Rights stating that Soering's extradition to a country that might impose the death penalty was a violation of the European Charter of Human Rights and the UK's legal obligations thereunder. Article 3 of the European Charter provides that "no one shall be subjected to torture or to inhumane or degrading treatment or punishment." Soering argued not only that the death penalty was inhumane but that incarcerating him and

9. 597 U.S. 215 (2022).

placing him on death row in the United States would constitute inhumane and degrading treatment in violation of the European Charter. The UK government argued at the European Court of Human Rights (located in Strasbourg, France) that it should not be held responsible for actions in another country, but the court concluded otherwise. In a unanimous decision, all 18 judges held that it would be a violation of the European Charter for Mr. Soering, a European citizen, to be extradited to the United States. The case raised many legal issues about the extraterritorial effects of international and regional treaties and legal judgments in addition to a host of other issues: What is "inhumane and degrading treatment"? (Consider, for example, the general state of American prisons, or whether a terminal AIDS sufferer should be extradited to a country that does not offer medical care in its prisons, *see D. v. United Kingdom*, 24 Eur. H.R. Rep. 423 (1997).) Could anti-terrorism treaties and national security issues serve as a countervailing defense? Whose courts have the final word on these and other questions?

Notes & Questions

1. What kinds of conditions of "inhumane and degrading treatment" might prevent other extraditions?
2. This case predated September 11, 2001, the "war on terror," and a series of international treaties in which countries pledged to cooperate on international criminal law enforcement with regard to extradition, and later, with regard to American acts of torture on foreign soil (i.e., Abu Ghraib). How should the actions of states be judged? And by what laws should they be judged—by the law of the committing state, the law of the state in which the acts take place, or the law of the victim's home state)?
3. What happened to Jens Soering? Ms. Haysom gave herself up, returned to the United States, and was given a life sentence. Eventually, after promising not to ask for the death penalty, the United States was able to extradite Mr. Soering, who was sentenced to several consecutive life imprisonment terms. One of the ironies of the case is that Ms. Haysom was educated in the UK, and Mr. Soering, the son of a German diplomat, had grown up in Atlanta, Georgia. Modern international conflicts, at both the individual and state levels, now involve a multinational composition of actors, which gives rise to very complex issues of conflicts of laws. This story has spawned a great deal of media and film interest, *see, e.g.*, *Killing for Love* (a 2016 documentary directed by Marcus Vetter and Karin Steinberger); *The Promise* (an Elsani & Neary Media and Mediawan Rights true-crime television series), and *Till Murder Do Us Part: Soering vs. Haysom* (a Netflix true-crime docuseries).

B. American Human Rights: Disappearances and Assassinations

Negotiations for a human rights treaty in the Americas was a long process, sponsored by what became the Organization of American States. The American Convention on Human Rights, which created the Inter-American Court of Human Rights, was signed in 1969 but did not enter into force until 1978 with 11 ratifications; there are currently 24 parties. Two countries have withdrawn from the convention (Trinidad and Tobago and Venezuela), and others have threatened withdrawal because of death penalty exceptions and claims that United States has politicized and dominated the Inter-American Court.[10]

Although the Inter-American Court of Human Rights is located in San Jose, Costa Rica, and the United States is not a signatory to the convention, the Organization of American States has a major office in Washington, D.C., the Inter-American Commission on Human Rights maintains an office there, and many North American human rights lawyers are active in litigation in the court (Claudio Grossman, a Chilean-born American lawyer and dean of American University Law School, was the lead lawyer on *Velasquez Rodriquez v. Honduras*, discussed below). Americans, including Thomas Buergenthal, a law professor and Holocaust survivor, have served as judges on the Court.

Following a series of dictatorships in Latin America in the 1980s through the 1990s (in Argentina, Brazil, Chile, Honduras, Guatemala, Bolivia, El Salvador, Paraguay, Uruguay), human rights activists have litigated many human rights issues including forced disappearances (even successfully campaigning for a new convention prohibiting disappearances), police brutality and torture, abuse against women, and other claims. Ironically, as the Bolivarian countries' (Venezuela, Bolivia, and Ecuador) recent leadership have denounced "universal" human rights as the importation of "colonial" values and argued in favor of increased sovereign independence, other countries that emerged from dictatorships have crafted new constitutions which explicitly incorporate all human rights and international treaties as part of their constitutional regimes (e.g., Argentina's 1994 constitutional reform). As of the time of this writing, Chile is undergoing a dramatic national process of writing a new constitution. Thus, many parties to the Inter-American Human Rights Convention are engaged in an active and complex process of examining the relationship of national rights to allegedly universal commitments. Where the European Court of Human Rights has had a relatively successful period of compliance, even in the face of controversial rulings, the Inter-American Court has suffered from more politicized variation in its acceptance as many countries in the region undergo difficult regime transitions (moving from one type of government—whether dictatorship, democracy, authoritarian constitutionalism, or presidential constitutionalism—to a different type) or frequent constitutional revisions to permit extensions of presidential terms.

---

10. *See* OQUENDO, *supra* note 8.

In the case below, the Inter-American Court of Human Rights addresses state responsibility for its own citizens as well as state responsibility for the protection of witnesses.

Velásquez-Rodríguez v. Honduras

IACHR Series C No. 4, Judgment of 29 July 1988 (Merits),
Inter-American Court of Human Rights

1. The Inter-American Commission on Human Rights (hereinafter "the Commission") submitted the instant case to the Inter-American Court of Human Rights (hereinafter "the Court") on April 24, 1986. It originated in a petition (No. 7920) against the State of Honduras (hereinafter "Honduras" or "the Government"), which the Secretariat of the Commission received on October 7, 1981.

2. In submitting the case, the Commission invoked Articles 50 and 51 of the American Convention on Human Rights (hereinafter "the Convention" or "the American Convention") and requested that the Court determine whether the State in question had violated Articles 4 (Right to Life), 5 (Right to Humane Treatment) and 7 (Right to Personal Liberty) of the Convention in the case of Angel Manfredo Velásquez Rodríguez (also known as Manfredo Velásquez). In addition, the Commission asked the Court to rule that "the consequences of the situation that constituted the breach of such right or freedom be remedied, and that fair compensation be paid to the injured party or parties."

3. According to the petition filed with the Commission, and the supplementary information received subsequently, Manfredo Velásquez, a student at the National Autonomous University of Honduras, "was violently detained without a warrant for his arrest by members of the National Office of Investigations (DNI) and G-2 of the Armed Forces of Honduras." The detention took place in Tegucigalpa on the afternoon of September 12, 1981. According to the petitioners, several eyewitnesses reported that Manfredo Velásquez and others were detained and taken to the cells of Public Security Forces Station No. 2 located in the Barrio El Manchén of Tegucigalpa, where he was "accused of alleged political crimes and subjected to harsh interrogation and cruel torture." The petition added that on September 17, 1981, Manfredo Velásquez was moved to the First Infantry Battalion, where the interrogation continued, but that the police and security forces denied that he had been detained....

10. By Resolution 22/86 of April 18, 1986, the Commission deemed the new information presented by the Government insufficient to warrant reconsideration of Resolution 30/83 and found, to the contrary, that "all evidence shows that Angel Manfredo Velásquez Rodríguez is still missing and that the Government of Honduras ... has not offered convincing proof that would allow the Commission to determine that the allegations are not true." In that same Resolution, the Commission confirmed Resolution 30/83 and referred the matter to the Court....

39. By note of November 4, 1987, addressed to the President of the Court, the Commission asked the Court to take provisional measures under Article 63 (2) of the Con-

vention in view of the threats against the witnesses Milton Jiménez Puerto and Ramón Custodio López. Upon forwarding this information to the Government of Honduras, the President stated that he "does not have enough proof to ascertain which persons or entities might be responsible for the threats, but he strongly wishes to request that the Government of Honduras take all measures necessary to guarantee the safety of the lives and property of Milton Jiménez and Ramón Custodio and the property of the Committee for the Defense of Human Rights in Honduras (CODEH)...." The President also stated that he was prepared to consult with the Permanent Commission of the Court and, if necessary, to convoke the Court for an emergency meeting "for taking the 8 appropriate measures, if that abnormal situation continues." By communications of November 11 and 18, 1987, the Agent of the Government informed the Court that the Honduran government would guarantee Ramón Custodio and Milton Jiménez "the respect of their physical and moral integrity ... and the faithful compliance with the Convention...."

40. By note of January 11, 1988, the Commission informed the Court of the death of José Isaías Vilorio, which occurred on January 5, 1988 at 7:15 a.m. The Court had summoned him to appear as a witness on January 18, 1988. He was killed "on a public thoroughfare in Colonia San Miguel, Comayaguela, Tegucigalpa, by a group of armed men who placed the insignia of a Honduran guerrilla movement known as Cinchonero on his body and fled in a vehicle at high speed."

41. On January 15, 1988, the Court was informed of the assassinations of Moisés Landaverde and Miguel Angel Pavón which had occurred the previous evening in San Pedro Sula. Mr. Pavón had testified before the Court on September 30, 1987 as a witness in this case. Also on January 15, the Court adopted the following provisional measures under Article 63 (2) of the Convention: 1. That the Government of Honduras adopt, without delay, such measures as are necessary to prevent further infringements on the basic rights of those who have appeared or have been summoned to do so before this Court in the "Velásquez Rodríguez," "Fairén Garbi and Solís Corrales" and "Godínez Cruz" cases, in strict compliance with the obligation of respect for and observance of human rights, under the terms of Article 1 (1) of the Convention. 2. That the Government of Honduras also employ all means within its power to investigate these reprehensible crimes, to identify the perpetrators and to impose the punishment provided for by the domestic law of Honduras.

42. After it had adopted the above Order of January 15, the Court received a request from the Commission, dated the same day, that the Court take the necessary measures to protect the integrity and security of those persons who had appeared or would appear before the Court.

43. On January 18, 1988, the Commission asked the Court to adopt the following complementary provisional measures: 1. That the Government of Honduras inform the Court, within 15 days of the specific measures it has adopted to protect the physical integrity of witnesses who testified before the Court as well as those persons in any way involved in these proceedings, such as representatives of human rights organizations.

2. That the Government of Honduras report, within that same period, on the judicial investigations of the assassinations of José Isaías Vilorio, Miguel Angel Pavón and Moisés Landaverde. 3. That the Government of Honduras provide the Court, within that same period, the public statements made regarding the aforementioned assassinations and indicate where those statements appeared. 4. That the Government of Honduras inform the Court, within the same period, on the criminal investigations of threats against Ramón Custodio and Milton Jiménez, who are witnesses in this case. 5. That it inform the Court whether it has ordered police protection to ensure the personal integrity of the witnesses who have testified and the protection of the property of CODEH. 6. That the Court request the Government of Honduras to send it immediately a copy of the autopsies and ballistic tests carried out regarding the assassinations of Messrs. Vilorio, Pavón and Landaverde.

44. That same day the Government submitted a copy of the death certificate and the autopsy report of José Isaías Vilorio, both dated January 5, 1988.

45. On January 18, 1988, the Court decided, by a vote of six to one, to hear the parties in a public session the following day regarding the measures requested by the Commission. After the hearing, taking into account "Articles 63 (2), 33 and 62 (3) of the American Convention on Human Rights, Articles 1 and 2 of the Statute of the Court and Article 23 of its Rules of Procedure and its character as a judicial body and the powers which derive therefrom," the Court unanimously decided, by Order of January 19, 1988, on the following additional provisional measures: 1. That the Government of Honduras, within a period of two weeks, inform this Court on the following points: a. the measures that have been adopted or will be adopted to protect the physical integrity of, and to avoid irreparable harm to, those witnesses who have testified or have been summoned to do so in these cases. b. the judicial investigations that have been or will be undertaken with respect to threats against the aforementioned individuals. c. the investigations of the assassinations, including forensic reports, and the actions that are proposed to be taken within the judicial system of Honduras to punish those responsible. 2. That the Government of Honduras adopt concrete measures to make clear that the appearance of an individual before the Inter-American Commission or Court of Human Rights, under conditions authorized by the American Convention and by the rules of procedure of both bodies, is a right enjoyed by every individual and is recognized as such by Honduras as a party to the Convention. This decision was delivered to the parties in Court....

149. Disappearances are not new in the history of human rights violations. However, their systematic and repeated nature and their use not only for causing certain individuals to disappear, either briefly or permanently, but also as a means of creating a general state of anguish, insecurity and fear, is a recent phenomenon. Although this practice exists virtually worldwide, it has occurred with exceptional intensity in Latin American in the last few years.

150. The phenomenon of disappearances is a complex form of human rights violation that must be understood and confronted in an integral fashion.

151. The establishment of a Working Group on Enforced or Involuntary Disappearances of the United Nations Commission on Human Rights, by Resolution 20 (XXXVI) of February 29, 1980, is a clear demonstration of general censure and repudiation of the practice of disappearances, which 27 had already received world attention at the UN General Assembly (Resolution 33/173 of December 20, 1978), the Economic and Social Council (Resolution 1979/38 of May 10, 1979) and the Subcommission for the Prevention of Discrimination and Protection of Minorities (Resolution 5B (XXXII) of September 5, 1979). The reports of the rapporteurs or special envoys of the Commission on Human Rights show concern that the practice of disappearances be stopped, the victims reappear and that those responsible be punished.

152. Within the inter-American system, the General Assembly of the Organization of American States (OAS) and the Commission have repeatedly referred to the practice of disappearances and have urged that disappearances be investigated and that the practice be stopped.

153. International practice and doctrine have often categorized disappearances as a crime against humanity, although there is no treaty in force which is applicable to the States Parties to the Convention and which uses this terminology (Inter-American Yearbook on Human Rights, 1985, pp. 368, 686 and 1102). The General Assembly of the OAS has resolved that it "is an affront to the conscience of the hemisphere and constitutes a crime against humanity" (AG/RES. 666, supra) and that "this practice is cruel and inhuman, mocks the rule of law, and undermines those norms which guarantee protection against arbitrary detention and the right to personal security and safety" (AG/RES. 742, supra).

154. Without question, the State has the right and duty to guarantee its security. It is also indisputable that all societies suffer some deficiencies in their legal orders. However, regardless of the seriousness of certain actions and the culpability of the perpetrators of certain crimes, the power of the State is not unlimited, nor may the State resort to any means to attain its ends. The State is subject to law and morality. Disrespect for human dignity cannot serve as the basis for any State action.

155. The forced disappearance of human beings is a multiple and continuous violation of many rights under the Convention that the States Parties are obligated to respect and guarantee. The kidnapping of a person is an arbitrary deprivation of liberty, an infringement of a detainee's right to be taken without delay before a judge and to invoke the appropriate procedures to review the legality of the arrest, all in violation of Article 7 of the Convention which recognizes the right to personal liberty by providing that: 1. Every person has the right to personal liberty and security. 2. No one shall be deprived of his physical liberty except for the reasons and under the conditions established beforehand by the constitution of the State Party concerned or by a law established pursuant thereto. 3. No one shall be subject to arbitrary arrest or imprisonment. 4. Anyone who is detained shall be informed of the reasons for his detention and shall be promptly notified of the charge or charges against him. 5. Any person detained shall be brought promptly before a judge or other officer authorized by law to exercise

judicial power and shall be entitled to trial within a reasonable time or to be released without prejudice to the continuation of the proceedings. His release may be subject to guarantees to assure his appearance for trial. 6. Anyone who is deprived of his liberty shall be entitled to recourse to a competent court, in order that the court may decide without delay on the lawfulness of his arrest or detention and order his release if the arrest or detention is unlawful. In States Parties whose laws provide that anyone who believes himself to be threatened with deprivation of his liberty is entitled to recourse to a competent court in order that it may decide on the lawfulness of such threat, this remedy may not be restricted or abolished. The interested party or another person in his behalf is entitled to seek these remedies ...

194. THEREFORE, THE COURT:

Unanimously

1. Rejects the preliminary objection interposed by the Government of Honduras alleging the inadmissibility of the case for the failure to exhaust domestic legal remedies. Unanimously

2. Declares that Honduras has violated, in the case of Angel Manfredo Velásquez Rodríguez, its obligations to respect and to ensure the right to personal liberty set forth in Article 7 of the Convention, read in conjunction with Article 1 (1) thereof. Unanimously

3. Declares that Honduras has violated, in the case of Angel Manfredo Velásquez Rodríguez, its obligations to respect and to ensure the right to humane treatment set forth in Article 5 of the Convention, read in conjunction with Article 1 (1) thereof. Unanimously

4. Declares that Honduras has violated, in the case of Angel Manfredo Velásquez Rodríguez, its obligation to ensure the right to life set forth in Article 4 of the Convention, read in conjunction with Article 1 (1) thereof. Unanimously

5. Decides that Honduras is hereby required to pay fair compensation to the next-of-kin of the victim. By six votes to one

6. Decides that the form and amount of such compensation, failing agreement between Honduras and the Commission within six months of the date of this judgment, shall be settled by the Court and, for that purpose, retains jurisdiction of the case. Judge Rodolfo E. Piza E. dissenting.

Unanimously

7. Decides that the agreement on the form and amount of the compensation shall be approved by the Court.

Notes & Questions

1. Why do you think the United States has not signed the American Convention or formally participated in the court? Why then does the United States support (in Washington, D.C.) and partially fund the activities of the commission and supply so many legal professionals to the court?

2. Should the Inter-American Court and European Court of Human Rights look to each other for legal guidance (precedent)?
3. It has been clearly established that the United States provided training and financing for, and perhaps even conducted, forced disappearances, executions, torture, and kidnappings (of adults and newly born children) in several Latin American countries. What remedies, if any, could be pursued in the Inter-American Court and Commission system?
4. Several victims of police brutality in a small town in Argentina petition the Commission on Human Rights for compensation and injunctions against their local police department. They allege that police beatings and lengthy detentions were conducted in violation of the American Convention on Human Rights, which establishes rights to humane treatment, due process, fair trial, freedom of movement, and other rights. The commission seeks to pursue an "amiable settlement" according to its procedures, in which some of the victims and their families would receive some compensation and the police department would be ordered to conduct enhanced human rights training for its officers. Some of the families want to accept this, while others want to proceed to a full hearing at the Inter-American Court because they would like to pursue a written precedent. You are the lawyer for the families. How do you deal with and counsel the families about how to proceed? What are the advantages and disadvantages of accepting a settlement or proceeding to a hearing?

IV. Hybrid and Special Courts

In the period between the creation of the International Criminal Tribunals for the former Yugoslavia and Rwanda in the mid-1990s and the creation of the International Criminal Court in 2002, several countries experienced violent civil wars and upheavals (Kosovo, East Timor, Sierra Leone, Liberia) and the leaders of former atrocity-driven regimes (e.g., the Khmer Rouge, which carried out genocide in Cambodia) were brought to account for their crimes. The international community and the UN Security Council recognized that while there was as yet no international criminal court, it could neither afford to stand by and do nothing, nor could it afford to create new international tribunals for every atrocity. As a result, an interesting era of experimentation involving what are called "hybrid" or "special" courts ensued. During this time, the UN and international lawyers attempted to facilitate criminal prosecutions and some civil and restorative justice efforts with the use of "mixed" legal personnel, that is, personnel chosen from both the local state or community as well as from the international sphere, to serve as judges, lawyers, and advisors. The idea was that international personnel could assist in capacity building, helping to design courts for newly democratic nations (see Chapter 9: Dispute System Design), and model and assist in the first set of cases.

Many eyes were turned to the Extraordinary Chambers in the Courts for Cambodia (ECCC), which was established to try the architects of the Cambodian mass killings and nationwide use of detention camps under the Communist dictator Pol Pot in the

1970s. But alas, most evaluations of that Chamber have concluded that it was not able to carry out its mission. In the long interim between the fall of the Pol Pot regime and the development of the ECCC, many witnesses had died or moved away, and many of those remaining still feared reprisal and potential assassination. Some other tribunals, such as Sierra Leone and East Timor, had some successes. In Liberia, for example, guerilla leader and former head of state Charles Taylor was eventually convicted in the Special Court of Sierra Leone for his role in abetting mass killings and inciting civil wars; he was sentenced to 50 years of imprisonment. After American forces captured Saddam Hussein in Iraq, he was tried in that country for crimes against humanity and genocide, in a "national" court known as the Iraqi Special Tribunal. His trial was carried out by the interim government and facilitated by the United States and other international justice lawyers. He received a death sentence and was executed on December 30, 2006, but many in the international human rights community were highly critical of what they believed was a "show trial" that failed to meet international standards of due process and did not assist in the development of a stable and legitimate rule-of-law judicial order.

Richard J. Goldstone & Adam Smith, International Judicial Institutions: The Architecture of International Justice at Home and Abroad

96 (2009)

Timeline of Post-Cold War institutions/Prosecutions

ICTFY	1993
ICTR	1994
Special Panels in East Timor	2000
Kosovo International Judges and Prosecutors	2000
Extraordinary Chambers in Cambodia	2001 (Agreement with UN; 2003)
ICC	2002
Special Court for Sierra Leone	2002
Iraqi Special Tribunal	2003
Special Chambers of Belgrade District Court	2003
State Court of Bosnia-Herzegovina	2005
Special Tribunal for Lebanon	2007

In addition there have been various domestic movements toward addressing (if not prosecuting) international crimes in countries including Ethiopia, Chile, Spain, France, Britain, Liberia, Ghana and elsewhere.

Notes & Questions

1. What current civil or international wars do you think would require a special court (think of nations that are not signatories to the Rome Statute/ICC)? Should such courts be used only for criminal prosecutions, or is there a role for special civil courts? How and by whom should such civil courts or tribunals be structured? For example, consider how to develop such a court in Sri Lanka to address suits relating to the civil war between the Tamil Tigers and the Sri Lankan Armed Forces, which formally ended in 2009?
2. Should there be special tribunals for the redress of older crimes or wrongs (e.g., slavery, colonialism) that precede the establishment of positive or customary law understandings? What should be the statute of limitations on such wrongs? Who could design or serve on such courts (e.g., on a reparations court)? Note that we will return to the issue of reparations when we consider dispute system design in Chapter 9.

V. Private International Litigation

The courts and tribunals discussed so far in this chapter all involve public disputes and public international law. But as you know from Chapter 4 on arbitration, private parties sue each other across borders regularly for breach of contract and other claims. International arbitration emerged after the First World War, when it was thought that increased commercial trade was good for the world, not only economically but in terms of increasing the likelihood of peaceful relations between countries. Litigating a dispute between citizens of different countries involves complex questions of civil procedure (jurisdiction over the persons, subject-matter jurisdiction), choice of applicable substantive law (called conflicts of law and choice of law), and ultimately enforcement of judgments. The International Chamber of Commerce, a private organization, helped to promote international arbitration as a less-complex alternative to litigation for private parties. As of May 2024, the New York Convention for the Recognition and Enforcement of Foreign Arbitral Awards has over 170 parties (countries); these countries have agreed to enforce the consent-based arbitration awards issued in each other's countries.

Some litigants still prefer court judgments, and there has been a decades-long effort to draft and approve an international Convention of the Enforcement of Foreign Judgments (like the New York Convention for arbitration). The issues are somewhat different here because judgments are acts of public states, and countries are less willing to enforce each other's judgments when there are substantive law and policy differences in formal law (which in common law countries can have precedential effect). There is also a question of reciprocity. Some nations have expressed willingness to sign such a convention from another country, but only if that other country also recognizes their judgments. Enforcement of foreign money judgments is quite different from enforcement of foreign arbitral awards. The United States is not (yet) a party to any fully ratified international treaty or convention controlling the enforcement of judgments, leaving the decision solely in the hands of the courts. After decades of negotiations, the United States has now signed but not ratified the 2019 Hague Convention on the Recognition and Enforcement of Foreign Judgments (Civil and Commercial), but very few other countries have ratified this treaty.

Because enforcement is a state law issue, the *Erie* doctrine dictates that federal courts must decide whether to enforce a foreign court's judgment based on state statute and common law. Each state has developed its own criteria for courts to use in granting enforcement, and the result is a lack of uniformity. Some states have enacted a uniform statute to address this problem, but the success has been mixed. Foreign judgment creditors are left with the possibility of facing different laws in each state. The Conference on Uniform State Laws has issued some guidance by promulgating a Uniform Foreign-Country Money Judgments Recognition Act, but not all U.S. states have adopted it. Meanwhile, other regions of the world have signed conventions to recognize and enforce each other's judgments, for example, the 1968 Brussels Convention, in which members of the EU agreed to recognize and enforce each other's civil judgments.

Another reason enforcement of judgments is different from enforcement of arbitration is that arbitration is consented to by both parties, while a foreign suit is filed only by the plaintiff. Unless the defendant consents to the foreign court's jurisdiction, any other court will examine whether the foreign court had personal jurisdiction over the defendant. A court will often not enforce a judgment if it feels that the foreign court did not have jurisdiction over the defendant, and the court will judge jurisdiction under its own standards, not those of the jurisdiction that entered the judgment. Similarly, in enforcing judgments (or even arbitral awards that are claimed to violate the enforcing country's public policy, per Article V 2(b) of the New York Convention), courts will look to the law and public policy of both the enforcing and issuing countries. This makes enforcement of a judgment subject to another layer of litigation.

For example, in *Laminoirs-Trefileries-Cableries de Lens, S.A. v. Southwire Co.*,[11] the district court refused to enforce an arbitration reward where the interest applied was considered usury:

> The Court concludes that the imposition of an additional 5% interest by the arbitrators in accordance with the French statute is penal rather than compensatory, and bears no reasonable relation to any damage resulting from delay in recovery of the sums awarded. Therefore, that portion of the award which purports to assess the rates of interest at 14½% and 15½% will not be enforced or recognized by this Court. 9 U.S.C.A. § 201, Art. V, par. 2(b), Convention on the Recognition and Enforcement of Foreign Arbitral Awards. The rates of 9½% and 10½%, as imposed by the arbitrators, will continue to accrue until the date of Judgment.

11. 484 F. Supp. 1063, 1069 (N.D. Ga. 1980).

Notes & Questions

1. On what laws does the court rely in considering whether to enforce this arbitral award?
2. How might the application of different laws affect whether private parties choose litigation or arbitration?
3. The Georgia court felt the additional 5 percent assessed by the French arbitrators was contrary to Georgia public policy, calling usury "odious, illegal, and immoral." Is it appropriate to apply domestic state law in these international cases?

There is great debate about whether courts fairly conduct litigation and enforcement when one of the litigants is foreign (see the materials on the *Loewen* case in Chapter 7). Scholars debate and study the issue empirically, but lawyers representing clients have to make decisions about where to bring their actions when they have a choice.

Ji Li & Carrie Menkel-Meadow, *Dispute Process Choices among Chinese Companies in the United States: Some Preliminary Data and Analyses*

27 Harv. Negot. L. Rev. 295, 303–05, 332–33 (2022)

Whether international commercial arbitration is a corrective for assumed biases against foreign litigants is now a contested terrain for academics and legal practitioners who must make strategic choices about what venue and process to use in business disputes.

For example, as the use of international arbitration grew in the 1980s, different nationals preferred different arbitration tribunals. But, in a series of empirical studies and articles, researchers Theodore Eisenberg and Kevin Clermont demonstrated that foreign litigants have little to fear from litigating in U.S. courts, at least in some matters and at some points in time. In their first study, utilizing data from the Administrative Office of the Courts from 1987–1994, Eisenberg and Clermont found that foreign defendants and plaintiffs won substantially more than domestic litigants in 92,142 cases with diversity or alienage jurisdiction. The domestic plaintiff win rate was 64% and the foreign plaintiff win rate was 80% with no significant case type variations. Foreign defendants also fared better than domestic. At the time of the study in 1996, Eisenberg and Clermont attributed this result to selection bias, as foreign litigants and their lawyers tend to bring strong cases to litigate in U.S. courts.

Following their seminal work, several other researchers sought to study this alleged judicial bias when foreign parties litigate in U.S. courts. One notable study suggested that American parties won 64% of patent cases against foreign defendants and that foreigners chose not to defend their U.S. acquired patents in U.S. courts. This finding was of jury trials, not bench trials, so Eisenberg and Clermont contend that there might be some anti-foreigner bias in some jury cases and that patent cases might be a special subset of cases. In another published study, foreign corporations did worse than domestic corporations in bench trials and suffered stock price losses when it was disclosed that litigation in U.S. courts was occurring, offering some suggestion of home court advantage bias.

Given the conflicting findings, Clermont and Eisenberg did another study after 9/11/2001 using data from the Administrative Office of the Courts up to 2005, which was comprised of 171,710 diversity and alienage cases. This data set also included many case outcomes in addition to completed trials, including terminations and conclusion of cases through summary judgment, consent, and default. Since trials serve an increasingly small role in U.S. courts, a broader definition of "case termination" was used. In this later study, the authors found some evidence of a declining advantage of foreign litigants, suggesting their win rates were virtually indistinguishable from domestic litigants. Clermont and Eisenberg suggest that in order to fully determine how these data can be explained, it would be necessary to watch data changes over a longer time period (to account for changes caused by major events such as 9/11) and to supplement statistical and quantitative analysis with interviews to determine whether lawyers and other advisors of foreign litigants have changed their assessments of venue advantage (based on data from such studies or other facts or assumptions). To supplement their study, Clermont and Eisenberg conducted a separate analysis of out-of-state litigants in diversity cases and found that out-of-staters did better than in-staters, suggesting "home court advantage was not strong in domestic litigation. However, all of this is possibly affected by a large increase in settlement rates and decrease in formal terminations or judgments in all federal cases, rendering any arguments about foreigners doing "worse" in courts hard to substantiate...."

The data from our survey suggest that there are factors, such as fees, access to American advice, views about judicial fairness, and preference in the selection of U.S. lawyers with Chinese backgrounds that militate in favor of placing arbitration clauses in Chinese business contracts in the United States. We also note some factors which do not seem to affect the choice of arbitration clauses, such as amount of revenue, whether or not the firm is state-owned, and whether or not the firm is listed. Since these findings come from a 2017 survey instrument, it would be important to expand on and supplement these data with more interviews with actual decision makers about dispute resolution clauses, such as contract drafters, Chinese business managers in the United States, and, where appropriate, Chinese government officials reviewing Chinese business practices in United States. Changes in U.S.-China business and trade relations in recent years may have had some effect on the newer contracts being drafted and different choices being made when disputes arose. Further studies of Chinese legal strategies with respect to disputes involving both government parties and private parties might suggest different approaches in different contexts, as well as in different business sectors....

Ultimately, the question of how Chinese business and legal decisions are made about what form of dispute resolution to use involving disputes in the United States may be independent from the choices Chinese entities (both state-owned and private) make about preferred dispute resolution mechanisms in other (international or Chinese domestic) venues. Chinese businesses in the United States, in some situations, may choose to adapt. As the saying "when in Rome, do as the Romans do" suggests, Chinese firms may defer to American conceptions of arbitration or litigation for dispute resolution when operating in the United States. However, as dispute resolution "with Chinese characteristics" (Belt and Road Initiative hybrid forms) becomes more prominent in other venues, will Chinese businesses make different choices, both contractually (pre-dispute) and during or after the ripening of disputes (ad hoc dispute resolution), and employ their own preferred form of dispute resolution? These questions are unanswerable at present but provide an interesting research agenda for the future. To what extent do we have national/domestic/cultural preferences for some forms of dispute resolution? To what extent do other factors (e.g., costs, trust in legal institutions, advice from legal and business professionals, sectors, and size of enterprise) control dispute resolution choices? We look forward to further research with more questions and more answers.

Notes & Questions

1. If you were advising a non-American client about whether to sue for a breach of contract that occurred in the United States, would you advise suing in an American court or going to arbitration? What factors would you be looking at?
2. If you were advising a non-American client about writing a dispute resolution clause into a contract with an American client (*see* Chapter 9), would you recommend an arbitration clause or another choice of dispute resolution clause? What factors would you be looking at?
3. You represent an American coffee chain, Starlight Coffee, that buys its cappuccino makers from an Italian company, LARAZZA. (See the simulation problem in Chapter 4.) This commercial arrangement worked very well for many years; however, over the last few years, there have been enormous shipping delays, and the last order (which was worth about $5,000,000) included many defective machines. Starlight wishes to commence a case against LARAZZA for its delays and defective supplies. What courts might you sue in? What remedies would you seek? Would you recommend litigation or another form of dispute resolution? Why?

Further Reading

Accountability for Atrocities: National and International Responses (Jane Stromseth ed., 2003).

Robert Ahdieh, *Between Dialogue and Decree: International Review of National Courts*, 79 NYU L. Rev. 2029 (2004).

Karen J. Alter, The New Terrain of International Law: Courts, Politics, Rights (2014).

Paul Schiff Berman, *Global Legal Pluralism*, 80 S. Cal. L. Rev. 1155 (2007).

Donald Childress III, Michael Ramsey, & Christopher Whytock, Transnational Law and Practice (2015).

Carla del Ponte, Madame Prosecutor: Confrontations with Humanity's Worst Criminals and the Culture of Impunity (2009).

Francis Fukuyama, The End of History and the Last Man (2006).

Mary Ann Glendon, A World Made New: Eleanor Roosevelt and the Universal Declaration of Human Rights (2002).

Jack L. Goldsmith & Eric A. Posner, The Limits of International Law (2011).

Richard J. Goldstone & Rebecca Hamilton, Bosnia v. Serbia*: Lessons from the Encounter of the International Court of Justice with the International Criminal Tribunal for the Former Yugoslavia*, 21 Leiden J. Int'l L. 95–112 (2008).

Richard J. Goldstone & Adam Smith, International Judicial Institutions: The Architecture of International Justice at Home and Abroad (2009).

Oona A. Hathaway & Scott J. Shapiro, The Internationalists: How a Radical Plan to Outlaw War Remade the World (2017).

Rosalind Higgins, *A Babel of Judicial Voices? Ruminations from the Bench*, 55 ICLQ 791 (2006).

Lynn Hunt, Inventing Human Rights: A History (2008).

Int'l Law Commission, *Conclusions of the Work of the Study Group on the Fragmentation of International Law: Difficulties Arising from the Diversification and Expansion of International Law*, *in* II Yearbook of the International Law Commission (2006), https://legal.un.org/ilc/texts/instruments/english/draft_articles/1_9_2006.pdf.

Carrie Menkel-Meadow, *In the Land of Blood and Honey: What's Fair or Just in Love and War Crimes? Lessons for Transitional Justice*, *in* Framing Law and Crime: An Interdisciplinary Anthology (Caroline Joan S. Picart, Michael Hviid Jacobsen, & Cecil Greek eds., 2016).

Susan Moller Okin et al., Is Multiculturalism Bad for Women? (1999).

John Noyes, Laura A. Dickinson, & Mark Janis, International Law Stories (2007).

Angel E. Oquendo, Through Thick and Thin: From Human Rights Principles to Politics across the Americas and Beyond (2022).

Public Int' Law & Pol'y Group, *Analysis of the Legal Options for Establishing a Tribunal for the Crime of Aggression under the Auspices of the Council of Europe and European Union* (June 2023).

Dinah L. Shelton, Advanced Introduction to International Human Rights Law (2014).

Yuval Shany, Assessing the Effectiveness of International Courts (2014).

Kathryn Sikkink, The Justice Cascade: How Human Rights Prosecutions Are Changing World Politics (2011).

Jane Stromseth, David Whippman, & Rosa Brooks, Can Might Make Rights?: Building the Rule of Law after Military Interventions (2006).

Chapter 7

Innovations in International Dispute Resolution— Hybrid Processes: Variations on Dispute Processes in Private, Public, and Mixed Settings

We have now looked at the foundational processes in international dispute resolution: negotiation, diplomacy, mediation, conciliation, arbitration, and adjudication. Modern conflicts that cross boundaries can be experienced in many different settings—across nations, within nations, in post-colonial conflicts, among and between private parties, and between public and private parties.

These foundational or pure dispute resolution processes are now often combined to form new hybrid processes. This chapter and the next one look at the hybridization of international dispute resolution processes in three senses: (1) *processes of hybridization*, that is, combinations (e.g., med-arb), adaptations (e.g., ombuds), or innovations of process (e.g., online dispute resolution (ODR)); (2) *combinations of private and public parties* and dispute processes (e.g., private investor-state investment disputes) and (3) *international or transnational forms of dispute processes* (e.g., the dispute resolution processes used by international organizations that are governed by treaties or agreements rather than by national or international law, such as the United Nations, World Trade Organization, and World Bank). Thus, hybrid dispute resolution in the international arena is both processual and substantive. The sources of law and procedural rules in these settings can be very complex and create a multilayered form of international *process and legal pluralism.*

International organizations are governed by their own internal rules (e.g., the World Bank, United Nations, International Red Cross) but also by treaties in their work in many countries, which may involve activities related to peacekeeping, trade (GATT and WTO), or state-investor disputes (Washington Convention of 1965 and its creation of the International Centre for the Settlement of Investment Disputes, a forum which primarily uses arbitral processes).

New legal regimes, like regional human rights treaties and institutions (e.g., European Court of Human Rights, Inter-American Court of Human Rights, and African

Court of Human Rights), utilize both formal adjudicatory processes and "amiable settlements." The Nuremberg and Tokyo tribunals at the end of World War II established some precedents for criminal prosecutions of war crimes and atrocities (see the discussion of the newer international criminal tribunals in Chapter 6). In the aftermath of more recent atrocities and wars and the fall of dictatorships in various countries, international justice seekers have developed new processes and institutions for other forms of dispute resolution, seeking broader remedies and attempting to encourage reconciliation, democracy, empowerment programs, and general legal and social-capacity building. Their endeavors have led to the formation of the new fields of transitional and restorative justice. These new processes raise important issues of process fairness; reparative relief; sub-national, national, and transnational jurisdiction; and substantive and representative equity.

Perhaps the newest development in international dispute resolution is the use of online dispute resolution (ODR) and other forms of computer-assisted, "virtual" judicial and non-judicial formats for conflict resolution. These formats raise novel issues involving literacy, capacity, access, jurisdictional authority, and enforcement.

The next three chapters introduce some of these processes as well as examples of new institutions developed to broaden and deepen the capacity of human beings to effectively deal with a variety of conflicts without having to resort to violence or even to formal and expensive tribunals. There are several major issues to consider as we study these processes:

- Is it a good thing to have many processes to choose from (whether from a *menu* (horizontal) of processes or a *tier* (vertical) of condition precedents), or is there a danger that this could lead to a babel of inconsistent outcomes? This is forum-shopping at the most complex and open-ended international level.
- Does each "pure" dispute resolution process have its own set of rules (or internal integrity) and ethical commitments (past rights adjudication versus future relationship governance) so that combining them into hybrids, such as med-arb or arb-med, risks causing confusion about how they should be conducted and what outcomes they produce?
- Should there be clear rules or customs of use, and vertical hierarchies of appeals, or does it make more sense to allow many fora to seek dispute and conflict settlement?
- How can these hybrid or newer forms of conflict resolution achieve compliance, enforcement, and sustainability of their outcomes, whether mutually agreed to, as in mediation and negotiation, or commanded by some other authority, as in truth and reconciliation commissions?
- What are the costs and benefits of combining private dispute resolution regimes like arbitration with public enforcement regimes requiring court orders for compliance?

- What should happen when disputants come from different jurisdictions, sectors of society, or legal traditions?
- When should conflict resolution formats be freely and voluntarily chosen, and when should they be prescribed or commanded?

I. Variations on Pure Processes: Med-Arb, Arb-Med, Public and Private, Mandatory or Consensual

The following article develops a definitional taxonomy of different kinds of dispute processes. These can be new processes arising from combinations or modifications of the basic ones, designed to fit different kinds of issues involving public law and state interests as well as private parties and interests. In the next chapter, we illustrate more of these using examples from other applications involving state and private parties, such as restorative justice and ombuds.

Carrie Menkel-Meadow, *Hybrid and Mixed Dispute Resolution Processes: Integrities of Process Pluralism*

in COMPARATIVE DISPUTE RESOLUTION 408–410; 412–413
(Maria F. Moscati, Michael Palmer & Marian Roberts eds., 2020)

Taxonomies of Hybridity: Public-Private; Consensual-Coercive; Formal-Informal; Binding-Non-Binding; Facilitative-Decisional; Rights-Interests-Needs

As the modern dispute resolution movement in the 1970s rediscovered mediation from ancient sources, redefined arbitration and negotiation processes, and critiqued the brittleness and inefficiencies of adjudication, a variety of "alternative" (we now say "appropriate") dispute resolution methods were often combined to encourage consensual, multiple-issue, party-empowered decision making (mediation) first, with decisional backdrop or default processes later available. Thus was born "*med-arb.*" The idea is to let the parties try to resolve their dispute on their own (with the facilitative help of a mediator first); and then, if their facilitated negotiation does not work, let the third party decide for them. Med-arb has probably been used for centuries in various forms of indigenous and historical communities, with local "headmen"—village elders and others (e.g., Communist party officials in China)—hearing the parties out, either alone or in front of the whole community. After encouraging consensual negotiation, bargaining processes and forgiveness or "self-criticism" ceremonies, those same village elders or party officials may then potentially command a decision—not only for the parties in dispute, but also for the "harmony" or better interests of the community.

Thus, despite [Lon] Fuller's analytic desires to keep processes "pure," it is more likely that human history has included more hybridized forms of dispute resolution, with variegated legal and cultural uses of law, custom, informal norms, power and self and community "interests" as governing rubrics. Older forms of "med-arb" are actually quite common in modern legal systems where judges attempt to mediate before they decide.... [M]odern dispute resolution theorists and practitioners have created taxonomies of characteristics of disputes and dispute processes in the hope of developing classification schemes to properly allocate disputes to appropriate fora. (See *Table* 7-1 below.)

But as with any taxonomy, even these categories may themselves be mixed or hybridized. Med-arb, as described above, has been a public process in community disputes historically; a private process of choice by parties electing to use it in commercial disputes; a common practice in labor disputes, which can be either private (collective bargaining agreement) or public (mandated by law); and culturally variable as different legal systems and communities adapt its use to their ends. In less populous counties of California, for example, a controversial variant of "med-arb" has been used in family disputes, where a mediator or family social worker investigates child abuse or custody and attempts to find consensual solutions with the parties, but then "turns" either expert reporter to a judge or the actual decision maker if the parties cannot agree. This sort of "role confusion" or mixing is precisely what disturbed [Lon] Fuller. When the mediator seeks to persuade the parties to provide all confidential information to him or her to help facilitate a solution, he or she breaks role ethics by then using that information in decisions if the information might not have been admissible in court. Mediators and adjudicators (or adjuncts of adjudicators) have different "moralities" and responsibilities to the parties and the system.

A new variation on the "med-arb" theme has been the development of informal "*arb-med*," also used in both public and private disputes. Parties may choose arbitrators (pre-dispute in contract or post-dispute by election or treaty in international disputes) who, before they decide anything, try informally to bring the parties together to negotiate a more consensual settlement. Disputes ranging from private commercial disputes (both domestic and international) to more public international investment disputes increasingly involve arbitrators who attempt settlement first, knowing that consensual agreements are more often complied with than command decisions (Schneider and Welsh 2013). [Recall the uses of these processes in the *Rainbow Warrior* dispute in Chapter 1—Eds.]

Even the simplest hybridization of mediation and arbitration processes raises important questions from these categories of classification and legitimacy. Must the parties consent (volunteer) to these changes in process; do they truly understand the differences?

Table 7-1 Characteristics of conflict processes and institutions

Private	Public
Consensual/voluntary	Compelled/mandatory
Nonbinding	Binding
Informal	Formal
Oral-written process and decision	Written rules, process, and decision
Temporary/contingent/variable outcome	"Permanent" decision or outcome
Parties only	Other participants (representatives or third-party neutrals)
Dyadic (two-party)	Multiparty
Competitive (distributional)	Collaborative, integrative
Rights based (public norms)	Interests based (private norms; trades)
Common-sense/community norms	Expertise—science, technical process
Pre-dispute contractual	Post-dispute election or assignment

Beyond the simple mixing of mediation and arbitration, as governments have used other hybrids—such as *facilitated public policy consensus-building processes* of negotiation, mediation and facilitation—for "*negotiated rule-making*" and policy formation (Susskind, McKearnan and Larner 1999; Podziba 2013), questions about the blending of the potentially conflicting values of public transparency with mediation's promise of confidentiality and secrecy demonstrate the Fullerian concern with process "morality." How these conflicting underlying values can be effectively and legitimately "mixed" presents difficult ethical dilemmas for the field (Menkel-Meadow 2009).

In other ways, the public sector in many countries has now borrowed from the private sector, requiring or encouraging the use of some form of more consensual dispute resolution within the context of command or coercive institutions, such as courts or administrative tribunals, thus mixing formal legal processes with less formal forms of dispute resolution. Many formal legal systems often now require the parties to attempt *mediation or conciliation* as a condition precedent to access to a court hearing (Steffek, Unberath, Genn, Greger and Menkel-Meadow 2013; Ali 2018). Whether the mediators are private or court based, compensated or not, permitted to evaluate cases and recommend solutions or not, all vary not only by country, but also by local court rules and practices....

At the decisional end of the spectrum, *private arbitration* has also been hybridized to encompass several models, from *binding* (and enforceable in international contexts through the New York Convention for the Recognition and Enforcement of Foreign Arbitral Awards), ... to *non-binding* and variations in between. In classic arbitration, the parties choose the decision makers (one or a panel of three); the procedural rules (often choosing those provided for by the major international tribunals, such as the International Chamber of Commerce or the London Court of International Arbitration); and usually the substantive legal rules to be applied (in contracts or treaties). Such contractually agreed-to arbitration proceedings are binding because the parties agree to be bound by the award and thus are still considered a "consensual" form of dispute resolution.

In recent years, adaptations of classic arbitration have included such things as *final offer* arbitration, where the parties make an offer to the arbitrators of what they would like or the arbitrator suggests what his or her (or the panel's) award is likely to be, and the parties can accept that or engage in further negotiations with each other. *Baseball arbitration*, taken from U.S. baseball salary disputes and used in some commercial disputes, requires the parties to make a final "best" (hoped to be more reasonable) offer to the panel, which must choose one of the offers as given, with no authority to change the final award. Although this process was designed to encourage the parties to come closer to each other in disputed matters, baseball arbitrators report that the final offers are often still quite far apart. Final offer arbitration is now also often the final stage of a mediation that comes to an impasse, as mediators provide a "final offer" [or "muscle mediation" in international contexts such as Presidents Carter and Clinton's efforts in N. Korea] (of what they think a good resolution might be), but this is a "non-binding" form of arbitration (unless the parties agree in advance to be bound by what is offered). These variations on arbitral themes (there are others) demonstrate the porousness of the categories: parties often alter their decisions to be non-binding or binding in mid-stream; and since arbitration is usually the product of party agreement in the first place, the parties can usually (not always) alter their procedures, processes and outcomes during the arbitration itself....

Arbitration has become the go-to process for many international disputes, including private commercial disputes, hybrid state-private party foreign investment disputes (through the International Centre for the Settlement of Investment Disputes, ICSID, which administers arbitrations, through an organ of the World Bank), public trade disputes, (through the World Trade Organization's legal procedures) and even international boundary and diplomatic disputes. Many boundary disputes (especially in the nineteenth century) have been arbitrated by kings, (Canada, US), popes (Argentina-Chile) or specially constituted bodies either within or outside of the Permanent Court of Arbitration set up for such purposes in the late 19th century. As arbitration is an agreed-to process by the parties (as is mediation), both private and public parties have molded this decisional process (rules, decision makers and outcomes) to their particular needs. At the international level, agreed-to arbitral proceedings may actually be more successful in compliance with awards than decisions of the relatively powerless international adjudicative bodies, including even the International Court of Justice (from which many parties, like the US, [see US withdrawal from jurisdiction in Nicaragua vs. United States (1986)—Eds.] have occasionally withdrawn as jurisdiction is consensual, not mandatory.) Arbitration has also become the process of choice in sports disputes ranging from the International Olympic Committee to the International Football Association (FIFA) which often call for a quick decision (doping, referee calls, contract issues, off field behavioral issues) during play, tournaments and other competitions).

In this chapter, we focus on how hybrid processes are used in commercial and economic interactions, between states, between private parties, and between states and private parties. In the next chapter, we turn to which of these processes can be utilized in the areas of human rights, transitional justice, and post-conflict reconciliation.

II. Hybrid Processes in Different Economic Fora: Investor-State and Trade Disputes (Courts, Arbitration, or Mediation) and Public or Private Dispute Resolution

Modern international economic relations are characterized by hybrid forms of dispute resolution. As we explored in Chapter 4, international arbitration is the most common form of dispute resolution in private commercial disputes between actors from different countries who buy and sell goods and services from each other and are citizens of countries who have signed on to the New York Convention for the Recognition and Enforcement of Foreign Arbitral Awards (1958). But, in addition to private-party commercial relations, nation-states have economic issues with each other, too. When states invite private investors into their countries, those investors want to be sure they will be treated fairly in terms of regulations, taxation, and the ability to take their profits. In the past, when a nation "nationalized" or "expropriated" private property (e.g., oil, agricultural products, communications, utility industries), as has occurred after socialist and communist political regime changes, the nation-state of the expropriated company would often use "gunboat diplomacy" (coercion, violence, or other means) to seek restitution or other remedies.

The 1965 Convention on the Settlement of Investment Disputes between States and Nationals of Other States (the Washington Convention) aimed to address these issues. Under this treaty, private investors and host countries with disputes about such actions would, if their countries were parties to bilateral or multilateral investor agreements, agree to use arbitration to resolve them, and the arbitral awards would be enforceable in the same manner as the New York Convention. The International Centre for the Settlement of Investment Disputes (ICSID), a part of the World Bank complex administers these cases. Several hundred cases of investor-state disputes have now been arbitrated, leading to much academic and practitioner commentary about whether this system is a "hybrid" public or mostly private system, since not all awards are published and there is no requirement of adherence to precedent (though there is now much cross-referencing by arbitrators). The jurisprudence which has developed from these arbitrated cases has helped to establish clear doctrine around some basic issues such as what constitutes expropriation and what compensation should be due when it occurs. There has also been a rich doctrinal development of what constitutes "fair and equitable treatment" of foreign investors in a host country.[1]

The Bretton Woods Convention in New Hampshire, held in 1944 following the end of World War II, is responsible for creating the basic international economic legal regime. It established the World Bank and the International Monetary Fund, and it also recommended lowering trade barriers and increasing trade in the hope that doing so would result in economic prosperity and world peace. This recommendation led to the proposed International Trade Organization (ITO), which would have encouraged international trade agreements through the reduction of tariffs, import-export taxes, and internal subsidies. Sadly, the onset of the Cold War prevented the development of a fully functional ITO, even as several major rounds of international meetings produced hundreds of agreements on trade and tariffs, known as the General Agreement on Trade and Tariffs (GATT). GATT has become the governing regime for resolving state-to-state disputes about tariffs and subsidies among and between nations. Finally, in 1994 at the "Uruguay Round," the World Trade Organization, headquartered in Geneva, Switzerland, was established to host and monitor international, bilateral, and multilateral trade agreements. The WTO established an elaborate dispute-settlement system with a Dispute Settlement Understanding (DSU), which provided for an arbitral-like system of decisions with expert panels subject to review by the Appellate Body of the WTO. These decisions would be accepted by all WTO members with a system that now requires a consensus to not recognize a particular award. This system, unlike the ICSID system, publishes its opinions, and it had been widely regarded as one of the most successful forms of international dispute resolution. Unfortunately, as United States-China trade relations began deteriorating in the latter half of the 2010s, then President Trump failed to appoint US members to the Appellate Body, and so the judicial (appellate review) process for many disputes has been moribund, with nations looking to create other fora for trade disputes (e.g., the EU and Canada have recently signed a treaty to develop a separate dispute resolution system to deal with any trade disputes they might have).

In recent years, the use of more or less "private" party-chosen arbitrators for investment disputes has come under great criticism and was part of the reason that two very comprehensive trade agreements, the Transpacific Trade Agreement and the Transatlantic Trade Agreement, were not supported by the United States.

This chapter introduces you to some complex issues that can arise in using these forms of hybrid dispute resolution so that you may consider the advantages and disadvantages of different processes. For more comprehensive treatment of these issues, you should consult the suggested readings at the end of this chapter or take a separate course on investor-state or international trade law.

---

1. Alec Stone-Sweet & Florian Grisel, The Evolution of International Arbitration: Judicialization, Governance, Legitimacy (2017).

The next article outlines how states set up different structures as they are creating hybrid processes, with a focus on economic interactions between states and between states and individuals. Consider the choices and policy priorities of each state as it engages in designing these processes. Later in the chapter, we examine how these hybrid processes have been amended, adapted, and ended as states shift in their goals and priorities.

Andrea Kupfer Schneider, *Getting Along: The Evolution of Dispute Resolution Regimes in International Trade Organizations*

20 Mich. J. Int'l L. 697, 700–02, 704, 705, 712, 713–23, 759–63 (1999)

I. Importance of Studying International Dispute Resolution Regimes

The creation of the North American Free Trade Agreement ("NAFTA") and the World Trade Organization ("WTO") in this decade has clearly shifted the focus on international trade from bilateral agreements to multilateral and global agreements. This historic trend towards the growth of international trade organizations was accelerated by the apparent success of the European Union's efforts in the 1990's to revitalize the European economy and create the internal market of 1992. The drive to mimic the European Union ("EU") (and combat its strength) was then seen in the proliferation of regional organizations such as NAFTA, MERCOSUR, Association of Southeast Asian Nations ("ASEAN"), and the proposed Free Trade of the Americas.

At the same time, and no doubt in conjunction with the growth of trade organizations, international trade has become increasingly important both economically and politically. With each year, states find that an increasing part of their economy is dependent upon international trade, and the ripple effect of economic troubles has become more and more apparent even in the last year....

These events have spurred and accompanied the evolution of a variety of different dispute resolution regimes. These regimes evolved from differences in the international organizations themselves, their members and their goals. As the number of international organizations continues to grow, it has become increasingly important to categorize and analyze these dispute resolution regimes. While it sometimes appears as if each new international organization is reinventing the wheel in trying to figure out the balance between negotiation and adjudication, between supremacy over domestic laws and sovereignty of member states, some guidelines and general rules can be detected. Systematizing the regimes of dispute resolution and understanding their differences and unique balances will assist in both advising new organizations in setting up their dispute resolution systems and advising existing organizations on improving their dispute resolution mechanisms....

The choice of regimes could look like this:

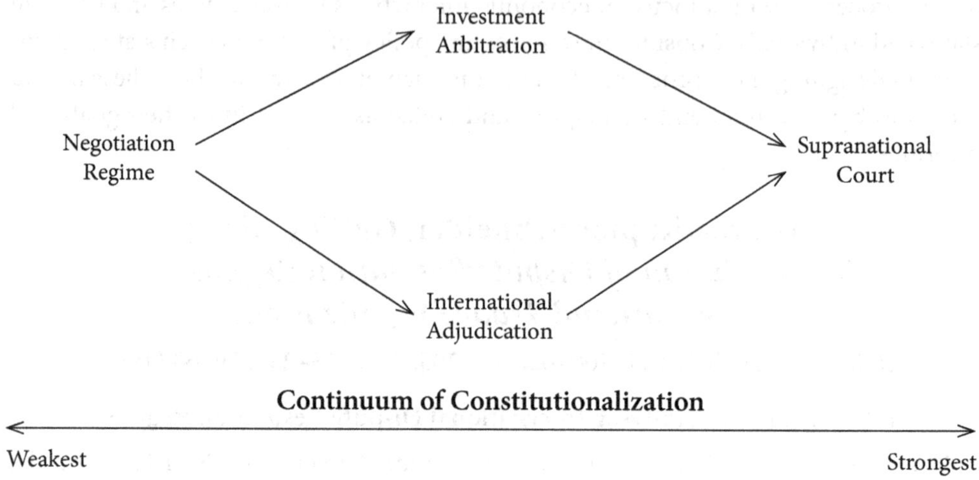

....

II. Differentiating Between Dispute Resolution Regimes

After reaching an understanding as to why the study of dispute resolution regimes is necessary and timely, we now turn to an examination of the legal factors that differentiate between these regimes. I have previously used these legal factors in an analysis of private involvement in international trade dispute resolution. Here we use these factors in order to categorize existing dispute resolution regimes....

Regimes/Factors	**Negotiation**	**Investment Arbitration**	**International Adjudication**	**Supranational Court**
Direct Effects	No	Yes	No	Yes
Standing for Private Actors	No	Yes	No	Yes, directly and indirectly
Supremacy	None	Only as to that award	Supreme, but not integrated into domestic law	Supreme and integrated
Transparency	Optional	Optional	Yes	Yes
Enforcement	Negotiation	Likely	Varying—None (NAFTA) to Retaliation (WTO)	Fines & Damages; Domestic Remedies also

B. Negotiation Regime

1. Individual Rights & Standing

The first type of regime of an international dispute resolution system is the Negotiation Regime. The Negotiation Regime is exemplified by the dispute settlement system of the General Agreement on Trade and Tariffs ("GATT") as it existed prior to the creation of the WTO as well as the current form of Chapter 20 of the NAFTA. In this regime, most of the factors we have discussed are on the lower end of the range. Typically, individuals are not granted rights under the organizations that use negotiation as their regime nor are individuals involved in the negotiation process. Disputes under this system are resolved informally using diplomacy between states. For example, in a disagreement over alleged dumping, two states might make an ad hoc agreement to change the particular system discussed. Historically, most disputes regarding trade, or anything else, have been resolved in this way.

2. Supremacy

Disputes under this regime are resolved by a negotiated agreement between states. This dispute resolution may result in changes to some law or practice in one or both states. More often, however, this type of dispute resolution agreement will not result in an amendment to an existing treaty or a new treaty itself, but rather will be a lesser type of commitment from the governments. Therefore, this dispute resolution will not be granted supremacy over domestic laws unless it, too, is considered international law under the respective domestic systems.

3. Transparency

In terms of transparency, a negotiated agreement may be publicized, particularly when governments are trying to please a domestic constituency. It may also provide an example for other negotiations over similar disputes, although this type of dispute resolution is clearly not precedent for any court. Nor do negotiated agreements create predictability for individuals or other states. Unlike a court case, where previous cases can be analyzed and decisions examined, an upcoming negotiation cannot be easily predicted based on previously negotiated agreements.

4. Enforcement

Enforcement under a negotiation regime of dispute resolution is left to the respective states. There is no oversight institution. Any noncompliance with the underlying trade agreement would put the parties back at the negotiation table in order to work out the dispute. In other words, a negotiation regime relies on "first-order" compliance at all times. States either follow the agreement or renegotiate a new agreement.

C. Investor Arbitration Regime

The Investor Arbitration Regime was specifically created to give private actors both rights and remedies under the relevant international treaty. The move toward investment arbitration began with the creation of the International Centre for the Settlement of Investment Disputes ("ICSID") under the aegis of the World Bank. A decade later, the UN Commission for International Trade Law ("UNCITRAL") drafted rules for ad hoc arbitration. This concept of permitting individuals to bring cases against states has since been copied in bilateral investment treaties in order to encourage foreign direct investment and outlined in NAFTA for investor disputes under Chapter 11B.

1. Individual Rights

Under treaties that establish investment arbitration, private actors are granted such rights as national treatment or a minimum standard of treatment in the host state.

These rights are directly effective. In other cases, domestic implementing legislation will provide for the rights to become directly effective. This makes sense because these types of treaties are specifically designed to encourage individual investment.

While an Investment Arbitration regime provides rights against the host government, none of these underlying treaties provide direct effect of rights against another individual. In other words, a private actor has no recourse against another private actor under this regime. Investment arbitration is established solely as a right and remedy between a private investor and the host state. Further, because investment arbitration is only available against a host state, nationals have no recourse against their own government. Finally, rights under this regime have limited scope. Investment Arbitration is provided for only the narrow right of national treatment in most regimes. Any state action falling outside those parameters is unreachable.

2. Individual Standing

In investment arbitration, private actors have the ability to bring cases directly against a state. This is quite a historic development in this century. First, individuals were historically seen as nationals of their state and, on the international plane, could only be represented by their government. Second, private suits against a government in domestic courts were also foreclosed due to laws that limited the grounds upon which states could be sued. This meant that foreign investors had little recourse to the host domestic legal system. Third, even if a private actor wanted to bring a suit in his own home court against the foreign state, most states had laws that provided foreign sovereign immunity.

In the meantime, international commercial arbitration had become a popular method for resolving commercial disputes between private disputants because it provided a more neutral, fairer, and potentially faster way of resolving disputes. This regime appealed to investors who were concerned with the potential bias, inefficiency, or unfamiliarity of foreign courts. By creating an international arbitration option between individuals and states, the creators of this regime hoped that investors would be more willing to bring their business to these states because disputes could be resolved through this international neutral body.

ICSID has jurisdiction over any legal dispute arising out of an investment between a Contracting State and a national of any other Contracting State. For a national of a Contracting State or a Contracting State to initiate proceedings under the ICSID, that party must submit a written request to the Secretary-General of ICSID detailing the issues in dispute, the parties, and consent to arbitration. After the dispute is certified by the Secretary-General of ICSID, an individual can have the case heard by an arbitral panel established by ICSID.

3. Supremacy & Transparency

Arbitration decisions generally provide for damages and not a change in domestic laws. Therefore, the issue of supremacy does not really arise because there is no new law created....

4. Enforcement

In terms of enforcement, an investment arbitration system does provide for relatively effective enforcement. The Convention on the Recognition and Enforcement of Arbitral Awards ("New York Convention") provides that all signatory states shall enforce arbitral awards in their domestic courts. As a result, if a state refuses to pay the arbitral award, the investor can go to the domestic court in that state or in any state where there are commercial assets in order to enforce the judgment. Although the investor still must go to the domestic court, the New York Convention provides for straightforward enforcement. In fact, many states that once ignored court orders from other states now willingly comply with arbitral awards....

D. International Adjudication Regime

The regime of international adjudication is the one that we are most familiar with under international law as the structure for resolving disputes between states. Evolving from the Permanent Court of Arbitration, and the Permanent Court of International Justice, the International Court of Justice ("ICJ") is the most recognized international court. In the trade arena, the WTO Dispute Settlement Understanding is closest to international adjudication.

1. Individual Rights & Standing

Under the International Adjudication Regime, private actors are neither granted rights directly by the treaty establishing the international court nor have any right of standing to bring cases before the court. This regime exists to resolve disputes between states—inter-national disputes—and therefore individuals have not had recourse to this regime....

2. Supremacy & Transparency

Under international law, the decisions of the international court are supreme to the domestic law and the relevant state must change its behavior or laws to comply. But the court's decision is not integrated into domestic law....

3. Enforcement

Perhaps the most controversial part of international adjudication is the question of compliance and enforcement. Because international courts have not thus far had armies to forcibly carry out their decisions, many critics of the international system focus on those cases where states have chosen to ignore the international court. Similarly, under GATT, states could delay the appointment of panels, effectively block adoption of panel reports and, on occasion, ignore panel decisions. For instance, after the U.S. asserted a complaint in 1981 under GATT against the European Community ("EC") concerning pasta export subsidies, the EC effectively blocked adoption of the panel report in favor of the United States. The United States resort to indirect retaliation efforts that sparked countermeasures by the EC. Without arguing as to whether an international court can ever truly "work," it is important to assess the level of enforcement a court can have.

Both GATT and the ICJ are examples of court systems that provide for no enforcement beyond censure of the international community. These systems stop at second-order compliance—states should obey the law and, if held to be violating the law, should pay the fine (or change their law). The WTO outlines more stringent enforcement measures by providing a menu of enforcement options. First, a state has the opportunity to follow the ruling and, usually, change the offending practice. Second, the state can continue the practice and pay damages to the harmed state. If neither of these options are taken, the harmed state can retaliate. The WTO provides that the harmed state must first retaliate in the same sector of trade. However, if this is not effective, the WTO provides that cross-sector retaliation is permitted. This newer evolution of the international adjudication regime has more teeth than its predecessors and attempts to correct some of the problems of the past....

Notes & Questions

1. We will turn shortly to examples of both international arbitration hybrids and international adjudication hybrids. What are the factors that states should consider when establishing these processes? How much attention should be paid to providing individual remedies versus meeting overarching national goals?
2. In examining these processes, how necessary is it that other states have similar underlying legal systems? Is capitalism a prerequisite? How about democracy?

A. Investor-State Arbitration

Nations make both bilateral and multilateral trade agreements, which lay out the rules for dealing with each other economically. The North American Free Trade Agreement (NAFTA), which has been superseded by the United States-Mexico-Canada Trade Agreement (USMCA), provided rules for foreign direct investment (FDI) and for trade (e.g., the fair and equitable treatment standard) between and among the United States, Canada, and Mexico. Examples of the equal treatment that should be accorded to foreign investors include no differential tax policy and no differential capital policy. These rules all impact the executive branch of government. What happens when unequal treatment occurs in the courts?

Imagine that a US investor has set up a business in Mexico where equal treatment is guaranteed under NAFTA and that a Mexican company sues the US company in a Mexican court for a breach of contract. When speaking to the jury, the Mexican lawyers use slurs and innuendo to suggest that the white northern colonizer should be punished. The judge does not stop the lawyers or admonish them for their biased language, and, sure enough, the jury awards millions of dollars to the Mexican plaintiffs. Should the US company be able to bring a case against the Mexican government for unequal treatment in its courts?

Consider your answer in reading the following case: In a very unusual dispute, Ray Loewen, a Canadian businessman who owned and operated a chain of hundreds of funeral homes, was sued in a Mississippi court for contract and antitrust actions by Jeremiah O'Keefe, the owner of eight funeral homes.[2] During the jury trial in Missis-

2. See the full and colorful report in Jonathan Harr, *The Burial*, THE NEW YORKER, Nov. 1, 1999, at 70–95.

sippi, some of the lawyers and the judge made comments which were "anti-foreign" and allegedly racist. The jury awarded millions of dollars of damages to O'Keefe, and Loewen then brought an action within the ICSID system claiming that the American legal system had denied him "fair treatment" under the NAFTA treaty. The case created international controversies on many levels.

In earlier proceedings, O'Keefe sued Loewen in a Mississippi trial court regarding a commercial dispute. Both parties were sizeable competitors in the funeral home and funeral insurance business in Mississippi. According to Loewen, the state trial judge repeatedly allowed plaintiff O'Keefe's attorneys to make numerous, irrelevant, and prejudicial references about Loewen's foreign nationality (he was Canadian), to make race-based distinctions between O'Keefe and Loewen, and to make class-based distinctions between the wealthy Loewen Group and the supposedly less wealthy family-business owner O'Keefe.

The trial judge refused Loewen's request to give a jury instruction admonishing jurors that nationality-, race-, and class-based discrimination were impermissible evidence. The original complaint sought $5 million in damages. The jury awarded O'Keefe $500 million in damages. Loewen was required to post a $625 million bond within seven days if he wished to appeal, in order to keep the plaintiff from immediately taking Loewen's property to satisfy the judgment. That procedural decision effectively foreclosed Loewen from being able to appeal the judgment against him on its merits. With the sale of his Mississippi assets scheduled to start the next day, Loewen entered into a settlement with O'Keefe, under great duress, whereby he agreed to pay $175 million.

Loewen filed this subsequent action in the ICSID tribunal, claiming that the Mississippi proceedings violated the NAFTA prohibition on prejudice against a foreign investor in the courts of a NAFTA nation. Because of the important issues involved in this case, the governments of Canada and Mexico (the other NAFTA nations) attended the hearing on the merits.

1. Jurisdictional Overlap

In the Proceeding between The Loewen Group, Inc., and Raymond L. Loewen (Claimants) and United States of America (Respondent)

ICSID Case No. ARB(AF)/98/3, 42 Int'l Legal Materials 811 (2003)

Tribunal's Opinion:

...

VII. THE NATURE OF CLAIMANT'S CLAIM

39.... Claimants argue that (1) the trial court, by admitting extensive anti-Canadian and pro-American testimony and prejudicial counsel comment, violated Article 1102 of NAFTA which bars discrimination against foreign investors and their investments;

(3) the trial court, by the way in which it conducted the trial ... by permitting extensive nationality-based, racial and class-based testimony and counsel comments, violated Article 1105 of NAFTA which imposes a minimum standard of treatment for investments of foreign investors, including a duty of "full protection and security" and a right to "fair and equitable treatment" of foreign investors;

...

(6) the discriminatory conduct, the excessive verdict, the denial of Loewen's right to appeal and the coerced settlement violated Article 1110 of NAFTA, which bars the uncompensated appropriation of investments of foreign investors.... Claimants allege that Respondent is liable for Mississippi's NAFTA breaches under Article 1105, which requires that the Parties to NAFTA shall ensure that all necessary measures are taken to give effect to the provisions of the Agreement, including their observance by State and provincial governments. Claimants also allege that, by tolerating the misconduct which occurred during the O'Keefe litigation, Respondent [US] directly breached Article 1105, which imposes affirmative duties on Respondent to provide "full protection and security" to investments of foreign investors, including "full protection and security" against third-party misconduct.

...

X. THE TRIAL

54. Having read the transcript and having considered the submissions of the parties with respect to the conduct of the trial, we have reached the firm conclusion that the conduct of the trial by the trial judge was so flawed that it constituted a miscarriage of justice amounting to a manifest injustice as that expression is understood in international law. Whether this conclusion results in a violation of Article 1105 depends upon the resolution of Respondent's submissions still to be considered, in particular the submission that State responsibility arises only when final action is taken by the State's judicial system as a whole. [Loewen settled for a lesser amount than the trial court judgment, rather than appeal.—Eds.]

...

(a) O'Keefe's nationality strategy

56. O'Keefe's case at trial was conducted from beginning to end on the basis that Jerry O'Keefe, a war hero and "fighter for his country," who epitomized local business interests, was the victim of a ruthless foreign (Canadian) corporate predator. There were many references on the part of O'Keefe's counsel and witnesses to the Canadian nationality of Loewen ("Ray Loewen and his group from Canada"). Likewise, O'Keefe witnesses said that Loewen was financed by Asian money, these statements being based on the fact that Loewen was partly financed by the Hong Kong and Shanghai Bank, an English and Hong Kong bank which was erroneously described by Jerry O'Keefe in evidence as the "Shanghai Bank." Indeed, Jerry O'Keefe ... depicted ... [his] business under American and Mississippi flags and Loewen under Canadian and Japanese flags, stat[ing] that the Japanese may well control both the "Shanghai Bank"

and Loewen but he did not know that [when entering into a business association with Loewen]. O'Keefe's strategy ... was linked to Jerry O'Keefe's fighting for his country against the Japanese.

This strategy was calculated to appeal to the jury's sympathy for local home-town interests as against the wealthy and powerful foreign competitor.

60. An extreme example of appeals to anti-Canadian prejudice was evidence given by Mr. Espy, former United States Secretary of State for Agriculture who, called to give evidence of the good character of Jerry O'Keefe, spoke of his (Espy's) experience in protecting "the American market" from Canadian wheat farmers who exported low priced wheat into the American market with which American producers could not compete and later, having secured a market, then jacked up the price....

61. The strategy of emphasizing O'Keefe's American nationality as against Loewen's Canadian origins reached a peak in Mr. Gary's closing address. He likened Jerry O'Keefe's struggle against Loewen with his war-time exploits against the Japanese, asserting that he was motivated by "pride in America" and "love for your country." By way of contrast, Mr. Gary characterized Loewen's case as "Excuse me, I'm from Canada."

...

62. ... Mr. Gary characterized Loewen as a foreign invader who "came to town like gang busters. Ray came sweeping through...." Mr. Gary likened Loewen to the Canadian wheat farmers. Loewen would "come in" and purchase a funeral home and "no sooner than they got it, they jacked up the prices down here in Mississippi."

...

(b) O'Keefe's racial politics strategy

65. Claimants' case that O'Keefe engaged in a strategy of racial politics is largely based on the efforts of O'Keefe to suggest that O'Keefe did business with black and white people alike whereas Loewen did business [only] with white people. [The trial judge, eight of twelve jurors, and both parties' lead lawyers were African American.—Eds.]

...

(c) O'Keefe's appeal to class-based prejudice

68. Claimants further complain that Mr. Gary repeatedly portrayed Loewen as a large, wealthy foreign corporation and contrasted Jerry O'Keefe as a small, local, family businessman.... There were a number of references by O'Keefe's counsel emphasizing this contrast. These references culminated in Mr. Gary's closing address in which he incited the jury to put a stop to Loewen's activities. Speaking of Jerry O'Keefe, Mr. Gary said: He doesn't have the money that they have nor the power, but he has heart and character, and he refused to let them shoot him down. You know your job as jurors gives you a lot of power.... You have the power to bring major corporations to their knees when they are wrong. You can see wrong, make it right. Suffering and stop it. Ray comes down here, he's got his yacht up there, he can go to cocktail parties and all

that, but do you know how he's financing that? By 80- and 90-year-old people who go to get to a funeral, who go to pay their life savings, goes into this here, and it doesn't mean anything to him. Now, they've got to be stopped....

Do it, stop them so in years to come anybody should mention your service for some 50 odd days on this trial, you can say 'Yes, I was there', and you can talk proud about it.

XVII. EVALUATION OF THE TRIAL

119. By any standard of measurement, the trial involving O'Keefe and Loewen was a disgrace. By any standard of review, the tactics of O'Keefe's lawyers, particularly Mr. Gary were impermissible. By any standard of evaluation, the trial judge failed to afford Loewen the process that was due....

121. ... The question is whether the whole trial, and its resultant verdict, satisfied minimum standards of international law, or the "fair and equitable treatment and full protection and security" that the Contracting States pledged in Article 1105 of NAFTA. This question is addressed in paras. 124–137....

123.... [W]e take it to be the responsibility of the State under international law and, consequently, of the courts of a State, to provide a fair trial of a case to which a foreign investor is a party. It is the responsibility of the courts of a State to ensure that litigation is free from discrimination against a foreign litigant and that the foreign litigant should not become the victim of sectional or local prejudice....

XVIII. NAFTA ARTICLE 1105

124. Article 1105 which is headed "Minimum Standard of Treatment" provides:

> 1. Each party shall accord to investments of investors of another party treatment in accordance with international law, including fair and equitable treatment and full protection and security." The precise content of this provision, particularly the meaning of the reference to "international law" and the effect of the inclusory [*sic*] clause has been the subject of controversy.

125. On July 31, 2001, the Free Trade Commission adopted an interpretation of Article 1105(1). The Commission's interpretation is in these terms: Minimum Standard of Treatment in Accordance with International Law

(1) Article 1105(1) prescribes the customary international law minimum standard of treatment of aliens as the minimum standard of treatment to be afforded to investments of investors of another Party. (2) The concepts of "fair and equitable treatment" and "full protection and security" do not require treatment in addition to or beyond that which is required by the customary international law minimum standard of treatment of aliens. (3) A determination that there has been a breach of another provision of the NAFTA, or of a separate international agreement, does not establish that there has been a breach of Article 1105(1)....

128. The effect of the Commission's interpretation is that "fair and equitable treatment", and "full protection and security" are not free-standing obligations. They constitute obligations only to the extent that they are recognized by customary international law....

129. It is not in dispute between the parties that customary international law is concerned with denials of justice in litigation between private parties. Indeed, Respondent's expert, Professor Greenwood QC, acknowledges that customary international law imposes on States an obligation "to maintain and make available to aliens, a fair and effective system of justice." ...

130. Respondent submits that, in conformity with the accepted standards of customary international law, it is for Loewen to establish that the decisions of the Mississippi courts constituted a manifest injustice....

131. In ... the International Court of Justice in Elettronica Sicula SpA (ELSI) United States v. Italy (1989) ICJ 15 at 76: "Arbitrariness is not so much something opposed to a rule of law, as something opposed to the rule of law.... It is willful disregard of due process of law, an act which shocks, or at least surprises a sense of judicial propriety."

132. Neither State practice, the decisions of international tribunals nor the opinion of commentators support the view that bad faith or malicious intention is an essential element of unfair and inequitable treatment or denial of justice amounting to a breach of international justice. Manifest injustice in the sense of a lack of due process leading to an outcome which offends a sense of judicial propriety is enough, even if one applies the Interpretation according to its terms.

133. In the words of the NAFTA Tribunal in Mondev International Ltd v. United States of America ICSID Case No. ARB (AF)/99/2, Award dated October 11, 2002, "the question is whether, at an international level and having regard to generally accepted standards of the administration of justice, a tribunal can conclude in the light of all the facts that the impugned decision was clearly improper and discreditable, with the result that the investment has been subjected to 'unfair and inequitable treatment'."

134. If that question be answered in the affirmative, then a breach of Article 1105 is established. Whether the conduct of the trial amounted to a breach of municipal law as well as international law is not for us to determine. A NAFTA claim cannot be converted into an appeal against the decisions of municipal [trial] courts.

135. International law does, however, attach special importance to discriminatory violations of municipal law.... A decision which is in breach of municipal law and is discriminatory against the foreign litigant amounts to manifest injustice according to international law [italics added].

136. In the present case, the trial court permitted the jury to be influenced by persistent appeals to local favouritism as against a foreign litigant.

137. In the light of the conclusions reached in paras. 119–123 (inclusive) and 136, the whole trial and its resultant verdict were clearly improper and discreditable and cannot be squared with minimum standards of international law and fair and equitable treatment. However, because the trial court proceedings are only part of the judicial process that is available to the parties, the rest of the process, and its availability to Loewen, must be examined before a violation of Article 1105 is established....

XIX. THE CLAIM OF BIAS

138. Claimants' argument that Judge Graves and the jury were actually biased against Loewen is not made out. There is no direct evidence of bias on the part of Judge Graves or the jury. Nor do the jury interviews demonstrate that the jury was biased. The interviews reveal that the jury took an adverse view of Loewen's conduct based on evidence which included testimony of Loewen employees and former employees. Nor does the evidence warrant the drawing of an inference of bias against the jury, though there is strong reason for thinking that the jury were affected by the persistent and extravagant O'Keefe appeals to prejudice. Although the trial judge's conduct of the trial is explicable by reference to bias, the evidence does not support a finding that he was biased against Loewen. We take the view that the judge, for reasons which do not clearly appear, failed to discharge his paramount duty to ensure that Loewen received a fair trial.

XX. NAFTA ARTICLE 1102

139. Article 1102 bars discrimination against foreign investors and their investments. Article 1102(1) and (2) requires each Party to accord investors and investments of another Party "treatment no less favorable than it accords in like circumstances to its own investors" or their investments. With respect to a state or province Article 1102(3) requires "treatment no less favorable than the most favorable treatment accorded, in like circumstances, by that state or province to investors, and to investments of investors, of the Party of which it forms part."

The effect of these provisions ... is that a Mississippi court shall not conduct itself less favourably to Loewen, by reason of its Canadian nationality, than it would to an investor involved in similar activities and in a similar lawsuit from another state in the United States or from another location in Mississippi itself. We agree also with Professor Bilder when he says that Article 1102 is direct only to nationality-based discrimination and that it proscribes only demonstrable and significant indications of bias and prejudice on the basis of nationality, of a nature and consequence likely to have affected the outcome of the trial.

140. A critical problem in the application of Article 1102 to the facts of this case is that we do not have an example of "the most favorable treatment accorded, in like circumstances" by a Mississippi court to investors and investments of the United States.

...

What Article 1102(3) requires is a comparison between the standard of treatment accorded to a claimant and the most favourable standard of treatment accorded to a person in like situation to that claimant. There are no materials before us which enable such a comparison to be made.

...

142. Having reached the conclusion that the trial and the verdict were improper and cannot be squared with minimum standards of fair international law and fair and equitable treatment, we must now consider the question whether, in the light of subsequent

proceedings, the trial and the verdict alone or in combination with the subsequent proceedings amounted to an international wrong.

...

XXVI. DOES THE SETTLEMENT AGREEMENT OPERATE TO RELEASE ALL CLAIMS AGAINST RESPONDENT?

205. It is convenient to deal here with an argument based on a release of claims provided for by the settlement agreement. Respondent submitted that, on its true construction, the settlement agreement operated to release all claims by Loewen, including the NAFTA claims in issue in this arbitration, against Respondent, notwithstanding that Respondent is not a party to the agreement.

206. ... The answer to Respondent's submission is that when the settlement agreement and the release are read in their entirety and in context, we do not regard them as releasing Loewen's NAFTA claims. They lie outside the ambit of the claims dealt with. [The tribunal here examines the various remedies which were available to Loewen's, before lodging this claim in an international tribunal.]

...

217. Accordingly, our conclusion is that Loewen failed to pursue its domestic remedies, notably the Supreme Court option and that, in consequence, Loewen has not shown a violation of customary international law and a violation of NAFTA for which Respondent is responsible.

...

XXXI. CONCLUSION

241. We think it right to add one final word. A reader following our account of the injustices which were suffered by Loewen [Group] and Mr. Raymond Loewen in the Courts of Mississippi could well be troubled to find that they emerge from the present long and costly proceedings with no remedy at all. After all, we have ... criticized the Mississippi proceedings in the strongest terms. There was unfairness here towards the foreign investor. Why not use the weapons at hand to put it right? What clearer case than the present could there be for the ideals of NAFTA to be given some teeth?

242. This human reaction has been present in our minds throughout but we must be on guard against allowing it to control our decision. Far from fulfilling the purposes of NAFTA, an intervention on our part would compromise them by obscuring the crucial separation between the international obligations of the State under NAFTA, of which the fair treatment of foreign investors in the judicial sphere is but one aspect, and the much broader domestic responsibilities of every nation towards litigants of whatever origin who appear before its national courts. Subject to explicit international agreement permitting external control or review, these latter responsibilities are for each individual state to regulate according to its own chosen appreciation of the ends of justice. As we have sought to make clear, we find nothing in NAFTA to justify the exercise by this Tribunal of an appellate function parallel to that which belongs to the

courts of the host nation [referring to the remedies that Loewen could have pursued, before coming to this tribunal]. In the last resort, a failure by that nation to provide adequate means of remedy may amount to an international wrong but only in the last resort. The line may be hard to draw, but it is real. Too great a readiness to step from outside into the domestic arena, attributing the shape of an international wrong to what is really a local error (however serious), will damage both the integrity of the domestic judicial system and the viability of NAFTA itself. The natural instinct, when someone observes a miscarriage of justice, is to step in and try to put it right, but the interests of the international investing community demand that we must observe the principles which we have been appointed to apply, and stay our hands.

Notes & Questions

1. How many different legal processes were used here?
2. If the ICSID panel found the trial proceedings so unfair, why did they not find for Mr. Loewen?
3. What should Mr. Loewen have done to preserve his case? From the perspective of NAFTA enforcement, what are the advantages and disadvantages of the *Loewen* decision?
4. Should international arbitration tribunals be able to review domestic judicial proceedings in the same way that they review the executive and legislative branches? How does this compare to the US courts' concern in the Chromalloy example you encountered in Chapter 4?
5. To what extent is the tribunal applying "international principles" of law or policy here?
6. Do you agree with how these international principles were applied to Mr. Loewen's case?
7. For a fuller and somewhat exaggerated treatment of this case, see the film *The Burial* (2023) and the New Yorker article on which it is based, Jonathan Haar, The Burial, THE NEW YORKER, Nov. 1, 1999, 70–95.

2. The Problem of Precedent in ICSID Arbitration

In 2000, Argentina suffered an economic crisis, and the government revalued the peso. It had been pegged to the US dollar, but after revaluation, the peso was worth about one-third its prior value. This revaluation resulted in enormous losses for many companies which had invested in Argentina, often in joint projects with the Argentine government. In the more than 20 years since the revaluation, dozens of suits claiming expropriation and failure to fully compensate and treat "fairly and equitably" the foreign companies which had lost millions of dollars have been filed by investors against the Argentine government, using ICSID arbitral processes (and a variety of different arbitral rules, including ICSID, UNCITRAL, and ad hoc arbitral rules).

The next two excerpts explain what happens in investor-state disputes and demonstrate what can happen when different arbitrators decide similar issues when there is no formal system of adherence to precedent or appeal. They show how different ICSID arbitral panels dealt with Argentina's "necessity defense" claims to justify its actions in revaluing the peso during an economic crisis, even if that meant losses for its private foreign investors.

Susan D. Franck, *The Nature and Enforcement of Investor Rights under Investment Treaties: Do Investment Treaties Have a Bright Future?*

12 U.C. Davis L. Rev. 47, 48, 52–55 (2005)

Investment Treaty Arbitration in a Nutshell

A BIT is an agreement between two Sovereigns that safeguards the investments made by investors from each country in businesses or projects located in the other's territories. These treaties have a common origin and function, where Sovereigns offer investors basic guarantees in the hopes of procuring foreign investment within their jurisdiction. These rights consist of a variety of general guarantees to substantive standards of protection for their investments, including appropriate compensation for expropriation, freedom from unreasonable or discriminatory measures, guarantees of national treatment, assurances of fair and equitable treatment of investments, promises that investments will receive full protection and security as well as treatment no less favorable than that accorded under international law, and a Sovereign's commitment to honor its obligations. These substantive guarantees create a new system of international rights and obligations for the signatories. As a practical matter, the substantive standards in BITs have become the fundamental source of international law in the area of foreign investment, displacing customary international law as well as, in some cases, relevant domestic law.

BITs also provide procedural rights that permit the enforcement of the substantive rights. Generally, two different types of parties can bring claims related to an investment treaty. First, Sovereigns can bring claims where a dispute arises about the interpretation or application of the treaty. This typically requires Sovereigns to settle disputes diplomatically and, as a last resort, through arbitration. Sovereigns infrequently utilize this option, perhaps in part because little difference exists between this option and the traditional method of espousing investment-related claims before the International Court of Justice. Second, investors can directly bring a claim against a Sovereign for violation of a treaty, functioning in a manner similar to private attorneys general in the protection of the public interest.

Investors now regularly bring investment claims, in part because this direct action lets investors choose where they will bring their claims. In what amounts to a sophisticated choice of forum clause, some treaties require investors to choose between litigating their treaty claims in national courts and arbitrating their investment claims before an arbitral panel in a neutral forum, such as the International Centre for Settlement of Investment Disputes (ICSID), the International Chamber of Commerce (ICC) or an *ad hoc* tribunal organized under the UNCITRAL rules. Other treaties require investors to arbitrate their claims, but let the investors choose the arbitral body that will administer the dispute.

Investors have overwhelmingly accepted Sovereigns' standing offers to arbitrate and have brought their claims before arbitral tribunals, which provide a neutral forum for resolving disputes against a Sovereign and render awards with streamlined enforcement mechanisms. The investor begins the process by submitting the requisite notice and request for arbitration. The investor and the Sovereign each select one arbitrator. Typically, the party-appointed arbitrators then together appoint a third arbitrator as a Chair. The claim resolution procedures then commence in earnest. The parties gather their evidence and make arguments in private; and the tribunal renders an award that is enforceable worldwide.

William W. Burke-White, *The Argentine Financial Crisis: State Liability under BITS and the Legitimacy of the ICSID System*

3 Asian J. WTO & Int'l Health L. & Pol'y
200–202; 202–210; 216–220 (2008)

More than forty of the cases presently pending before ICSID have been brought against the Republic of Argentina and asserted that the Argentine government's response to the catastrophic financial crisis that hit that country in late 2001 and 2002 impaired investor rights secured under a number of Argentina's BITs. These cases are of extraordinary importance, not just because of the immense financial liability to which they expose Argentina, but also because, in response, Argentina has invoked a broad set of legal arguments about the rights of states to craft policy responses to extraordinary situations such as a massive financial collapse. Argentina has asserted two separate arguments that go to the heart of the sovereign prerogative of states to develop fundamental policies to address exceptional circumstances, one based on treaty law and the other based on customary international law. Argentina's treaty law argument invokes the non-precluded measures (NPM) provisions of Argentina's BITs that exempt certain actions taken by states in response to extraordinary circumstances from the substantive protections of the treaties. Argentina's customary international law argument has asserted that the doctrine of necessity precludes the wrongfulness of Argentina's actions in response to the crisis. These arbitrations thus test both the limits of state freedom of action and investor protections under the BIT regime in exceptional circumstances.

The resulting jurisprudence of the ICSID Tribunals in four cases against Argentina decided by early 2008 is deeply problematic, due in part to poor legal reasoning and questionable treaty interpretation and, in part, to the contradictory holdings in the awards issued to date. In fact, three of the four Tribunals have held Argentina fully responsible for harms to investors notwithstanding the extreme financial crisis it faced, whereas the remaining Tribunal absolved Argentina of much of its responsibility for those acts. This article asserts that the three ICSID Tribunals that have held Argentina liable failed to fully recognize the treaty-based exceptions provided for in the NPM clauses of Argentina's BITs and have interpreted the customary law doctrine of necessity extremely narrowly—so narrowly as to make it essentially unavailable to any state. Particularly when taken in light of the Decision of the Annulment Committee in *CMS* which rejected the legal reasoning of the arbitral tribunal in that case but failed to overturn the substantive outcome of the Tribunal's award, this problematic jurisprudence presents a serious challenge to the legitimacy of the BIT regime and the ICSID system more generally. While scholars have long noted a legitimacy deficit in investor-state arbitration and predicted a crisis in the system, the Argentine cases may well be precipitating that crisis both because these cases touch on the most fundamental policy choices of states and because, for the first time, a *CMS* Annulment Committee appears to be catalyzing a rethinking of investor-state arbitration more generally through its own jurisprudence.

The Argentine Financial Crisis and the Government's Response

In the last weeks of 2001, Argentina experienced a financial collapse of catastrophic proportions. In one day alone, the Argentine peso lost 40% of its value. As the peso collapsed, a run on banks followed. According to *The Economist*, throughout the collapse, "income per person in dollar terms ... shrunk from around $7,000 to just $3,500" and "[u]nemployment [rose] to perhaps 25%." This economic chaos meant that, by late 2002, over half the Argentine population was living below the poverty line. The crisis soon spread from the economic to the political sphere. In December 2001, one day of riots left 30 civilians dead and led to the resignation of President Fernando de la Rua and the collapse of the government. A "tragicomic spectacle of a succession of five presidents taking office over a mere ten days" followed.

In response to the crisis, which has been likened to the Great Depression of the 1930s in the United States, Argentina adopted a number of measures to stabilize the economy and restore political confidence. Among these efforts was a significant devaluation of the peso through the termination of the currency board which had pegged the peso to the U.S. dollar, the pesofication of all financial obligations, and the effective freezing of all bank accounts through a series of measures known collectively as the *Corralito*.

Though these measures offered a long-term prospect of restored economic confidence and stability, they also imposed immediate and painful costs on all participants in the Argentine economy, including foreign investors. While Argentine citizens had little legal recourse, many foreign investors who were harmed by Argentina's response to the crisis sought legal protection under the regime of BITs, which Argentina had entered into during the 1980s and 1990s. Such treaties offered investors guarantees including the internationalization of contractual breaches, national treatment, and most-favored-nation protections. In addition, these treaties often provided investors the possibility of direct investor-state arbitration before the ICSID.

For investors harmed by Argentina's response to the economic crisis, the possibility of direct arbitration against the Argentine government for breaches of BITs offered a potentially promising means to recoup losses suffered during the crisis. Claims framed as a violation of a BIT could be brought directly against Argentina through ICSID. Only limited means are available to challenge ICSID awards and such awards are generally perceived as enforceable in national courts. Not surprisingly, then, Argentina has become subject to no fewer than forty-three ICSID arbitrations brought by investors who assert that Argentina's response to the crisis harmed investments protected by various BITs. Argentina's potential liability from these cases alone could be greater than eight billion U.S. dollars, more than the entire financial reserves of the Argentine government in 2002. Some have speculated that the total value of potential claims against Argentina could reach eighty billion U.S. dollars.

Argentina's Legal Arguments for Policy Flexibility in Response to an Economic Crisis

In response to this onslaught of ICSID arbitrations, Argentina has, not surprisingly, denied that its actions in fact caused the harms asserted by investors. Argentina's legal approach has also gone considerably further, asserting two broad arguments which raise deeper structural questions about the rights of states to respond to extraordinary situations such as a massive financial crisis. Specifically, Argentina has invoked the NPM clauses of its BITs and has asserted that the state of necessity in customary international law precludes the wrongfulness of its actions. These arguments suggest, first, as a matter of treaty law and, second, as a matter of customary law, that states in circumstances such as that which Argentina faced in 2001 and 2002 have a legal right to take actions that could harm investors and that would in ordinary circumstances violate BIT obligations. In an ever more globalized world in which exceptional circumstances such as financial crises, terrorist threats, and public health emergencies—are all too common, the ability of states to craft viable policy responses becomes ever more critical. In that context, the Argentine ICSID cases test the extent of state freedom to craft critical policy choices and the reach of investor protection under BITs and customary law in the face of exceptional, but far from uncommon, emergencies.

Argentina's first legal response has been to invoke a long-dormant treaty clause in the BITs under which investors brought their claims against Argentina and that appeared perfectly tailored to deal with just such a situation. Argentina's BITs with the United States, Germany, and the Belgian-Luxembourg Economic Union (BLEU) each contain an NPM provision that limits the applicability of investor protections under the BIT in exceptional circumstances. These NPM clauses allow states to take actions otherwise inconsistent with the treaty when, for example, the actions are necessary for the protection of essential security, the maintenance of public order, or to respond to a public health emergency. NPM provisions effectively "permit host-state impairment of covered investment" and, in turn, weaken the BIT "as an instrument for regulating host-state governments." As long as the host-state's actions are taken in pursuit of one of the permissible objectives specified in the NPM clause, acts otherwise prohibited by the treaty do not constitute breaches of the treaty and states should face no liability under the BIT. The lawyers in Argentina's *Procuración del Tesoro de la Nación* have argued that the economic collapse of 2001–2002 triggered the NPM clauses of many of its BITs and thereby relieved the state of liability and any duty to compensate investors.

A few examples of NPM clauses offer an overview of their form and legal implications for state freedom of action in response to extraordinary crises such as the Argentine financial collapse. The first U.S. BIT, signed with Panama in 1982, stipulates in Article X that "[t]his treaty shall not preclude the application by either Party of any and all measures necessary for the maintenance of public order, the fulfillment of its obligations with respect to the maintenance or restoration of international peace and security, or the protection of its own essential security interests." Over the years, the United States has developed new versions of its Model BIT and, hence, variations in the form and structure of the NPM clause have appeared over time. One of the more notable modifications occurred in the late 1990s when the United States clarified its position on the self-judging nature of the NPM clauses in its BITs by including explicit language to that effect, now stating that a party was not precluded from taking any measures that "it considers necessary" for the protection of the stated permissible objectives. The NPM clause in the U.S.-Argentina BIT, drafted before this clarification of the self-judging nature of the treaty, provides: "[t]his treaty shall not preclude the application by either Party of any and all measures necessary for the maintenance of public order, the fulfillment of its obligations with respect to the maintenance or restoration of international peace and security, or the protection of its own essential security interests."

NPM clauses, such as that found in the U.S.-Argentina BIT, contain three basic elements. First, they provide for a nexus requirement. NPM clauses require that measures taken by a state that would otherwise deviate from a treaty obligation must be sufficiently related to the permissible objectives specified in the clause. This relationship is termed the "nexus requirement." One widely used phrasing of the nexus requirement found, for example, in the U.S.-Argentina BIT, requires that for measures to be covered by the clause they have to be "necessary" for the attainment of one of the specified permissible objectives. Second, NPM clauses specify their scope of applicability, in that they either apply to an entire BIT or can be written in a more limited form so that they apply only to a subset of the treaty's substantive provisions. The NPM clauses in U.S. BITs provide that "*[t]his Treaty* shall not preclude" the application of the subsequently specified measures. As a result, the successful invocation of the NPM clause precludes the existence of a violation with respect to any and all substantive treaty provisions. In contrast, NPM clauses of a more limited scope, such as those found in German BITs, apply only to certain substantive clauses of the BIT, for example the guarantee of no "treatment less favourable." Finally, NPM clauses establish a list of permissible objectives, toward which a state's actions must be directed if they are to be covered by the exception provided for by the NPM clause. Permissible objectives in BIT NPM clauses include security, international peace and security, public order, public health, and public morality, among others. The U.S.-Argentina BIT, for example, specifies three permissible objectives: essential security, public order, and international peace and security.

Despite the fact that NPM clauses are, in fact, relatively widespread in BIT agreements and occur in most, if not all, BITs of the U.S., Germany, India, Canada and the BLEU, the Argentine cases present the first test of such cases in investor-state arbitration. In each of the cases arising under the U.S.-Argentina BIT, Argentina has argued that its actions in response to the financial crisis of 2001–2002 were justified as measures necessary to protect essential security and public order and that, because those actions fell within the provisions of the NPM clause, they did not violate the substantive protections accorded investors under the U.S.-Argentina BIT. As a result, Argentina has claimed that no internationally wrongful acts were committed, and no state liability should attach.

In arguing that the NPM clause of the U.S.-Argentina BIT precludes Argentina's liability under the treaty, Argentina has asserted that the NPM clause should be interpreted as self-judging. Although the U.S.-Argentina BIT did not include expressly self-judging terms such as *which it considers necessary*, found in later U.S. BITs, Argentina has relied on a mutual understanding of the term evidenced in the treaty's context and *travaux preparatoires* from a consistent U.S. practice that such NPM clauses are understood as self-judging. In the alternative, Argentina has asserted that, even if the NPM clause in the U.S.-Argentina BIT is not found to be self-judging, the terms of the clause were satisfied by the situation in Argentina in late 2001 and 2002.

In addition to the treaty-based defense provided by the NPM clauses in its BITs, Argentina has also invoked the doctrine of necessity in customary international law to preclude liability for harms to investors. The customary defense of necessity provides that a state may not be liable for actions taken to "safeguard an essential interest against a grave and imminent peril." According to the International Law Commission (ILC) Draft Articles on the Responsibility of States for Internationally Wrongful Acts (Draft Articles):

> 1. Necessity may not be invoked by a State as a ground for precluding the wrongfulness of an act not in conformity with an international obligation of that State unless the act:
>
> (*a*) Is the only way for the State to safeguard an essential interest against a grave and imminent peril; and
>
> (*b*) Does not seriously impair an essential interest of the State or States towards which the obligation exists, or of the international community as a whole.
>
> 2. In any case, necessity may not be invoked by a State as a ground for precluding wrongfulness if:
>
> (*a*) The international obligation in question excludes the possibility of invoking necessity; or
>
> (*b*) The State has contributed to the situation of necessity.

A successful invocation of the necessity defense precludes the wrongfulness of a state's actions and thereby allows the state to possibly avoid both responsibility and liability. As the Draft Articles explain, the defense of necessity is a secondary rule of customary international law that governs "the circumstances in which the wrongfulness of conduct under international law may be precluded." Argentina has argued that the financial crisis of 2001 and 2002 impaired the country's essential interests and that the various legislative measures Argentina took in response thereto were the only available response to that crisis. As a result, Argentina has asserted that the criteria for customary law defense of necessity were met, precluding the wrongfulness of its actions independently from its argument with respect to the treaty based NPM exception.

Argentina's plea of necessity under customary law represents the first modern necessity claim in investor-state arbitration. While the International Court of Justice (ICJ) recognized the validity of the necessity defense in *Gabčíkovo-Nagymaros Projects*, the Court found the defense inapplicable in the case as Hungary was deemed to have other means available to address the environmental threats to its essential interests. In its submissions to ICSID, Argentina has also relied on a number of earlier cases before arbitral tribunals and the Permanent Court of International Justice (PCIJ), in which necessity was claimed on the basis of a state's financial problems and in which tribunals applied a more lenient standard than did the ICJ in *Gabčíkovo-Nagymaros Projects*, including *Société Commerciale de Belgique* and *Serbian Loans*.

The four arbitrations against Argentina decided thus far and the remaining claims still pending provide a critical test of both the interpretation and applicability of NPM clauses and the availability of the customary law defense of necessity in response to a major economic crisis. In so doing, these cases test the flexibility available to states to craft policy responses to emergencies and the scope of investor protections in such circumstances.

The Jurisprudence of the ICSID Tribunals

The four awards handed down in the Argentine cases as of early 2008 consider both the NPM exception and the necessity defense advanced by Argentina and reach contradictory and, at times, legally questionable conclusions. Whereas the Tribunals in *CMS, Enron* and *Sempra* found both the NPM clause and the necessity defense inapplicable, the Tribunal in *LG&E* found the NPM clause properly invoked and the necessity defense potentially applicable to Argentina.

Significantly, however, both the jurisprudence and legal reasoning of these ICSID Tribunals is often problematic. Not only do these Tribunals essentially ignore the treaty-based NPM exception and restrict the necessity defense, the findings of at least three of the Tribunals appear to overlook the basic bargain between investor protection and state freedom of action inherent in a BIT and, thereby, limit the state's ability to respond to exceptional situations, such as financial crises, in ways that that may threaten the long-term willingness of states to participate in investor-state arbitration and, perhaps, the legitimacy of that system itself....

The ICSID Tribunals and the Customary Defense of Necessity

In addition to asserting the exception to the substantive protections of the BIT provided for by the NPM clause, Argentina has also invoked the separate defense of necessity under customary international law in each of the ICSID arbitrations against it. Despite the fact that the four Tribunals that have issued awards in the Argentine cases have improperly conflated the treaty based NPM clause with the customary law defense of necessity, each Tribunal does offer an opinion on the applicability of the necessity defense to the Argentine financial crisis. Although the *LG&E* Tribunal found that the necessity defense might be available to Argentina, the *CMS, Enron* and *Sempra* Tribunals all held the necessity defense inapplicable and the wrongfulness of Argentina's actions not precluded. All four Tribunals accept the ILC Draft Articles as the definitive interpretation of the necessity defense in customary law and apply the criteria specified in the Draft Articles to determine the applicability of the necessity defense. While the *CMS, Enron* and *Sempra* Tribunals suggest somewhat different standards for the invocation of necessity under customary law, all three offer such narrow interpretations of necessity so as to make the defense essentially unavailable to a state attempting to devise a policy response to a severe crisis or other emergency.

As an initial matter, the *CMS*, *Enron*, and *Sempra* Tribunals find that the economic crisis, which befell Argentina, was not of a sufficient magnitude to threaten Argentina's essential interests and, thereby, open the door to a necessity defense. The *CMS* Tribunal, for example, notes that: "[t]he Tribunal is convinced that the crisis was indeed severe.... However, neither could it be held that wrongfulness should be precluded as a matter of course under the circumstances." Similarly, while acknowledging that Argentina faced a severe crisis, the *Enron* Tribunal opines that "the argument that such a situation compromised the very existence of the State and its independence so as to qualify as involving an essential interest of the State is not convincing." In contrast, the *LG&E* Tribunal found that the financial crisis in Argentina was sufficient to imperil an essential interest and, thereby, open the door to the necessity defense: "[a]s evidence demonstrates, economic, financial or those interests related to the protection of the State against any danger seriously compromising its internal or external situation, are also considered essential interests."

A second issue considered by all four Tribunals arises from article 25(1)(a) of the Draft Articles, according to which the defense of necessity is only available if the actions taken by the state were "the only way for the State to safeguard an essential interest against a grave and imminent peril." As the ILC's commentaries to the Draft Articles provide: "[t]he plea is excluded if there are other (otherwise lawful) means available, even if they may be more costly or less convenient." The key question facing the four Tribunals in this regard was how to interpret the no other available means requirement. Would it be sufficient to invalidate the plea of necessity if, for example, there were some other policy choices open to Argentina or would it have to be shown that there was an equally effective policy response open to Argentina that would not have breached the substantive protections of the BIT? At its core, that is a question of how much deference to give the Argentine government's determination that its policy choice was the only or best available response to the crisis.

Again, the *CMS*, *Enron* and *Sempra* Tribunals offer extremely narrow interpretations of the necessity defense, essentially second-guessing Argentina's policy choices and suggesting that, because some other means was available to Argentina to respond to the crisis, the necessity defense was legally unavailable. The *CMS* Tribunal, for example, finds that the ILC's comment "that the plea of necessity is 'excluded if there are other (otherwise lawful) means available, even if they may be more costly or less convenient,' is persuasive in assisting this Tribunal in concluding that the measures adopted were not the only steps available. Similarly, the *Enron* Tribunal notes: "[a] rather sad world comparative experience in the handling of economic crises, shows that there are always many approaches to address and correct such critical events, and it is difficult to justify that none of them were available in the Argentine case." The *CMS*, *Enron* and *Sempra* Tribunals all fail to suggest alternative courses of action Argentina could have followed or to consider the counterfactual argument of the results such alternative policies might have entailed for both the state and investors. The three Tribunals simply assert that if any alternative policy choice is available—regardless of its likely effectiveness—the necessity defense is unavailable. Since states always face a range of policy choices in response to any issue, whichever policy a state chooses is, by definition, not the only available response to the crisis. The three Tribunals thus give no deference whatsoever to Argentina's policy choices and, essentially, vitiate the necessity defense as a matter of law.

In contrast, the *LG&E* Tribunal gives considerable deference to Argentina's own policy choices in response to the crisis, recognizing that an *ad hoc* arbitral tribunal is poorly positioned to second-guess the policies of the government. The *LG&E* Tribunal observes: In this circumstance, an economic recovery package was the only means to respond to the crisis. Although there may have been a number of ways to draft the economic recovery plan, the evidence before the Tribunal demonstrates that an across-the-board response was necessary, and the tariffs on public utilities had to be addressed.

The *LG&E* Tribunal does not ask if a slightly different recovery package could have been employed, but merely determines that some across-the-board recovery package was needed. It pays deference to Argentina's determination that the specific policies adopted by the country were the most appropriate in the circumstances and finds that the criteria for invocation of the necessity defense in customary law were satisfied. This approach is far more appropriate in that it leaves open the necessity defense as long as some other clearly available and less restrictive policy alternative would not have provided an obviously adequate response to the crisis with less harm to the interests of investors.

The final issue with respect to the invocation of the necessity defense in customary law considered by all four Tribunals is whether Argentina contributed to the situation of necessity. The four Tribunals ask what level of contribution by a state to a crisis would be necessary to render the necessity defense inapplicable. In *Gabčíkovo-Nagymoros Projects*, for example, the ICJ found the plea of necessity inapplicable because Hungary had "helped, by act or omission to bring" into being the situation of necessity. According to the ILC's commentaries, "the contribution to the situation of necessity must be sufficiently substantial and not merely incidental or peripheral."

The *CMS*, *Enron*, and *Sempra* Tribunals all found that any contribution by Argentina whatsoever, including long range economic planning, was sufficient to invalidate the plea of necessity. In the words of the *Enron* Tribunal: Although each party claims that the factors precipitating the crisis were either endogenous or exogenous, the truth seems to be somewhere in between with both kind of factors having intervened.... This means that to an extent there has been a substantial contribution of the State to the situation of necessity and that it cannot be claimed that the burden falls entirely on exogenous factors.

Similarly, the *CMS* Tribunal notes: The crisis was not of the making of one particular administration and found its roots in the earlier crisis of the 1980s and evolving governmental policies of the 1990s that reached a zenith in 2002 and thereafter. Therefore, the Tribunal observes that government policies and their shortcomings significantly contributed to the crisis and the emergency and while exogenous factors did fuel additional difficulties, they do not exempt the Respondent from its responsibility in the matter.

As a result, these three Tribunals determined that the necessity defense was unavailable to Argentina because the state had contributed to the crisis.

Again, the *LG&E* Tribunal took a very different approach to the level of contribution necessary to exclude the plea of necessity, finding that even if Argentina had contributed to the underlying economic crisis, that contribution was neither significant nor intentional. In this respect, the *LG&E* Tribunal found that "in the first place, Claimants have not proved that Argentina has contributed to cause the severe crisis faced by the country; secondly, the attitude adopted by the Argentine Government has shown a desire to slow down by all the means available the severity of the crisis." The *LG&E* Tribunal thus left the plea of necessity open to Argentina.

With respect to the applicability of the necessity defense, there is a clear split in the jurisprudence of the ICSID Tribunals to date. While the *CMS*, *Enron*, and *Sempra* Tribunals significantly limit the availability of the necessity defense and find it unavailable to Argentina, the *LG&E* Tribunal offers a far more deferential analysis of the state's invocation of necessity and finds the defense to apply in the case of the Argentine financial crisis. The approach taken by the majority of the tribunals thus far is, again, problematic because the analysis used by these three Tribunals essentially renders the necessity defense a legal nullity as a state will, almost without exception, have contributed at least in some indirect way to whatever emergency it may face and such a state will also, in almost every circumstance, have more than one possible policy response to such a situation. If this majority line of jurisprudence is followed, a state responding to any crisis, with the possible exception of a truly unforeseeable natural disaster, despite the technical availability of the necessity defense, will be unable as a matter of law to successfully invoke the defense and liability will attach to whatever policy the state may choose to respond to the crisis. Again, as with the Tribunals' flawed interpretation of the NPM clause, the result may be to chill states' willingness to enter into BIT obligations or to subject themselves to ICSID jurisdiction.

Notes & Questions

1. What sources of law do these arbitral panels rely on? Note the use of language and analysis from both bilateral investment treaties and the GATT.
2. What attention is paid to precedent? Do the different tribunals rely on the same or similar legal sources or not? How do the different tribunals formulate their findings on the facts?
3. With which opinions and decisions do you agree? Why?
4. What is the effect of these different rulings on how "necessity" should be construed in subsequent cases?
5. Argentina's economic struggles continue. Since 2000, there have been other instances of the Argentine government's seizing foreign investment entities (e.g., Spanish investment in the natural gas industry) or failing to share contractually agreed-to profits. At what point does an economic emergency end? The COVID-19 pandemic uprooted much of the world economy, and there are now pending many international arbitrations (and formal litigation proceedings) on whether the pandemic justified *force majeure* or *necessity* relief from both contractual (private) and treaty (investment and trade) obligations. When there is a national or worldwide crisis, do you think it is better to have multiple arbitral or mediational venues for resolution, or should there be a "world court" deciding these issues for uniformity and precedential value?

B. Adjudication under GATT and the World Trade Organization

We now turn to the hybrid processes created to handle trade versus foreign investment. As described earlier in the text, the GATT process had elements of both negotiation and adjudication. Only member states had standing and could negotiate with other member states or bring cases to the GATT panels (a more adjudicatory process). However, as described below, these panel decisions could be vetoed by the very state against which the decision was rendered, reverting this back to a negotiation regime. In the face of this lack of enforcement, states created the World Trade Organization, with a clear adjudicatory process. Yet there have still been challenges. The articles below cover two well-known cases: one about tuna and dolphins (where the United States tried to protect dolphins from tuna fishers in Mexico) and the other about the import of bananas to the European Union (a multiyear, multi-regime process involving the EU's favoring of imports from certain banana-producing countries at the expense of others).

Diana Hurwitz, *Fishing for Compromises through NAFTA and Environmental Dispute-Settlement: The Tuna-Dolphin Controversy*

35 Nat. Resources J. 502–504; 507–509 (1995)

Introduction

Market liberalization has been pursued by free traders primarily through the General Agreement on Tariffs and Trade (GATT), which attempts to diminish protectionist trade barriers throughout the world. The tuna-dolphin conflict peaked in the GATT international trade dispute resolution panel in 1991. However, despite a formal panel ruling on this issue, the distinction between environmental protection laws and protectionist trade barriers is still blurred....

Thus, understanding the tuna-dolphin conflict and finally resolving this ongoing controversy could facilitate the creation of a framework for the eventual harmonization of trade and environment issues. However, the tuna-dolphin conflict is a complicated matter with a long history of disagreement.

On September 7, 1990, the U.S. government implemented an import embargo on tuna caught by the Mexican tuna-fishing fleet. According to this court order, the Mexican vessels were not meeting the dolphin-mortality quotas established by the U.S. Marine Mammal Protection Act of 1972, as amended. Imports of tuna from Panama, Ecuador, Venezuela, and Vanuatu were also terminated. Sixty days after the original embargoes, the U.S. government followed with a secondary ban on imports of tuna from 20 nations that import Mexican tuna as a raw material, package it, and export it to the United States. As a result of these embargoes, Mexico has been effectively shut out of one of the largest tuna markets in the world.

The United States and Mexico share a 2,000-mile border over which thousands of people and products flow daily. This stretch of land is the only area of the world in which an advanced industrial country shares an extensive border with a less developed country. Given the cultural and historical differences between these two countries, not to mention clear asymmetries of power, the possibilities for conflict are great. However, the United States and Mexico also share strong and increasing environmental, social, and political ties. Most notably, the economies of these two nations and Canada have recently been cemented together by the North American Free Trade Agreement (NAFTA), which took effect on January 1, 1994. This agreement created the largest trading block in the world—with a $6 trillion market.

Thus, the tuna-dolphin controversy has created animosity between the United States and Mexico at a time when the increasing interdependence of these bordering nations necessitates multilateral collaboration on mutually important policy issues. Beyond its bilateral importance:

> rooted in the tuna-dolphin controversy are the major philosophical and environmental questions of the day. Preservation versus management; the rights of

human beings versus the rights of other creatures; the needs of many versus the demands of the few; feeding the hungry versus conserving natural resources; and one nation's power position versus another's attempts to rise from poverty.

A review of the history of this conflict and the different perspectives on this issue reveals that traditional dispute-settlement procedures have been inadequate in resolving this disagreement and therefore must be improved. In particular, the GATT conflict resolution panel has failed to provide an adequate solution. The embargoes and the animosity among the various parties in this conflict act as a thorn in the side of policy makers seeking collaboration today. We must look elsewhere for a remedy.

NAFTA provides two potential avenues for solving this dilemma: a framework for dispute-settlement and a trilateral Commission on Environmental Cooperation (CEC). However, the wording of the Supplemental Agreements to NAFTA creates substantial obstacles to bringing the tuna-dolphin issue to the dispute resolution panel. Thus, by bringing together the various players in international disputes under the cloak of a mutually agreed-upon commitment to environmental cooperation, the CEC could provide the better means for resolution of the tuna-dolphin conflict.

Economic integration among countries at divergent levels of economic and political development inevitably produces the potential for conflict on a variety of issues. However, a solution that can effectively bring an end to the unilateral U.S. embargoes against Mexico while also diminishing Mexican dolphin-mortality rates to zero is both vitally necessary and within our reach. If properly utilized, NAFTA can act as a major stepping-stone in institutionalizing procedures for the resolution of current trade and environmental disputes. Moreover, in addition to ending the bilateral tuna-dolphin conflict, NAFTA can also act as a model for structuring future multilateral trade agreements in an environmentally sustainable manner.

A Recent History of the Tuna-Dolphin Controversy

The GATT Panel Decision

On January 25, 1991, the Mexican government challenged the legality of the MMPA through the GATT dispute resolution panel. GATT serves as the primary international trade agreement in existence today, in which both the United States (1948) and Mexico (1986) are members. While its primary focus is on facilitating trade liberalization among nations, the GATT also contains a dispute-settlement panel to resolve international trade disagreements.

On August 16, 1991, the GATT panel ruled in favor of Mexico, while specifically allowing the United States to use voluntary labeling for "dolphin-friendly" tuna, as long as it was applied evenly to imports and American-caught tuna. "Dolphin-safe" or "dolphin-friendly" tuna, as defined by the U.S. Dolphin Protection Consumer Information Act, includes any tuna not harvested by using purse seine nets and tuna not caught with high-seas drift nets.

The GATT panel's decision rested on many criteria, but the two most controversial and fundamental principles invoked were: Imported products must be treated in a manner that is no less favorable than that of domestic products, and the method of production or "production process" cannot be taken into account in determining equal treatment under GATT regulations. In addition, subsections (b) and (g) of Article XX of GATT were ruled not to apply to this situation, which effectively meant that the protection of animal life or the conservation of natural resources are justifiable trade barriers only when they occur within a state's own borders.

Despite this favorable outcome, former President Salinas de Gortari of Mexico did not pursue the implementation of the GATT ruling and, to date, no further GATT action has been taken on this decision. It appears that Salinas did not want environmental issues, such as the tuna-dolphin panel ruling, obstructing the prospect of a \$6 trillion North American market through NAFTA. As Juanita Darling, a reporter for the *Los Angeles Times,* wrote at the time, "Salinas sees a trade pact as his best weapon for fighting Mexico's nagging inflation rate, widespread unemployment, poverty, and mounting trade imbalance." Given the amount of political collateral invested in NAFTA by the Mexicans, failure to secure this agreement would have significantly damaged Salinas' personal reputation, not to mention the harsh repercussions that a "no-NAFTA" outcome would have had for the Institutional Revolutionary Party (PRI) presidential candidate in the 1994 election. Thus, while Salinas might have preferred U.S. markets to be opened to Mexican tuna, the adverse consequences of forcing the United States to retract the embargoes might not have been worth the fight.

To lessen tension after the GATT ruling, Salinas unveiled a ten-point program on September 24, 1991, specifically designed to protect dolphins. This program represented an advance in two respects. First, international inspectors would be present on every tuna vessel of the Mexican fleet, as contrasted with previous regulations allowing them on only one-third of the boats. In addition, Salinas set aside \$1 million for research into dolphin-safe fishing practices. While there have been no high technology breakthroughs in stopping dolphin deaths from tuna-fishing since the drafting of this proposal, the mere presence of inspectors has undoubtedly contributed to the decreasing Mexican dolphin-mortality rates by encouraging Mexican fisherman to be more careful about killing dolphins.

The U.S. Congress followed these Mexican efforts by wielding a major blow to any hopes that the tuna embargoes might soon be lifted. To further protect the dolphins, on October 8, 1992, Congress passed the International Dolphin Conservation Act, which amended the MMPA. This unilateral law strengthened regulations on both domestic and foreign tuna fleets that want to sell tuna in the United States. Under this law, dolphin kills by U.S. fleets were not to exceed 800 total for the period January 1, 1993 to March 1, 1994, while the quota thereafter was to be zero. Regarding foreign fleets, this legislation authorized the Secretary of State to negotiate a global moratorium on the setting of tuna nets on dolphins:

> [The law] imposes strict non-discretionary embargoes and sanctions against countries failing to abide by the global moratorium. These will include fish

product sanctions that, for example, could reach $100 million per year if Mexico pledges to enact a moratorium, but then fails to abide by its pledge.

As of May 1994, Mexico had not pledged to participate in this global moratorium.

Given the sharp drop in the number of dolphin deaths caused by Mexican tuna harvesters over the last decade, it is likely that the quota-based embargoes on Mexican tuna would have been lifted. However, the International Dolphin Conservation Act squelches the possibility of ending the bans. On March 1, 1994, the moratorium-based embargoes of Mexican tuna went into effect. Thus, it appears that the conflict and animosity surrounding the tuna-dolphin controversy will continue until an adequate dispute resolution apparatus is established and implemented.

Notes & Questions

1. What actually ended up happening?

   P.S. The report was never adopted.

   Under the present WTO system, if WTO members (meeting as the Dispute Settlement Body) do not by consensus reject a panel report after 60 days, it is automatically accepted ("adopted"). That was not the case under the old GATT. Mexico decided not to pursue the case and the panel report was never adopted even though some of the "intermediary" countries pressed for its adoption. Mexico and the United States held their own bilateral consultations aimed at reaching an agreement outside GATT.

   In 1992, the European Union lodged its own complaint. This led to a second panel report circulated to GATT members in mid-1994. The report upheld some of the findings of the first panel and modified others. Although the European Union and other countries pressed for the report to be adopted, the United States told a series of meetings of the GATT Council and the final meeting of GATT contracting parties (i.e. members) that it had not had time to complete its studies of the report. There was therefore no consensus to adopt the report, a requirement under the old GATT system.

   Mexico etc. versus U.S.: "Tuna-Dolphin," WTO, https://www.wto.org/english/tratop_e/envir_e/edis04_e.htm (last viewed June 2, 2024).

2. How should countries balance their desires for national priorities (e.g., protecting dolphins) at the expense of free trade? Is a dispute resolution process an appropriate place to weigh these priorities? Consider also the Argentina cases, where the arbitral panels weighed issues of national economic policy and security against investor protections.

Recall the discussion of international adjudication from Andrea K. Schneider's article earlier in the chapter. Under the WTO (an example of a system of international adjudication), any country can make a complaint about violations of free trade. The *Bananas* case is one of the most complicated examples of the WTO's trying to regulate the EU's restrictions on bananas.

The bananas dispute centers around the EU's regulatory regime for imported bananas, which was enacted in 1993 and which subjected the import of bananas to one of two two-tier tariff rate quotas depending on the country of origin. In February 1996, the United States, in addition to Ecuador, Guatemala, Honduras, and Mexico, filed a complaint against the EU's banana import regime. The countries argued that the regime violated several of the GATT 1994 Articles as well as the Agreement on Import Licensing Procedures, the Agreement on Agriculture, the General Agreement on Trade in Services (GATS), and the Agreement on Trade-Related Investment Measures. In May 1997, the WTO panel found that the regime "was discriminatory and as such was inconsistent with the GATT 1994, the WTO agreement on Import Licensing and the GATS." On appeal, the Appellate Body found additional violations. In January 1998, the European Commission announced a modified banana regime it purported was WTO-compatible.[3]

Simon A. B. Schropp & David Palmeter, *Commentary on the Appellate Body Report in EC-Bananas III (Article 21.5): Waiver-Thin, or Lock, Stock, and Metric Ton?*

9 World Trade Rev., Mar. 2010, at 7–8; 12–13; 53

Introduction

The trade dispute over the European Community's banana importation regime is one of the longest-standing cases in the history of the WTO. The fact-load of this case is mind-boggling, and through the years *Bananas* has left a long trail of panels, arbitrations, and procedural battles. The Appellate Body (AB) Report on the second compliance Panel under Article 21.5 of the Dispute Settlement Understanding (DSU) is the presently last stage in the *Bananas* saga.

The AB was summoned by the EC to assess substantial findings made by the compliance Panel under Articles II and XIII of the GATT, as well as a host of procedural issues. Sadly, for the researcher charged with commenting on this case (but fortunate for the practitioner), there is little scope for criticism against the findings of the AB. Nevertheless, the compliance proceedings in *Bananas III* offer some interesting general legal and economic aspects, for example on the legal nature of Panel suggestions, the economics of tariff quotas, and the relationship between Article 21.5 Panels and arbitrations under Article 22.6 of the DSU....

---

3. Eliza Patterson, *The US-EU Banana Dispute*, Am. Soc'y of Int'l Law (Feb. 27, 2001), https://www.asil.org/insights/volume/6/issue/4/us-eu-banana-dispute.

2.3 Arguments by the complainants and findings by the compliance Panel

Both Ecuador and the United States initiated Article 21.5 proceedings claiming continued WTO inconsistency of EC Regulation 1964/2005 and related measures (the Bananas Import Regime). Ecuador—for the second time—claimed that the EC had 'failed to implement the rulings and recommendations of the DSB in the original dispute and continues to be in breach of its obligations as a WTO Member'. In particular, Ecuador requested that the Panel find that the EC measures are inconsistent with: (i) GATT Article I, 'because the European Communities applies different and more favourable duties to bananas originating in ACP countries than those applied to bananas originating in Ecuador and most or all other WTO members'; (ii) GATT Article II, 'because the European Communities applies a tariff (currently E176/mt) on the import of bananas originating in Ecuador (and other WTO Members) that is above the EC bound rate of duty under Article II, which is E75/mt'; and (iii) GATT Articles XIII:1 and 2, 'because the European Communities continues to provide a tariff rate quota system reserved exclusively for bananas of ACP origin, while Ecuador is denied any share of the preferential quota, let alone the share to which it is entitled under Article XIII'.

The US also claimed that the EC had 'failed to implement the rulings and recommendations of the DSB in the original dispute and continues to be in breach of its obligations as a WTO Member'. Specifically, the United States requested that the Panel find that the EC measures are inconsistent with: (i) GATT Article I, 'because the European Communities applies a zero tariff rate to imports of bananas originating in ACP countries in a quantity up to 775,000 mt, but does not accord the same duty-free treatment to imports of bananas originating in all other WTO Members'; and (ii) GATT Articles XIII:1 and 2, 'because the European Communities reserves the 775,000 mt zero-duty tariff quota for imports of bananas originating in ACP countries and provides no access to this preferential tariff quota to imports of bananas originating in non-ACP substantial or non-substantial supplying countries'.

The compliance Panel rejected various procedural arguments and preliminary issues brought forth by the EC and found violations of GATT Articles I, II, and XIII. It recommended that the DSB request the EC to bring its inconsistent measures into conformity with its obligations under the GATT 1994.

Conclusion

At first glance, the Appellate Body Report in *Bananas III* (Article 21.5; Second Recourse) does not seem to be a case for the Guinness Book. The EC should not have appealed the Panel Report, and the AB did a good job upholding most of the Panel's findings. It is at second sight that the AB Report reveals its interesting facets. Practitioners may be interested in the role of estoppel in WTO litigation, the legal effect of Panel suggestions, the relevance of modalities papers as interpretative tools, and other legal aspects we discussed. Readers more interested in law and economics theory may find food for thought in our examination of the economics of tariff quotas and the inherently discriminatory nature of Article XIII: our assessment of temporary opt-outs in the WTO, or our discussion of the relevance of compliance proceedings for the damage calculation under Article 22.6 of the DSU.

Notes & Questions

1. Consider how many different processes were used to try to resolve this particular dispute? States engaged in direct negotiations, used arbitration panels, used adjudication panels, and utilized sanctions and retaliatory trade measures but were still unable to agree on a regime "fair" to all parties. Might there be disputes for which no process will work? (We will revisit this idea in Chapter 11.)
2. Under President Trump, the United States was highly critical of the WTO for failing to deal with China's alleged abuses of the international trade regime. While President Biden has spoken of the WTO more favorably, he has not counted on the WTO to resolve trade disputes. *See* James McBride & Anshu Siripurapu, *What's Next for the WTO?*, Council on Foreign Rels. (updated June 10, 2022), https://www.cfr.org/backgrounder/whats-next-wto. The *Bananas* dispute highlights some of the issues with the structure of the process. What reforms would you suggest to make the WTO more effective? Is this an issue of dispute resolution design (see Chapter 9) or the underlying legal regime?

Further Reading

Shahla Ali, Exploring Court Mediation Reform: Insights from Court Mediation Reform: Efficiency, Confidence and Perceptions of Justice (2018).

Comparative Dispute Resolution (Maria F. Moscati, Michael Palmer, & Marian Roberts eds., 2020).

Philip H. Gulliver, Disputes and Negotiations: A Cross-Cultural Perspective (1979).

Stuart Hampshire, Justice is Conflict (2000).

John Howard Jackson, The World Trading System: Law and Policy of International Economic Relations (1989).

Carrie Menkel-Meadow, *Are There Systemic Ethics Issues in Dispute System Design? And What We Should (Not) Do about It: Lessons from International and Domestic Fronts*, 14 Harv. Negot. L. Rev. 195–231 (2009).

Carrie Menkel-Meadow, *Regulation of Dispute Resolution in the United States of America: From the Formal to the Informal to the Semi-Formal*, *in* Regulating Dispute Resolution—ADR and Access to Justice at the Crossroads (Felix Steffek, Hannes Unberath, Hazel Genn & Carrie Menkel-Meadow eds., 2013).

Susan Podziba, Civic Fusion: Mediating Polarized Public Policy Disputes (2013).

THE PRINCIPLES OF SOCIAL ORDER: SELECTED ESSAYS OF LON L. FULLER (Kenneth Winston ed., 2002).

REGULATING DISPUTE RESOLUTION—ADR AND ACCESS TO JUSTICE AT THE CROSSROADS (Felix Steffek, Hannes Unberath, Hazel Genn & Carrie Menkel-Meadow eds, 2013).

Frank E.A. Sander & Stephen Goldberg, *Fitting the Forum to the Fuss: A User-Friendly Guide to Selecting an ADR Procedure*, 10 NEGOT. J. 49–68 (1994).

GREGORY SHAFFER, EMERGING POWERS AND THE WORLD TRADING SYSTEM: THE PAST AND FUTURE OF INTERNATIONAL ECONOMIC LAW (2021).

ALEC STONE-SWEET & FLORIAN GRISEL, THE EVOLUTION OF INTERNATIONAL ARBITRATION: JUDICIALIZATION, GOVERNANCE, LEGITIMACY (2017).

LAWRENCE E. SUSSKIND, SARAH MCKEARNAN, & JENNIFER THOMAS LARMER, THE CONSENSUS BUILDING HANDBOOK: A COMPREHENSIVE GUIDE TO REACHING AGREEMENT (2019).

Nancy A. Welsh & Andrea K. Schneider, *The Thoughtful Integration of Mediation into Bilateral Investment Treaty Arbitration*, 18 HARV. NEGOT. J. 71–144 (2013).

Chapter 8

Contexts and Examples of Hybrid Processes: Ombuds, Internal Organizational Dispute Resolution, Transitional and Restorative Justice, and Reparations

Now that you are more familiar with hybrid dispute resolution processes, we turn our attention to more specific examples in which individuals or groups have sought some form of hybrid dispute resolution or reparative justice. The first part of the chapter focuses on labor and employment rights and how individuals can pursue these rights in a variety of hybrid ways within international organizations. The second part of the chapter focuses on broader issues of human rights and post-conflict restorative redress for individuals and whole societies. We look at how international organizations and national governments have, through a mix of negotiation, mediation, and adjudication, developed particular dispute resolution processes to provide justice and reconciliation for internal conflicts, including civil war and atrocities carried out by governments on their own people. The fields of organizational and transitional justice are modern sites for hybridizing the basic forms of dispute resolution, often with broader goals such as compensation, apologies, the creation of new relationships, and new forms of both political and social, if not economic, orders. As new conflicts occur in our modern world, new adaptations of these processes are likely to be developed to provide even newer forms of reparative relief.

I. Ombuds (and Internal Dispute Resolution)

This first section on hybrid processes focuses on how international, regional, and even domestic organizations deal with internal complaints. These complaints are predictable in that every organization has disputes between employees and management. And, in fact, the field of dispute system design, which we discuss in the next chapter, stems from organizations' using best practices to create processes responsive to predictable, regular, and iterative disputes. In the following excerpts, we first look at the creation of an ombuds, someone who manages disputes while providing transparency and accountability throughout the organization, before turning to how national courts view the internal dispute resolution processes adopted by international organizations.

Carrie Menkel-Meadow, *Hybrid and Mixed Dispute Resolution Processes: Integrities of Process Pluralism*

in COMPARATIVE DISPUTE RESOLUTION 414–415
(Maria F. Moscati, Michael Palmer, & Marian Roberts eds., 2020)

Modern Innovations in Hybridized Dispute Resolution: Organizational, Governmental, Technological and International

Some modern innovations and adaptations of the *basic* dispute resolution processes are derived from older forms of dispute resolution, but now vary with context and culture. The Scandinavian institution and process of *Ombuds*, as a neutral investigator of complaints against governments and international organizations, like the United Nations and the World Bank, has evolved into several separate strains of governmental complaint handling and private organization dispute resolution. The Ombuds role is diverse and can vary from simple investigation of complaints against government agencies, public services (health, welfare benefits, human rights, and private (and in some countries, regulated) industry (airlines, energy, banking and finance) to counseling complainants, negotiating on their behalf and in many settings now, actually deciding and "resolving" claims of certain values.

In some countries, such as Germany, the UK, and Italy, Ombuds offices maintained either by the government or by a financed consortium of providers of services or products (energy, telecommunications, banking) are authorized to settle (usually with cash or apologies, less often with some kind of "injunctive" relief) complaints in what is close to an adjudicative model, without a formal court decision. The EU requires that all regulated industries provide some form of "ADR" making Ombuds services a common option. In Germany, some of the Ombuds are retired judges, both granting some legitimacy to the process and also preserving a more adjudicative model.

Many large and multinational corporations (e.g., Coca-Cola, United Technologies), public entities (e.g., the National Institutes of Health in the US), universities, and international organizations now also maintain internal Ombuds offices for resolution of employment and management disputes and grievances, preferring to keep conflict resolution "in the family" (and to avoid public litigation).

The Ombuds role is itself a hybrid and mixed one—offering investigation, counseling, negotiation, mediation, and adjudicative services depending on the particular remit of the office in different companies and legal systems. In theory, Ombuds are to be neutral and report only to the leader of the organization (or to consumer or governmental watchdog groups), they have developed their own codes of ethics in their international professional association, but they are still controversial in some settings for "internalizing" and privatizing disputes, except in those cases where Ombuds have some authority to report on systemic patterns of disputes, raising the possibility of more extensive remedial measures or legal reform (Sturm & Gadlin, 2007).

In the governmental arena, combinations of mediation, negotiation and facilitation have been used in the United States to facilitate public administrative regulation (negotiated rule-making) and policy formation in such areas as environmental regulation, worker safety, product, and drug safety, relations with indigenous groups and civil rights (Susskind et al. 1999 and Podziba 2013), with controversies about participation, transparency, and efficiency leading to more critical receptions of this process elsewhere, as in the UK (Bingham Center Report 2016). In the private sector, such combinations of processes have been used in highly intractable disputes (abortion, gun rights, animal rights, civil rights, police abuse) to at least stop violence, promote lawsuit settlement, and occasionally to reach accommodations of very disparate interests. The methodology of a private NGO, Public Conversations (now Essential Partners, www.whatisessential.org), in facilitating dialogue across differences (by exploring differences, commonalities, and points of "curiosity" in group meetings) has been very successful in some of these social and community conflicts, drawing on community organizing, social work, conflict resolution, and peace activism principles and practices.

As indicated above, many of the world's international and regional organizations, including the World Bank, UN, International Monetary Fund, International Red Cross, WTO, and European Union, operate in Washington, D.C., New York, Geneva, Brussels, Paris, and other major cities. These organizations are created by treaty (agreements with multiple nations) and are not generally governed by the laws of the nations in which they are located. As you might imagine, these organizations have conflicts and disputes themselves. These disputes may be internal (e.g., employment/labor disputes, policy disputes) or external, with their constituents or third-parties (e.g., UN peacekeeping forces, suppliers, vendors), or even with their beneficiaries (e.g., in environmental disputes where private investment or World Bank loans are used to "develop" property or resources at the expense of local communities). Many of these institutions have created their own internal dispute resolution bodies, for example, the World Bank's Inspection Panel and its Accountability Mechanism, which use a variety of dispute resolution processes to deal with complaints about World Bank-financed projects.[1] Most of these organizations use some form of ombuds or internal dispute resolution (IDR) mechanisms to handle complaints and issues from employees and some independent contractors.[2] The World Bank, for example, utilizes a "menu" of internal dispute resolution services which includes mediation, ombuds

1. *See Inspection Panel*, The World Bank, https://www.inspectionpanel.org/; *Accountability Mechanism*, The World Bank, https://www.worldbank.org/en/programs/accountability.

2. *See, e.g., Internal Justice Services*, The World Bank, https://www.worldbank.org/en/about/unit/internal-justice-services.

(counseling, advice, and informal resolution), an ethics office (for complaints about possible ethics violations and corruption in the workplace), peer counseling (maintained by a staff association), and a more formal adjudicative process (an Administrative Tribunal) for complaints regarding discrimination or retaliation. This menu was developed to better address cultural and legal system differences that exist in international and multicultural organizations as well as the absence of more formal legal rules and processes. Disgruntled World Bank employees who were unable to find full satisfaction of their disputes internally have attempted to lobby the US Congress to withhold US contributions to the World Bank until certain internal issues are dealt with (e.g., complaints about internal sexual harassment). This is yet another form of "alternative" dispute resolution—appeals to international funding sources. These efforts have not been successful thus far.

All of these international organizations, established as "supra-national" organizations without legal sovereign identity, claim to be legally immune from litigation. When they are sued in national courts for employment issues—or worse, for injuries, negligence, or even killings—these organizations claim that their internal processes are the sole form of recognized process for redress (as you will see in the cases below).

The World Bank Internal Justice Services

https://www.worldbank.org/en/about/unit/internal-justice-services

The Internal Justice Services (IJS) offers World Bank Group staff support ranging from counseling to formal review of concerns to preserve fairness in the workplace. IJS services are available to staff in addressing their workplace concerns.

IJS CORE SUPPORT SERVICES

The Respectful Workplace Advisors (RWA) Program consists of volunteer peers in Bank Group work units in Washington and in-country Offices. RWAs serve as an informal avenue of assistance to staff facing harassment, disrespectful behaviors, or other sources of stress at work. RWAs do not become directly involved in resolving the issues brought to them by colleagues. The RWA Program is overseen by the Ombuds Services office.

Ombuds Services is a confidential, impartial and informal service independent from the World Bank Group's formal management channels that facilitates the resolution of workplace issues. An Ombudsman helps staff analyze problems and assists in identifying options and can, only if requested by the visitor, become involved in trying to resolve issues. Ombuds Services also provides information to staff members on the Bank Group's policies and procedures. Additionally, Ombuds Services alerts management to systemic trends and issues and makes recommendations for change.

The Office of Mediation provides World Bank Group staff with processes for resolving workplace disputes, including mediation and group facilitation. In mediation, an impartial mediator helps parties better understand their issues, concerns, needs, and interests. The mediator also helps parties make decisions on how to resolve their matter. The mediation process is informal and confidential. When issues are settled through mediation, a memorandum of understanding sets out the specific agreements reached by the parties, and the parties' agreement is final and binding.

The peer review process is an independent review of managerial decisions, actions, or inactions affecting a Bank Group staff member by a panel of impartial volunteer staff members. The Peer Review panel considers whether the Bank Group's actions are consistent with the staff member's contract of employment and/or terms of appointment, including the pertinent Bank Group rules and policies. The Peer Review panel may recommend that the Bank Group award relief to the staff member and/or take other corrective measures.

Notes & Questions

1. Why is it in an organization's interest to create an ombuds office? How does the role of an ombuds, as described by the readings above, differ from other types of neutrals you have read about? Consider who pays the salary of the ombuds.
2. Why is an ombuds office considered a hybrid process? What are the different varieties of dispute resolution processes that an ombuds can utilize?

Case Study: Angelique Cleuseau

Angelique Cleuseau is an employee at the World Bank. She is a French national but has worked at the World Bank for over 15 years, both in its headquarters in Washington, D.C., and in its various field offices. Recently she has become suspicious that one of her supervisors is perhaps taking bribes from one of the World Bank's loan recipients in a French-speaking country in the Caribbean. When she asks her supervisor's supervisor to initiate an investigation, he responds by suggesting that "instead of making trouble," she should go out to dinner with him and discuss the promotion she will receive if she "cooperates." As she leaves his office, he pats her on the back and says, "We can be friends and much more in this office, as we do good in the world." What can Angelique do about this situation?

Considering the World Bank processes outlined above, what options does she have regarding (1) the possible ethics/corruption complaint and (2) a possible sexual harassment claim? What internal process would you recommend she use? What remedial powers would an ombuds have? What legal or other recourse does she have? What do you think the appropriate process should be here?

The two cases below[3] present contrasting decisions on how national courts treat the internal dispute resolution processes of international organizations. In the first case,

3. Translations by Caterina Cesario.

Belgium's *Cour de Cassation* reviews an employment dispute in the Western European Union (this organization ceased to exist in 2011). In the second case, which took place only one year later, France's *Cour de Cassation* reviews a case from the Organization for Economic Cooperation and Development. The *Cour de Cassation* of Belgium and of France are the highest judicial bodies, serving as the final court of appeal for civil and criminal matters. Neither court reexamines the facts of a case but instead reviews a case for the correct application of law and legal procedure.

Cour de Cassation de Belgique

S.04.0129.F/1 (21 Decembre 2009)

On December 21st, 2009, the Belgian Cour de Cassation, rendered a decision (Cour de Cassation de Belgique—21 Decembre 2009—S.04.0129.F/1) refusing to recognize the Western European Union ("WEU") jurisdictional immunity for a conflict with one of its employees.

The case involved an employee of the WEU who was terminated and took legal action against the international organization to obtain a judgment that would require the organization to pay her a sum of money as compensation in lieu of notice. During the internal process, the WEU tribunal rendered a judgment awarding her an amount of money that she deemed insufficient, and as a consequence, she filed a case with the Belgian Tribunal de Travail de Bruxelles, which ruled against the WEU. The WEU subsequently appealed this decision to the Cour de Travail de Bruxelles.

The Cour de Cassation rejected the WEU's appeal against the judgment of the Cour de Travail de Bruxelles that denied jurisdictional immunity to the organization, thereby confirming the conclusions of the Cour de Travail de Bruxelles, which determined that the case against the WEU could proceed in the local Belgian courts.

The Cour de Cassation initiated its analysis by saying that:

> Article 6, § 1, of the Convention for the Protection of Human Rights and Fundamental Freedoms guarantees everyone the right to have any dispute concerning their civil rights and obligations heard by a court. This right of access to the courts is not absolute. [...] However, the limitations imposed cannot unduly restrict an individual's access to the extent that the right itself is significantly impaired. Moreover, such limitations are compatible with Article 6, § 1, only if they serve a legitimate purpose and exhibit a reasonable proportionality between the means employed and the objectives pursued.
>
> Granting privileges and immunities to international organizations is crucial for their proper functioning, without unilateral interference by governments. States generally grant jurisdictional immunity to international organizations under their founding agreements or additional accords, which has been a long-standing practice aimed at ensuring the smooth operation of these organizations. This practice's significance is further emphasized by the trend of increasing and intensifying international cooperation across various sectors of

> contemporary society. In these circumstances, the principal of jurisdictional immunity for international organizations serves a legitimate purpose. While measures adhering to widely recognized principles of international law regarding the immunity of international organizations generally do not constitute an excessive restriction on the right of access to a court as protected by Article 6, § 1, it remains essential to evaluate the question of proportionality in each case, taking into account the specific circumstances.
>
> To determine whether the infringement on fundamental rights is acceptable under Article 6, § 1, it is crucial to examine, in accordance with the jurisprudence of the European Court of Human Rights, whether the individual against whom jurisdictional immunity is invoked has other reasonable means to effectively safeguard the rights guaranteed by the Convention. [...]
>
> When, in the process of assessing whether the jurisdictional immunity invoked by an international organization is admissible under Article 6, § 1, of the Convention for the Protection of Human Rights and Fundamental Freedoms, the judge handling the dispute determines that the person facing this immunity has the option to bring the dispute before an appeals board, the judge cannot simply note that the instruments establishing this board qualify it as independent.

The ruling acknowledges that the plaintiff had the opportunity to pursue internal remedies within the organization and that the internal appeals board "indeed held a judicial role and possessed the competence to resolve disputes." However, it pointed out that "the appointment of its members is vested in the intergovernmental committee, which appoints the board members for a two-year term." The ruling emphasized that "the method of appointment and the short tenure carry the risk that the board members may have excessive ties to the organization," highlighting that "judicial immutability (/judicial security of tenure) is a necessary corollary of the concept of independence."

With these statements, the ruling, without disregarding the authority of the interpretation provided by the European Court of Human Rights, legally justifies its decision that the internal appeals board of the plaintiff lacks independence. Consequently, it deems the infringement on the rights guaranteed to the defendant by the aforementioned Article 6, § 1, as impermissible.

Cour de Cassation—Chambre Sociale

No. 09-41.030 (29 Septembre 2010)

On September 29th, 2010, the French Cour de Cassation, rendered a decision (Cour de Cassation—Chambre sociale—29 Septembre 2010—No. 09-41.030) recognizing the jurisdictional immunity of the Organization for Economic Co-operation and Development ("OECD") in a conflict involving one of its employees.

The Plaintiff was a consultant for the OECD and filed a case with the Conseil de Prud'hommes in Paris, the French local court that handles labor disputes, to contest her termination and request the requalification of her contract.

The Cour de Cassation upheld the decision of the Cour d'Appel, which recognized the OECD's jurisdictional immunity and dismissed the Plaintiff's appeal. The court affirmed that, based on the circumstances of the case, it was evident that the OECD could assert its jurisdictional immunity given that "OECD personnel, who have not adhered to the Convention for the Protection of Human Rights and Fundamental Freedoms, have a judicial recourse for the resolution of their labor disputes which includes guarantees of impartiality and fairness. Therefore, it can be deduced that the procedure established by the international organization does not contravene the French concept of international public order."

The Court particularly considered what was highlighted by the Cour d'Appel, which noted that "according to Regulations 16 and 22 of the OECD staff regulations, the OECD has established within the organization an administrative tribunal tasked with adjudicating individual disputes. This tribunal consists of three judges appointed by the Council, a body composed of representatives from the OECD member states. These judges are selected from individuals outside the OECD who provide guarantees of impartiality and possess high qualifications in labor law, public service, or labor relations, in accordance with Article 8 of Annex II of the regulations, which states that they "shall be impartial and completely independent in the exercise of their duties". Furthermore, the tribunal's sessions are public unless the tribunal decides otherwise or at the request of the parties. The dates of the sessions are published on a list accessible to employees, delegations, and the staff association, and that the judgments are rendered in writing."

OECD Regulation 22

Advisory Bodies

a) The Secretary-General shall establish an Advisory Board comprising a Chairman from outside the Organisation, and six other members, three of whom shall be nominated by the Staff Association. Unless, under a specific provision, another body is responsible for giving its opinion in a particular field, this Board shall advise the Secretary-General, at the request of the official concerned, on any individual dispute arising from a decision of the Secretary-General and which an official, former official or the duly qualified claimants to their rights consider inequitable to themselves or contrary to the terms of the appointment or to the provisions of these Regulations or of applicable Rules.

b) The Secretary-General shall establish a Re-evaluation Commission comprising a Chairman and two members nominated by him/her. This Commission shall advise the Secretary-General, at the request of an official, on any individual dispute arising from a decision of the Secretary-General relating to the official's performance evaluation, periodic advancement or post classification and which the official considers contrary to the terms of the appointment or to the provisions of these Regulations or of applicable Rules. Prior referral to this Commission is a precondition for filing an application with the Administrative Tribunal mentioned in paragraph c) of this Regulation.

Administrative Tribunal

c) There shall be established an Administrative Tribunal which shall decide individual disputes arising from a decision of the Secretary-General, which he/she has taken on his/her own authority or in application of a decision of the Council and which officials, former officials or the duly qualified claimants to their rights consider as prejudicial to themselves. The Tribunal shall have jurisdiction to resolve, with due regard to vested rights, all questions regarding the interpretation and application of these Regulations, of any applicable Rules and of the terms of appointment. The Tribunal may annul such decisions of the Secretary-General as are contrary to the terms of appointment of the official concerned or the provisions of these Regulations or to any applicable Rule. It may also order the Organisation to redress the damage resulting from any irregularity committed by the Secretary-General.

d) The Tribunal shall be composed of three judges and three deputies, who shall not be members of the staff of the Organisation and shall be appointed by the Council for a period of three years from among persons of proven impartiality and who are jurists or otherwise highly qualified in labour law or civil service law or in the field of labour relations at the national or international level. The Council shall appoint the Chairman from among the judges, having regard to their judicial experience. The members of the Tribunal shall be of different nationalities and, overall, their selection shall ensure that the main legal systems of the Member countries of the Organisation are represented.

e) The other provisions relating to the Statute and operation of the Administrative Tribunal are set out in a Council Resolution annexed to these Regulations.

Notes & Questions

1. Can you reconcile the two contradictory decisions based on the internal processes set up by each organization?
2. Having read how consensual dispute resolution processes often provide participants with finality as well as a voice, what is the danger of allowing appeals from internal dispute resolution processes?
3. Should national courts be in a position to oversee international organizations?
4. What precedents, if any, are created within organizations' own dispute resolution processes?
5. What precedential value do the cases above have for other employment or internal disputes taken to national courts? What precedential value do they have within the same country? What precedential effects do they have for other countries (with the same international or regional organizations)?

II. Transitional and Restorative Justice

After the Second World War ended, international tribunals to try perpetrators of war crimes were established in Nuremberg and Tokyo during the mid- to late-1940s (*see* Chapter 7). Apart from the Korean War in the 1950s and various struggles in Algeria, Kenya, Uganda, and other African countries for post-colonial independence in the 1960s, the post-WWII world was marked by relative peace. But turbulent times returned in the 1970s, with the ascendancy of dictatorships in Central and South America and in Cambodia, many of which used violent means ("disappearances") to control the populace. In South Africa, the legalization of racism through the doctrines and policies of Apartheid continued decades-long anti-democratic and repressive regimes. In the 1980s, as some dictatorships fell and were replaced by more democratic elections, human rights actions were filed in the human rights courts (*see* Chapter 7). These cases sought not only compensation but also legal precedents prohibiting various human atrocities. International human rights lawyers and democracy activists promoted a new form of political and legal consciousness: transitional and restorative justice. The idea was that post-colonial, post-dictatorship, post-civil war, and post-apartheid societies would need more than legal proceedings to right past wrongs; they would need processes to guide their "transition" to democracy and "restorative" or "reparative" measures to repair the harms done to individual victims and whole societies.

Bolivia was the first country to develop a truth and reconciliation commission (TRC); its TRC was established to uncover "the truth" about the actions of its dictatorship[4] and to consider what processes might be needed to "reconcile" a bitterly divided society. After the fall of the Pinochet dictatorship in Chile and the Videla dictatorship in Argentina, both countries developed different models of society-wide processes to (1) investigate the truth of *los desaparecidos* (the disappeared), murders, torture, and imprisonment; (2) provide some compensation for victims; and (3) raise society's consciousness of human rights in future democratization and maintain political vigilance against dictatorships. Argentina's process was a relatively public one, in large part because of the *Nunca Más* report, an official report summarizing the research of Argentina's National Commission on the Disappearance of Persons that was made available to all citizens. Chile's truth commission, though less public, eventually resulted in a new more stable government (and currently, Chile is in the process of trying to create and pass a new constitution). But it was the South African Truth and Reconciliation Commission, created by legislation in the post-Apartheid regime of Nelson Mandela and inspired by Christian teachings and South African communitarian principles of *ubuntu* (being human together), that gained world attention and has inspired a number of processes for dealing with post-conflict transitions to more democratic societies. There remain great controversies about the "justice" of these processes, including too little focus on past atrocities, too little actual compensation for harmed victims, too much

---

4. Priscilla Hayner, Unspeakable Truths: Transitional Justice and the Challenge of Truth Commissions (2d ed. 2010).

"forgiveness" or amnesty for wrong-doers, a lack of attention to economic equality, and a lack of capacity to deal with both formal and informal processes.

The excerpts below describe some variations of restorative and transitional justice, and the questions that follow ask you to think about how the competing issues and values of different alternative processes can be combined (or not) to deal with past injustices, future reconciliation, and individual and social healing.

Pumla Gobodo-Madikizela, A Human Being Died That Night: A South African Story of Forgiveness

117–20, 126–29 (2003)

Although forgiveness is often regarded as an expression of weakness, the decision to forgive can paradoxically elevate a victim to a position of strength as the one who holds the key to the perpetrator's wish. For just at the moment when the perpetrator begins to show remorse, to seek some way to ask forgiveness, the victim becomes the gatekeeper to what the outcast desires—readmission into the human community. And the victim retains that privileged status as long as he or she stays the moral course, refusing to sink to the level of the evil that was done to her or to him. In this sense, then, forgiveness is a kind of revenge, but revenge enacted at a rarefied level.

Truth and Healing

"If the affirmative case for truth commissions rests on the goal of healing, then the working hypothesis is that testimony of the victims and perpetrators, offered publicly to a truth commission, affords opportunities for individuals and the nation as a whole to heal. With the aim of producing a fair and thorough account of the atrocities, a truth commission proceeds on the assumption that it helps individuals to tell their stories and to have them acknowledged officially. Also assumed here is the premise that a final report can create a framework for the nation to deal with its past. Echoing assumptions of psychotherapy, religious confession, and journalistic muckraking, truth commissions presume that telling and hearing truth is healing." Martha Minow. *Between Vengeance and Forgiveness* 61 (1998).

The question is no longer *whether* victims can forgive "evildoers" but whether we—our symbols, language, and politics, our legal, media, and academic institutions—are creating the conditions that encourage alternatives to revenge. We have come to rely too narrowly on retribution as the only legitimate form of justice and on the Nuremberg trial model as the only one capable of adequately addressing state-orchestrated atrocities. Tellingly, recent international tribunals such as the International Criminal Tribunal on the genocide in Rwanda and the tribunal in The Hague on the former Yugoslavia have run into problems. In Rwanda, for example, victims have felt largely excluded from a process that is supposed to help heal their wounds and restore some normality in their society. Our knowledge of the dynamic between victims and perpetrators have further been influenced by narratives from the Holocaust experience. Although a few Jewish German groups have been established to try to build positive relationships between children of Holocaust survivors and descendants of Nazi perpetrators, Holocaust discourse has sometimes emphasized remembering but not so clearly dialogue, which is critical if victims are to live again with perpetrators in the same society or indeed if they are to live in greater harmony with themselves.

Dialogue, of course, will not solve every problem faced by a society that has suffered sustained violence on a large scale. But dialogue does create avenues for broadening our models of justice and for healing deep fractures in a nation by unearthing, acknowledging, and recording what has been done. It humanizes the dehumanized and confronts perpetrators with their inhumanity. Through dialogue, victims as well as the greater society come to recognize perpetrators as human beings who failed morally, whether through coercion, the perverted convictions of a warped mind, or fear.

Far from relieving the pressure on them, recognizing the most serious criminals as human intensifies it, because society is thereby able to hold them to greater moral accountability. Indeed, demonizing as monsters those who commit evil lets them off too easily.... Sustained, engaged, ordered dialogue thus forces an offender to unearth what moral sensibilities he has buried under a facade of "obedience to orders" or righteous "duty to my country" and to face what he has done, not in the heady climate of the period of mayhem but in the sobering atmosphere of reflection on ordinary human lives now shattered. But it also thereby invites him, if he can, if he dare, to negotiate the chasm between his monstrousness and the world of the forgiven. It thus encourages him to stop denying the suspected truth: that all along, he knew that he was human and knew right from wrong. The act of humanizing is therefore at once both punishment and rehabilitation. Finally, dialogue creates the possibility of setting the persons actions, through testimony and witnessing, in the broader framework of the political-ideological context that may have supported and even directed his deeds. It is this component of the crime, the one that resides at the systemic, institutional, and policy levels rather than at a personal level, that is notoriously difficult to substantiate within the strict evidentiary rules of a purely judicial process. Thus, the politics of abuse that were enshrined in the policies of an oppressive system can be acknowledged and confirmed in ways that the more rigid, adversarial relationship of courtroom exchanges cannot....

What enables some victims to forgive heinous crimes? What distinguishes them from those who feel unable to do so? In addition to an external context that makes reconciliation normative through the language of restoration—a truth commission, for example, or a counseling agency that focuses on victim-offender encounters, or a national dialogue that begins to put in place the symbols and vocabulary of forgiveness and compromise—there are internal psychological dynamics that impel most of us toward forming an empathic connection with another person in pain, that draw us *into* his pain, regardless of who that someone is. The possibility of making an empathic connection with someone who has victimized us, as a response to the pain of his remorse, stems significantly from this underlying dynamic. The power of human connectedness, of identification with the other as "bone of my bone" through the sheer fact of his being human, draws us to "rescue" others in pain, almost as if this were a learned response embedded deep in our genetic and evolutionary past....

This is not a statement about whether it "makes sense" for the victimized to respond with empathy, nor an evaluation of the propriety of extending forgiveness. It is a tracing of what makes it possible for enemies to connect in a way that might otherwise seem unimaginable. There is another dimension to the internal dynamic that motivates many to connect with those who have victimized them. A broad consensus exists in the literature that in order to torture, kill, and maim, perpetrators must first exclude their victims from the moral obligations they feel toward the world in general and, in particular, toward those with whom they are socially and politically connected. Moral exclusion of a victim from the community of those who deserve to be treated humanely, in effect, effaces his pain....

When perpetrators express remorse, when they finally acknowledge that they can see what they previously could not see, or did not want to, they are revalidating the victim's pain—in a sense, giving his or her humanity back. Empowered and revalidated, many victims at this point find it natural to extend and deepen the healing process by going a step further: turning around and conferring forgiveness on their torturer.

The motivation to do this does not stem only from altruism or high moral principles. The victim in a sense *needs* forgiveness as part of the process of becoming rehumanized. The victim needs it in order to complete himself or herself and to wrest away from the perpetrator the fiat power to destroy or to spare.... Reciprocating with empathy and forgiveness in the face of a perpetrators remorse restores to many victims the sense that they are once again capable of affecting a profound difference in the moral community.

Notes & Questions

1. Is the language of healing compatible with notions of justice? Can therapeutic mediation substitute for adjudication when terrible human rights violations have occurred?
2. Is truth-telling enough for building coexistence, a new nation, and a new culture? Do the different vocabularies or techniques of mediation, therapy, and adjudication, as well as the different remedies produced by these different processes, limit what each process can offer?
3. Is it possible for the same events, both within and between nations, to be processed in different ways?

The next excerpt focuses on the transitional justice needs in Latin America to help illustrate how cultural variations and different histories can be reflected in the processes adopted for reconciliation and dispute resolution.

Carrie Menkel-Meadow, *Process Pluralism in Transitional/Restorative Justice: Lessons from Dispute Resolution for Cultural Variations in Goals Beyond Rule of Law and Democracy Development (Argentina and Chile)*

3 INT'L J. CONFLICT RESOL. & ENGAGEMENT
4; 8; 12–14; 16–18; 22–23 (2015)

The Gulag commissars had retired long ago, with medals and pensions. Not one had been arraigned. Russia had turned its back on the past. And I, how could I understand? Since the Holocaust, my world had made a duty of remembrance. Russia, like China, had chosen forgetfulness. That, said the writer Shalamov, was how people survived. A nation was not built on truth. Thubron (2007: 204–205)

This essay will use the examples of post-military dictatorships in Argentina and Chile to illustrate how transitional justice itself must be sensitive to change, cultural, historical, political and local differences, and the social and political learning that has come from the observations of our field—by scholars, practitioners and the civil society in which such processes are embedded. As I will conclude at the end of this essay, we need process pluralism and variations in different contexts to respond to the differences of circumstances, but most importantly, we need layers of social-cultural, as well as legal, pluralism (courts, truth tribunals, testimonies, compensation, memorials and museums, governmental and interpersonal training, mediation, cultural activities, therapy and use of local and indigenous practices) in the design and practice of those processes. However named, transitional justice processes will not ultimately succeed unless the 'acted upon' (the civil or not-so-civil society) are a part of the construction and implementation (and legitimacy) of any particular transitional justice structure. As some critics of transitional justice have pointed out, the human atrocities and violations that cause the conditions that require 'transitional' justice do not leave a level playing field of equals—'transitions' are often constructed in continuing conditions of unequal political, economic and social power, with disparate abilities and conditions for participation in that construction of the 'transition'. Transitional justice is not only governmental and legal; it is social and cultural as well, and different processes and institutions may be necessary, even within single societies, to interweave the elements of a flourishing or at least peaceful social order....

Illustrations from Chile and Argentina: Variable Transitions within the Transitions

On 11 September 1973 a coup, led by Augusto Pinochet (and other military leaders), against the elected socialist leader, Dr. Salvador Allende, in Chile, led to a dictatorship lasting more than 15 years in which thousands were 'disappeared', murdered, tortured, brutally treated, threatened, surveilled, detained and attacked, both physically and emotionally. Estimates of those killed (about 3,000) and tortured still vary, although the Jesuit brothers at Universidad Alberto Hurtado kept the best records they could. Of those who were not killed or detained, many exiles fled the country to agitate for justice from other ports in South America (ironically, including Argentina, with its own military dictatorship), Europe and the United States (whose government was fully implicated in Pinochet's coup). Unlike many dictators, Pinochet eventually sought the legitimacy of election-plebiscite, which, to his surprise, he lost! In 1988 Patricio Alywin was elected President, and a truth and reconciliation process was begun with a human rights investigation that included human rights activists and Chilean exiles, including Jose Zalaquett, now a professor of law and human rights at the Universidad de Chile. The jurisdiction of the commission in Chile only extended to cases of "torture resulting in death", and was criticized for failing to treat the cases of the up to 200,000 (a significant percentage of Chile's population) who were allegedly tortured and then released. The report of this commission was completed in 1991 (1,800 pages, with few copies initially printed, of proceedings that had been held mostly in private, with relatively little public comment at the time). In 1978 an amnesty law was passed granting amnesty to those who participated in these acts ('in defence of the state'), and Pinochet became a 'senator for life', even as he 'voluntarily' stepped down from his country's leadership.

Ten years later, in a period characterized by many of us in the transitional justice field as the 'peace versus justice' dilemma, Chile provided a 'classic' example of the bargain made for 'peace' as the transition to a more democratic state allowed many former office holders and military officers to remain in place, with relative impunity (at least until much later). As is now well known, in 1998 Pinochet, en route to London for medical treatment, was indicted in Spain for human rights violations of those with Spanish citizenship (and on the basis of some universal jurisdiction legal principles) for human rights crimes committed in Chile. After groundbreaking litigation in the British courts, Pinochet was allowed to return (without extradition to Spain for trial) to Chile, where despite efforts to indict him for tax claims and other legal wrongs, he died without coming to trial. Soon thereafter, amnesty laws were repealed (mostly through judicial interpretation), and some prosecutions (most notably of Catholic priests complicit in the regime) began and are ongoing. The Inter-American Court of Human Rights, which had pioneered the recognition of the human rights violation of state enforced 'disappearances' and the state's duty to investigate all such claims in *Velasquez Rodriguez v. Honduras* (1988), found that the amnesty laws passed in Chile could not override the state's duty to investigate, prosecute and punish those responsible for such wrongful acts (see *Luis Alfredo Almonacid Arellano et al. v. Chile* [2006]) (forced disappearances by the state now being a violation of the International Convention on the Protection of All Persons from Enforced Disappearance [2006]). Over one thousand have now been tried, and about 250 found guilty, but only of the worst 'crimes' of torture and death and not for more common forced 'detentions'.

In 1976 a military coup in Argentina, including Jorge Videla and others, used several alleged left-wing bombings to seize power from Isabel Peron (the widow of Juan Peron), and proceeded to engage in forced disappearances, murders, torture, detentions, surveillance and other human rights violations, now labeled 'the Dirty War'. Estimates of those murdered now exceed 30,000 (comparable as a percentage of the population to

Chile). After losing the Falklands/Malvinas War against the United Kingdom in 1983, the military dictatorship fell, and Raul Alfonsin assumed the presidency. Like Alywin in Chile, he announced the formation of a Truth and Reconciliation Commission (CONADEP), which researched, investigated and reported on (in the now readily available report Nunca Mas! now in multiple printings) the forced disappearances and other acts of detention and torture. Carlos Nino (in exile in the United States), a distinguished philosopher of law and one of the intellectual fathers of transitional justice, became advisor to Alfonsin to assist in the development of a new democratic state. Unlike Chile, Argentina began compensating some victims, especially given the persistent activism of the Madres de Plaza de Mayo (a human rights group of mothers and grandmothers of the disappeared who continued to march in front of the Casa Rosada during and after the military dictatorship to demand accountability and information on their disappeared children). Videla was eventually prosecuted (and died under house arrest), as were other military officials, until both Alfonsin's and, later, Carlos Menem's regime issued new pardon (amnesty or 'Full Stop') laws. In 2003, under President Nestor Kirchner, the Argentine Congress revoked the pardon laws, while the Argentine Supreme Court declared them unconstitutional. The new Argentine Constitution in 1994 incorporated several international human rights treaties as part of its law (making it a 'monist' regime of international law), making legal action possible in national courts for international legal claims. Argentina is actively prosecuting some surviving perpetrators, not only through official state prosecutors, but also with the representation of victims by the civil law procedure of 'victim's counsel' or private prosecutors, including law clinics in some of Argentina's law schools....

Side by side, two Spanish-speaking post-military dictatorship countries separated by the Cordillera de los Andes seemed worlds apart in their post-conflict reactions to somewhat similarly suffering regimes (fighting 'communism and leftwing politics' with US-supported repressionary tactics). Why? Although many were to observe the 'cultural' features described in the Colin Thubron quote that opens this paper (a 'European' [Argentinean historical identification with Europe]) focus on the past in Argentina (with the highest per capita representation of psychiatrists in the world!) as a cultural difference in the two nations' demographic and psychic make-up, with Chileans more focused on 'the future' (both economic and nation 'rebuilding'), there are structural differences as well. Ironically, for Chile the military dictatorship was somewhat of a 'one-off', if longer, aberration in an otherwise more democratic and judicially passive state. The Truth and Reconciliation process and investigation was less transparent, restricted in jurisdiction and not fully circulated to the public when completed.

In contrast, when organized by internationally renowned legal theorists, the Argentine TRC was more public and observed by thousands as *Nunca Mas*! became a domestic and then international bestseller. Argentina's human rights community was supported and activated by international networks, and when exiles returned with European and North American rights consciousness, despite the back and forth of amnesty laws, both the courts and the legislature actively revamped the pardon laws. In

Chile, the amnesty laws were more 'circumvented' than overruled, until more recently. The interaction of the larger social and political 'culture' (perhaps more 'diverse' in European origin) in Argentina, and legal culture in these two nations thus produced, at least in the first decade after the military dictatorships, quite different social, if not, legal, post-conflict societies....

Thus, in different ways, Argentina and Chile demonstrate some examples of process pluralism—as different processes (Truth, not Reconciliation, Commissions and different concepts of amnesty, prosecutions and some financial reparations) were created immediately after the collapse of the military dictatorships, and then later (now, over two decades later) prosecutions continue and historical excavation of the 'truth' (in both legal and other forms, e.g., movies, novels, art forms, museums) continues to be differentially experienced by survivors, victims and bystanders of the events themselves.... At the same time, critics of transitional justice practices, both of TRCs and courts, have suggested that the definitions of wrongs have often excluded those perpetrated against women or children or ethnic or religious minorities, and that even seemingly 'human rights-sensitive' organizations and processes re-perpetuate existing (national? gender? class? religious?) hierarchies by harm definition and official actors within the processes of transition. And, as noted by Colin Thubron above, some societies, like China, have not even acknowledged their genocides or mass atrocities, such as the Cultural Revolution or the Great Leap Forward, which may turn out to have killed the most human beings in actions taken by a government in the twentieth century. And among those many unacknowledged modern atrocities, there is Japan's refusal to apologize for their use of Korean "comfort women". New critics of some transitional justice processes have argued for less "westernized" legalistic categories, suggesting that even the most truth-seeking TRCs still individualize presentations of harm and narrative, rather than allowing another form of "collective memory" to be developed, used or created in such settings—the telling of and acknowledgment of "collective memories of wrongfulness" or group harms and group narratives.

There will be many opportunities for transitional justice institutional design as more and more nations begin to acknowledge their wrongdoing under civil society and international pressure (or after the effective date (2002) of the Rome Treaty makes signatories responsible for enforcing international criminal laws in their national courts). As post-conflict-atrocity societies attempt to transition to a new society, the challenge is to compensate, remember and correct for the past, with an eye towards what might be created for the future. This too may be culturally varied—are human/political rights enough? What of economic opportunity or justice? Land allocations? Property return or compensation? Fear of revenge and retribution? Cultural values certainly vary in tolerance of difference and "living together" or preferred separation? Many designs of transitional justice presume that the individuals constituting a particular society can be encouraged to share enough common 'values' (peace, coexistence, human well-being) to create and sustain a new society after great harm has produced hostile separation.

Notes & Questions

1. Consider how two different neighbors dealt with similar issues. What cultural differences can explain the process differences?
2. Now compare the truth and reconciliation process used in South Africa versus in Latin America. Do you notice any best practices or consistencies? In the next chapter, we turn to issues of system design—might there be particular lessons from these examples you would suggest to future problem-solvers trying to help their countries transition?

III. Reparations

In recent decades, the world community has begun to assess the human costs of major international atrocities and harms caused by the world slave trade and colonialism. Various proposals for different kinds of reparations have been made, whether for the descendants of enslaved people; for citizens of post-colonial states whose human and material resources have been depleted or abused by empires and private foreign entities (e.g., atrocities committed by the British East India Company, British colonists' abuse of Aboriginal people); for harms caused by wars fought on "proxy" shores; for the looting of property, art, and other items, such as natural herbs and agricultural products which are being exploited by multinational pharmaceutical companies); and for the victims of sexual abuse at the hands of religious figures (e.g., the Catholic Church sexual abuse cases).

Consider whether processes for these complex issues should grant relief of some kind to individuals (and what degree of proof should be required), to groups of people (such as to aboriginal groups for colonizers' stealing their land and committing personal and cultural abuses), or to whole nations (such as what Britain "owes" to India and Pakistan, what Britain and Spain "owe" to conquered territories in North and South America and Australia, or what China "owes" to Central and Southeast Asia). What is the relationship of past wrongs to what can be accomplished for present and future justice among the peoples of the world? The next excerpt uses the example of indigenous claims in Canada to illustrate another hybrid process.

Carrie Menkel-Meadow, *Unsettling the Lawyers: Other Forms of Justice in Indigenous Claims of Expropriation, Abuse, and Injustice*

64 U. Toronto L.J. 621–623; 625–639 (2014)

Introduction: Unsettling the Lawyers— What Processes for What Injustice?

What role can the legal profession, law, and legal processes play in the search for justice, reconciliation, and restoration of humanity after great (mass) harm has been done? This is a question faced by any lawyer in human rights, personal injury, civil and constitutional rights, criminal, discrimination, and international law. The twentieth century and the legacies of nineteenth (and earlier) centuries of colonization, genocides, expropriations of land, culture, homes, bodies, souls, and human dignity have now forced us to reconceive how we deal with the past (in the present and for the future) when harm has been caused, not only to individuals, but to whole groups of people, in numbers that challenge our western legal conceptions of individualism and in content that challenges our conceptions of what wrongs or injustice consist of. To what extent must conventional legal processes (lawsuits, judgments, damage awards, and injunctions) expand or give way to include a different set of processes and remedies for the recognition and acknowledgement of harm and hurt, where full restitution or compensation cannot be made, where injured victims cannot be 'made whole' in the conventional way our (Anglo-American-Canadian) adversarial system provides for? What can lawyers contribute to alternative legal processes to attempt to deal with (if not right) the wrongs that have been done to others, especially as conceptions of right and wrong are themselves changeable over time?

In the present article, I hope to draw on my life's work as a process pluralist both to commend the Canadian Indian Residential Schools Settlement for its attempt to provide models of different processes to deal with a gross and mass injustice done to the Indigenous peoples of Canada and to reflect on what this process might teach us about how legal processes and lawyers must be able to reconceive how they attempt to achieve justice in situations, like this, when great wrongs are done to many. It is my view (and argument) that current legal institutions and legal education are inadequate to deal with more modern recognition of different claims of value and loss (e.g., loss of culture, loss of homeland, loss of language, loss of family, and intergenerational injustice) and more diverse claims for justice, restoration, reparation, or restitution, after great harm has been done. The Indian Residential Schools Settlement is one illustration of how conventional legal processes (individual lawsuits, class actions) in a variety of different levels of courts and jurisdictions evolved into national, regional, and local sets of processes to attempt to deal with personal and group harms by drawing on both conventional legal processes (lawsuits, discovery, negotiations and settlement, compensation) and more modern (and local and Indigenous) processes of restorative justice, through truth and reconciliation processes, testimonies, apologies, commemoration, and ongoing care and counselling. My hope here is to spur us on to reconceive the role of the lawyer in designing more tailored or 'bespoke' processes and institutions for the necessary processes of recognizing, taking responsibility for, and apologizing for past wrongs, while at the same time, focusing on more complex remedies for moving from the past to the future, including compensation, apologies, and affirmative action to improve and repair the lives of those who suffer from the legacies of great harm. This must, in my view, include both victims and perpetrators (or their descendants)—in current terminology, both the 'settlers' and those who were here 'first'—as we now must live together with our histories and our futures.

As many now write about 'unsettling' the settlers (whether Canadian, Australian, American, British, French, or other colonizers) so they take responsibility for what they or their ancestors have done to the original inhabitants of the lands they conquered or settled, I want here to unsettle the lawyers about how they (we) deal with these past injustices—old methods of lawsuits, trials, and affixing (through the legal necessity of individualized proof) of blame may not be adequate to repair the harms that have been done in the past, if we who inhabit these lands in the present hope to live together, more reconciled to our future shared fates....

So, in the last few decades, both individuals and groups of people have sued in domestic, international, and even private (arbitration) tribunals for both civil (damages and injunctions) and criminal remedies (imprisonments, punishment, fines, etc.). Modern legal claims include demands for compensation for lost lives, limbs, health, property, wages, consortium, dignitary rights, pain and suffering, emotional harm, torture, opportunity costs, and more recently, for such things as group harms and collective losses. Modern litigation has produced some more modern remedies in the form of medical monitoring and treatment for some health claims, injunctions to monitor organizational compliance with discrimination claims or monitor prison conditions, 'coupons' and new forms of economic compensation for some consumer and anti-trust claims as well as the controversial affirmative actions of setting goals and quotas for job hiring and promotion or other benefits in both private and public settings. The Indian Residential Schools litigation has been significant for many reasons, but among those reasons are newly stated claims for loss of language, loss of culture, and the intergenerational harm that have come from the forced displacement of children away from their parental homes, raising important questions about what claims can or should be recognized in courts.

The claims brought by former residents of Indian Residential Schools in Canada were brought both individually and collectively as class actions for claims of abuse (physical, mental, and sexual) and of loss of home, culture, language, and family over a period of years. In Canada, Australia, and the United States (my own country has not yet formally apologized or taken any formal action with respect to similar claims), Indian children were removed from their homes, beginning in the seventeenth century and continuing until well into the present. In my own country, for example, it is estimated that the peak year for enrolment in Indian boarding schools was 1973, when an estimated 60,000 children remained in such schools. The justifying ideology of such schools was the claim that Natives or Indigenous people needed to be 'civilized.' As early as 1634, Fr Andrew White of the Society of Jesus established a mission to 'extend civilization and instruction to this ignorant race and show them the way to heaven.' While both Harvard College (as early as 1665) and later Dartmouth College admitted Indigenous students to their colleges for education along with the colonists in the East, later schools in the Western regions of the colonies were initially founded by missionaries. Thus, modern litigants have sued both governmental bodies and a variety of Protestant and Catholic churches that established schools in the name of 'civilizing' the local 'savages.' Reflecting typical comments of the time, a United States Army officer, Richard Henry Pratt, is reported to have said famously, in 1892 (serving as a model for policies developed by the Bureau of Indian Affairs): 'A great general has said that the only good Indian is a dead one. In a sense, I agree with the sentiment, but only in this: that all the Indian there is in the race should be dead. Kill the Indian in him and save the man.' Pratt developed a policy of assimilation 'through total immersion.' Curricula in Indian boarding or residential schools depended on learning English and English/American/Canadian/Australian history and culture and silencing and prohibiting all use of Native languages and practices. Long hair was cut; religious or tribal customs were prohibited and severely punished, often with harsh physical discipline. Physical conditions in the schools themselves were substandard, deficient in sanitary and heating and other health conditions. The modern lawsuits also alleged (and proved) sexual assault on both male and female students as well as harsh corporal punishment and mental degradation and anguish. Compulsory conversion to Christianity was part of most schools, whether religiously or governmentally funded and managed. In the early 1920s and 1930s, some government reports indicated there were infectious disease (including tuberculosis and other communicable diseases) and physical and mental abuse, and the first demands of activists and some government officials that the schools be reformed or eliminated began.

In Canada, the residential schools for First Nations (including Métis, Inuit, and other groups) were funded by the Canadian government's Department of Indian Affairs but mostly administered by Christian churches. Attendance at a day industrial or residential school for First Nations children was mandatory and often enforced by compulsory assignment to a residential school, especially, but not exclusively, in more rural regions. Estimates range, but suggest that close to 150,000 students passed through these schools before they were closed in the 1990s. In addition to claims of abuse within the institutions themselves, modern lawsuits also made claims for the 'intergenerational harms' of higher rates of alcoholism, drug use, and domestic violence within communities in which family and Indigenous social structures were destroyed and disrupted by the effects of compulsory removal to residential schools. The media brought attention to this issue in a variety of ways, aided by the efforts of the litigation lawyers representing victims and the courageous actions taken by First Nations victims of these schools, as well as by some documentary films and published narratives, children's stories, novels, and plays.

In an important, but seen by many still to be a purely 'symbolic' act, Prime Minister Stephen Harper publicly apologized in Parliament on 11 June 2008 on behalf of the Canadian government for this long-standing policy, following on from a March 1998 Statement of Reconciliation issued by the government for those who were sexually or physically abused. The government established an Aboriginal Healing Foundation and allocated some $350 million to fund community-based healing programs. In 2003, in response to both lawsuits and increasing publicity about the schools and their legacy, the government launched an alternative dispute resolution (ADR) process for compensation and psychological support for those who could prove some form of physical or sexual abuse or other conditions of 'wrongful confinement.' The ADR process was itself quite controversial: there were claims that the high standard of proof demanded for particular claims did not address all the actual experiences of harm, differences in awards, and arguments that the government used this process to obtain 'legal certainty and closure' and not to fully acknowledge Indigenous demands for apologies and other kinds of reparations. Kathleen Mahoney, in this issue, describes in greater detail how inadequate the ADR process was, risking re-victimizing claimants and giving the lie to the meaning and ideology behind alternative dispute resolution processes which are intended to be more, not less, sensitive to people's needs when they are making claims such as these.

The Truth and Reconciliation Commission born out of the Indian Schools Settlement, discussed more fully below, documented deaths, disease, forced sterilizations, sexual abuse, corporal and harsh punishments, inadequate and poorly heated facilities, poor sanitation, inadequate education, and some forced labour, particularly agricultural work. In Canada, some of the government reports issued in the 1940s criticized much Indian policy and eliminated some of the compulsory policies, but existing schools remained underfunded, and lawsuits have demonstrated that abuse continued well into the 1990s. As more fully reported in other articles in this issue and in the full report of the Indian Residential Schools Settlement, a series of successful lawsuits led to large monetary payments of damages from the Canadian government and from the major churches (Catholic, Anglican, United Church, and Presbyterian) which administered and ran the schools. Settlement talks began in the early 2000s, as some feared the lawsuits might actually bankrupt the Canadian government and cause serious financial difficulties for the churches.

In stories and reports featured at this conference, Assessing Canada's Indian Residential Schools Litigation and Settlement Processes, we learned how activist National Chief Phil Fontaine, representatives of the Ministry of Justice, and government mediators met with the lawyers, claimants, and representatives of First Nations, churches, and government bodies in a series of mediated meetings to arrive at what is still the largest (in dollars) settlement of a claim against the Canadian government. The Indian Residential Schools Settlement provided for $5 billion dollars in total allocation for

- 'common experience payments' to be paid to all former students who resided in a school;
- an independent assessment process for individualized claims of sexual, physical, or other abuse;
- a truth and reconciliation commission, mandated to hold seven national events, create a public historical record, and provide awareness about the school system and its impact;
- a commemoration initiative, with an allocation of $20 million to support local, regional, and national activities to honour, remember, memorialize, and pay tribute to former students, their families, and communities; and
- other measures to support healing, through the Aboriginal Healing Funds and Indian Residential Schools Resolution Health Support Program.

This settlement began to operate on 19 September 2007, after approval by the participating parties and relevant courts.

While the motivations to come to a mediation table and seek negotiation and settlement of such mass injustices are many and vary among the parties who choose to participate in such events (and we can never really know them all, especially in a confidential process, often protected by formal undertakings of secrecy and confidentiality, whether by contract, legislation, or informal agreement), the fact that so many diverse actors came together to forge this multi-faceted settlement of compensation, apology, hearings, ceremonies, documentation, truth telling, commemoration, treatment, and healing is historically important and significant, not only for Canada and its many peoples, but for what this process might teach others who suffer similar group-focused but individually suffered injuries.

What lessons can we learn from what we do know about the processes and ultimate settlement of these grievous wrongs? What can lawyers and the legal system bring to these issues? What might lawyers and legal systems learn from what has been accomplished here?

The Present and Future: Restorative, Reconciliative, and Transitional Justice as Additions to Legal Justice

Make no mistake about it, conventional litigation strategies were, in my view, absolutely essential for some rectification of the Indian Residential Schools' harms and claims. It is also my view that they alone should not be the sole or even primary way of attempting to 'resolve' (or as I prefer to say") 'deal with' or 'handle' this dark chapter in Canadian history.

Litigation, whether individual or, in this case, collective (class action), frames the legal issues and calls the attention of the defendant(s) (in this case, the government and the churches) and the public to the fact that a claim has been made in a public forum with demand for remedial action. Lawsuits serve the function of clarifying legal claims, asserting demands for redress, and in the course of discovery and information exchanges, often produce the evidence necessary to prove claims (as long as the legal claims are already recognized in law). In the case of the Indian Residential Schools litigation, these functions were performed, with information produced and enough successful verdicts for large amounts of money to provide the motivation to seek what is known in aggregate litigation as a 'global settlement.' That is, the Canadian government and the churches feared economic loss and the continued anger and resentment of various parts of the polity (including both First Nations peoples and others who both acknowledged or denied the claims). That the mediation (which resulted in the ultimate settlement) was achieved is a momentous event for Canada, legal history, and for the legal profession, but it is not without its lessons and cautions. I comment here on a few, based on my work as a conflict resolution and legal profession scholar and mediation practitioner.

At its best, the Indian Residential Schools Settlement is one exemplar of what I have come to call a 'transformative moment' in the development of the legal system, a further evolution from the days of trial by fire or ordeal to adversarial (or inquisitorial) trial and now to more hybrid forms of justice, which include mediation, multi-party dispute resolution, transitional justice, restorative justice, and more responsive and inclusive forms of justice."‘ Injured parties can request and often receive remedies or outcomes not available in conventional litigation, which focuses on the past, not the future. So modern developments in restorative justice permit, indeed encourage, apologies and commitments by the parties to undertake changes in their future relationship, and in some cases, particular actions or recompense (or services provided). In addition, restorative justice processes often involve whole communities, not just the litigation parties, and are themselves often derived from Indigenous, local, and alternative dispute resolution processes.

If our conventional adversarial system requires plaintiffs and defendants (the latter the doers of bad acts to the plaintiff) to prove their duties and obligations and failures to each other by proof and evidence, then they may have a remedy prescribed by legal principles of liability—in these cases, damages for abuse, physical, and mental harm. But in the Indian school litigation, we also see the limits of the traditional adversarial model—many of the doers of bad acts (or non-feasance as well as malfeasance) are no longer with us and many, if not most, of the victims are also now gone. How do we remedy past harms to those currently living who continue to suffer from those harms but cannot confront or claim against the individuals responsible? How do we remedy the group harms? And although our modern legal system has, for the most part, abolished the doctrines of sovereign or charitable immunity, the institutional wrongdoers—the government and the churches—would, at common law, have been immune from suit for the policies they developed and implemented. If we now allow claims against governments, churches, and charities in particular settings, we still do not formally or legally recognize some of the claims actually experienced as harms by the victims—loss of family (consortium?), loss of language, loss of culture, loss of group belongingness. So the lawsuits are useful in framing new categories of claims as lawyers transform the narrative expressions of their client's stories and pain into legally cognizable claims that still have not been fully accepted by the formal legal system.

To the extent, however, that participation of First Nation representatives, as claimants, lawyers, mediators, and judges, allowed the expression of and demand for recognition of claims beyond those formally recognized by the legal system, the mediation of actual claims with multiple parties (not just two sides to the dispute) permitted the development of more than conventional compensation—some recognition of more Indigenous forms of remedies in apologies, truth commissions, reconciliation, and commemoration events and activities.

As a process of conflict resolution, mediation creates room for more a direct expression of claims, narratives, and human desires, including demands for justice and principles, and it provides a forum where feelings can be recognized and demands for moral, religious, and ethical attention to the issues be confronted (as well as authorizing the statement but not adjudication of legal claims). Mediation allows (at great risk and with difficulty, requiring a different form of professional training and skill) more direct confrontation and discussion among and between those involved in the claims than do formal rules of evidence and testimony in court, but it also promises more direct understanding, transformation, and mutual knowledge. Mediation of all kinds of disputes, both in the courts, criminal and civil, and outside (including in the family, workplace, commercial, labor, business, and diplomacy), has now inspired the development of alternative processes in a wide variety of settings including mass harms, post-conflict transitional justice, criminal justice, and human rights violations. As in the Indian Schools Settlement, different forms of restorative, restitutionary, apologetic, and compensatory processes have now been used to document truth (e.g. the many truth and reconciliation commissions in a variety of post-conflict settings), offer apologies, reintegrate offenders into the community, grant forgiveness, prescribe future-oriented restitutionary behavior, adapt and recraft contingent outcomes, and revisit the agreed-on terms of any agreement. In short, new forms of restorative or transitional justice are evolutionary developments supplementing and adding to our more conventional justice system. Such forms of justice, providing both permanent institutions and more temporary ones, allow different rules of engagement (narrative without cross-examination, evidence without formal rules, and more direct communication, often with professional intercessions) and different outcomes (not only damage awards or injunctions, but apologies, commitments to future undertakings, and the creation of new monitoring, counselling, health, or educational programs). Most importantly, these forms of justice can provide both individual and group opportunities for expression of harm, acknowledgement of guilt, confession, apology, and forgiveness. The Indian Residential Schools Settlement, by allocating funds for commemoration and truth commission activities, demonstrates just how other forms of (more responsive) justice can be tailored to particular situations.

Yet the processes of restorative justice in general and the Indian Residential Schools Settlement in particular are not without dangers and problems as well. Authenticity of participation is essential if apologies and forgiveness are to be taken seriously. Critics of the South African truth and. reconciliation process noted that many of the key actors—for example, the lawyers and judges who enforced the apartheid regime—did not fully participate. Earlier efforts to involve Indigenous peoples in Canadian law making have been similarly criticized. The pre-Settlement ADR process (and some of the language) in the final settlement document reflects the co-opting of alternative processes by conventional legal language and requirements—what seemed alternative instead required conventional proof at a hearing and the process was considered by many to be over-professionalized and legalized, even when hearing officers were not lawyers or were First Nations people. The danger of co-optation by legal concepts and legal language of even the most alternative processes remains a danger in many efforts to craft tailored processes for particular situations and has been noted by some critics of the Canadian Indian Schools Settlement process, dominated by the Canadian legal establishment.’ The same has been notable in the use of ADR by many formal court systems. Individualized hearings intended to provide compensation for those specifically injured have devolved into conventional, legal evidentiary hearings, inflicting the pain of reliving abuse on rape victims, who often complain that trials become a second rape, and demonstrating just how difficult it is to truly change a legal process.

In Australia, the path-breaking case of *Mabo v Queensland* (1992) recognized, for the first time, the legitimacy of land claims of Aboriginal people, but in the twenty years since, new legislation and the reassertion of conventional colonial conceptions of proof of land claims has not much altered the landscape. Aboriginal critics in both Australia and Canada continue to lament the failure of the colonials to really engage in true dialogue and work towards understanding the different conceptions of justice and the meaning of those communities. True healing and forgiveness cannot be commanded. Critics claim that postcolonial governments still seek closure (whether of compensation amounts or land title) of conventionally framed legal claims and are not willing to reopen or revisit earlier settlements. Others are concerned that even commemorative events and truth and reconciliation commissions do not engage the whole society. Prime Minister Stephen Harper apologized at a brief session in Parliament in 2008; Australia had a full Apology Day, with expectations that the entire nation would participate in public places; the United States has yet to offer any formal recognition of the many harms it has inflicted on its Indigenous population. Yet, despite these very public and symbolic events, underlying resentment may continue. How can such issues be resolved and the different perspectives be reconciled if economic, educational, health access, and other conditions that transcend the legal issues of the residential school cases are not ameliorated?

Thus, it can be said that the Canadian Indian Residential Schools Settlement Agreement has been momentous, in many respects. It arises from what is probably the first truth and reconciliation process *within a* nation, not in connection with a violent ongoing conflict or civil war, and one of the largest compensatory settlements by a former colonial power (including both governmental and religious bodies); it acknowledges wrongdoing and attempts to rectify some harms through both material and more non-material acts, with the desire to correct, account for, and change a nation's history and its relationship to its first citizens and inhabitants. Yet the settlement is both honored and criticized for what it has accomplished and what it has not. Aboriginal life in Canada, as in much of the rest of the colonized world, is still distorted by poverty, dislocation, abuse, alcoholism, health and education deficiencies, experiences of inequality and discrimination, and ambivalence about relations with the larger polity.

At the same time, there are many valuable lessons to be learned as well as questions still to be resolved about both the process and the substantive settlement itself:

1. Litigation may be necessary, but not sufficient, to deal with mass (group) harms. Litigation frames issues, publicizes bad acts, generates information, and provides the initial framework for legal liability.
2. Legal liability is not enough to acknowledge deeper moral and historical claims. To the extent that legal doctrines (such as proof and evidentiary requirements, legal fees rules, immunity, and the limitations of remedial imaginations and powers) limit what courts can do, litigation may be inappropriate for the handling,

management, and resolution of complex, multi-party, long-term, and complex social, political, and legal issues.

3. Even collective (class actions, consolidations) or other forms of aggregate litigation' may be inadequate for the resolution of complex group and individually-based claims that rely on both individual proof and collectively or group-based or experienced harm. Some claims and harms require more complex hybridized treatment.
4. Litigation may be a starting point, but is inadequate for the recognition of 'harms' experienced that are not yet recognized as legal claims (e.g. loss of language/culture/family/group).
5. Conventionally trained lawyers and judges may be limited in how they conceive of legal claims and harms and be unable to enter into the subjective experience of those who experience harms and claims not yet recognized by formal legal systems. As some have noted, the Indian Residential Schools Settlement is still Western and legal in conception—a settlement of lawsuits and legal issues, not the reintegration and healing of communities.
6. Those harmed in such group/mass settings may have a great variety of experiences that cannot easily be fit into legal remedies; thus more flexible, tailored, and 'bespoke' processes (and outcomes) may be necessary to deal with the human variation in injurious experiences.
7. Process pluralism (drawing on meditational, restorative justice as well as litigation) may be a better way to conceive of managing such complex claims. There may be preferred orders for such processes: litigation to frame claims; negotiation and mediation to explore deeply felt needs, interests, preferences, applicable principles, motivations, emotional, group, ethical, religious, and other concerns in order to search for a variety of different kinds of outcomes and solution. Some processes may need to be public for educational and judicial (justice-seeking) purposes; others may require some confidentiality, to provide protection for individuals, and to explore potentially controversial solutions.
8. Group and mass claims require a menu of choices for processes and outcomes—some of those who have been injured will want public hearings; others will prefer privacy and secrecy to reveal what happened to them and to seek accountability from those who caused harm. Some will want compensation; others will want apologies. Some will be willing to forgive (if not forget); others never will. One size will not fit all. Our legal system requires more diverse processes than binary legal hearings with win/lose outcomes. The Indian Residential Schools Settlement has at least attempted to create a menu of some choice and differentiated processes for different purposes.
9. Those who engage in the legal work affecting large groups of people with great injury will require training and skills which may be quite different from or additional to conventional legal training—negotiation, mediation, problem-

solving, responsive dialogue, dispute system design, counseling, healing, and non-legal forms of communication. It may be that alternative or more appropriate forms of justice will require differently skilled professionals at different stages of these processes.

10. Complex, historically based, and group claims may require processes that are more susceptible to change and modification ('contingent' solutions) than conventional legal processes provide for. This is part of the development of the newer legal processes of deliberative democracy and consensus building as methods of managing and handling modern complex legal (and human) disputes that do not lend themselves so easily to final resolutions. (Consider here environmental, scientific, medical, family, and some business issues, where change may affect resolution so that re-opener clauses and other opportunities for re-negotiation are required.) What do we do when new information comes to light, during, or even after, the resolution of some claims?
11. Finally, when do seemingly *sui generis* claims of harms, like the often repeated (US, Australia, Canada, UK, and other perpetrators of similar harms) practices of abuse, require their own particular, culturally specific processes, with a mixture of legal, historical, and emotional healing, with both backward-looking and forward-facing concerns? Will it ever be possible to plan for and design such processes in advance or to use similar processes in different settings, or must such mass and group and culturally specific claims always be designed *sui generis?*

It is my view that the Indian Residential Schools Settlement demonstrated use of a variety of legal and non-legal processes that attempted, in an imperfect but very human way, to face up to a shameful period in the national history of Canada and the equally shameful human behavior of most colonial powers. If we can learn anything from what has been accomplished thus far, it is that human frailty and bad behavior evolves and changes over time. As we now acknowledge the wrongs we have done, we must continue to explore and experiment with new ways to attempt to reconcile and reintegrate ourselves with each other. For me, this means that law, lawyers, and legal processes will have to evolve to improve our relations with each other, to enable us to really hear the needs and demands of others, like First Nations peoples, on their own terms and with their own values, and to create new forms of process and new remedial ideas to reach new understandings of each other and true healing, especially, as here, where we can never achieve full compensation and remediation.

Notes & Questions

1. Consider how the substantive results of this settlement might be a reflection of the process used. Would other types of processes result in different settlements?
2. Pick one of these typical reparations issues: post-war, post-colonial, post-dictatorship, post-slavery, art or agricultural looting, or Catholic priest sexual abuse. Consider what kind of process should be developed to deal with past injustices or to create

appropriate fora to develop rules of engagement for the future. Consider such examples as Korean "comfort women" for Japanese soldiers in World War II; children kidnapped in Ukraine, Israel, and Argentina during wartime/military dictatorship; Indigenous children in "Indian schools" in the United States, Canada, and Australia as described above; and all civilian victims of war.

3. Consider the following new efforts to provide reparative or restorative justice:
   a. University College of London's new program to provide scholarships specifically for Indian (Asian) students to study in London, in recognition of Britain's history of colonization in India. *See* Grace McCabe, *Scholarship of the Month: New Scholarships for Indian Students to Study in the UK*, Times Higher Educ. (Dec. 4, 2023), https://www.timeshighereducation.com/student/advice/scholarship-month-new-scholarships-indian-students-study-uk.
   b. Georgetown University's establishment of a large scholarship fund intended to "compensate" descendants of enslaved people owned by Georgetown and sold as property by the university for financial gain. *See* Susan Svrluga, *Jesuits, Georgetown Give $27 M to Fund for Descendants of Enslaved People*, Wash. Post (Sept. 13, 2023), https://www.washingtonpost.com/education/2023/09/13/georgetown-jesuits-enslaved-descendants-fund/.
   c. Various state programs providing financial payments to those wrongfully convicted of crimes and then released. *See, e.g.*, Cal. Penal Code § 4900 (statute granting relief to those erroneously convicted and imprisoned, where a successful claim results in recommendation to the legislature to provide compensation in the amount of $140 for each day of claimant's wrongful imprisonment). Other states (e.g., Massachusetts and Pennsylvania) are considering whether to provide some form of claims adjudication in court or in alternative forms of dispute resolution as has been done in other mass torts (e.g., victims of terrorism, crimes, or weather disasters, or those injured by vaccines). *See* Victor Cohn, *U.S. Agrees to Pay Those Paralyzed By Swine Flu Shots*, Wash. Post (June 20, 1978), https://www.washingtonpost.com/archive/politics/1978/06/21/us-agrees-to-pay-those-paralyzed-by-swine-flu-shots/26c65a54-e3c9-4e4c-a23f-b8a411b563b3/.
4. Think about the kinds of harms the government should provide compensation for. Think also about the kinds of harms private companies should provide redress or compensation for. Consider the current controversy surrounding bankruptcy court settlements for victims of opioid addiction:

   > It has been 27 years since the prescription opioid OxyContin first came on the market. The manufacturer of the drug, Purdue Pharma, promoted the drug as less susceptible to abuse, but OxyContin proved instead to be highly addictive. The result was a public health crisis and, eventually, thousands of lawsuits seeking trillions of dollars against Purdue Pharma and the Sackler family, which principally owns the company and controlled it until recently, accusing them of having deceptively marketed the drug.

> At the Supreme Court on Monday, the justices appeared conflicted over whether to allow a multi-billion-dollar bankruptcy plan for Purdue Pharma to move forward. The federal government is seeking to block the plan because it releases members of the Sackler family from civil liability for opioid-related claims, but the company's creditors—which include state and local governments and victims of the opioid crisis—broadly support the plan as the only way to ensure that they will receive compensation and funding for opioid recovery projects.
>
> Monday's oral argument was the latest chapter in four years' worth of litigation over the efforts to seek a fresh start in the face of the opioid lawsuits. Purdue Pharma—but not the Sacklers—filed for bankruptcy in 2019, and a bankruptcy court in New York put lawsuits against both the company and the Sackler family on hold shortly after that.

Amy Howe, *Court Conflicted over Purdue Pharma Bankruptcy Plan that Shields Sacklers from Liability*, SCOTUSBLOG (Dec. 4, 2023), https://www.scotusblog.com/2023/12/purdue-bankruptcy-sacklers/. See the Supreme Court's rejection of the Pharma bankruptcy settlement in *Harrington v. Purdue Pharma*, 603 U.S. ___ (2024).

5. What other kinds of harms do you think should be dealt with through some form of restorative or reparative justice?

Further Reading

ELAZAR BARKAN, THE GUILT OF NATIONS: RESTITUTION AND NEGOTIATING HISTORICAL INJUSTICES (2000).

COMPARATIVE DISPUTE RESOLUTION (Maria F. Moscati, Michael Palmer, & Marian Roberts, eds. 2020).

PRISCILLA HAYNER, UNSPEAKABLE TRUTHS: TRANSITIONAL JUSTICE AND THE CHALLENGE OF TRUTH COMMISSIONS (2d ed. 2010).

JAN KLABBERS, ADVANCED INTRODUCTION TO THE LAW OF INTERNATIONAL ORGANIZATIONS (2015).

Carrie Menkel-Meadow, *Restorative Justice: What Is It and Does It Work?*, 10 ANN. REV. L. & SOC. SCI. (2007).

MARTHA MINOW, BETWEEN VENGEANCE AND FORGIVING: FACING HISTORY AFTER GENOCIDE AND MASS VIOLENCE (1998).

Martha Minow, *Do Alternative Justice Mechanisms Deserve Recognition in International Criminal Law? Truth Commissions, Amnesties and Complementarities at the International Criminal Court*, 60 Harv. Int'l L.J. 1–45 (2019).

Mayo Moran, *Cardinal Sins: How the Catholic Church Sexual Abuse Crisis Changed Private Law*, 21 GEO. J. GEN. & L. 95 (2019).

Susan Podziba, CIVIC FUSION: MEDIATING POLARIZED PUBLIC DISPUTES (2012).

A RESTORATIVE JUSTICE READER: TEXTS, SOURCES, CONTEXTS (W. Gerry Johnstone ed., 2003).

Susan Sturm & Howard Gadlin, *Conflict Resolution and Systemic Change,* 2007 J. Disp. Resol. 1 (2007).

Lawrence Susskind et al. THE CONSENSUS BUILDING HANDBOOK: A COMPREHENSIVE GUIDE TO REACHING AGREEMENT (1999).

RUTI G. TEITEL, GLOBALIZING TRANSITIONAL JUSTICE (2014).

TRUTH VS. JUSTICE: THE MORALITY OF TRUTH COMMISSIONS (Robert Rotberg & Dennis Thompson, eds. 2000).

COLIN THUBRON, THE SHADOW OF THE SILK ROAD (2007).

DESMOND TUTU, NO FUTURE WITHOUT FORGIVENESS (1999).

Chapter 9

Dispute System Design (DSD)

Some conflicts are so sufficiently complicated or unique that it makes sense to design structures just for them. In the previous chapter, for example, you read about the international community's attempts to create processes for reconciliation for countries coming out of civil war or dictatorship. Other disputes are repetitive, and so it makes sense to create processes that are not only fair but also efficient. This thinking underlies the processes discussed in Chapter 7: ombuds regularly deal with institutional disputes, and investor-state arbitration standardizes the processes for disputes between individuals and states. In either case, theories of how to design a system are often applied.

In this chapter, we explore the processes and frameworks that are used in designing dispute systems. We review both the evolving theory of dispute system design (DSD) and provide examples of how it has been applied in a variety of international contexts. The first part of this chapter explains the field of dispute system design and outlines the different frameworks for creating dispute resolution processes. The second part turns our attention back to hybrid processes, covered in the previous two chapters, and shows how specific dispute system design processes have been implemented.

I. DSD Frameworks

This first excerpt, from a textbook on DSD, provides a history of dispute system design. Further sections outline frameworks and specific questions that need to be asked when creating these systems.

Lisa Blomgren Amsler, Janet K. Martinez, & Stephanie E. Smith, Dispute System Design: Preventing, Managing, and Resolving Conflict

10–11; 13 (2020)

Throughout history humans have developed systems for managing conflict, but the modern language for DSD emerged from labor-management relations more than thirty years ago as a way to think about improving how organizations, their employees, and other stakeholders address disputes. At the same time, scholars discussed conflict management related to human resources management and non-union employment conflict. "Conflict" is the broader term, encompassing arenas within which disputes occur. Scholars from diverse disciplines—for instance, anthropology, psychology, sociology, law, and economics—have studied the causes and responses to conflict and developed a discipline of conflict analysis.

Now, DSD most often occurs within or in relation to an organization, whether a private company, public agency, international institution, or nonprofit entity. A systems approach to problem definition and resolution of a stream of similar disputes has emerged in, for example, engineering, social science, and natural science but has become notably prominent in organizational development. Historically, organizations only *reacted* to conflict—they did not systematically plan how to manage it. However, organizations became dissatisfied with time-consuming and costly disputing processes that did not produce satisfactory outcomes.

In its initial usage, DSD applied to systems for managing explicit, or "ripe" disputes, such as when unions submit breach of contract claims to a grievance procedure culminating in the quasi-judicial forum of labor arbitration. William Ury, Jeanne Brett, and Stephen Goldberg examined how to improve this system in collective bargaining by inserting a new, mediation step (a third party who helps disputants negotiate) before arbitration (a private adjudication). Would this addition change the dynamics of the system? Would it help parties resolve disputes faster and save money by reducing cases requiring a costly outside arbitrator? They found that providing mediation in unionized coal mines within twenty-four hours of a grievance both resolved disputes more quickly and produced substantial participant satisfaction with the mediation process and outcome.

Grievance mediation as a process focuses on interests (basic human, social, or economic needs and concerns). Ury, Brett, and Goldberg recommended that systems focus on interests instead of rights or power to address conflict. Rights-based dispute resolution requires a neutral third party to apply agreed-on rules from law, policy, or contract to a set of facts to determine who wins. It includes arbitration, administrative adjudication, or a court trial. Power-based processes use dominance in physical force or financial resources to impose an outcome—for example, strikes and lockouts in collective bargaining. Ury, Brett, and Goldberg suggested that a healthy system should use rights-based approaches (such as arbitration or litigation for law or contract) only as a fallback when disputants reach impasse; generally, parties should not resort to power (use of force or strikes).

Cathy A. Constantino and Christina Sickles Merchant focus on principles for organizational systems to determine whether designers can tailor some form of ADR to a specific category of disputes. They seek to ascertain whether prevention (not just dispute resolution) is available, the system is accessible with minimal bureaucracy and maximal choice over the processes and selection of third parties, and the organization supports the DSD. In evaluation, they find that higher-quality systems are more efficient (in terms of cost and time) and lead to more satisfaction with the process, outcome, and ongoing relationship between disputants. They include in the notion of effectiveness the durability of the resolution, the nature of the outcome (quantity and character of dispute recurrence), and the effect on the organizational environment.

Notes & Questions

1. Early DSD focused on the difference between rights-based dispute resolution (adjudication), power-based dispute resolution (strikes or, in the international context, gunboat diplomacy), and an interest-based dispute resolution process (mediation, conciliation, or negotiation). How do these different categories of disputes play out in the international arena? Reflect back on some of the case studies you read in earlier chapters—which type of process was used in each?
2. Consider that dispute systems have been created by international organizations (the UN, OECD, ICSID) bilaterally (between individual countries) or internally. How might the concepts of multiparty negotiation (discussed in Chapter 5) play out in the application of creating dispute systems?

A. Frameworks for DSD

In the next excerpt, Stephanie Smith and Janet Martinez propose a framework for organizing and guiding the analysis and design of dispute systems. This section dives deeper into the key elements of an analytical framework for DSD.

Stephanie Smith & Janet Martinez, *An Analytic Framework for Dispute Systems Design*

14 HARV. NEGOT. L. REV. 123, 129–32 (2009)

Goals

The element of *goals* consists of two parts: to identify which types of conflicts the system seeks to address and what goals the system intends to accomplish. A dispute resolution system within an organization may address one, few or many categories of conflicts. For instance, a company could design a system intended to resolve only internal employee disputes. Alternatively, the company could design a broader system that addresses disputes with external actors, such as clients or suppliers. At its most extensive, an integrated conflict management system (ICMS) could address all or almost all of an organization's conflicts, among internal stakeholders and between internal and external actors. The more integrated approach could include goals on prevention and management as well as resolution, and provide multiple access points for process intervention.

Once the scope of conflict is defined, it is important to consider what the system intends to accomplish. Desired outcomes, and the priorities among them, need to be established, both to clarify the policy direction ex ante, and to assess the system's success ex post. The range of possible objectives is extensive:

- Conflict prevention? Management? Resolution?
- Efficiency/resource savings: Minimize time of stakeholders, institution and/or neutrals; Minimize cost for institution and/or stakeholders? Reduction of number or type of conflicts?

- Relational: Transform or restructure relationships? Whose?
- Safety: Prevent violence against parties? Protect property?
- System operation: Enhance access to the system? Decrease caseload?
- Public recognition: Protect privacy? Provide public vindication? Create precedent?
- Substantive outcome: Increase "justice"? How defined?
- Fairness: Procedural? Substantive?
- Reputation (of individuals, organization)?
- Compliance: To sanction or punish? Deter future disputes?
- Satisfaction: Of all, or fewer than all, stakeholders? Durability of resolution?
- Organizational improvement: To identify institutional weaknesses or injustices and correct them

Ultimately, the designer of the system has the power to define the goals of that system and their relative priority. The trade-offs required among competing goals may affect the quality of the resulting system. A significant tension can be one between the goals of efficiency and fairness or justice.

Process and Structure

Many different types of processes can be used to prevent, manage, and resolve conflicts. Some organizations offer one formal process, such as mediation or arbitration, while others develop a range of processes for one or more types of disputes. If multiple options are offered, those options may be linked together in an integrated system or they may exist ad hoc, as discrete, unlinked processes that evolved in different parts of the organization over time, often without centralized or strategic thought. Either way, the available processes may have different incentives (financial, timing, or other) that encourage or discourage their use by different stakeholders.

An organization's freedom to design its internal conflict prevention, management, and resolution processes as it wishes may be constrained by courts, legislatures, or administrative bodies. Existing law may prohibit use of certain processes or require that specific due process elements be included. Once designed, an organization's dispute system may be challenged in a court or legislative body if some stakeholders believe the processes included run afoul of legal or other societal norms.

Stakeholders

The third element is identification of various *stakeholders* and their relative power. For existing systems, it will be worthwhile to learn which stakeholders were involved in the system's design and whose interests are represented.

Stakeholders may be the immediate parties in conflict, individuals, or entities subsidiary to or constituents of those parties, or others directly or indirectly affected by the dispute's outcome. In creating a system, it is usually best to identify as many stakeholders as possible in order to understand and create a system that takes into account all significant interests, has legitimacy, and is therefore more likely to garner credibility and produce durable outcomes. System dysfunction can often be attributed to failure to adequately involve and acknowledge the interests of key stakeholder groups.

Resources

A system can only achieve its goals if it is adequately supported. To avoid creating an elaborate set of processes with inadequate resources, however, may require making hard decisions that as noted above can have impacts on fairness, justice, and likelihood of success.

Also central to understanding the funding issue is the question of who pays. Financing of the system by some parties and not others may create bias or a perception of bias. While having only one side pay increases the risk of bias, imposing financial costs on lower income parties may create burdens that effectively deny access in some cases.

Success and Accountability

The last element to assess is *success*. At the first level, one can ask to whom is the system accountable? Is the system transparent in terms of its operation, access to processes, and its results, and to whom? Second, does the system include an evaluation component, and if so, what is studied, when, and by whom, and to whom are the results made available? Finally, is the system successful when measured against its intended goals, as well as other relevant legal and societal norms?

A system's success is best judged if outcomes are made available to and studied by independent evaluators. Unfortunately, barriers such as cost, privacy concerns, difficulty, and wariness to exposure often preclude meaningful evaluation from taking place.

Evaluation is important in three primary respects. First, evaluation is necessary for system operators to ascertain whether the system is functioning effectively. Are key stakeholder groups staying out of the system? Are costs proving to be far in excess of projections? Are neutrals failing to deliver quality services or violating ethics rules? Are users satisfied with the options and services provided? Second, ongoing evaluation enables improvement of the system. Without ongoing evaluation, system operators would be unable to identify shortcomings in an organization's dispute resolution processes. Third, it is important for users to understand how and how well the system operates. Transparency increases credibility and therefore participation, and encourages further feedback from participants to system operators.

At a minimum, evaluation should begin with internal monitoring, including some combination of data collection on usage, surveys, and focus groups designed to obtain candid feedback from key stakeholder groups. Of course, independent external review is preferable and provides more detailed and objective assessment.

The Analytic Framework

1. ***Goals***
   a) *Which types of conflicts does the system seek to address?*
   b) *What does the system's designer seek to accomplish?*
2. ***Process and Structure***
   a) *Which processes are used to prevent, manage and resolve disputes?*
   b) *If there is more than one process, are they linked or integrated?*
   c) *What are the incentives and disincentives for using the system?*
   d) *What is the system's interaction with the formal legal system?*
3. ***Stakeholders***
   a) *Who are the stakeholders?*
   b) *What is their relative power?*
   c) *How are their interests represented in the system?*
4. ***Resources***
   a) *What financial resources support the system?*
   b) *What human resources support the system?*
5. ***Success and Accountability***
   a) *How transparent is the system?*
   b) *Does it include an evaluation component?*
   c) *Is the system successful?*

The next article examines dispute system design in the context of transitional justice and human rights violations and how it can result in a variety of hybrid structures (*see* Chapter 8).

Andrea Kupfer Schneider, *The Intersection of Dispute Systems Design and Transitional Justice*

14 Harv. Negot. L. Rev. 289, 290–292; 297–298; 302–306; 312 (2009)

Among the many challenges that dispute systems designers face when dealing with human rights violations are the following:

1. Should we be setting up a DSD at all? How can we design systems that both acknowledge the need for justice and promote peace on the ground as soon as possible?

2. Who designs and implements the DSD? How can we design systems that are almost inevitably implemented from the top down while recognizing that the best healing occurs from the bottom up?
3. How is the system designed? How can we as designers be efficient and use the best practices of the past while still customizing each dispute system to take unique account of each individual conflict?
4. What values are promoted by the DSD? How can we explain the push for judicialization of international disputes at the same time that trial rates in the U.S. continue to drop?
5. What remedies are provided by the DSD? How can we design systems for the future while recognizing that the people most affected often need to cope with the past violations before looking to the future?...

II. Should a Dispute System Be Set Up at All?—
Justice v. Peace

As conflicts end, politicians often wonder whether we need an official response or structure to resolve disputes or, perhaps, other responses would be more appropriate. After World War II, Stalin famously suggested that instead of the Nuremberg Tribunal, the Allies could just take the Germans out back and shoot them. On the other hand, in many countries, it seems to be enough if the political leadership changes, perhaps amnesty is granted, and the population at least appears to be willing to move on. Due primarily to cold war politics, blanket amnesty for dictators and war criminals was the norm prior to 1993. In Argentina, Chile and several other South American countries, amnesty was granted to the military leadership in exchange for stepping down. As Professor Carlos Nino has stated, "a legal duty selectively to prosecute human rights violations committed under a previous regime is too blunt an instrument to help successor governments who must struggle with the subtle complexities of re-establishing democracy."

Today, the need for immediate peace between the parties, the desire for swift justice, and the long-term goal of a more lasting peace among the warring groups regularly provides conflicting concerns for scholars and international dispute systems designers alike. Is it more important to stop the violence or to pursue justice by punishing those responsible for human rights violations? In the quest to end conflicts, can the international community achieve peace and justice without granting amnesty to war criminals? The tension arises because, arguably, oppressive dictators and war criminals will not want to give up power (and thus stop the violence) if they will be hauled into court the next day....

III. Who Actually Designs & Implements the System?—
Top-Down v. Bottom-Up

A second conflict in international DSD is the problem of introducing solutions from the designer's top-down perspective, when the process must take place from the bottom up. After all, the impact of any structure will be measured by more than its effect on the international community but rather how the DSD affected the post-conflict society.

In international DSD thus far, the most well-known structures have been designed by an international elite. The various ad hoc courts established by the UN for Yugoslavia and Rwanda are a clear example and have been criticized for their distance—physically and psychologically—from the affected countries. Even in the more recently created courts, this concern has not been fully met. Recognizing already some of issues raised by the ICTR and ICTY, the Sierra Leone hybrid court was designed to try to meet some concerns by creating a mix of international and local judges with a mix of international and local law. But with only a few Leoneans at the top levels of the court and many of the local legal community avoiding it altogether, there were questions as to whether the decisions of the court will have any precedence within Sierra Leone or be enforceable at all. Similarly, the tribunal for Khmer Rouge in Cambodia, designed by the international community, has also been unsuccessful in their battle for public perception The tribunal faced many challenges early on, including widespread allegations that some judges and staff were required to kick back part of their salary in order to keep their jobs. Some have even argued that the UN did not investigate these claims in an attempt to keep the court moving forward.

This top-down design has also been an issue for truth commissions. The truth commission in El Salvador, created relatively early in 1992, consisted entirely of international commissioners and staff members, purposely excluding Salvadoran natives because of the civil war. The truth commission was not trusted initially by the Salvadorans because it lacked the local perspective, having a staff that was totally international, and had to work hard to overcome that suspicion. Other times, these DSD's are established by the domestic elite—South Africa's Truth & Reconciliation Commission is an early example where the politicians created the system for the populace to use. The larger point is that the victims are often spread throughout the country, come from lower economic classes, while the structures are created by concentrated or foreign elite groups. At the same time, without international support, these structures will not be created at all....

IV. How Is the System Designed?— Standardization v. Customization

A third challenge in creating international DSD is that as these models of tribunals and truth commissions are used, a conflict can arise between standardization and customization. The challenge is how to deal with large scale violations and problems where each case and crime is painfully individual. Legal models transferred with little thought from one crisis to the next will not work, as the evolution to hybrid tribunals demonstrates. Hence, we can see the evolution of Nuremberg to Yugoslavia and Rwanda to locally hosted hybrid tribunals. However, customizing each aspect of a tribunal or TRC is time-consuming and expensive. And, as we can see from the various financial crises faced by the newer ad hoc courts, the international community has a funding limit. The standing ICC may relieve some of the funding burden but might not be able to meet the broader healing needs of each community. We can examine both domestic and international dispute systems for lessons in dealing with striking the right balance between efficiency and individuality....

**V. What Values Are Promoted by Different Systems?—
Trials v. Consensual Processes**

After examining the challenges outlined above—peace v. justice, top-down v. bottom-up, efficiency v. individuality—the challenge of what structure works best for the conflict is clearly influenced by navigating all of those. This section of the essay notes that while the structure is important, the values promoted by the system are far more important....

**VI. What Remedies Are Provided by the System?—
Past v. Future**

A final issue that arises in DSD is that the design itself must look prospectively to future remedies in order to be effective, yet the participants, victims, and others are inherently looking backward to the incident. This tension exists in almost every kind of DSD. Inevitably, we end up designing systems that respond to problems already created—unhappy customers, litigation with employees, an explosion of medical mistakes, etc. In international conflicts, this tension between the past and future is even more profound. Often there are grave violations of human rights about which to testify—in fact we argue that the ability to be heard, to tell the story, to establish the historical record, and to set the truth are all crucial parts of the process. Yet as we design the process or processes, we focus on what will be needed for the future—the record, the effect of deterrence, the ability to set the law, remedies that meet the victims' needs. Different processes will, inevitably, provide different remedies. Often, in examining transitional justice cases, the tension appears to be between trials and truth commissions.

Notes & Questions

Review the questions asked in the previous article and think about how you would apply them to different claims, for example, American Indians suing for their loss of land and other injuries (e.g., Indian boarding schools), descendants of enslaved people seeking reparations, or victims of U.S. weather disasters bringing suit on account of receiving inadequate federal, state, or local attention/support (e.g., Hurricane Katrina). Feel free to consider any other mass injury claims you can come up with.

B. Modification and Considerations

In the next excerpt, author Dan Shapiro reimagines DSD as a reconciliation system in which the process is harnessed specifically for healing purposes. The second excerpt discusses the ethics that must be considered when creating such systems.

Daniel L. Shapiro, *Reconciliation Systems Design: A Systemic Approach to Collective Healing in Post-Conflict Societies*

26 Harv. Negot. L. Rev. 198–206; 211–212; 218 (2021)

Reconciliation Systems Design is a methodical approach to conceptualize, operationalize, and synergize reconciliation interventions within post-conflict societies. A large body of research examines individual reconciliation interventions such as the structure of a truth commission. Reconciliation Systems Design, in contrast, focuses on the meta-processes through which a society develops a coordinated set of interventions. The three fundamental components of this method—reconciliation, systems, and design—require explication.

Reconciliation. Reconciliation is the process of fostering harmonious coexistence between opposing individuals and groups. Ideally, a divided society is made whole through political, social, legal, and economic measures that enable individuals and groups to (1) come to terms with grievances, (2) live and work together in dignity and harmony, and (3) address differences through peaceful means. Reconciliation does not produce a conflict-free society, for discord is inevitable—and desirable—in a democratic society where people's voices matter. Instead, society actuates its capacity to resolve differences nonviolently through political means, economic development, and dispute resolution mechanisms including law, negotiation, mediation, and arbitration. A vibrant, interconnected society emerges in which stakeholders cooperate on issues of common concern, manage differences effectively and fairly, and avoid the human and financial costs of interpersonal, intergroup, and structural violence. Political and psychological reality is not always so kind to this vision, but the ideal is important for society to keep in mind to motivate a proactive stance toward collective healing.

Relational Identity Theory provides insight into the process of reconciliation by differentiating between core identity and relational identity. Core identity refers to the set of characteristics that define who one is as an individual or member of a group, ranging from one's beliefs and values to self-categorization as a representative of a social, spiritual, or political group. Because core identity is central to our sense of personal continuity and worldview, it is extremely resistant to change; any reconciliation program that seeks to convert our deepest beliefs is likely to fail. A much more fluid type of identity is what I call relational identity—the characteristics that define who we are in relation to another individual or group. Herein lies the power of reconciliation. Whereas violent conflict pits core identities against one another—Hutu versus Tutsi, Northerner versus Southerner—reconciliation weaves people's relational identities into an interconnected whole.

Reconciliation must address two basic dimensions of relational identity: affiliation and autonomy. Affiliation is the quality and degree of our emotional connection to individuals, groups, and institutions—the extent to which we feel close to them and included within social, economic, political, and legal structures. Autonomy refers to the quality and degree to which we feel free to make independent decisions about what to think, feel, and do in relation to an individual, group, or institution. Do we feel pressured to publicly reveal our stories of victimization? Are we treated as second-class citizens with constrained freedom to contribute to, and benefit from, the political, economic, and legal system? Fundamentally, the challenge of reconciliation is to achieve cross-group affiliation and mutual respect for everyone's autonomy, but innumerable complications arise. Should society grant amnesty to perpetrators of violence and guarantee them seats in a new government, expanding their political autonomy but disaffiliating people who oppose this inclusive policy? Or should society enact punitive measures that affirm hard-edged justice at cost to cross-group affiliation? How should society re-affiliate youth soldiers who have experienced the front lines of battle and the agency of combat?

Because reconciliation is a relational process, it has no definitive endpoint. While some scholars argue that it is an outcome—a state of restored relations—I assume there is no moment that can be hailed as the finale to societal divides. Relational identity is fluid, organic, and dynamic, and conflict narratives and collective emotional memories can reemerge serendipitously or deliberately at a later point in time. Serious intergroup divides can bury deep within society's collective psyche and reemerge in new forms years or generations later, implying that reconciliation is an on-going process. Although its methods vary across cultures and contexts, they typically involve a range of state-organized and community-initiated activities to come to terms with the widespread impact of war crimes, crimes against humanity, and individual and institutional violence, as well as efforts to cultivate inclusive attitudes, social norms, and institutions.

Political negotiation and reconciliation are distinct, complementary, and at times overlapping processes. The purpose of political negotiation is to bridge political divides through a mutually acceptable political agreement that meets stakeholder interests to the extent feasible. In contrast, the purpose of reconciliation is to bridge relational divides to the extent feasible, ranging from increased behavioral cooperation to internalization of positive relations. Put succinctly, "politics is a process to deal with the issues that have divided us in the past. Reconciliation is a parallel process that redesigns the relationship between us." Political negotiations are usually private and prolonged, during which negotiating agents better understand each other's perspectives—in effect undergoing a degree of interpersonal reconciliation—but society at large is rarely privy to these sessions, and taboos against affiliating with the enemy keep the negotiators' amicable relations hidden from the public eye.

System. Addressing structural disparities and entrenched narratives of victimhood requires a multi-level, multi-dimensional set of coordinated interventions to work through grievances, revise structural tensions, and restore positive intergroup relations. The specific interventions—which I refer to as healing mechanisms—range from local social and educational activities to society-wide economic and political reform. Because justice can foster societal healing, I also categorize justice-oriented interventions as healing mechanisms. Reconciliation happens at many levels within a society, and the interaction of these healing mechanisms forms systems of interdependence. Neighborhood projects can improve national unity just as a national truth commission can soothe local tensions. Furthermore, local interventions typically nest within national ones. A national healing mechanism can inspire a neighborhood reconciliation project which, in turn, can energize national bridge-building efforts.

Design. Reconciliation Systems Design explores optimal processes for designing an integrated system of collective healing mechanisms. How should healing mechanisms be developed, by whom, and how can society synergize multiple interventions? A major task of Reconciliation Systems Design is to create what I call templates for action—guides for developing and coordinating tailored healing mechanisms within specific post-conflict contexts. In the immediate aftermath of mass violence, it is much easier for policymakers to review these illustrative reconciliation design processes and adapt the most relevant ones to their situation than to start from scratch and move forward on instinct alone....

Three categories of obstacles hamper a reconciliation system: (1) a poorly formed design team; (2) a poorly laid conceptual foundation for reconciliation; and (3) a poorly constructed healing system. These three broad groups and specific obstacles that fall within each are summarized in Table 1....

Table 1: Key Obstacles to Reconciling Relations and Strategies to Address Them

Obstacle	Strategy
Forming the Design Team	
1. Nobody starts the process	Establish the convenor
2. Limited awareness of stakeholders	Map the stakeholders
3. Non-credible design team	Assemble a representative design team
4. Team members compete	Build affiliation as working partners
5. Clash of values	Formulate ethical guidelines
Building the Blueprint for Reconciliation	
6. No societal vision of coexistence	Develop a shared vision of harmonious coexistence
7. Incomplete understanding of societal divides	Identify emotional and structural factors impeding reconciliation
8. No shared theory of collective healing	Clarify strategic healing objectives
Designing the System	
9. Cookie-cutter approach to reconciliation	Build transitional, enduring, and symbolic healing mechanisms
10. System fragmentation	Synergize healing mechanisms
11. Emotional chasm threatens the system	Boost system resilience
12. A deficit of public will	Mobilize public will toward reconciliation

Ambassador Sergio Jaramillo Caro, former High Commissioner for Peace in Colombia and a key architect of his country's reconciliation process, recently told me that the government had designed its sophisticated reconciliation process "by studying every reconciliation case we could locate from around the world and then creating our own, homegrown approach that met our specific needs." When I asked him pointblank whether his team followed any sort of systematic roadmap or theory to guide the design process, he responded, "No." This anecdote highlights the objective of Reconciliation Systems Design: providing a conceptual and practical roadmap to facilitate the design of a high-impact, integrated reconciliation system that benefits from analysis of previous conflicts and reconciliation systems. This Section presents major tenets of Reconciliation Systems Design and details twelve strategies, outlined in Table 1, that can achieve this objective.

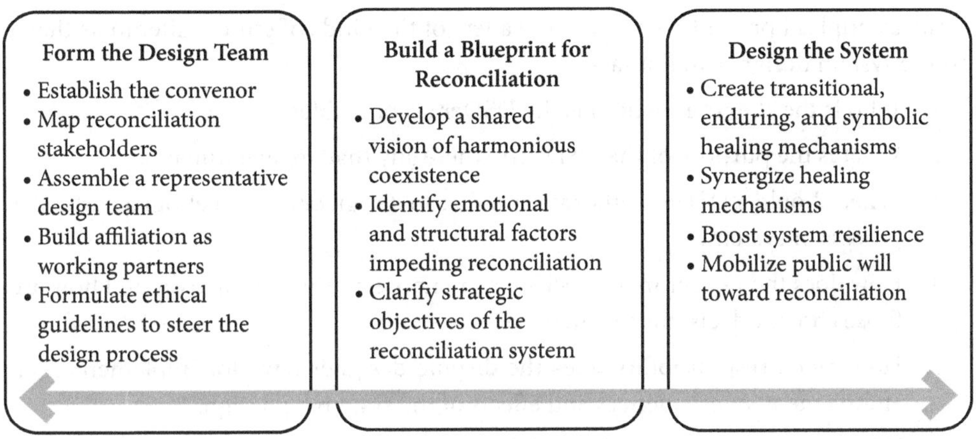

Notes & Questions

1. What do you think may be the most common and difficult part of reconciliation?
2. Recall the examples of governments abusing their own citizens, civil wars, and external conflicts that were discussed in the previous chapter. How would the reconciliation processes in each of these situations differ?
3. Chapter 3 explored the Northern Ireland conflict and how Senator George Mitchell mediated the Good Friday Accords. That agreement, which at least halted much of the bloodshed, also left room for possible reconciliation. Consider how the debates in the last section of this chapter (on peace versus justice and the past versus the future) are still ongoing in Northern Ireland, where some parties want to end inquiries into human rights violations and focus instead on moving forward, while others want to continue to pursue fact-finding and the truth. How would the Reconciliation System Design model deal with these tensions?

So far we have covered the questions that need to be asked and an analytical framework that should be followed when designing a dispute resolution process. But there is another key element that must be considered when deciding on which process to use and implement: ethics, specifically the ethics and values of the field and of the individual designers. In the next excerpt, Carrie Menkel-Meadow tackles the question of whether there are core principles in the field.

Carrie Menkel-Meadow, *Are There Systemic Ethics Issues in Dispute System Design—and What We Should [Not] Do about It: Lessons from International and Domestic Fronts*

14 Harv. Negot. L. Rev. 195, 211–213; 220–21 (2009)

Deductive Ethics: Are There Core Principles in the Field?

The examples I present above are only a few of the kinds of ethical dilemmas that a dispute system designer might face:

1. Who is the client? To whom is the DSDer accountable?
2. What is the purpose of the DSD? Are there any that are illegitimate?
3. When should a DSDer withdraw or refuse to design or consult about a particular process or system?
4. How does the DSDer make decisions or choose among alternatives and how are those choices/decisions justified?
5. How much responsibility does the dispute designer have for implementation, enforcement, consequences and effects of the system he designs?
6. What responsibility does the DSDer bear for most efficient and fair use of organizational/institutional/governmental resources? (How should DSD be weighed against competing organizational and individual needs and resources?)
7. How much independence does the DSDer have from the client? (When is the DSDesigner being used for illegitimate ends?) When does a DSDer have a conflict of interest (because of different or competing needs within the client organization or because of other work for other clients or other professional commitments)?
8. What are the sources of "values," norms, ethics or good practices in DSD?

These general questions then, suggest some general principles for developing a set of "best practices" or ethics for the field of DSD centered around responsibility, accountability, fairness, independence, judgment, participation (of affected parties) and pursuit of legitimate goals. These "general" principles could be used to derive, deductively, some general norms for the profession of DSD.

Nevertheless, I suggest that the tension of universality or generality and particularity or cultural differences may make agreement on ethics principles difficult in DSD.

If modern ADR theory and practice has taught us anything, it is that modern process is plural. Claimants, victims, parties, defendants, law reformers, judicial officers and other decision makers, and policy analysts all may desire different things from a legal or dispute resolution system. Some want vindication, others want apologies and forgiveness; some want clear legal rules, others want more subtle terms for ongoing relationships. Some desire punishment and retribution.

As Lon Fuller so clearly described and anticipated in his many articles on legal process, DSD is based on the idea that different processes are necessary for different kinds of contexts and party needs. So mediation is appropriate in ongoing relationships for its flexibility, ability to tailor solutions to the particular needs of parties, and opportunity for open-ended narratives and human interaction. Arbitration is most appropriate when decisions and final settlements are required, but choice of law (contract provisions), decision makers (chosen by parties), privacy and flexibility on rules of procedure or evidence are consensually desired by the parties. Some processes are private (most forms of mediation and arbitration); other legal processes are intended to be public (courts, international tribunals, truth, and reconciliation commissions) and parties may have different needs and desires with respect to the transparency and privacy of the legal harms they have suffered. Consider the case of discrimination claimants, some of whom desire to "go public" and make big statements on their cases and others who prefer some privacy (AIDS victims, gays or transsexual claimants, some rape and war crimes victims).

Thus, in a modern world characterized by "process pluralism," is it possible to develop generalized, universal and robust ethics principles across process differences? Is the act of "designing" processes sufficiently coherent and uniform to allow general principles, even if the processes designed are themselves different or pluralistic?...

More importantly, in international contexts we may not have agreement on some of the most basic, core values: peace at any cost, punishment of wrong doers, forgiveness, precedent setting, standard articulation, private vs. public proceedings, formal vs. informal mechanisms and institutions, local (indigenous) vs. national, regional or international locuses of dispute resolution fora, compensation, apologies, rights of past (right of return) vs. present (compensation) vs. future (affirmative action, land rights, social welfare, etc.).... If I had only several "canons of ethics" to suggest they would be:

1. Be truly sensitive to local conditions and "thick descriptions of cultures" in all their variety;
2. Do no harm; and
3. Make no assumptions about what people want.

Notes & Questions

1. How can claims processes be developed in an international context with different legal systems and different standards of liability?
2. Is it possible to think of recompense without "proof" of individual injury? Is "group" injury enough? When? How should such claims be decided?

3. It has been proposed that the UN develop a single fund (which would have to be huge) to compensate the victims of unlawful wars, humanitarian disasters, and similar occurrences (e.g., famines, floods, droughts). Think of what kinds of injuries should qualify and what kinds of processes could be designed to deal with such situations.

II. DSD in Action

In this second part of the chapter, we look at dispute system design in several different contexts. The first section focuses on how the United Nations has designed specific tribunals to handle a multitude of individual cases with claims against a country. The second section explores ombuds, discussed in Chapter 8, as a mini-system of dispute design. The third section also uses examples from the previous chapter but focuses on DSD in transitional and restorative justice. The final section examines dispute system design in the investor-state arbitration system, a system that is discussed in detail in Chapter 7.

A. The United Nations and Claims Tribunals

David D. Caron, *The Nature of the Iran-United States Claims Tribunal and the Evolving Structure of International Dispute Resolution*

84 Am. J. Int'l Law 104, 151–56 (1990)

III. The Evolving Structure of International Dispute Resolution

In 1914 and 1916, Mr. Mavrommatis obtained concessions from the Ottoman Empire to provide certain public services in Jerusalem and Jaffa. After the First World War, the British Government granted duplicate concessions to a different person. Predictably, a dispute ensued. The Government of Greece eventually espoused the claim of Mavrommatis, its national, against the British Government on the basis of diplomatic protection. Ultimately, the claim was addressed on the public international law level by the Permanent Court of International Justice.

In the early 1920s, Mavrommatis had few, if any, other options for pursuing his claim. Today, in contrast, he would likely include, as a part of his concession, a clause providing for international commercial arbitration in, for example, Geneva under the UNCITRAL Rules of Arbitration or Paris at the International Chamber of Commerce. In contrast to settlement by the Permanent Court of International Justice, this proceeding would not require the cooperation of the other party and could result in an award enforceable and recognizable around much of the world under the New York Convention.

Many arbitrations at the turn of the century, like the Mavrommatis case, involved claims of individuals based on diplomatic protection. That is, many of the disputes were not truly between the two states named as parties.

Today, depending upon the circumstances, similar claims likely would be handled through lump sum settlement or international commercial arbitration. Thus, the aggregate effect of the change in options described for Mavrommatis is that there quite plausibly has been a shift in dockets....

IV. Conclusion

The arbitral proceedings before the Iran-United States Claims Tribunal involving claims of nationals are governed by the legal system of the Netherlands. This conclusion does not sit easily with the prevailing tendency to think that the proceedings of a tribunal formed by treaty to resolve a crisis between two countries are an interstate process not subject to interference by municipal legal orders. The tension between this conclusion and intuition is all the more striking, as the support for the former is extensive, if not overwhelming. The prevailing tendency nonetheless persists because it rests upon a categorical distinction between public and private international dispute resolution that in the past reflected practice quite faithfully. This distinction, however, no longer adequately describes the variations in international dispute resolution. The inadequacy of the distinction is problematic particularly for the interpreters of treaties because it may lead them unconsciously to force the innovative features of a treaty into the pigeonholes of the past. Thus, unconscious reliance upon this distinction should be replaced with a case-by-case examination of the mechanism the parties intended to create. Where this is done, innovation through treaty is protected, and a means for the development of international organization preserved.

The desire to innovate is driven by the perception that existing mechanisms do not fulfill the needs of the parties. To the parties, the various mechanisms are not separate doctrines but, rather, alternatives that should be measured against their needs. In this way, the parties' needs fuel the evolution of these mechanisms. Two particularly important dimensions to international dispute resolution in which innovation has occurred are the means of reviewing the validity of the result and the means of gaining enforcement of the result. The emergence of specific machinery such as the Tribunal and ICSID, and the increasing incidence of transnational litigation involving states and international commercial arbitration with state parties—all concurrent with an arguably decreasing need to rely on diplomatic protection—indicate that the various private, state and interstate mechanisms for the resolution of international disputes should not be viewed as operating in isolation, but as competing with, and evolving in response to, one another.

Francis E. McGovern, *Dispute System Design: The United Nations Compensation Commission*

14 Harv. Negot. L. Rev. 171–176; 188–189 (2009)

I. Introduction

The Security Council of the United Nations established the United Nations Compensation Commission ("UNCC") with its Resolution 687 on April 3, 1991. It was the first compensation system established under the authority of Chapter VII of the U.N. Charter and was designed to process and pay claims arising from the Iraqi invasion of Kuwait in 1990. Resolution 687 confirmed that Iraq was liable "for any direct loss, damage, including environmental damages and the depletion of natural resources, or injury to foreign Governments, nationals and corporations...." Resolution 687 also created a fund to pay those claims and a commission to administer that fund. The details of the compensation fund and the commission were established by Security Council Resolution 692 on May 20, 1991.

The goals of the UNCC were (1) to effect a speedy, fair, and efficient evaluation of the claims made against Iraq and to process them in accordance with the various resolutions of the U.N. Security Council, and (2) to make payments to claimants from the funds obtained from Iraq in accordance with the procedures and priorities decided by the Security Council.

The progress of the UNCC was speedy by international standards. After its conception in April of 1991, the Secretariat of the UNCC was established on July 29, 1991, the first decisions of the Governing Council were made in August, 1991, and claim forms were distributed that December. The first Commissioners were appointed on March 30, 1993, and the first report by Commissioners of claims was submitted to the Governing Council on April 14, 1994. The UNCC completed the entire claim review process by June of 2005.

Eventually, the staff of the Secretariat grew to over 300 employees. There were eighteen panels of Commissioners who made recommendations on the 2.68 million claims that were submitted for a total claimed amount of $352.5 billion. Roughly 15% of those claims were recommended for payment and approximately $20 billion has been paid to claimants from funding out of Iraq's oil export revenues.

II. Historical Background

Iraq invaded Kuwait on August 2, 1990. After a series of United Nations Security Council resolutions condemning the invasion, demanding withdrawal, and imposing an arms embargo and economic sanctions, the Gulf War was commenced on January 16, 1991. On March 2, 1991, U.N. Security Council Resolution 686 demanded compliance with its previous resolutions and that Iraq "[a]ccept in principle its liability under international law for" losses, damages, and injuries as a result of its invasion and occupation of Kuwait. Iraq agreed to comply with Resolution 686 the following day. Security Council Resolution 687 reaffirmed that Iraq "is liable under international law for any direct loss, damage, including environmental damage and the depletion of natural resources, or injury to foreign Governments, nationals, and corporations, as a result of Iraq's unlawful invasion and occupation of Kuwait." The same resolution created a fund to pay the claims for these losses and directed the Secretary-General to develop recommendations for implementing the resolution.

The Report of the Secretary-General Pursuant to Paragraph 19 of Security Council Resolution 687 on May 2, 1991 proposed the UNCC. The historic model for reparations has been a lump sum payment by the vanquished to be distributed by a sovereign victor. The amount of the payment was generally related to punitive intensity and the ability to pay. The distribution was usually a political process and the beneficiaries could vary considerably. The UNCC, although not inconsistent with its war reparations ancestry, drew on three more recent models: (1) the Iran-U.S. Claims Tribunals, (2) a variety of government-sponsored compensation programs, (3) and a broad range of claims resolution facilities from other contexts.

The Iran-U.S. Claims Tribunal ("the Tribunal") was established in 1981 as part of the Algiers Accords, which resolved Iran's November 4, 1979 seizure of the American Embassy in Tehran and retention of U.S. Embassy personnel as hostages, and the subsequent freezing by the United States of Iranian assets in the U.S. It is a bilateral adjudicative body located in The Hague, The Netherlands. After more than 26 years of operations, the end of its work is not yet in sight. The Tribunal is based upon an international arbitration model with full equality of representation and consequential adversarial processes. It consists of full-time judges who work together to resolve cases one-by-one with full deliberations. These judges ostensibly are not part of a political process and are required under the Tribunal's rules, which are modified UNCITRAL rules of arbitration, to act independently. The initial focus of the Tribunal was on the business and government claims rather than individual claims. The funding for these claims was secured by a requirement in the Algiers Accords that Iran post a $500 million security account to pay any claims against it.

The authors of the UNCC were intimately involved in the Iran-U.S. Claims Tribunal and were insistent on avoiding its perceived failings: the bias toward business and governments, the obstructive potential of party-appointed judges operating against the backdrop of often hostile relations between the two sponsoring states, the pitfalls of the same judge's ruling on the same issues presented by repeat players, the expense, the slow pace, and the general frustration of powerlessness for the political process to operate in an open and transparent manner.

A second source of authority for the UNCC arises from numerous government sponsored claims processes detailed in Appendix A. These generally statutory or litigation-oriented programs were created in response to perceived governmental or corporate wrongs that had not been adequately addressed. While each process was substantively different, they shared many similarities. They each had a rationale, a source of authority and funding, and a defined administrative scheme and mechanism for managing costs. Each process also required a definition of beneficiaries, proof for an award, and a predetermined computation method for determining the amount of an award. Although some processes provided for an opt-out right, most were designed to be global. A review of these various designs reveals common elements for reparation that focus on "rough justice" in the distribution process. They have a legal and political approach to the calculation of damages as well as elements of individualization in the distribution process.

Appendix B focuses on a third series of claims resolution approaches: common U.S. procedures for compensation. An overview of these facilities by the method for calculating a distribution, or the model, the decider, implementation, size, funding, and rationale, narrative, metaphor, or paradigm provides some insight into the thinking of the designers of the UNCC. There are several varieties of valuation methodologies:

flat payment, a grid, selected variables, a formula based upon surrogate variables, or all potential variables. The decider can vary from legislature to judge to jury to the parties themselves. Implementation is by third party administrator, a judicial administrator, or the litigation process. Size varies from less than 1,000 to over 5,000. Funding can be limited or unlimited, public or private. The metaphor can be disaster, reparations, welfare, tort, or contract.

An analysis of these designs reveals little consistency except in the relationships of the metaphor to the valuation methodology. The more the metaphor seems to reflect fate and collective harm, the more the valuation methodology seems to be the same for the claimants. The more there seems to be accountability or blame for the harm, the more the valuation methodology becomes individualized....

IV. Conclusion

The design of the United Nations Compensation Commission was, in some respects, well within the tradition of war reparations facilities and, in other respects, unique. Its political governance structure within the U.N. and the Governing Council ensured that it was responsive to the demands of its founders. Its quasi-judicial elements—rules of procedure, independent Commissioners, evidentiary standards, inquisitorial style—made it a hybrid entity, neither purely political, nor purely adjudicatory. One of the most striking aspects of its procedure was its lack of adversarialness with restrictions on Iraq's ability to participate in its decision-making processes. Probably the most legitimizing aspects of its procedure related to the transparency of its proceedings. Notwithstanding the political oversight, the operation of the UNCC was consistent with the well-established tradition of claims resolution facilities—inquisitorial process, horizontal and vertical equity in the application of its rulings, and a reasoned elaboration of those rulings.

What distinguishes the UNCC most from its predecessors is the quantity and variety of the claims before it. The UNCC was able to process and pay millions of disparate claims within a record time frame. This accomplishment was achieved by the disaggregation of claims into more digestible segments, and the application of state-of-the-art decision-making tools to assist the Commissioners in reaching their decisions. The hallmark of the UNCC was pragmatism: the assimilation of "rough justice" into judicial proceedings without destroying the legitimacy of the enterprise in the eyes of the international community. There will be a continuing debate in the context of the UNCC regarding the concept of legitimacy and the concept of rough justice, as well as the interaction between them. Hopefully, the design of the United Nations Compensation Commission will serve as a model, or at least a yardstick, for future claims facility designs.

The UNCC will remain unique, particularly because of the open-ended nature of its funding and the *lex specialis* necessitated by its governance. The UNCC should, however, be a model for the design of future claims resolution facilities because of its tailoring of decision-making techniques to different types of claims. By adopting the processes to the claims, rather than vice versa, the UNCC has become a model of rough justice that will have long-lasting precedential impact.

Notes & Questions

1. What are key components of the UNCC that make it a model for DSD systems? Could this model work for more current disputes with Iran?
2. How might this model be used in other contexts?

B. Ombuds as Its Own Mini-DSD

The next article turns back to the ombuds system, introduced in Chapter 8, and explains further how ombuds can be used in and are part of a larger framework for dispute resolution within an organization.

Mary P. Rowe, *The Ombudsman as Part of a Dispute Resolution System*

mitsloan.mit.edu/shared/ods/documents?PublicationDocumentID=7793
87–94 (1990)

Contemporary theory and practice suggest that organizations should design and build dispute resolution *systems*—rather than just one or another dispute resolution structure—in circumstances where people will be working together or dealing with each other over time. Twenty years of experience suggests that an ombudsman office is one desirable and cost-effective element for an efficient system (and ombudsman offices are proliferating quite rapidly). This article discusses the ombudsman as part of an intra-institutional system. Much of the discussion is equally appropriate for ombudsmen who serve clients such as citizens, students, newspaper readers, patients, vendors, taxpayers, etc....

Definition of an (Internal) Ombudsman

I define an internal ombudsman as a neutral or impartial manager within an organization, who may provide informal and confidential assistance to managers and employees in resolving work-related concerns, who may serve as a counselor, informal go-between and facilitator, formal mediator, factor-finder, upward-feedback mechanism, consultant, dispute prevention device and change agent, and whose office is located outside ordinary line management structures. An often-quoted sentence about ombudsmen states that "*ombudsmen may not make or change or set aside a law or policy; theirs is the power of reason and of persuasion.*" Ombudsmen thus have all the functions of any complaint-handler except that of judge or arbitrator. Ombudsmen do not "deliver due process" in the sense of a court system. They encourage practices that are fair and just and respectful. They work to foster whatever responsible process is "due under the circumstances" (in the ideal situation, this process is one chosen, or at least agreed to, by the parties).

Functions and Characteristics of Dispute Resolution Systems

An effective dispute resolution system includes all of the following functions:

- **Expressing respect for feelings**, especially rage, fear or retaliation and grief. Helping people deal with their feelings—so they will be able to make responsible decisions and be able to deal effectively with their problems or complaints—may be the most cost-effective element of a dispute resolution system. This is true in part because providing respect and dealing with feelings cost very little. It is also because respect is the parent of productive work relations, and because humiliation is the parent of destructive behavior. In my experience, this is the function most likely to fail in a dispute resolution system.
- **Giving and receiving information** on a one-to-one basis (making referrals, telling people how the system works, receiving whistleblowing complaints, etc.). Many people overestimate how much information disputants have. Nearly everyone overestimates how much information top managers have, especially when things are going wrong.
- **Consultation to help people help themselves**: counseling with employees and managers, inventing new options, listing all possible options for the choice of the person(s) with a problem, consulting and coaching on how a person or group may deal with the problem directly (problem-solving, role-playing, teaching negotiation skills, anticipating possible outcomes, etc.); helping review the strengths and weaknesses of previous dispute resolution efforts. This is the function that helps to define what process is "due under the circumstances."
- **Shuttle diplomacy** by a third party, back and forth among those with a problem, to resolve the matter at hand (sometimes called "conciliation" or "caucusing," as a form of "mediation"). Shuttle diplomacy and mediation both may include offering advice as to what may happen if informal problem-solving fails, including advisory arbitration.
- **Mediation**: having a third party bring together the people or groups with a problem, so they reach their own settlement or are helped by a third party to reach their own settlement. The settlements of mediation may be formal or informal and on file or off-the-record.
- **Fact-finding or investigation**: this may be done either formally or informally. Reports may be made either with or without recommendations from the fact-finder to one or more decision-makers.
- **Decision-making, arbitration or adjudication**: where a person or body with power and/or formal authority decides a dispute. This may be structured as (part of) a formal complaint-and-appeals channel or formal grievance procedure. As Ury, Brett and Goldberg have pointed out, it is often useful to consider a variety of mechanisms to provide rights-based and power-based decisions.

- **Upward feedback, dispute prevention, and systems change**: designing a generic address to a problem, or a single complaint, or a pattern of dispute; fostering change in policies, procedures or structures as a result of inquiry, suggestion, complaint or dispute, or as a result of evaluating the handling of a previous dispute; providing group training in dispute resolution skills.

An effective internal dispute resolution system also has the following characteristics:

- **The system is taken seriously**. It has strong support from top management. It is widely publicized. Managers and employees hear discussion and receive some training in conflict resolution. The system reports back aggregate statistics, to top management and the community, as an integral part of the organization's management information system.
- **The system provides significant evidence of change**, (including reversal of some management decisions), as a result of complaints and disputes.
- **Policies against retaliation are taken seriously by all**. Managers are not punished for reversals of decisions they made in good faith; employees are not punished for raising questions or for responsible disputing.
- **The system provides** *loopsback*, from adjudicative options to problem-solving options, **and also** *loopsforward*, so that people with problems can at any stage choose investigation and adjudication of their complaints, so long as they do so in good faith.
- **The system is available to everyone**, managers and employees alive, for every type of problem.
- **The system provides in-house, designated neutrals** or impartial persons, to help people to deal with the system, to legitimate the asking of questions and raising of concerns, to minimize retaliation against those who complain, to provide consultation on options, to review how conflicts have been handled in the past (especially patterns of conflict), to be alert for new problems, to be available for bizarre, delicate, distasteful or frightening problems, to provide individualized coaching on negotiation skills, and where appropriate, to keep disputants focused on interests and on cost-effective modes of disputing.
- **The system provides, if possible, more than one available neutral**, so that people with problems have a choice. Ideally, people should have the choice of dealing with an impartial complaint-handler or mediator of the same gender and race as themselves. Providing more than one neutral or impartial person also helps in cases where the first such person is no longer appropriate or available, and where there is a wide variety of disputes requiring a variety of skills.
- **The system guarantees confidentiality** to all who approach an in-house, designated neutral off the record (e.g., for consultation, counseling, and mediation), except in the rare case where there is a duty to protect. The practice and perception of absolute confidentiality is utterly essential to building trust in a system that is going to handle delicate and difficult disputes.

The Role of the Ombudsman in a Dispute Resolution System

An ombuds office may be seen by itself as a mini-system, since the internal ombuds practitioner has all the functions of any complaint handler except that of formal investigator or arbitrator (and research indicates that internal ombudspeople do in fact perform all their allotted functions). In addition, the ombuds practitioner typically works closely with supervisors and with other dispute resolution structures within an organization.

An internal ombudsperson is often the first person approached for very difficult problems within a given workplace. In these cases the ombuds office is the point of entry into the system rather than the only person of contact. However many managers and employees who seek out an ombudsperson come in just to blow off steam, or find out a fact or two, or to learn how to help themselves. In these common cases, the ombudsperson may be the only complaint-handler, and also does not intervene.

Many workplaces also have other offices where people may go to express or sort out their feelings off the record, give or receive information include sensitive supervisors, employee assistance, equal opportunity officers, human resources personnel, the appropriate medical department, religious counselors. Ombudspeople quite regularly refer visitors to such offices and receive referrals from these colleagues, as all these practitioners seek to build an effective support network for those with problems.

Ombudspeople also intervene as third parties. Ombudsmen are sometimes asked to pursue shuttle diplomacy between peers, and it is common for an ombuds practitioner to be asked to go back and forth between the person with a concern and his or her supervisor. Many ombudspeople are mediators (formal mediation is more common between peers than between supervisor and supervisee within a workplace). Here again most workplaces also have other people who serve these functions; skilled supervisors, human resource managers, and outside consultants. Ombuds people make and accept referrals to and from these other helping resources.

Informal investigation is a very common function for an ombudsman. Frequently the practitioner will get permission from a visitor to look into and pursue a concern. This often entails an inquiry. Thereafter the ombudsman may make informal recommendations to a decision-maker and/or lobby quite stubbornly for change. It is, however, quite rare for an ombudsman to be asked to do a formal investigation in a formal grievance process. (The common belief that ombudspeople are formal investigators applies perhaps more appropriately to classic public ombudsmen than to internal practitioners.)

Informal and formal investigation are of course functions also shared with labor-relations, and other human resource personnel, active supervisors, and some other specialized personnel such as safety, equal opportunity, security and audit professionals. As noted above, it is common for referrals to come to the ombuds office and be made from the ombuds office to these colleagues. In particular, an ombudsman who is the recipient of a whistleblowing report will likely be working with line managers and other staff offices to see the matter properly investigated by appropriate persons.

In some workplaces, ombudsmen are so much a symbol of "interest-based" dispute resolution that some people presume that these practitioners function mainly as a *loop-back* process from adjudication to problem-solving. Looping back is in fact common. However, most ombudsmen also facilitate and support *looping forward* (to rights-based, formal investigation and adjudication) on important (if uncommon) occasions where this is the option responsibly chosen by a visitor. Ombudsmen also may serve as non-voting managers of a peer review process and in other ways support formal complaint and appeals channels. Research indicates that internal ombudsmen typically spend a quarter to a third of their time as internal management consultants, trainers and change agents. This may occur in many ways. Sometimes the only way to deal with a specific problem is through a generic response, where the ombuds practitioner will be working with the relevant line manager or personnel specialist. Sometimes the ombudsman will suggest new policies or changes in policies and procedures. Sometimes the ombudsman will be called to conduct training programs on conflict management or negotiation skills, for people or groups that will be working together.

Notes & Questions

1. Individuals who experience harassment may care more about stopping the harassment and prefer to avoid processes that expose them to publicity even if those processes might punish the offender. In designing a dispute resolution system to deal with these issues, how would you weigh (1) the preferences of the complainants and (2) community interests related to establishing justice and tracking repeat offenders?
2. What if the corporate client prefers to avoid any confidential processes because it fears that this will be perceived as trying to hide—rather than address—a problem?

C. DSD and Transitional Justice

This next section looks at some of the DSD questions in the context of transitional justice. The first article examines the questions asked in the development of truth and reconciliation commissions, and the second discusses the issue of standardizing these responses to human rights violations.

Carrie Menkel-Meadow, *Process Pluralism in Transitional/Restorative Justice: Lessons from Dispute Resolution for Cultural Variations in Goals Beyond Rule of Law and Democracy Development in Argentina and Chile*

2015 Int'l J. Conflict Engagement & Resol. 3, 10–11 (2015)

The Thesis: Process Pluralism & Cultural Imperatives

Different histories, cultural formations, group and national memberships and identities, and individual human variations will not allow a single conception of 'transitional', 'restorative' or 'reparative' justice to function adequately in the many ways we need to move from the past of mass harm to a future of greater well-being or healing. In the words of the American novelist William Faulkner (1951), "the past is never dead; it's not even past". How we deal with the past varies with human experience. Among the challenges of any regime of transitional justice is how to reconcile the "pain of past suffering" (prosecution, punishment, deterrence, and recompense) with the "present and future needs" (peaceful coexistence, new governmental structures, political and economic equity, reconciliation) of any post-conflict/atrocity society, where different societies and cultures may have different hierarchies of values, preferences and desires.

Whatever the goals of formal governmental transitional justice design, actual transitional justice will be performed, enacted, and delivered by members of civil society, unless state control is totalistic. In Habermassian political terms, the "acted upon" must have a say in the rules and processes that are intended to govern them; in realist-sociological terms, they will 'perform' transitional justice as cultural and social, as well as political and legal, forces elucidate and constrain those values and practices.

The first 'Truth and Reconciliation' commission (TRC) was not the now famous and most public process in South Africa, inspired by Desmond Tutu's particularly 'religious' (both Christian and indigenous values) conceptions—but in Central America, followed by South America. TRCs have become the most common 'face' of involving the larger society in transitional justice, which may also include the prosecution of harm doers; lustration or purges of former officials; development of new governmental and civil society institutions; compensation for injuries and lost property; rebuilding of infrastructure, homes, schools and other major institutions; as well as the more subtle and difficult task of 'reintegrating' a nation torn apart by civil war, atrocities, genocides, and other grievous wrongs. For those of us who study transitional justice the basic questions remain difficult, both in theory and in institutional design and practice:

How much 'truth' and accountability is necessary to move forward for a new legitimate regime to be born?

1. What should be the consequences of past wrongdoing (prosecution and punishment, compensation, confession, apology, narrative, amnesty, lustration, forgiveness)?
2. What should be the relation of a new state to the old? (How much dismemberment of old institutions and removal of officials? How much continuity is required, for social functioning, with often competing claims for legitimacy?)
3. How does a civil society 'reconceive' (or 'reintegrate' or 'reimagine') itself? (Formal institutions, memorials, museums, media, cultural activities and exchanges, economic development projects, etc.)
4. What processes/institutions are best used to accomplish the above (should they be ad hoc/temporary or permanent)?
5. How are legal/governmental/political processes deployed within societies or communities with varying emotional, religious, ethical and cultural cohesion and commitments?

6. What is or should be the role of non-governmental processes or institutions in reconciliation/peacebuilding?

Most discussions of transitional justice focus on the international, governmental, and institutional processes often developed from the 'top-down' (whether internationally developed or domestic). More recently, we have focused on the role of 'civil society'—the people who live in and constitute society, whether or not they are in engaged in formal governmental positions (and whatever their roles in the relevant conflict, harms or atrocities). As in all discussions of transitional justice, one of the most difficult questions is what should be the proper 'recipe' for the relation of peace (the civil society's probable current desire) to justice (the need for rectification of past harms to the development and establishment of important and future-guiding standards of wrongdoing and rectification in order to ensure political and social legitimacy of authority, among other goals).

Modern transitions from military dictatorships, civil wars, genocides, and post-Communist, post-military dictatorships, or other post-authoritarian regimes have varied in the last 50 years, as cultures, polities and people vary in what they value and who grabs control of the 'transitional narrative'. Even given our hope for some more 'universal' understandings of basic human rights and notions about what is required for human flourishing, I think a close study of successful (or fragile, but peaceful transitions, such as current Northern Ireland) recent transitions demonstrates that we must describe, account for, and allow 'plural transitional' strategies, at both the national and the individual levels. We need, in transitional justice, what has been argued for in some forms of domestic and international procedural law—'process pluralism'—different kinds of disputes and different kinds of parties may require different kinds of processes. How we design and choose among them for what purposes in which kinds of political and social environments is a difficult and complex issue of modern jurisprudence. Just as formal court adjudication has been supplemented or supplanted by mediation and arbitration, and hybrids of these processes, in both court-annexed public settings and in choices to resolve some disputes in private and legal settings, some transitional societies move from prosecution to reconciliation, and others add layers at the same time (TRCs plus prosecutions for some) or change over time (Argentina alternated from prosecutions to amnesties and then back to prosecutions over time). And transitional justice regimes of any kind must be studied, monitored and observed over time for calibration, 'correction' and change as they may themselves create new issues of conflict, human rights violations and violence.

In recent human history, transitional justice, including TRCs, special criminal courts, hybrid courts, local courts, and indigenous peace and adjudication processes (such as gacaca and ubuntu), has been incremental and iterative—we need to learn something, but not too much, from each one that has gone before. The nature of divisions within societies (religious, political, class, whether sharing land or competing for it, degree of integration) varies too much to allow a single design or order of process for transition from danger to relative safety. Noted political scientist and historian and theorist of transitional justice, Jon Elster, has said, "I have found the context-dependence of the phenomena [of transitional justice] to be an insuperable obstacle to generalizations." In addition, transitions themselves are incremental and iterative—Chile and other Latin American nations have recently gone from immunity-granting processes to some prosecutions of those formerly granted amnesty, and Spain is currently re-examining its own post-Fascist past. Transitional justice, within particular post-conflict sites, may evolve as people (and generations) change with the transition itself and what they learn from watching others grapple with similar, but also different, dilemmas. In short, transitional justice is itself transitional and should be flexible and capacious enough to include pluralistic forms of process and institutions.

Andrea Kupfer Schneider, *The Intersection of Dispute Systems Design and Transitional Justice*

14 Harv. Negot. L. Rev. 289, 304–06 (2009)

We also need to learn from past international examples. The Yugoslavia and Rwanda tribunals are similar in their laws, jurisdiction, requirements for proof, etc., and started with the basis of Nuremberg. The next evolution was to ad hoc tribunals like in Sierra Leone culminating in the standing tribunal of the ICC. Similarly, truth commissions have developed a common model over the past decades as they too have been implemented around the world. Truth commissions tend to have four main characteristics: (1) a focus on the past, (2) an investigation of a pattern of abuse, (3) a temporary body, and (4) are sanctioned or empowered by the state.

How can we reconcile the joint need for standardization and customization? We can create default legal frameworks—for courts, tribunals, and truth commissions—with best practice manuals for the lessons gleaned from around the world. This should at least include a few basic principles. First, what is our best advice for jurisdictional time frame? We learned that having only six months to investigate a twenty-year civil war in Guatemala was too short for the truth commission. Also, Designers must recognize that closed versus open sets of victims must be handled differently. The 9/11 Commission had the advantage of a closed set of cases (the victims were known, the event was known, future plaintiffs were unlikely to emerge) and could plan for a determined future with a clear ending date. In an international DSD dealing with a limited time period (like Rwanda) or a limited segment of the population is affected (like Guatemala), the DSD may be able to act more like the 9/11 Commission and establish a set ending date. On the other hand, one could imagine a DSD set up for Israeli-Palestinian claims at some point which would have the potential to involve huge swaths of population and take large amounts of time. Further, and seemingly obviously, certain pieces of the process need to be customized by asking questions. Who committed the atrocities (segments of the population, race, ethnicity, the leadership etc.) How geographically widespread were the pattern of violations? Who is currently in power? What type of atrocities were committed (murder, disappearances, rape, imprisonment, torture, etc.)? For example, in Chile, the truth commission could only investigate disappearances and murders. Torture victims who survived had no recourse through the commission, thus opening the commission to harsh criticism for missing a crucial part of the story. Disappearances need to be dealt with by searching for truth and finding out what happened. Other violations may not be in that vein—we know the information and we just need to have it properly recorded. Continuing, who led the violators? Who carried out the violations and why? In Sierra Leone, for example, victims want to know why the war became so brutal. Why did mutilation become so common?

Aside from the legalistic and factual questions above, cultural differences also must be taken into account when customizing the DSD. A revealing story told by Professor Jane Stromseth from the establishment of the East Timorese tribunal reflects this concern. When setting up the tribunal for East Timor, UN experts found themselves in a quandary. In Timorese culture, defendants were expected to confess to the crimes truthfully with the expectation that sentences would be determined with compassion. In order to train the Timorese in the adversarial, Western model that is typical for criminal law, "the UN experts had to train the Timorese to lie." In setting up the Khmer Rouge tribunal, commentators have worried that the tribunal does not match the values of the Buddhist Cambodian population. And even the basic difference between civil law and common law countries must be recognized when setting up courts to understand how precedent and international law will interact with the domestic legal system. Another practical issue is thinking about even where to set up offices for the tribunal or truth commission. Priscilla Hayner relates the story of how the truth commission in El Salvador set up its offices in the heart of the capital's wealthiest neighborhood causing serious stress to those victims visiting the offices.

Notes & Questions

1. In light of the historical international examples provided above as well as the identified principles, what suggestions do you have for future designers of dispute systems?
2. Think about what kinds of transitional or restorative-justice processes and reconciliation processes could be designed for each of the following conflicts:
    a. Israel-Palestine War
    b. Syrian civil war
    c. Sudanese civil war
    d. Russia's invasion of Ukraine

    Are there any other ongoing conflicts/civil wars/atrocities/mass human rights violations you can think of, and if so, what transitional/restorative/reconciliation processes could be created for them?
3. Explain how the following values can be expressed in any process you might design:
    e. Accountability for wrongdoing (punishment, amnesty, apology)
    f. Compensation for human injury or property loss or damage (reparations, restitution)

g. Reconciliation
h. Democracy capacity-building (consider future governance structures)
i. Commemoration (memorials, museums, holidays, rituals)
j. New institutions (consider whether they are needed, also consider constitutional or other reforms)
k. Evaluation, compliance, and enforcement
l. Social, cultural, and educational issues

D. DSD and Investment

Chapter 7 discussed the hybrid process of investor-state arbitration, a process created to encourage foreign direct investment, provide efficient resolution of disputes, and protect the national interests of countries. But what happens when this goes wrong?

The next excerpt pertains to a series of disputes that occurred between the Republic of Ecuador and Chevron Corporation regarding an investment and development agreement that was signed in 1973. That agreement allowed Chevron, an energy industry giant, to develop oil fields in Ecuador in exchange for giving the Ecuadorian government below-market rate oil. A group of Ecuadorians sued for both personal injuries and environmental damages tied to this arrangement in a case that has now become infamous.

Christopher Whytock, *Some Cautionary Notes on the "Chevronization" of Transnational Litigation*

1 Stanford J. Complex Litig. 467–468; 483–485 (2013)

Introduction

In 1993, residents of the Lago Agrio region of the Ecuadorian Amazon sued Texaco, Inc. alleging extensive environmental damage and personal injuries caused by Texaco's oil extraction operations there. The U.S. District Court for the Southern District of New York dismissed the suit on forum non conveniens grounds in favor of the courts of Ecuador, and the U.S. Court of Appeals for the Second Circuit affirmed in 2002. Meanwhile, Chevron Corp. had acquired Texaco in 2001. After the forum non conveniens dismissal, the Lago Agrio plaintiffs sued Chevron in an Ecuadorian court, which entered a $17.2 billion judgment against Chevron. Since then, the parties have been engaged in an extensive litigation and public relations battle over the enforcement of the judgment, a battle that has reached beyond the United States and Ecuador to countries including Argentina, Brazil and Canada. According to the Second Circuit, this story of conflict "must be among the most extensively told [stories] in the history of the American federal judiciary."

Although the Chevron-Ecuador case raises many interesting legal issues, this Essay sounds a note of caution about the lessons of the case for transnational litigation.

On the one hand, the case usefully highlights two important transnational litigation trends: the growing multipolarity of transnational litigation, and the increasing interaction between the transnational litigation system and other international legal sub-systems....

Investor-State Arbitration Versus Conflict of Laws

As noted above, in September 2009, Chevron initiated arbitration against the Republic of Ecuador pursuant to the Ecuador-United States BIT. Among other things, Chevron is seeking an order and award requiring Ecuador to inform the court in the Ecuadorian proceedings that Chevron has been released from liability and that Ecuador or Petroecuador is "exclusively liable for any judgment that may be issued in the Lago Agrio Litigation." The arbitral tribunal has issued interim awards ordering Ecuador "to take all measures to suspend or cause to be suspended the enforcement and recognition within and without Ecuador" of the Lago Agrio judgment. In February 2013, the tribunal found that Ecuador was in violation of those awards.

As one experienced practitioner puts it, "While we think of BIT claims as mechanisms whereby foreign investors can directly seek and recover damages from host states, the [Chevron-Ecuador] case is striking for its emphasis on non-monetary relief. Indeed, its principal goal appears to be to prevent recognition and enforcement of any award outside Ecuador ... [and to obtain] declaratory relief that Chevron and Texaco have no liability." Given the stakes and the seriousness of Chevron's allegations regarding the Ecuadorian proceedings, it is no surprise that the panel of arbitrators in the case has been inclined to provide this sort of relief—at least pending a final award on the merits.

But there is a bigger looming policy question: Is it a good thing to make the investor-state arbitration system available as a mechanism for enjoining the enforcement of domestic court judgments? Again, there is a risk that case-specific imperatives may cause careful policy deliberation to be a short-circuited system for judgment enforcement, which is based on a highly decentralized conflict-of-laws framework, can be very messy and uncertain. A judgment creditor identifies a jurisdiction where the judgment debtor has assets, and seeks enforcement there under the judgment enforcement law of that jurisdiction. In the Chevron-Ecuador case, this is already under way. The judgment creditors have filed enforcement actions in Argentina, Brazil, and Ontario, Canada. What judgment debtor in Chevron's shoes wouldn't prefer a more centralized solution?

However, there are at least two concerns that should be fully addressed before rushing to investor-state arbitration as a solution. First, the arbitral tribunal's order that Ecuador "take all measures at its disposal to suspend or cause to be suspended the enforcement or recognition within and without Ecuador of any judgment against [Chevron] in the Lago Agrio Case" obviously has an adverse impact on the judgment creditors—the Lago Agrio plaintiffs. Yet the Lago Agrio plaintiffs are not parties to the arbitral proceedings. In its Third Interim Award on Jurisdiction and Admissibility, the arbitral tribunal noted the *Monetary Gold* principle, according to which a tribunal should not exercise jurisdiction if the decision would determine the rights and obligations of a non-party, but held that it was not applicable. Thus, parties who will be directly and seriously affected by the arbitral tribunal's decision are not parties to the process that could determine the fate of the judgment under which they are beneficiaries. Second, as Ralph Steinhardt has argued, arbitral awards ordering a state to suspend enforcement of a judgment issued by one of its courts would seem to be in tension with principles of judicial independence. As a matter of general policy, would the United States, for example, be comfortable with a system where, pursuant to an investor-state arbitral award, the United States may be required to nullify a decision of its independent judicial branch? As Steinhardt argues, this concern may be especially acute when a domestic court's judgment is implementing other obligations of states, such as international human rights obligations. One might argue that this isn't what's happening in the Chevron-Ecuador case—but that itself would highlight the need to be cautious about proposals for legal change that are driven by alleged facts in a particular case but not necessarily sensible from a more general policy perspective.

My point is not that the existing conflict-of-laws system is ideal, and my point is not that there categorically should not be a role for the investor-state arbitration system in the realm of judgment enforcement. But there is reason for skepticism. The risk is that a movement in this direction in the Chevron-Ecuador case may be driven by case-specific imperatives rather than objective general policy analysis with widespread participation by different affected constituencies, and that this use of investor-state arbitration would nevertheless become a new model for avoiding judgments.

Notes & Questions

1. Using the questions and the framework from earlier in the chapter, consider how you would design a system from scratch to resolve these types of disputes. How does the investor-state arbitration system serve interested parties? What or who might have been overlooked?
2. Suppose you work for an oil company that would like you to design a simplified claims process to be available in case of an oil spill. What would be the advantages and disadvantages of using a claims process that fits local traditions? How might the claims process differ (if at all) if the spill occurred off the East Coast of the United States as opposed to somewhere in the Persian Gulf?

The next article focuses on the use of community consent processes in the design of foreign-investment projects.

Lisa J. Laplante & Suzanne A. Spears, *Out of the Conflict Zone: The Case for Community Consent Processes in the Extractive Sector*

11 YALE HUM. RIGHTS & DEV. L.J. 69, 84–85, 87, 91 (2008)

IV. The Community Consent Model for Overcoming Conflicting and Promoting Sustainable Development

Second-generation CSR [corporate social responsibility] efforts are largely defensive, meaning that they are strategies to protect companies against legal and reputation risk. Today, some companies see opportunities for those who lead the industry by example. Third generation CSR is based on the idea that, if approached strategically, responsible engagement with society creates value and forms part of a company's competitive advantage. Aside from risk reduction, harmonious relations with a host community will produce financial benefits, as others will prefer to do business with a company that has a community's support. Harmonious relations will also produce developmental benefits for host communities—an objective embraced by many extractive industry companies.

There is a long road ahead, but the idea that behaving responsibly increases profits may well be able to prompt a true transformation in how businesses behave. Even if companies embraced sustainable development out of a sense of charitable philanthropy at the outset, they will be required to make progress on the issue in order to maintain not only their social license to operate, but also their competitive advantage. The following two Parts examine the emergence of sustainable development as a core strategic issue for the extractive industries and introduce FPIC as a third-generation model of stakeholder engagement.

A. Emergence of Sustainable Development as a Core Strategic Issue for the Extractive Industries

Two trends combined to make "[d]oing well by doing good ... a fashionable mantra" for businesses today. First, financial markets have created rankings and indices of various kinds to measure and reward the positive impact of effective CSR strategies on a company's value.... Second, proliferating news reports of extractive industry companies engaged in ugly confrontations with host communities and governments are driving companies to get out ahead of their competitors in making peace with local communities.

B. Free, Prior, and Informed Consent (FPIC)

In recent years, indigenous peoples and other vulnerable communities have begun to demand some form of prior and informed consent to the extractive industry projects that impact them. The passage of the United Nations Declaration on the Rights of Indigenous Peoples in September 2007 has strengthened their case, as it recognizes the right of indigenous peoples to give "their free and informed consent prior to the approval of any project affecting their lands or territories and other resources, particularly in connection with the development, utilization or exploitation of their mineral, water or other resources." Like the passage of the Declaration, general acceptance of the concept of FPIC is long-overdue, as more than ten years have passed since the organizer of a World Bank-sponsored conference on mining and the community predicted "that the move from consultation to participation in decision-making is the next logical (albeit difficult) step in the evolution of [extractive industry]-community relations."

FPIC envisages that local communities are informed about development projects in a timely manner and given the opportunity to approve or reject a project prior to the commencement of operations. This includes "participation in setting the terms and conditions that address the economic, social, and environmental impacts of all phases of mining and post-mining operations." FPIC differs importantly from consultation in the way decision-making authority is exercised and legitimated. Whereas consultation processes require only that extractive industry companies hear the views of those potentially affected by a project and take them into account when engaging in decision-making processes, consent processes require that host communities actually participate in decision-making processes. Consent processes give affected communities the leverage to negotiate mutually acceptable agreements under which projects may proceed, thereby ensuring that projects stand a better chance of producing results that benefit them....

V. Challenges Facing Community Consent Processes

A number of extractive industry associations, initiatives and companies have endorsed FPIC. However, a number of other extractive industry participants continue to resist the principle. The Extractive Industries Review, a multi-year review of the extractive industries commissioned by the World Bank, endorsed the principle; but the governors of the World Bank ultimately refused to do so. Instead of adopting FPIC, they mandated that an extractive industry project must secure the "broad support" of affected communities through a process of "free, prior, and informed consultation" in order to be eligible for Bank financing. Following a comprehensive review of its own environmental and social policies, the IFC also adopted the broad community support standard, and the Equator Principles Banks (EPBs) followed suit. In its 2006 Draft Position Statement on Mining and Indigenous Peoples Issues, the ICMM stated that its members "may ... seek consent for [their] activities" as part of a process of gaining and maintaining broad community support. It remains to been seen whether the final position statement, due to be released this year, will go further to require FPIC in all instances, retain the text as drafted, or retreat from this principle.

Extractive industry companies and their financial institutions appear to have three principal concerns with the concept of FPIC: that it is a direct challenge to sovereignty, that it is not well enshrined in law, and that it is difficult to operationalize.

Notes & Questions

1. Compare the dispute system designs that may have resulted if the parties in the Chevron example had accepted free, prior, and informed consent (FPIC) versus if they had not.
2. How might you suggest building community consent processes into the DSD frameworks outlined earlier in the chapter?

Further Reading

LISA BLOMGREN AMSLER, JANET MARTINEZ, & STEPHANIE SMITH, DISPUTE SYSTEM DESIGN: PREVENTING, MANAGING AND RESOLVING CONFLICT (2020).

Lisa Bernstein, *Opting Out of the Legal System: Extralegal Contractual Relations in the Diamond Industry*, 21 J. LEGAL STUD. 115–57 (1992).

GABRIELA BLUM, ISLANDS OF AGREEMENT: MANAGING ENDURING ARMED RIVALRIES (2007).

Amy Cohen, *Dispute System Design, Neoliberalism, and the Problem of Scale*, 14 HARV. NEGOT. L. REV. 51–80 (2009).

CATHY COSTANTINO & CHRISTIANA SICKLES MERCHANT, DESIGNING CONFLICT MANAGEMENT SYSTEMS: A GUIDE TO CREATING HEALTHY AND PRODUCTIVE ORGANIZATIONS (1996).

NAOMI CREUTZFELDT, OMBUDSMEN AND ADR: A COMPARATIVE STUDY OF INFORMAL JUSTICE IN EUROPE (2018).

LAUREN EDELMAN, WORKING LAW: COURTS, CORPORATIONS AND SYMBOLIC CIVIL RIGHTS (2016).

JON ELSTER, CLOSING THE BOOKS: TRANSITIONAL JUSTICE IN HISTORICAL PERSPECTIVE (2004).

KENNETH FEINBERG, WHAT'S LIFE WORTH? THE UNPRECEDENTED EFFORT TO COMPENSATE THE VICTIMS OF 9/11 (2005).

Valerie Jenness & Kitty Calavita, *"It Depends on the Outcome": Prisoner's Grievances and Perceptions of Justice*, 52 L. & SOC. REV. 41–71 (2018).

Carrie Menkel-Meadow, *Are There Systemic Ethics Issues in Dispute System Design? What Should We (Not) Do About It? Lessons from International and Domestic Fronts*, 14 HARV. NEGOT. L. REV. 195–212 (2009).

Carrie Menkel-Meadow, *Taking the Mass Out of Mass Torts: Reflections of a Dalkon Shield Arbitrator on Alternative Dispute Resolution, Judging, Neutrality, Gender, and Process*, 31 LOY. L.A. L. REV. 513–50 (1998).

NANCY ROGERS, ROBERT BORDONE, FRANK E.A. SANDER, & CRAIG MCEWEN, DESIGNING SYSTEMS AND PROCESSES FOR MANAGING DISPUTES (2d ed. 2019).

Frank E.A. Sander & Stephen Goldberg, *Fitting the Forum to the Fuss: A User-Friendly Guide to Selecting an ADR Procedure*, 10 NEGOT. J. 49–68 (1994).

Andrea Kupfer Schneider & Natalie C. Fleury, *There's No Place Like Home: Applying Dispute Systems Design Theory to Create a Foreclosure Mediation System*, 11 NEV. L.J. 368–96 (2011).

LAWRENCE SUSSKIND, SARAH MCKEARNAN, & JENNIFER THOMAS-LARMER, THE CONSENSUS BUILDING HANDBOOK: A COMPREHENSIVE GUIDE TO REACHING AGREEMENT (1999).

WILLIAM URY, JEANNE BRETT, & STEPHEN GOLDBERG, GETTING DISPUTES RESOLVED: DESIGNING SYSTEMS TO CUT THE COSTS OF CONFLICT (1988).

Rory Van Loo, *The Corporation as Courthouse*, 33 YALE J. ON REG. 547–602 (2016).

Chapter 10

Online Dispute Resolution and Artificial Intelligence in Dispute Resolution

This chapter on modern technology in dispute resolution pulls together the themes of the last several chapters. In chapters 7 and 8, we discussed how dispute resolution processes can be adapted to the needs of a particular dispute through hybridization. And in the previous chapter, we discussed the theories and choices that designers of new systems face. This chapter expands upon this foundation with an exploration of additional dispute resolution hybrids and the particular choices that online dispute resolution (ODR) creators and providers make as they design new systems.

In recent decades, technological innovations have been increasingly used in dispute resolution processes. Technology use in dispute resolution started with email, but other technologies soon followed: computer-assisted negotiation and mediation programs, which offered asynchronous as well as synchronous forms of communication; online legal libraries and searchable legal materials; data analysis and mining; online crowd-sourcing for solution-devising and for reputational sanctions (e.g., Yelp, Trip Advisor); the blockchain; document sharing; and, as a result of COVID-19 restrictions' severely limiting in-person interactions, full online dispute resolution in all its forms, including mediation, arbitration, negotiation, and even adjudication (with and without juries in some systems). In dispute resolution, if two disputants are the first two parties, and the mediator or arbitrator is the third-party neutral, then the computer or technology used can be considered the fourth party—and in fact, many believe there is a fifth party to consider as well, the online platform designer (*see* Chapter 9), whose existence raises new ethical and bias concerns in conflict resolution.

The use of technology in dispute resolution is hybrid because it involves human-machine interactions. It also clearly crosses legal jurisdictions, thus making its use and possible regulation subject to many competing interests and jurisdictions—security, confidentiality, legal rules, ethics, lay or professional action, access, transparency, safety, and fairness, as well as substantive law differences (re-contracting and enforcement of agreements and judgments). All of these issues are now the subject of concern, debate, and calls for regulation. As with any technological innovation (from cave paintings to the printing press to radio, film, and now computer technology) there are advantages and efficiencies as well as potential disruptions of human well-being (e.g., hacked information, pornography, child abuse, and instruments for human trafficking). This field is currently in a state of great experimentation and innovation, and there are contestations of many issues.

Some jurisdictions are now mandating ODR for all low-value court cases,[1] to increase access and to eliminate the costs of utilizing physical buildings and courts. Others are offering ODR as an option, and there are even proposals to create online platforms for cross-national consumer disputes (e.g., European Directives and Regulation on ODR in Consumer Disputes, UNCITRAL Framework for Online Dispute Resolution (currently deadlocked due to legal system differences)). Whatever one's view about online dispute resolution among and between different kinds of disputants, whether within the same legal system or across different systems, it is undeniable that the COVID-19 pandemic greatly expanded its use. And as artificial intelligence continues to advance, it is expected to lead to further innovations in mechanisms, processes, solutions, and outcomes.

This chapter starts by addressing how ODR builds on ADR theories to create new dispute resolution options through technology, and then it looks at how ODR designers have utilized DSD theories in practice to create these new structures and processes. It then turns to concerns about ODR, not only in terms of technological obstacles but also in terms of how to meet the challenges of providing access to justice and justice itself as we create these new dispute resolution processes across a multitude of contexts.

I. ODR as ADR

Carrie Menkel-Meadow, *Hybrid and Mixed Dispute Resolution Processes: Integrities of Process Pluralism*

in COMPARATIVE DISPUTE RESOLUTION CH. 28
(Maria F. Moscati, Michael Palmer & Marian Roberts eds., 2020)

Another modern hybrid, *online dispute resolution*, began by harnessing foundational processes of mediation, arbitration, negotiation (e.g., see Cybersettle) and adjudication to computer and now internet services, allowing both synchronous and asynchronous communication between parties and third-party helpers in seeking resolution of a wide variety of disputes, including commercial, family, torts and injuries, consumer and public benefits. Now online dispute resolution offers its own forms of "digital justice", by providing specialized platforms for dispute resolution where parties can interact directly or through intermediaries to resolve disputes through Internet communication. eBay resolves over 60 million disputes a year between buyers and sellers of goods and now also includes a "crowdsourced" online court to adjudicate disputes about reputational reviews, which have immediate economic consequences for users. In the United Kingdom and Canada, recent initiatives announced by the governments will

1. RICHARD SUSSKIND, ONLINE COURTS AND THE FUTURE OF JUSTICE, 2019.

move all civil cases below a certain value to an "Online Court". Private (non-lawyer) providers and designers are programming and revisioning the entire justice system (e.g., Modria), causing at least one commentator to pronounce on the "end of lawyers."

In what promises to be a very creative hybridization of digital and interpersonal dispute resolution, a new computer site in the Netherlands allows divorcing parties to negotiate online for child custody, visitation and family support; but also to choose counselors and mediators to meet with in person. This harnessing of "mixed" forms of communication is an attempt to combine the efficiency and "safe" distance of online dispute resolution with the possibility of interpersonal interaction. Whether such mixed modalities will be translated and used in other forms of dispute resolution (civil disputes and even criminal law—they are now used for traffic violations in some nations) remains to be seen.

The European Union and the United Nations Commission on International Trade Law (UNCITRAL) have sponsored and promoted a plan for online dispute resolution for transborder consumer disputes (now deadlocked in committee; UNCITRAL 2016). Issues of the digital "divide" and language literacy remain for the young, elderly, poor, language-challenged and other potential users. It may be that in the future, public libraries, providing access to public computers, will become more central to dispute resolution than courts. Whether ODR is ADR or requires its own standards of ethics and practice (who will inform consumers and users how best to access and use these services?) is a topic of much concern.

Carrie Menkel-Meadow, *Is ODR ADR?: Reflections of an ADR Founder from 15th ODR Conference, the Hague, the Netherlands,* 22–23 May 2016

3 Int'l J. Online Disp. Resol., 2016, at 4–6

I am left asking the question do ODR and 'A' DR (now 'appropriate,' not 'alternative') dispute resolution have the same goals? Access to justice? Efficiency and transparency of dispute resolution? Quality of solutions? Satisfaction with dispute resolution? Justice?...

Online Dispute Resolution is just a bit younger than the ADR movement. Twenty years ago, founders of ODR, Ethan Katsh, Janet Rifkin and Colin Rule all had a hand in online dispute system design by creating and working with e-Bay's online dispute resolution system which now handles over 60 million disputes a year between online vendors and buyers of goods by a private innovative company that wanted to create a world-wide network with a quality reputation. Imagine if all those cases went to court!

While parts of the private sector have advanced with uses of online complaint systems and customer service (Amazon is reported to have better customer service than any bricks and mortar business, but recent newspaper reports suggest that is due to exploitation of Amazon workers—if the customer is always right, maybe it is the employee who is making it possible!)

The caseloads of modern life cannot be sustained in a paper filled legal system. Courts, unlike, hospitals, businesses and even schools, have resisted change in design and function as we move to an electronically based communication society. Lord Fulford (Lord Chancellor of the UK) suggested we would dispense with buildings and consumers and complainants would indeed have access to computers, smartphones and could go to local community libraries to get online to deal with their cases, as physical courts move into 'Virtual' courts of streamlined case management and document filing and access, and decisions.

I still have my doubts. The digital divide is still profound—language, both linguistic and computer logic language, age (sight and typing and comprehension for the elderly or those alone), income, access to equipment and learning of constant updates and an inability to talk to a real person to give and get advice about legal matters that don't lend themselves to tick boxes are issues that continue to worry me.

I am most impressed by the Dutch Rechtwijzer divorce platform which combines great computer design and human interfaces—parties will be able to file for divorce and then use financial and calendar programs to figure out support and child custody schedules on their own, but also to access a counselor or mediator if they prefer some real-life human interaction. Watching how this program can work has converted me somewhat to thinking the future of ODR is a combination of a well-designed computer platform where some interactive possibilities still allow human and more flexible and tailored advice and information to come through....

As one who has been studying the challenges of regulating the new platform economies of Uber and Airbnb as they both offer new access to services, but also challenge labor, health and safety regulations, and tax payments, I wonder how the regulation of advice giving online will play out in different legal regimes—much will depend on the power of that great profession of monopolization—the lawyers.

Nancy Welsh and Leah Wing reminded [us] of the importance of "procedural justice" and ethics of online dispute resolution design. In my personal interviews of several of the platform developers it is clear that ethics and quality is a concern of many. But, what about those entrepreneurial outliers who seek to make money without participating in these voluntary meetings of sharing the state of the art and knowledge at the cutting edge of the field?.... But what about those who weren't there to hear these exchanges and proposed codes of conduct in an unregulated field?

... What I wonder about is what drove me to ADR in the first place—where in the tick boxes and the email communications will there be room to brainstorm and create a different solution, give an apology, come to understand someone else's perspective, and improve, rather than just 'resolve', relations and disputes. For me Online Dispute Resolution may be one tool for some 'access' to dispute resolution of some kind, but I wouldn't over claim the 'justice' part. I recently resolved an ongoing dispute with one of my airlines online—what I felt was relief it was over and done, not any sense that 'justice' had been served and it was very clear that at the other end of my computer was not someone with the power or discretion of a mediator or judge to consider a more creative and tailored solution. I got what the tick boxes or company policy allowed. Will we be getting small claims or civil justice in a programmed set of legally required tick boxes? I thought the common law allowed more flexible rulings and mediators and negotiators working in the 'shadow of the law' could still fashion new and creative remedies that looked to the parties' futures, as well as past conflicts.

Notes & Questions

1. Consider the advantages and disadvantages of technology in the realm of dispute resolution—what might be a positive for courts? For parties? For companies? And what concerns do you have?
2. Have you had a consumer complaint resolved online? Was it efficient/successful in your view? Would you have preferred some other form of dispute resolution, such as in person or on the phone? Have you used online dispute resolution services in any way for an international transaction?

In the next article, Professor Amy Schmitz examines how online dispute resolution has evolved in the last decade to address a multitude of disputes, likely in contexts you have already experienced.

Amy J. Schmitz, *Evolution and Emerging Issues in Consumer Online Dispute Resolution (ODR)*

in The Cambridge Handbook on Emerging Issues at the Intersection of Commercial Law and Technology
(Stacy-Ann Elvy & Nancy Kim eds., forthcoming 2024)

The New Handshake

The pandemic shined a light on technology's potential to connect us in this rapidly changing global society. Furthermore, new technologies like smart contracts and NFTs, or non-fungible tokens, have helped us reimagine how we transact and assess value. These technologies also generate new disputes and more need for ODR to address these disputes. Consumers may enjoy new opportunities to purchase goods from around the world and invest in new forms of value such as cryptocurrencies. However, they may be left with no remedy when unscrupulous sellers disappear or cryptocurrencies plummet in value despite fraudulent promises. At the same time, some companies delegate their customer service to robo-chat mechanisms that often fail to provide real remedies. Many companies have nearly eliminated their in-person or even telephone customer service, and it can sometimes feel that unhappy customers have nowhere to go in this "race to the bottom" in customer service....

ODR in B2C Commerce

A. Reasons for B2C ODR

ODR can be especially helpful for consumers to access remedies in what I have termed the "squeaky wheel system" (SWS) in consumer exchanges. This conception of the SWS builds on the notion that the "squeaky wheels"—who are proactive in pursuing their needs and complaints—are most likely to get the assistance, remedies, and other benefits they seek. Meanwhile, those who remain silent because they lack the knowledge, experience, and/or resources to artfully and actively pursue their interests usually do not receive the same benefits. This means that the individuals who already enjoy disproportionate power due to social or economic status are usually the squeaky wheels that receive the disproportionate benefits—thus perpetuating the divide between the consumer "haves" and "have-nots." Additionally, this SWS thwarts proper market regulation for fairness, as the squeaky wheels that get the benefits are unlikely to share information with the majority in order to prompt consumers to "vote with their feet" by refusing to purchase from unscrupulous sellers. This creates a need for expanded and equalized access to remedies in order to promote consumer protections.

ODR can help address the SWS by lowering the costs and burdens of pursuing purchase complaints in the B2C markets so that all consumers, regardless of power and resources, can access remedies. Online complaint systems are usually less expensive and more convenient than face-to-face dispute resolution processes due to the ease and flexibility of text, online messaging, and other computer-mediated communication (CMC). Simple asynchronous systems are especially appropriate with respect to smaller dollar claims or smaller infractions, such as parking tickets and driving misdemeanors, when individuals do not necessarily need to "vent" or spend a great deal of time discussing an issue. It often makes sense to allow each side to input their facts and arguments on their own schedules, without the need to arrange for a meeting during business hours.

At the same time, some parties may want synchronous video discussion, which is also possible with ODR. In this way, ODR processes open a new avenue for individuals to vent and share their concerns—without the time and expense of travel. Furthermore, ODR may go beyond merely providing portals for consumers to post complaints or discuss claims via chat or video platforms. It can be configured to use third-party neutrals to facilitate resolutions, again without costs of time and travel. ODR systems may also use automated negotiation processes, powered by data analytics and algorithms built on gathered data around similar disputes. These systems can be especially effective where they are user-friendly, allowing consumers to quickly fill out standard forms and upload related documents to obtain timely resolutions.

These systems are essential for consumers, who generally lack access to remedies. We have a justice crisis, and the justice gap is increasing. Those without educational and economic resources tend to have the least and worst access to remedies, especially because they usually lack legal assistance. This highlights the need for user-centric dispute system designs, which consider individual needs and allow for self-empowerment.

ODR has the capacity to provide this type of access to remedies for those with sufficient comfort with, and access to, technology.

That said, there are no enforceable ethics standards in place for ODR, and not all individuals have sufficient access to technology. Online communications also come with dangers. There is always fear that information shared will be "hacked" or that the anonymity of CMC may inspire use of abusive language individuals would not use in person. CMC also may diminish empathy and create misinterpretations in online discussions. At the same time, individuals may be more civil online because they know their communications are preserved. Also, we have become increasingly adept at expressing ourselves online through standardized textual cues and emotive characters. Individuals have developed means for building rapport over the Internet. Furthermore, the relative anonymity and comfort of communicating through a computer or smartphone may ease some of the social and power pressures of face-to-face (F2F) communications. This is especially true for consumers who fear stereotypes or biases.

B. Evolution of Private ODR in B2C Contexts

ODR started in ecommerce, with companies like eBay and Amazon creating ODR processes for consumer disputes as means for quickly dealing with complaints and building goodwill. eBay learned that it could actually make money off of consumer disputes, as consumers who used eBay's ODR process were prone to make more purchases. Today, eBay encourages users to attempt to work out seller/buyer issues with one another before moving to next steps. If a buyer/seller cannot get a resolution directly with the seller/buyer, the party is able to file a claim in the eBay Resolution Center. This will spark online negotiations between the seller and the buyer. If the parties cannot resolve the case through negotiations or a party fails to answer a complaint after three days, the aggrieved party has twenty-one days to report it to eBay to have them step in through a type of online mediation. If the goods do not arrive or are not as promised, the buyer usually gets her money back. As a seller, the typical complaint is that a buyer has not paid for the item. If the parties do not reach a resolution on their own, the seller can use the online Resolution Center, where things are usually settled through negotiation.

Amazon also provides ODR under its Buyer Dispute Program. Buyers who do not receive goods or receive goods not as described may file a claim against the merchant through Amazon. Complaints must be filed within thirty days of final payment and start a process that begins with online negotiation. Amazon aims to resolve all complaints within forty-five days. Amazon sets certain parameters for denying buyer claims, but most legitimate complaints result in the buyers getting their money back. In the case that a claim is denied, the buyer may appeal. If a seller loses a complaint, the seller has thirty days to file an appeal. If a merchant is uncooperative, Amazon may restrict or terminate their account.

Not to be outdone, Facebook also has created an ODR process to handle disputes between buyers and sellers on its site. This is through Commerce Manager that is available to customers who buy from merchants who have a "Facebook Page Shop" and facilitate purchases through Facebook or Instagram. This applies under its Purchase Protection plan, which is fairly narrow. This would not apply to a business that just has a general Facebook Page, an individual selling on Facebook Marketplace, or merchants outside of the U.S. Per Facebook's information page, "Purchase Protection only applies when you purchase an item with shipping or checkout on Facebook. This means that items purchased with local pickup or with a peer-to-peer payment method (example: PayPal, payments in Messenger, Venmo) aren't covered." Claims are limited to $2,000 with a $10,000 lifetime coverage limit.

Under this policy, when a customer makes an inquiry, the seller has two business days to respond through either the Commerce Manager Inbox or through the business's email provided to the Commerce Manager. If the business does not correct the issue, the customer has forty-five days from the date of delivery to create a dispute claim for Facebook to review. Facebook then notifies the business to let them know a claim has been filed. Facebook considers the following when evaluating a claim: (1) the order details; (2) communication between the parties; (3) information provided by the parties; and (4) the customer's past refund requests and purchase activity indicating fraudulent behavior. This appears to be an online arbitration process, allowing for appeals within ten days from the notification of the decision.

Importantly, ODR is not merely a function within private e-commerce. That may be where ODR started, but it has expanded immensely into the public sector. The next section will discuss this expansion in the courts.

C. ODR in the Courts

Consumers in commercial contexts have also seen ODR in the courts—especially for traffic tickets and small claims. For example, Michigan was one of the first U.S. states to launch an ODR pilot program in collaboration with Matterhorn, a private ODR provider, for resolving traffic disputes. Today, ODR may also include small claims, which are quite common in B2C contexts. In 2019, Michigan implemented a large-scale ODR system called MI-Resolve, available to all state citizens. It is an asynchronous ODR process that allows parties to negotiate directly with one another with or without a mediator. MI-Resolve was implemented through Michigan's seventeen Community Dispute Resolution Program (CDRP) centers. In 2022, a survey was published of mediators, board members, and courts/attorneys who made referrals to mediation, which indicated that six out of ten said MI-Resolve was at least somewhat effective in resolving disputes. These respondents indicated that it was most effective for small claims and debt collection.

The Michigan program was not specifically court-annexed, however, in the same way as other court ODR projects. For example, Utah implemented an ODR program for small claims cases statewide under the direction of an ODR Steering Committee that was formed by the Utah Judicial Council in June 2016. The goal was to create means for improving access to remedies in small claims cases. Then Justice of the Utah Supreme Court, Deno Himonas, took the lead in supporting the effort and became a champion for innovation. The ODR program follows a stepped process, beginning with "Education and Evaluation," moving to direct negotiation and then allowing for mediation if the parties are unable to resolve their dispute on their own. Nonetheless, as will be discussed in Part III, the program has faced criticism for failing to address shortcomings and caving to repeat players.

Another ODR pilot aimed at helping consumers access remedies is the Franklin County Municipal Court Dispute Resolution Department's ODR program in Ohio. It began with a focus on addressing individuals' disputes with the City of Columbus Division of Income Tax. Again, this was the type of dispute for which in-person alternatives were inconvenient and costly considering the small sums often at stake. Early surveys regarding the Ohio project revealed that 94% said that they would recommend ODR to others. Additionally, the Department reported that the ODR program shortened the time from case filing to resolution significantly in comparison with in-person litigation. Matterhorn, the company Ohio hired as the ODR software provider, also reported that the intervals between filing and commencing ODR were much shorter than similar intervals for cases outside of the ODR program. The provider also notes that the ODR pilot has created conveniences for consumers and has increased the City's collection of unpaid taxes.

Since the pandemic, there has been even more growth in state ODR. For example, Florida launched its Online Dispute Resolution 2020 Pilot Program, and has now given it the green light to expand beyond the pilot counties. A comprehensive report on the pilot program was prepared and provided to the Florida Supreme Court in January 2021. The report discusses uneven results and shows the difficulties of working with private ODR vendors to implement state programs. Florida's program covers mainly small claims cases, as well as traffic tickets and family dissolution in particular jurisdictions. According to the Florida court dispute resolution director in the Eighteenth Judicial Circuit, 1,800 cases were referred to online dispute resolution in 2021, resulting in negotiated settlements for about 40% of them. In contrast, the Florida Ninth Judicial Circuit court piloting ODR reported that only 5% of its ODR cases resulted in settlements. Throughout the pilot, the Ninth Judicial Circuit worked closely with their vendor to work out issues, but participation was very low.

In sum, judicial ODR projects have impacted consumers by creating a virtual door to the courthouse in small claims, traffic tickets, dissolution, landlord/tenant, and other generally smaller and less complex cases. This can benefit consumers where it makes seeking remedies less expensive and more convenient. However, it can also curb access to remedies, and justice, for those without adequate access to technology. Furthermore, ODR programs can empower repeat players when not properly designed. For example, it can make it easier for debt collectors to go after consumers.

Notes & Questions

1. Now that you've read about the evolution of eBay, Amazon, Facebook, and court usage of ODR, consider again the advantages and disadvantages of technology in the realm of dispute resolution. Does its use differ in private versus public contexts?
2. Given any concerns you might have, how and what should we consider in terms of designing ODR moving forward?

II. ODR as DSD

This section explores how ODR fora and venues can/should be designed (for more on this topic, see Chapter 9). Consider issues of top-down (tribunals, international organizations, managers) or bottom-up (users) developers and designers. What should be the relative roles of legal actors (lawyers, legislators), managers, engineers, and technical professionals in designing online dispute resolution? (We consider some ethical issues in the final section of the chapter.)

Orna Rabinovich-Einy & Ethan Katsh, *Technology and the Future of Dispute Systems Design*

17 Harv. Negot. L. Rev. 151, 164–65 (2012)

DSD, even in fairly recent writing, has devoted very little attention to the role, value, and impact of technology. Thus, in those instances when practitioners have found some software application to be useful, they have rarely found it embedded in the dispute resolution system designed for their organization. This is unfortunate but not surprising. Attention to the larger system in which some activity occurs is likely to happen only after the activity proves itself to be of some value. "Getting Disputes Resolved" [Ury, Brett & Goldberg 1988] was a response to an ADR movement that had been growing for more than a decade. By the time the book was published, there had been increasingly widespread experience with ADR, and perhaps the most influential book about ADR, "Getting to Yes," had been published seven years earlier. "Getting Disputes Resolved" not only had a title that began with the same word (and was written by one of the same authors), but was a work that extended and built upon the earlier book's emphasis on an interest-based approach to negotiation and mediation.

DSD, in other words, emerged as an attempt to understand how ADR might be used most effectively in an organization and to provide a coherent framework for its use. The focus of DSD on how different ADR models might best be employed in different contexts was an appropriate and even predictable development for a field that had already been accepted, was expanding in use, and was looking toward the future. We are, to some extent, at a similar point in the history of ODR, a time when its value in individual cases has been confirmed and when it is appropriate, therefore, to consider its impact, uses, and the potential applicability it has in the design of other systems.

While those interested in DSD have mostly ignored ODR, it is also true that those involved in ODR have given relatively little thought to the differences between systems and tools or to the value of thinking about the systems in which the tools are being used. In general, and as might be expected at an early stage of technological use, the concern of those interested in or using ODR has been very practical and aimed at identifying and experimenting with any and all software that could be used fruitfully at some stage in a mediation process. ODR today may be used in a narrower range of disputes than ADR was in 1988, but it is likely to be employed in larger numbers of disputes. ODR is providing increasing numbers of useful tools and the more they are employed on- and offline, the greater the need to understand how they might be of value in different contexts.

The future of ODR is assumed by many to lie in an expanding array of tools that will open up new options for third parties. Perceived in this way, ODR is not in itself a distinct field, but more of a support system for mediators and arbitrators addressing individual disputes. As mediators have become more comfortable generally in the use of technology, they have increasingly been looking for software applications that could perform discrete functions and could be plugged into their practice in some way. From such a perspective, the future of ODR would seem to lie in an ongoing evolution of more and more powerful software that could be employed in more and more complicated contexts. In this view at least, technology is a force that is moving the field in the same direction it has been moving, rather than generating a change in direction or a change in conceptualization.

The Web, in its "disruptive" guise, is an innovative force, not only accelerating change but accelerating changes in direction, moving in formation in new ways, new patterns, and among groups who might not have communicated before at all. It is in the nature of an emerging communications network to involve new participants and stakeholders and to generate links and connections among users that could not have been made before. Accordingly, the view that we suggest in this article considers technology as more than a new tool; we see technology as a force that will deeply touch the field of dispute resolution, both on- and offline.

The following discussion of several key examples of ODR is meant to illustrate how and why this is likely to occur and how software can be both a tool and a system. These examples are well known in the literature of ODR, but are generally examined only through the lens of tools. Our purpose is to broaden the discussion and examine what they reveal about the use and impact of technology at the system level and what implications these case studies may have for the future of DSD.

A. The First Decade of ODR: Some Illustrative Examples

1. eBay

eBay is the most cited example of a successful and very high-volume ODR. It is also an example of innovative use of technology in addressing disputes from a systems perspective with purposeful design that has challenged the boundaries of both existing ADR concepts and practices and ODR's tool-focused approach. eBay's use of ODR began in March 1999 when the Center for Information Technology and Dispute Resolution (now the National Center for Technology and Dispute Resolution) was asked to conduct a pilot project to see if it was feasible to mediate disputes between eBay buyers and sellers. The approach decided upon was to use the traditional ADR model of a trained human mediator communicating with the parties. In this situation, instead of communicating face to face, email was used. The pilot project handled two hundred disputes in a two-week period, by far the largest number of disputes mediated online up to that date and was successful in that it demonstrated that agreements satisfactory to both sellers and buyers could be achieved online.

eBay decided to continue to offer mediation to its buyers and sellers and turned over dispute resolution to an Internet start-up, SquareTrade. SquareTrade's challenge was two-fold. It needed an ODR process that could handle large numbers of cases, which email and a human mediator alone could not satisfy. In addition, because it was a private company, it needed a sustainable business model. eBay disputes predominantly involved small sums of money that could not be expected to generate sufficient revenue to compensate mediators and still generate a profit.

The solution to the twin goals of scale and revenue was to place dispute resolution within a larger system, which held open the possibility of an appeal to a human mediator but that had a required first step of a software-driven process that could lead to settlement without any human third-party intervention. The solution to the revenue issue was to offer eBay sellers a seal or trustmark to include on the screen when their product was being offered for sale. The seal, sold for a small fee, was meant to build trust in an environment where buyers did not know sellers, where there were no real brand names, and where fear of fraud was significant. The SquareTrade seal guaranteed that the seller actually existed and, most relevant for this discussion, that the seller promised to engage in dispute resolution should the buyer have a problem with the item. From the beginning, therefore, SquareTrade had a dispute resolution tool but understood that it was intimately connected to a larger process of trust building as well as revenue generation. It also understood that technology had thrust it into a larger environment, one in which the stakeholders were numerous and expectations about speed of resolution were very high.

SquareTrade built its ODR process by identifying components of the traditional mediation process and building them into software, essentially reengineering the entire process. What made this feasible was that mediation, and indeed all dispute resolution processes, rely on the communication, management and processing of information. When mediators "work with the parties" they do so by managing the flow of information. Various stages of a mediation process (for example caucusing, brainstorming, option generating, and drafting) are communications processes that the mediator encourages and structures.... Mediators may, of course, differ in exactly how they manage the use and flow of information. Some may simply want an agreement and an exchange of promises about future actions that are acceptable to both parties. Other mediators may seek an agreement that goes deeper and transforms a relationship. What all traditional mediators have available to them, however, when meeting face to face are the multiplicity of communication channels. Their skill resides in when and how to use those channels.

SquareTrade understood that mediation revolves around communication and information processing, and also realized that it could not duplicate the richness or flexibility of a face-to-face exchange. It was confronting an environment in which some subtleties of interaction could not be guaranteed and in which the likelihood of very large numbers of disputes was high. At the same time, it also knew that software can be programmed to ask questions in a structured way and then provide other questions based on the answers given. In addition, compared to a negotiation via email (or face-to-face) where there is little or no structure in exchanges, other forms of web-based communication could be shaped in ways that would move or guide a dialogue in a certain direction.

The UMass project mentioned above tried to mimic the face-to-face process by using email and managed to do so with some success. Yet that process was found to be not only very labor intensive, but also one that relied on a specific software application, email, which was not particularly helpful to a mediator who wanted to carefully manage the flow of information. Even if labor intensiveness had not been a problem, SquareTrade realized that it was in an environment which called not only for a better way, but for a different way as well.

SquareTrade's goal was not to make available a machine version of a human mediator, but rather to design something that revolved around an exchange of information about positions and interests, and that resembled mediation in that the outcome would be consensus-based, even if the exact route taken to reach the final agreement was not the same. It knew that there could not be a human mediator present to shape the communication in most cases, but it also wanted the resolution to result from an online negotiation and be one that the parties felt was fair and unbiased. While software could not duplicate the skill of a human mediator interacting with the parties, software could provide some structure to the communication and to the flow of information between the parties. Indeed, the very definition of software is something that manages the flow of information and the work of a programmer is to specify how this will occur and how it will appear on the screen. The software SquareTrade developed that would eventually handle millions of disputes appropriated many elements of traditional mediation. For example, SquareTrade and its software had to be viewed as being fair and not likely to induce settlements favoring either buyer or seller. It had to be trusted not only as being impartial but also as being effective in terms of cost, time to settlement, and enforcement. Lastly, it needed to lead to settlements that were acceptable to both sides.

In the traditional mediation context, the mediator tries to elicit particular interests of the parties and ideas about preferred and acceptable outcomes via exchanges with the parties, together or separately. SquareTrade's software strategy was to discover the preferences of parties by presenting the parties with forms and choices they could select from. In the context of buyer-seller disputes on eBay, this was possible because the problems likely to arise with an eBay transaction (e.g., the item broke, was delivered late, etc.) are both predictable and limited in scope and, therefore, can usually be identified ahead of time. More importantly, SquareTrade acquired data from each case as to which choices were being made and how information on the screen was being understood and used, providing the basis for ongoing changes and refinements.

SquareTrade needed effective tools but it also viewed dispute resolution as a contributor to other parts of its business. It understood that in order for every part of the company to improve, every part of the company needed to both use data and generate data that might be used by other parts. It promised confidentiality to parties but it also used data from every dispute to improve all of its services. Like other online companies, it wanted to find some valuable piece of information in every click of the mouse. In this instance, the data it derived from resolving disputes allowed for enhancements to that process and to the larger and more challenging goal of generating trust online.

The use of information in this manner was radically different from the use of information by offline mediation or ombuds offices. Those offices might accumulate data for statistical purposes and for learning about the number of cases handled, successes and failures, etc. Typically, data that might possibly reveal something about the parties or about a particular case is discarded. Online systems have capabilities for managing data in a way that can overcome the traditional operational boundaries and practices of mediation. If not done carefully, designing systems that use data from individual cases in ways that would not have occurred before creates a very sensitive challenge for DSD. It is also one that will be faced frequently as more and more links are established between the system and the tools used to further the goals of the system. It is a challenge not rooted in the traditional confidentiality concern, namely that data about a party may escape, but in a more likely concern that data about individuals could be constructed out of multiple seemingly trivial pieces of data.

The availability of rich data, together with the capabilities for mining and analyzing digitally stored information, allowed SquareTrade to continuously improve its dispute resolution system. In five years they came to handle over two million disputes. One way in which SquareTrade used newly available data for improvement and learning was to analyze party input in open text boxes to uncover problems in the dispute and solution typologies. Another area of improvement was mediator performance. First and foremost, the online process allowed SquareTrade to monitor mediator performance without undermining their authority vis-a-vis parties. But the principle means for monitoring and improving the functioning of mediators was through the collection and analysis of data on success stories (what made for "good" mediators) and failures (analyzing patterns of complaints on mediators).

In 2003, several years after the launch of the SquareTrade system, eBay decided to develop in-house ODR systems and hired Colin Rule as Director of ODR. In the years that followed, eBay launched an internal automated negotiation system for specific types of disputes: item not as described, item not received, unpaid item and feedback related dispute. In all those cases, eBay discovered that disputes primarily arise due to miscommunication and that the transfer of key information can clarify the nature of the problem and assist in assigning responsibility and devising a solution. Under this system, parties are asked to answer questions and supply documents that have been found to shed light on the type of conflict in question. Recently, the volume of such disputes was estimated at 60 million each year. Again, the volume of transactions and the repetitive, simple nature of these disputes have allowed eBay to formulate fixed formats that can be programmed and do not require human intervention for addressing these problems. Most importantly, eBay's move in developing these systems internally represents an understanding that handling disputes that arise out of eBay transactions has become an inherent component of what eBay does.

Since the launch of the internal automated negotiation processes, eBay has continued to develop its ODR services, expanding initially to PayPal and, more recently, broadening the scope of dispute resolution processes offered by developing an online community court. This latest dispute resolution mechanism addresses feedback removal disputes. Instead of an external third-party expert deciding whether to remove negative feedback, a "crowd sourcing" mechanism was developed where a disinterested jury of 21 eBay users decides the issue. In all of these dispute resolution avenues, eBay has been a pioneer in understanding digital technology's impact on DSD. This can be evidenced in eBay's and SquareTrade's defiance of the limits on the conceptual boundaries, separating process types (technology-assisted negotiation as a new mix of mediation and negotiation, and crowd sourcing as a substitute for an expert third party) and questioning the necessity of core features traditionally associated with ADR (broad confidentiality and individualized tailoring of process structure). In many of their decisions, eBay and SquareTrade understood and faced similar questions to those posed in the DSD literature with respect to face-to-face dispute resolution. Their answers, however, were often quite different from the answers that might have been given in considering an offline process.

Janet K. Martinez's discussion of ODR in the following excerpt stems from her role as a commentator for a panel discussion at a session of the Association of American Law School's annual meeting in New Orleans in January 2019. The conference served to assess what ODR is, its functions, and how it can be improved. The panelists showcased their respective studies of consumer, commercial, and judicial ODR.

Janet K. Martinez, *Designing Online Dispute Resolution*

J. Disp. Resol., no. 1, 2020, at 135, 135–36

DSD Analytical Framework

Dispute system design offers academics and practitioners alike the opportunity to examine how disputes are handled in different resolution domains, which processes within a given system are effective, and what variables can make a difference. The DSD Framework is built on a series of assessment questions around the following elements: goals, stakeholders, context and culture, processes and structure, resources, and success and accountability....

A. Goals

Our panel presented different kinds of disputes, different kinds of people (disputants and neutrals), and different kinds of processes (facilitative and evaluative). Alyson Carrel and Noam Ebner organized around functional goals: administrative, communicative, substantive, and educational. Aylet Sela examined small claims (including those handled by the British Columbia Civil Claims Tribunal and Her Majesty's Civil Money Claims (Beta)) to access justice, efficiency, and quality of process that engaged parties to deliberate on interest-based options. David Larson devoted his research and development toward a court system focused on protecting consumers, delivering efficiency, and providing accessibility to justice for credit card collection cases. Orna Rabinovitch-Einy and Ethan Katsh, as well as Amy Schmitz and Colin Rule, focused on smart contracts on the blockchain, which have distinctive characteristics; they are decentralized, immutable, and anonymous to achieve democratic decision-making and automatic enforcement of resolutions. Thus, the more emphasis on consumer cases, e.g., civil claims and credit debt claims, the more that access to justice, efficiency, and interest-based process options may be valued as goals by some affected stakeholders. Thus, the balance of user and stakeholder participation in the design process is critical. In the newer case category of smart contracts on the blockchain, as more trust is vested in the technology, the more valued are predictable outcomes and enforcement.

B. Stakeholders

The second framework element is identification of stakeholders and analysis of their interests, representation, relationships, and relative power. Stakeholders include the people and organizations that create, host, use, and are affected by DSD. The more stakeholders, including users, are involved in the dispute system's design and continuous improvement, the more likely the system is to be sustainable in the long term. Larson described an extensive stakeholder engagement process that took thousands of hours interviewing court staff, creditors, creditor organizations, debtors, debt buyers, consumer representatives, legal service providers, and others. After a rigorous RFP process, the ensuing proposal was not ultimately adopted by the court, in part due to resistance by vocal legal service providers (both participants and nonparticipants in the stakeholder process) and the absence of judge leadership and early participation. Rabinovitch-Einy and Katsh, Carrel and Ebner, and Sela all noted the centrality of the fourth party, the technological-intermediary. This may be the heart of ODR. How do the case category and system goal(s) integrate with an ODR process? Who has the power to design the technology to bridge the gap and serve as the fourth party, whether serving in an administrative, communicative, or substantive function?

C. Culture and Context

ODR was spurred by the context of e-commerce and the development and expansion of information, communication, and AI technology. Smart contracts on the blockchain represent a leap of capacity to achieve additional functionality. Cultural expectations of various stakeholders users, designers, administrators, and provider have a critical influence on how, and for what purpose, ODR continues to expand. Just as the fourth party is an important stakeholder (both as an actor whose role may evolve with machine learning, as well as the owners of that technology), the culture surrounding it is an important background condition. Sela's research on the effect of digital architecture contributes to our understanding of the causes and effects by which ODR molds our decision making.

D. Process and Structure

The spectrum of processes designed and used has expanded with the newest versions of ODR. Carrel and Ebner and Larson note progress within mediation, as well as from mediation to collaborative decision making *supplemented* by technology used for communicating, information sharing, and accessing information. Now, processes are integrated *with* technology. Larson, in the court RFP, contemplated an expert system with a solution explorer.

Smart contracts on the blockchain emphasize rights-based resolutions with anonymous, crowdsourced jurors to deliver inclusive and democratic outcomes, arbitration-utilizing game theory, and AI algorithms that suggest solutions based on big data. Nevertheless, Sela points out that the bias introduced even magnified with AI can anchor the user's experience of digital choice-architecture.

E. Resources

A system's success will be substantially determined by the financial and human resources available at the design stage. Whether internal advisors or outside consultants design the system, the amount of money and staff time devoted to implementation will be important for educating users, training administrators and providers, and ultimately shifting perceptions of fairness, justice, and overall success. This issue of resources is intertwined with the goals of cost efficiency for the institution (which is often the driver for ODR) and cost efficiency for the user. Thus, resources indirectly impact access to justice.

The New York Consumer Debt project aimed to provide a more efficient, less costly case process; the ABA Enterprise Fund Award enabled creation of a pilot ODR system. The intention was to prepare a financial model that would build and maintain a system that valued transparency. Rabinovitch-Einy and Katsh describe the complex dispute handling options for smart contracts on the blockchain and detail which processes may involve crowdsourcing of jurors who need to be paid by any party, all parties, or a third party.

F. Success, Accountability, and Learning

System procedures should be transparent and accountable to all stakeholders and provide fair, just, balanced, unbiased, and effective means for managing conflict and resolving disputes. Nevertheless, transparency is not unbounded; a parallel goal for the DSD may be maintaining privacy of case details, so a balance must be struck. Systems have traditionally been deemed effective if they achieved the goals of lessening transaction costs, increasing satisfaction with the outcome, building relationships among the disputants, and reducing recurrence of the disputes.

Larson reviewed lessons learned with the New York Consumer Debt project, including the value of a pre-assessment to collect stakeholders' perspectives and interests, the necessity of engaging judges' support early on, and carefully picking the case category and process options (e.g., ODR). Sela sketched out an overview of digital choice architecture that synthesizes the motivations and the goals in tension: justice and efficiency. Her proposed evaluation methodology would provide evidence to find the relationship between implementation of targeted digital nudges and user behavior in the online court setting. Rabinovitch-Einy and Katsh and Schmitz and Rule describe the specific dispute category of smart contracts on the blockchain. There are a number of process options and numerous providers of such options, but a few cross-cutting concerns: cultural, legal, and technological. The uncertainty of the law and what the shadow of the law means in the online context poses a significant problem. But even more so:

> At the heart of dispute resolution lies the concept of legitimacy, which is ultimately premised on trust in the system, trust in the process, and trust in its fairness and therefore a willingness to abide by outcomes. In the blockchain context, on the other hand, there is a belief that trust is generated through technology by creating a secure enough environment that trust in anything but the blockchain itself becomes unnecessary. This creates a problem when the technology fails to deliver, as it has, and trust is broken, but no mechanisms for re-establishing it are available.

The shift in what constitutes trust interpersonal relationships leveraged with legal mechanisms, or an airtight coding structure may pose the most important challenge with ODR. The answer will likely vary with the parties and circumstances and reflect their unique priorities.

G. ODR Design Examples

The following table (1) sketches out an array of systems that incorporate ODR, and (2) identifies their unique DSD Framework elements.

DSD Element	eBay	Court and Tribunals	NextDoor Social Media	Kleros
Goals	Fast and fair resolutions for transaction problems.	Efficiency, streamlined user experience, and justice.	Intervene on fake news and bullying; promote civility, politeness, and neighborliness.	Fair, transparent, scalable, and self-administering.
Stakeholders	eBay, consumers, sellers, and regulators.	Courts, court staff, judges, the public, counsel, and litigants.	Citizens/ neighbors, journalists, and regulators.	Commercial disputants, employment or insurance smart contracts, and coders.

Context and Culture	High volume, low value; international or cross-border; transactional relationship.	Public; diverse; formal; various levels of literacy, education, and comfort with technology.	Geographic proximity; personal relationships; different races, ages, and income levels.	Online-first; international diversity; informality; high comfort with technology.
Processes	Diagnosis, negotiation, facilitation, and evaluation.	Settlement, mediation, and trial.	Discussion forums, technology-based coaching and advice, facilitative process.	Online evaluation, crowd-sourced jurors, and incentivized participation.
Resources	eBay investments in the software and case management staff.	Public funds, public employees, supporting non-profits.	NextDoor investments in the software and case management staff.	Kleros overall management, but designed to be self-sustaining.
Evaluation	eBay teams using surveys, user experience research, and data capture and monitoring.	Internal and external evaluation programs and court satisfaction data.	Surveys and user experience monitoring.	Overall usage and growth of the Kleros caseload and user base.
Designer	eBay	Court with external vendors and partners.	NextDoor	Kleros and the worldwide developer community.
Process Selection for Individual Case	Specified in user agreement; initiated by consumer.	Opt-in by filer/ plaintiff.	Required by NextDoor software.	Can be initiated by either complainant or respondent.

The primary goals of the above examples overlap significantly and are mostly compatible, but there exists a tension between giving primacy to fairness (eBay, Kleros, and NextDoor) or efficiency (courts). Each example is comprised of multiple stakeholders with likely differentiated goals. The notion of process pluralism underscores the importance of multiple processes that would each meet some goals better than others. Both facilitative and evaluative options are offered, with a tilt toward facilitative with NextDoor and evaluative with Kleros. Context and culture capture both public and private interests, again calling for process options according to parties' priorities. In an individual case, process choice is usually made by the user/consumer with eBay, courts, and NextDoor. Resources and design leadership are primarily provided by the dispute resolution provider. A combination of engaged stakeholder goal assessment, process choice according to rights or interests, and substantive and procedural transparency all contribute to system success.

Observations and Conclusion

... To start, working tips for the use of ODR as a dispute resolution option might include:

- Issues are relatively clear;
- Both the user and the administrator benefit from efficiency;
- Stakeholders (including actual users and decision-makers) are involved in the design and implementation process;
- Intervention is made upstream (during the policymaking process) to help prevent disputes (for example, with improved case information access and diagnosis process options);
- Multiple ODR processes are offered, including consensual on parties' interests, and adjudicative options to assess parties' rights;
- Adequate resources are available for training neutrals, administrators, and providers, and educating users;
- Process and outcomes are transparent (subject to private individual case information); and
- Independent evaluators conduct periodic reviews.

Depending on the transparency of the design, ODR may work less well when: legal parameters are unclear, precedent-setting is important, participants do not recognize the other side's rights, the process is used as a means to delay or hinder the other side's rights, algorithms that guide or make decisions are non-transparent, or designers make obscure tradeoffs across goals.

These tips reflect not only ODR, but process design overall. The ones that are especially a function of ODR seem to be: clearly defined issues with a premium on efficiency for both user and administrator, coupled with focus on prevention that can be achieved with AI; participatory design including users and all key stakeholders; both interest-based (mediation) and rights-based (adjudicatory) processes, especially as ODR includes increasing use of AI and algorithms; and processes and outcomes that are transparent, again, especially around the data inputs that produce algorithms.

On the contra-tips, if precedent-setting and clarity of legal parameters become more important with the need to test enforcement of smart contracts on the blockchain, the pressure for transparency in ODR design may increase. The trajectory of user skills and dependence on mobile and internet use may veer toward increased ODR, while it may also induce a backlash against a process perceived as insufficiently human-based and psychologically grounded. People's goals, cultural preferences for the use of ODR or other processes, reliability of data, and complexity of underlying legal issues in dispute will pose continuing challenges to the legal field of researchers and practitioners.

Notes & Questions

1. Now that you have read about so many kinds of dispute resolution processes, can you develop any guidelines for the processes that should be used in different kinds of disputes?
2. Should processes be chosen voluntarily? What if the parties involved don't agree?
3. Do you think it is a good idea to have a menu or tier of choices for dispute resolution?
4. What are the possible dangers of having different outcomes in different dispute resolution settings?
5. Which types of cases or subject matter should have appellate boards or another mechanism for review and precedent generation?
6. A Swiss manufacturer of winter sports equipment produces a new line of chic and streamlined skis. After one year of sales, it emerges that over 45 people from different countries have been injured by a malfunctioning boot mechanism on the skis. You have been asked by the manufacturer to design an efficient online dispute resolution system for prompt and confidential resolution of these claims. What are the issues you will need to consider in designing such a dispute resolution platform?

III. Considerations and Obstacles in ODR

In this section, we turn our attention to the challenges of ODR. We start by examining the technology that provides the platform for these processes and then consider how access to this technology could impact the ethics of using ODR.

A. Technical Difficulties

This section outlines some of the ongoing issues and concerns with communicating about conflict. Technology provides many choices for how we talk to one another, so it is crucial to understand the implications of each mode of communication. The following article discusses concerns with email communication and outlines the skills that are needed to use it most effectively.

Noam Ebner et al., *You've Got Agreement: Negoti@ting Via Email*

in Rethinking Negotiation Teaching 91, 94–106
(Christopher Honeyman, James Coben, & Giuseppe de Palo eds., 2009)

Part I: Negotiation via Email: Yes, It *Is* Different!

In negotiation, communication media influence not only what information is shared and how that information is communicated, but also how information is received and interpreted. Some information may be easy to communicate face-to-face, but difficult to convey in an email. Other information might be laid out clearly in an email message but misconstrued in a face-to-face setting. We can understand these differences more clearly by comparing face-to-face and email negotiations with reference to two dimensions of communication media: *media richness* and *interactivity*. Media richness is the capacity of the medium to transmit visual and verbal cues, thus providing more immediate feedback and facilitating communication of personal information. Interactivity is the potential of the medium to sustain a seamless flow of information between two or more negotiators. Both characteristics account for differences across media in the structure of information exchanged, the number of social context cues transmitted, and the social presence of negotiators....

Part II: Media Effects: Implications of Email Communication for Negotiation

The foregoing comparison of face-to-face negotiation and email negotiation gives rise to five major implications—incorporating both challenges and opportunities for parties negotiating by email:

1) Increased contentiousness

2) Diminished information sharing

3) Diminished process cooperation

4) Diminished trust

5) Increased effects of negative attribution

1) Increased Contentiousness

Even before the advent of Internet-based e-communication, research showed that communication at a distance via technological means is more susceptible to disruption than face-to-face dialogue....

In Internet-based communication, these findings not only hold true, they are intensified. Communication in cyberspace tends to be less inhibited; parties ignore the possible adverse consequences of negative online interactions because of physical distance, reduced social presence, reduced accountability and a sense of anonymity). The lack of social cues in e-communication causes people to act more contentiously than they do in face-to-face encounters, resulting in more frequent occurrences of swearing, name calling, insults, and hostile behavior.

Research shows that these findings on e-communication also hold true in e-negotiation. Early research showed that negotiators are apt to act tough and choose contentious tactics when negotiating with people at a distance. As researchers began to focus on e-negotiation, they discovered the effects of diminished media richness in e-negotiation: the social presence of others is reduced and the perceived social distance among negotiators increases). Thus, negotiators' social awareness of each other may be seriously diminished when communicating through email. This might explain why e-negotiators feel less bound by normatively appropriate behavior than face-to-face negotiators apparently do. This weakening of the normative fabric translates into an increased tendency to make threats and issue ultimata to adopt contentious, "squeaky wheel" behavior, to lie or deceive, to confront each other negatively, and to engage in flaming.

Hence, email negotiators are contending on a much rougher playing field than face-to-face negotiators. Still, the better we understand the nature of email as described in the previous section, the greater our abilities to turn the potentially hazardous characteristics of email to good use—i.e., *reducing* contentiousness. Used properly, lean media may facilitate better *processing* of social conflict exactly because these media do *not* transmit visual and verbal cues. First, the visible, physical presence of an opponent can induce arousal which leads to more aggressive behavioral responses. Therefore, the absence of visual and verbal cues in email may defuse such triggers. Second, email may also reduce the salience of group differences. By masking or deemphasizing gender, race, accent, or national origin, to name just a few, email may actually reduce the impact of unconscious bias on negotiation. Deemphasizing group membership may also suppress coalition formation. In addition, because negotiators are physically isolated and the social presence of others is diminished, they can take time to "step out" of the discussion and thoughtfully respond rather than merely react to the other party's behavior, potentially limiting the escalation of social conflict even further.

2) Diminished Inter-party Cooperation

Experiments in email negotiation have explored two connected concepts: the measure of inter-party cooperation throughout the negotiation process, and the degree to which resulting outcomes are integrative at the end of the negotiation. The connection between the two is obvious: the potential for integrative outcomes grows as parties become more aware of each other's needs and capabilities, and areas of potential joint gain emerge.

Email negotiations make information exchange likely to be constrained, analytical, and contentious. This diminishes negotiators' ability to accurately assess differential preferences and identify potential joint gains. Indeed, one comparison of face-to-face and computer-mediated negotiations revealed that negotiators interacting electronically were less accurate in judging the other party's interests....

However, when used properly, email could *increase* information exchange. Lean media may work to promote more equal participation among negotiators. Diminished social context cues and resulting reduction in the salience of social group differences can reduce social influence bias among individuals and encourage lower-status individuals to participate more.... Attention to this "new" information may subsequently enable negotiators to identify optimal trades and create more integrative agreements....

3) Reduction in Integrative Outcomes

As previously mentioned, reduced process cooperation is expected to result in a lower level of integrative agreements. Many experiments measuring these two indicators—cooperative behavior and integrative outcomes—have shown that in e-negotiation, as opposed to face-to-face negotiation, one is less likely to encounter cooperation in the process, and less likely to achieve integrative outcomes. Additionally, the potential for impasse appears to be greater than in face-to-face negotiation....

On the other hand, the media effects of email negotiation include one feature that might promote integrative thinking and outcomes. As we have seen, negotiators tend to exchange long messages that include multiple points all in one "bundle" when using asynchronous media like email. Argument-bundling may facilitate integrative agreements by encouraging negotiators to link issues together and consider them simultaneously rather than sequentially. This can promote log-rolling, a classic tool for reaching integrative outcomes. However, negotiators should avoid "over-bundling" [because] too many issues and too much information delivered at one time can place higher demands on the receiver's information processing capabilities....

4) Diminished Degree of Interparty Trust

Trust between negotiating parties has been identified as playing a key role in enabling cooperation, problem-solving, achieving integrative solutions, effectiveness, and resolving disputes.

Communication via email, however, is fraught with threats to trust that are inherent in the medium and in the way parties approach and employ it. It has been suggested that lack of trust in online opposites is the factor responsible for the low levels of process cooperation and of integrative outcomes.

5) Increased Tendency Towards Sinister Attribution

The media effects of email negotiation exacerbate the tendency toward the sinister attribution error: the bias toward seeing negative events as the outgrowth of others' negative intentions rather than unintended results or conditions beyond their control. The lack of social presence and of contextual cues lends a sense of distance and of vagueness to the interaction. The asynchronous dynamic of email negotiations adds to this challenge. Research shows that e-negotiators ask fewer clarifying questions than face-to-face negotiators do. Instead of gathering information from their counterparts, email negotiators may be more likely to make assumptions; if those assumptions later prove unfounded, the negotiators may perceive the other's inconsistent actions or preferences as a breaking of trust. The power of the sinister attribution error in e-negotiation is clearly demonstrated by experiments showing that e-negotiators are more likely to suspect their opposite of lying than are face-to-face negotiators, even when no actual deception has taken place.

Part III: Repacking the Negotiator's Toolbox: Recommended Skill-Sets for Email Negotiators

In this section, we will briefly introduce four basic skill sets that email negotiators need to acquire in order to cope with the media effects of email discussed in the last section. These four skills are discussed as initial proposals and are certainly not suggested as an exhaustive list; no doubt, others will emerge.

Skill-Set #1: Writing Ability

A central skill that may seem both so obvious and so crucial that we need not address it is the ability to write—clearly, persuasively, and (at times) movingly.... Particularly when it comes time to establish rapport, defuse tension, or even apologize, some email negotiators may find that their writing skills are simply not up to the task at hand.

Skill Set #2: Message Management

Managing Our Own Anxiety

The art of negotiating solely by exchanging written messages through postal mail is a long-forgotten one. We have become accustomed to exchanging opinions through synchronous communication, either face-to-face or over the telephone. Email negotiators need to relearn the art of asynchronous communication. This may not be intuitive, for one of the Internet's promises is instant access to anything and anyone. Our synchronous-communication upbringing, combined with our expectations of instant access, clashes with the basic nature of asynchronous communication. As a result, email communication often involves an anxiety that blends distrust of the channel with distrust of the other. When we send messages and do not receive responses promptly, not only do we question whether our counterparts received the messages, we begin to wonder why (if indeed they *have* received them) they are taking so long to respond. To manage this anxiety and prevent a downward spiral of distrust, e-negotiators need to understand and bear in mind the limitations of the medium they are using.

Managing the Other's Anxiety

Research has shown that frequent message exchanges, as opposed to communication broken by intervals, are conducive to trust-building within groups. This is also true for the dyadic group formed by two people negotiating. Responding to an email within 24 hours, even if only to say that we are considering what a negotiation counterpart has written, might be a useful standard. On the other hand, delivering a strongly negative response or a total rejection of the counterpart's proposal should not be done too hastily.

Utilizing Asynchronicity

Once we become aware of, and overcome, the challenging characteristics of asynchronous communication, we can focus on the potential it offers for improved communication dynamics. It can be a very conducive channel for reasoned discussion, careful responses, and trust-building moves. It can help control our response time—to our own advantage. Asynchronous communication allows us to avoid knee-jerk reactions or escalatory cycles of contentious behavior, and to think proactively. The slower pace allows us to fashion and frame our response thoughtfully and productively. It enables us to verify details instead of giving off-the-cuff responses that may later turn out to be inaccurate—providing for more exact information sharing. Email creates a searchable thread of exchanged email messages so that we can hold others accountable for representations and commitments. And we can check our own past communications if they over-claim something we have allegedly promised. We can read a received message twice, or ask a colleague to take a look at it and tell us what she thinks, before we reply to it, lowering the effect of sinister attribution. We can do the same with a message we have written, before sending it. By learning when *not* to click "Reply," and when to delay clicking "Send," email negotiators can use the medium to maximum effect.

Skill-Set #3: Relationship Management

Setting the Stage: Unmasking

As we have seen, the mutual invisibility inherent in email negotiation facilitates adversarial, contentious, and trust-breaking behavior. It is easier to cause damage to a faceless other, particularly when we feel protected by a shield of anonymity and physical distance. The sense of anonymity and distance created between email negotiators leads both to assumptions that one can get away with aggressive or trust-breaking behavior, and to a lowering of moral inhibitions against doing so. This necessitates that negotiators consciously adopt a proactive agenda of unmasking themselves *toward* the other. The more negotiation counterparts perceive us as *people they know* rather than anonymous, faceless email addresses, the more likely they are to share information, rely on us, and trust in us.

Building Rapport

The concept of using pre-negotiation social interaction to create a positive and unmasked environment for an upcoming negotiation process is widely discussed and advocated in the negotiation literature that focuses on face-to-face interactions.

In face-to-face encounters, introductions and light, social conversations come naturally; in e-negotiation, this tendency diminishes. As we have discussed, negotiators tend to remain on topic, task-oriented, and analytic, leaving little room for social lubrication. As a result, e-negotiators need to *consciously* dedicate time and effort to the unmasking process. Experiments have indicated that even minimal pre-negotiation contact, at the most basic level of "schmoozing" via preliminary email introductory messages or brief telephone exchanges, has the potential for building trust, improving mutual impressions, and facilitating integrative outcomes. By inviting the other to reply, we are initiating a cycle of unmasking which not only transcends physical distance but also reshapes the process into one allowing for recognition and empathy, which can continue to develop as the negotiation progresses.

We would suggest building rapport through words rather than emotions. A negotiator could write the business part of the email first—working for absolute clarity and thoroughness—and then go back to insert the schmooze factor at the beginning of the email, e.g., "lovely to see you last week," "thanks much for getting back to me," etc.

Showing E-empathy

Demonstrating empathy is universally described as a powerful tool and an important skill for any negotiator. This has been found to hold true in online communication as well: e-negotiators who show empathy are trusted by their negotiation opposites more than those who do not. This trust might cause the empathic negotiator's actions and intentions to be construed more positively, diminishing the tendency towards sinister attribution. Negotiators will be more likely to share information with a trusted counterpart, opening the door for more integrative agreements.

Skill-Set #4: Content Management

The absence of contextual cues focuses email negotiators on the actual *content* of messages. This necessitates particular skills with regard to three issues:

Clarity

As we have seen, message clarity helps avoid sinister attribution and allows for precise information sharing. Clear messages allow e-negotiators to focus on what their counterparts have written, reply to their points, and consider their proposals. Clarity in reply creates a virtuous cycle.

Bundling

Email negotiators tend to bundle multiple points and multiple arguments in a single message. While on the one hand, we have noted how this tendency might potentially facilitate the identification of integrative agreements by encouraging negotiators to link issues together and consider them simultaneously rather than sequentially, it might also clash with basic message clarity. Additionally, even if clearly written, an excessive amount of data might send the message recipient into an information overload. Email negotiators need to learn and practice balanced bundling. Judicious use of the "subject" line in an email helps both negotiators and their counterparts to search for and to frame the content of emails they receive. Thus, negotiators should craft subject lines that are sufficiently general that a broad search will produce a list that includes them (e.g., "Smith v. Jones") but also specific enough that they alert the recipient to what they contain and facilitate targeted searches (e.g., "Smith v. Jones—concerns about Smith deposition").

Framing

With the bulk of a message's impact shifted to its content, language and wording become paramount. This is especially important in the framing of issues and discussion topics. Asynchronous communication allows for careful framing of issues and well-thought-out revision of frames proposed by the other party.

Part of framing is also thinking about the formatting of the email, which affects the perceptual frame through which the other recipient takes in the message content. In the body of the email, negotiators should alter default settings for style and font with caution and only for good reason. A negotiator should also think carefully about using all caps—IT IS THE EQUIVALENT OF SCREAMING in an email. Finally, we would suggest not using too many!!! to make a point or too many ☺ to try and lend "tone" to a particular comment—unless negotiators are certain that the relationships they have with their opposites make this suitable.

Notes & Questions

1. What are the most common challenges you have faced in relying on email communication as opposed to face-to-face communication? Why do you think most of us use email despite some drawbacks?
2. Note the particular strategies that you might adopt to improve your own email communications, and consider how we might build those skills into ODR structures. How can we support users of ODR?
3. Have you had any experience using some form of ODR for a dispute with a party in another country? What happened?

In the next essay, adapted from a keynote speech for Singapore Mediation Week, Andrea Schneider considers how the pros and cons of each mode of communication should affect the choices we make. During the COVID-19 pandemic, we increased our technological skills but also our reliance on technology for communication. How do we choose the most effective mode (email, text, video, phone, or face-to-face)? Building on the concepts outlined in the previous article regarding rapport and trust building (through social intuition), this excerpt outlines considerations for each of these modes.

Andrea Kupfer Schneider, *The Next Wave of Effective Dispute Resolution: Developing Emotional and Social Intelligence*

2003 ASIAN J. MEDIATION 5–9

D. Translating to an Online Medium

Now, we need to think about how to translate [social intuition and rapport-building skills] when we are not face-to-face. Face-to-face is the gold standard. Our first question has always been to ask whether it is worth getting on a plane and flying to our destination to talk face-to-face. But now, we have all these other ways of communicating. The way that we communicate makes a difference. Once again, social intuition can help us figure out how we are sending information. So, as we think about the ways that we communicate, we are going to use the media richness approach.[2] The approach asks us to consider the extent to which we are received by the other party through any communication platform. For example, in messaging, WhatsApp will give little checkmarks that someone has read the message. Even if you did not respond, I know that you have read it. In contrast, most of us do not know if our email was read after sending unless somebody responds.

---

2. Noam Ebner, *The Human Touch in ODR: Trust, Empathy and Social Intuition in Online Negotiation and Mediation*, *in* ONLINE DISPUTE RESOLUTION: THEORY AND PRACTICE (Daniel Rainey, Ethan Katsh & Mohamed Abdel Wahab eds., 2d ed. 2021).

When we think about technology, we must think about another set of factors. For instance, we should ask about timing. Are you communicating at the same time? We also need to consider the communication channels involved. An example is texting somebody to tell them that there is an email that I want them to respond to. Another example is when too many emails were sent and I must pick up the phone or get on video to explain why the emails should have been clearer. Our creativity in conflict also plays a role. If you are texting with emojis, your creativity is limited to ability to convey meaning through the emojis. Emotions matter as well when it comes to determining how soon we reply to our emails.

E. Adapting to a Post-pandemic Environment

Whatever I would have said in February 2020 has now been completely upended. Consider how you were once not very comfortable on Zoom, or your usage of Cisco and WebEx was limited by how technological you were, and times when you did not get to make eye contact or were looking in the wrong place. Now, we are all comfortable for better or worse with Zoom and everything else.

We need to consider the challenges of trust in online negotiation and mediation. In terms of email, we tend to have low expectations of trust that typically end up as self-fulfilling.[3] We do not have contextual clues. We read emails as if somebody is yelling at us even when it is not written in all caps. If you send emojis, the other system does not necessarily pick it up. Without tone, you do not have peace of mind because you are not hearing anything other than the voice potentially yelling at you. We may tend to misinterpret things and think the worst of somebody else. All these things are problematic. We assume that when we send emails, they are perfectly clear with a lovely tone of voice. We absolutely intend to be supportive, kind, and clear. Yet, when somebody else sends us an email in response, we are shocked by the fact that they did not read the email the way that we intended.

It is social intuition that can help recognize and dig us out of this. We should look towards applying the skills of factoring in tone and voice, and the need to create rapport and trust to help us choose the different ways that we communicate. At the end of the day, we want to take advantage of a multimedia approach to know when we should use email, get on the plane, or talk on the phone. The next Part will therefore be spent going through the different modes of communication.

IV. Evaluation of Modes of Communication

A. Emails

I can read emails during any occasion, like while on the soccer field as I watch my children play. I can read them at night or in the morning. The choice and flexibility to read them wherever I want is great. I can also read and reflect before writing back in email. In particular, we get to reflect on the huge benefit of what information we received before replying. Emails are also terrific for task-oriented communication. How-

3. *Id.*

ever, emails incorporate neither contextual cues nor tone. We thus tend to misread the social cues. Emails are often asynchronous. It is not only that somebody might not have read it, but by the time they read it, there are three more emails ahead. We sometimes read them in backwards order, and other times we are hopping into a conversation that is five to ten emails deep. The mirroring skills that we have talked about are impossible to be applied. The time to develop trust tends to be more difficult. It is hard to demonstrate empathy in most of our emails: every tool that we have been taught about active listening or developing empathy sounds strange on email.

B. Texting

We move on to texting. I used to think that text messaging was only for casual communication. Yet, there are prosecutors and defense attorneys in the US who are now plea bargaining via text. We see that texts are being used increasingly in a professional setting. Compared to emails, texts are also more likely to be in sync. On the other hand, you can lose the thread. Until very recently, you could not mark your messages as unread. Many would find it hard to remember responding to previously opened texts, or instead responding too quickly without slowing down to think.

C. Phones

There are some of us that look at a picture of a phone and think of it as just a social media tool. Instead, it is also useful for emails and text messages. Phones have also been shown for years to have advantages in terms of conveying tone and pace. There are studies showing that even in the primary use of email, the usage of phones would at least allow parties to hear each other's voice once and set a tone for how they are reading the email afterwards.[4] This is indeed more effective at building rapport. At the same time, the lack of visual cues may lessen the impact of negative cues that were not intended. Talking on the phone enables mobility: one can be walking around all over their house, right up and down the block. However, you are still not seeing body language and eye contact so it is again harder to build rapport.

D. Video Conversations

We are getting much better at reading cues over video conversation. Technology is much better in terms of eye contact. In terms of body language, at least you can see more cues such as hand movements and facial expressions. Depending on the technology, most of our social intuition cues are coming through. We are all more comfortable in ways that we were previously not in terms of using a new mode of communication. As we saw during the pandemic, we are all equal in terms of the size of our video box. And so, in conflict, it is nice that everybody has the same equal space occupied on the screen. On the other hand, we are not necessarily operating at the same time in terms of synchronization. Also, there are some interesting studies showing that there was still

4. *See, e.g.*, Michael Morris et al., *Schmooze or Lose: Social Friction and Lubrication in Email Negotiations* 6 Group Dynamics 89, 90 (2002).

a gap in expectations online when it came to gender, race, and age.[5] Looking at others on the screen can also be distracting. Some people experience "Zoom fatigue" because staring at yourself, as much fun as it is, is also tiring.

E. Face-to-Face Conversations

Regarding the tracking of cues, this is the gold standard when we think about how social intuition is used. On the other hand, if we are in a conflict and talking face-to-face, there may be times when you may be caught off guard. Your response then may not be better than one thought of during your car ride home afterwards.

After talking about the different modes, let us think about how it all matters. There tends to be a moving target in terms of the different ways we communicate when we reflect either on our nonverbal cues, *i.e.*, visual, audio, or paraverbal. When it comes to timing, we must ask what are the advantages and disadvantages of communicating at the same time with somebody against having more time to reflect? How does everything then wrap itself up into trust and building a relationship? [The table below shows all of these considerations for each mode.]

Differences in Modes of Communication

	Content	Nonverbal Cues	Timing	Trust/ Relationship
Face-to-Face	All things personal and/or professional	High level of verbal and nonverbal cues	Simultaneous	Easy to build rapport
Phone	All things personal and/or professional	Paraverbal only	Simultaneous	More challenging
Email	Tends to be more task-oriented	Only if added deliberately	Dependent on access & and promptness of reply	More challenging
Text	Tends to be more personal but …	Easy to add emojis to language; and lots of casual language	Can be simultaneous	More challenging if professional
Video Conferencing	Depends on platform expectations (i.e., FaceTime v. Zoom)	High in verbal and nonverbal cues (but technologically dependent)	Simultaneous	Can be easier, but technologically dependent

5. *See, e.g.*, Allison S. Gabriel, Daron Robertson, & Kristen Shockley, *Research: Cameras On or Off?*, Harv. Bus. Rev. (Oct. 26, 2021), https://hbr.org/2021/10/research-cameras-on-or-off (last visited Oct. 16, 2023).

V. The Future of Remote Dispute Resolution

We now link back to negotiation effectiveness. The first question is, what are we comfortable with? What is your communication default and is it the same in conflict? Why are we comfortable with the skill and use of that default? At the same time, we need to start figuring out the person with whom we are negotiating or mediating. What is their default? What is their comfortable communication mode? For most of us, these conflicts are repeated. We repeatedly deal with the same people whom we work with. We should be able to start figuring out what are the better ways to communicate with them. My previous Dean had a harder time saying "no" in person but would very easily say "no" via email. So, I stopped emailing. However, he loves email whereas I do not. So, I would go and see him face-to-face before following up with an email. In the end, we are figuring out how that works for the both of us.

We know that negotiations and mediations are moving online. We have hosts of judges, lawyers, clients, and mediators who are comfortable online. However, we need to be cognizant of the strengths and weaknesses of doing our work online. Is it serving your client? Is it serving you in the best way to get the parties together? If you have a few lawyers working on the conflict, it is not only about who has the area of expertise but also who is good at reading cues face-to-face, or these days, on Zoom. For the latter, it can boil down to the little changes to the virtual settings that create rapport. We must think about the pros and cons of the process itself.

In the dispute resolution field, we know that it can be more efficient and more effective for clients if they do not have to travel and spend time doing so. However, when technology is required, depending on your clients and what their access to technology is, holding the negotiation or mediation remotely may exacerbate the divide. While court processes go online, as many did during the pandemic, it assumes that people have access to computers and internet connection. Trying to file a court document on your smartphone from the parking lot of Walmart is not effective.

I have heard from more than one divorce mediator that they are very excited about never having to be in the same room as their clients again. Yet, if your client is someone who wants to be heard by the mediator and needs to be able to tell their story in person, that is something to be considered as well. It should not be an automatic assumption that we are never going to have anybody together in the same room. We also know that both lawyers and mediators in the last couple of years have not been as effective on Zoom in creating as much rapport. Parties are leaving less satisfied. While we do not have to commute and it is very "comfy", it is not necessarily serving our primary purpose.

VI. Conclusion

We must recognize that we still need social intuition in whatever mode of technology we are using. It is meant to help us choose the modes. When we think about all the different ways, we want to know ourselves and know what advantages there are. We want to embrace the multimedia approach. When it comes to email, start adding in rapport-building elements so that you are aware of the social intuition that aids both parties. Text can be good for casual signaling. Using the phone is still useful for taking advantage of the paraverbal. Video conversations are great for building a connection. And of course, face-to-face is still the gold standard.

B. Issues of Ethics and Access to Justice in Use and Design of ODR

In this final section of the chapter, we turn to various issues surrounding the use of ODR—unequal access to justice on account of the "digital divide" that exists in almost every country; ODR's consequent variable legitimacy and acceptance; and concerns about how ODR is designed and practiced. The first article you will read outlines how technological and legal capacities intersect in the ODR space, the second presents empirical data on income disparities in perceptions and uses of ODR, and the third proposes an ethics code. This section also includes the European Regulation on Online Consumer Dispute Resolution to help you see what other jurisdictions are implementing in an effort to protect consumers in the ODR space. Compare this to what Professor Menkel-Meadow says about ethics in general dispute system design in Chapter 9, and think about whether online *international* dispute resolution presents different or additional ethical issues.

Some have suggested that the use of online dispute resolution reflects a transformation in legal thinking and reasoning—that there is a new "digital legal consciousness" that may separate those who have computer literacy and access from those who don't. Consider the taxonomy Naomi Creutzfeldt presents in the following excerpt and how it should/might impact the development of both domestic and international online dispute resolution (including cross-border issues).

Naomi Creutzfeldt, *Towards a Digital Legal Consciousness?*

12 (3) European J.L. & Tech. (2021)

How do people make sense of digital justice and what is their relationship with it? In a rapidly growing and constantly developing digital justice space, there is a need to explore (theoretically and empirically) emerging patterns on how people (dis)engage with this space. The purpose of this article is to contribute a framework for this task. To do this, I build on my previous work where I have called these developing patterns digital legal consciousness. I argue below that our digital legal consciousness develops by us combining our attitudes and capabilities towards the law with our attitudes and capabilities towards the digital. In other words, in order to explore how the digital turn of the justice system is being experienced, I bring theories of legal consciousness to digital justice. The starting assumption of digital legal consciousness is that people approach the digital justice system with a mixture of expectations they learned and developed through a combination of their (dis)engagement with the offline justice system and their (un)ease of everyday engagement with the digital space. Therefore, people approach a digital justice system with two sets of expectations. First, expectations that the justice system will operate as it does in the offline space (as humans we cannot avoid making sense of the activities we are engaged in by drawing on our previous history of activities and learning; and second through their expectations and experiences of the digital space. Most people have more experience with online transactions and interactions than they do with legal settings. In other words, the way in which people are able to engage with the digital justice system depends on both sets of capabilities: legal capabilities and digital capabilities....

Access to Justice in the Emerging Digital Justice Space

Digital justice is the space that people have to access when engaging with a court, tribunal or legal advice to resolve their problems online. Perceptions of justice are contingent and multiple. In this article I conceptualize digital justice as a space, as opposed to justice as effect of spatialization and material dynamics (e.g. digital media), in which the idea of efficiency is bound up with the definition of a working justice system (see below) even though efficiency and needs of users of these systems are often at odds. Many parts of justice systems around the world have gradually been upgraded to deliver their services online. This upgrade comes with a promise of fewer delays, greater efficiency and better access to justice. The worldwide *digital turn* of justice systems occurs at different paces and is at different levels of evolution in each country....

Conceptualizing Digital Legal Consciousness

Digital legal consciousness sets itself apart from legal consciousness through the space in which law is experienced and takes place. Digital legal consciousness takes place online whereas legal consciousness has been developed in the mundane face-to-face (offline) space. I argue here that we base our initial engagement and expectations of digital justice on our legal consciousness but then we need additional skills to enter, and act confidently, in the digital space. In the online justice space, we have to negotiate both legal and digital skills and capabilities. The digital space provides opportunities for those who are at ease with operating online, and obstacles for those who are digitally less able than others. In other words, the online justice space, replacing the physical justice space, requires us to learn and to negotiate different skillsets. This means that our digital legal consciousness develops by us combining our attitudes and capabilities towards the law with our attitudes and capabilities towards the digital. I offer four profiles of people's attitudes to consider when exploring engagement with the digital justice space.

5.1 Four Profiles

The four profiles offered below are constructed as ideal types for the purpose of building a theoretical model to understand people's (dis)engagement with the digital justice system. This model needs to be empirically tested and in reality, these types can overlap and do not have the clear-cut distinctions as outlined below. Nevertheless, the four profiles constructed in this model help to start to explore how people engage with digital justice, as a combination of their digital and legal capabilities. As mentioned above, there will be different levels in which each of the capabilities present themselves and thus influence our engagement with and access to the digital justice system.

		Digital capabilities +	Digital capabilities –
Legal capabilities	+	1. Digitally and legally literate/enabled	2. Digitally agnostic/ Legally able
Legal capabilities	–	3. Digitally assisted/ Legally unable	4. Digitally and legally abandoned/excluded

5.1.1 Digitally and Legally Literate, Enabled

People in this category are aware of the law, identify with the law, and choose to do everything online. They are confident to use the justice system online and possess both digital and legal capabilities. A report by the Carnegie Trust UK (2017) explored questions about how people, once digitally engaged, navigate the online world. Digitally literate citizens know how to access technology and are open to using technology to deal with all aspects of their lives.

Digitally Agnostic, Legally Able

People in this category are aware of the law, identify with the law, but choose not to use the internet for justice matters. Although they are able to use the online justice system, they draw a line and believe that justice needs to remain in an offline space. This group of people uses the internet with ease for other transactions as a routine part of their lives. They have legal capabilities and choose not to use their digital capabilities to engage with the legal system online.

Digitally Assisted, Legally Unable

People in this category are aware of the law, have a low identification with the law, and are not able to digitally access the justice system themselves—they need assistance. Typically, this group of people will have regular engagement with the state welfare system and possibly designated advisers to assist them. They are not able to identify that the problems they are facing might be legal ones and where to get help. This group is on the margins of being digitally excluded but if they manage to seek help then they will obtain assistance in legal and digital access. Although these people have low digital capabilities and low legal capabilities, with assistance, they can access the digital justice system.

Digitally and Legally Abandoned/Excluded

People in this category have a limited legal awareness and are not able to access the digital justice system. They have turned their backs to the law, usually due to the lack of assistance or capabilities. This group has lost trust in justice and thinks that it is just not for them. They suffer the most as they do not have access to technology and do not know if their problems are legal problems or where they can go to seek help. These people are digitally excluded, they lack the skills and confidence to use online technology, and usually do not have access to devices or stable internet connections. This is just one layer of social and economic problems that are also related to social exclusion.

These described four profiles provide a starting point to explore digital legal consciousness empirically in the real world. The profiles are not as empirically distinct from each other as proposed in the taxonomy, rather this approach offers a theoretical paradigm to grasp the complex and multidimensional understanding of access to digital justice. Legal consciousness is three-dimensional and complex, it has helped me to think about how people make sense of law and legality and inform the taxonomy.

This taxonomy of ideal profiles can be put to the test to explore how they overlap in reality. We can argue that a person can be, for example, against the law and digitally literate. Further people can be, and feel, alienated from the law. This opens up the complexity that lies behind the taxonomy and needs to be explored when empirically tested. Further, the relationship between the digital options and the legal options needs to be empirically disentangled. This entails asking how people self-identify: digitally or legally capable, and also what the administrators and creators or these systems experience them to be. Profiles 1–3 can be empirically captured through surveys, for example, whereas profile 4 needs interviews and participant observations.

Notes & Questions

1. Where in this taxonomy of those who use online dispute resolution do you see yourself? Most Americans? Most people in India? China? Europe? Nigeria? How can international dispute resolution online fora be developed for people of "different" digital and legal consciousness? How do national legal systems affect digital legal consciousness?
2. Can you see ODR used in and adapted for different international claims and disputes? Could you design an international online platform for human rights abuses, migration and refugee issues, post-disaster food aid, or fundraising?
3. What kinds of "justice" or remedies can ODR deliver in the international conflict space?

The next article analyzes whether online proceedings bridge the access-to-justice gap associated with in-person hearings. It examines the applicability of the traditional procedural justice model to the setting of online courts and also discusses whether procedural justice and access-to-justice perceptions are predictors of perceived system legitimacy in online proceedings.

Avital Mentovich, J.J. Prescott, & Orna Rabinovich-Einy, *Legitimacy and Online Proceedings: Procedural Justice, Access to Justice, and the Role of Income*

57 L. & Soc'y Rev. 189, 203–207; 209 (2023)

To summarize, our analysis uncovers evidence of heterogeneity across socioeconomic status in two key determinants of perceived legitimacy. First, we estimate a significant coefficient on our procedural-justice-by-income interaction variable, which translates to procedural justice being more weakly related to legitimacy perceptions on average for participants in the lower-income group versus the higher-income group. Second, we estimate a significant access-by-income interaction coefficient for the higher-income group that offsets the main positive access relationship, implying that access-to-justice perceptions are a stronger predictor of legitimacy for the lower-income group. For the sake of completeness, we add that our estimated outcome-favorability-by-income interaction coefficient is small and statistically insignificant. Overall, these patterns are consistent with our hypothesis that lower-income individuals place greater relative weight on access-to-justice considerations in their evaluation of the legitimacy of the legal system relative to higher-income individuals....

First, despite the thin nature of online communication, we find that procedural-justice perceptions are a strong predictor of legitimacy perceptions even in online proceedings. This result may tie to particular traits of online communication (Ebner & Greenberg, 2020). While some lament the lack of rich, real-time physical communication when interacting online (Sternlight, 2020), certain features of online exchanges may actually enhance a party's experience and thus their procedural-justice perceptions. For example, limiting physical interaction also mitigates negative features of in-court proceedings, such as long waits and a rushed process, which can convey disrespect and inhibit voice. In addition, some litigants may find it uncomfortable to address a judge face to face and would prefer to "voice" their story in writing. Indeed, rather than a "second-class" procedural scheme, online asynchronous proceedings may amply serve litigant procedural-justice needs and, for some people, even be an improvement. Another explanation may lie in people having different expectations for online proceedings—that is, people may experience proceedings in light of what is possible given the medium, and no one expects rich, physical interaction in an easy-to-access forum for written exchanges. Expectations, preferences, and values underlying procedural-justice experiences may be undergoing transformation (Turkle, 2011). Future research should explore the precise components of procedural-justice experiences in online settings (and indeed in each type of online setting).

Second, consistent with our hypothesis, we find no evidence that instrumental concerns in the form of outcome-favorability perceptions predict legitimacy perceptions in online proceedings. This finding may be surprising because online spaces may seem especially conducive to instrumental motivations. Our results nevertheless mirror research in face-to-face settings that show, at most, the marginal importance of instrumental concerns to legitimacy. Perhaps the explanation lies in legitimacy perceptions being rooted in deep-seated psychological needs and motivations that are unlikely to be satisfied by news of a favorable outcome.

Third, our study adds a new angle to the familiar normative versus instrumental lens on legitimacy by incorporating access to justice, a more structural dimension of the legal system. Online dispute resolution seems like a natural setting to examine the role of access in generating legitimacy because increasing access has been one of the driving forces behind the design and adoption of online proceedings. Our data confirm the potential importance of access-to-justice perceptions in predicting legitimacy perceptions. Thus, accessibility may not only be a core consideration in how to design online proceedings but also in how users experience those proceedings. One important question is whether access-to-justice perceptions, which may naturally attach to the unique features of online proceedings, will also prove central to how people experience traditional procedures, a possibility future research should explore.

Fourth, we present tentative evidence of a connection between access-to-justice perceptions and intent to comply with traffic laws, hinting that innovations in access may offer an additional route toward improving compliance. We also detect some indication that, for lower-income parties, higher outcome-favorability perceptions may positively correlate with compliance intentions. Both patterns appear to hold even when accounting for legitimacy perceptions. We also uncover a connection between perceived legitimacy—as shaped by procedural-justice and access-to-justice perceptions—and intentions to comply. However, we advise against relying on these results without corroborating studies using better data and measures—after all, we measure compliance using self-reported intentions, which are susceptible to social-desirability bias and may not be useful predictors of actual behavior. However, we hope these patterns will motivate future rigorous work on compliance, including attempts to replicate these patterns—testing, for example, whether access-to-justice perceptions predict compliance and whether people with below-average incomes place some weight on instrumental concerns in their compliance behavior, possibly a function of relative economic disadvantage....

Our research also has implications for the connection between dispute system design and party perceptions. While design questions are not limited to online proceedings, the online setting lends itself to "design thinking" and gives rise to more design options than typical face-to-face justice settings. Thus, we should understand our findings in the context of the design of the proceedings we study. The impact of the change in medium on party perceptions is likely to be multi-directional and highly dependent on the precise design choices of the specific online proceeding in question. To understand procedural-justice, access-to-justice, and legitimacy perceptions in online legal proceedings, we should systematically study a wide-range of online court processes and explore how variations in system design influence party perceptions.

Conclusion

Despite the rapid growth in online court proceedings, research into how users experience these proceedings is just beginning. Analysis of legitimacy perceptions and their determinants online is almost nonexistent. This study is the first to provide empirical insight into how changes from centuries-old, face-to-face hearings to novel online proceedings may matter for the underpinnings of legal legitimacy. We find that positive assessments of access to justice and procedural justice in online proceedings predict more robust legitimacy perceptions. We also find that access-to-justice perceptions appear relatively more important in explaining legitimacy views among lower-income litigants. Our results suggest that technology can generate novel procedural options that are at least compatible with and may advance access to justice, procedural justice, and system legitimacy. Technology is no panacea, but thoughtful design choices accompanied by careful attention to litigant experiences may give rise to new and exciting opportunities for justice while enhancing the legitimacy of our legal institutions.

In the next article, Leah Wing, one of the most prominent ODR and tech ethicists, proposes an ethics code for ODR design. As you read, consider how Professor Wing would be concerned with or applaud the findings above from the Michigan traffic courts. How might her proposed code change some of the elements of the court ODR system?

Leah Wing, *Ethical Principles for Online Dispute Resolution: A GPS Device for the Field*

3 Int'l J. Online Disp. Resol. 23–29 (2016)

The Benefits of Non-Rules-Based Ethical Principles

The value of ethical principles and ethical standards has been debated across the disciplines and a wide range of professional organizations, illuminating useful roles that non-rules-based principles can play, specifically because they provide the opportunity to be flexible while still being robust. Such a set of ethical principles

- provides guidance that can be applied to the infinite variations in circumstances that arise in practice
- can cope with rapid changes of the modern […] environment
- prevents the development of a mechanistic, 'box-ticking' approach to decision making and the use of legalistic loopholes to avoid compliance with guidance
- focuses on the spirit of the guidance and encourage[s] responsibility and the exercise of professional judgement, which are key elements of professions.

Principles can set a higher level framework than rules may set, articulating expectations in broader language and allowing for responsiveness to specific contexts. Rules and standards can play invaluable roles in enforcement and accountability to assist in providing ethical and high-quality systems and services. However, they may work well in tandem with higher level ethical principles, since "even when a specific circumstance is addressed by a rule, compliance is often with the letter of the rule, not its spirit. What is needed is a principles-based approach to decision-making, which encourages deliberation, judgement and responsibility."

Shared principles do not negate the need for rules and standards by which processes, platforms, practitioners and their practices can be held accountable. In fact, the latter are strongest when they are also tied to the former—principles that can set out the shared expectations upon which rules or standards can be built. It is in the spirit of contributing to the contours of those developments that the National Center for Technology and Dispute Resolution, its Fellows and many others in the field have, for over a decade and a half, been discussing ODR and ethics through scholarship and in a variety of venues such as the annual International ODR Forums, the annual Cyberweek online public discussion fora and webinars, and other international conferences. At the most recent ODR Forum in September 2016 it was agreed: "The time is ripe for the articulation of, and the commitment to, a set of ethical principles specifically designed for developing and conducting ODR. The adoption of principles would further increase trust in ODR and the e-commerce setting and ensure the delivery of high quality ODR processes."

5 Ethical Principles for Online Dispute Resolution

5.1 Preamble

The Ethical Principles for Online Dispute Resolution (ODR) are designed to enhance the quality, effectiveness and scope of dispute resolution processes with technological components. Taken together, they can provide a touchstone for best practices, standards, rules, qualifications and certification efforts in dispute resolution and related fields that address dispute resolution processes and practices. This document builds on previous work by the National Center for Technology and Dispute Resolution on principles and standards of practice, as well as the growing body of literature and the standards of numerous professional, governmental and commercial bodies concerning ODR and dispute resolution more generally. There is no priority to be implied by the sequence of the principles that are list alphabetically. They are meant to be taken as a framework that is interlocking and interdependent.

With the rapidly growing adoption of ODR in a number of sectors, it is timely to produce a living document of ethical principles integral to the design, structure, practices and implementation of online dispute resolution systems. Therefore, while debate will likely continue over time about the definition and scope of ODR and what practices and standards should be formalized, if any, it is hoped that the creation of these Ethical Principles for Online Dispute Resolution can provide a benchmark for these discussions and for systems development, usage and the integration of ODR into existing institutions.

With the knowledge that there is a diversity of perspectives and practices, and that there will be a constant innovation of new technologies impacting the ways we use, foster and transform conflict, it is worthwhile to formulate and continue to revisit ethical principles to inform, guide and inspire best practices. Articulating a set of principles shared across jurisdictions simultaneously requires a recognition that their manifestation will also be necessarily grounded in legal jurisdictional requirements and in sectorally and culturally specific ways.

It is intended that the Ethical Principles for Online Dispute Resolution will find a wide audience, instilling further confidence in the integration of ODR into systems and institutions as the stakeholders in systems of ODR become more expansive and inclusive.

They are designed to guide and foster ethical ODR systems and practice in both the public and private spheres. It is likely that more specific or additional principles may be articulated in the future from within particular sectors and jurisdictions. These, instead, are offered as core, shared values and as a living document that can respond to new conditions, technologies, stakeholders and knowledge—to prove sustainable to those relying on it.

5.2 Accessibility

The design and implementation of efficient and effective processes provide for their usage, not only to the broadest range and number of people, but also by accounting for the reality of cultural differences within and between jurisdictions, as well as differential access to resources and experiences of marginalization that can hinder access to dispute resolution and justice processes, whether formal or informal. ODR systems and processes effectively facilitate and do not limit the right to representation for parties in processes of dispute resolution.

5.3 Accountability

The development and implementation of ODR systems, processes and practices are accountable to the institutions, legal frameworks and communities that they serve.

5.4 Competence

ODR systems, processes and practitioners will be competent in or provide access to relevant technological or human competency required for the effective implementation of the dispute resolution process that they undertake to assist with. This includes but is not limited to relevant dispute resolution, legal, and technical knowledge; languages; and culture.

5.5 Confidentiality

The development and implementation of ODR systems, processes and practitioners maintain confidentiality in accordance with all legal obligations and in a manner that is consistent, in particular, with the principles of Legal Obligation, Informed Participation, Security and Transparency.

5.6 Empowerment

ODR systems and processes are designed and implemented in ways that seek to enable growth and positive change for individuals, relationships, systems and society, thereby increasing access to justice and enhancement of choices and effective decision making opportunities.

5.7 Equality

ODR processes are designed and implemented in ways that treat all participants with respect and human dignity; that system design and processes enable silenced or marginalized voices to be heard and actively seek to ensure that privileges and disadvantages are not replicated in the experience of participation; that no participant is placed at a higher risk than others; and, therefore, that ODR processes are designed to respond effectively to the reality that some contexts may put some at more risk than others.

5.8 Fairness

ODR processes are designed and implemented to facilitate and uphold due process, without bias or benefits for or against individuals or groups, including those based on algorithms. They are responsive to and reflective of the communities and stakeholders they serve.

5.9 Honesty

ODR processes are designed and implemented with the intention that data is gathered, managed, and presented in ways to ensure it is not misrepresented or presented out of context.

5.10 Impartiality

ODR processes are designed and implemented, and practitioners function with commitment to reducing bias in the delivery of the process. This includes accounting for technological and other conditions that could structure patterns of privilege in process and outcome for repeat players with particular attention tithe principles of Accessibility, Fairness and Transparency.

5.11 Informed Participation

In the development and implementation of ODR systems and processes active effort is made to ensure (1) explicit disclosure to participants of all information about risks and benefits of the process, (2) the competency of participants to evaluate the information about participation in the process, (3) understanding by participants of the information, (4) whenever possible, the voluntary acceptance by the participants of the risks of participating; and whenever voluntary consent is not possible due to the mandatory nature of participation than that is made transparent.

5.12 Innovation

Online dispute resolution continues to innovate to improve the delivery of dispute resolution services and benefits more fairly, effectively, and efficiently in ways that increase peace, trust, and access to justice.

5.13 Integration

ODR processes are effectively integrated both internally within a system and externally with other systems, networks, and entities. Technology serves the dispute resolution process as seamlessly as possible. The application of technology and of dispute resolution is designed and implemented in the context of their linkages with other existing systems and networks and of knowledge that new ones will emerge. This is implemented with special attention to the integration with public entities to enhance inclusiveness and access to justice.

5.14 Legal Obligation

The design and implementation of ODR systems and processes uphold the laws of relevant jurisdictions and ensure that relevant laws are known and followed in the context of the principles of Accessibility, Informed Participation, and Transparency.

5.15 Neutrality

ODR systems and practitioners function with independence from the disputing parties, and any conflicts of interest are made transparent.

5.16 Protection from Harm

ODR design and implementation seek to prevent and minimize harm and risk for those involved in dispute resolution processes, with particular attention to those most marginalized and with the least access to justice.

5.17 Security

All reasonable efforts are made to ensure that the data and communication between the parties and other entities linked to ODR processes are secure to the fullest extent of the law, making transparent any known limitations.

5.18 Transparency

All reasonable efforts are taken to make transparent the true purposes, risks and legal obligations inclusive of but not limited to the form and legal jurisdiction of dispute resolution processes; the identities, affiliations, obligations and conflicts of interest of the parties, entities and systems; and the data security, confidentiality and privacy policies and systems involved.

Conclusion

Ethical principles for online dispute resolution, serving as a GPS device, can assist us in seeing where we are as a field and where we want to travel, providing a guide for that journey. There are many ways to cross the terrain, and there are modes of travel yet to be invented. However, with articulation of our shared values, it can assist us in navigating both the expected and the unexpected dilemmas we will face.

As noted earlier, there are a number of challenges that both ADR and ODR have faced for more than a generation, including unequal access to resources, power imbalances, privileging of repeat players, and other access to justice issues. Employing ethical principles may assist in finding strategies for tackling some of these concerns, especially with the help of technology. The principle of Impartiality, for example, could point platform designers toward considerations of how algorithms could be used to prevent gaming the system for repeat players. The ethical principles could serve as a resource for the development of best practices for practitioners regarding vulnerable populations who could be more at risk online. For example, the Protection from Harm principle could stimulate guidelines on the selection of apps to use with disputants who have risks regarding stalking and domestic violence or who are negotiating in the context of other conditions in the shadow of violence. The ethical principles of Competency, Integration, and Legal Obligation could highlight the need for contextualization. As a result, ODR systems designers and providers might develop a set of protocols relevant to their particular sector, client base, and form of dispute resolution that can be used to consider important issues of contextualization before employing a technological feature or commissioning its development; this could include a multilingual tool or a particularized training for parties who are unfamiliar with certain technologies.

A benefit of framing a set of ethical principles as interlocking and interdependent is that they mutually support one another. For example, consider the principles of Accessibility, Equality and Informed Participation: they each address different aspects of fostering increased access to a fair process, and together they reinforce other principles such as Empowerment and Transparency. Another example also demonstrates how the interdependency of the principles can provide for a more ethical practice. Consider an ODR practitioner who reflects on her process through the lens of each of these principles. The Informed Participation principle can prompt her to re-examine each step in the process where disputants are communicating or submitting data. Are the risk levels different at different phases of the process or depending on the types of technological features she may ask parties to employ (i.e., video conferencing, chat features, email, document uploads to a cloud, utilization of an app with location features, etc.)? The Accessibility principle can prompt an examination of whether all parties will know how to use each technological feature she may use during the process. The Equality principle encourages her to consider whether the risks are higher for some disputants based on their backgrounds, experiences, resources, and relationships with those with whom they are disputing (i.e., based on domestic violence, finances or repeat player status). Seeking to address the important issues regarding Informed Participation, Accessibility, and Equality can also lead to responding to concerns that would be raised by Confidentiality. However, the reverse is not necessarily the case. For example, if the ODR intervenor had used only the Confidentiality principle when reflecting on her practice, she may have outlined at the outset of the case the general perimeters of confidentiality and required a disputant to agree with one click at that time; however, this may not be sufficient to meet the ethical issues that actually exist in a case as raised by the questions outlined above. The disputant might only have anticipated the use of email and document exchange when agreeing to the process but, later, when video conferencing is proposed he could have concerns that the other party could tape the encounter for use elsewhere. The principle of Informed Participation could help the conflict intervenor to consider this possibility more clearly in advance and provide the necessary information about the technological tools to be used as part of informed consent for participation in the dispute resolution process. These examples illustrate some of the benefits of viewing the principles as interdependent while engaging each of them to foster ethical best practices for ODR.

The efforts to construct ethical principles applicable specifically to ODR is a continuous work in progress, one necessary to sustain a healthy ecosystem of dispute resolution processes across a spectrum of fields and professions. Further scholarship, reflective practice, and ongoing engagement with an ever-increasing number of stakeholders as well as the explicit use of them are required to enhance their relevance and applicability. As Ethical Principles for Online Dispute Resolution are put to use, as the field continues to grow, and as technology changes, our ongoing engagement is vital to enhance and strengthen them to ensure that they provide an effective GPS for moving forward on our journey.

Notes & Questions

1. Are there any other principles you would want to add?
2. Can you imagine these ethical principles being adapted for cross-national (international) use? What body or bodies or treaties would be necessary to draft such a statement, and how might it be "enforced"? Contrast and consider the various efforts to provide ethical standards in international arbitration presented in Chapter 4.

Below is the European Regulation on Online Consumer Dispute Resolution. As you read it, refer back to the principles described by Wing and also consider how this regulation attempts to meet some of the concerns outlined by Creutzfeldt.

European Regulation on Online Consumer Dispute Resolution

Regulation (EU) No. 524/2013 of the European Parliament and of the Council of 21 May 2013 on online dispute resolution for consumer disputes and amending Regulation (EC) No. 2006/2004 and Directive 2009/22/EC (Regulation on consumer ODR)

CHAPTER II

ODR PLATFORM

Article 5
Establishment of the ODR platform

1. The Commission shall develop the ODR platform (and be responsible for its operation, including all the translation functions necessary for the purpose of this Regulation, its maintenance, funding and data security. The ODR platform shall be

user-friendly. The development, operation and maintenance of the ODR platform shall ensure that the privacy of its users is respected from the design stage ('privacy by design') and that the ODR platform is accessible and usable by all, including vulnerable users ('design for all'), as far as possible.

2. The ODR platform shall be a single point of entry for consumers and traders seeking the out-of-court resolution of disputes covered by this Regulation. It shall be an interactive website which can be accessed electronically and free of charge in all the official languages of the institutions of the Union.

3. The Commission shall make the ODR platform accessible, as appropriate, through its websites which provide information to citizens and businesses in the Union and, in particular, through the 'Your Europe portal' established in accordance with Decision 2004/387/EC.

4. The ODR platform shall have the following functions:

(a) to provide an electronic complaint form which can be filled in by the complainant party in accordance with Article 8;

(b) to inform the respondent party about the complaint;

(c) to identify the competent ADR entity or entities and transmit the complaint to the ADR entity, which the parties have agreed to use, in accordance with Article 9;

(d) to offer an electronic case management tool free of charge, which enables the parties and the ADR entity to conduct the dispute resolution procedure online through the ODR platform;

(e) to provide the parties and ADR entity with the translation of information which is necessary for the resolution of the dispute and is exchanged through the ODR platform;

(f) to provide an electronic form by means of which ADR entities shall transmit the information referred to in point (c) of Article 10;

(g) to provide a feedback system which allows the parties to express their views on the functioning of the ODR platform and on the ADR entity which has handled their dispute;

(h) to make publicly available the following:

(i) general information on ADR as a means of out-of-court dispute resolution;

(ii) information on ADR entities listed in accordance with Article 20(2) of Directive 2013/11/EU which are competent to deal with disputes covered by this Regulation;

(iii) an online guide about how to submit complaints through the ODR platform;

(iv) information, including contact details, on ODR contact points designated by the Member States in accordance with Article 7(1) of this Regulation;

(v) statistical data on the outcome of the disputes which were transmitted to ADR entities through the ODR platform.

5. The Commission shall ensure that the information referred to in point (h) of paragraph 4 is accurate, up to date and provided in a clear, understandable and easily accessible way.

6. ADR entities listed in accordance with Article 20(2) of Directive 2013/11/EU which are competent to deal with disputes covered by this Regulation shall be registered electronically with the ODR platform.

7. The Commission shall adopt measures concerning the modalities for the exercise of the functions provided for in paragraph 4 of this Article through implementing acts. Those implementing acts shall be adopted in accordance with the examination procedure referred to in Article 16(3) of this Regulation.

Article 10

Resolution of the dispute

An ADR entity which has agreed to deal with a dispute in accordance with Article 9 of this Regulation shall:

(a) conclude the ADR procedure within the deadline referred to in point (e) of Article 8 of Directive 2013/11/EU;

(b) not require the physical presence of the parties or their representatives, unless its procedural rules provide for that possibility and the parties agree;

(c) without delay transmit the following information to the ODR platform:

(i) the date of receipt of the complaint file;

(ii) the subject-matter of the dispute;

(iii) the date of conclusion of the ADR procedure;

(iv) the result of the ADR procedure;

(d) not be required to conduct the ADR procedure through the ODR platform.

Article 12

Processing of personal data

1. Access to information, including personal data, related to a dispute and stored in the database referred to in Article 11 shall be granted, for the purposes referred to in Article 10, only to the ADR entity to which the dispute was transmitted in accordance with Article 9. Access to the same information shall be granted also to ODR contact points, in so far as it is necessary, for the purposes referred to in Article 7(2) and (4).

2. The Commission shall have access to information processed in accordance with Article 10 for the purposes of monitoring the use and functioning of the ODR platform and drawing up the reports referred to in Article 21. It shall process personal data of the users of the ODR platform in so far as it is necessary for the operation and maintenance of the ODR platform, including for the purposes of monitoring the use of the ODR platform by ADR entities and ODR contact points....

Article 14
Consumer information

1. Traders established within the Union engaging in online sales or service contracts, and online marketplaces established within the Union, shall provide on their websites an electronic link to the ODR platform. That link shall be easily accessible for consumers. Traders established within the Union engaging in online sales or service contracts shall also state their e-mail addresses....

Notes & Questions

1. How do you think the EU did in incorporating the principles outlined by Wing?
2. Refer to Schmitz's article on the evolution of online consumer dispute resolution. Compare and contrast the EU's regulation to the examples described by Schmitz. Does the EU meet the challenges outlined? Would you suggest that the United States adopt a similar regulation?

Further Reading

Sarah R. Cole & Amanda Spangler, *Virtual Mediation: The Only Door Needed in the Multi-Door Courthouse?*, 52 STETSON L. REV. 477–506 (2023).

PABLO CORTÉS, THE LAW OF CONSUMER REDRESS IN AN EVOLVING DIGITAL MARKET: UPGRADING FROM ALTERNATIVE TO ONLINE DISPUTE RESOLUTION (2018).

Catrina Denvir & Amanda Selvarajah, *Safeguarding Access to Justice in the Age of the Online Court*, 85 MODERN L. REV. 25–68 (2022).

Noam Ebner & Elayne Greenberg, *Strengthening Online Dispute Resolution Justice*, 63 WASH U. J.L. & POL'Y 65–118 (2020).

Noam Ebner & John Zeleznikow, *No Sheriff in Town: Governance for the ODR Field*, 32 NEGOT. J. 297–323 (2016).

Florian Grisel, *Canceling Disputes: How Social Capital Affects the Arbitration of Disputes on Wikipedia,* Law & Soc. Inquiry (June 2023); https//doi 10.1017/lsi.2023.15.

I, DANIEL BLAKE (Sixteen Films 2016, Ken Loach dir.; Paul Laverty, writer).

ETHAN KATSH & ORNA RABINOVICH-EINY, DIGITAL JUSTICE: TECHNOLOGY AND THE INTERNET OF DISPUTES (2017).

David Larson, *Designing a State Court Small Claims ODR System: Hitting a Moving Target in New York During a Pandemic*, 569–80 (2021).

Janet Martinez & Mayu Watanabe, *ODR System Design: An Analytical Framework with Examples*, 10 INT'L J. ONLINE DISP. RESOL. 55–59 (2023).

Nick O'Brian, *Administrative Justice in the Wake of* I, Daniel Blake, 89 POL. Q. 82–91 (2018).

ONLINE DISPUTE RESOLUTION—THEORY AND PRACTICE: A TREATISE ON TECHNOLOGY AND DISPUTE RESOLUTION (Daniel Rainey, Ethan Katsh, & Mohamed S. Abdel Wahab eds., 2d ed. 2021)

Orna Rabinovich-Einy, *Process Pluralism in the Post-COVID Dispute Resolution Landscape*, 10 TEX. A&M L. REV. 55–73 (2022).

Orna Rabinovich-Einy & Ethan Katsh, *Artificial Intelligence and the Future of Dispute Resolution*, *in* ONLINE DISPUTE RESOLUTION-THEORY AND PRACTICE (Mohamed Abdel Wahab, Daniel Rainey, & Ethan Katsh eds., 2021).

Daniel Rainey, *Third Party Ethics in the Age of the Fourth Party*, 1 INT'L J. ONLINE DISP. RESOL. 37–56 (2014).

Jean R. Sternlight, *Pouring a Little Psychological Cold Water on Online Dispute Resolution*, 2020 J. DISP. RESOL., Winter 2020, at 1.

RICHARD SUSSKIND, ONLINE COURTS AND THE FUTURE OF JUSTICE (2019).

WILLIAM L. URY, JEANNE M. BRETT, & STEPHEN B. GOLDBERG, GETTING DISPUTES RESOLVED: DESIGNING SYSTEMS TO CUT THE COSTS OF CONFLICT (1988).

Janet Martinez, Leah Wing, Ethan Katsh, & Colin Rule, *Designing Ethical Online Dispute Resolution Systems: The Rise of the Fourth Party*, 37 NEGOT. J. 49–64 (2021).

Chapter 11

Wicked Problems

This chapter covers some of the most intractable and difficult conflicts in the world. No book on dispute resolution processes would be complete without highlighting some of the instances where knowledge, expertise, and even good intentions have failed to bring about resolution. These intractable issues help to demonstrate the limits of the processes outlined in this text, and they are also a good reminder that humility is required in analyzing and thinking about the tough international conflicts around the world. Pundits and commentators who claim they have the answers are likely missing something; otherwise, these disputes would already be resolved. And so these "wicked problems" help to illustrate that rules and processes are only part of the complex system of humankind and that some elements will remain murky.

We start with an exploration of what makes a problem wicked, according to policy and planning analysts, and what tools we have for responding to these kinds of problems. We then analyze three different examples of wicked problems—art repatriation, conflict in the Middle East, and hybrid warfare—in an attempt to figure out what makes each so difficult to solve and what tools may be applied to help us understand these disputes at a different level. Is it too optimistic to think that there is hope for the future? If Germany and France can be close allies and together form the backbone of the European Union after fighting against each other in three hugely destructive wars in the span of 70 years, is it also possible that other countries could experience seismic (positive) shifts in relations? Can you think of other seemingly intractable conflicts that have been "solved"?

I. What Makes a Wicked Problem

This first reading outlines what makes a problem wicked in terms of public policy planning. The readings after that then turn to systems-design and conflict-management theory from international relations, public policy, and politics to highlight the tools that might be utilized in trying to solve these dilemmas.

Horst W. J. Ritell & Melvin B. Webber, *Dilemmas in a General Theory of Planning*

4 Pol'y Sci., June 1973 159–161

By now we are all beginning to realize that one of the most intractable problems is that of defining problems (of knowing what distinguishes an observed condition from a desired condition) and of locating problems (finding where in the complex causal networks the trouble really lies). In turn, and equally intractable, is the problem of identifying the actions that might effectively narrow the gap between what-is and what-ought-to-be. As we seek to improve the effectiveness of actions in pursuit of valued outcomes, as system boundaries get stretched, and as we become more sophisticated about the complex workings of open societal systems, it becomes ever more difficult to make the planning idea operational.

Many now have an image of *how* an *idealized* planning system would function. It is being seen as an on-going, cybernetic process of governance, incorporating systematic procedures for continuously searching out goals, identifying problems, forecasting uncontrollable contextual changes, inventing alternative strategies, tactics, and time-sequenced actions, stimulating alternative and plausible action sets and their consequences, evaluating alternatively forecasted outcomes, statistically monitoring those conditions of the publics and systems that are judged to be germane, feeding back information to the simulation and decision channels so that errors can be corrected—all in a simultaneously functioning governing process. That set of steps is familiar to all of us, for it comprises what is by now the modern-classical model of planning. And yet we all know that such a planning system is unattainable, even as we seek more closely to approximate it. It is even questionable whether such a planning system is desirable.

Planning Problems Are Wicked Problems

The kinds of problems that planners deal with—societal problems—are inherently different from the problems that scientists and perhaps some classes of engineers deal with. Planning problems are inherently wicked.

As distinguished from problems in the natural sciences, which are definable and separable and may have solutions that are findable, the problems of governmental planning—and especially those of social or policy planning—are ill-defined, and they rely upon elusive political judgment for resolution. (Not "solution." Social Problems are never solved. At best they are only re-solved—over and over again).

The problems that scientists and engineers have usually focused upon are mostly "tame" or "benign" ones. As an example, consider a problem for mathematics, such as solving an equation, or the task of an organic chemist in analyzing the structure of some unknown compound, or that of the chess player attempting to accomplish checkmate in five moves. For each the mission is clear. It is clear, in turn, whether or not the problems have been solved.

Wicked problems, in contrast, have neither of these clarifying traits, and they include nearly all public policy issues—whether the question concerns the location of a freeway, the adjustment of a tax rate, the modification of school curricula, or the confrontation of crime.

There are at least ten distinguishing properties of planning-type problems, i.e. wicked ones, that planners had better be alert to and which we shall comment upon in turn. As you will see, we are calling them "wicked" not because these properties are themselves ethically deplorable. We use the term "wicked" in a meaning akin to that of "malignant" (in contrast to "benign") or "vicious" (like a circle) or "tricky" (like a leprechaun) or "aggressive" (like a lion, in contrast to the docility of a lamb). We do not mean to personify these properties of social systems by implying malicious intent. But then, you may agree that it becomes morally objectionable for the planner to treat a wicked problem as though it were a tame one, or to tame a wicked problem prematurely, or to refuse to recognize the inherent wickedness of social problems.

Consider which conflicts covered thus far fall into any of these categories: malignant, vicious, tricky, or aggressive. Is the Russian invasion of Ukraine malignant or aggressive? Would we consider climate change "vicious" since it seems to cycle? The next excerpt builds on the public policy definition of wicked to explain how negotiation or dispute resolution fits into this analysis.

Calvin Chrustie, James Richard Coben, & Christopher Honeyman, *Negotiating Wicked Problems: Five Stories*

in VENTURING BEYOND THE CLASSROOM: VOLUME 2 IN THE RETHINKING NEGOTIATION TEACHING SERIES 449, 451–54 (Christopher Honeyman, James Coben, & Giuseppe De Palo eds., 2010)

The concept of tame versus wicked problems is imported from public planning; we find the distinction also useful for thinking about why negotiation works well in some situations but not in others. However, the terms cause difficulty, because while "wicked" problems have a flavor all their own, the term "tame" seems insulting as well as inaccurate for problems that can include the negotiation of multi-million-dollar deals or the settlement of complex litigation. It is important to acknowledge that "tame" is not a synonym for easy, and "wicked" is not a synonym for complex.

A more useful way to think about negotiating tame versus negotiating wicked problems is to consider the types of changes negotiators need to make when dealing with a problem. Tame problems can be very complex, but they are still amenable to "technical" solutions. To the extent that "Negotiation 1.0" focuses on linear movement through identifiable steps and stages (which of course has never been *entirely* the case), it can be analyzed largely in terms of "technical" change—with the negotiator or intervener applying an external set of tools to solve a problem. Wicked problems, on the other hand, require "adaptive" responses that require negotiators or interveners to modify their own views and behaviors, rather than merely applying tools to a problem outside themselves. To the extent that "Negotiation 1.0" was originally "developed in large part by relatively affluent Western white males culturally situated in a free-enterprise context" with a focus on managing transactions rather than managing ongoing relationships), it does not lend itself to dealing with problems that require the negotiators to change themselves and their relationships in order to address problems. It is also important to acknowledge that "tame" is not another word for "nonviolent" and "wicked" is not another word for "violent." Three of the authors work in situations dominated by violence or the potential for violence. The other authors do not deal regularly with violence. Yet we all deal with problems that appear to be wicked; each of the cases exhibits some combination of the following features:

- The problem is ill-defined and resists clear definition as a technical issue, because wicked problems are also social, political, and moral in nature. Each proposed definition of the problem implies a particular kind of solution which is loaded with contested values. Consequently, merely defining the problem can incite passionate conflict.
- Solutions to a wicked problem cannot be labeled good or bad; they can only be considered better or worse, good enough or not good enough. Whether a solution is good enough depends on the values and judgment of each of the parties, who will inevitably assess the problem and its potential solutions from their respective positions within the social context of the problem.
- Every wicked problem is unique and novel, because even if the technical elements appear similar from one situation to another, the social, political, and moral features are context-specific.
- A wicked problem contains an interconnected web of sub-problems; every proposed solution to part or the whole of the wicked problem will affect other problems in the web.
- The only way to address a wicked problem is to try solutions; every solution we try is expensive and has lasting unintended consequences. So, although we have only one shot to solve *this* wicked problem, we will have plenty of opportunities to develop our skills as we deal with the wicked problems that we create with our attempted solutions.

A tame problem, by contrast, can be—more or less—separated from the surrounding context and dealt with as a discrete issue. (Again, we must emphasize, this does *not* mean that "tame" should be confused with "easy"; problems meeting this definition can include the settlement of complex litigation or the negotiation of multi-million-dollar deals.) ... A tame problem:

- Has a relatively well-defined and stable problem statement.
- Has a definite stopping point, i.e., we know when a solution is reached.
- Has a solution which can be objectively evaluated as being right or wrong.
- Belongs to a class of similar problems which can be solved in a similar manner.
- Has solutions that can be tried and abandoned.

Wicked problems cannot be separated from the surrounding context; any engagement with a wicked problem has its own implications for the larger social, political, and cultural order. But contexts are not all alike. Some are more or less stable while others are highly unstable. Consequently, we see wicked problems at work in several differing contexts in our stories.

Some wicked problems arise in situations where the context surrounding the specific problem for which one might consider using negotiation is unstable and, in some cases, prone to violence. Other wicked problems arise in situations where the context is more stable—perhaps even too stable. In other cases, the context is a complicated mix of unstable and overly stable (or "stuck") features. Contextually driven factors that should be investigated when dealing with a wicked problem include:

- It is difficult for the parties to sustain a stable definition of the problem.
- It is also hard to demarcate the boundaries of the negotiable problem in ways that prevent other issues from encroaching on the negotiation process.
- The negotiating parties find it difficult to reach agreement about the relative goodness or badness of the proposed solutions.
- Individually, the participants have difficulty articulating their best and worst alternatives to a negotiated agreement because it is difficult to calculate risk and opportunity against an uncertain future.
- Deep-seated problems exist, but they are not being addressed.
- Individuals who "see" the problem are dismissed as doom-sayers, comparable to the hysterical protagonist in the Chicken Little fable who keeps proclaiming "the sky is falling!"
- The system or parts of the system may have to be destabilized—by leaders, mass movements, violence, or catastrophic events—before the wicked problem will be adequately recognized.
- The beneficiaries of the unsustainable or violent systems resist change or threaten to resist change that alters their privileges.

Common to all wicked problems is the need for negotiators to proceed with careful attention to both the processes and the ethical implications of social negotiations which they choose to engage, as well as an appreciative mindfulness of those social negotiations which are already in play....

Peter T. Coleman & Robert Ricigliano, *Getting in Sync: What to Do When Problem-Solving Fails to Fix the Problem*

in THE NEGOTIATOR'S DESK REFERENCE Ch. 83
(Chris Honeyman & Andrea Kupfer Schneider eds., 2017)

Operation Impact: Using a Screwdriver to Fix a Cloudy Day

Top-down, unilateral, strong-arm responses to dangerous problems feel right and can make good sense.... Heightened surveillance and security measures are therefore a necessary but insufficient response. Too often, we are attracted to such short-term, seemingly efficient, hardline solutions to complex local problems. The likelihood is that the solutions will show some immediate effect and signal to our constituents that we are in control of a difficult situation. However, such effects are usually not sustainable, and can contribute to making the problems worse.

Why do we respond like this? Because as a culture we are conditioned to believe that if it's "broke, fix it." If schools are suffering from high levels of violence, then make them more secure. However, this sensible, direct, and occasionally effective approach makes a critical, though unstated assumption about how the world works. It assumes that problems, even complex and intractable ones like urban school violence, are mechanical in nature—that a set of knowable causes create, in a predictable way, a certain set of impacts. For example, take the belief that safe schools are the result of proper discipline, accountability for administrators, and adequate security personnel. Conversely, if one or more of these causes is missing, then you will have higher levels of school violence. And, if so, then the "fix" for an unsafe school is to add in discipline, accountability, and/or security personnel as needed.

This way of looking at the problem of school violence—as what is known as a "Clock Problem"—is sensible and valid, but is not the only way of thinking about the problems we face and how to address them. Karl Popper, probably the most influential philosopher of science of the last century, offered a key distinction between what we termed clock problems and cloud problems. *Clock problems* are those, like clocks, that are of a more mechanical, knowable, controllable, and predictable nature. Such problems can be readily disassembled and analyzed—broken down to their components parts and systematically studied to reveal the source of the problem. The "mechanism" can then be repaired and reassembled to resume its original functionality. Typically, problems with automobiles, jet engines, computers and even traffic planning can be solved by approaching them as clock problems. Similarly, many problems negotiators and mediators face are relatively clock-like, such as contractual obligations and disputes, legal and procedural matters, and many aspects of interpersonal or community disputes that are responsive to standard forms of problem analysis and problem solving (Popper 1972).

In contrast to these analysis-friendly problems are what Popper termed *cloud problems*. These are problems like chronic patterns of urban violence, which are of a much more complex, murky, uncontrollable, and unpredictable nature.... These are problems of a highly irregular and disorderly nature, which typically prove unresponsive to standard, proven solutions or attempts at problem solving. These are not simply more complicated problems, but are considered *complex* because many aspects of these problems interact over time in unpredictable ways, and therefore evidence erratic behavior and outcomes. As a result, our good faith attempts to address them can have no identifiable effects, can result in problems going away in the short-term but reemerging in the longer-term, or can even serve to make matters worse.

In short, if school violence is really a cloud problem and not a clock problem, then thinking we can "fix it" directly by administering one or more mechanical solutions is like thinking we can "use a screwdriver to fix a cloudy day." The "fix" is totally inappropriate for making the change we want to see in the world. But the insight that "clock tools" are ineffective, or even counterproductive, when dealing with cloud problems, albeit true, is not enough. We are much more familiar and comfortable with "clock tools" like linear planning models and reductionist thinking that give us a feeling of being in control of seemingly uncontrollable problems. On the other hand, we lack the same level of familiarity and comfort with "cloud tools." And, without a sturdy set of cloud tools, we are doomed to the "fix or flee" dilemma described at the beginning of this chapter.

In response, we are offering a framework for how to think about and take action in the face of cloud problems like urban school violence. While no set of cloud tools will be as precise as our more familiar clock tools, we hope that this framework will give negotiators new ways of thinking and working that will help us understand and get in sync with the complex realities we face.

Working in Sync: The Approach

Based on years of work with practitioners trying to make change in complex and dynamic environments around the world, we developed the "Sync" framework—named as such because we are proposing that rather than trying to impose solutions, negotiators should learn to work in sync with the people and forces that make up a complex system....

Mastery is the belief that we have the capacity and responsibility to attempt to control nature, society and the world around us. In contrast, *Submission* is based on the belief that the natural (and the supernatural) world is so immensely complex and mysterious that it is ultimately unknowable and unfixable. Somewhere between pure Mastery and pure Submission is *Harmony* or the belief that humans can exercise partial but not total control of nature by living in balance with our surrounding social and environmental forces.

When applied effectively to the right types of clock problems, the Mastery approach can be powerful, effective, responsible, and efficient. In these cases, the role of the problem-solver is that of the expert—like a physician or mechanic—and our job is to apply our expertise to help remedy the problem. However, when Mastery is applied to more complex cloud-like problems, it can lead to a great deal of frustration....

Similarly, the Submission approach has the virtue of us not making the situation worse when dealing with complex problems. However, the imperative to *do no harm* can often lead us to prematurely decide that we are powerless. Worse yet, it can breed a strong sense of helplessness, inferiority and bitterness in people and communities, leading to a type of malaise or depression. And as the Holocaust survivor Elie Wiesel famously noted, sometimes inaction is, in fact, collusion with tyranny.

Fortunately, there is a better way. The Harmony response to cloud problems, like urban school violence, is what we call working in Sync—rather than working against or fleeing from complex problems, the Sync framework is intended to help us work with a system to leverage how it is evolving in order to facilitate desired outcomes (e.g.

more justice, less violence, better quality of life, etc.). Accordingly, it reorients the basics of conflict resolution significantly (e.g. how we set goals, focus our work, and take effective action). The Sync approach is composed of five principles that offer a more effective alternative to Mastery and Submission when dealing with cloud problems:

Table 1: The What, Where and How of Conflict Resolution

The Question	Mastery	Sync	Submission
What is our goal?	Fix the problem	Improve the system dynamics	Do no harm
Where do we focus?	Zoom in on the problem	Understand the evolving problem in context	Zoom out to see the full chaos
How do we engage?	Impose control Implement solutions Lead change, be the hero	Work with the energy in the system Employ adaptive action Enable change, be a guide	Relinquish control Minimize risk Avert disaster, be cautious

Working in Sync: What Is Our Goal?

Guideline 1: Develop goals for how you want the dynamics of the system (family, organization, community, etc.) to eventually be qualitatively different—and produce different outcomes—even if you cannot articulate the specific end states you hope to achieve.

In contrast to the more focused objectives of the Mastery approach (fix the problem, resolve the dispute), or the objectives of Submission (do no harm, avoid making matters worse), the Harmony approach aims more generally to improve the functioning and well-being of the broader system (relationship, family, organization, community, environment, etc.) over the long term. This shift in goal is not small or inconsequential: It moves us from problem-centered outcome goals to systemic-process goals.

This guideline most likely contradicts everything you were taught about goal setting (i.e. identify moderately difficult, achievable, measurable goals). These remain true with clocks, but the game changes with clouds. Cloud problems are the products of an ever-changing and interconnected collection of diverse forces. For example, urban school violence is a product of economics, geography, environmental health, community and family health, cultural norms, public policy, government effectiveness, etc. As such, it is less important to make a short-term dent in the amount of school violence, than to influence the underlying forces that produce the levels of violence that currently exist in our schools. This formulation of the goal will direct us to engage the systemic causes rather than just the symptoms. And because cloud problems inherently take time to affect, a "systemic goal" is better able to support constant adaptation and experimentation than an outcome goal (e.g. a 10% reduction in violence), which we either hit or miss....

Working in Sync: Where Do We Focus?

Guideline 2: Understand the evolving problem in context. Resist the tendency to prematurely oversimplify threatening problems by becoming familiar with the complex forces operating in the context and how they interact over time to create the problem of concern. This "leaning into complexity" will help clarify opportunities for high-leverage impact, gateways, and patterns otherwise disguised by the urgency and complexity of the problem.

Orienting our work toward broad, temporally distant goals will necessitate a shift in perspective on where we focus our work as well. A Mastery approach encourages zooming in to analyze, isolate, and focus in on the target problem and what we can best change, while a Submission approach emphasizes zooming out to note the overwhelming complexity and unpredictability of the constellation of forces operating in the system. Sync recommends employing both lenses in an iterative sequence. It means developing a holistic understanding of the complex and dynamic relationship between the issue we care about (e.g. urban school violence) and the surrounding environment—both physical and social. It requires that we become skilled at *seeing the problem in the context of time and space:* learning to first step back and consider the many complex factors that are operating at different levels (people, groups, and institutions) and at different time scales (immediate effects, delayed effects, and trends over time) in the context which drive and constrain the problem—and only then focus in on those aspects of the constellation of forces that are important, high-impact and actionable.

Most of us were educated through the paradigm of the scientific method, which privileges analysis (the process of separating something into its constituent elements) and short-term, linear cause-and-effect relationships between variables. This has taught us a great deal, but it tends to blind us from seeing the whole: noticing how constellations of variables interact in complex ways and form patterns that evolve and stabilize over time. It is like we are trying to make sense of a really long and complicated movie with nothing but still photography as our lens.

Negotiators will benefit from developing new tools that allow them to see how complex dynamics unfold over time to establish, maintain, and transform patterns. Imagine if we could put on a visor and it would reveal how dynamic patterns flow over time in a social system—like time-elapsed photography. This would help us begin to understand the differences between 1) problems, 2) the multiple causes of problems, 3) the relations between these causes, and 4) understanding how these many relationships affect the *dynamics* of a system which results in *patterns* that emerge in the system (chronic violence, chronic poverty, thriving communities, etc.)....

Working in Sync: How Do We Engage the System?

Guideline 3: Locate and work with the energy for change that resides within the system.

In contrast to a Mastery approach of imposing unilateral control over problematic situations and a Submission approach of relinquishing control, the Sync approach starts with the assumption that it is the system that is in control. People can't "fix" or control complex systems. The best we can do is to find those areas in the system where there are people, ideas, or other forces that are creating change in the system and then work with them to affect the direction of that change so the system produces more of the outcomes we want (e.g. less violence, more peace, more justice, better economic development, etc.)....

Guideline 4: Employ adaptive action: Constantly improve your ability to work effectively for change in your system by pursuing a range of strategies and tactics that will promote effective learning about how the system works and adapting to more effectively engage it.

The dominant (Mastery) approach to seeking social change in the world of peacebuilding and development is to determine a logical framework which sets out a series of steps that will lead to a desired objective. This plan is usually based on "proven" solutions and success is determined by how well an organization is able to execute the plan. This might work quite well in the "clock world" but less so when dealing with cloud problems. Because cloud problems are difficult or impossible to fully understand, and are constantly changing, the best you can do is try multiple strategies and tactics as long as you are able to minimize the potential costs of failure and maximize your ability to learn effectively and adapt accordingly (also known as "smart fail"—Ricigliano 2012). In the cloud world, you have to learn your way into having impact....

Guideline 5: Enable change: Use your role (your skills, relationships, and knowledge) to create the conditions for the system to change itself, rather than implementing or leading the change directly.

Finally, what about us? What role do we, the negotiator, mediator, facilitator or change agent, play in this new, harmonious approach to conflict management? In contrast to the hero role most associated with the fix-it Mastery approach, and the cautionary role most associated with do-no-harm Submission, Sync requires us to create and adopt a new role.

We like to think of the Sync role as a guide or enabler—someone who helps take people on a long journey; who knows the territory well and is good with mapping and navigation; who understands the local terrain, the flora and fauna and the dangers that lurk; who delights in their surroundings—appreciating the interconnectedness and splendor of the natural world and who's joy is contagious; and who is adaptive to sudden changes in the weather or local conditions, but who also knows how to use the stars to navigate successfully. Working in Sync with systems requires that we play the role of enabling the people within the system to make change for themselves and their environment. Our standard conception of leadership defines a good leader as someone who leads others—who knows the better way and helps others get there. The Sync role of an enabler of change is new and foreign to many of us trained as Masters of clocks. It will require a new set of competencies and skills unfamiliar to most of us.

Notes & Questions

1. Of the processes we have covered, how might each solve clock problems and cloud problems?
2. What model might we need to shift our tools?
3. How can dispute system design help with this?

II. The Problem of "Stolen" (Looted) Art

Here we examine several examples of wicked problems. As you read, consider what makes them wicked, intractable, or "cloudy." The first case study is the "Elgin" or "Parthenon" marbles. The facts and the parties are relatively clear, like a clock problem, yet because a solution continues to evade the disputing parties, it may in fact be a cloudy problem.

An historical record spanning centuries is often one of the most difficult issues parties face in international dispute resolution. Nations did not always have the borders they do today; ancient and indigenous peoples were conquered and colonized; victors of war plundered villages, cities, and countries. Objects of art that are considered part of a culture's patrimony have been removed from their original locations or taken from their original owners, only to be owned, possessed, or exhibited by foreign nations or by private bona fide purchasers for value.

We outline here perhaps the most famous of the ongoing controversies—the British Museum's holding of the Parthenon Marbles, also known as the Elgin Marbles. The Parthenon Marbles are a collection of friezes, free-standing sculptures, and pediments "taken" from Greece in the early 19th century by Lord Elgin, the British ambassador to the Ottoman Empire (at the time, Greece belonged to the Ottoman Empire). This ongoing dispute presents legal, moral, and cultural claims that currently have no clear avenue/process for resolution.

But the Parthenon Marbles are only one example of art objects' being taken from one land to another by any of various means (e.g., war and conquest, theft, sale, bribery, manipulation, fraud, economic power). Each incident raises different kinds of issues, which makes developing any single process of restoration, reparation, or "sharing" difficult. In addition to the International Council of Museums (ICOM) Code of Ethics (an international agreement among museums, not nations), there are currently several treaties and conventions dealing with art disputes: UNESCO Convention on the Means of Prohibiting and Preventing the Illicit Import, Export, and Transfer of Ownership of Cultural Property (1970); UNESCO Convention concerning the Protection of the World Cultural and Natural Heritage (1972); UNIDROIT Convention on Stolen or Illegally Exported Cultural Objects (1995, applying to Europe); and Hague Convention for the Protection of Cultural Property in the Event of Armed Conflict (1954). However, most of these conventions do not apply to many of the world's most significant art disputes, sometimes because of statutes of limitations (because events often took place long before these laws and conventions came into effect), but mostly because there is little in the way of enforcement mechanisms for many of the provisions of these documents.

Over the years, there have been many claims of art being "stolen" or "looted" after wars (e.g., Napoleon and the Louvre collection; Italian takings of Egyptian artifacts; the Benin Bronzes (taken from current-day Nigeria and which can be found in museums in France, Germany, the United States, and the United Kingdom)) and through acquisitions, legitimate and contested (e.g., the contested provenance of Italian art objects (which have since been returned) acquired by Marian True, former curator of the Getty Museum), and a lengthy conflict over Yale's holdings of Peruvian objects taken by a Yale archeologist (which have since been voluntarily returned)).[1] In fact, an entire area of law focused entirely on recovering "Holocaust art," that is, Jewish art seized by or forcefully sold to the Nazi regime, has even developed in the years following a complex and ultimately successful lawsuit brought against the Austrian government by the heirs of the original owner of Gustav Klimt's "The Lady in Gold," who sought its return from Vienna's leading art museum.[2] Other lawsuits seeking to retrieve "stolen" art have been proceeding apace in American and some European courts.

We set out the Parthenon Marbles case below as an exemplar of the difficulties of combining complex legal issues, knowable and unknowable contested facts, history, moral and ethical claims, and a complex set of parties. Greece, as a country, is the party seeking return of the Marbles to the Parthenon from where they were taken. The British Museum (not the United Kingdom) is the current possessor, whose ownership is authorized by statute and is claimed to be legitimated by a long investigatory and approval process carried out by the British Parliament in 1815 and by a Select Committee, which concluded that Lord Elgin had "lawfully" purchased and paid for the Marbles (as granted by a *firman*, a legal document signed by some Ottoman officials, if not the Sultan), which he then sold for value and approval to the British Museum. The Marbles have been on display in a main room in the British Museum since the early 19th century, and despite many claims—formal, legal, diplomatic, political, cultural, moral, ethical, and historical—by Greece, the museum claims it is barred by law from moving

---

1. *See* Hugh Eakin, *Marion True on Her Trial and Ordeal*, The New Yorker (Oct. 14, 2010), https://www.newyorker.com/news/news-desk/marion-true-on-her-trial-and-ordeal; Stephanie Swanson, *Repatriating Cultural Property: The Dispute between Yale and Peru over the Treasures of Machu Picchu*, 10 San Diego Int'l L.J. 469–91 (2009); Julia Zorthian, *Yale Returns Final Machu Picchu Artifacts*, Yale Daily News (Nov. 12, 2012), https://yaledailynews.com/blog/2012/11/12/yale-returns-final-machu-picchu-artifacts/.

2. *See* Lynn H. Nicholas, The Rape of Europa: The Fate of Europe's Treasures in the Third Reich and the Second World War (1994); Anne-Marie O'Connor, The Lady in Gold: The Extraordinary Tale of Gustav Klimt's Portrait of Adele Bloch-Bauer (2012); *Altmann v. Austria*, 541 U.S. 677 (2004) (holding that Sovereign Immunities Act applied retroactively so that Maria Altmann could use an exception to the Act to proceed with a civil lawsuit against the country of Austria to obtain return of her family's painting, which was eventually returned through an arbitral proceeding and is now on display in a New York museum). (The lawyer for Maria Altmann was Randy Schoenberg, a graduate of USC law school and now a specialist in the legal complexities of international and domestic art return law, *see Lady in Gold* (BBC Films, Origin Pictures 2015), directed by Simon Curtis.

or transferring the artworks. (How might this "claim" be remedied?) The legal claims turn on the validity of the *firman*; whether Lord Elgin was self-dealing as an ambassador; whether the *firman*, even if valid, permitted their removal; and whether shipping from the port of Piraeus was properly authorized. Moral, political, and ethical claims turn on arguments that cultural heritage belongs where it was created and recovered from and that the Greeks were subject to occupation of the Ottoman Turks and should be given their own patrimony back, given its historical and political importance and value. The arguments and claims continue as of the time of this writing—in November 2023, for instance, the Greek Prime Minister refused to meet with the British Prime Minister after UK Prime Minister Rishi Sunak again stated that the Marbles would not be returned to Greece.

In the last few years, there have been major efforts at mediation, direct diplomatic negotiation, and sponsored conferences by UNESCO and other international bodies to resolve this dispute. As you read the excerpts below, consider what processes you think could be used to resolve this issue and what substantive solutions you see.

A. Case Study: The Parthenon Marbles

John Henry Merryman, *Thinking About the Elgin Marbles*

83 Mich. L. Rev. 1881–1882;1889–90; 1893–95;
1903; 1911–1913; 1915; 1918; 1921 (1985)

In the early nineteenth century, a British Lord removed much of the sculpture from the Parthenon and shipped it to England. Housed in the British Museum and named after their exporter, the Elgin Marbles have become a source of international controversy. The Greeks wish to see the Marbles returned to the Acropolis and their position is supported by a growing movement seeking the repatriation of cultural property. The Elgin Marbles are representative of the many works of art in the world's museums and private collections that could be subject to repatriation. Rejecting the emotional appeal of the Greek position, Professor Merryman analyzes the controversy and the proper disposition of the Marbles on reasoned, principled grounds. He concludes that the Greeks do not have a legal claim to the Marbles and that moral arguments fail to justify the return of the Marbles to Greece. Professor Merryman then turns to general principles that should govern the allocation of cultural property. He rejects cultural nationalism as a basis for the disposition of the Marbles, because cultural nationalism expresses dubious values and is founded on sentiment. The concerns of cultural internationalism—preservation, integrity, and distribution/access—do not clearly support the Greek position. Under the general principle of repose, the Elgin Marbles should remain in the British Museum until the Greek government can offer more compelling reasons for their return.

"This is our history, this is our soul."—Melina Mercouri

Between 1801 and 1812 Thomas Bruce, 7th Earl of Elgin and, from 1799 to 1803, British Ambassador to the Sublime Porte of the Ottoman Empire, removed many of the surviving sculptures on the Parthenon and shipped them to England. He sold them in 1816 to the British Museum, where they are now displayed and are known as "The Elgin Marbles." In 1983 the Greek Government, represented by Melina Mercouri, the famous actress who is also the Greek Minister of Culture, requested that the Elgin Marbles be returned to Greece. The plea has been made before, but Minister Mercouri's appears to be the first official request by the Greek Government for return of the Parthenon sculptures. The current request was officially declined by the British Government in 1984....

Despite national laws limiting the export of cultural property, some of it still finds its way abroad. There has been much discussion and a significant amount of international and national legislation about this traffic in recent years. Where cultural property from nation A illegally makes its way to the territory of nation B, a variety of responses is possible. The smuggler may be criminally prosecuted by the authorities of nation A if they can catch him. If the stolen cultural property is brought into the United States, the smuggler may be tried for violation of the Interstate Stolen Property Act. If the illegally removed property was taken without the owner's consent, a civil action for damages is another possibility. In most cases, however, the remedy sought will be restitution or, as it is more often called when dealing with cultural property, repatriation. Punishment of the offender is desirable, and money damages would help to assuage the loss, but repatriation is often the preferred objective. In theory, repatriation should be easy. Cultural property is, for most legal purposes, like other property: the owner can recover it, subject to the possible rights of good faith purchasers. The courts of all nations are open to such actions. If X steals my painting and takes it to Mexico, I can sue in a Mexican court for its recovery. Thus, to refer to the case of the Marbles, if Greece believes that they were stolen, it can sue the British Museum in a British court for their return.

Where the object was not stolen, however, the law is different. Suppose X, the owner of a Titian painting in Genoa, sells it to a Swiss collector who hides it in his luggage and smuggles it out of Italy. Under Italian law such a painting cannot legally be removed from Italy without a permit that, in the case of a work by Titian, would almost certainly not be granted. In addition, since the work would not be going to a European Economic Community member country, an ad valorem tax would be due. The smuggler has thus violated Italian law twice. In such "illegal export" cases, the legal situation differs significantly from that in the theft cases. Italy may wish to have the painting returned to Italy, but it is not the owner. Accordingly, Italy would have no standing before a foreign court to recover the Titian. X, the Genoese seller of the painting, obviously cannot recover it, since he sold it....

Politically, there is increasing activity within UNESCO and, more recently, the Council of Europe, to encourage the voluntary repatriation of cultural property, independently of any legal obligation to do so. UNESCO became actively involved with cultural property issues in the 1960s. Its first major effort, culminating in the 1970 Convention, was prospective, and did not attempt to deal with events occurring before its implementation. More recently UNESCO and the United Nations General Assembly have focused on the question of restitution of previously acquired cultural property. In 1973, at the request of Zaire, the United Nations General Assembly considered the question of "restitution of works of art to countries victims of expropriation." Since then the Secretary General, in collaboration with the Director-General of UNESCO, has submitted two progress reports on the implementation of United Nations Resolutions on the question. In 1978, UNESCO formed an Intergovernmental Committee for Promoting the Return of Cultural Property to its Countries of Origin or its Restitution in Case of Illicit Appropriation. The Parliamentary Assembly of the Council of Europe issued an order and a resolution on the subject in 1983. Public and private sensitivity to the desire of Third World nations for the return of artifacts has led to a number of often unpublicized cases of voluntary repatriation. As the pressure for repatriation grows, the necessity for a framework for discussion of cultural property questions grows with it....

Why Do We Care?

A preliminary question: what difference does it make to us (i.e., to non-British and non-Greeks) whether the Marbles stay in Britain or are returned to Greece? It is easy to see why the British want to keep them and to understand why the Greeks want them back, but why should the rest of us care? We care about the Elgin Marbles for three reasons. First, they are monuments of human culture, an essential part of our common past. They tell us who we are and where we come from, give us cultural identity. Second, we enjoy them as great art. Like literature and music, they enrich our lives. Third, the Marbles dramatically illustrate an important fact: the Metropolitan Museum in New York, the British Museum in London, the Louvre in Paris, the Hermitage in Leningrad and indeed all of the great Western museums contain vast collections of works from other parts of the world. If the principle were established that works of foreign origin should be returned to their sources, as Third World nations increasingly demand in UNESCO and other international fora, the holdings of the major Western museums would be drastically depleted. The Elgin Marbles symbolize the entire body of unrepatriated cultural property in the world's museums and private collections. Accordingly, the preservation and enjoyment of the world's cultural heritage and the fate of the collections of the world's great museums are all in some measure at stake in a decision about the Marbles....

The moral question is much harder to resolve than the legal question because moral norms are imprecise and their applicability is controversial. That is one reason for legal rules: to provide definitive and practically workable solutions to otherwise troubling and unruly questions. There is a trade-off; something is gained, but something is also lost. As a result, it occasionally happens that what is legal seems morally wrong, even to those making the legal decision. The preceding discussion concludes that the removal of the Marbles was legal. The question now is whether, even if legal, it was immoral....

To whom should such arguments be addressed? We have shown that the Greeks could sue for the return of the Marbles in a British court. Even if they should do so,

however, the range of argument that the British court could properly hear and decide is quite narrow, limited to determining the legality of the removal. The kind of question we here wish to pursue is different, and there is at present no tribunal competent to consider it. We must therefore supply our own hypothetical supranational tribunal, one charged with making informed, principled decisions concerning the proper allocation of disputed cultural property. Assuming that such a tribunal existed and that the Greek claim to the Marbles was properly submitted to it, how should it decide?

Cultural Nationalism

The most obvious argument is that the Marbles belong in Greece because they are Greek. They were created in Greece by Greek artists for the civic and religious purposes of the Athens of that time. The appealing implication is that, being in this sense Greek, they belong among Greeks, in the place (the Acropolis of Athens) for which they were made. This argument, which I will call the argument from cultural nationalism, requires careful examination, since it is basic to the Greek position and because arguments like it are frequently made by other governments calling for the return of cultural property (and is strongly implied in their use of the term "repatriation"). Public attitudes toward the campaign for restitution of cultural property are based to a large extent on uncritical acceptance of the cultural nationalism argument. Its validity is assumed in much of the dialogue in the United Nations, UNESCO, and the Council of Europe, as well as in the process of policy formation within a number of nations....

In bare form, the argument from cultural nationalism is more an assertion than a reason. It is not self-evident that something made in a place belongs there, or that something produced by artists of an earlier time ought to remain in or be returned to the territory occupied by their cultural descendants, or that the present government of a nation should have power over artifacts historically associated with its people or territory. Our first task is to discover whether there is more to the cultural nationalism argument than a mere self-serving assertion. In its truest and best sense, cultural nationalism is based on the relation between cultural property and cultural definition: (1) For a full life and a secure identity, people need exposure to their history, much modern creation for which there is little historical basis before the nineteenth century; (2) the Parthenon only became a symbol of Greek nationality in the 1820s; and (3) the assertion by modern Greeks of their identity with ancient Greeks is in this sense a national myth of the modern Greek state which is represented or illustrated by objects. Such artifacts are important to cultural definition and expression, to shared identity and community. They tell people who they are and where they come from. In helping to preserve the identity of specific cultures, they help the world preserve texture and diversity. Works of art civilize and enrich life. They generate art (it is a truism among art historians that art comes from art) and nourish artists. Cultural property stimulates learning and scholarship. A people deprived of its artifacts is culturally impoverished.

The difficulty comes in relating the notion of cultural deprivation to the physical location of the Marbles. If the British had attempted to appropriate the identity of the Marbles, disguising or misrepresenting their origin, then the Greeks, and all the rest of us, would rightly object to such falsification of the culture. If such misrepresentation were encouraged or justified by their location in England, then one could see the basis for an argument that the Marbles should be returned to Greece. But in fact, the British have from the beginning presented the Marbles openly and candidly as the work of Greek artists of extraordinary genius and refinement. Presented as they are, spectacularly mounted in their own fine rooms in one of the world's great museums, the Marbles honor Greece and Greeks. No visitor to the British Museum could come away with any other impression. By their removal to London and exposure in the British Museum, they have brought admiration and respect for the Greek achievement. As we have seen, that was one of Lord Elgin's intentions. In the most important sense the Greek cultural heritage has been preserved, arguably enhanced, by the British acquisition and display of the Marbles. It is not clear that enjoyment of cultural value (as distinguished from economic and political value, which are discussed below) requires possession of the Marbles. Greeks need access to their cultural heritage, and access would be easiest and most direct if the Marbles were in Athens, but writings about the Marbles are widely published and well-illustrated, and excellent reproductions exist. In that sense the Marbles are, or could easily be made to be, as accessible to the Greeks through reproductions as through the originals. There must be some cultural magic inherent in the authentic object, and not in an accurate reproduction, that speaks only to Greeks, or the argument fails. Authentic objects have many times the market value of even the most convincing reproductions....

The final component of the nationalism argument is political: the belief that the presence of the Marbles in England, or in any place other than Greece, is an offense to Greeks and to the Greek nation. Here the demand for the return of the Marbles is based on national pride. That sort of sentiment is close to cultural deprivation of the sort just discussed, but it is worlds away from it in a very important sense.

I conclude that the argument from cultural nationalism fails to make the case for the return of the Marbles. It fails because it expresses values not clearly entitled to respect (political nationalism), because it is founded on sentiment and mysticism rather than reason, and because it is a two-edged argument that is equally available to the British. One can admire the Greekness of the Marbles and respect their specific cultural importance to Greeks without concluding that they belong in Greece.

Cultural Internationalism

The Hague Convention for the Protection of Cultural Property in the Event of Armed Conflict of May 14, 1954, states in its preamble that "cultural property belonging to any people whatsoever" is "the cultural heritage of all mankind." These words, appearing for the first time in any major piece of international legislation, announce the important principle that everyone has an interest in the preservation and enjoyment of all cultural property, wherever it is situated, from whatever cultural or geographic source. There is still, regrettably, an exception for military necessity, and nations sometimes do violate their legal obligations toward cultural property, but the principle is clearly accepted. All of us, from every country, have an interest in the preservation and disposition of the Marbles; the matter does not touch only on Greek and English interests. The Marbles are "the cultural heritage of all mankind." It is early in the development of cultural internationalism to suggest that it applies to all cultural property in all circumstances or that, in a conflict between a sovereign nation's preference and the international interest, the latter will prevail. For present purposes a more modest approach will serve: if the legal and moral arguments are treated as evenly balanced, and if the argument from nationalism is also inconclusive, are there considerations from the point of view of cultural internationalism (which the Hague Convention language expresses) that indicate the proper way to allocate the Marbles?

There are three such considerations: preservation, integrity, and distribution. Preservation takes priority for obvious reasons. If the Marbles are destroyed, people of all cultures will be deprived of an important part of their cultural heritage, and the problem of allocation disappears. Damage short of destruction—whether through inadequate care, the action of the elements, or the hazards of war, terrorism, or vandalism—threatens the same value. It is essential that the Elgin Marbles be protected from damage or destruction, but it can hardly be argued that they are exposed to such danger in London. On the contrary, they are well mounted, maintained, and guarded. There is no reason to suppose that they would be safer in Athens. Indeed, if one compares the record of care for works on the Acropolis and in the British Museum since 1816, it is clear where the greater danger has lain. The sculptural reliefs remaining on the Parthenon and the Caryatids on the Erechtheion have all been badly eroded by exposure to a variety of hazards, including the smog of Athens. The Marbles in the British Museum have fared much better. If one had to make a decision based solely on concern for the physical preservation of the Marbles, it would be difficult to justify moving them to Athens. Even if, as is probable, they would be placed in a museum there, rather than reinstalled on the Parthenon, what reason would there be to expose them to the danger involved in removal and transport? What reason would there be to expect that they would be safer in Athens, over the next 170 years, than they have been in London, over the past 170 years? If the time should come when they would be safer in Greece, then the preservation interest would argue for their return. Under present conditions, the preservation concern favors leaving the Marbles in the British Museum. We must also consider the concern for the preservation of the records of a civilization. It is important to our understanding and appreciation of the artifact that we properly associate it with the time, place, and manner of its origin and with its functions and significance within the culture. But such understanding and appreciation are not necessarily advanced by returning articles to their original sites. It is true that the removal of an artifact from its site can destroy vital information....

The argument for return is an argument for restoration of the integrity of the Parthenon, and that is not (at present) possible without exposing the Marbles to unacceptable hazards. Accordingly, although the "integrity of the work of art" or "rememberment" argument is persuasive, present conditions make it inapplicable. Should it become possible to reinstall the Marbles safely on the Parthenon, then the integrity argument would favor their return. The other international interest is distributional; a concern for an appropriate international distribution of the common cultural heritage, so that all of mankind has a reasonable opportunity for access to its own and other people's cultural achievements. There is a tendency for works of art to flow from the poor to the wealthy nations, and one can imagine the unpleasant extreme of a Third World denuded of cultural property in order to stock the museums and the private collections of a few wealthy nations. The motivating force for the movement of art is today primarily economic. Dealers, collectors, and museums in wealthy countries are prepared to pay well for artworks, and it is not unreasonable for art-rich but otherwise poor countries to express concern about the flow. The prospect of a world in which all major artworks are concentrated in a few nations, with the rest culturally impoverished as a result, is unpleasant to contemplate. How should this distribution/access consideration affect the allocation of the Marbles? It is true that Greek antiquities can be found in major museums and private collections throughout the world and that some of the greatest Greek antiquities are found abroad. But it is difficult to argue that Greece itself is in this sense impoverished. One of the reasons people go to Greece is to enjoy its wealth of antiquities. One of the informed and concerned traveler's preoccupations is with the future of the many works that remain in Greece; like most art-rich nations, Greece faces enormous problems of expense and cultural organization in order to protect, conserve, and display what it has. The distribution interest actually has another and quite different aspect. There is an international interest in the accessibility of cultural property to all people. That policy is advanced by distribution, rather than retention in one place, of the works of a culture. If all the works of the great artists of classical Athens were returned to and kept there, the rest of the world would be culturally impoverished. That is not specifically an argument for retention of the Marbles by the

British; it is a refutation of the notion that all of the works of a culture belong at that culture's situs.

Criteria for an appropriate international distribution of the artifacts of a culture do not yet exist; the dialogue until now has been dominated by demands for repatriation and by deference to cultural nationalism. But as a general matter, it seems difficult to argue convincingly for the return of the Marbles to Athens on distributional grounds. If we focus instead on the question of access, there seems little reason to suppose that the Marbles would be more accessible to the world's peoples in Athens than they are in London.

Reviewing the arguments made to our hypothetical supranational tribunal, we find the following: cultural nationalism is a dubious argument at best, entitled to little weight. In any event, it supports both the Greek and the British cases and is inconclusive. Economic nationalism merely reargues the question of who has the legal property in the Marbles, and the British seem to win that one. Political nationalism is difficult to employ in a convincingly principled way, since it seems to urge values that are of dubious desirability. The values of cultural internationalism—preservation, integrity, and distribution/access—lead in different directions. The most powerful of them, preservation, does not under present circumstances advance the Greek cause, since there is no basis for arguing that the Marbles would be safer in Athens. The integrity argument favors reuniting the Marbles with the Parthenon, but at present that is not possible without exposing them to unacceptable hazards. There are no developed criteria for applying the distribution/access concern, but it does not appear that the present distribution of Greek antiquities argues strongly for returning the Marbles to Athens. Accordingly, under present circumstances, the tribunal should leave the Marbles where they are.

As you read the next article, think about whether you ever totally changed your views about something. How did it happen?

Carrie Menkel-Meadow, *Why We Can't "Just All Get Along": Dysfunction in the Polity and Conflict Resolution and What We Might Do About It*

J. Disp. Resol., no. 1, 2018, at 5, 12

A recent such moment for me came on a return visit to Athens. I spent a full year living next door to the Elgin Marbles in the British Museum in London some years ago and often taught with the formal document used by the Museum to explain the "dispute" and why the Elgin Marbles were "better off" being taken care of and displayed in London, rather than Athens. Many of my students had written papers and made dispute resolution proposals for a variety of contested art ownership issues (post-colonial, contested provenance, Nazi art looting, University and archeological "thefts" some now governed by treaty.) It took a visit *in situ* to the new museum across from the Parthenon (where the other "half" of the Marbles are displayed) to change my mind completely. The newly architected building, with archeologists permanently available for conversation, and the "epiphany" of seeing the sublime friezes in their "natural" home, made the "return" of all of them to their historical home seem the best outcome to me. (There are of course, very expensive other outcomes for such disputes—e.g. "rotation" of displays etc., but this time I think I have totally changed my mind). I was moved by the natural and historical habitat and the care with which Greek archeologists and scientists were managing their heritage.

Notes & Questions

1. As explained above, there is now a grand and new museum in Athens, beautifully architected and prepared to accept the Marbles when they are brought back. The museum is across the street from the Parthenon, where all the other friezes and sculptures are, and where the Marbles are to be kept indoors, protected from the elements. What effect does this new development have on Merryman's argument about preservation in this dispute?
2. Can you lay out the legal claims that Greece might make to seek restitution or repatriation of the Marbles? In what venue(s)? With what likely outcomes?
3. What are your own views about "cultural nationalism" versus "cultural internationalism"? Do you think general views of these concerns and claims have changed over time? How should international dispute resolution deal with changing political, social, and cultural values? Can legal regimes adapt to such changes?
4. What process do you think might most effectively deal with the Parthenon Marbles dispute? In considering the DSD principles we have studied, what other process might you design?
5. Consider how the problem of art theft could be a clock problem—we pick a legal principle, and we apply it. (In some ways, this has been the solution for Holocaust art reparations, where US courts have usually required the return of the artwork once it has been proven that it was wrongfully taken.)
6. Yet this is a cloud problem, not a clock problem, since there are several competing principles, all are valued, and all are interconnected. Which of the advice you have read about so far might help to unstick this dilemma? What possible solutions do you see? Many solutions have been suggested in the literature and in behind-the-scenes, ongoing negotiations. See ALEXANDER HERMAN, THE PARTHENON MARBLES DISPUTE: RESOLVING THE DISPUTE CH. 10 (2023).
7. What other cultural heritage, stolen, or looted art disputes are you aware of? How might they be resolved?
8. Do you think there should be a special international formal tribunal to deal with such disputes, or do you think it is better to leave these disputes to ad hoc, case-by-case

negotiation, mediation, or resolution? What are the issues in precedent-setting in this kind of dispute?

III. Israel-Palestine

The "classic" wicked problem of the last 75 years (and even that timing is debated) is the Israeli-Palestinian conflict. We note that this was not always the case—in fact, Jewish communities flourished under Arab and Ottoman rule. To many of us alive today, it may seem inconceivable that the Sultan of the Ottoman Empire, Bayezid II, welcomed Jews (and of course, Muslims) expelled by Spanish rulers Ferdinand and Isabella in 1492. (Bayezid II even noted how short-sighted Ferdinand was: "'You venture to call Ferdinand a wise ruler,' he said to his courtiers, 'he who has impoverished his own country and enriched mine!'"[3]) Other Arab rulers and the Ottoman Empire would continue to welcome Jewish citizens for centuries. Salonika (now Thessaloniki), Greece, under the Ottoman Empire was over 50 percent Jewish as recently as 1920. But, as the Ottoman empire neared its end in the early 20th century, the dueling populations within it which were vying for a state of Palestine brought an end to this long history of co-existence, eventually leading us to the current Israeli-Palestinian conflict.

The following two articles examine the history of Israel-Palestinian peace negotiations in the 1990s and 2000s, a period in which the greatest number of such negotiations were attempted.

Robert H. Mnookin, Ehud Eiran, & Sreemati Mitter, *Barriers to Progress at the Negotiation Table: Internal Conflicts among Israelis and among Palestinians*

6 Nev. L.J. 317–325; 362–366 (2006)

The Intractability of Both Issues [Palestinian "right of return" and the Israeli settlements]

As noted above, the conflict over the Palestinian refugees dates back to the creation of Israel in 1948, while the conflict over the Jewish settlements arose in the aftermath of the 1967 Six Day War. For years, each side asserted its positions, and there were no negotiations, as neither side recognized the legitimacy of the other. When direct negotiations between the Israelis and the Palestinians finally began in 1991, both sides agreed to defer any meaningful discussion of the substantive issues to a later phase of the Oslo process. The first serious attempt to even discuss these issues took place only in the spring of 2000, during what came to be known as the "Swedish channel."

During the short negotiation history, which begins at the first direct talks in 1991 and culminates at the last official attempt at bilateral negotiation in the winter of 2001

---

3. 2 The Jewish Encyclopedia: A Descriptive Record of the History, Religion, Literature, and Customs of the Jewish People from the Earliest Times to the Present Day 460 (Isidore Singer & Cyrus Adler eds., 1912).

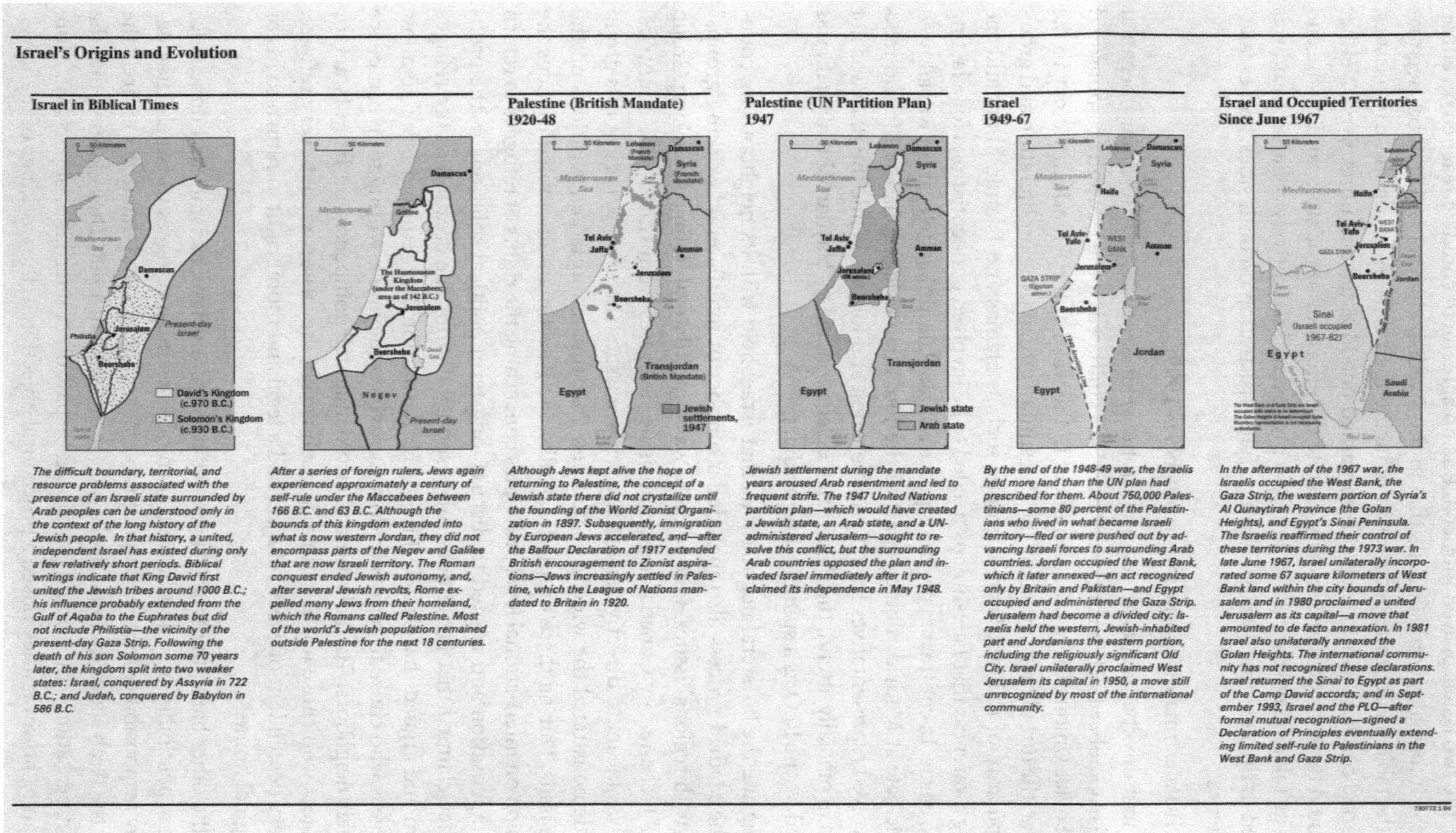

United States Central Intelligence Agency. Directorate of Intelligence. The Gaza Strip & West Bank: a map folio, https://www.loc.gov/item/2011591411/.

at Taba, the two issues proved intractable as no agreement could be reached on either. While the informal record suggests that in the Swedish channel and at Taba, negotiators at the table made some progress in reducing their differences on these two issues, the internal conflicts within each side remained unaddressed and unresolved. Neither issue could be resolved satisfactorily despite the efforts of negotiators, and by the end of talks at Taba in February 2001, the Oslo process had definitively collapsed, and was followed in the next three years by intensifying frustration on both sides, and escalating violence.

1. Israeli-Palestinian Negotiations from 1991–1999

The first direct attempts at negotiation between Israelis and Palestinians began at Madrid in October 1991 during multilateral talks initiated by the U.S. and co-sponsored by the Soviet Union. These talks were held in the wake of the American victory in the Gulf War, the turbulence caused by the Palestinian intifada, the proliferation and growing popularity of militant Islamic groups such as Hamas and Islamic Jihad, and the growing awareness that Palestinians needed to be involved in negotiations for a lasting peace to ensue. In contrast to previous peace talks, a Palestinian delegation was allowed to participate at Madrid, albeit as part of the Jordanian delegation. The Madrid talks also involved representatives from Syria, Lebanon and Jordan. While the PLO was not allowed to officially attend, the Palestinian delegation, led by Haydar 'Abd al Shafi, was accepted by the PLO as a suitable intermediary.

Alongside the bi-lateral negotiations that Israel held with its neighbouring countries, the Madrid process also included a number of multilateral "working groups" to deal with regional issues. One of these was a multilateral Refugee Working Group ("RWG"), chaired by Canada and comprising delegates from thirty-nine countries, which was meant to directly discuss the refugee issue. The proceedings of this group amply demonstrated the wide gaps between Palestinian and Israeli positions on the refugee issue. During these multilateral talks, the Palestinians attempted to focus the discussion on international legal principles concerning the rights of refugees to return and compensation and wished to discuss long-term political solutions to the problem. They claimed that Israel bore full responsibility for the creation of the refugee problem and argued that Article 11 of U.N. Resolution 194 required Israel to allow all refugees who chose to return to do so, provided they were willing to live in peace with their neighbors. The Palestinians also demanded compensation from Israel for all refugees who chose not to return; and, above all, they asserted that every refugee, and every descendant of every refugee, had a legal and moral right to return to his or her original home.

On the other hand, the Israeli delegates rejected outright, as Israel had done since 1949, any possibility of a significant return of Palestinian refugees to Israel. They denied any responsibility for the refugee problem, arguing instead that it was entirely the fault of the Arab states that had declared war on Israel in 1948. They claimed that the only compensation Israel would pay would be part of an international package. More importantly, however, they raised a procedural objection to the workings of the RWG, insisting that the refugee issue could never be solved in a multilateral framework. They demanded instead that the RWG talks be restricted to technical and humanitarian concerns (e.g., job creation, vocational training, public health, and child welfare for the Palestinian refugees in their host countries) as well as on policies of adaptation (i.e., better social and economic integration of the refugee communities into their host surroundings).

While the RWG meetings continued to flounder in irrelevance, Israel and the PLO reached a breakthrough agreement on mutual recognition which culminated in the joint "Declaration of Principles" at Oslo in 1993. Inspired by the nascent hope that permeated the region at the time, Yossi Beilin, then the Israeli Deputy Foreign Minister, announced his government's willingness to double the number of annual licenses granted to Palestinian refugees through the family reunification program from 1000 to 2000.

Meanwhile, the historic mutual recognition between the PLO and the state of Israel had led to the commencement of bilateral talks, which meant, for the first time, a direct negotiating channel between the two parties. However, these talks were carefully circumscribed to discuss only "interim" issues, with talks about long-term political solutions to the refugee issue relegated, with other major issues such as borders and settlements, to the planned "final status" talks that were to be concluded by the end of a five-year interim period in May 1999.

As such, the three agreements that were arrived at between the Israelis and the Palestinians over the course of the next few years (The Declaration of Principles on September 13, 1993, the Gaza-Jericho Agreement on May 4, 1994, and the interim agreement on September 28, 1995) contained nothing of relevance to the refugee issue. Instead, buried in Article XII of the "Declaration of Principles," now known as the "Oslo Accord" under a subheading titled "Liaison and Cooperation with Jordan and Egypt," was a sentence that established a multi-lateral committee that would decide "the modalities of admission of persons displaced from the West Bank and Gaza Strip." This provision, agreed to by the PLO leadership, related to persons "displaced" from their West Bank homes as a result of the 1967 war, not refugees of 1948.

The Oslo Accord and the other interim agreements signed during this period must be considered nothing short of pivotal in the context of the larger history of the Arab-Israeli conflict. But the accords placed a higher priority on taking steps towards Palestinian autonomy (and its promise of eventual statehood) in Gaza and the West Bank over a resolution of the refugee issue. Those Israelis who supported the Oslo process assumed that the creation of a Palestinian state, to which refugees could return, would be the solution to the refugee problem.

Likewise, no concrete discussions ensued at Madrid about the settlements. What discussion there was about territorial issues was limited strictly to the scope of autonomy in the territories. Similarly, there was no discussion in the Declaration of Principles of settlements or borders, which were relegated to "final status talks" that were meant to be held at the end of an interim period of five years. One clause of "Oslo 2" (Sept 28,

1995, Ch. 2, Art. 10, section 2) vaguely implied a withdrawal of Israeli troops from the West Bank over a period of time, but the scope of this troop withdrawal was ambiguous, and no mention was made of settlements or settlers.

2. Final Status Negotiations—The Swedish Channel (Spring 2000)

Although final status talks were meant to begin in 1996, the peace process entered a crisis in 1995, and the ensuing stalemate was not broken until Ehud Barak led the Labor Party back to power in 1999 on the strength of a campaign promise to end the conflict and usher in peace. Implied in this promise was his willingness to attempt to solve permanently the refugee issue, and, to that end, he demonstrated a willingness on Israel's part to allow the refugees of the 1967 war (though not the 1948 refugees) to re-enter the territories now administered by the Palestinian Authority (previously, Israel had demanded repatriation of all "displaced persons" to Egypt or Jordan). While Barak remained adamant that there would be no return of refugees to Israel, and while he insisted that Israel would accept no responsibility for the creation of the refugee problem, many considered these to be "opening positions" at the negotiation table when final status talks formally began in September 1999. Serious final-status negotiations finally got underway in the spring of 2000, in secret talks that came to be known as the "Swedish Channel" or "Stockholm Talks."

By this time public opinion polls indicated that Israeli, Jews, and Palestinians held diametrically opposite views about the appropriate resolution to the conflict. The vast majority of Palestinians in the West Bank and Gaza (no polls were conducted at the time of refugees in Lebanon, Jordan, and Syria) wanted a full right to return to Israel, while the vast majority of Israelis rejected any solution that would allow large numbers of Palestinians to be admitted to Israel and insisted that it was Israel's sole right to decide "who should be allowed to return, if at all."

In the secret negotiations that occurred in the Swedish Channel, it appeared that the representatives at the table made some progress with respect to the refugee issue. There was little change in the Israeli position. The Israelis proposed accepting up to 10,000 refugees within a humanitarian "family reunification scheme." The Palestinians proposed that an international commission ask all refugees where they wished to reside, with the questions framed in such a way that the probable result would be that only a limited number would settle in Israel. The parties agreed to try to create what would be a vaguely worded historical recapitulation on the right of return that would somehow be consistent with both people's historical narratives. And they also discussed the creation of a twenty billion dollar fund by the international community to settle refugee claims and financially aid those countries that shouldered the burden of accepting and rehabilitating them.

According to some Israeli sources, the talks on refugees were sufficiently promising so that the impression on the Israeli side was that the question of the right of return could be "satisfactorily resolved."‘ According to the same sources, however, the Palestinian delegates, while unofficially admitting that the Swedish Channel had resulted in agreement in principle that the right of return would never be fully implemented, were unhappy with the vague wording of the statement that was meant to resolve the contradictory narratives. They believed Israel should assume moral and legal responsibility for the situation of the refugees and issue an apology, demands that had been rejected by the Israeli delegates. Most fundamentally, it was not clear whether President Arafat was aware of concrete proposals that were discussed, much less whether he had agreed to them.

3. Final Status Negotiations—Camp David (2000)

While the underlying reasons are not clear, during the Camp David summit in July 2000, the refugee issue did not receive as much attention as did other divisive issues, such as Jerusalem, security, and borders. Indeed, some participants suggested there was something of a regression between the Swedish Channel and Camp David on the refugee issue. Whatever the reason, it is clear that nothing more was achieved than had already been achieved at Stockholm. Barak continued to refuse the notion that Israel should accept any responsibility, legal or moral, for the refugee problem, and he continued to oppose any recognition of the principle of the right of return. However, he also agreed to express Israel's regret for the suffering of the refugees, to absorb "tens of thousands" under the family reunification plan, and to make financial contributions to an international organization that would be established for the rehabilitation of the refugees outside Israel.

Yasser Arafat and his delegates, for their part, continued to insist on the moral and legal bases of the right of return but also agreed on practical grounds that there could be no full return of refugees to Israel. And, for the first time in the negotiating history of the issue, Arafat's team referred to a non-literal interpretation of U.N. Resolution 194, which marked a departure from the very literal interpretation on which they had traditionally grounded their claim. The Palestinian position demanded that Israel accept the principle of a right of return that would give individual Palestinians a choice, but it would be understood that the right would be somehow implemented so that only a limited number of Palestinian refugees would actually return to Israel. As the PLO Negotiations Affairs Unit put it:

> [A]n Israeli recognition of the Palestinian right of return does not mean that all refugees will exercise that right. What is needed in addition to such recognition is the concept of choice. Many refugees may opt for (i) resettlement in third countries, (ii) resettlement in a newly independent Palestine (though they originate from that part of Palestine which became Israel) or (iii) normalization of their legal status in the host country where they currently reside. In addition, the right of return may be implemented in phases so as to address Israel's demographic concerns.

For Israel, no deal was possible unless it was entirely clear that the numbers would be limited and that Palestinians would give up all future claims with respect to return.

While both the Israelis and the Palestinians had traveled some ways from the days when they clung to a fierce denial of all return to Israel or a fierce demand for a full return to Israel, the parties were clearly unable to resolve the refugee issue at Camp David. The Palestinian delegation had accepted a non-literal interpretation of the right of return, although the issue of Israel's acceptance of moral responsibility remained central and non-negotiable for them; the Israelis had increased the numbers of refugees they would allow in under family-reunification schemes, although any acceptance of responsibility on their part, and any uncontrolled return of large numbers of refugees, remained for them equally non-negotiable.

By all accounts, the territorial/border/settlement discussion consumed much time and attention at Camp David, but again, no agreement emerged and the discussions ended in acrimony. The Israelis and Americans claimed that the final proposal offered by Barak and Clinton to the Palestinians would have involved Israeli annexation of nine to ten percent of the West Bank, encompassing many current settlement blocs, but leaving the Palestinian territory in one contiguous piece. In addition, a narrow strip comprising fifteen percent of the length of the border along the Jordan River valley would be kept by Israel for security purposes on a "long-term lease" for an interim period. In return, the Israelis would cede one to three percent of their territory in the Negev to Palestine.

The Palestinians claimed that this proposal aimed to divide the would-be state of Palestine into four separate and non-contiguous cantons surrounded by Israel—the Northern West Bank, the Central West Bank, the Southern West Bank, and Gaza. This division, they charged, would prohibit freedom of movement of goods and persons within the Palestinian state, and subject Palestinian nationals and the Palestinian economy to Israeli control, thereby depriving the state of any semblance of sovereignty and independence. Lastly, they objected to the fact that the final proposal sought to leave Israel in control of all Palestinian borders. However, they also stated that they were not opposed to discussing further the solutions that had been proposed by the Israelis during the talks, but they proposed that such swaps should "be based on a one-to-one ratio, with land of equal value and in areas adjacent to the border with Palestine and in the same vicinity as the lands to be annexed by Israel." They claimed that the Camp David proposal envisioned a nine-to-one land swap in Israel's favour, which was not only unfair but also detrimental to the principle of fair territorial compromise for peace.

4. The Clinton Proposal (December 2000)

The Clinton proposal was an attempt, on the part of President Clinton, to bridge the gaps that still existed between the sides at the end of Camp David. With respect to the refugee issue, President Clinton stated, "I sense that the differences are more relating to formulations and less to what will happen on a practical level,"‘ and this sense led Clinton to believe that the gap on the refugee issue concerned not the actual return (he believed that the Palestinians were ready to "give it up") but the handling of the history of the issue, and the question of the apology. This led in turn to a proposal that was not materially different on the refugee issue from what had been discussed at Camp David, but one that employed different language. Clinton said, for instance, that "we need to adopt a formulation on the right of return that will make clear there is no specific right of return to Israel itself but that does not negate the aspiration of the Palestinian people to return to the area." The Clinton proposal suggested individual Palestinians would not have a right to choose to come to Israel, but they would have a right to "return" to a new Palestinian homeland which would become a state. The Clinton plan also specified that "the agreement will make clear that the return to the West Bank, Gaza Strip and area acquired in the land swap would be a right to all Palestinian refugees, while rehabilitation in host countries, resettlement in third countries, and absorption into Israel will depend upon the policies of those countries." Lastly, the plan mentioned the need to prioritize the refugee population in Lebanon.

While the Israelis accepted the Clinton Plan within forty-eight hours of its publication with some reservations (which had to do with security clauses and the sovereignty to be assigned to the Temple Mount), the Palestinians responded on January 1, 2001, with a stern document titled "The Palestinian Position Regarding Clinton's Proposal" which declared the plan objectionable primarily on account of its ambiguity, and which stated:

> The United States proposals were couched in general terms that in some instances lack clarity and detail. A permanent status agreement, in our view, is not merely a document that declares general political principles. It is, rather, a comprehensive instrument that spells out the details, modalities, and timetables of ending the Palestinian-Israeli conflict. For such an agreement to be effective, it must be backed by clear, effective international implementation guarantees. We believe that a general, vague agreement at this advanced stage of the peace process will be counter-productive.... The permanent status agreement must be a truly final agreement rather than an agreement to negotiate.

With respect to refugees, the official Palestinian position on the Clinton proposal was not much different from the negotiating position of the Palestinians at Camp David. They claimed the substitution of the word "home" with the word "homeland" was unacceptable and not in keeping with international law, and they claimed Palestinian refugees must be given the option to choose where to settle. However, they also claimed they were "prepared to think flexibly and creatively about the mechanisms for implementing the right of return," and that they were willing to accommodate Israel's demographic and security concerns. In the Palestinian view, the Clinton proposal did less than what had already been agreed to at the Swedish Channel almost a year ago, and in this view they perhaps did not differ too much from their Israeli counterparts.

The Palestinians had a series of objections to the territorial issue:

> a) The proposal was unaccompanied by a map, which made it difficult to see how Palestinian contiguity would or would not be affected and which settlement blocks would be annexed to Israel;
>
> b) The proposal had not made clear what was the total of annexed land for purposes of the calculation (i.e., it was unclear whether East Jerusalem and the Dead Sea area were considered to be part of the West Bank when calculating

the three to four percent that would be annexed to Israel, or whether those were in addition to the other portions that would be swapped, which would bring the "percentage annexed" number closer to the ten percent range);

c) The proposal did not contain any provisions to ensure direct Palestinian access to its international borders or even Palestinian control over movement of goods and people within the new state of Palestine;

d) The proposal envisioned that an additional ten percent of Palestinian territory would be placed under Israeli control under what they called "ill-defined security arrangements;"

e) The proposal had not made clear which areas would be swapped in return for the settlements (the Palestinians desired that annexed land be swapped with land of equal size and value, and not, for example, with arid desert regions in the Negev).

Despite these substantial objections, the Palestinians agreed to reconvene talks with the Israelis at the end of the month and to take as their starting point the Clinton proposal.

5. Taba (January 2001)

Israeli and Palestinian negotiators met for a final time officially in what was described as a "last-ditch effort" to secure an overall permanent-status agreement before the prime-ministerial elections in Israel which were scheduled for February 2001 and were widely believed to hold slim chances of success for Ehud Barak's by-then-very beleaguered government.

The talks at Taba ended inconclusively, with no agreement between the parties on any of the issues discussed. These talks were probably doomed from the outset because Prime Minister Barak's government had fallen, elections had already been scheduled for February 2001, and the second intifada was raging. Unlike Camp David, neither Barak nor Arafat was present, and it is unclear whether either leader in fact authorized the unrecorded proposals that were discussed by the negotiators at the table. Moreover, even if the Palestinians had accepted the Israeli proposals, which they did not, it appeared at the time that Barak would have faced significant difficulties ratifying and implementing an agreement.

There is no official record of the negotiations at Taba, but an EU Special Representative later created a report, never officially made public but in fact later released ("EU non-paper"), suggesting that concessions appeared to have been offered by both sides....

Conclusion

Our introduction suggested the paradoxical nature of the Israeli-Palestinian conflict from the perspective of a negotiation analyst: while a majority within each community tells pollsters that it accepts the basic notion of a two-state solution, Israeli and Palestinian leaders seem unable to reach an agreement notwithstanding the fact that the essential terms of a two-state deal are reasonably clear. The explanation, we suggest, relates to internal "behind-the-table" conflicts among Israeli Jews about the settlements project and among Palestinians about the scope and meaning of the right of return.

Since the lecture on which this paper is based was delivered in March of 2005, a great deal has transpired: Prime Minister Sharon successfully implemented the "unilateral" evacuation of Gaza; Sharon and his former nemesis Shimon Peres launched Kadima, a new centrist political party; Sharon became incapacitated by a stroke, and Ehud Olmert became acting Prime Minister; and Hamas won a surprising political victory in the Palestinian legislative elections. By the time this article appears there will be a new government both in Israel and for the Palestinian Authority.

The quick condemnations of the third-track initiatives by some Israelis and Palestinians and the recent electoral success of Hamas serve as a useful reminder that there are some within each community who explicitly and vehemently reject the idea that there should be two states in the land between the Mediterranean Sea and the Jordan River. The charter of Hamas explicitly calls for the destruction of Israel and the restoration of all of "Palestine" to the Palestinian people. Some Israelis would have Israel annex all of the West Bank and dream of sending its Palestinian population to Jordan or elsewhere in the Arab world.

In addition to those who explicitly reject a two-state solution, there are many more within each community who pay lip service to the idea but take positions that, as a practical matter, are profoundly inconsistent with what would be required to make such a solution viable. On the Palestinian side, this group includes those leaders and individuals who publicly declare their support for the two-state solution but who at the same time insist on an individual and collective right of return that might permit large numbers of Palestinian refugees to return to Israel and thus threaten the continued existence of Israel as a democratic Jewish state. Given the PLO's competition with Hamas, that the PLO leadership persists in rhetorically claiming a broad right of return becomes more understandable. It allows the PLO to support the idea of a two-state solution while undercutting one of the most powerful objections to it by those refugees who still dream of going "home."

What is problematic about this stance, however, is that it reinforces unrealistic expectations among some refugees. Moreover, no Israeli leader would conceivably accept a deal granting a broad "right of return" because of the demographic and security risks entailed and because of the ideological consequences. Today a substantial minority of Israeli citizens (about twenty percent) are Palestinian Arabs. Israeli Jews fear that broad recognition of a Palestinian right of return would soon create an Arab majority within what is now Israel. In the eyes of most Israelis, this demographic change would mean Israel would no longer remain the Jewish homeland and a Jewish state.

Instead, what is now a Jewish democratic state would either become a second state controlled by Palestinians or an undemocratic state that limited Palestinian political participation.

On the Israeli side, there are also those who pay lip service to the two-state solution but persist in taking positions that would make its durable implementation impractical. This group includes those within Likud's leadership who declare their support for the two-state solution but who continue at the same time to insist that Israel must retain and even expand settlements that would make impossible the creation of a Palestinian state with a contiguous region in the West Bank.

No Palestinian leader could conceivably accept a deal unless it provides for a contiguous state encompassing nearly all of the West Bank (along with, of course, East Jerusalem and Gaza). As a practical matter, this deal would require that all the settlements be evacuated. While some have suggested that Jewish settlers should be allowed to remain but be subject to the protection and control of a new Palestinian state, this seems unlikely to create a stable solution. There is widespread Palestinian hostility towards the Jewish settlers who are seen as having illegally dispossessed Palestinians of their land. If a Jewish settlement came under attack and was not adequately protected by the new Palestinian state, Israel would face irresistible pressure to intervene and come to its aid. Within Israel, there is a widely shared notion that the state has a duty to the extent possible to defend Jews anywhere in the world. Israeli intervention in a neighboring state on behalf of former Israeli citizens, many of whom would have relatives or co-workers in Israel, would seem inevitable. Knowing this, a Palestinian negotiator is likely to insist on the evacuation of the Jewish settlers.

The recent evacuation of the Jewish settlements in Gaza offers some hope but also serves as a sobering reminder of the difficulties inherent in these internal conflicts. There are grounds for both optimism and pessimism. The good news relates to the basic fact that Israel was able to evacuate without bloodshed over 8500 Jewish settlers, notwithstanding fierce internal political opposition. Israel did prove to itself that it had the capacity, through its political institutions, to relocate settlers. After fierce internal debate in Israel regarding disengagement, the conflict was resolved through the formal political process. The plan was approved by the cabinet and the Parliament and stood the test of judicial review by the Israeli Supreme Court.

The sobering news relates to how difficult this relatively small evacuation proved to be, and to the demands it imposed on Israel's material resources, political institutions, and leadership. Today there are more Jewish settlers remaining in the Occupied Territories than there were when Sharon first announced his initiative in December 2003. While the Sharon government was relocating settlers from Gaza and the northern West Bank, it was simultaneously expanding settlements in other parts of the West Bank. A day after the last Israeli soldier left Gaza, both Prime Minister Sharon, and Defense Minister, Shaul Mofaz, vowed to "strengthen the settlement blocks." In this sense, far from resolving the internal conflict, the Gaza evacuation can be seen as a continued form of deferral which may make the internal questions more difficult to resolve in the long run.

The events leading up to the Gaza withdrawal as well as its aftermath suggest the monumental leadership challenges on both sides. The Israeli withdrawal was not a consequence of any across-the-table negotiations between Israel and the Palestinians, but rather a unilateral act initiated and implemented by Israel alone. No Palestinian leader was required to take any actions that required diminishing the scope of a right of return.

On the Israeli side, it took Sharon, the former champion of the settlement movement and a leader known to have a will of iron, to pull off this important but modest evacuation of settlements. That Prime Minister Sharon would survive the challenge, either politically or physically, was by no means clear. The Israeli security services took very seriously the threat that a Jewish assassin might try and kill Sharon to prevent the implementation of the plan. Nor was his political survival assured. If following the March 2006 elections, Ehud Olmert becomes Prime Minister, it remains open to question whether he will have the political capital to bring about further settlement evacuations in the West Bank. He plainly lacks Prime Minister Sharon's national security credentials.

The Gaza evacuation serves as a useful reminder that the evacuation of Jewish settlements in the West Bank and the resolution of the Palestinian refugee issue will require extraordinary amounts of resources and government institutional capacity to implement decisions involving the relocation of large numbers of people. The costs of resettling those Palestinians who now reside in refugee camps outside of the West Bank and Gaza, let alone the costs of fairly compensating those Palestinians for their loss of property when they fled Israel will amount to untold billions of dollars. Unwinding the settlement project in Gaza was far greater than the costs of creating it in the first place: avoidance and deferral are expensive. The Gaza evacuation required an enormous investment of resources to relocate less than four percent of the settlers. Israel deployed five Army divisions to carry out the operation and evacuate less than 10,000 settlers and Israel earmarked over a billion dollars to relocate these settlers and to fund various other activities related to the relocation.

The impressive fashion in which the Israeli police and military combined empathy and assertiveness in evacuating the Gaza settlers has important implications for the broader internal conflicts. In Gaza, the soldiers and police charged with physically removing the settlers were unarmed but deployed in overwhelming numbers. They were patient, sympathetic and sometimes even tearful but also firm and purposeful. In resolving the broader internal conflicts, national leadership will also need to combine both empathy and assertiveness.

Israeli leaders must show empathy for those West Bank settlers who will need to leave their houses and dismantle their communities. Palestinian leaders will need to show empathy for those refugees who will need to give up the dream of ever returning to their ancestral homes. Leaders on both sides also need to be assertive. The Israelis should, as they did in the summer of 2005, signal to the settlers that if a democratic government should decide to relocate them, the decision will be carried out. The Palestinian leaders must also be assertive. Most of all, they need to say in public what they admit in private: most refugees, after sixty years of dispossession, will never be able to regain their lands in what is now Israel. For too long, Palestinian and Israeli leaders have fed false hopes: that the refugees will be able to choose to return and that Jews would be able to settle Eretz Israel. It is time to end this pattern.

Andrea Kupfer Schneider, *The Day after Tomorrow: What Happens Once a Middle East Peace Treaty Is Signed?*

6 Nev. L. Rev. 401, 402–19 (2006)

The Graveyard of Good Ideas—A.K.A. The Current Situation

Numerous excellent political scientists and legal scholars have written multiple explanations of what is preventing peace in the Middle East. These theories can be divided into three categories: solution-focused, party-focused, and international community focused.

A. Solution-Focused Barriers to Peace

Scholars examining the Israeli-Palestinian conflict have taken different views of what has prevented peace thus far.

1. It's a Question of a Solution

Early writings about the Israeli-Palestinian conflict pointed out the difficulty of finding a solution to such a complex situation. There were borders, religious sites, reparations, and mixed populations to be negotiated. And, of course, if one viewed the negotiation as sovereignty versus security, solutions would appear even more difficult.

Even here, we now know that the negotiation teams made excellent progress at Taba, coming close on borders for Israel and the Palestinian state, solutions for the right of return, and border control. In fact, most commentators would now agree that a lack of solution is not the problem here.

2. It's a Question of BATNA

Linked to the question of solution is the question of the parties' alternatives to that solution. Russell Korobkin has written here and elsewhere that each side's BATNA determines how they can negotiate in the current situation. As long as the respective BATNAs look better than the expected outcome, the current situation will continue.

Korobkin writes that without an overlapping zone of agreement, agreement cannot occur. Of course, as he notes, part of the problem here could well be that the zone *does* exist and the battle is to divide the "surplus" of the agreement. This battle to divide the surplus leads to hard bargaining on both sides and, in the end, stalemate.

The problem with BATNA analysis in this particular conflict is that this requires the assumption that there are rational players with a rational view of the entire situation. Outlining zones of agreement does not take account of cognitive and psychological barriers to settlement, cultural and language barriers that keep parties apart, and team divisions so that the BATNA actually appears differently to different entities on the same side. While zone analysis might work in economic transactions with "rational" businesspeople, it is hard to argue that this approach on its own is sufficiently rich and nuanced for longstanding ethnic conflict.

3. It's a Question of Ripeness

Another theory examining the solution versus alternatives is William Zartman's theory of ripeness [excerpted in Chapter 3—Eds.]. He explains that conflicts need to reach a mutually hurting stalemate before each side will be willing to sit and talk. The stalemate is defined as a place where further escalation would not be expected to result in gains. If either side thinks that they can escalate the violence and make more progress that way, the stalemate (and thus the opportunity for progress) does not exist. In some ways, this is the international relations interpretation of the bargaining zone/BATNA analysis—a mutually hurting stalemate exists because the BATNA is lousy for one or both sides.

The problem with this theory, as Zartman acknowledges, is that waiting for this stalemate to end can be lengthy and guessing when that magically occurs can be difficult. One could have assessed a stalemate in 1994 before the Oslo Accords. One might have thought that there was a mutually hurting stalemate prior to Taba with Israeli elections looming and Sharon likely to invalidate most concessions made by Barak. Nonetheless, there is no good way to move the parties along while waiting if one thinks that only a mutually hurting stalemate will move the parties to peace. Professor John Paul Lederach has also commented on this dilemma, noting that the concept of mutually hurting stalemate creates an analogy to cherry-picking (as if the solution was only waiting there to be carried out) rather than recognizing the hard part of *cultivating* solutions to international conflict [*see* Chapter 3—Eds.]. Lederach's vision of cultivation may be more realistic in these long-term intractable conflicts, albeit unsatisfying in terms of the amount of patience needed.

B. Party-Focused Barriers to Peace

The second group of theories to explain peace or the lack thereof focuses on the parties themselves.

1. It's a Question of Leadership

Many columnists and opinion leaders wrote during the course of the last twenty years that if only the leadership could be changed—in both Israel and in the Palestinian territories—we would be able to achieve peace. Looking at the Palestinian side, many believed that if moderates were in charge of the PLO or if Yasser Arafat was no longer in charge, then the PLO would be able to move forward toward peace. On the other side, there were many critics of Sharon's leadership as well.

Of course, both of these predictions have proven false. The death of Yasser Arafat and the change in PLO leadership has not yet resulted in any dramatic change in policy nor in moving the peace process forward. Similarly, (and ironically), it has been under the more conservative Likud party leadership that significant deals have been made (Rabin) and the first actual land withdrawals have occurred (Sharon). Sharon's new party, Kadima, seems to have been created with the goals of continuing withdrawals that would have been fought by Likud. While there have been times in history where the peaceful change in leadership has made dramatic progress in peace among neighbors, more often the change is not as dramatic as expected or does not produce the policy change that others might have expected. Abbas has not been able to control the extremist elements in the Palestinian territories and now, with Hamas in power, it is unclear that there ever will be a willingness to confront those elements and make true progress.

2. It's a Question of Internal Conflict

The thesis of the Mnookin article is a failure of centrism among the two sides and a concurrent failure by leadership to control and mitigate the extremists. Without leadership willing to control the extremists who support either the attacks on Israel or the expansion of settlements, true progress in the conflict cannot be made. This internal tendency to move toward the extreme has been seen in numerous other situations as well. Groups, talking primarily to themselves, support more extremist thinking than if they were forced to spend time with the other side of the dispute. The most successful example we have in recent times about the centrist push toward peace is in Northern Ireland with George Mitchell's procedure for mediation [excerpted in Chapter 3—Eds.] In the way that he managed the process, Mitchell built trust and power with the center and enabled the centrists on both sides to move forward without letting extremists on either side derail the process.

Mnookin's prescriptive advice is that we need both empathy and assertiveness in order to deal successfully with this move to the extremes. Part of the problem with this advice is the timing of "empathy," let alone how to measure it. How does "empathy" turn into a procedure for peace? First, how long must the empathy with the other side last? The goal is obviously to build lasting empathy both within and across groups but, in the meantime, what can we expect from citizens? Should empathy trump new bombings? Harassing delays at border crossings? Second, how do we measure this empathy? If empathy is measured by eliminating suicide bombing or by holding off on responsive attacks, we can realistically expect this to be violated. The problem is that the restraint will not be perfect nor last for a significant period of time.

3. It's a Question of Diplomacy

Building on both the theories of bargaining range and dealing with domestic constituencies, political scientist Robert Putnam explains international negotiations as "Two-Level Games." In other words, in negotiations between countries X and Y with their domestic constituencies represented by x and y, there are three negotiations going on.

$$\begin{array}{cccc} \uparrow & X \longleftrightarrow Y & \uparrow \\ | & x \qquad\quad y & | \end{array}$$

Constituencies x negotiate with government X in order to set the negotiation range. Constituencies y negotiate with government Y in order to set their negotiation range. Then governments X and Y must negotiate on the basis of the range they have already negotiated domestically. As we might hypothesize, the bargaining range for any international agreement is significantly narrowed by the domestic level negotiations prior to any international negotiation.... Negotiators must consider not only good policy but what is good politics.

4. It's a Question of Teams

A fourth theory looking at the parties examines how the teams have operated in actual negotiations. David Matz has outlined a situation in which, fed by the internal conflicts explained above, the miscommunication among the negotiation team seriously hampered the negotiation. In his analysis of the Taba negotiations, Matz explains that both the Israelis and Palestinians had designated team members to negotiate by issue. Each issue team actually made impressive progress at Taba but without coordination and general oversight of the teams, the progress was to no avail. Of course, as he notes, this is also a question of leadership. To move forward, the teams themselves must better coordinate their communications within the team and, most importantly, with their own leadership.

C. International Community & Systemic Barriers to Peace

The third group of barriers to peace is more systemic and, in part, has to do with third parties.

1. It's a Question of International Pressure

Early in the Israeli-Palestinian conflict (and even now) some argue that external pressure or superpower pressure is what is needed to move the parties to peace. This was clearly the situation that ended both the 1967 and 1973 wars between Israel and its Arab neighbors (where the United States pressured Israel to stop its military actions) so it would not be illogical to assume that a similar approach would work today.

Of course, it would be hard to argue that there has not been sufficient international attention to this conflict, particularly given the focus of the Clinton administration through multiple summits and meetings. Even with a four-way push for peace (the contact group) it appears that neither party is likely to bow to outside pressure without all other interests being met.

2. It's a Question of How We Negotiate

Another barrier to peace could be the way most international negotiations are conducted. Much international relations analysis has traditionally viewed the world through the theory of realism. More recently, liberal international relations theory has been used to analyze relations. Realists would argue that conflict resolution will occur when parties find it in their best interests to end violence, while liberal theorists would argue the impact of international organizations in pushing and encouraging member states to end conflict for the good of many states. An example of liberal international relations theory in practice is the Andean Pact trade organization's requirement that its member states all are democratic. While arguably a democracy is unnecessary for a free trade agreement, this provision has proven useful in maintaining democracy in the region. The even greater economic incentive to join the EU has pushed many former communist countries to democracy as well.

Terrence Hopmann [1995] has explored the parallels between international relations and styles of negotiation. The realist approach to the world tends to be reflected in "hard bargaining" while the liberal approach would be reflected in "problem solving." Hoppman argues that perhaps the reason we see so much hard bargaining in the international arena is the prevailing view of realism in international relations. (And since hard bargaining leads to more stalemates and intransigence, this style default has implications). On the other hand, if we were to adopt a more liberal view of international relations where countries act together to meet their interests, perhaps we would see more problem solving in the negotiations among countries.

3. It's a Question of Our Goals

Another systematic problem found in conflict resolution theory is balancing interests in peace versus interests in justice. [discussed in Chapter 8] In other words, is it more important to stop the violence or to pursue justice (often punishment) for those perpetrators of human rights violations? John Paul Lederach has labeled this dilemma as one of the primary paradoxes of conflict resolution. As discussed earlier, many South and Central American countries chose "peace" (and moving toward democracy) over "justice" and granted the military amnesty for violations carried out under its regime. The resolution to the Bosnian civil war was a good example of pursuing peace (getting the Serbs to stop killing Muslims and Croats) rather than pursuing justice (although the tribunals are supposed to be accomplishing one aspect of justice) since the carving up of Bosnia into two states was, in some ways, handing the Serbs the division for which they had clamored. Formerly mixed areas are now almost completely divided by ethnicity. The question of what values to pursue can also be paralyzing. In the Israeli-Palestinian case, from the Israeli perspective making peace seems to reward terrorism. From the Palestinian perspective, making peace means an entire shift in identity and relinquishing much of the past.

By understanding how there are multiple barriers to peace, it is easier to understand why—even with an overlapping zone of agreement, mutually hurting stalemate, apparent solutions, and outside pressure—this conflict has not yet been resolved. All of the barriers in all three areas—solution, parties, and the international community—need to be removed before there will be peace in this situation. Similarly, as we think about what will happen after peace, problems can occur along these same three axes-solution, parties and international community.

What Needs to Happen as Part of a Peace Treaty

The International Center for Transitional Justice has outlined five potential areas to be addressed in moving countries out of conflict and into peace (the process called transitional justice). While each area might not be needed in each conflict, it is a useful framework of analysis to see what is needed here. The Center examines: (1) prosecuting individual perpetrators (justice); (2) establishing truth-seeking initiatives;

(3) providing reparations; (4) reforming institutions (like the police or the courts); and (5) facilitating reconciliation processes. As we examine what is needed in this conflict, perhaps all of these elements except (4) could be included in a peace treaty between Israel and the Palestinian Authority. Furthermore, as discussed above, it is more helpful in this conflict to include truth-seeking as part of the reconciliation process rather than have a separate entity to perform that function.

A. Justice—Should There Be Prosecutions?

Justice is a loaded word, and even more so in this conflict. What could this mean? Acknowledgement of wrongs committed? Expulsion of Arabs? Expulsion of Jews? State-supported terrorism? In many conflicts, international law (or at least the international community) has a relatively clear narrative of the aggressor and the victim, the human rights violator, and the population that suffered. As others have already pointed out, that narrative is much more complex here, both from the inside and the third-party perspective.

Furthermore, while international law is often seen as the savior for the weak, in the Israeli-Palestinian conflict, both sides remain highly skeptical of international law. From the Israeli perspective, the UN has had no credibility dating to at least the infamous 1973 General Assembly resolution that Zionism was a form of racism. The UN refugee agency, UNWRA, has long been suspected of backing the Palestinians while ignoring violations, and allowing itself to be used as a political tool. More recent accusations include ignoring the kidnapping of Israeli soldiers carried out in front of UN observers, and insufficiently condemning suicide bombing. Most recently, the General Assembly brought a case against Israel to the International Court of Justice ("ICJ") regarding the building of the barricade between Israel and the Palestinian territories. The ICJ case itself and the decision, which condemned the building of the barricade without acknowledging that the fear of terrorist attacks might have been a partial (or complete) motivation, was yet another example of what Israelis see as a hopeless UN bias against them. The case against Israel brought by the General Assembly to the ICJ two years ago, was merely the most recent example of where, in the Israelis' eyes, the UN is hopelessly biased against Israel—condemning the building of the barricade between Israel and the West Bank, while not acknowledging the reason for the barricade—the impact of terrorism in Israel. The Palestinians could also be suspicious of international law which, aside from popular backing in the UN, has not brought them much. With the United States as the primary power broker in the region, the Palestinians could view their victories in the General Assembly as completely hollow.

More important than the view of law, however, is what a tribunal or court would actually be able to accomplish in this situation. Most courts that have been set up try to accomplish one of several purposes: compensation (as in the Iran or Swiss claims tribunals); getting out the facts of the situation (as in Rwanda, Bosnia, and Nuremberg); and/or punishing the perpetrators. In the Israeli-Palestinian situation, it is unclear that any of these purposes is necessary or even helpful. First, truth finding through a court is highly suspect. We do need more understanding of each side in this conflict, but the adversarial procedures of prosecution are not the best way to accomplish this because of the obvious conflict between the procedural narrowing of the issues to provide for fair trials and the wide-ranging investigation that is needed to promote understanding.

Second, punishment and prosecution will clearly not be agreed to by either side in this conflict. Could we imagine prosecuting the PLO for its links to suicide bombing? Could we imagine individual Israelis suing the Palestinian government for injuries or deaths? Since terror victims are compensated by the Israeli state, (although they could clearly use and deserve more money for their injuries) the traditional tort case seems unnecessary. And, since almost all the Fatah leadership, let alone Hamas, at one time or another condoned suicide bombing (if only by failing to speak out against it) a prosecution of those responsible could cripple the Palestinian leadership. Similarly, are we going to have trials of Israeli government officials for increasing the number of settlements during the last decades, demolitions of homes on the West Bank, or actions taken in 1948 to force Arabs to leave?

One could imagine a limited claims commission, much like the Iranian or Swiss claims tribunals, in which Palestinians present evidence of their losses (land taken from their family, olive groves destroyed for the barrier, etc.) for recompense by the Israeli government. However, this also has potential for breakdown for at least two reasons. First, Israelis might protest a claims commission that only hears claims from Palestinians for economic loss without equally allowing Israelis to bring claims for their own economic losses. Israelis could claim losses due to Jewish expulsions from Arab lands after 1948 (estimates range up to one million Jews who were expelled forcibly from Arab countries) as well as economic losses from terrorism. Second, if, in fact, the commission hears both sides, there may be the strong potential to try to even out the payments so that both governments are happy. In the case of the Eritrean-Ethiopian claims commission, for example, the commission seemed to value even-handedness over accuracy. The commission's attempt at balance and at making both parties happy undercuts its own legitimacy. Rather, the primary needs of reconciliation and economic growth need to emerge from different structures established in the peace treaty.

B. Reparations—The Need for Economic Growth

One of the primary determining factors of post-conflict resolution is the economic well-being and stability of the participants. While much aid has flowed to the Palestinian authority, economic growth needs to be spread out among the entire Palestinian population and maintained. In the long term, this economic growth will most likely occur by opening borders with Israel (which has long employed thousands of Palestinians) as well as by developing markets in Europe. The importance of economic growth for the entire population cannot be underestimated.

First, economic growth provides jobs, money, and respect. While lack of jobs does not lead directly to political instability, there is no question that a high unemployment rate among a population is not the best thing for peace. The riots in Paris in November 2005 are just the latest example of this phenomenon. Economic growth will also demonstrate to Palestinians that they are better off maintaining peaceful relations with Israel. Finally, as we have seen in other post conflict resolutions, populations are unable to move past the conflict if their primary needs are still not being met. Similar to Maslow's argument about a hierarchy of needs, reconciliation and understanding are unattainable if food and housing are still a primary concern. Finally, economic growth will demonstrate the workability of the refugee issue. If refugees still feel unfairly treated and still believe that they would be better off with a return of their land (however romantic and unrealistic that vision might be), the treaty itself will be suspect.

The needs for economic growth and stability are similar for the Israelis even though the Israeli economy is quite strong. There will be serious budgetary pressures from moving thousands of settlers back into Israel. The government will be responsible for housing and finding new employment for many of these citizens. While Israel might be better able economically to handle this, attention must also be paid to the economic equation on this side. Many settlers, as Mnookin has pointed out, moved to the settlements because of economic opportunities and incentives. Replacement communities will have to be built in new regions of Israel to house the settlers and offer similar opportunities for economic development. Aid to Israel and other types of development will be needed. Similar to the Palestinians' position on a peace treaty, any peace treaty will have far more credibility in Israel if affected Israelis feel that their lives have improved or at least remained more or less the same. If settlers are left in a much worse economic situation after their removal, this important political bloc is more likely to continue to advocate expansion rather than withdrawal.

C. A New Narrative—Reconciliation

In the end, peace and economic growth will be best fostered by increased peaceful contacts among the populations and better understanding from each side of the stories told about the conflict. Many organizations, both governmental and otherwise, have already started good work on cross-cultural exchanges and joint projects. Seeds of Peace (which does youth exchange and camps), Hand-in-Hand (which focuses on joint Jewish-Arab schools), and other exchanges continue to help build contacts and understanding.

The media can also play an important role in this understanding. For example, Al Jazeera covered the withdrawal of settlers from the Gaza Strip. As many articles noted, while Palestinians and other Arabs were in favor of their removal, the media aired coverage of Israelis crying at their losses and succeeded in humanizing the other side. Another example is that most Israeli textbooks now are more balanced in their coverage of the 1948 war and discuss how some Palestinians were forced from their homes. These stories of loss on both sides need to be taught. A wonderful example of this in practice is the Parents Circle, comprised of families who have lost a loved one in the Israeli-Palestinian conflict. The Parents Circle is based on restorative justice principles and focuses on using stories of loss to move toward peace. Broadening this opportunity for dialogue will only be helpful as the parties move forward after a peace treaty.

As part of this reconciliation, each side needs to create a new narrative for itself and its role in the future. Part of domestic opposition to Israeli occupation, for example, always came from the fact that many Israelis could not view themselves as "occupiers." A narrative of democracy in action will continue to hold weight among Israelis. More importantly, the narrative of the Palestinians must be dramatically changed. The narrative for the Palestinians begins primarily with their expulsion from Israel and, thus, has primarily been one of victimhood. This narrative of victimhood must be replaced by another narrative so that the populations can feel part of creating their own future. The narrative should include a successful Arab democracy with a free and open economy—and describe a people in charge of their own destiny. Ironically, the Palestinians could use the example of the Israelis, changing their own narrative from one of victims of the Holocaust to builders of a nation.

Notes & Questions

1. Note how many of the theories discussed in other chapters have already been tried in this wicked conflict. Are there other tools we can utilize here? *See* Carrie Menkel-Meadow and Irena Nutenko, *The Next Generation: Creating a New Peace Process in the Middle East*, 24 NEGOT. J. 567–84 (2009).
2. Consider some of the approaches outlined in Coleman & Ricigliano, *Getting in Sync*, excerpted in Part I above (work with the energy in the system; employ adaptive action; enable change, be a guide). How should these be utilized? How are these different from the approaches that have already been tried?
3. Has this wicked problem become even more wicked in light of the most recent events in Israel and Gaza? Are there new risks of an escalating war in the Middle East that involve more issues, more parties, and more danger? *See* ITAMAR RABINOVICH, MIDDLE EASTERN MAZE: ISRAEL, THE ARABS, AND THE REGION 1948–2022 (2023), and Thomas Friedman, *A Titanic Geopolitical Struggle Is Underway*, NEW YORK TIMES (Jan. 25, 2024), https://www.nytimes.com/2024/01/25/opinion/israel-gaza-war-ukraine.html. In his article, Friedman argues that the Ukraine and Israel-Gaza wars are linked. Russia and Iran have the common goal of destabilizing the West; Friedman calls this the "Resistance Network." Meanwhile, the United States, part of what Friedman refers to as the "Inclusion Network," is trying to create "a web of economic and technological interdependence" in the hope of promoting regional stability. How might reflecting on this linkage impact our choices of dispute resolution? As we turn to our third wicked problem in the next section, note that Russia, China, and Iran have all been linked to hybrid warfare as a means of achieving their goals.

IV. Hybrid Warfare

The third type of wicked problem is not necessarily violent; it is wicked because the parties and goals are unclear. The next two articles outline what makes hybrid warfare challenging and which negotiation and dispute resolution theories may lead to better responses.

Cynthia Alkon & Sanda Kaufman, *A Theory of Interests in the Context of Hybrid Warfare: It's Complex*

24 Cardozo J. Conflict Res. 583–584; 588–592; 583–584 (2023)

A. How Is Hybrid Warfare Different than Other Conflict Contexts?

Negotiation is conducted in a variety of contexts. Legal disputes range from traditional to contract negotiations to starting or ending a business relationship. Negotiation is also the means by which we arrive at public decisions and resolve conflicts in planning, policy, public administration, and environmental conflicts. International conflicts also involve negotiations.

For the purposes of our discussion, hybrid warfare is "covert subversion, disinformation, cyberattacks" and various illicit ways of collecting information about opponents. A number of possible hybrid warfare scenarios fit this broad definition. One example is cyber-attacks that include ransom demands to release databases frozen by malware. Hybrid warfare attacks could (and do) target key public services such as electricity or water supplies, or other municipality operations, with profoundly disrupting effects (which can be similar to those caused by natural disasters) on targeted communities. Another example is kidnappings—often of people in key organizational positions or believed to have access to resources. To contrast hybrid warfare to other negotiation contexts, we will examine scenarios where the direct parties making demands are identifiable, their actions go beyond simple criminal behavior, and they may have some kind of state actor or larger political group behind the action. We include cases where the identity of the attackers may not be fully known, as is common in cyber-attacks, but they have made a demand, such as to pay a certain amount of money to secure deblocking a computer system. In a traditional negotiation context, the counterparts are known, as are most or all parameters of the conflict or dispute. In hybrid warfare instances, such as a ransomware attack, we may not have the name, address, or role of the counterparts, or ways to reach out to them outside the parameters they specify. Therefore, at times, victims cannot act in ways beyond those dictated by their attackers and are forced to work within their timeline. Negotiators need to be aware of what to look for, both to realize when they might be in a hybrid warfare context and to devise better strategic decisions about how to handle hybrid warfare negotiations....

ii. Hybrid Warfare Context

Hybrid warfare presents several challenges, in part because the classical or expected negotiation conditions are unlikely to be present.

1. Parties

In a hybrid warfare situation, the attacked targets are unlikely to know the decision-making parties and their proxies. For example, the anonymous contact behind a ransomware attack may never become known. In an early 2023 ransomware attack targeting servers in multiple countries, the ransomware note said "Security Alert! We hacked your company successfully ... send money within 3 days otherwise we will expose some data and raise the price." The initial request was for $23,000 to be paid to a bitcoin wallet. Reportedly, the bitcoin wallet was different in each attack, and there was no website for the group. Under these circumstances, it is nearly impossible to find out who the attacker is. What country are they operating from? Is it just one? Are they part of a hacking group in Russia operating with full Russian governmental support, or are they rogue criminals in some other location or locations? In a kidnapping, it may be impossible to know who is behind the kidnappers themselves if the operation seems highly resourced. Who provided their weapons, their safehouses, and their transportation? There may be more than one responsible party or entity, and the relationships may be so layered that it is difficult or impossible to fully, or even partially, unwrap them.

In addition, in hybrid warfare, even when negotiators believe they have built a relationship with their counterparts, the relationship is illusory or unreliable due to the absence of expectations on either side that they will meet again and will be able to retaliate if deceived. An anonymous ransomware attacker may never be found. Even when the kidnappers have faces or names, negotiators can't trust any relationship they think they are building.

2. No Engagement Rules

Unlike in a classical negotiation environment, there are no engagement rules. Hybrid warfare happens across borders and legal systems and largely outside the protections that legal systems can provide, at least in terms of classical rules of engagement. There is no guarantee or way to enforce an agreement. For example, once a ransom is paid, there is no assurance that the attackers will release the data from a frozen computer system and no recourse if they do not. The cyber attacker could decide to double the demand or take the money and not release the key to unfreeze the system. The lack of rules particularly plagues cases where attackers succeed in remaining anonymous.

3. Time Horizon Unknown and Layered

If the attackers are unknown, then their ultimate goals are unknown, which means the time horizon is also unknown. Hybrid warfare operates with an unknown time horizon which may be layered—part of a broader, longer-term scheme—in unknown ways. A cyber-attack on a water treatment plant could be a first step in such a scheme, testing vulnerabilities and responses that will be foiled in later attacks on other utilities, municipal or state government websites, or databases.

4. Agents May Represent Their Own Interests

Negotiations in a hybrid warfare context may include agents and sometimes self-appointed agents. A known go-between for an insurgent group may negotiate on behalf of kidnappers or cyber-attackers. But are go-betweens fully, or even partially, representing the interests of their principal and guaranteeing that the principal will come through on commitments the agents promise? Or are they benefiting themselves? Duplicitous middlemen in ransomware attacks are so common that attackers have been known to warn their targets against using them. There are no ethical codes binding the attackers and no organizations such as bar associations to protect principals and to ensure that agents are working on their behalf. They may be, or they may just as well have an entirely different agenda. The uncertainty and risks can be overwhelming. However, professional hostage negotiators can be trustworthy agents for the victims.

5. Intervenors Not Available/Reliable

In a ransomware attack or kidnapping by an insurgent group, there may be no option other than direct negotiation under conditions dictated by the attackers. The anonymous ransomware attacker issues a take-it-or-leave-it offer which excludes engaging the services of a mediator (whose work usually depends on the ability to identify the parties' interests—not an option in hybrid warfare) or moving into an arbitration process (which also relies on conditions unavailable in hybrid warfare). Intervenors may be available, for example, in a kidnapping by a local insurgent group. But, as with concerns about who agents really work for, those representing themselves as mediators for a kidnapping negotiation may or may not be reliable. They could have an entirely different agenda.

6. Assume Deception, Not Good Faith

Hybrid warfare has the opposite characteristics of good-faith negotiations. It may be difficult or impossible to know what the attackers' final goals are, and they may include intangible elements such as destabilizing a government. In contrast, researchers have found Somalian pirates engaging in criminal kidnapping (for money rather than for larger political goals) could, and reportedly do, rely on "mutual assumption of good faith" as the kidnappers get an "expected rate of return." Likewise, in criminal ransomware attacks, there might be an increasing regularization of the practices; hacker groups, in response to criticism, have even promised not to target schools, hospitals, or non-profits. But whatever "standard" practices may emerge around some of these criminal practices, negotiators cannot rely on them holding true in every case when these same acts (kidnapping or ransomware attacks) are actually acts of hybrid warfare. Just as there are no ethical rules, codes, or licensing bodies to enforce rules in hybrid warfare scenarios, there should be no expectation that parties will operate in good faith. Instead, negotiators should prepare for and assume their counterparts are likely to be deceptive and are not bound by concerns about trust or reputation that could temper behaviors in other contexts.

7. Preparation Possibilities Are Limited

Due to all the unknowns—counterparts, rules of engagement, time horizon, agent and intervenor trustworthiness—negotiators cannot expect that they can prepare for a hybrid warfare negotiation as well as they might in classical negotiations. Moreover, in many hybrid warfare situations, negotiators have to assume deception and bad faith from their counterparts. All combined, this is a negotiation environment that does not lend itself to traditional preparation since the information which skilled negotiators usually seek (such as indications of the counterparts' interests) is mostly unavailable. This does not mean that negotiators shouldn't fully prepare, but the information they should seek will be different. They should strive to be as prepared as possible to face these kinds of situations. They should know their objectives, what they can agree to (i.e., the real monetary limits to ransom pay-offs), and bottom lines, if any. For example, in a ransomware attack, there might be a point at which the demands exceed the value of the blocked data or the cost of functional recovery by other means. Negotiators should also know as much as possible about the decision factors under their control. Negotiators should know the full range of options available to them, as well as what is out of their reach. However, they face serious limitations in terms of how prepared they can be going into a hybrid warfare negotiation regarding their counterparts and anyone beyond themselves and the party they are representing. And since each hybrid warfare attack is different, negotiators cannot draw on precedent or best practices as they can more reliably in classical negotiations.

Nancy A. Welsh, Sharon Press & Andrea Kupfer Schneider, *Negotiation Theories Engage Hybrid Warfare*

24 Cardozo J. Conflict Resol. 546–549; 569–570; 577–579 (2023)

II. Reframing the Response to Hybrid Warfare as Hybrid Conflict Management

Hybrid warfare and gray zone conflict are two terms that have arisen recently to highlight that in the relations between rival nations, "the space between war and peace is not an empty one—but a landscape churning with political, economic, and security competitions that require constant attention." This basic concept—nations will engage in constant, intense, and sometimes quite underhanded efforts to disrupt and destabilize each other—is not at all new. History is replete with examples of competing sovereigns working to erode each other's national economics, undermine their governments', and key institutions' legitimacy, encourage internal discord, and weaken their alliances with other sovereigns.

In recent years, though, following the fall of the Soviet Union and the rise of the United States as the only real superpower with overwhelming, military advantage and a tendency to engage in global policing, military and political scholars began to express fear that the U.S. had become less vigilant, less cognizant of the existence and threat of a still-churning, intensely competitive international landscape. According to some scholars. This inattention has the potential to reduce American foreign policy to a dangerously "reactive and tactical emphasis" on the use of military forces "by default."

At the start of the Cold War, U.S. diplomat George Kennan observed a similar state of affairs—i.e., a mode of conflict occurring in the midst of a time of peace—and coined the term "political warfare" to describe it:

> In the broadest definition, political warfare is the employment of all the means at a nation's command, short of war, to achieve its national objective. Such operations are both overt and covert. They range from such overt actions as political alliances, economic measures, and "white" propaganda to such covert operations as clandestine support of "friendly" foreign elements, "black" psychological warfare and even encouragement of underground resistance in hostile states.

Anyone who has read a John LeCarre novel has entered into a morally ambiguous netherworld of political warfare between nations. But a novel is not real, the experience is vicarious, and the world of real-life spies is quite distant from the lives of most of us. What differentiates gray zone conflict or hybrid warfare is that it is very real, very potent and it can—and does—strike quite close to our homes. This is due to two widely heralded developments—the pervasiveness of international trade and the amazing power and connection of the internet. Notice how all the following examples of hybrid warfare weaponize the connectivity of international trade or the internet.

- China regularly pressures foreign companies into sharing trade secrets and intellectual property with Chinese corporate partners, with particularly negative impacts on the U.S. companies whose business is based on specific technology rights, know-how, and data. These practices have weakened the U.S. economy while allowing China to accelerate the growth of its technology sector.
- China has made opportunistic investments in core U.S. companies when those companies required fresh capital to withstand the negative effects of the COVID pandemic.
- In December 2022, the U.S. agreed to a prisoner exchange that enabled the Russian government to gain the release of convicted Russian arms dealer Victor Bout, who was serving a prison sentence for conspiracy to kill Americans. This was in return for Russia's release of basketball star Brittney Griner, who was arrested for possession of a small amount of cannabis oil as she traveled from New York to join her off-season basketball team in the Russian Premier League
- Russian businessman and Putin Ally, Yevgeny Prigozhin, admitted recently that he had interfered in U.S. elections and would continue to do so "[c]arefully, accurately, surgically and in our own way, as we know how to do." Prigozhin has previously been accused of sponsoring Russian-based "troll farms" that seek to affect U.S. politics.

- In 2017, a computer virus traced back to the Russian government brought down Ukraine's computer systems and harmed many multinational firms, including US pharmaceutical manufacturer Merck. The firm then was unable to fulfill orders for its vaccine against human papillomavirus and had to borrow the U.S. government's entire emergency vaccine supply....

It seems to us that the kinds of problems raised by hybrid warfare situations are exactly what were contemplated by those who developed the term "wicked problem." As those of us engaged in this project grappled to understand what we were talking about—and even debated whether to use the terms hybrid warfare or hybrid conflict management—it was clear that the problem was most definitely ill-defined and was not just a technical issue but one that often includes social, political and moral aspects. Further, how one chooses to define the problem to be addressed—i.e., warfare vs. conflict management—implies a particular solution with contested values. Thus, this situation meets the first feature listed above.

Second, solutions to this issue often cannot be labeled good or bad; they can only be considered better or worse, good enough or not good enough. Whether a solution is good enough depends on the values and judgment of each of the parties, who will inevitably assess the problem and its potential solutions from their respective positions within the social context of the problem. In fact, many of the negotiation experts gravitated to describing this project in terms of hybrid conflict management as opposed to hybrid warfare, for this very reason. Managing these issues is not like traditional "warfare" where there is a winner and a loser. Instead, it will be more typical for the issues to unfold over time and even a "win" in one area may lead to a "loss" in another aspect.

Third, every hybrid warfare problem is unique and novel, because even if the technical elements appear similar from one situation to another, the social, political, and moral features are context specific.

Fourth, these problems contain an interconnected web of subproblems; every proposed solution to a part or the whole of the problem will affect other problems in the web. This is especially true given that the world is so interconnected. Decisions made in one area or context will almost certainly have a ripple effect in another unrelated area. For example, when a nation's government discovers a weakness in software, a decision must be made whether to reveal the weakness (to protect the nation's industries) or not reveal it to be able to exploit it later for its own cyberattacks.

Finally, we accept the last element in the definition of a wicked problem, which is that the only way to address it is to try solutions knowing that every solution is expensive and has lasting unintended consequences....

IV. Conclusion

As this Article has considered the application of negotiation theories, concepts and skills in response to hybrid warfare—in other words, as it has considered how these theories, concepts and skills might facilitate effective engagement in hybrid conflict management—the following have become clear: First, situations involving hybrid warfare are complex—not just complicated—and are only a component part of larger systems and dynamics. Second, these situations often trigger panic and a sense of crisis that can impede clear thinking. Third, both in anticipation of a hybrid warfare attack and after such an attack, these situations involve many potential players—i.e., internal and external constituents and coalition partners—not only the aggressor and the target. Fourth, working with those internal and external constituents and coalition partners before an attack can enable a potential target to develop more favorable BATNAs. Fifth and relatedly, preparation—which includes identifying internal and external constituents and coalition partners—is key.

This last point deserves additional elaboration. Hostage negotiation teams prepare for the crises that they know they will face, even though they do not know the specifics of what they will encounter. Firefighters similarly prepare, with the right equipment and with practice. Pilots use simulators and practice flights to prepare for all sorts of adverse conditions and emergencies they may face. In each of these instances, professionals are internalizing what they will need to do when a crisis emerges—as it inevitably will. In a sense, they are developing their "muscle memory" or their automatic response systems so that they will be able to fully attend to the larger context and situational specifics they will face. With practice, they can become "part of the flow," just as the wicked problem theorists recommend.

A nascent form of such practice is already beginning to emerge. We have become aware that some corporations are conducting internal trainings to prepare for hybrid warfare attacks, using simulations, engaging different parts of their organizations, identifying teams, establishing lines of communication and authority. The negotiation theories we have examined here affirm the value of this sort of preparation and also suggest additional avenues for exploration and preparation. Among the most important is identifying external constituencies and potential coalition partners including insurers, government agencies, and even industry competitors.

The authors of this Article also have been struck that the advice to be gleaned from this exploration of negotiation theories varies for different groups of people and organizations affected by hybrid warfare. For businesses that have been the victims of hybrid warfare—or fear that they could be:

- Do not assume the ability to respond effectively "on the fly." Be humble—and if we have not yet repeated this enough—prepare.
- Build internal teams and include outside advisors who work regularly with the business. Train/conduct simulations on responses. Understand lines of communication and authority. Identify and share interests, objective criteria, options, and BATNAs.
- Build networks of communication with industry peers and with appropriate government agencies. Share information on attacks and responses. Share information on training.

- Think broadly regarding relevant constituencies, identify influencers and begin reaching out and developing networks and coalitions.
- Slow down and pay attention to the system as a whole rather than rush to make an intervention in one area. Think about the presenting issue or example of hybrid warfare in the context of a system.

For governmental actors that have been the victims of hybrid warfare—or are assisting business or others who have been victims—these are some of the important lessons:

- Consider creating the hybrid conflict management equivalent of hostage negotiation teams, perhaps even by industry, to consult with and assist targets. And then, just as firefighter units provide backup to each other in the event of really huge and complex fires, these teams could provide backup to each other in the event of particularly widespread and complex examples of hybrid warfare.
- Develop expertise and collaborative relationships at all levels—federal, state and local—because all of these systems will also face attacks.

Last, the negotiation theories, concepts and skills discussed here suggest that the governmental actors responsible for preparing for or reducing susceptibility to hybrid warfare should:

- Start preparing early because many of the hybrid conflict management tools described here will require time and development.
- Promote laws that reduce the incentives to conceal attacks or blame others for an attack or fail to share information.
- Ensure that the agencies responsible for implementing diplomatic, informational, military, and economic tools of state power are in communication and coordination with each other.
- Network with other levels of government.
- Network with governments around the world facing similar threats to share best practices and build capacity.
- Identify citizens as important constituents and increase national awareness of hybrid warfare and its consequences—pointing out, for example, its impacts on social media, elections, supply chains—and train citizens to be ready to respond, just as many citizens are now trained in CPR to be ready to respond to an emergency until an ambulance arrives.
- Consider the larger system of which hybrid warfare is just one part. Perhaps governments around the world—many of which engage in some form of aggressive competition with other nations—could be interested in placing mutual limits on these competitive behaviors, negotiated and ratified through a treaty as has occurred with other powerful, mutually-destructive weapons.

Notes & Questions

1. Consider how different dispute resolution processes need to be engaged to deal with the different elements of hybrid warfare—internal negotiations within the target, collaborative processes with the government, other direct action with the perpetrator. Would you even consider some of these to be under the rubric of dispute resolution?
2. Can you imagine other kinds of "hybrid" or "grey" warfare or conflict? Can you match up particular possibilities with particular kinds of processes or remedies? Is that "clock-like" thinking? What kinds of preparation can you imagine doing for more "cloud-like" problems?

Further Reading

Abdel Monem Said Aly, Shai Feldman, & Khalil Shikaki, Arabs and Israelis (2022).

Gershon Baskin, The Negotiator: Freeing Gilad Schalit from Hamas (2013).

Gabriella Blum, Islands of Agreement: Managing Enduring Armed Rivalries (2007).

Encounter Point (Just Vision Pictures 2006).

Mark Galeotti, The Weaponization of Everything: A Field Guide to the New Way of War (2023).

Alexander Herman, The Parthenon Marbles Dispute (2023).

Alexander Herman, Restitution: The Return of Cultural Artefacts (2021).

Christopher Hitchens, The Elgin Marbles: Should They be Returned to Greece? (1987).

P. Terrence Hopmann, *Two Paradigms of Negotiations: Bargaining and Problem Solving*, 542 Annals Am. Acad. Pol'y & Soc. Sci. 24 (1995).

Russell Korobkin, *Exploring the Link Between Domestic Conflicts and Negotiation Failure in the Middle East*, 6 Nev. L.J. 388 (2006).

Daniel Kurtzer & Scott Lasensky, Negotiating Arab-Israeli Peace (2008).

John Merryman, *Two Ways of Thinking of Cultural Property*, 80 Am. J. Int'l L. 831–53 (1986).

One Day after Peace (Erez Laufer Films 2012).

Karl Popper, Objective Knowledge: An Evolutionary Approach (rev. ed. 1972).

Promises (Promises Film Project 2001).

Itamar Rabinovich, Middle Eastern Maze: Israel, The Arabs, and the Region 1948–2022 (2023).

Robert Ricigliano, Making Peace Last: A Toolbox for Sustainable Peacebuilding (2012).

Dennis Ross, The Missing Peace: The Inside Story of the Fight for Middle East Peace (2004).

Robert I. Rotberg, Israeli and Palestinian Narratives of Conflict: History's Double Helix (2006).

Side by Side: Parallel Histories of Israel-Palestine (Sami Adwan et al. eds., 2012).

Catharine Titi, The Parthenon Marbles and International Law (2023).

Sharon Waxman, Loot: The Battle over the Stolen Treasures of the Ancient World (2009).

Chapter 12

Ethics and Cross-Cultural Issues in International Dispute Resolution

By now you have learned about the many different kinds of international conflict resolution: formal (adjudication), less formal (arbitration), informal (negotiation), and mixed processes (mixed in terms of their formality and type of decisional process—e.g., hybrid, voluntary, command). You have seen that different forms of conflict resolution involve different kinds of parties from different kinds of national, ethnic, political, group, and individual cultures. This chapter reviews some of the issues in trying to develop guidelines and standards for ethical and best practices for parties, representatives, and third-party mediators, arbitrators, and judges when different processes and different legal systems and traditions are involved. There are no simple answers to some of the questions raised here, but it is important that participants in conflict resolution be attuned and sensitive to different cultures and traditions when acting in cross-cultural and national settings.

As you will see below, even formal legal systems (e.g., civil or common law) come to different conclusions on some important procedural and substantive issues. At philosophical and sociological levels we can ask if ethics are universal, including consideration of means, ends, and effects on others (Kantian); relative (utilitarian); focused on the consequences of those affected; or situational (variable by context). Some ethical issues that are impacted by cultural variability, and here there are questions about the appropriate units of analysis—national cultures, professional cultures (e.g., legal versus business), ethnic cultures, organizational cultures, and ultimately the fact that ethical decisions are made in a particular context (court, mediation, arbitration, diplomacy) by individuals acting either for themselves or as agents for others (countries, organizations, or clients). As you can see, there are many layers of ethical decision-making in international conflict resolution!

I. Introduction: Universal, Relative, or Situational Ethics

Thomas Donaldson, *Values in Tension: Ethics Away From Home*

Harv. Bus. Rev. (Sept.–Oct. 1996) 49; 52; 53; 55; 60; 61

When we leave home and cross our nation's boundaries, moral clarity often blurs. Without a backdrop of shared attitudes, and without familiar laws and judicial procedures that define standards of ethical conduct, certainty is elusive....

According to cultural relativism, no culture's ethics are better than any other's; therefore there are no international rights and wrongs. If the people of Indonesia tolerate the bribery of their public officials, so what? Their attitude is no better or worse than that of people in Denmark or Singapore who refuse to offer or accept bribes....

At the other end of the spectrum from cultural relativism is ethical imperialism, which directs people to do everywhere exactly as they do at home. Again, an understandably appealing approach but one that is clearly inadequate. Consider the large U.S. computer-products company that in 1993 introduced a course on sexual harassment in its Saudi Arabian facility. Under the banner of global consistency, instructors used the same approach to train Saudi Arabian managers that they had used with U.S. managers: the participants were asked to discuss a case in which a manager makes sexually explicit remarks to a new female employee over drinks in a bar. The instructors failed to consider how the exercise would work in a culture with strict conventions governing relationships between men and women....

The theory behind ethical imperialism is absolutism, which is based on three problematic principles. Absolutists believe that there is a single list of truths, that they can be expressed only with one set of concepts, and that they call for exactly the same behavior around the world.... The second problem with absolutism is the presumption that people must express moral truth using only one set of concepts. For instance, some absolutists insist that the language of basic rights provide the framework for any discussion of ethics. That means, though, that entire cultural traditions must be ignored. The notion of a right evolved with the rise of democracy in post-Renaissance Europe and the United States, but the term is not found in either Confucian or Buddhist traditions. We all learn ethics in the context of our particular cultures, and the power in the principles is deeply tied to the way in which they are expressed. Internationally accepted lists of moral principles, such as the United Nations' Universal Declaration of Human Rights, draw on many cultural and religious traditions. As philosopher Michael Walzer has noted, "There is no Esperanto of global ethics."

The third problem with absolutism is the belief in a global standard of ethical behavior. Context must shape ethical practice. Very low wages, for example, may be considered unethical in rich, advanced countries, but developing nations may be acting ethically if they encourage investment and improve living standards by accepting low wages. Likewise, when people are malnourished or starving, a government may be wise to use more fertilizer in order to improve crop yields, even though that means settling for relatively high levels of thermal water pollution....

But there are some hard truths that must guide managers' actions, a set of what I call *core human values*, which define minimum ethical standards for all companies. The right to good health and the right to economic advancement and an improved standard of living are two core human values. Another is what Westerners call the Golden Rule, which is recognizable in every major religious and ethical tradition around the world. In Book 15 of his *Analects*, for instance, Confucius counsels people to maintain reciprocity, or not to do to others what they do not want done to themselves.

Although no single list would satisfy every scholar, I believe it is possible to articulate three core values that incorporate the work of scores of theologians and philosophers around the world. To be broadly relevant, these values must include elements found in both Western and non-Western cultural and religious traditions.... Despite important differences between Western and non-Western cultural and religious traditions, both express shared attitudes about what it means to be human. First, individuals must not treat others simply as tools; in other words, they must recognize a person's value as a human being. Next, individuals and communities must treat people in ways that respect people's basic rights. Finally, members of a community must work together to support and improve the institutions on which the community depends. I call those three values *respect for human dignity*, *respect for basic rights*, and *good citizenship.*

Codes of conduct must be explicit to be useful, but they must also leave room for a manager to use his or her judgment in situations requiring cultural sensitivity. Host-country employees shouldn't be forced to adopt all home-country values and renounce their own. Again, Motorola's code is exemplary. First, it gives clear direction: "Employees of Motorola will respect the laws, customs, and traditions of each country in which they operate, but will, at the same time, engage in no course of conduct which, even if legal, customary, and accepted in any such country, could be deemed to be in violation of the accepted business ethics of Motorola or the laws of the United States relating to business ethics." After laying down such absolutes, Motorola's code then makes clear when individual judgment will be necessary. For example, employees may sometimes accept certain kinds of small gifts "in rare circumstances, where the refusal to accept a gift" would injure Motorola's "legitimate business interests." Under certain circumstances, such gifts "may be accepted so long as the gift inures to the benefit of Motorola" and not "to the benefit of the Motorola employee."

Striking the appropriate balance between providing clear direction and leaving room for individual judgment makes crafting corporate values statements and ethics codes one of the hardest tasks that executives confront. The words are only a start. A company's leaders need to refer often to their organization's credo and code and must themselves be credible, committed, and consistent....

The French pharmaceutical company Rhône-Poulenc Rorer has allowed foreign subsidiaries to augment lists of corporate ethical principles with their own suggestions. Texas Instruments has paid special attention to issues of international business ethics by creating the Global Business Practices Council, which is made up of managers from countries in which the company operates. With the overarching intent to create a "global ethics strategy, locally deployed," the council's mandate is to provide ethics education and create local processes that will help managers in the company's foreign business units resolve ethical conflicts....

Many people think of values as soft; to some they are usually unspoken. A South Seas island society uses the word *mokita*, which means, "the truth that everybody knows but nobody speaks." However difficult they are to articulate, values affect how we all behave. In a global business environment, values in tension are the rule rather than the exception. Without a company's commitment, statements of values and codes of ethics end up as empty platitudes that provide managers with no foundation for behaving ethically. Employees need and deserve more, and responsible members of the global business community can set examples for others to follow.

Notes & Questions

1. Can you identify "core values" for all processes of international dispute resolution?
2. Do ethical principles vary by type of process? (Recall from Chapter 7 Lon Fuller's claims that every dispute resolution process has its own special "integrity.")
3. You are counsel to a company which has a dispute with a middle-eastern oil producer. You agreed by contract to use international arbitration and the ICC (International Chamber of Commerce) as the administering tribunal. You are in the process of selecting arbitrators, and you choose one of the leading international arbitrators, a Swiss neutral, who has done dozens of cases for the ICC. The oil company strikes her selection, saying that they will not comply with any decision rendered by a woman adjudicator under their own national laws and traditions, and thus no arbitral award would be enforceable as they would object on public policy grounds (New York Convention, Art V 2(b)) to any enforcement of such an award in their country. What do you do? Do you go along with their choice to make sure any arbitral award would ultimately be enforceable? What else could you do? *See* Jan Paulsson, *Arbitration in Three Dimensions* (London School of Econ., Working Paper No. 2/2010), doi:10.2139/ssrn/1536093.

II. Formal Ethical Codes for International Lawyers

Leslie C. Levin, Lynn Mather, & Leny de Groot-van Leuwen, *The Impact of International Lawyer Organizations on Lawyer Regulation*

42 FORDHAM INT'L L.J. 407, 436–40 (2018)

While much of the scholarly attention devoted to lawyer regulation focuses on state or national actors, the impact of international lawyer organizations has been largely ignored. Increasingly, however, a number of such lawyer organizations influence the regulation of lawyers, including, inter alia, the International Bar Association ("IBA"), the Union Internationale des Avocats ("UIA"), the Council of Bars and Law Societies of Europe ("CCBE"), the Inter-American Bar Association ("IABA"), and the Pan-African Lawyers Union ("PALU"). So, too, do a few national lawyer organizations with an international reach, such as the American Bar Association ("ABA"). Thus, the term "international lawyer organization" is used here to include not just organizations with a truly international membership, but transnational lawyer organizations, as well as national lawyer organizations with a substantial international mission. These organizations are playing an important role in shaping lawyer admission requirements and ethical standards for lawyers, the structure of lawyer regulatory systems, and attitudes about the role of lawyers in civil society....

Commercial and political interests play a role in international organizations' efforts to influence lawyer regulation. International lawyer organizations seek to encourage the development and adoption of common rules of practice to insure predictability in commercial transactions and dispute resolution. These organizations also work to develop common rules that permit cross-border practice. Cross-border practice creates increased economic opportunities for lawyers (both domestically and internationally) and makes it easier for their clients to increase their profitability and efficiency by doing business abroad. Efforts to enable cross-border practice can also have a distinctly political objective. For example, for actors who strongly favor further European integration, facilitating the mobility of lawyers across the EU Member States advances that goal. Many international lawyer organizations also seek to influence lawyer regulation to promote the rule of law or human rights. Nations that are post-conflict or transitioning to democracies receive help from international lawyer organizations in developing national laws and institutions to advance these goals. Organizations like the International Commission of Jurists ("ICJ") work to establish the rule of law, in part by bolstering the ethics and independence of lawyers and judges. The International Legal Assistance Consortium ("ILAC"), which includes more than fifty national and international lawyer organizations, helps to coordinate efforts by international actors to build justice systems in post-conflict countries. The development of lawyer regulation consistent with the rule of law not only strengthens governments and their institutions, but can provide increased predictability and protection for businesses that are considering investing in those countries and may need to use local lawyers and courts....

At the same time, by exporting these standards, the international lawyer organizations are facilitating the increasing convergence of the law governing lawyers in different countries. This includes regulatory models that place significant responsibility for regulation of the profession within lawyer organizations rather than government institutions. These standards also impose substantial educational requirements on lawyers, including, in some cases, university-level training before licensing individuals to practice law. Lawyers must also maintain client confidentiality, avoid conflicts of interest, and perform their work honestly and competently. They can face discipline—often administered by lawyer organizations—if they do not....

Codes, Principles, and Guidelines for Conduct

All three organizations place great importance on developing professional standards of conduct for lawyers. They did not develop in isolation from one another, and it is useful to look at their evolution. The ABA was the first of the organizations to develop standards for lawyers, in its 1908 Canons of Professional Ethics. The original thirty-two canons varied greatly in their level of specificity and did not have the force of law unless they were adopted by a state. The ABA replaced the Canons in 1969 with the Code of Professional Responsibility, which was a mix of aspirational statements and specific disciplinary rules. The Code was replaced again in 1983 with the ABA Model Rules of Professional Conduct, which are detailed rules that have been adopted in some form by every US jurisdiction. Efforts to create an ethical code on the international level began in 1956, when the International Bar Association adopted its International Code of Ethics, a relatively short document that was designed for lawyers engaged in cross-border practice. It was intended as a "guide" as to what the IBA "considered to be a desirable course of conduct by all lawyers engaged in international practice." As Mary Daly noted, the IBA Code was "essentially a statement of norms" similar to the ABA Canons. The IBA revised the code in 1988, again in 2011 as the IBA International Principles on Conduct for the Legal Profession (the IBA Principles), and efforts are underway to substantially revise the code again. The IBA Principles were drafted with the assistance of Americans with deep knowledge of the ABA Model Rules. Each of the ten IBA Principles includes "commentary on how it could be used as a basis to establish codes of conduct for lawyers within different jurisdictions." The IBA Principles expressly state that they are not to be used to impose disciplinary sanctions and lack any enforcement mechanisms. But they do "serve as a basis on which codes of conduct may be established by the appropriate authorities for lawyers in any part of the world." And indeed, many jurisdictions have adopted the principles for their legal professions. The CCBE [Council of Bars and Law Societies of Europe] attempted to articulate standards of cross-border practice for EU lawyers starting with its 1977 Declaration of Perugia on the Principles of Professional Conduct of the Bars and Law Societies of the European Community. The Declaration contained eight ethical standards and was similar in style and format to the 1956 IBA Code. In 1982, the CCBE began to explore the feasibility of drafting a code of conduct that would articulate a set of principles that could be adopted as codes in the Member States. The CCBE was assisted by work done by the IBA, the UIA, and "in particular" by work done by the ABA on its codes of conduct. In 1988, the CCBE adopted a Code of Conduct for European Lawyers ("CCBE Code") to clarify ethical rules for European lawyers doing business across European borders....

The standards articulated by all three organizations share important commonalities. The IBA Principles are titled: independence, honesty/integrity/fairness, conflicts of interest, confidentiality/professional secrecy, clients' interest, lawyers' undertaking, clients' freedom, property of clients and third parties, competence, and fees. These issues are also addressed in the CCBE Code, the CCBE Charter, and the ABA Model Rules. Nevertheless, the content of lawyers' obligations in areas such as conflicts of interest, fees, confidentiality, and advertising differs. Concepts such as "lawyer independence" or "conflicts of interest" have different meanings or interpretations across jurisdictions. Moreover, the ABA Model Rules are much longer and more detailed than the IBA Principles or the CCBE Code. In the United States, lawyer codes are law-like rules, while elsewhere—and especially in civil law countries—such codes have been understood as "general norms of professional behavior."

Harry Arthurs, *A Global Code of Legal Ethics for the Transnational Legal Field?*

2 (1) Legal Ethics 66 (1999)

But however successful it may be in making the world safe for transnational law firms and legal practice, however reassuring for clients, governments, the public of traditional professional bodies, a global code of legal ethics is not likely to do much to enhance the honesty, diligence or civil mindedness of lawyers in the transnational legal field. To be effective, such a code after all must ultimately constrain the activities and challenge the interests of the powerful law firms which dominate the field. However, these same firms also dominate the IBA, and to a lesser extent, the CBBA; they can draft a global code in their own interests, and they can administer it in any way they find convenient. If they were really interested in an effective regulatory regime, these firms might have exhibited more diligence in using their national codes to enhance professional standards in the transnational field, in seeking sanctions against lawyers for conduct outside their home jurisdiction, or in accepting vicarious responsibility for the unethical acts of firm members stationed abroad.

III. Case Study: Ethics in International Arbitration

Carrie Menkel-Meadow, *Ethical Ordering in Transnational Legal Practice? A Review of Catherine A. Rogers's* Ethics in International Arbitration

29 Geo. J. Legal Ethics 207, 217–19 (2016)

In the last few decades, several organizations have drafted non-compulsory (because there is no formal enforcement mechanism) ethical standards for international arbitration, particularly, but not exclusively, in relation to issues of possible conflicts of interest of arbitrators and more recently for "attorney misconduct" in international practice.... In addition to the International Bar Association's Guidelines on Conflicts of Interests for International Arbitrators, several of the international arbitral institutions that have now promulgated their own rules or ethical guidelines (e.g., International Institute for Conflict Prevention and Resolution("CPR"), LCIA, the ICC and the International Centre for the Settlement of Investment Disputes ("ICSID")), have been urged to promulgate such standards. Even the ICC, the institution that most resisted development of ethical guidelines because of objections reviewed here, has now contemplated its own process of ethical guideline development. This may be a reaction to the claims that the arbitral institutions are engaged in a competition over the delivery of dispute resolution services and ethical standards are one of the distinguishing features of the competition.

Finally, when and if parties seek enforcement, non-recognition, vacatur, or annulment of an arbitral award under the New York Convention, national courts may rule on challenges to the award, implicating ethical issues, such as "evident partiality," or "corruption or bias" of the arbitrator or other grounds for non-recognition under the treaty and its applicable case law. Thus, those who may be asked to rule or opine on ethical issues include arbitration institutions, panels of or individual arbitrators, national courts, some international tribunals(ICSID), the World Trade Organization (WTO), formal governmental disciplinary bodies (national or state in the case of federal countries), non-governmental professional associations (e.g. International Bar Association) and other international or transnational bodies, or domestic bar associations and disciplinary bodies, and even private law firms or other practice units.

Thus, any regime of international arbitration ethics is likely to be "plural," both in substantive content (different legal regimes and different subject matter disputes) and in the bodies or institutions that may ultimately rule on whether some ethical standard, rule or guideline has been transgressed....

In what long has plagued international arbitral practice, American ethical and professional malpractice rules of witness preparation (and likely testimonial rehearsal and coaching) have openly collided with several legal traditions of explicitly prohibiting this practice. To varying degrees, France, Belgium, Germany and the United Kingdom have placed restrictions on how much pre-testimonial contact a lawyer may have with witnesses. Professor Rogers reviews the variations in treatment of this issue through national rules and practice and then explores "the elusive international consensus" that has gradually emerged from deliberations in the non-governmental International Bar Association. She then deftly explores how often compromise language in multi-system legal ethics formulations does not fully deal with the problem. Does the permitted witness "interviewing" allow payment for expert testimony? Does it permit access to confidential information held by an employee or former employee of an organizational client? Professor Rogers digs deep when she describes a simple solution recognized by bar rules in Switzerland, Paris and Brussels, which, recognizing this conflict of laws problem, allows an exception to the no preparation of witness rules if the lawyer is appearing in an international tribunal that has different rules. Professor Rogers describes these international "compromises" as too often taking a "binary" view of an issue without more fully exploring its complexity and possible variations. Disclosure of documents or "American-style" discovery is another such example explored here. While American lawyers (and increasingly British lawyers too) are permitted to "root around" in the documents, even if adverse, of the other party, most civil lawyers are not, and many such documents are independently protected by corporate and general privacy laws in Europe. Another product of our differentially technologized world includes variable duties to return documents (whether paper or electronic) that have inadvertently been delivered to the wrong parties, with different ethical and procedural traditions of document production. This too raises legal and cultural differences that probably require more specific, rather than more general, drafting in ethical standards.

Similar ethical cultural divides are explored in the book with respect to conflicts of interests. The United States has the most detailed and particularized rules about what constitutes a conflict (prior clients, former government service, law firm imputation conflict if one member has a conflict, business dealings with clients, acceptance of gifts or payments for legal services by third parties, organizational conflicts). Other nations have either a different conception of "conflicts of interest" (France's notion of avoidance of "indelicacy") or an absence of formal regulation and sanction. Different configurations of practice in different countries, including Asia, South America, and Europe with smaller units of practice or shared office arrangements without stringent conflicts rules have led in recent years to more complicated challenges to international arbitrators coming from the same legal "chambers" or offices as some of the advocating lawyers. At the level of award enforcement and challenges, some national systems discipline such conflicts (as does the U.S. in some contexts) only when actual harm has been shown (e.g., revelation of confidential information, disloyal conduct, rulings in favor of former clients, actual financial interests in outcomes). As Professor Rogers suggests, some arbitral bodies are reluctant to rule on such challenges, claiming lack of authority or lack of standards in international settings. I would suggest they are also reluctant to rule on this issue because they are often implicitly ruling on their own potential conflicts of interest (of either the past, or the future, as they contemplate further work in the field, as either arbitrators or representatives, known as "upstream" conflicts). Another area of different understandings of basic principles occurs with client confidentiality and attorney-client privilege, especially as it affects representatives of corporate or organizational bodies. In many civil law countries confidentiality is both broader and narrower than in the United States. Corporate or trade secrets communicated from client to lawyer are often protected from disclosure by the lawyer, but the advice from the lawyer to the client is not. Also contrary to American rules and practices, in some jurisdictions, lawyers may have to keep their own communications with each other across adversary lines confidential from their own clients! And, not unlike the variations among states in the United States, different national systems require different responses from lawyers who learn about client wrongdoing. Issues of what can be argued or treated as evidence in international arbitrations may turn on different ethical rules and practices in different national systems which require international arbitrators to make evidentiary rulings that may, in fact, implicate ethical requirements, with potential for discipline or other penalty within a lawyer's (or witness's) home country.

Perhaps the trickiest and most common ethical differences have over time been the rules and practices of ex parte communication. American parties and lawyers have moved into international arbitration with their domestic customs of choosing partisan arbitrators with whom they continued to have private and advocacy conversations during the arbitration proceedings. The tradition of international arbitration most often requires "impartiality" or "neutrality" at least after all the arbitrators are chosen. Over time even the American arbitration institutions, such as the American Arbitration Association and its international arm, International Center for Dispute Resolution, have moved to a notion of "impartiality" and prohibition of most ex parte communication between representatives and arbitrators. Ironically, ex parte communications continues to be a cultural issue as tradition and practice has not generally prohibited meals and social contacts among arbitrators, lawyers and parties in Continental practice. Now, in some cases involving China and other Asian countries, blurring of roles from mediator to arbitrator or other function has blurred some of the lines of communication, both prohibited and permitted. Just as in American med-arb (mediation-arbitration hybrids) dispute resolution practice, there can be issues with separate meetings (caucuses) with mediators who try to settle cases and then later serve as arbitrators deciding matters on the basis of secret or non-shared or responded to information. These issues, described with several case examples, demonstrate the great variety of practices and confusion that may occur when different nationals, subject to different, or no rules at all, participate in an international hearing. Particular arbitral tribunals can set their own single case "rules" for their proceedings. Increasingly, the rules of each of the arbitration institutions may provide for default rules on the issue of ex parte communications and expectations of impartiality. However, if the lawyers have different cultural expectations about what is appropriate (conversations, sharing a meal, staying in the same hotel), there may be different behaviors with respect to communications that can have an effect on outcomes, and can lead to post-award challenges.

Professor Rogers does not offer a specific solution to these issues, but she demonstrates how cultural practices may differ, but also may be converging, in practice, if not in formal rules or decisions.

Harder to regulate in any realistic way is the issue Professor Rogers calls "creativity, aggression and bad manners." These are the different cultural practices in the legal profession and within different corporate cultures. Non-Americans complain both about the aggressiveness of American lawyers generally and about cross-examination practice in particular in international arbitration. Non-Americans also are often surprised by the "creativity" of legal arguments, departing from formal rules, contracts and laws, with creative interpretations of evidence and contract terms as "zealous representation" of clients. As Professor Rogers notes, arbitrators and American courts in enforcement proceedings are now more likely to "sanction" with fines or other penalties (including reduced attorney's fees) particularly outrageous behaviors. Still, it remains unclear what powers arbitrators or arbitration institutions have to either curb this behavior or socialize for greater "civility." Related to using sanctioning powers is the issue of variations in how attorney's fees are provided for in different national cultures, including American style contingent fees or British and some Continental "loser pays" attorneys' fees shifting rules. These kinds of fee issues are more likely to be dealt with explicitly in international institutional rules but the effects of attorneys' fees rules on different behavioral assumptions in practice is less easily reconciled....

What other models of ethical regulation of arbitration might there be? What are comparisons to the current efforts at ethical regulation of counsel and judges in international tribunals? Are there other examples of transnational professional regulations such as international pilots, admiralty rules, public health professionals (World Health Organization), private international medical and emergency service providers, e.g. International Red Cross, Medicens Sans Frontiers, Antarctic and other research scientists, Interpol, anti-terrorism transnational professionals, amongst others, we should look to?

In my own work on legal ethics over the decades it has been instructive to look not only at the pluralism within our own profession (differences for prosecutors, big firm lawyers, mediators) but to see how other professions within our own country deal with similar issues (accountants for disclosure of economic fraud, doctors and nurses for informed consent and patient-client counseling, engineers and architects for substantive liability and outcome assessment, clergy for confidentiality protections, etc.). To what other professions might international arbitrators be compared? Is there a danger that American legal ethics, more developed in both codifications and case law, will "dominate" the development of international legal ethical standards, as American adversary practice has affected the conduct of arbitration practice? How can we insure full international participation in the creation and implementation of ethical standards for international arbitration?

Case Study: Ethical Dining

You are conducting a hotly contested arbitration under ICC Arbitration Rules. You represent an American manufacturer who claims a French supplier has provided substandard goods. So far there have been three days of lawyer arguments and the beginning of testimony from expert witnesses. You schedule a dinner with your next expert witness at a nice restaurant near your hotel, and when you get there, you see that the lawyer for the French company is having dinner with two of the three arbitrators—the one arbitrator that the lawyer selected and the "neutral" chair (you selected the third arbitrator according to ICC Rules). The next day, the French lawyer objects to the arbitral panel that you were inappropriately preparing a witness before testimony, and then you protest to them about the dinner two of them had with your opposing counsel. What should the arbitral panel do about these objections? By what standards and authority?

IBA Guidelines on Conflicts of Interest in International Arbitration

(2014)

(2) Conflicts of Interest

(a) An arbitrator shall decline to accept an appointment or, if the arbitration has already been commenced, refuse to continue to act as an arbitrator, if he or she has any doubt as to his or her ability to be impartial or independent.

(b) The same principle applies if facts or circumstances exist, or have arisen since the appointment, which, from the point of view of a reasonable third person having knowledge of the relevant facts and circumstances, would give rise to justifiable doubts as to the arbitrator's impartiality or independence, unless the parties have accepted the arbitrator in accordance with the requirements set out in General Standard 4.

(c) Doubts are justifiable if a reasonable third person, having knowledge of the relevant facts and circumstances, would reach the conclusion that there is a likelihood that the arbitrator may be influenced by factors other than the merits of the case as presented by the parties in reaching his or her decision.

(d) Justifiable doubts necessarily exist as to the arbitrator's impartiality or independence in any of the situations described in the Non-Waivable Red List.

Explanation to General Standard 2:

(a) If the arbitrator has doubts as to his or her ability to be impartial and independent, the arbitrator must decline the appointment. This standard should apply regardless of the stage of the proceedings. This is a basic principle that is spelled out in these Guidelines in order to avoid confusion and to foster confidence in the arbitral process.

(b) In order for standards to be applied as consistently as possible, the test for disqualification is an objective one. The wording 'impartiality or independence' derives from the widely adopted Article 12 of the United Nations Commission on International Trade Law (UNCITRAL) Model Law, and the use of an appearance test based on justifiable doubts as to the impartiality or independence of the arbitrator, as provided in Article 12(2) of the UNCITRAL Model Law, is to be applied objectively (a 'reasonable third person test'). Again, as described in the Explanation to General Standard 3(e), this standard applies regardless of the stage of the proceedings.

(c) Laws and rules that rely on the standard of justifiable doubts often do not define that standard. This General Standard is intended to provide some context for making this determination.

(d) The Non-Waivable Red List describes circumstances that necessarily raise justifiable doubts as to the arbitrator's impartiality or independence. For example, because no one is allowed to be his or her own judge, there cannot be identity between an arbitrator and a party. The parties, therefore, cannot waive the conflict of interest arising in such a situation.

(3) Disclosure by the Arbitrator

(a) If facts or circumstances exist that may, in the eyes of the parties, give rise to doubts as to the arbitrator's impartiality or independence, the arbitrator shall disclose such facts or circumstances to the parties, the arbitration institution or other appointing authority (if any, and if so required by the applicable institutional rules) and the co-arbitrators, if any, prior to accepting his or her appointment or, if thereafter, as soon as he or she learns of them.

(b) An advance declaration or waiver in relation to possible conflicts of interest arising from facts and circumstances that may arise in the future does not discharge the arbitrator's ongoing duty of disclosure under General Standard 3(a).

(c) It follows from General Standards 1 and 2(a) that an arbitrator who has made a disclosure considers himself or herself to be impartial and independent of the parties, despite the disclosed facts, and, therefore, capable of performing his or her duties as arbitrator. Otherwise, he or she would have declined the nomination or appointment at the outset, or resigned.

(d) Any doubt as to whether an arbitrator should disclose certain facts or circumstances should be resolved in favour of disclosure.

(e) When considering whether facts or circumstances exist that should be disclosed, the arbitrator shall not take into account whether the arbitration is at the beginning or at a later stage.

Explanation to General Standard 3:

(a) The arbitrator's duty to disclose under General Standard 3(a) rests on the principle that the parties have an interest in being fully informed of any facts or circumstances that may be relevant in their view. Accordingly, General Standard 3(d) provides that any doubt as to whether certain facts or circumstances should be disclosed should be resolved in favour of disclosure. However, situations that, such as those set out in the Green List, could never lead to disqualification under the objective test set out in General Standard 2, need not be disclosed. As reflected in General Standard 3(c), a disclosure does not imply that the disclosed facts are such as to disqualify the arbitrator under General Standard 2. The duty of disclosure under General Standard 3(a) is ongoing in nature....

(6) Relationships

(a) The arbitrator is in principle considered to bear the identity of his or her law firm, but when considering the relevance of facts or circumstances to determine whether a potential conflict of interest exists, or whether disclosure should be made, the activities of an arbitrator's law firm, if any, and the relationship of the arbitrator with the law firm, should be considered in each individual case. The fact that the activities of the arbitrator's firm involve one of the parties shall not necessarily constitute a source of such conflict, or a reason for disclosure. Similarly, if one of the parties is a member of a group with which the arbitrator's firm has a relationship, such fact should be considered in each individual case, but shall not necessarily constitute by itself a source of a conflict of interest, or a reason for disclosure.

(b) If one of the parties is a legal entity, any legal or physical person having a controlling influence on the legal entity, or a direct economic interest in, or a duty to indemnify a party for, the award to be rendered in the arbitration, may be considered to bear the identity of such party....

(7) Duty of the Parties and the Arbitrator

(a) A party shall inform an arbitrator, the Arbitral Tribunal, the other parties and the arbitration institution or other appointing authority (if any) of any relationship, direct or indirect, between the arbitrator and the party (or another company of the same group of companies, or an individual having a controlling influence on the party in the arbitration), or between the arbitrator and any person or entity with a direct economic interest in, or a duty to indemnify a party for, the award to be rendered in the arbitration. The party shall do so on its own initiative at the earliest opportunity.

(b) A party shall inform an arbitrator, the Arbitral Tribunal, the other parties and the arbitration institution or other appointing authority (if any) of the identity of its counsel appearing in the arbitration, as well as of any relationship, including membership of the same barristers' chambers, between its counsel and the arbitrator. The party shall do so on its own initiative at the earliest opportunity, and upon any change in its counsel team.

(c) In order to comply with General Standard 7(a), a party shall perform reasonable enquiries and provide any relevant information available to it.

(d) An arbitrator is under a duty to make reasonable enquiries to identify any conflict of interest, as well as any facts or circumstances that may reasonably give rise to doubts as to his or her impartiality or independence. Failure to disclose a conflict is not excused by lack of knowledge, if the arbitrator does not perform such reasonable enquiries....

Part II: Practical Application of the General Standards

1. If the Guidelines are to have an important practical influence, they should address situations that are likely to occur in today's arbitration practice and should provide specific guidance to arbitrators, parties, institutions and courts as to which situations do or do not constitute conflicts of interest, or should or should not be disclosed. For this purpose, the Guidelines categorize situations that may occur in the following Application Lists. These lists cannot cover every situation. In all cases, the General Standards should control the outcome.

2. *The Red List* consists of two parts: 'a Non-Waivable Red List' (see General Standards 2(d) and 4(b)); and 'a Waivable Red List' (see General Standard 4(c)). These lists are non-exhaustive and detail specific situations that, depending on the facts of a given case, give rise to justifiable doubts as to the arbitrator's impartiality and independence. That is, in these circumstances, an objective conflict of interest exists from the point of view of a reasonable third person having knowledge of the relevant facts and circumstances (see General Standard 2(b)). The Non-Waivable Red List includes situations deriving from the overriding principle that no person can be his or her own judge. Therefore, acceptance of such a situation cannot cure the conflict. The Waivable Red List covers situations that are serious but not as severe. Because of their seriousness, unlike circumstances described in the Orange List, these situations should be considered waivable, but only if and when the parties, being aware of the conflict of interest situation, expressly state their willingness to have such a person act as arbitrator, as set forth in General Standard 4(c).

3. *The Orange List* is a non-exhaustive list of specific situations that, depending on the facts of a given case, may, in the eyes of the parties, give rise to doubts as to the arbitrator's impartiality or independence. The Orange List thus reflects situations that would fall under General Standard 3(a), with the consequence that the arbitrator has a duty to disclose such situations. In all these situations, the parties are deemed to have accepted the arbitrator if, after disclosure, no timely objection is made, as established in General Standard 4(a).

4. Disclosure does not imply the existence of a conflict of interest; nor should it by itself result either in a disqualification of the arbitrator, or in a presumption regarding disqualification. The purpose of the disclosure is to inform the parties of a situation that they may wish to explore further in order to determine whether objectively—that is, from the point of view of a reasonable third person having knowledge of the relevant facts and circumstances—there are justifiable doubts as to the arbitrator's impartiality or independence. If the conclusion is that there are no justifiable doubts, the arbitrator can act. Apart from the situations covered by the Non-Waivable Red List, he or she can also act if there is no timely objection by the parties or, in situations covered by the Waivable Red List, if there is a specific acceptance by the parties in accordance with General Standard 4(c). If a party challenges the arbitrator, he or she can nevertheless

act, if the authority that rules on the challenge decides that the challenge does not meet the objective test for disqualification.

5. A later challenge based on the fact that an arbitrator did not disclose such facts or circumstances should not result automatically in non-appointment, later disqualification or a successful challenge to any award. Nondisclosure cannot by itself make an arbitrator partial or lacking independence: only the facts or circumstances that he or she failed to disclose can do so.

6. Situations not listed in the Orange List or falling outside the time limits used in some of the Orange List situations are generally not subject to disclosure. However, an arbitrator needs to assess on a case-by-case basis whether a given situation, even though not mentioned in the Orange List, is nevertheless such as to give rise to justifiable doubts as to his or her impartiality or independence. Because the Orange List is a non-exhaustive list of examples, there may be situations not mentioned, which, depending on the circumstances, may need to be disclosed by an arbitrator. Such may be the case, for example, in the event of repeat past appointments by the same party or the same counsel beyond the three-year period provided for in the Orange List, or when an arbitrator concurrently acts as counsel in an unrelated case in which similar issues of law are raised. Likewise, an appointment made by the same party or the same counsel appearing before an arbitrator, while the case is ongoing, may also have to be disclosed, depending on the circumstances. While the Guidelines do not require disclosure of the fact that an arbitrator concurrently serves, or has in the past served, on the same Arbitral Tribunal with another member of the tribunal, or with one of the counsel in the current proceedings, an arbitrator should assess on a case-by-case basis whether the fact of having frequently served as counsel with, or as an arbitrator on, Arbitral Tribunals with another member of the tribunal may create a perceived imbalance within the tribunal. If the conclusion is 'yes', the arbitrator should consider a disclosure.

7. *The Green List* is a non-exhaustive list of specific situations where no appearance and no actual conflict of interest exists from an objective point of view. Thus, the arbitrator has no duty to disclose situations falling within the Green List. As stated in the Explanation to General Standard 3(a), there should be a limit to disclosure, based on reasonableness; in some situations, an objective test should prevail over the purely subjective test of 'the eyes' of the parties.

8. The borderline between the categories that comprise the Lists can be thin. It can be debated whether a certain situation should be on one List instead of another. Also, the Lists contain, for various situations, general terms such as 'significant' and 'relevant'. The Lists reflect international principles and best practices to the extent possible. Further definition of the norms, which are to be interpreted reasonably in light of the facts and circumstances in each case, would be counterproductive.

1. Non-Waivable Red List

1.1 There is an identity between a party and the arbitrator, or the arbitrator is a legal representative or employee of an entity that is a party in the arbitration.

1.2 The arbitrator is a manager, director or member of the supervisory board, or has a controlling influence on one of the parties or an entity that has a direct economic interest in the award to be rendered in the arbitration.

1.3 The arbitrator has a significant financial or personal interest in one of the parties, or the outcome of the case.

1.4 The arbitrator or his or her firm regularly advises the party, or an affiliate of the party, and the arbitrator or his or her firm derives significant financial income therefrom.

2. Waivable Red List

2.1 Relationship of the arbitrator to the dispute

2.1.1 The arbitrator has given legal advice, or provided an expert opinion, on the dispute to a party or an affiliate of one of the parties.

2.1.2 The arbitrator had a prior involvement in the dispute.

2.2 Arbitrator's direct or indirect interest in the dispute

2.2.1 The arbitrator holds shares, either directly or indirectly, in one of the parties, or an affiliate of one of the parties, this party or an affiliate being privately held.

2.2.2 A close family member[1] [3] of the arbitrator has a significant financial interest in the outcome of the dispute.

2.2.3 The arbitrator, or a close family member of the arbitrator, has a close relationship with a non-party who may be liable to recourse on the part of the unsuccessful party in the dispute.

2.3 Arbitrator's relationship with the parties or counsel

2.3.1 The arbitrator currently represents or advises one of the parties, or an affiliate of one of the parties.

2.3.2 The arbitrator currently represents or advises the lawyer or law firm acting as counsel for one of the parties.

2.3.3 The arbitrator is a lawyer in the same law firm as the counsel to one of the parties.

2.3.4 The arbitrator is a manager, director or member of the supervisory board, or has a controlling influence in an affiliate[2] [4] of one of the parties, if the affiliate is directly involved in the matters in dispute in the arbitration.

2.3.5 The arbitrator's law firm had a previous but terminated involvement in the case without the arbitrator being involved himself or herself.

---

1. [3] Throughout the Application Lists, the term 'close family member' refers to a: spouse, sibling, child, parent or life partner, in addition to any other family member with whom a close relationship exists.

2. [4] Throughout the Application Lists, the term 'affiliate' encompasses all companies in a group of companies, including the parent company.

2.3.6 The arbitrator's law firm currently has a significant commercial relationship with one of the parties, or an affiliate of one of the parties.

2.3.7 The arbitrator regularly advises one of the parties, or an affiliate of one of the parties, but neither the arbitrator nor his or her firm derives a significant financial income therefrom.

2.3.8 The arbitrator has a close family relationship with one of the parties, or with a manager, director or member of the supervisory board, or any person having a controlling influence in one of the parties, or an affiliate of one of the parties, or with a counsel representing a party.

2.3.9 A close family member of the arbitrator has a significant financial or personal interest in one of the parties, or an affiliate of one of the parties.

3. Orange List

3.1 Previous services for one of the parties or other involvement in the case

3.1.1 The arbitrator has, within the past three years, served as counsel for one of the parties, or an affiliate of one of the parties, or has previously advised or been consulted by the party, or an affiliate of the party, making the appointment in an unrelated matter, but the arbitrator and the party, or the affiliate of the party, have no ongoing relationship.

3.1.2 The arbitrator has, within the past three years, served as counsel against one of the parties, or an affiliate of one of the parties, in an unrelated matter.

3.1.3 The arbitrator has, within the past three years, been appointed as arbitrator on two or more occasions by one of the parties, or an affiliate of one of the parties. It may be the practice in certain types of arbitration, such as maritime, sports or commodities arbitration, to draw arbitrators from a smaller or specialised pool of individuals.

3.1.4 The arbitrator's law firm has, within the past three years, acted for or against one of the parties, or an affiliate of one of the parties, in an unrelated matter without the involvement of the arbitrator.

3.1.5 The arbitrator currently serves, or has served within the past three years, as arbitrator in another arbitration on a related issue involving one of the parties, or an affiliate of one of the parties.

3.2 Current services for one of the parties.

3.2.1 The arbitrator's law firm is currently rendering services to one of the parties, or to an affiliate of one of the parties, without creating a significant commercial relationship for the law firm and without the involvement of the arbitrator.

3.2.2 A law firm or other legal organisation that shares significant fees or other revenues with the arbitrator's law firm renders services to one of the parties, or an affiliate of one of the parties, before the Arbitral Tribunal.

3.2.3 The arbitrator or his or her firm represents a party, or an affiliate of one of the parties to the arbitration, on a regular basis, but such representation does not concern the current dispute.

3.3 Relationship between an arbitrator and another arbitrator or counsel.

3.3.1 The arbitrator and another arbitrator are lawyers in the same law firm.

3.3.2 The arbitrator and another arbitrator, or the counsel for one of the parties, are members of the same barristers' chambers. frequently appoint the same arbitrator in different cases, no disclosure of this fact is required, where all parties in the arbitration should be familiar with such custom and practice.

3.3.3 The arbitrator was, within the past three years, a partner of, or otherwise affiliated with, another arbitrator or any of the counsel in the arbitration.

3.3.4 A lawyer in the arbitrator's law firm is an arbitrator in another dispute involving the same party or parties, or an affiliate of one of the parties.

3.3.5 A close family member of the arbitrator is a partner or employee of the law firm representing one of the parties, but is not assisting with the dispute.

3.3.6 A close personal friendship exists between an arbitrator and a counsel of a party.

3.3.7 Enmity exists between an arbitrator and counsel appearing in the arbitration.

3.3.8 The arbitrator has, within the past three years, been appointed on more than three occasions by the same counsel, or the same law firm.

3.3.9 The arbitrator and another arbitrator, or counsel for one of the parties in the arbitration, currently act or have acted together within the past three years as cocounsel.

3.4 Relationship between arbitrator and party and others involved in the arbitration

3.4.1 The arbitrator's law firm is currently acting adversely to one of the parties, or an affiliate of one of the parties.

3.4.2 The arbitrator has been associated with a party, or an affiliate of one of the parties, in a professional capacity, such as a former employee or partner.

3.4.3 A close personal friendship exists between an arbitrator and a manager or director or a member of the supervisory board of: a party; an entity that has a direct economic interest in the award to be rendered in the arbitration; or any person having a controlling influence, such as a controlling shareholder interest, on one of the parties or an affiliate of one of the parties or a witness or expert.

3.4.4 Enmity exists between an arbitrator and a manager or director or a member of the supervisory board of: a party; an entity that has a direct economic interest in the award; or any person having a controlling influence in one of the parties or an affiliate of one of the parties or a witness or expert.

3.4.5 If the arbitrator is a former judge, he or she has, within the past three years, heard a significant case involving one of the parties, or an affiliate of one of the parties.

3.5 Other circumstances

3.5.1 The arbitrator holds shares, either directly or indirectly, that by reason of number or denomination constitute a material holding in one of the parties, or an affiliate of one of the parties, this party or affiliate being publicly listed.

3.5.2 The arbitrator has publicly advocated a position on the case, whether in a published paper, or speech, or otherwise.

3.5.3 The arbitrator holds a position with the appointing authority with respect to the dispute.

3.5.4 The arbitrator is a manager, director or member of the supervisory board, or has a controlling influence on an affiliate of one of the parties, where the affiliate is not directly involved in the matters in dispute in the arbitration.

4. Green List

4.1 Previously expressed legal opinions

4.1.1 The arbitrator has previously expressed a legal opinion (such as in a law review article or public lecture) concerning an issue that also arises in the arbitration (but this opinion is not focused on the case).

4.2 Current services for one of the parties

4.2.1 A firm, in association or in alliance with the arbitrator's law firm, but that does not share significant fees or other revenues with the arbitrator's law firm, renders services to one of the parties, or an affiliate of one of the parties, in an unrelated matter.

4.3 Contacts with another arbitrator, or with counsel for one of the parties

4.3.1 The arbitrator has a relationship with another arbitrator, or with the counsel for one of the parties, through membership in the same professional association, or social or charitable organisation, or through a social media network.

4.3.2 The arbitrator and counsel for one of the parties have previously served together as arbitrators.

4.3.3 The arbitrator teaches in the same faculty or school as another arbitrator or counsel to one of the parties, or serves as an officer of a professional association or social or charitable organisation with another arbitrator or counsel for one of the parties.

4.3.4 The arbitrator was a speaker, moderator or organiser in one or more conferences, or participated in seminars or working parties of a professional, social or charitable organisation, with another arbitrator or counsel to the parties.

4.4 Contacts between the arbitrator and one of the parties

4.4.1 The arbitrator has had an initial contact with a party, or an affiliate of a party (or their counsel) prior to appointment, if this contact is limited to the arbitrator's availability and qualifications to serve, or to the names of possible candidates for a chairperson, and did not address the merits or procedural aspects of the dispute, other than to provide the arbitrator with a basic understanding of the case.

4.4.2 The arbitrator holds an insignificant amount of shares in one of the parties, or an affiliate of one of the parties, which is publicly listed.

4.4.3 The arbitrator and a manager, director or member of the supervisory board, or any person having a controlling influence on one of the parties, or an affiliate of one of the parties, have worked together as joint experts, or in another professional capacity, including as arbitrators in the same case.

4.4.4 The arbitrator has a relationship with one of the parties or its affiliates through a social media network.

Notes & Questions

1. How does this set of guidelines compare to the ABA Model Rules of Professional Conduct or the ACR/ABA/AAA or CPR Model Standards or Codes of Conduct for lawyers, arbitrators, and mediators?
2. How are these guidelines enforced?

IV. Ethics, Implicit Bias, and Best Practices for Online Dispute Resolution

Elayne E. Greenberg, *Zooming In on Neutrals' Implicit 'isms*

15 NYSBA New York Disp. Resol. Law., no. 2, 2022, 9–11

Video conferencing, extolled for its economic and efficiency benefits, has now become an accepted option in the "new normal" of dispute resolution practice. Consequently, our professional discussions about video conferencing have advanced from sharing the mechanics of "how to" conduct an arbitration or mediation on Zoom to more nuanced explorations about the appropriate use of video conferencing. This column contributes to this exploration by questioning how dispute resolution processes conducted via video conferencing might trigger the implicit biases of arbitrators and mediators and compromise a neutral's ethical obligation to be impartial. *When a neutral conducts their dispute resolution processes via video conferencing, how might communicating via video conferencing amplify a neutral's existing implicit biases or create new implicit biases that shape a neutral's assessment of the participants?*

Many neutrals, as part of their professional training, may have taken implicit bias training to learn debiasing strategies that help mitigate their implicit biases when conducting in-person dispute resolution processes. However, emerging research and anecdotal reports reveal that video conferencing, as a different communication channel, may also trigger implicit biases, albeit in a different context.

One glaring example about how context matters took place in March 2020, when the court, in response to COVID-19 health concerns, shifted those court-connected dispute resolution processes previously conducted in-person to video conferencing. Those participants who did not have computers, reliable access to broadband, and technological competence had to participate via their cell phones. In this unfamiliar context, were different biases evoked than those that might be anticipated if the dispute resolution process took place in-person? Chief Judge Janet DiFiore had adopted a "zero tolerance" policy for discrimination and a commitment to equitable justice for all in the New York State courts and responded quickly to these concerns. The chief judge appointed the Honorable Edwina Mendelson to serve as deputy chief administrative judge for justice initiatives, who, with the chief judge's support, took affirmative steps to narrow this digital divide and ensure meaningful participation in dispute resolution processes for those participants who needed it. Could this fix address unconscious reactions and implicit bias?...

Video conferencing as a communication channel allows all participants to see each other from the shoulder up. However, as neutrals try to equate this video conference "seeing" with the "in-person" seeing, neutrals experience a depletion of their cognitive resources, or Zoom fatigue. As one illustration, neutrals make eye contact with the participants on video conferencing by looking at the camera, not directly at the parties on the screen. Many neutrals, including this author, still find looking into the camera instead of directly in the eyes of the participants counterintuitive, requiring conscious energy. A second cognitive burden is that the mediators and arbitrators observe themselves and adjust their reactions when they are participating via video conferencing. Third, we have all experienced the added energy drain of trying to discern participants who are in poor light or have uneven connections. If participating in video conferencing creates Zoom fatigue, neutrals may find they have less energy available for combating implicit biases....

Another visual that might trigger a neutral's implicit biases is the background that participants are using, whether virtual or the participant's natural backgrounds. When we are all together in a conference room, we all have the same "background." One neutral acknowledged that when a mediation participant uses a virtual background, the mediator can't help but wonder what that person is hiding. In another example, my esteemed colleague Edna Sussman reported on how affiliation and affinity might be unconscious drivers that influence an arbitrator's decision-making. The question deserving further exploration is how cues or other visuals in a participant's background might trigger a neutral's implicit bias.

One unanswered question among the many about the impact of video conferencing on implicit bias is: do those participating in our dispute resolution processes via video conferencing assess *us as impartial*? Proceduralist Tom Tyler reminds us that even when participants in dispute resolution processes receive an unfavorable outcome, they are still more likely to be satisfied with process if *inter alia* they found the neutral overseeing the process to be impartial. Professor Donna Shestowsky reinforces the importance of learning from the process users whether they perceive the process as fair. Given all these unanswered questions, how might a neutral who has scheduled a mediation or arbitration via video conferencing tomorrow ethically proceed?

In many ways, you've taken the first step. Awareness and acknowledgement. Hopefully, by reading this column, you will continue to heighten your sensitivity and awareness about how your implicit biases might be triggered by different cues and contexts when conducting dispute resolution processes via video conferencing, As part of that awareness and acknowledgement, you can make sure to schedule mental breaks before and during the dispute resolution process to help avoid the cognitive depletion that will make it more likely for your implicit biases to compromise your ethical mandate of impartiality. As part of a more reflexive practice, I welcome your insights about whether you have noted new implicit biases or have observed your pre-existing biases amplified when you have conducted your dispute resolution processes via video conferencing. What affirmative steps have you taken to mitigate these implicit biases?

Notes & Questions

1. Think about how biases might be worse or better in international online dispute resolution.
2. What steps would you take to "de-bias" yourself as an advocate or third-party neutral in an online international mediation, arbitration, or negotiation?
3. What might be some of the issues in a formal court hearing in an international matter conducted online?
4. To the extent that online dispute resolution is a less "rich" medium (restricted visuals with audio), how might it affect dispute resolution adversely? Are there any positives?

V. Cross-Cultural Issues in International Dispute Resolution

"American Westerns are about taking culture to the west, it's about one culture going to another place; they're taking law and order to the west. A Chinese Western is totally different. It's about exchange between different cultures."[3]

Cheryl Rivers, *Lying, Cheating Foreigners!! Negotiation Ethics across Cultures*

12 INT'L NEGOT. 1, 3, 5, 8–9, 14, 16, 20, 23 (2007)

Ply your average international business negotiator with a glass or two of wine and it won't be long before you hear a negotiation story that involves "those lying cheating #*&%$s!!" from one or other country. When foreigners breach ethical expectations they elicit potent negative emotions such as appalled, unhappy, angry and frustrated. These emotions are contradictory to cultivating the trust that we know helps achieve integrative potential in a negotiation....

Arguably, it is harder to deal with ethically ambiguous negotiation tactics when they are perpetrated by a foreigner because the negotiator lacks certainty about the rules

3. He Ping, Chinese film director, to Peter Hessler, in PETER HESSLER, ORACLE BONES: A JOURNEY THROUGH TIME IN CHINA 350 (2006).

of negotiation in a foreign land. Although there is growing evidence that there are cultural differences in the use and perceived appropriateness of ethically ambiguous negotiation tactics, this work can be extended by explaining how culture influences ethical decision making in negotiation....

The dominant view in the business ethics literature is also that ethical decision making is situationally specific and it is notable that the situation has a feature role in the main models in this literature. The definition of ethics adopted in this paper also emphasizes the situation: ethics are the 'rules, standards, codes or principles which provide guidelines for the morally right behaviour and truthfulness in specific situations'....

Empirical evidence of cultural differences in perceived ethicality of tactics emerged in a series of studies since the mid-90s. In the process of developing a scale to measure perceptions of appropriateness of EANTs [ethically ambiguous negotiation tactics], Lewicki & Robinson (1998) and Robinson et al., (2000) reported that perceived appropriateness of negotiation tactics is sensitive to cultural differences. There were significant differences in the mean rating of the tactics grouped as traditional bargaining between the U.S./U.K. students and Asian students, and significant differences between Asian students' ratings of appropriateness and USA and Canadian students' ratings of appropriateness in two factors called 'false promises' and 'inappropriate information gathering'. Perhaps it is not surprising that Asian students rated so-called 'inappropriate' information gathering tactics as more appropriate than Western students. These tactics include 'gain information about an opponent's position by cultivating his/her friendship through expensive gifts, entertaining or personal favours' which are common relationship building practices in Asian cultures....

Zarkada-Fraser & Fraser (2001) also compared negotiators' perceptions of ethicality in a comparative study of the U.S.A., the U.K., Japan, Greece, Russia and Australia. They found that there was greater variance between rather than within the national groups with the Japanese the most different in their ratings from all the other nationalities but 'generally closer to the Greeks and the Russians in their evaluations than to Americans, British and Australians' (Zarkada-Fraser & Fraser, 2001, p:283). They found that Japanese rated the tactics as less acceptable than the other groups.

Although all these findings support the existence of cultural differences in perceptions of ethicality of negotiating tactics, it is hard to generalise the findings because they do not explain what aspect of culture is causing the difference.... The main cultural value used in ethical decision research is individualism and collectivism (I/C) following Hofstede's (1980) argument that I/C is the value dimension that is most closely associated with moral dimensions because it reflects individual's relationships with society.... The dominant view is that individualists are interested in themselves, so they are more likely to act in a way that supports individual achievement and be less concerned for others. In other words, collectivists will be more ethical than individualists because collectivists are more concerned about others....

I have argued that a culture in context perspective will help unravel the influence of culture on ethical decision making.... A situational factor is one that is characteristic of the decision setting (as compared to being characteristic of the decision maker) and that is expected to influence the decision making process and outcome.... In the current model of ethical decision making process by Lewicki et al. (2003) eight situational/contextual variables are identified. These are a) past experiences of the negotiator; b) incentives; c) relationship with the other party; d) the relative power between the negotiators; e) mode of communication; f) whether or not the negotiator is acting as an agent; d) the group and the organisational norms, and; e) the cultural norms....

Acknowledging that goals are motivational, I propose that negotiators in cross-cultural negotiations are likely to find organisational goals influential in their ethical decision making. For example, if a company is desperate to get a sale in a new market because profits have been weak, the negotiator may be more inclined to use EANTs if they help him or her achieve the goal.... Organisational goals will vary with each negotiation and are likely to be directly influenced by culture....

My model proposes that the legal environment is a salient situational factor for negotiators' ethical decision making. The legal environment is widely considered the first hurdle to be cleared in ethical decision making and has been included in ethical decision making models. There are national differences in legal systems and cross-cultural research shows that managers differentially apply rules according to whether they believe in applying a rule uniformly to all situations or applying the rule according to the particular circumstances....

The ultimate test of negotiation theory is perhaps whether it makes any sense, and is of any use to the negotiation practitioners who have to craft deals across cultures. A raft of research has succeeded in identifying cultural differences in perceived appropriateness of ethicality of tactics, yet none has succeeded in explaining why there are differences.

Sharon Press & Ellen Deason, *Mediation: Embedded Assumptions of Whiteness*

22 Cardozo J. Conflict Resol. 453, 477–79 (2021)

[O]ne must acknowledge that the commitment to impartiality and neutrality are based on Western (white) ideology. As Wing explains:

> These values are imbedded in a Western ideology of positivism that assumes it is possible for the observer to be separate from the observed; that one can conduct an intervention (whether it be as a scientist leading an experiment or as a judge, jury, or mediator engaged in a proceeding) without having one's own experiences or values permeate the process. This outlook does not take into account that valuing distance between a conflict intervener and disputing parties is a cultural belief; it does not consider the impact the intervener has

on the course of a mediation as he guides the process by asking certain questions and not others.

Other Western (again, white) assumptions are also incorporated into mediation through our way of viewing negotiation. There is a tendency to think of mediation as, "negotiation in presence of a neutral third person," whose role is to assist the parties in developing a settlement. Michelle LeBaron and Mario Patera have identified the following assumptions underlying the current approach to training in interest-based negotiation:

- Explicit communication and direct confrontation;
- Individualist perspectives on agency and autonomy;
- Competitive assumptions that people will act to maximize individual gains, and can be assisted to extend this behaviour to maximizing joint gains if their own interests are not compromised;
- Action-orientation at the expense of a focus on "being" or inaction;
- Analytic problem-solving;
- Sequential orientation to time;
- Universalist ideas about the international applicability of "interest-based" negotiation;
- Agreement as a central measure of success.

The problem is that this conception of conflict, and of ways to resolve it, is not universal. Culture affects both how individuals experience conflict and how they approach it. It creates "the mental and emotional structures through which people understand their actions and those of others in the conflict." The characteristics LeBaron and Patera identify are "representative of dominant U.S. American culture and other groups influenced by Western thought." The framing of mediation as "negotiation with assistance" embeds the Western, rational, linear approach to negotiation and conflict in the mediation process. Certainly, these white assumptions about conflict manifest themselves in mediation as generally practiced in court annexed programs.

Notes & Questions

1. Do you think that mediation is "Western" or "white"? (See the readings in Chapter 3.)
2. Are mediators really "neutral" or unbiased? Impartial? Are these the same things, or are they different?
3. What can be done to deal with cultural assumptions in mediation, negotiation, and adjudication models?

John Barkai, *What's a Cross-Cultural Mediator to Do? A Low-Context Solution for a High-Context Problem*

10 Cardozo J. Conflict Resol. 47–49; 53–57; 60; 66; 70; 82; 87–89 (2008)

How Different Is Different?

How extreme and important can cultural differences be? When we encounter people from different cultures, their language and nonverbal communication may be different, and they can be very different in other fundamental ways that impact their behavior, view of life, values, the way they see and solve problems, and make decisions. For example, in religion, they may worship other gods, more than one god, or no god. They may read books by starting at what westerners would consider the "back" and ending at the "front." They may read printed words on a page from right to left, instead of left to right, or even read words in lines down the page, rather than across the page. Even when parties speak the same language and use a relatively similar international driving system to stop at red traffic lights and go at green ones, they might spell the color of those lights in different ways ("color" and "colour") and drive on the "wrong" side of the road. It is no wonder that cross-cultural negotiation and mediation is challenging.

Popeye's Problem

Although I write this article with the hope of offering a cross cultural mediation guide for all mediators, I am sure that I am a bit like "Popeye the Sailor Man" in this situation. Popeye said, "I am what I am and that's all that I am." Popeye's words remind me that I am an American, who is an American-trained mediator, who speaks only one language (English), and who, despite rather extensive travel, has lived outside the United States for less than one year. To use terms further developed later in this article, this means that, in many ways, my behavior is that of the typical American stereotype in that I am an individualist, egalitarian, informal, low-context communicator who makes extensive use of jokes and humor, and uses a rationally-based, problem-solving approach to resolve conflicts. Because of our culture, myself and most other American mediators have a difficult time (and perhaps a true inability) radically shifting our cultural perspective and behavior ninety degrees or more to see and do mediation differently. This is what I call "Popeye's Problem": lacking the ability to be what you are not and consequently not being able to relate to people from other cultures as they might prefer to be related. As Popeye says, "I am what I am and that's all that I am." For cross-cultural mediation, as I will explain in greater depth later, I am a low-context communicator, and I cannot relate or communicate well in a high-context manner. However, as I shall also explain, I believe that reaching wise, desirable, and long-lasting solutions to cross-cultural problems can be accomplished by using a low-context communication approach even with high-context communicating disputants....

Although the formal use of the informal process of mediation is only about 30 years old in the United States, mediation is as old as time. Ever since there were three people on earth, it is likely that one of them, at times, mediated between the other two. In traditional societies, wise old men probably mediated in business, social, and religious disputes. Most Asian nations have a long tradition of alternative dispute resolution (ADR) going back long before there was a United States of America....

A pre-mediation face-to-face meeting or phone conversation between the mediator and one or more parties to a mediation is quite common in commercial mediation (and a rarity in community mediation). The meeting can be a joint meeting between the mediator and all of the parties to the dispute, or a private, ex parte meeting between the mediator and one party. The mediator can have several reasons for such a meeting, such as performing administrative tasks like signing a mediation agreement or confidentiality agreement, ensuring that the right people are at the mediation, developing a working relationship with the parties, and even starting to mediate. A party, or lawyer representing a party, may also have reasons for wanting a pre-mediation meeting, such as to determine or reconfirm the mediator's style and approach, to advance the party's case, to use the mediator to educate a resistant or less-experienced party or advocate, to verify that the necessary parties will be attending the mediation, or to ensure that there will be sufficient time available to resolve the case....

[A] cross-cultural mediator's assessment during a pre-mediation meeting might indicate that the substantive issues are much less important than the less explicit, yet equally or more important issues related to such factors as race, harmony, sovereignty, national pride, or a host of other issues. Although Asian businesspeople might see the importance of establishing (or re-establishing) a good working relationship between the negotiators at the mediation, some Americans might be reluctant to spend time in such a pre-meditation stage....

My friend and sometime co-teacher, David Day, describes cross-cultural mediation as "put[ting] Humpty Dumpty back together," suggesting that a fragile, egg-like relationship has been cracked and needs to be somehow repaired. Of course, it is very difficult to put fragile Humpty Dumpty back together again, unless there is an understanding of how the Humpty Dumpty business deal was put together in the first place. Americans think of business deals as simple, negotiated agreements. Much of the rest of the world, on the other hand, thinks of business deals in terms of introductions by mutual friends or business associates, the presentation and receiving of gifts, the calling upon of old favors, the forming of trust-based relationships, business relationships formed in entertainment settings, and business arrangements based upon a handshake, not a written contract....

Especially if one of the parties is not aware of or does not appreciate the importance of cultural differences, a soft, Socratic method approach of teaching through questions asked by the mediator and answers given by the parties can be very effective....

High and low context refers to how people interact and communicate with other members of their culture. In low-context cultures, people communicate directly and explicitly and rely on verbal communication, as opposed to non-verbal communication to express themselves. In low-context cultures, the discussion is direct and straightforward, like an arrow. Important issues are explicitly discussed no matter how sensitive the subject matter is. In high-context cultures, the information lies in the context, is not always verbalized, and the talk goes around the points like a circle. The main issues may only be inferred or not discussed at all. A cultural outsider could easily fail to understand the major issues because they are not stated explicitly. Most observers would say that people in the United States, Canada, Australia, New Zealand and most Northern and Western European countries use direct, explicit, low-context communication and that Asian countries, along with most of the rest of the world, use indirect, implicit, high-context communication.

Even those of us who live in low-context national cultures, such as the U.S., have some experience in high-context subcultures. For example, our homes, our families, family gatherings, and groups of close friends represent high-context subcultures. In these situations, people sometimes use high-context communication within the group. An "insiders' joke" would be an example of such communication. Every national culture has its high and low context aspects. In high-context subcultures there are clear "insiders" compared to "outsiders." High-context cultures are more past-oriented and value traditions over change. On the other hand, low-context cultures are more present and future-oriented, and value change over tradition. Individualism is usually a characteristic associated with low-context cultures....

If the parties employ direct, low-context communication the mediator will work best by also being direct and saying exactly what is meant. For example, if in the mediator's opinion a person offering money is not offering enough money in a mediation to reach a settlement, the mediator could directly say, "That amount of money will not bring us to an agreement. You probably will have to offer more to end this dispute." When working with parties who are indirect and who use high-context communication, the mediator might say, "Perhaps you should reconsider your offer" or "It might be difficult to reach a settlement under present conditions." The belief is that the high-context communicating parties will understand these communication signals and consider changing their positions. The mediator might need to act as a translator between high context and low-context parties. Although there is some risk that high-context communicators might be insulted or otherwise put-off by the low-context communication, without translation and interpretation, low-context communicators may well completely miss the intended, implicit message of the high-context communicators. Mediators can bridge these communication and understanding gaps, usually in caucuses, to clarify the messages and help the parties to save face. Furthermore, the mediator might move quickly to get the parties into a caucus to preserve any "wa" or harmony....

Formality in the informal process of mediation can take on other forms. In the Hawaiian dispute resolution process of Ho'oponopono, the parties usually are encouraged to speak directly to the mediator or "haku," who is a high status elder, and not to speak directly to each other even in joint mediation sessions. Sometimes the formality can be increased by the use of high status language. For example, Japanese parties to a mediation might well call the mediator "sensei," a title used to refer to a teacher, but which is used for any person to whom you are trying to show respect. The status of mediators comes to play in several ways. A serious cultural mistake in cross-cultural negotiations with a negotiator from a high Power Distance culture is the failure to match the status of individuals who are negotiating with each other. It is an insult to not send an equally high status person to a mediation. In other words, if the president of one company goes to meet another company, the second company should also make sure its president is also at the meeting and not send a lower status individual. The same could be said about mediators. It might be important to have a mediator of the same (or higher) status level as the parties....

Decision-making varies markedly across cultures and can have a great impact on a mediation. In some cultures, there is an expectation that a single individual will make the decision (although the individual may welcome the input of others). In other cultures, there is often an expectation of group decision-making. Classically western business teams have individual decision makers and are teams that are given the authority to make the final decision at the bargaining table. On the other hand, some groups, particularly Asians, rely on group decision making. Asian negotiation teams usually do not have authority to make a concession to reach a final agreement. There might have been many rounds of consensus building that were necessary to reach the initial negotiation demand, and any concession will need to have an organizational decision to support and change the position. Everyone in the affected group has some input, sometimes called the "nemawashi" or "ringi" process. A mediator should always try to clarify the decision-making procedures for the parties at the mediation. Such clarity eliminates some of the frustration often felt towards authority when dealing with teams without authority....

In international negotiations, the negotiators may hold different values, objectives, and may play the game of negotiation by different rules. However, it is my view that the *Getting To Yes* concept of "interests" can encompass all those different values....

Conclusion

Cross-cultural mediations are more complex than domestic mediations because of cultural differences. However, mediators who find themselves in cross-cultural mediations can apply some basic principles and strategies to improve the likelihood of success based upon the application of cultural dimension interests (CDIs) to their mediation. The direct application of these ideas can be used as part of a four-stage approach for cross-cultural mediation:

1. Learn the cultural stereotypes about the culturally different parties who will come to the mediation.
2. Investigate the actual people involved, as well as the problem.
3. Be flexible and understand that the parties may well act differently than the stereotypes, and that the stereotypes still are useful in planning for the mediation, and
4. Use the template to apply a variety of approaches in mediation based upon the Cultural Dimension Interests (CDI's) to resolve the dispute.

The International Mediation Institute (based in Europe) provides training and criteria for certification in intercultural competency.

Criteria for Qualifying Assessment Program (QAP) Intercultural Competence

https://imimediation.org/orgs/cag-icc/

I. General Requirements	II. Substantive Criteria	Cultural Focus Areas
A. Methodology	**A. Knowledge**	1. Relatedness and Communication Styles
B. Transparency	1. Cultural Framework (s)	2. Mindset towards Conflict
C. Integrity	2. Self-Awareness	3. Mediation Process
D. Diversity	3. Multi-Cultural Perspectives	4. Orientation Toward Exchanging Information
	B. Skills	5. Time Orientation
	1. Communication	6. Decision Making Approaches
	2. Preparation	
	3. Managing Process	

Notes & Questions

1. What credence do you give to generalizations about culture (national, religious, ethnic, racial, gender affinity group, social status, class)?
2. Do you think there should be cultural competency training requirements for all international or cross-national lawyers, judges, and third parties (mediators, arbitrators)?
3. How can such competency be assessed?
4. To what extent is culture malleable, individual, or based on factors such as one's role (professional) or personal history (multiracial, well-traveled or educated, non-unitary or binary)?
5. Do some conflict resolution formats have greater affinity for use in particular cultures? Which ones? Why?
6. Do you think globalization in business, education, the arts, trade, mass entertainment, or travel is producing more convergence in conflict resolution modalities? Or has the recent increase in nationalism and authoritarianism in some political regimes reduced the likelihood of universalizing less formal forms of dispute resolution?
7. You have been asked to mediate a business conflict between a state-owned Chinese producer of electronics and a European company which assembles the components into a highly sophisticated sound system for performance arenas and for individual hearing assistance devices. The companies had done business together for several

years under contract without much difficulty. Lately, however, there have been delays in production, and so payments have also been delayed, making management at both companies unhappy. It is not clear whether they will want to terminate or continue the relationship. How would you prepare for the mediation?

8. You have been asked by a major philanthropic organization to investigate whether a collective comprising different indigenous groups would productively benefit from receiving a major grant from the organization for use in various development projects. You don't know much about either the individual groups or how well they work with each other. How would you structure meetings or sessions to explore whether the groups can work together so that you can advise your client organization whether to invest in this project?

Further Reading

SIMON BLACKBURN, ETHICS: A VERY SHORT INTRODUCTION (2d ed. 2021).

THE CONFLICT & CULTURE READER (Pat K. Chew ed., 2001).

ETHICS AND INTERNATIONAL AFFAIRS: EXTENT AND LIMITS (Jean Marc Coicaud & Daniel Warner eds., 2001).

Isabelle Gunning, *Diversity Issues in Mediation: Controlling Negative Cultural Myths*, 1995 J. DISP. RESOL., no. 1, 1995, at 55.

THE HANDBOOK OF NEGOTIATION AND CULTURE (Michele J. Gelfand & Jeanne M. Brett eds., 2004).

GEERT HOFSTEDE, CULTURE'S CONSEQUENCES: INTERNATIONAL DIFFERENCES IN WORK RELATED VALUES (1980).

Carol Izumi, *Implicit Bias and the Illusion of Mediator Neutrality*, 34 WASH. U. J.L & POL'Y 71 (2010).

Michelle Le Baron & Mario Patera, *Reflective Practice in the New Millennium*, *in* RETHINKING NEGOTIATION TEACHING: INNOVATIONS FOR CONTEXT AND CULTURE 45 (Christopher Honeyman, James Coben, & Giuseppe De Palo eds., 2008).

Roy J. Lewicki & Robert J. Robinson, *Ethical and Unethical Bargaining Tactics: An Empirical Study*, 17 J. BUS. ETHICS 665–82 (1998).

CARRIE MENKEL-MEADOW & MICHAEL WHEELER, WHAT'S FAIR: ETHICS FOR NEGOTIATORS (2004).

WILLIAM HERNANDEZ REQUEJO & JOHN L. GRAHAM, GLOBAL NEGOTIATIONS: THE NEW RULES (2008).

CATHERINE ROGERS, ETHICS IN INTERNATIONAL ARBITRATION (2013).

M. Schwartz, *The Nature of the Relationship between Corporate Codes of Ethics and Behaviour*, 32 *J. Bus. Ethics* 247–62 (2001).

Robert Toscano, *The Ethics of Modern Diplomacy*, *in* ETHICS AND INTERNATIONAL AFFAIRS: EXTENT AND LIMITS (Jean-Marc Coicaud & Daniel Warner eds., 2001).

Anna Zarkada-Fraser & Campbell Fraser, *Moral Decision Making in International Sales Negotiations*, 16 J. BUS. & INT'L MKTG. 274–93 (2001).

Chapter 13

International Conflict Resolution Processes and Peace, Justice, and the Rule of Law

In this book, we have explored many different processes for handling conflict in the international arena. Some of these processes involve formal court proceedings (*see* Chapter 6 on adjudication), while others utilize formal legal procedures and arguments but are not formal courts (*see* Chapter 4 on arbitration). Other processes involve less formal ways of negotiating or mediating international disputes, either assisted by third parties or organizations (like the United Nations) or with direct party or diplomatic interactions (*see* Chapters 2 and 3). We have touched on some of today's most difficult international issues: climate change; ongoing wars in several regions; attempts to reconcile past wars, atrocities, and internal conflicts (*see* Chapter 8); and the challenges brought by new forms of technology (*see* Chapter 10 on ODR and the discussion of hybrid warfare in Chapter 11).

The tools covered in this text should enable you to assess which processes may be appropriate for different kinds of international conflicts—whether between nation-states, between private parties from different countries, or between public and private parties (*see* Chapters 5, 7, and 8, respectively). They should also enable you to assess which conflicts are best handled confidentially, and which require public transparency. You should now have the analytical tools to examine the elements, parties, and issues involved in disputes and conflicts among and between parties of different legal systems and different cultures. This book is about both more and less than an international law book—we have looked at processes that may be governed by international law (treaties, customary law, and "soft law"), invoking issues about how far the Rule of Law extends across borders and includes complex issues regarding enforcement in the international arena. But we have also looked at dispute resolution processes that may not require the law or that may seek more consensual forms of international problem-solving such as mediation and negotiation. As someone who is interested in international conflict resolution, you should now know about and be able to participate in an array of different processes.

The 20th century witnessed horrific world wars and civil wars as well as violent struggles for independence from colonial rule, all of which resulted in great disruption and created even more conflicts. Death, mass injuries, atrocities, property destruction, and human suffering, became visible to all through modern technology, films, news coverage, or instant viewing on social media. On the other hand, these terrible situations have also produced major developments in international law—the creation of new international institutions, such as the United Nations, the International Court of Justice, and the World Bank; treaties (humanitarian, human rights, anti-terrorism, anti-discrimination, declarations of rights and cooperative agreements on the environment, air travel, commerce, trade and investment); and new international processes and tribunals, such as the International Tribunal for the Law of the Sea and the International Centre for Settlement of Investment Disputes (ICSID). New regional treaties and agreements have also created new entities for adjudication and economic cooperation, such as the European Union, the European Court of Human Rights, the InterAmerican Court of Human Rights, Mercosur, and ASEAN.

The 21st century has produced newer forms of conflict resolution, through new forms of technology and easier travel for face-to-face meetings such as large climate change conventions. Some of the less formal processes we have studied here are now recognized more formally (*see* the UN Convention on International Settlement Agreements Resulting from Mediation (the Singapore Convention) (2019)). Additionally, there has been considerable critique of the 20th century's institutions, much of it coming from Third World Approaches to International Law (TWAIL), a decentralized network comprising international law scholars. TWAIL asserts that much international law is the creation of the "victors" of 20th-century wars or systems of colonialization, which has in turn created a "Western" or "Northern" global world order. A group of countries collectively known as the Global South has emerged to challenge some of the institutions and processes we have studied here (e.g., international investment dispute resolution). Progress is being made in recognizing and using new and creative ways of achieving a more peaceful and prosperous world, and every new challenge is an opportunity to spark even more creative solutions.

At the same time, the world continues to face enormous difficulties—ongoing wars and conflict; cybercrime; the physical and mental abuse of migrants; the mistreatment of minority populations in their home countries and abroad; the mistreatment of women, children, and other vulnerable populations; increasing political polarization and the rise of autocratic, non-democratic regimes; and the ongoing destruction of our planet and its resources.

This chapter presents both optimistic and less optimistic (i.e., more realistic) takes of some of the challenges facing our world. The excerpts raise big questions: What is the relationship of peace-seeking to justice-seeking? Are these goals always compatible? What should our goals for conflict resolution be? Is the Rule of Law a necessary or sufficient requirement for effective conflict handling? Is democracy a necessary political system for effective conflict resolution? How can we manage conflicts across different legal and cultural systems and traditions? Is it possible to specify "universal" standards of human rights or justice?

We hope to leave you thinking about the processes that might be used to manage some of the world's seemingly intractable issues. As you read, consider which processes you believe have the potential to contribute to the ongoing quest for peace and human flourishing. Also think about how you might be able to contribute, whether by participating in these processes or perhaps by inventing some new ones. So, even as we offer the following assessments from experts in our field, we ask you to consider what might be done to achieve peace, justice, and well-being in the world.

I. Challenges to International Conflict Resolution

Our first excerpts here focus on challenges to the basic concepts underlying this book and field—that interest-based and problem-solving-based negotiated processes can facilitate good outcomes in conflict situations, with consensual processes that seek to meet the needs of the parties. Roger Fisher, William Ury, and Bruce Patton's *Getting to Yes*, now in its third edition, was first published in the early 1980s. It inspired several generations of diplomats, lawyers, academics, and political scientists to reorient us away from adversarial and conflictual thinking to seeking mutual gains and creative problem solving, through a process that is based on information sharing, learning, and curiosity and that attempts to expand resources and reach agreements that are accepted by all parties. While millions of copies have been sold, the authors and their followers (such as the authors of this book) have long wondered why the cultural change the book advocates has not resulted in a complete cultural change toward negotiated creative problem solving. Carrie Menkel-Meadow, in a review essay from the 25th anniversary of the book's publication, seeks to understand this. Sanda Kaufman, Christopher Honeyman, and Andrea Kupfer Schneider ask why international relations practitioners (diplomats and professional negotiators) and the general public have not paid more attention to the teachings of modern negotiation theorists.

Carrie Menkel-Meadow, *Why Hasn't the World Gotten to Yes? An Appreciation and Some Reflections*

4 Negot. J. 497–500 (2006)

The Way Forward: The Continuing Legacy of Getting to Yes

So, with all of this intellectual ferment and practical activity, why has the world not been more successful at "getting to yes?" The legacy of *Getting to Yes* operates on several different levels. It functions on the ideational or theoretical level; that is, what ideas did it give us? It also functions on the practical level: do we achieve more consensual and better-executed settlements than we used to? Is this a good model of negotiation to teach people? Finally, the book's legacy has a moral dimension: should we continue to try to "get to yes" with those whom we have profound disagreements with or whom we are trying to make something new with?

At the level of ideas, *Getting to Yes* was nothing short of a plea for a major cultural change. To focus on underlying interests and to approach another party in a negotiation with the idea of forging a joint agreement that would meet the needs of both parties was—and, I am afraid, still is—countercultural to the way in which most parties approach negotiations. Rather than thinking of the other side as someone to be bested, *Getting to Yes* asks us to think about seeing the other party as a partner in creating new entities, new or better relationships, or new resources, even if we are in disagreement (or worse, engaged in litigation or war) with the other party.

Getting to Yes provided some of the techniques for trying to achieve this (brainstorming, one-text procedures, side-by-side planning), and subsequent scholarship and popular writing provided more. Lax and Sebenius (1986), for example, wrote about the analytics of trading, and making contingent and sequential agreements. More recently, negotiation scholars have broadened the intellectual agenda to consider under what conditions integrative or principled bargaining will be mostly likely to succeed, whether negotiation is best studied as a rational process of thinking and planning or a more chaotic human behavioral improvisational art, and under what circumstances negotiation is the best process to use and which circumstances are better suited to a different process.

In the last two decades, teachers of negotiation from varied disciplines have created thousands of simulations to be used in teaching particular techniques (listening, brainstorming, trading for differences, value creation, resource expansion, dovetailing differential goals) in arenas as diverse as management, international relations, environmental studies, public policy, labor relations, and all areas of litigation. (See, e.g., Menkel-Meadow, Schneider, and Love 2006 [and 4e 2025—Eds.].)

Periodically, we meet and exchange research findings and pedagogical ideas. And, over the years, we have implemented efforts to bring theorists and practitioners together to bridge the theory-practice divide. And, although there has been spirited debate about the times when negotiation is not appropriate or right (see, e.g., Mnookin 2010), most of us doing this all believe that "getting to yes" is a morally good thing to do. But, as Roger Fisher asked several years ago, if all of this is such a good idea, why have these ideas not had a greater cultural impact or more of an effect on international relations, in the media, in the schoolyard, our universities, workplaces, or in Congress?

Is there something in human nature that prevents us from seeing those opposite us at a negotiation table as a partner with whom we might create a joint venture, or, at the very least, an agreement to stop disagreeing? Are we socialized in a competitive society to consider "the other" as an antagonist? Is the world really one of scarce resources that makes sharing or making new things virtually impossible? Does the larger zeitgeist in which we live (Cold War, economic boom and bust, globalization, the War on Terror) affect how we conceptualize the world and what we do? Is *Getting to Yes* and its progeny a product of its time or a more universal expression of what might be possible, of what might be achieved?

These difficult questions merit deep exploration. We must ask to what extent the *Getting to Yes* model is situated in a larger culture over which it has attempted to exercise some influence and to what extent it is a product of a particular time as Mary Parker Follett (the 1920s) and the game theorists (1940s–1960s) were of theirs? I also wonder why the negotiation theorists, teachers, and practitioners among us are not more often consultants to nations in conflict, to litigants in dispute, to government agencies. Moreover, when we have had these opportunities, what have we learned about our own effectiveness? I am reminded of Michael Ignatieff's (1995) eloquent lament in the introduction to his book *Blood and Belonging* in which he expressed the hope that the fall of the Berlin Wall and the Soviet state signaled the dawn of an era of cosmopolitanism, to be characterized by an appreciation for cultural differences within a world of peaceful exchange and democratic governance. But as ethnic wars broke out in rapidly disintegrating nation states, Ignatieff wrote that he learned an important lesson: that some degree of nation-state security and economic self-sufficiency is necessary to prevent the scarcity and suspicion that breed the fear and insecurity that lead to death and destruction.

When I think of *Getting to Yes* and the world of integrative negotiation that I too have embraced, I wonder sometimes if we have been naïve about the social structural conditions under which integrative negotiation can most optimally occur. So, while social psychologists and game theorists look at strategic and interactive behavior at the individual, dyadic, or group level, I wonder whether we negotiation theorists need to spend more time on the macro questions surrounding our work: under what socioeconomic and political conditions can we actually get to yes by negotiating fairly, equitably, and wisely to achieve joint and mutual gain with those we negotiate with? What do we owe to others—both those inside and outside our negotiations—when we negotiate? Should we work to "get to yes" only for the parties inside a negotiation or should we think about how what we do affects the rest of the world?...

Despite the current War on Terror and fighting in the Middle East, the Dayton Accords and the Oslo Accords exemplify the use of negotiation and mediation-based principles in international diplomacy and violence reduction. Negotiation principles are now explicitly discussed in transactional work (contracting, entity creation) and governmental and policy decision making.

Some might argue that negotiation and conflict resolution theory is part of the backbone or foundation of recent efforts to enhance deliberative democracy in our own nation, as well as abroad. Perhaps most importantly, many of us have discovered that friends, acquaintances, and colleagues from outside our areas of expertise will sometimes display an awareness of the principles of *Getting to Yes*; in the midst of a disagreement and in an unlikely place, we will sometimes discover someone who "speaks our language." These ideas are increasingly well exposed, and some of my students and younger colleagues report that in many settings (childcare, sports teams, schools), one can expect people to solve problems and approach each other differently than they did, say thirty years ago. Of course, we can all rattle off a list of places in which this thinking has not taken hold—from Columbine High School and all the other tragic school shootings in the U.S. to the horrifically violent ethnic conflicts that continue to rage around the world. And, many of us have met lawyers, as well as real estate, entertainment, and sports brokers and agents who still prefer to "shoot first, talk later" or who continue to act as if the world is only made up of scarce resources. Clearly, there are groups of people who have vested interests in perpetuating conflict and adversarial and competitive approaches to its resolution. We must study further the incentives and disincentives for choosing particular approaches to conflict and problem solving, and their costs and benefits in both the long and short run.

But I also think that for those of us who seek to make the world a better, more peaceful place through negotiation ("as long as they are talking, they are not killing"), we owe it to Roger Fisher, Bill Ury, and Bruce Patton to rigorously explore when and how getting to yes can be made more possible in the world. In short, it is time for us to rigorously study those situations of success (where and when the tenets of *Getting to Yes* have worked) and failure (what has not worked in particular settings and why). And, of course, each of us should ask ourselves every day, what have we done today to get to yes (or not) in our own lives?

Sanda Kaufman, Chris Honeyman, & Andrea Kupfer Schneider, *Should They Listen to Us? Seeking a Negotiation/Conflict Resolution Contribution to Practice in Intractable Conflicts*

2017 J. Disp. Resol., no. 1, 2017, 75–78

The accumulated negotiation wisdom from research and practice might be expected to at least affect its initial domains of politics and international affairs. Yet in both contexts, large-scale conflicts such as those plaguing the Middle East, some African and some Latin American regions, and the countries neighboring the South China Sea have resisted theoretical analysis, prediction, or prescriptions for practice. To say this of intractable conflicts borders on tautology and should not surprise, since they are by definition resistant to resolution within time periods comparable to human life spans. However, even in situations not necessarily diagnosed as intractable, interventions remain challenging to design, implement, and evaluate. Granted, one major obstacle is the uniqueness of each case, and the relatively small number of instances in each class, which together tend to defeat useful generalizations. But the fact remains that negotiation theorists have not reshaped meaningfully the practices of the decision-making bodies and institutions managing societal conflicts....

There have also been some international successes. In South Africa, a large-scale conflict was resolved in ways consistent with negotiation prescriptions and was followed by a reconciliation process. More recently, in 2016, the Colombian government managed to negotiate an end to its longstanding conflict with the Revolutionary Armed Forces of Colombia (FARC) guerrilla movement.

In contrast, by 2007, the 1993 and 1995 Oslo Accords, aiming to bring peace to the Middle East and rooted in prescriptions dear to negotiation scholars, had already shown signs of weakness; they have since unraveled under a thousand cuts. Civil war replaced the brief negotiated peace respite in Darfur. Negotiations had limited, if any, impact in several other protracted, long-drawn conflicts around the world. Examples can be found on several continents: Rwanda, Zimbabwe, Tibet, Nepal, Kashmir, Indonesia, Spain, Yugoslavia, Cyprus, Sierra Leone, Congo, Uganda, and much of Latin America. In some of these places negotiation wisdom has been largely ignored, while in others conflict persists despite repeated interventions. In still other places, such as Sierra Leone, East Timor, Guatemala, and El Salvador, post-conflict institutions have fallen short of their promise to provide peace and justice. Even in relatively successful cases like Bosnia and Kosovo, the ethnic groups remain divided and there is an unstable equilibrium among contending groups....

A key observation guiding our 2007 analysis is that public and international conflicts are complex and "wicked:" they typically involve multiple, layered relationships among numerous parties—individuals, interest groups, public, private and nonprofit organizations, and governments. Stakeholders act unilaterally and jointly in environments that are themselves in flux and not well-understood. "Wickedness" means that solutions to any specific problem are bound to interact in both known and unexpected ways with the systems in which they are embedded, sometimes resulting in the desired outcomes, but often also generating unwanted side-effects, which can sometimes be worse than the presenting problem and spur renewed conflict.

To generate some helpful steps toward linking negotiation theory and practice in public and international negotiations, we turned to psychologist Dietrich Dörner's book, *The Logic of Failure*, for an analysis of antecedents of decision-making failure in complex situations. His findings offered a useful framework for our purposes because they use some of the cognitive shortcomings discovered experimentally but combine them—often experimentally—with situational features of complex situations to inform us of their interplay in individual and joint decision making.

Dörner identified several reasons why analyses of complex situations are predictably flawed, yielding problem-solving approaches that are doomed to fail. Such are: (1) decision makers' lack of attention to context, (2) ignoring scale and uniqueness, (3) failure to predict outcomes and anticipate decision side effects and long-term repercussions (due to a focus on isolated cause-and-effect relationships), (4) the cumulative effects of numerous small judgmental mistakes, over-generalizations, and rigid mental models of reality, (5) frozen frames, with low tolerance for uncertainty, (6) a tendency to solve the problem we can solve instead of the one we ought to solve, (7) the conviction that everyone's intentions are unquestionably good, (8) and impatience with low-feedback systems. In Dörner's words:

> "Failure does not strike like a bolt from the blue; it develops gradually according to its own logic. As we watch individuals attempt to solve problems, we will see that complicated situations seem to elicit habits of thought that set failure

in motion from the beginning. From that point, the continuing complexity of the task and the growing apprehension of failure encourage methods of decision making that make failure even more likely and then inevitable."

Notes & Questions

1. Why do you think international dispute resolution professionals have not been more influenced by integrative problem-solving negotiation models? Is it ignorance/lack of education or training? Inexperience or fear? Inability to "change the negotiation culture"?
2. How important do you think the philosophical orientation to integrative, interest-based, negotiated problem-solving is for resolving or managing international conflict?
3. Do you agree with Dörner that the problem with negotiating "wicked problems" is mostly cognitive? Or are there other factors that prevent the use of an integrative problem-solving approach to difficult international conflicts?

II. The Role and Rule of Law in Conflict Resolution

Here we consider the role of law as an underpinning of conflict resolution processes. Is a functioning democracy necessary to create and support the processes we have discussed in this book? Is capitalism a necessary prerequisite? It appears obvious that the answer to these questions is no, as numerous countries have adopted and signed on to the processes we have described—from multinational courts and treaties to commercial arbitration. And yet, at what point, does respect for individual rights need to be built into the national-level system? Moreover, is this a Western conception in the first place?

In the first excerpt, Andrea Schneider examines the phenomenon of a seemingly contradictory impetus to trial at the international level with a push to dispute resolution in the United States. She finds that similar desires—for voice and fairness—motivate these concurrent developments. In the second excerpt, Greg Shaffer and Wayne Sandholtz worry about what has happened to commitments to the Rule of Law at both national and international levels. Consider how these processes and substantive developments affect what kinds of processes are available for current international conflicts and disputes. In the final excerpt in this section, New York Times foreign affairs correspondent Thomas Friedman opines on the issue of good and bad choices made in international relations, with a focus on the importance of the role of leaders in decision-making that affects the world order.

Andrea Kupfer Schneider, *Bargaining in the Shadow of (International) Law: What the Normalization of Adjudication in International Governance Regimes Means for Dispute Resolution*

41 N.Y.U. J. Int'l L. & Pol. 817–819; 821–822 (2009)

One possibility arising from the normalization of international adjudication is that we start to see a voluntary move away from adjudication. As the law becomes more standardized, transparent, predictable, and understood, countries might turn to consensual dispute processes attached to courts or adjudicatory bodies—they will be bargaining in the shadow of (International) Law. As the rights of human rights victims vis-a-vis their governments become clear, will we see victims (or NGOs on their behalf) negotiating settlements in advance of adjudication?

This has great possibility, but the rush to dispute resolution cannot be too fast. For international disputes, particularly those dealing with transitional justice, the rule of law must first be established in courts before the values of procedural justice can be realized in consensual processes. We cannot promote consensual dispute resolution or create a court-connected ADR system as in the United States without an established government, human rights protections, and a working court system. The process of dispute resolution does not inherently provide these values unless the settlements are based on core values of justice and equality. Otherwise, consensual dispute resolution is just another set of processes to be abused by those with power. This is similar to the understanding (not always recognized) that democracy is not achieved by elections alone. The process does not create democracy, but rather the laws upon which the process operates do so. For democracy, we need the equivalent of the Bill of Rights (rights for minorities, freedom of speech, freedom of association, protection from arbitrary detention, etc.). Similarly, a voluntary process like dispute resolution without the backdrop of a court system that operates to protect rights is unlikely to be a step forward.

In the United States, we are generally quite sure that the law will be enforced. So, even when we use ADR, we know that we are bargaining in the shadow of a longstanding body of law we can count on. As we create international systems, we need to think carefully about the underlying legal structures, the law, and how it is implemented. Where the rule of law already exists, perhaps more domestic and consensual processes can be used. But where inequality and a lack of rights permeate the legal landscape, international courts and hybrid tribunals are a necessary first step. Nonetheless, as international criminal and human rights law evolves, we can expect to see a return to diplomacy, a return to negotiation, and a likelihood of increased bargaining in the shadow of international law....

Conclusion

As the streams of international criminal law and human rights law have increasingly utilized international adjudication in the last ten years, this pattern has created interesting comparisons with a similar increase in domestic consensual dispute resolution. The analogous goals of increased voice, procedural justice, and fairness are being accomplished in both arenas. Using dispute resolution theory, we can also see how certain challenges faced by the international systems have been handled. Rather than creating systems that provide either truth or justice, we now employ various processes to provide multiple remedies and meet the goals of victims, societies, and the international community. Rather than designing systems solely by the elite to the citizens, we now have more integrated and creative processes to ensure both external and internal commitment to recovery. And, rather than providing only individual litigation or individual prosecution to protect rights, we now have systems that can hear individual stories while efficiently operating to provide larger remedies. This suggests a potential for continued evolution of international adjudication and dispute resolution in at least two different ways. As the law is increasingly transparent and enforceable, countries and individuals will likely turn back to traditional diplomacy and be able to bargain in the shadow of international law. In addition, the cross-fertilization among human rights courts, truth commissions, and even domestic courts have the opportunity to push increasingly creative and responsive remedies for victims based on restorative justice. As international human rights adjudication moves out of its adolescence in the next ten years, its maturity could be even more revolutionary.

Gregory Shaffer & Wayne Sandholtz, *The Rule of Law under Challenge: The Enmeshment of National and International Trends*

Geo. U. L. Ctr., Res. Paper No. 2023/14, 2023, https://ssrn.com/abstract=461788

These are difficult times. Populist and authoritarian leaders are dismantling rule-of-law norms domestically, and they are working to do so internationally. Although political actors increasingly deploy rule-of-law discourse, they frequently abuse it to legitimate authoritarian rule, often in the name of law and order. How to measure these shifts is a challenge given the variety of institutional means to advance or undermine the rule of law, yet both qualitative and quantitative analyses indicate overall declines in rule-of-law protections, which are essential for individuals to lead lives not subject to domination. In this introductory framework essay, we conceive of the rule of law as an ideal—or meta principle—under which individuals are not to be subject to the arbitrary exercise of power. We examine the interaction of domestic and international factors in eroding the rule of law, including the rise of populist, authoritarian leaders in traditionally democratic countries, and the relative decline of Europe and the United States in relation to an authoritarian China and other emerging powers. These shifts weaken the diffusion and settling of rule-of-law norms within states, which, in turn affects normative development and institutional practice internationally. They also are generating robust responses that we evaluate....

We posit that the rule of law is a normative ideal that should be viewed teleologically in terms of its ends. The goal of the rule of law is to oppose the arbitrary exercise of power by setting boundaries on, and channeling, power's exercise through known legal rules and institutions that apply to all. The rule of law aims to limit, through legal rules exercise of power by some persons over others. Arbitrary power can be terrorizing. People internalize its threat. Through self-suppression and self-protective collaboration, individual freedom and civil society wither. The goal is thus to create restraints on government, as well as private power, together with channels for cooperative and coordinative activities, which provide security and predictability so that people can plan and organize their pursuits and do so without fear. Power can be used for good or ill. For us, as for theorists ranging from Judith Shklar in the last century to Montesquieu earlier, "the fear of violence and the threat of arbitrary government provides an essential context in which the rule of law takes its meaning." As a goal, the rule of law is best viewed as a principle and not simply as a set of rules because rules can be manipulated to subvert goals. As an ideal, the rule of law will never be fully attained given human failings, but that does not make the principle any less important. In this essay, we focus predominantly on public power, while noting that effective state power also is required to temper the arbitrary exercise of private power, particularly as states delegate and outsource traditional public tasks to private actors. Ultimately, for the rule of law to become effective, it must be institutionalized as part of a culture of conduct. It must become a practice. It is for this reason that we apply a broader conception of law that includes institutionalized practice. From a socio-legal perspective the rule of law provides restraints on arbitrary state and private behavior through norms that enable people to reasonably know what is required of them, what is prohibited, what they may do, and what can be done to them, combined with the institutionalization of these norms so that they "count as a source of restraint and a normative resource." These restraints facilitate the advancement of multiple social goals. Where institutionalized, the rule of law becomes a habit or routine....

We see no reason to create a distinct conception of the "international rule of law." Rather, we maintain that the concept of the rule of law ultimately addresses the relation of authorities to individuals, but that international law's horizontal dimension of governing interstate relations is critical directly and indirectly for protecting individuals from power's arbitrary exercise. We thus retain our conception of the rule of law in terms of goals—to protect individuals from arbitrary power through legal rules and institutionalized practices, while providing channels for cooperative and coordinative activities. We nonetheless contend that international law is critical for advancing the rule of law in multiple direct and indirect ways that affect individuals and societies. At a minimum, the recognition of state boundaries and prohibition of the use of force except in self-defense helps ensure international peace and reduce the violence of war, thus benefiting individuals and communities from power's arbitrary exercise. Going further, states can be viewed as agents or trustees in advancing rule-of-law goals, and not simply as subjects and beneficiaries of international law. International law creates norms, institutions, and mechanisms that aim to protect individuals from arbitrary power, whether directly or indirectly. At the same time, international institutions, multinational companies, and foreign states can wield power arbitrarily in ways that affect individuals. International law is thus critical for tempering their unbridled exercise of power as well....

There is parallel evidence of decline in international law and institutions, which some now call a "crisis," a decline that implicates rule-of-law protections. The evidence that we present is largely of a qualitative nature. It concerns challenges to, and constraints placed on, international courts, a turn away from treaties to informal agreements and understandings, the neutering of international institutional scrutiny of human rights and rule-of-law violations, and the distortion and harnessing of international law to support repression, such as in the name of suppressing "terrorism," "separatism," and "extremism" to maintain "public order." States have negatively responded to international courts over the last decade, and in particular international human rights courts. To start, there has been considerable backlash against the flagship human rights court—the European Court of Human Rights....

The backlash is not limited to human rights courts. China rejected a ruling of the Permanent Court of Arbitration against its claims in the South China Sea, calling the decision "wastepaper." The United States neutered the Appellate Body of the World Trade Organization by blocking the appointment of new members after existing members' terms expired, a tactic that Zimbabwe (under President Mugabe) earlier used against the South African Development Community Tribunal following unfavorable rulings regarding its land seizures. The United States then increasingly deployed its economic power unilaterally to challenge foreign practices it did not like, in violation of WTO law, a tactic that China also adopted. Similarly, a number of states terminated (or allowed to expire) bilateral investment treaties instituting investor-state dispute settlement (including India, Indonesia, South Africa, and the United States regarding NAFTA's investment chapter), and some withdrew from the International Centre for Settlement of Investment Disputes, which provides a procedural framework for such arbitrations. Investor-state arbitral tribunals themselves have raised rule-of-law challenges given their asymmetric nature where only investors can bring claims, and investors appoint one of the three arbitrators. Still, if the goal is enhanced rule-of-law protections within states, international venues offer a more reliable forum than do national courts, especially as national rule-of-law indicators decline....

What Might Be Done

The rising challenges to democracy and the rule of law, however, are more than economic. They also reflect cultural backlash against the relative success of liberal, pluralist norms from those who feel a loss of status or a sense that their ways of life are under threat. Immigration becomes an easy target, reflecting rising social cleavages in the United States and Europe. Norms of social community, solidarity, and cooperation decline. Minorities and foreigners become scapegoats, creating social conditions ripe for authoritarianism. Hannah Arendt's analysis of the rise of totalitarianism in the twentieth century is chillingly foreboding: "The preparation has succeeded when people have lost contact with their fellow men as well as the reality around them; for together with these contacts, men lose the capacity of both experience and thought.

The ideal subject of totalitarian rule is not the convinced Nazi or the convinced Communist, but people for whom the distinction between fact and fiction (i.e., the reality of experience) and the distinction between true and false (i.e., the standards of thought) no longer exist.... It [totalitarianism] bases itself on loneliness, on the experience of not belonging to the world at all, which is among the most radical and desperate experiences of man." Today, populist, nativist politicians and partisan media capitalize on and stoke anxieties through a politics of fear, anger, and resentment, giving rise to Schmittian friend-enemy politics of social identity. Climate change, political repression, war, and other crises will spur further migration, potentially heightening social conflict. The policy implications are challenging. Economists generally maintain that societies economically benefit from increased migration, but the domestic politics continue to raise barriers, indeed physical walls. To start, policies addressing rising economic inequality and social precarity could help stem such cultural backlash. Yet, those policy changes also face political blockages.

History is not linear. It involves cycles of advances and retrenchments in light of ongoing struggles. Rule-of-law protections that temper the arbitrary exercise of power are under challenge globally. In contrast, rule by law—the deploying of legal rules to serve the interests of autocratic power-holders—is on the rise. One of the critical challenges is how to stabilize and then revitalize rule-of-law principles and institutions within countries where they are under assault. An interlinked challenge is to reinforce and recalibrate regional and international legal norms and institutions, which are also under stress, in order to support the rule of law domestically.

Thomas L. Friedman, *What Is Happening to Our World?*

New York Times (Dec. 29, 2023),
https://www.nytimes.com/2023/12/29/opinion/israel-hamas-war.html

I've been The Times's foreign affairs columnist since 1995, and one of the most enduring lessons I've learned is that there are good seasons and bad seasons in this business, which are defined by the big choices made by the biggest players. My first decade or so saw its share of bad choices—mainly around America's response to Sept. 11—but they were accompanied by a lot of more hopeful ones: the birth of democracy in Russia and Eastern Europe, thanks to the choices of Mikhail Gorbachev. The Oslo peace process, thanks to the choices of Yitzhak Rabin and Yasir Arafat. China's accelerating opening to the world, thanks to the choices of Deng Xiaoping. India's embrace of globalization, thanks to choices initiated by Manmohan Singh. The expansion of the European Union, the election of America's first Black president and the evolution of South Africa into a multiracial democracy focused on reconciliation rather than retribution—all the result of good choices from both leaders and led. There were even signs of a world finally beginning to take climate change seriously.

On balance, these choices nudged world politics toward a more positive trajectory—a feeling of more people being connected and able to realize their full potential peacefully. It was exciting to wake up each day and think about which one of these trends to get behind as a columnist.

For the last few years, though, I've felt the opposite—that so much of my work was decrying bad choices made by big players: Vladimir Putin's tightening dictatorship and aggression, culminating in his brutal invasion of Ukraine; Xi Jinping's reversal of China's opening; Israel's election of the most right-wing government in its history; the cascading effects of climate change; the loss of control over America's southern border; and, maybe most ominously, an authoritarian drift, not only in European countries like Turkey, Poland and Hungary but in America's own Republican Party as well....

But before we become too pessimistic, let us remember that these choices are just that: choices. There was nothing inevitable or foreordained about them. People and leaders always have agency—and as observers we must never fall prey to the cowardly and dishonest "well, they had no choice" crowd. Gorbachev, Deng, Anwar el-Sadat, Menachem Begin, George H.W. Bush and Volodymyr Zelensky, to name but a few, faced excruciating choices, but they chose forks in the road that led to a safer and more prosperous world, at least for a time. Others, alas, have done the opposite.

Notes & Questions

1. How important is a commitment to the Rule of Law for productive international dispute resolution? How are international conflict resolution processes or institutions dependent, or not, on Rule of Law conceptions?
2. What other underlying principles other than the Rule of Law influence the practices of international conflict resolution?
3. Is democracy a necessary condition for successful conflict resolution? Can you think of examples where peaceful outcomes were achieved without democracy?
4. How important are decisions made by national or world leaders to the culture of conflict resolution?

We now turn to the issue of how to define the Rule of Law and whose law it is. The excerpts below illustrate some of the current conflicts about whether all legal or decision-making principles in international conflicts are culturally based. Anthropologist Fernanda Pirie is optimistic about law, even if it is culturally variable. But Makau Matua and M. Sornarajah, international scholars of TWAIL (Third World Approaches to International Law), are more critical and suggest that much of modern international law and the institutions it created are "Western" or "Northern" or "colonial" or based on the values of the "victors" of the two 20th-century world wars. As you read these excerpts, ask yourself whether it is possible to have "universally" applicable law or processes. What is culturally based in what we have studied in this text? Can you think of alternatives?

Fernanda Pirie, The Anthropology of Law

210–11 (2013)

Marti Koskenniemi (2001) suggests that international law both creates power and delimits it, offering a language for the defence of both hegemonic and anti-hegemonic power. Like Barkun, he argues that we should not think of law as primarily controlling the actions of bad men. International law is created in part to advance the repertory of substantive values, preferences and practices that those in the dominant positions seek to realize in the world, but it also gives voice to those who have been excluded from decision-making positions; it provides a platform on which claims about violence, injustice and social deprivation may be made. Its formalism brings political antagonists together as they involve contrasting understandings of rules and institutions, providing a shared surface for debate and allowing them to disagree within a structure of assumed universality. More than that, international law exists as a promise of justice: law describes the world of a legal community, in which questions of just distribution and entitlement are constantly on the agenda, where claims of legal subjects receive an equal hearing and where acts of public officials are assessed by a language of community standards.

Makau Matua, *What Is TWAIL?*

94 Proceedings of the ASIL Ann. Meeting 31 (2000)

The regime of international law is illegitimate. It is a predatory system that legitimizes, reproduces and sustains the plunder and subordination of the Third World by the West. Neither universally nor its promise of global order and stability make international law a just, equitable, and legitimate code of global governance for the Third World. The construction and universalization of international law were essential to the imperial expansion that subordinated non-European peoples and societies to European conquest and domination. Historically, the Third World has generally viewed international law as a regime and discourse of domination and subordination, not resistance and liberation. This broad dialectic of opposition to international law is defined and referred to here as Third World Approaches to International Law (TWAIL).

TWAIL is not a recent phenomenon. It stretches back to the decolonization movement that swept the globe after World War II. Bandung was the symbolic birthplace of TWAIL, although the North-South confrontation draws heavily from Latin American opposition to the domination of the Third World by the industrialized West. This confrontation has its roots in the anticolonial movement. TWAIL is a response to decolonization and the end of direct European colonial rule over non-Europeans. It basically describes a response to a condition, and is both reactive and proactive. It is reactive in the sense that is responds to international law as an imperial project. But it is proactive because it seeks the internal transformation of conditions in the Third World.

TWAIL is driven by three basic, interrelated and purposeful objectives. The first is to understand, deconstruct, and unpack the uses of international law as a medium for the creation and perpetuation of a racialized hierarchy of international norms and institutions that subordinate non-Europeans to Europeans. Second, it seeks to construct and present an alternative normative legal edifice for international governance. Finally, TWAIL seeks through scholarship, policy, and politics to eradicate the conditions of underdevelopment in the Third World.

M. Sornarajah, *On Fighting for Global Justice: The Role of the International Lawyer*

in Third World Approaches to International Law: On Praxis and the Intellectual (Usha Natarajan, John Reynolds, Amar Bhatia, & Sujith Xavier eds., 2018) 31–32; 38; 45

The origin of the Third World lies in the resistance of its people to the norms of international order that justified their subjugation. From initial European contacts first with Latin America and then with Asia and Africa, the norm that supported the subjugation of the cultures of these people has been driven by the superiority of Europe and its self-assumed civilizational responsibility to lift the peoples of these regions to Europe's level. The assumption of this civilizational responsibility was an altruistic cloak to plunder the wealth of the people of Africa and Asia.... The resistance that led to the decolonization involved in an assertion of the norm of self-determination.... The ending of imperial control over Asia and Africa, the consequent creation of new states, the coming together in conferences like the Bandung Conference and the formation of the Non-Aligned Movement resulted in the possibility of the use of collective power to change the legal order.[1] [1] The first generation of Third World international lawyers was active in bringing about change. They believed that international law could be changed so that it benefited the whole of humanity, not just the people of former colonial states. This may be because they believed in universality and the possibility of a plurality of laws for the whole of mankind based on justice and equality.... Third World leaders chose to remain within the system [after the collapse of the socialist system] and to make changes to the existing system without seeking to replace it. This is a paradox, for it was the very system that had been used to exploit them in the past that they sought to continue.... The founding of the United Nations and the rise of Third World power within the General Assembly were factors that contributed to this strategy, one that may have worked to their detriment later.

---

1. [1] [Editor's note: The Bandung Conference in 1955 was a meeting of African and Asian states, most of which were newly independent, organized by Indonesia, India, Ceylon, now Sri Lanka, Pakistan, and others for consideration of the development of economic and political cooperation and opposition to colonialism. It was one of several efforts to create a "third way" or "non-aligned" pact during the Cold War and after independence for many nations. Some of the participants wanted to create more "alternative" and more socialist economic and political joint action and new rules of engagement, challenging establishment international law and institutions, favoring poverty amelioration and other priorities.]

The Rule of Law Argument

The rule of law, redefined to suit neo-liberalism, takes the form of ensuring the protection of property and contract, on the grounds these are sacrosanct concepts without which international business cannot function. Devices such as global administrative law, and international constitutional principles extracted from systems of Europe, are brought in to construct this understanding of the rule of law. When it comes to comparative public law, there does not seem to be agreement, even among Europe's legal systems about the extent to which protection should be given to property and contract....

TWAIL must set itself the agenda of resisting international law norms based on power by setting up a system of norms based on justice. Justice has countervailing power, particularly when people support the changes that are sought. History has demonstrated the power of justice-based norms to affect change.

Notes & Questions

1. Do you agree with Pirie that international institutions provide a place for claims of the less powerful to be granted an "equal hearing"? In which of the processes we have studied is this possible?
2. Do you think TWAIL has a valid critique of the founding of international law and its processes by colonial powers? How does this impact what type and structure of dispute resolution you would suggest?
3. M. Sornarajah is a distinguished international lawyer and scholar (he has been a professor at the National University of Singapore for many years) and a major critic of the international investment arbitration system. Can you take up his "agenda" and imagine international legal processes that could be based on principles of "justice" and "equality" instead of "power"? How would you construct an international investment dispute resolution system or process?

III. Case Study: Universal Human Rights?

One of the basic hopes of international lawyers focused on justice and reparative claims, especially after the atrocities of World War II, was to create both rules and legal processes granting basic human rights to all individuals. The creation of regional (not yet international) human rights conventions and treaties was intended to provide both substantive claims and causes of action as well as venues for vindication of those "rights." New wars and forms of conflict, including civil wars; dictatorships; displacement resulting from climatic conditions; demands for reparations for earlier harms (e.g. slavery, colonization, and exploitation); and recognition of new claims (e.g. rape as a war crime) have led to the proliferation of both norms and possibly relevant (and overlapping) venues for the hearing of such claims.

Consider as an example the issues of violence against women and children in Ukraine, Israel, and Gaza, and before that, in Bosnia-Herzegovina, Nigeria (Boko Haram), and Mexico. Consider the following possible venues or processes for treating such claims, and also consider what is represented by the interlocking circles of potentially overlapping or exclusionary jurisdictional principles in the image below:

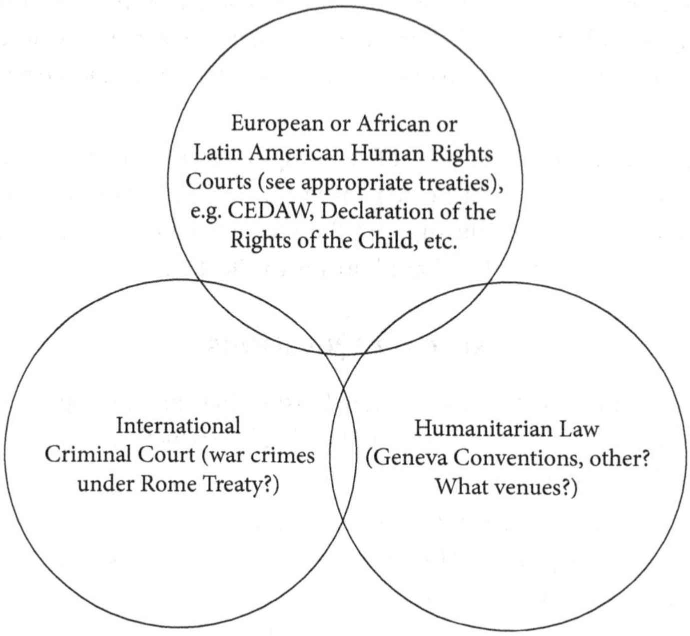

Notes & Questions

1. Consider adding other circles, for example, truth and reconciliation proceedings, civil tort actions (national or international?), or national/domestic criminal (and military) proceedings.
2. Where and in what venues should each of the following consider filing a claim: harmed individuals, family members of harmed individuals, the state, or harmed groups?

Some harms may be clearly defined in international law (whether by treaty or customary law). But what happens when one country's laws or customs conflict with another's, as is the case with issues such as veiling, female genital mutilation, and the death penalty?

Below is a case study implicating both universal norms and mediation norms. Consider how Susan Moller Okin answers the question in the framework of a Rule of Law, and then consider how Carrie Menkel-Meadow addresses the same question using an understanding of mediation ethics.

Case Study: Ziba and Ahmed's Iranian-American Divorce

Seventeen-year-old Ziba and her forty-four-year-old husband Ahmed have come to you for mediation services. Ziba and Ahmed have been married for four years. They have two sons, ages three and two. Ziba wants a divorce, but both she and her husband want to remain part of the local mosque and surrounding community. To ensure that the divorce is handled in accord with Quranic principles and meets the approval of their peers and community elders, Ziba and Ahmed met with their imam to learn how to properly dissolve their marriage contract in accord with local interpretations of Islamic law. Their imam advised them that while a husband can ask for and obtain a divorce for any reason, he is obliged to support his children until they reach the age of majority, regardless of who has primary custody. If the wife remains in the husband's home to observe a mandatory waiting period of seclusion, then he must provide for her needs during that time. In addition, he is obligated to pay the amount stipulated in their marriage contract that becomes due if the marriage ends. Ziba and Ahmed's marriage contract calls for a payment of $40,000. The imam also tells Ziba that she cannot receive a divorce without Ahmed's consent. If she initiates the divorce, she loses her right to the marriage contract payment, although Ahmed's financial obligations toward the children will still stand. As far as custody of the children goes, local understandings of Islamic law presume that young children should stay with their mother, but that once sons reach their seventh birthday, custody reverts to the father.

Ziba is miserable in the marriage. Ahmed is controlling and rigid in his notions of what Ziba can do. He monitors her movements, allowing her outside only to shop for groceries and run errands for the house. In addition, he has taken a second wife (in accord with his privileges pursuant to Islamic law) and has begun to pay less and less attention to both Ziba and their children. Angry and humiliated, Ziba insists she must have permission for the divorce from her husband and without it cannot move on with her life. Ahmed says that he will not grant her request unless she forfeits her marriage dissolution payment and any other financial support for herself and agrees to give up custody of each child at age five. Ahmed says that by asking for a divorce, Ziba is demonstrating that she is an unfit mother and that his sons should thus revert to his care at the earlier age. Ahmed says that it is fitting that his sons should be taken into his care and raised by his female relatives. At the mediation, Ziba capitulates and tearfully says she will waive all rights to financial support and agree to his requests regarding the transfer of custody at the given ages so long as Ahmed grants her request for a divorce. Although Ziba has agreed to relinquish her children two years earlier than traditional Islamic law would warrant, privately negotiated deviations from default rules are not uncommon.

Ahmed is very unhappy with the prospect of divorce and strongly feels Ziba's behavior compromises her ability to parent. He has stated to you in private that the only reason he is not demanding immediate transfer is that he doesn't think Ziba will agree and doesn't believe he would receive support from his community. He is confident, however, that the agreement as contemplated is broadly supportable and within the norms of the Iranian community in which they live.

As mediator, do you help the parties with their divorce?

Susan Moller Okin, *Is Multiculturalism Bad for Women?*

Boston Rev. (Oct. 1, 1997), https://www.bostonreview.net/forum/susan-moller-okin-multiculuralism-bad-women/

Until the past few decades, minority groups—immigrants as well as indigenous peoples—were typically expected to assimilate into majority cultures. This assimilationist expectation is now often considered oppressive, and many Western countries are seeking to devise new policies that are more responsive to persistent cultural differences. The appropriate policies vary with context: Countries such as England with established churches or state supported religious education find it hard to resist demands to extend state support to minority religious schools; countries such as France with traditions of strictly secular public education struggle over whether the clothing required by minority religions may be worn in the public schools. But one issue recurs across all contexts, though it has gone virtually unnoticed in current debate: What should be done when the claims of minority cultures or religions clash with the norm of gender equality that is at least formally endorsed by liberal states (however much they continue to violate it in their practice)?...

During the 1980s, the French government quietly permitted immigrant men to bring multiple wives into the country, to the point where an estimated 200,000 families in Paris are now polygamous. Any suspicion that official concern over headscarves was motivated by an impulse toward gender equality is belied by the easy adoption of a permissive policy on polygamy, despite the burdens this practice imposes on women and the warnings issued by women from the relevant cultures. On this issue, no politically effective opposition galvanized. But once reporters finally got around to interviewing the wives, they discovered what the government could have learned years earlier: that the women affected by polygamy regarded it as an inescapable and barely tolerable institution in their African countries of origin, and an unbearable imposition in the French context. Overcrowded apartments and the lack of each wife's private space lead to immense hostility, resentment, even violence both among the wives and against each other's children.

In part because of the strain on the welfare state caused by families with 20–30 members, the French government has recently decided to recognize only one wife and consider all the other marriages annulled. But what will happen to all the other wives and children? Having neglected women's view on polygamy for so long, the government now seems to be abdicating its responsibility for the vulnerability that women and children incurred because of its rash policy.

The French accommodation of polygamy illustrates a deep and growing tension between feminism and multiculturalist concerns to protect cultural diversity. I think we—especially those of us who consider ourselves politically progressive and opposed to all forms of oppression—have been too quick to assume that feminism and multiculturalism are both good things which are easily reconciled. I shall argue instead that there is considerable likelihood of tension between them—more precisely, between feminism and a multiculturalist commitment to group rights for minority cultures.

Demands for such group rights are growing—from indigenous native populations, minority ethnic or religious groups, and formerly colonized peoples (at least, when the latter immigrate to the former colonial state). These groups, it is argued, have their own "societal cultures" which—as Will Kymlicka, the foremost contemporary defender of cultural group rights, says—provide "members with meaningful ways of life across the full range of human activities, including social, educational, religious, recreational, and economic life, encompassing both public and private spheres." Because societal cultures play so pervasive and fundamental a role in the lives of members, and because such cultures are threatened with extinction, minority cultures should be protected by special rights: That, in essence, is the case for group rights.

Some proponents of group rights argue that even cultures that "flout the rights of [their individual members] in a liberal society" should be accorded group rights or privileges if their minority status endangers the culture's continued existence. Others do not claim that all minority cultural groups should have special rights, but rather that such groups—even illiberal ones, that violate their individual members' rights, requiring them to conform to group beliefs or norms—have the right to be "let alone" in a liberal society. Both claims seem clearly inconsistent with the basic liberal value of individual freedom, which entails that group rights should not trump the individual rights of their members; thus, I will not address the problems they present for feminists here. But some defenders of multiculturalism largely confine their defense of group rights to groups that are internally liberal. Even with these restrictions, feminists—anyone, that is, who endorses the moral equality of men and women—should remain skeptical. So, I will argue.

Gender and Culture

Advocates of group rights for minorities within liberal states have not adequately addressed this simple critique of group rights, for at least two reasons. First, they tend to treat cultural groups as monoliths—to pay more attention to differences between and among groups than to differences within them. Specifically, they give little or no recognition to the fact that minority cultural groups, like the societies in which they exist (though to a greater or lesser extent), are themselves *gendered*, with substantial differences of power and advantage between men and women. Second, advocates of group rights pay no or little attention to the private sphere. Some of the best liberal defenses of group rights urge that individuals need "a culture of their own," and that only within such a culture can people develop a sense of self-esteem or self-respect, or the capacity to decide what kind of life is good for them. But such arguments typically neglect both the different roles that cultural groups require of their members and the context in which persons' senses of themselves and their capacities are first formed *and* in which culture is first transmitted—the realm of domestic or family life....

Consider, too, the practice—common in much of Latin America, rural Southeast Asia and parts of West Africa—of encouraging or even requiring a rape victim to marry the rapist. In many such cultures—including fourteen countries of Latin America—rapists are legally exonerated if they marry or (in some cases) even offer to marry their victims. Clearly, rape is not seen in these cultures primarily as a violent assault on the girl or woman herself, but rather as a serious injury to her family and its honor. By marrying his victim, the rapist can help restore the family's honor and relieve it of a daughter who, as "damaged goods," has become unmarriageable. In Peru, this barbaric law was amended for the worse in 1991: the co-defendants in a gang rape are now all exonerated if one of them offers to marry the victim (feminists are fighting to get the law repealed). As a Peruvian taxi driver explained: "Marriage is the right and proper thing to do after a rape. A raped woman is a used item. No one wants her. At least with this law the woman will get a husband." It is hard to imagine a worse fate for a woman than being pressured into marrying the man who has raped her. But worse fates do exist in some cultures—notably in Pakistan and parts of the Arab Middle East, where women who bring rape charges are quite frequently charged with the serious Muslim offense of *zina*, or sex outside of marriage. Law allows for the whipping or imprisonment of such a woman, and culture condones the killing or pressuring into suicide of a raped woman by relatives concerned to restore the family's honor.

Part of the Solution?

It is by no means clear, then, from a feminist point of view, that minority group rights are "part of the solution." They may well exacerbate the problem. In the case of a more patriarchal minority culture in the context of a less patriarchal majority culture, no argument can be made on the basis of self-respect or freedom that the female members of the culture have a clear interest in its preservation. Indeed, they *may* be much better off if the culture into which they were born were either to become extinct (so that its members would become integrated into the less sexist surrounding culture) or, preferably, to be encouraged to alter itself so as to reinforce the equality of women—at least to the degree to which this is upheld in the majority culture. Other considerations would, of course, need to be taken into account, such as whether the minority group speaks a different language that requires protection, and whether the group suffers from prejudices such as racial discrimination. But it would take significant factors weighing in the other direction to counterbalance evidence that a culture severely constrained women's choices or otherwise undermined their well-being.

What some of the examples discussed above show us is how culturally endorsed practices that are oppressive to women can often remain hidden in the private or domestic sphere. In [one] Iraqi child marriage case, if the father himself had not called in agents of the state, his daughters' plight might well not have become public. And when Congress in 1996 passed a law criminalizing clitoridectomy, a number of US doctors objected to the law as unjustified, since it concerned a private matter which, as one said, "should be decided by a physician, the family, and the child." It can take more or less extraordinary circumstances for such abuses of girls or women to become public or for the state to be able to intervene protectively.

Thus, it is clear that many instances of private sphere discrimination against women on cultural grounds are never likely to emerge in public, where courts can enforce their rights and political theorists can label such practices as illiberal and therefore unjustified violations of women's physical or mental integrity. Establishing group rights to enable some minority cultures to preserve themselves may not be in the best interests of the girls and women of the culture, even if it benefits the men.

When liberal arguments are made for the rights of groups, then, special care must be taken to look at within-group inequalities. It is especially important to consider inequalities between the sexes, since they are likely to be less public, and less easily discernible. Moreover, policies aiming to respond to the needs and claims of cultural minority groups must take seriously the need for adequate representation of less powerful members of such groups. Since attention to the rights of minority cultural groups, if it is to be consistent with the fundamentals of liberalism, must be ultimately aimed at furthering the well-being of the members of these groups, there can be no justification for assuming that the groups' self-proclaimed leaders—invariably mainly composed of their older and their male members—represent the interests of all of the groups' members. Unless women—and, more specifically, young women, since older women often become co-opted into reinforcing gender inequality—are fully represented in negotiations about group rights, their interests may be harmed rather than promoted by the granting of such rights.

Carrie Menkel-Meadow, *Mediating Multiculturally: Culture and the Ethical Mediator*

in MEDIATION ETHICS: CASES AND COMMENTARIES 305, 320–23, 326–27 (Ellen Waldman ed., 2011)

Comments on Case 12.2

Whose culture? Whose laws? Whose ethics? Yours or mine?

Ziba and Ahmed's divorce mediation raises very difficult issues of cross-cultural mediation. My response to the dilemma presented here is easy for me, but likely to be seen as very controversial and unacceptable by many other mediators. I will explain why.

Self-determination (by both the parties and the mediator), capacity and consent to any agreements, "true" understanding of possible alternatives, and my own legal and social justice concerns all militate against my deferring to the parties' claimed desire to use religious law and principles to resolve their dispute.

Suitability for Mediation? Clash Between Religious/Communitarian and Legal Systems. Many ethnic, religious, and other affiliated communities have their own systems of rules, laws, and customs that they may seek to "enforce" through private mediation. Some have argued that mediation is particularly appropriate in such settings where communities seek to enhance their shared community values by their own systems of dispute resolution, away from the state or other cultures that they do not recognize or that do not recognize them. If Ziba and Ahmed had contacted me with their desire to use Shari'a law, I would likely have made a referral to a specialized religion-based mediation center. I would not take their case. Here's why:

First, Ziba, now seventeen, has, according to the facts, been married for four years. That means she was thirteen when she married. The facts as given do not specify whether her marriage took place in the United States or in another country, but by no measure of "full faith and credit" would I regard a marriage made at thirteen to be a legal marriage in the United States. And wherever they live in the United States, a state court will have to finalize their "legal" divorce. Most states require evidence of a marriage certificate to certify the marriage when the divorce is judicially approved. A marriage certificate of a girl of thirteen would not be valid in virtually all states of the United States. Thus, in my view, the marriage is not "legal" under American domestic law (and American law is still required to make the divorce legally binding here) and legally could be annulled. In addition, it is also possible that, given the absence of a legal marriage, Ahmed might even be guilty of statutory rape under American law. Ziba could possibly file charges against him if she wanted to (or she might choose to use this information to prevent him from further abusing her or to "bargain" for her "rightful" financial and custody rights).

As a lawyer mediator with some experience in domestic relations (in litigation and in mediation), I would tell Ziba and Ahmed this together in a joint premediation session, as well as in any separate caucus that I would have with both parties. I would give legal advice and counsel to both of them at the same time and tell them what American law provides. I would, in the presence of both parties, tell Ziba that if she consulted an American lawyer, she would likely be entitled to financial support, as well as custody of both of her children. Other mediators might fear doing this because of possible domestic abuse or other negative actions that Ahmed might take when he sees his wife being so advised, but in my view, as long as she is living in the United States, she has the right to legal information according to the rules of this country.

Whose Self-Determination? While I fully acknowledge all of our profession's norms and platitudes about self-determination (Standard I, Self-Determination, Model Standards of Conduct for Mediators, 2005), I do not believe that a thirteen-year-old girl had the capacity to "self-determine" when she married Ahmed, and thus the whole premise of the termination of the marriage is in question (for me). In addition, as long as we are looking at the platitudinous standards (which seldom help resolve really difficult questions), I would decline this case also for several other reasons:

- I am obviously not "impartial." I am judging the validity of the marriage and giving advice to one of the parties that at least one, if not both, of them is likely to view as "partial" (Standard II, Impartiality, Model Standards of Conduct for Mediators).
- I do not have the "competence" to mediate a case involving Shari' a law since I know not much about it, except as a legal educator and scholar. I do know that its teachings are actually subject to much controversy, change, and interpretation, and I do not entirely trust what the parties tell me their mullah has told them (Model Standards of Conduct for Mediators, Standard IV, Competence).
- I do not believe that a mediation that would sanction or permit these results would be one with the requisite "quality of process" (Standard VI, Quality of the Process, Model Standards of Conduct for Mediators), which, in my view, requires "safety" of the parties (including the affected children), full presence and participation of the parties, party competency (including noninterference by third parties), and "mutual respect" among all participants.
- I have a conflict of interest (Standard III, Conflicts of Interest, Model Standards of Conduct for Mediators) because I have spent a great deal of my legal career as a feminist advocate for equality in marriage, self-determination, and the rights of women to no-fault divorce, as well as to adequate child and spousal support, and thus could not possibly be seen as neutral or impartial by Ahmed (and maybe by Ziba as well). In addition, I am committed in print, as well as in my practice, to tolerance and appreciation of diversity, in culture and religion, but I am a secular humanist, who, while acknowledging the importance of plural systems of law and culture, could not myself "preside" over a mediation that used a set of norms and customs that institutionalizes deep structures of inequality, even if seemingly "consented to." ...

More complex issues actually underlie these "easy" answers from the Model Standards. One is that, as the hypothetical is intended to reveal, mediations like this pit significant cultural differences against each other: the couple's desire to use Shari' a law, which does not grant Ziba the same rights as domestic laws would, versus the mediator's own sense of legal entitlements and "justice." In cases of radically different cultural understandings, whose cultural understandings should govern? Isabelle Gunning has written eloquently on this point, in several relevant contexts, first in how "Western" feminists should deal with the religious or ethnic practice of "female genital mutilation" in the face of "international" standards of human health and safety (Gunning, 1991–1992, 1995) and, second, in seeing mediation as a site for self-empowerment for groups that are not recognized by or likely to be disadvantaged in formal court proceedings. The problem of cultural relativism or cultural hegemony is very significant in many modern mediations where parties choose to avoid formal law and legal systems and elect to apply other sources of social norms that they (and their mediators) may or may not share. There are no easy answers to the question of "whose culture" should govern....

Mediation is a process, not a separate justice system that automatically dismisses or renders inapposite "the law." At the same time, if a party is fully knowledgeable about the legal entitlements or arguments the law may provide, that party (indeed, both parties) may well decide to reach agreement or settle on the basis of other values (or nonlegal principles), seeking to apply his or her own sense of justice or fairness within his or her own relationship or community. Law or legal principles are not always determinative, and parties may and often do seek to do "real," if not "legal," justice between themselves. If, as a mediator, I am convinced they fully understand what they are doing, the parties may agree to depart from what the law might grant them. Laws are passed by legislatures for "the general public" and are interpreted by judges in particular situations. Mediation offers the parties a more democratic, nuanced, individualized, and self-empowering opportunity to interpret the law for themselves, as long as they agree and as long as the agreement is not legally voidable (by being unlawful). However, as a lawyer mediator I will not participate in or "preside" over an agreement that is "unlawful" under applicable law. In this case, the secular law of divorce is still necessary to grant the parties a legal divorce in a state court of appropriate jurisdiction.

Conclusion. In this case, beyond the question of "whose culture" and "whose law" is the (for me) ethical question of "whose justice." Mediation is a process; it has no substantive commitments except knowing consent of the parties (and is backed up by the legal system's enforcement of legally acceptable contracts that can be enforced in courts) and an aspiration to do individualized and legitimate justice for the parties as they see it. For me, however, a mediator is also a party to a mediation, and thus the agreement that is reached must also be one that I can be accountable and responsible for as a participant in the process. My sense of ethics, culture, and yes, even justice is also at stake, for I am a party too. I would honestly and completely tell the parties everything I have just told you, the reader, and would (1) advise them to seek legal advice and counsel about what is necessary for a legal divorce in my community; and (2) withdraw and ask them to find another mediator if they insist on applying a set of norms I am not competent to enforce, even as I have views about whether they do justice or not. This, of course, raises the next difficult issue of whether I am at all responsible for an outcome reached by someone other than myself (another mediator who agrees to let the parties use the agreement they have framed in the hypothetical, which you can see I think is unfair and unjust to Ziba). But that is a question for another day.

Notes & Questions

1. Susan Moller Okin wrote her piece over 20 years ago (she is now deceased) as a philosopher trying to integrate liberal notions of cultural and group rights with feminist principles of equality and individual self-determination. Based on her examples, what are the international legal human-rights implications when one country (e.g., France, the UK, or the United States), enforces its laws against immigrants or minority groups who adhere to religious or cultural practices that violate the country's laws? What do the different human rights conventions (European, African, Inter-American)

say about the adjudication of these issues? (Remember that the United States is not a signatory to any of these human rights conventions.) There has been a lot of litigation in many countries about various religious and cultural practices (e.g., polygamy, female circumcision, veiling and clothing generally, turbans) that run afoul of domestic laws. Is it possible to have universal rules here?

2. "The case of Ziba asks us to think about how we would balance competing concerns—neutrality of the mediator versus informed self-determination for the parties; party self-determination versus gender fairness; respect for cultural values and identity versus our outside view of fairness and rights; and a mediator's responsibility to carry out the parties' wishes versus a mediator's responsibility for the fairness of the outcome." Andrea Kupfer Schneider, *Carrie Menkel-Meadow and Dispute Resolution in a Feminist Voice*, 10 TEX. A&M L. REV. 151 (2022). What do you think? Do the guidelines on mediator neutrality rules (*see* Chapter 3) present an overly narrow and perhaps masculine version of dispute resolution in which neutrality is heralded above other values (hearkening back to feminist theory which says that equal treatment or neutrality under the law does not actually serve women)? And should this narrow view of neutrality be held over and above other values of dispute resolution that are important, including informed consent, justice, and fairness? How should we deal with competing norms of law, culture, and justice?

3. What would you do if Ziba and Ahmed asked you to mediate their divorce?

4. These issues of human rights, the "cultural defense" in some criminal matters (*see* ALISON DUNDES RENTELN, THE CULTURAL DEFENSE (2005)), and varied religious and cultural practices raise issues of legal pluralism—which legal, cultural, or religious system should govern? What process can be used to adjudicate or resolve such claims between states and individuals, or between individuals from different states or value systems? Is this a domestic or international dispute?

IV. The Promise and Opportunities of International Conflict Resolution

Despite all of the challenges to international dispute resolution, we remain hopeful that the creation and use of different processes, called process pluralism, will continue to allow us to seek peaceful settlements of many kinds of disputes and conflicts. Below we provide excerpts from the more hopeful and optimistic literature suggesting that we might still seek peace and justice simultaneously, using different kinds of methods for different kinds of conflicts. As you read, think about what you have learned about different processes, but also think about which processes would be most appropriate for the different kinds of international conflicts we are facing now or might face in the future. You will be the lawyers and process designers creating and implementing conflict resolution processes for the rest of this century.

In the first excerpt, Carrie Menkel-Meadow outlines the need for process pluralism, that is, the need for lawyers to be creative and deliberate in meeting the needs of parties, contexts, and society. In the second excerpt, Steven Ratner and his co-authors outline, in the human-rights context, how process pluralism could actually play out, inspiring the next generation of human-rights lawyers to view themselves as architects of future dispute systems.

Carrie Menkel-Meadow, *Peace and Justice: Notes on the Evolution and Purposes of Legal Processes*

94 Geo. L.J. 553, 555–56, 557, 576–79 (2006)

Process pluralism means paying attention to a variety of different systemic values (some of which may seem oppositional to each other) and party needs at the same time and offering variegated possibilities of process for engagement and decision making. Such values include the attempt to achieve peace with justice, choice and self-determination of the individual with care and responsibility for others, and recognition of the harms of the past with hopes for reconciliation in the future.... Some of the nettlesome issues to explore here include: (1) the relation of principle and social justice to compromise and consensus; (2) the need to include at least three forms of human discourse in human problem solving and legal decision making: principled argument, traded or bargained for preferences, and passionate commitments of emotion, religion, and moral values; (3) the tensions presented by needing rules of process and (perhaps different) rules of decision; and finally, (4) what I call the Oscar Wilde problem—if socialism takes up too many evenings,[2] [10] imagine what process pluralism and participatory democracy will do to our social lives. Do we have the time, desire, and commitment to fully participate in the processes of our polities and personal lives?...

The British social philosopher Stuart Hampshire, in what turned out to be his last major work, *Justice Is Conflict*, (2000) opined that because we are unlikely ever to reach any real, uniform consensus on what constitutes the "substantive good" in a deeply pluralist and divided world, perhaps we can, at best, arrive at some close-to-universal principles for processes that enable us to live together within these differences. For him, this process is *audi alterum partum* ("hear the other side," or the Anglo-American adversary principle). For me, ... it is closer to "understand all sides" of our modern multi-partied and multi-issued disputes. So, I substitute "understand" for Hampshire's "hear" (a deeper level of human engagement and empathy, as well as reason) and "all" sides for Hampshire's "other" or "two" sides. Modern social and legal life needs to get beyond the binary, adversarial idea that there are only two sides to an argument or the "truth." "Understanding" and "coexistence" as aspirational values of peace give us some goals and end-states but do not tell us much about how to get there. Political theorists and philosophers over the years have elaborated many theories of political and social organization, from Hobbes's *Leviathan* and Rawls's "veil of ignorance"[3] [18]

2. [10] Oscar Wilde, A Life in Quotes 238 (Barry Day ed., 2000)....
3. [18] John Rawls, A Theory of Justice 136–42 (1971).

to Habermas' "ideal speech conditions for uncoerced communicative action."4 [19] Most recently, a movement and plea for "deliberative democracy" harkening back to Aristotelian notions of participatory democracy and argument have inspired much writing on how we can achieve legitimate and fair consensus and good decisions at all levels of human interaction and conflict, even when we have deep conflicts about facts and values. These recent efforts seek to provide a legitimating and explanatory framework for how to seek fair and "just" outcomes in highly conflictual situations of disputes, conflicts, policy, and law-making. It is my hope to marry this work on deliberative democracy to conflict resolution theory and practice so that we might seek peace and justice (always provisional and evolving in a postmodern world) simultaneously....

The Way Forward

In the last ten years or so we have seen the flowering of process creativity in attempts to create whole new processes for human governance. Out of the horrors of apartheid, political oppression, genocide, and civil and ethnic wars, we, as a species, have created truth and reconciliation commissions and have adapted traditional community justice systems like *gacaca* in Rwanda, while using more traditional forms of adjudicated justice in the international war crimes tribunals of the former Yugoslavia, Rwanda, and other sites.

These new processes are intended to work on the levels of the most aspirational—of what could be best in our human species, often after what has been the worst—terrible violence. Intended to provide "truth" and "answers" for those who have been killed or seriously harmed (and their families), these processes "triage" cases so that the "least" serious can be dealt with by offering forgiveness, healing, and the possibility of reconciliation and the creation of a new and more peaceful society. These processes are the first I have seen to really take the emotional life of humans seriously. By use of narrative, storytelling, and some confrontation, victims and perpetrators meet head-on in a protected setting in which they are called to account on legal, emotional, and, ultimately, human levels.

These new processes are also quite controversial, and their successes and limits are being explored by participants and scholars. Nevertheless, political scientist James Gibson has concluded, after rigorous public opinion research, that those who participated in (or even only watched) the South African truth and reconciliation processes, even with all their weaknesses, were more likely to have internalized a "human rights consciousness" with an enhanced belief (or hope) in the rule of law to improve human relations and achieve justice.5 [102] This is consistent with decades of research in what is called "procedural justice," by social psychologists Tom Tyler and Allan Lind, finding

4. [19] 2 Jürgen Habermas, A Theory of Communicative Action 72–74 (Thomas McCarthy trans., 1985).

5. [102] ... *See generally* [James L.] Gibson, [Overcoming Apartheid: Can Truth Reconcile a Divided Nation? (2004)].

that people judge their satisfaction with legal processes by their participation in and perceptions of fairness of those processes, irrespective of the outcomes.

In many settings, these new processes of forgiveness, reconciliation, and new-constitution-drafting have come from new participants in the process design. Women and disempowered racial, ethnic, or religious groups are increasingly finding their voices, after great catastrophe, in the creation of new communities and governments, and seeking new processes to participate in, so that old factions and patterns of power domination will not be repeated. Those who are creating these new processes are interested in justice, but they also want peace—to live together with mutual respect, to have sufficient resources to be free from want or illness and to be able to seek their own forms of human flourishing. But many of these processes have still come too late—post hoc or after terrible conflict and violence and injustice. Can we imagine the use of such processes before the terrible conflict, violence, and injustice happens, preventing the Rwandan genocide, the Holocaust, Darfur, and more unnecessary killing in the Mideast? What processes can we develop for preventative dispute resolution, when our legal education and processes are so currently focused on the past (lawsuits and judicial decision making from past disputes)?...

The challenges for us are many in creating and sustaining new forms of processes with which to seek peace and justice:

1. What should the role of emotions/passions/beliefs be in our conflicts and deliberations with each other? Transformative empathy is among the most significant and important ways of grounding justice and moving people to new places. (Think Martin Luther King, Jr., the Civil Rights Movement, and parents of gays whose love for their children teaches them to change their views; think contra the emotional appeals of fascists and demagogues that tap into the baser forms of group identity and values).
2. How do we reconcile the need to adjudicate and punish the past, with correction of injustice, with reintegration of the future with peace and forgiveness, if not forgetfulness?
3. Do we need "rules" of process and decision rules "laid down" in advance, or can we negotiate and deliberate about the very processes we will use to achieve peace and justice in different contexts (historically, geographically, and culturally)?
4. How do we deal with the tyranny of the majority in a democracy and the needs of minorities for recognition and fulfillment (whether temporary, by issue or politics, or more permanent, by group or other identification)?

Steven R. Ratner, Jason S. Abrams, & James L. Bishoff, *Striving for Justice: The Prospects for Individual Accountability*

in Accountability for Human Rights Atrocities in International Law: Beyond the Nuremberg Legacy 372–378 (3d ed. 2009)

The Process for Pursuing Justice

[A]ccountability serves goals for the international community as a whole. International crimes violate the most central norms of humanity, and all states should have a moral and political interest in seeing an effective remedy. Accountability, whether through prosecutions or otherwise, also serves a preventive purpose. It can signal to future violators of human rights that their actions will not simply be forgotten in some political compromise. The exact form of accountability is less important than the existence of some process for stigmatizing the offender, aiding the victim, informing the society, and ensuring that political settlements and transitions take account of human rights abuses. We recognize that accountability alone is no deterrent to future atrocities....

[I]nternational law imposes duties on states to address various atrocities—duties that have arisen from the very moral and political concerns noted above. The treaty-based obligations in international criminal law are the most central, and various human rights treaties also contain provisions regarding accountability. In addition, recent actions by states, international organizations, and international courts suggest that a general norm requiring investigation and punishment of gross abusers is emerging. We are not overly sanguine as to whether this in fact reflects the actual expectations of most stares today, or whether most states that choose accountability do so out of any sense of legal obligation. Indeed, governments and international organizations have thus far proved quite deferential to the choices by individual stares in this area. But at the very least, the actions of states and international organizations in recent years—from the creation of diverse commissions of inquiry, to trials based on universal jurisdiction, to the creation of the ad hoc and hybrid tribunals and the ICC—suggest that the international legal process is now encouraging the establishment of mechanisms of accountability....

Choice of Mechanisms

The fora for holding individuals accountable for gross human rights abuses represent an amalgam of the old, the new, and the speculative, each with its promise and drawbacks. Each mechanism serves differing goals. Criminal proceedings best accomplish punishment and deterrence, with the accused facing a tribunal in public and the guilty imprisoned for their conduct. All the mechanisms, but especially investigatory commissions, serve to acknowledge the plight of the victims and promote transitions from times of trauma. As the most flexible mechanism, these panels are also in the best position to encourage specific reforms. Criminal or civil proceedings could conceivably result in financial reparation. The issues of selectivity noted earlier clearly affect and are affected by the relative weight states will assign to achieving each goal.

In choosing the means by which to advance these goals, societies must balance the legal, ethical, and social imperatives served by each approach against its political risks and other costs. Moreover, and significantly, they must differentiate between legal obstacles, on the one hand, and practical and political barriers, on the other. The legal impediments to all of the options considered are, relatively speaking, quite limited. Most choices will be dictated by concerns of practicality and a hefty dose of political realism.

With this in mind, some general principles for consideration can be elaborated:

- National tribunals are most likely to be successful in situations where a country's judicial system possesses the four critical prerequisites to the administration of justice—a legal framework of criminal law and procedure; a trained cadre of judges, lawyers, and other experts; adequate infrastructure; and a culture of respect for the fairness and impartiality of the process. This has meant some successful trials in Germany, Argentina, South Korea, Chile, Bosnia, Croatia, Serbia, and elsewhere. Where that system is dysfunctional or non-functional, local trials risk becoming a forum for settling personal and political vendettas, or may become mired in endless delays without regard for the human rights of the accused. In those situations, significant international assistance should be deployed to lay the groundwork for prosecutions meeting some minimum standards of fairness. This can rise to the level of dispatching foreign judges and prosecutors, thereby creating a hybrid tribunal under domestic law.
- Where defendants are located outside the state of the atrocities and for some reason cannot face justice at home, national trials by other states represent an appealing method of accountability. Such trials can both deliver justice for victims and perpetrators and embolden prosecutors and judges in the most affected state to initiate prosecutions. Success depends upon the extent to which the state is prepared to assert its prescriptive jurisdiction over crimes under international law, as well as its willingness to try a particular defendant. Many states will find the circumstances giving rise to the offenses too distant to justify prosecutions; but atrocities committed in states with a special connection to the forum states, e.g., a neighbor or former colony, may merit the attention of authorities. Nonetheless, the distance from the scene creates clear drawbacks both in terms of access to evidence and the impact of the trial on the society. Moreover, trials abroad might not guarantee respect for the defendants' rights, private plaintiff-prosecutors can bring politically motivated cases and, in some cases, the prosecutions might aggravate interstate relations in a manner than overshadows their general utility.
- Trials before an international criminal tribunal are more of a realistic possibility with the full functioning of the ICC. The ICC can encourage states to prosecute under complementarity and take a case itself if individual states cannot or do not wish to prosecute offenders. Stares with suspects will be able to hand them over to the Court, and those concerned with combatting impunity should put pressure on them to do so. Those refusing to transfer defendants may face binding

orders to comply. But the ICC will always limit itself to the worst offenders in the most calamitous atrocities. Future ad hoc international courts seem less likely now that the Security Council can refer situations to the ICC, but the Council will only refer a case (or conceivably create a new court under Chapter VII) if its members are convinced of the need for immediate action. The Darfur referral was such a case, but other equally egregious atrocities will not galvanize the Council without significant NGO and governmental lobbying. The work of the ICC or any new tribunal will demand substantial investment of political effort by members who deem such prosecutions worthwhile. Additional hybrid courts should be created by or with the UN as a way to keep justice local, but subject to some international oversight.

- Although a suit or advisory opinion in the International Court of Justice or before a regional human rights court cannot directly assess individual responsibility, it might support other methods of accountability under limited circumstances, by pressuring a state to fulfil obligations to prosecute individuals or supporting a demand from an international or domestic court for the surrender of an offender. But the option may also prove a confrontational way to encourage a government to pursue prosecutions.
- An investigatory commission can represent a highly effective method of accountability, preferably as a predecessor or complement to criminal trials. Where criminal trials are not feasible for the foreseeable future, commissions would appear indispensable. The key to their success will be in the mandate, resources, and time they are given. A thinly stretched staff, or an inability to name names, can easily undermine the restorative purposes of these panels. The political elites involved in setting up these bodies must allow them to work independently and agree to honor their findings and recommendations.
- Victims living in states that offer civil remedies can consider institution of civil actions both as a form of punishment as well as a possible source of some small compensation for the victim. The prime model here remains the US Alien Tort Claims Act. In order to prevail, a victim would need to identify a particular abuser. However, courts typically need to have jurisdiction over the defendant; there are few analogues outside the United States; US law is somewhat unsettled; and monetary damages remain extraordinarily difficult to collect.
- If offenders have traveled overseas since the time of the abuses, other states can bring immigration measures to bear to deprive them of safe havens. Deportation both removes offenders and can support prosecutions and other legal action.
- If former human rights abusers have stowed assets overseas, governments can consider instituting legal proceedings to retrieve them. This may prove extremely onerous given bank secrecy laws and the requirements for international cooperation, as the government of the Philippines discovered in its search for, and attempt to retrieve, the assets of Ferdinand and Imelda Marcos. It will also require substantial assistance from experts on money laundering.

- Lustration serves to both cleanse post-atrocity governments of those responsible for abuses as well as mete out a form of accountability. It can serve as a clear message that the state has turned a page in its history. But its greatest risks are the absence of due process to those subjected to loss of employment and the possibility that the new regime will extend the lustration too broadly, to the detriment of both the state and numerous citizens.
- The success of domestic, international, or hybrid tribunals depends critically upon gaining custody over the defendants. If they have fled the country (in the case of national or hybrid tribunals) or remain in havens or in hiding within the country, their apprehension becomes the critical issue for the forum, as seen with the impunity enjoyed by Mengistu Haile-Mariam, Ahmad Harun, and Ratko Mladic. International law enforcement cooperation is required to arrest these fugitives, including through a warrant that effectively prevents the accused's international travel.
- All the mechanisms depend upon access to usable evidence. It is a truism, though an important one, that those attempting accountability must obtain control of physical evidence as speedily as possible and ensure its preservation and locate witnesses and ensure their protection from retaliation for their testimony.
- The feasibility of any option will hinge on the amount of resources devoted to it. Any mechanism will also have to set priorities for the crimes it chooses to investigate. Efforts to bring people to justice face diminishing returns after a certain point. Investigations of sporadic or otherwise less important violations thus seem an inefficient use of resources.
- Once decision-makers choose one or more mechanisms, they will often have to manage the process in a highly volatile political environment. They will have to ensure that accountability measures do not turn into a free-for-all or excuse for vengeance against political enemies. To ensure impartiality, political leaders muse keep their rhetoric in check and refrain from interfering in the proceedings. Outside participants, in particular NGOs, will have to be sensitive to the constraints on a polity to undertake any form of accountability.
- Any mechanism can only work with the support of the people of the particular state. Although the crimes concern all mankind, it is ultimately the people of a state—past, present, and future—who remain most affected. If they have a democratically elected government, it must be their primary voice on this question. If that government rejects accountability in favor of a compromise with former abusers, amnesty, or other forms of impunity, or seeks to use accountability as a weapon against political enemies, almost any effort at accountability seems crippled, if not stillborn. Although international law imposes some duties on states to refrain from such policies, proponents of accountability may end up bearing the burden of persuading a government to foreswear impunity.

- If the state asks for international support for its own efforts, the global community can offer significant assistance at relatively low cost. Loans of law enforcement officials, forensic experts, legal advisors, and other specialists represent an immediate and tangible contribution to the state's efforts.

The Fate of Individual Accountability: A Word of Caution

The global community's attempt to erect an architecture of individual accountability from the ashes of World War II presents an opportunity to enforce human rights in the most direct way possible—by assigning responsibility to those who abuse human rights in the belief that they do so with impunity. The duty of states, international organizations, and nongovernmental organizations in this regard is thus clear.

On the one hand, the work of states, international institutions, and NGOs since the 1990s has yielded an impressive body of treaties, judicial opinion, and doctrine. Although we still lack a coherent codification of international criminal law concerning human rights abuses, domestic courts, international and hybrid tribunals, and investigatory commissions have created significant case law to elaborate the substantive norms of accountability. Yet, these implementation mechanisms, while greater in variety and now quite active, do not operate with full vigor and regularity, leaving individual accountability inconsistent and, in many ways, exceptional....

Thus, the traditional strategies to secure compliance with international human rights and humanitarian law remain highly pertinent as states and international organizations continue the experiment with individual accountability. These means turn on making the state or non-state entity overseeing abuses the target of opprobrium for the actions of its agents through the glare of publicity thrown on abuses by international organizations and NGOs, through diplomatic isolation, through economic sanctions and suspension of foreign aid, and, in exceptional cases, through military intervention to prevent or bring a halt to large-scale atrocities. Alongside these strategies to respond to abuses, governments, international organizations, and NGOs must also deploy preventive processes to keep political differences from turning into atrocities. It was, after all, not the threat of individual culpability that brought an end to apartheid in South Africa, military rule in Haiti, and civil wars in Latin America, but concerted and united, if too often delayed, action against states and other authorities. The centrality of these strategies was confirmed in 2005 by nearly all heads of state and government, when they adopted the Responsibility to Protect doctrine in a landmark General Assembly resolution. The concept places a new moral marker on the political landscape—but follow-up to its commitments remains weak. Given the state of enforcement mechanisms for international criminal law, those contemplating or committing human rights abuses may not yet fear individual accountability; but they should know that outside actors remain prepared to make robust use of other sanctioning devices. Until individuals can be caught, tried, and otherwise uncovered, their sponsors must feel the heat of the abuses they commit.

Notes & Questions

1. Is it a good thing that there are so many possible avenues and venues for attempting redress of human-rights atrocities and violations of international law, or is it problematic?
2. Would you advocate a single, *civil* law-based international court for human-rights violations to provide specific civil remedies? Would this be possible, given what we have seen about cultural variations in human-rights law?
3. What are the various enforcement mechanisms for each of the processes described above? Is weak enforcement a concern? Is it enough to have these processes and institutions as "symbolic" justice? Do they contribute to peace, democracy, or other values?

You might recall from Chapter 3 the debate between William Zartman, who writes about how we should wait for disputes to ripen, and John Paul Lederach, who asks us to think of peace work and dispute resolution as a process of "cultivation" that takes a long time and requires care and hard work over generations. Think about which processes here are suitable for developing a culture of cultivation of dispute resolution and reconciliation and which are more incident- or episode-based.

John Paul Lederach has been a leader in conflict resolution and peace for decades, working on many continents and in many countries. In one way or another, he says, he "can touch the hands of both his grandparents and grandchildren to see a span of over 100 year of human struggle with conflict—perhaps, little by little, each generation will learn from the one that went before."[6] We end with repeating his comments from Chapter 3 on the importance of optimistic "cultivation" of peace (and justice).

John Paul Lederach, *Cultivating Peace: A Practitioner's View of Deadly Conflict and Negotiation*

in CONTEMPORARY PEACEMAKING: CONFLICT, VIOLENCE AND PEACE PROCESSES 36, 36–38, 40–44 (John Darby & Roger MacGinty eds., 2d ed. 2008)

When I played basketball many years ago our coach had a phrase with which he provoked us whenever we missed an easy shot, "I can't believe you missed that cherry picker." Essentially it meant that a lot of work had gone into place and then just when everything was right and a giveaway opportunity was presented, the basket was missed.

There are times when I have the impression that the metaphor of ripeness leads towards an emphasis on mediator action as if it were "cherry picking." The impression

---

6. From John Paul Lederach, Preparing for Peace: Conflict Transformation across Cultures (1995), cited in Carrie Menkel-Meadow, *The Historical Contingencies of Conflict Resolution*, 1 Int'l J. Conflict Engagement & Resol. 32–55 (2013).

emerges from two understandings about mediation that I believe have significant limitations and implications.

What the ripeness metaphor does not provide is a sense of the long-term nature of the process, the building and sustaining of the relationships, nor the multiplicity of roles, activities and functions that may be necessary to make a sustained dialogue and change in the relationships possible.

It is not a metaphor that provides a vision of cultivating the soil, planting the seeds or nourishing the seedling in the face of winds, burning sun or icy storms, all of which speak to process, relationship and sustainability rather than a momentary action.

Alternative Metaphors to Ripeness …

Cultivation: The Building of Long-Term Authentic Relationships

The cultivation metaphor suggests that a deep respect for, and connection to, the context is critical for sustaining a change process that is moving from deadly expressions of conflict to increased justice and peace in relationships. The context of protracted deadly conflict, like soil, is the people, commonly shared geographies but often sharply differing views of history, rights and responsibilities, and the formation of perception and understandings based on cultural meaning structures. Cultivation is recognizing that ultimately the change process must be taken up, embraced and sustained by people in these contexts. The cultivator, as a connected but outside element in the system, approaches this soil with a great deal of respect, the suspension of quick judgment in favor of the wisdom of adaptation, and an orientation towards supporting the change process through highs and lows, ebbs and flows of violence and thawing of tensions, whether or not the situation appears ripe. The cultivator gives attention to the well-being of the ecosystem, not just the quick production of a given fruit.

Epilogue

So what do I say when the journalist asks, "And do you really believe it is possible to talk about negotiation and peace when war is raging?" I say hope is not negotiated. It is kept alive by people who understand the depth of suffering and know the cost of keeping a horizon of change as a possibility for their children and grandchildren. Quick fixes to long-standing violent conflict are like growing a garden with no understanding of seeds, soils and sweat. This conflict traces back across decades, even generations. It will take that long to sort out.

Journalists generally do not quote me in their papers. Sound bites about ripeness, people coming to their senses, and the need for realism and pressure seem to find their way into print more often. But I believe in cultivation. Cultivation as a metaphor suggests that the core of the peacebuilding work—fostering and sustaining committed, authentic relationships across the lines of conflict over time—does not rise and fall with the temporal ups and downs of the conflict cycles. It answers the question—is it possible to pursue peace when things are bad—with a resounding "Yes!" just as it also suggests that when things are suddenly headed towards an agreement the work is hardly over. It has only begun.

Notes & Questions

1. We close here by inviting you to embrace process pluralism and design your own systems:

   > Imagine yourself a person grievously wronged—a terminated employee, an abandoned spouse, a victim of an urban American police beating, a victim of discrimination, a released political prisoner from an opposition party in a dictatorial state, a family member of a murder victim, a property owner in a former Communist state whose property was confiscated, an aged surviving Korean "comfort woman," or a survivor of the German Holocaust or the Rwandan genocide. What kind of process would you want to feel you had been "justly" dealt with?

   Carrie Menkel-Meadow, *Remembrance of Things Past? The Relationship of Past to Future in Pursuing Justice in Mediation*, 5 Cardozo J. Conflict Resol. 97, 105 (2004).

2. Would you want a public process to give testimony? A private ceremony of grief? Would you require compensation, an apology, retribution, and/or a formal determination of guilt with punishment? Would you want to create your own process, or would you be willing to use the same process as other people who suffered the same wrongs? How likely do you think it will be that all people who suffer these injuries would agree to the same process?

We hope you will go forth and use your conflict resolution skills and analysis to seek peace and justice.

Further Reading

Accountability for Atrocities: National and International Responses (Jane Stromseth ed., 2003).

Christine Bell, On the Law of Peace: Peace Agreements and the *Lex Pacificatoria*, (2008).

Suzanne Buckley-Zistel & Stefanie Schafer, Memorials in Times of Transition (2014).

Building Peace: Reflections from the Field (Craig Zelizer & Robert Rubenstein eds., 2009).

Bruce W. Dayton & Louis Kriesberg, Constructive Conflicts: From Emergence to Transformation (6th ed. 2022).

Dietrich Dörner, The Logic of Failure: Recognizing and Avoiding Error in Complex Situations (1997).

Lois Edmond, Introduction to Peace and Conflict Studies (2021).

Isabelle Gunning, *Arrogant Perception, World Traveling and Multi-Cultural Feminism: The Case of Female Genital Surgeries*, 23 Columbia Human Rts. L. Rev. 189 (1991–92).

Isabelle Gunning, *Diversity Issues in Mediation: Controlling Negative Cultural Myths*, 1995 J. Disp. Resol. 55.

Stuart Hampshire, Justice Is Conflict (2000).

Michael Ignatieff, Blood and Belonging: Journeys into the New Nationalism (1995).

Sanda Kaufman, Chris Honeyman, & Andrea Kupfer Schneider, *Should They Listen to Us? Seeking a Negotiation/Conflict Resolution Contribution to Practice in Intractable Conflicts*, 2017 J. Disp. Resol., no. 1, 2017, at 73.

Sven M. G. Koopmans, Negotiating Peace: A Guide to the Practice, Politics, and Law of International Mediation (2018).

Martti Koskenniemi, The Gentle Civilizer of Nations: The Rise and Fall of International Law 1870–1960 (2001).

Will Kymlicka, Multi-Cultural Citizenship (1995).

David A. Lax & James K. Sebenius, The Manager as Negotiator: Bargaining for Cooperation and Competitive Gain (1986).

Inga Laurent, *An Absence of Accountability*, 54 Seton Hall L. Rev. 137–200 (2024).

John Paul Lederach, Building Peace: Sustainable Reconciliation in Divided Societies (1998).

John Paul Lederach, The Little Book of Conflict Transformation (2003).

Carrie J. Menkel-Meadow, Lela P. Love, Andrea Kupfer Schneider, Michael L. Moffitt, & Kristen Blankley, Dispute Resolution: Beyond the Adversarial Model (4th ed. 2025).

Robert Mnookin, Bargaining with the Devil: When to Negotiate, When to Fight (2010).

Sarah M. H. Nouwen, *Peacemaking* in Eyal Benvinisti & Dino Kritsiotis ed., Cambridge History of International Law Vol. XII (2024).

Angel Oquendo, Through Thick and Thin: From Human Rights Principles to Politics Across the Americas and Beyond (2022).

Alison Dundes Renteln, The Cultural Defense (2005).

Oliver P. Richmond, Peace: A Very Short Introduction (2014).

Amartya Sen, The Idea of Justice (2009).

Andrea Kupfer Schneider, *Bargaining in the Shadow of International Law*, 41 N.Y.U. J. Int'l L. & Pol. 789 (2009).

Third World Approaches to International Law: On Praxis and the Intellectual (Usha Natarajan, John Reynolds, Amar Bhatia, & Sujith Xavier eds., 2018).

Yoshifumi Tanaka, The Peaceful Settlement of International Disputes (2018).

Bibliography

Articles & Books

SAMI ADWAM, ET AL., SIDE BY SIDE: PARALLEL HISTORIES OF ISRAEL-PALESTINE (Prime 2012).

Robert B. Ahdieh, *Between Dialogue and Decree: International Review of National Courts*, 79 N.Y.U. L. REV. 2029–2163 (2004).

NADJA ALEXANDER, INTERNATIONAL AND COMPARATIVE MEDIATION: LEGAL PERSPECTIVES (2009).

SHAHLA ALI, EXPLORING COURT MEDIATION REFORM: EFFICIENCY, CONFIDENCE AND PERCEPTIONS OF JUSTICE (2018).

Cynthia Alkon & Sanda Kaufman, *A Theory of Interests in the Context of Hybrid Warfare: It's Complex*, 24 CARDOZO J. CONFLICT RESOL. (2022).

KAREN J. ALTER, ET AL., INTERNATIONAL COURT AUTHORITY (2017).

ABDEL MOENM SAID ALY, ET AL., ARABS AND ISRAELIS (2nd ed. 2022).

LISA BLOMGREN AMSLER, ET AL., DISPUTE SYSTEM DESIGN: PREVENTING, MANAGING, AND RESOLVING CONFLICT (2020).

Harry Arthurs, *A Global Code of Legal Ethics for the Transnational Legal Field*, 2 LEGAL ETHICS 59–99 (1999).

ROBERT AXELROD, THE EVOLUTION OF COOPERATION (1984).

John Barkai, *What's a Cross-Cultural Mediator to Do? A Low Context Solution for a High Context Problem*, 10 CARDOZO J. CONFLICT RESOL 43 (2008).

ELAZAR BARKAN, THE GUILT OF NATIONS: RESTITUTION AND NEGOTIATING HISTORICAL INJUSTICES (2000).

GERSHON BASKIN, THE NEGOTIATOR: FREEING GILAD SCHALIT FROM HAMAS (2013).

CHRISTINE BELL, ON THE LAW OF PEACE: PEACE AGREEMENTS AND THE LEX PACIFICATORIA (2008).

JACOB BERCOVITCH, STUDIES IN INTERNATIONAL MEDIATION (2003).

Paul Schiff Berman, *Global Legal Pluralism*, 80 S. CAL. L. REV. 1155–1238 (2007).

Lisa Bernstein, *Opting Out of the Legal System: Extralegal Contractual Relations in the Diamond Industry*, 21 J. LEGAL STUD. 115–157 (1992).

Simon Blackburn, A Very Short Introduction to Ethics (2nd ed. 2021).

Christopher Blattman, Why We Fight: The Roots of War and the Paths to Peace (2022).

Gabriella Blum, Islands of Agreement: Managing Enduring Armed Rivalries (2007).

Gary Born, International Arbitration: Cases and Materials (2021).

Jeanne M. Brett, Negotiating Globally: How to Negotiate Deals, Resolve Disputes, and Make Decisions Across Cultural Boundaries (3rd ed. 2014).

Edward Brunet, *Replacing Folklore Arbitration With a Contract Model of Arbitration*, 74 Tulane L. Rev. 39 (1999).

Suzanne Buckeley-Zistel & Stefanie Schafer, Memorials in Times of Transition (2014).

William Burke-White, *The Argentine Financial Crisis: State Liability Under BITS and the Legitimacy of the ICSID System*, 31 AJWH 200 (2008).

David Caron, *The Nature of the Iran-United States Claims Tribunal and the Evolving Structure of International Dispute Resolution*, 84 Am. J. Int'l L. 151–56 (1990).

The Conflict & Culture Reader (Pat Chew ed., 2001).

Donald Childress III, et al., Transnational Law and Practice (2015).

Calvin Chrustie, et al., *Negotiating Wicked Problems: Five Stories, in* Venturing Beyond the Classroom: Volume 2 of the Rethinking Negotiation Teaching Series (C. Honeyman, J. Coben, & G. de Palo eds., 2010).

Amy Cohen, *Dispute System Design: Neoliberalism and the Problem of Scale*, 14 Harvard Neg. L. Rev. 51 (2009).

Ethics and International Affairs: Extent and Limits (Coicaud Jean Marc & Daniel Warner eds., 2001).

Tony Cole & Pietro Ortolani, Understanding International Arbitration (2020).

Sarah Cole & Amanda Spangler, *Virtual Mediation: The Only Door Needed in a Multi-door Courthouse?*, 52 Stetson L. Rev. 477–506 (2023).

Peter T. Coleman & Robert Ricigliano, *Getting in Sync: What to Do When Problem-Solving Fails to Fix the Problem, in* The Negotiator's Desk Reference (Chris Honeyman & Andrea Kupfer Schneider eds., 2017).

Pablo Cortés, The Law of Consumer Redress in an Evolving Digital Market: Upgrading from Alternative to Online Dispute Resolution (2018).

Cathy Costantino & Christiana Sickles Merchant, Designing Conflict Management Systems: A Guide to Creating Healthy and Productive Organizations (1996).

NAOMI CREUTZFELDT, OMBUDSMEN AND ADR: A COMPARATIVE STUDY OF INFORMAL JUSTICE IN EUROPE (2018).

Naomi Creutzfeldt, *Towards a Digital Legal Consciousness*, 12 EUROPEAN J. OF L. & TECHNOLOGY (2021).

Moty Cristal, *Negotiation in A Low-to-no-trust Environment*, *in* THE NEGOTIATOR'S DESK REFERENCE (Christopher Honeyman & Andrea Kupfer Schneider eds., 2017).

Daniel Curran, et al., *Case Analysis: Two Paths to Peace: Contrasting George Mitchell in Northern Ireland with Richard Holbrooke in Bosnia-Herzegovina*, 20 NEGOTIATION J. 513–31 (October 2004).

BRUCE W. DAYTON & LOUIS KRIESBERG, CONSTRUCTIVE CONFLICTS: FROM EMERGENCE TO TRANSFORMATION (6th ed. 2022).

CARLA DEL PONTE, MADAME PROSECUTOR: CONFRONTATIONS WITH HUMANITY'S WORST CRIMINALS AND THE CULTURE OF IMPUNITY (2009).

Catrina Denvir & Amanda Selvarajah, *Safeguarding Access to Justice in the Age of the Online Court*. 85 MOD. L. REV. 25–68 (2022).

MORTON DEUTSCH, THE RESOLUTION OF CONFLICT: CONSTRUCTIVE AND DESTRUCTIVE PROCESSES (1973).

YVES DEZALAY & BRYANT GARTH, DEALING IN VIRTUE: INTERNATIONAL COMMERCIAL ARBITRATION AND THE CONSTRUCTION OF A TRANSNATIONAL LEGAL ORDER (1996).

Jayne Seminare Docherty, *Culture: Culture and Negotiation: Symmetrical Anthropology for Negotiators*, 87 MARQ. L. REV. 711 (2004).

Thomas Donaldson, *Values in Tension: Ethics Away From Home*, HARVARD BUSINESS REV. (1996).

DIETRICH DÖRNER, THE LOGIC OF FAILURE: RECOGNIZING AND AVOIDING ERROR IN COMPLEX SITUATIONS (1997).

Christopher Drahozal, et al., *Challenging and Enforcing International Arbitral Awards in U.S. Federal Courts: An Empirical Study* VA. J. INT'L L. (2023).

DANIEL DRUCKMAN, NEGOTIATION: IDENTITY AND JUSTICE: PATHS TO AGREEMENT (2023).

JEFFREY DUNOFF, ET AL., INTERNATIONAL LAW: NORMS, ACTORS, PROCESS (4th ed. 2015).

Noam Ebner, et al., *You've Got Agreement: Negoti@Ting Via Email*, *in* RETHINKING NEGOTIATION TEACHING 91–106 (Christopher Honeyman, James Coben, and Giuseppe de Palo eds., 2009).

Noam Ebner & Elayne Greenberg, *Strengthening Online Dispute Resolution Justice*, 63 WASH. U. J. OF LAW & POLICY 65–118 (2020).

Noam Ebner & John Zeleznikow, *No Sheriff in Town: Governance for the ODR Field*, 32 NEG. J. 297–323 (2016).

LAUREN EDELMAN, WORKING LAW: COURTS, CORPORATIONS, AND SYMBOLIC CIVIL RIGHTS (2016).

LOIS EDMOND, INTRODUCTION TO PEACE AND CONFLICT STUDIES (2021).

JON ELSTER, CLOSING THE BOOKS: TRANSITIONAL JUSTICE IN HISTORICAL PERSPECTIVE (2004).

Matthew S. Erie, *The New Legal Hubs: The Emergent Landscape Of International Commercial Dispute Resolution.* 60 VA. J. INT'L L. 228–266 (2020).

STUART E. EIZENSTADT, THE ART OF DIPLOMACY: HOW AMERICAN NEGOTIATORS REACHED HISTORIC AGREEMENTS THAT CHANGED THE WORLD (2024).

KENNETH FEINBERG, WHAT'S LIFE WORTH? THE UNPRECEDENTED EFFORT TO COMPENSATE THE VICTIMS OF 9/11 (2005).

William Felstiner, et al., *The Emergence and Transformation of Disputes: Naming, Blaming and Claiming,* 15 L & SOC'Y REV. 631–654 (1980–81).

ROGER FISHER, ET AL., BEYOND MACHIAVELLI: TOOLS FOR COPING WITH CONFLICT (1994).

ROGER FISHER, ET AL., GETTING TO YES: NEGOTIATING AGREEMENT WITHOUT GIVING IN (3rd ed. 2011).

Mary Parker Follett, *Constructive Conflict, in* MARY PARKER FOLLETT—PROPHET OF MANAGEMENT: A CELEBRATION OF WRITINGS FROM THE 1920S (Pauline Graham ed., 1995).

Susan D. Franck, *The Diversity Challenge: Exploring the 'Invisible College' of International Arbitration,* 53 COLUMBIA J. TRANSNAT'L L. 451–505 (2015).

Susan D. Franck, *The Legitimacy Crisis In Investment Treaty Arbitration: Privatizing Public International Law Through Inconsistent Decisions.* 73 FORDHAM L. REV. 1525–1580 (2005).

Susan D. Franck, *Predicting Outcomes In Investment Treaty Arbitration.* 65 DUKE L.J. 470–526 (2015).

Susan D. Franck, *The Nature and Enforcement of Investor Rights Under Investment Treaties: Do Investment Treaties Have a Bright Future?* 12 UC DAVIS L. REV. 48–55 (2005).

Thomas Friedman, *A Titanic Geopolitical Struggle is Underway,* N.Y. TIMES (2024).

Thomas Friedman, *What's Happening to Our World,* N. Y. TIMES (2023).

FRANCIS FUKUYAMA, THE END OF HISTORY AND THE LAST MAN (2006).

LON L. FULLER, THE PRINCIPLES OF SOCIAL ORDER: SELECTED ESSAYS OF LON L. FULLER (Kenneth I. Winston ed., 1981).

MARK GALEOTTI, THE WEAPONIZING OF EVERYTHING: A FIELD GUIDE TO THE NEW WAY OF WAR (2023).

THE HANDBOOK OF NEGOTIATION AND CULTURE (Michele Gelfand & Jeanne Brett eds., 2004).

JAMES GIBSON, OVERCOMING APARTHEID: CAN TRUTH RESOLVE A DIVIDED NATION? (2004).

MARY ANN GLENDON, A WORLD MADE NEW: ELEANOR ROOSEVELT AND THE UNIVERSAL DECLARATION OF HUMAN RIGHTS (2002).

PUMLA GOBODO-MADIKIZELA, A HUMAN BEING DIED THAT NIGHT: A SOUTH AFRICAN STORY OF FORGIVENESS (2003).

JACK L. GOLDSMITH & ERIC A. POSNER, THE LIMITS OF INTERNATIONAL LAW (2011).

Richard J. Goldstone & Rebecca Hamilton, Bosnia *v.* Serbia*: Lessons from the Encounter of the International Court of Justice with the International Criminal Tribunal for the Former Yugoslavia*, 21 LEIDEN JOURNAL OF INTERNATIONAL LAW 95–112 (2008).

RICHARD J GOLDSTONE & ADAM SMITH, INTERNATIONAL JUDICIAL INSTITUTIONS: THE ARCHITECTURE OF INTERNATIONAL JUSTICE AT HOME AND ABROAD (2009).

Elayne E Greenberg, *Zooming in on Neutrals' Implicit 'isms*, 15 NYSBA NEW YORK DISPUTE RESOLUTION LAWYER 9–11 (2022).

Florian Grisel, *Canceling Disputes: How Social Capital Affects the Arbitration of Disputes on Wikipedia*, 49 LAW & SOC. INQUIRY 1–22 (2023).

PHILIP H. GULLIVER, DISPUTES AND NEGOTIATIONS: A CROSS CULTURAL PERSPECTIVE (1979).

Isabelle Gunning, *Diversity Issues in Mediation: Controlling Negative Cultural Myths*. J. DISP. RESOL. 55 (1995).

Isabelle Gunning, *Arrogant Perception, World Traveling and Multi-cultural Feminism: The Case of Female Genital Surgeries*, 23 COLUMBIA HUMAN RTS. L. REV. 189 (1991–1992).

JURGEN HABERMAS, A THEORY OF COMMUNICATIVE ACTION (1981).

STUART HAMPSHIRE, JUSTICE IS CONFLICT (2000).

OONA A. HATHAWAY & SCOTT J. SHAPIRO, THE INTERNATIONALISTS: HOW A RADICAL PLAN TO OUTLAW WAR REMADE THE WORLD (2017).

PRISCILLA HAYNER, UNSPEAKABLE TRUTHS: TRANSITIONAL JUSTICE AND THE CHALLENGE OF TRUTH COMMISSIONS (2nd ed. 2010).

ALEXANDER HERMAN, THE PARTHENON MARBLES DISPUTE (2023).

ALEXANDER HERMAN, RESTITUTION: THE RETURN OF CULTURAL ARTIFACTS (2021).

GLEIDER HERNANDEZ, INTERNATIONAL LAW (2019).

Rosalind Higgins, *A Babel of Judicial Voices? Ruminations from the Bench*, 55 INT'L & COMPAR. L.Q. 791 (2006).

CHRISTOPHER HITCHENS, THE ELGIN MARBLES: SHOULD THEY BE RETURNED TO GREECE? (1987).

GEERT HOFSTEDE, CULTURE'S CONSEQUENCES: INTERNATIONAL DIFFERENCES IN WORK RELATED VALUES (1980).

Terence Hopmann, *Two Paradigms of Negotiations: Bargaining and Problem Solving*, 542 ANNALS AM. ACAD. POL & SOC. SCI. 24 (1995).

MEDIATION: PRINCIPLES AND REGULATION IN COMPARATIVE PERSPECTIVE (Klaus J. Hopt & Felix Steffek eds., 2013).

LYNN HUNT, INVENTING HUMAN RIGHTS: A HISTORY (2008).

Samuel P. Huntington, *The Clash of Civilizations? The International System After the Collapse of the East-West Order*, *in* THE INTERNATIONAL SYSTEM AFTER THE COLLAPSE OF THE EAST-WEST ORDER (Armand Clesse, et al. eds., 1994).

Diana Hurwitz, *Fishing for Compromises through NAFTA and Environmental Dispute-Settlement: The Tuna-Dolphin Controversy*, 3 NAT. RES. J. (1995).

MICHAEL IGNATIEFF, BLOOD AND BELONGING: JOURNEYS INTO THE NEW NATIONALISM (1995.

International Law Commission, *Conclusions of the Work of the Study Group on the Fragmentation of International Law: Difficulties Arising From the Diversification and Expansion of International Law*, YEARBOOK OF THE INTERNATIONAL LAW COMMISSION (2006).

Carol Izumi, *Implicit Bias and the Illusion of Mediator Neutrality*, 34 WASH. U. J.L. & POL'Y 71–99 (2010).

JOHN HOWARD JACKSON, THE WORLD TRADING SYSTEM: LAW AND POLICY OF INTERNATIONAL ECONOMIC RELATIONS (1989).

IRVING JANIS, GROUPTHINK: PSYCHOLOGICAL STUDIES OF POLICY DECISIONS AND FIASCOS (2nd ed. 1982).

Valerie Jenness & Kitty Calavita, *It Depends on the Outcome: Prisoner's Grievances and Perceptions of Justice*, 52 LAW & SOC'Y REV. 41–71 (2018).

A RESTORATIVE JUSTICE READER: TEXTS, SOURCES, CONTEXTS (Gerry Johnstone ed., 2003).

ENCOUNTER POINT (Just Visions Pictures 2006).

Miles Kahler, *Multi-lateralism with small and large numbers*, 46 INT'L ORG. 681–694 (1992).

Sanda Kaufman, et al., *Should They Listen to Us? Seeking a Negotiation/Conflict Resolution Contribution to Practice in Intractable Conflicts*, J. DISP. RESOL. (2017).

ETHAN KATSH & ORNA RABINOVICH-EINY, DIGITAL JUSTICE: TECHNOLOGY AND THE INTERNET OF DISPUTES (2017).

HENRY KISSINGER, WORLD ORDER (2015).

JAN KLABBERS, ADVANCED INTRODUCTION TO THE LAW OF INTERNATIONAL ORGANIZATIONS (2015).

MICHAEL KLARE, *The New Geography of Conflict*, 80 FOREIGN AFFAIRS 49 (2001).

SVEN M. G. KOOPMANS, NEGOTIATING PEACE: A GUIDE TO THE PRACTICE, POLITICS, AND LAW OF INTERNATIONAL MEDIATION (2018).

Russell Korobkin, *Exploring the Link Between Domestic Conflicts and Negotiation Failure in the Middle East*, 6 NEVADA L.J. 388 (2005–2006).

INTERNATIONAL NEGOTIATION: ANALYSIS, APPROACHES ISSUES (Victor Kremenyuk ED., 2002).

MARTTI KOSKENNIEMI, THE GENTLE CIVILIZERS OF NATIONS: THE RISE AND FALL OF INTERNATIONAL LAW 1870–1960 (2001).

DANIEL KURTZER & SCOTT LASENSKY, NEGOTIATING ARAB-ISRAELI PEACE (2008).

WILL KYMLICKA, MULTI-CULTURAL CITIZENSHIP (1995).

Lisa J. Laplante & Suzanne A. Spears, *Out Of The Conflict Zone: The Case For Community Consent Processes In The Extractive Sector*, 11 YALE HUM. RTS. & DEV. L.J. JOURNAL 69 (2008).

David Larson, *Designing a State Court Small Claims ODR System: Hitting a Moving Target in New York During a Pandemic*, 22 CARDOZO J. CONFLICT RESOL. 569–580 (2021).

MIRI LAUFER & EREZ LAUFER, ONE DAY AFTER PEACE (2012).

Inga Laurent, *An Absence of Accountability*, 54 SETON HALL L. REV. 137 (2023).

DAVID A. LAX & JAMES K. SEBENIUS, THE MANAGER AS NEGOTIATOR (1986).

Michelle Le Baron & Mario Patera, *Reflective Practice in the New Millennium*, *in* RETHINKING NEGOTIATION TEACHING: INNOVATIONS FOR CONTEXT AND CULTURE (C. Honeyman, et al. eds., 2008).

JOHN PAUL LEDERACH, BUILDING PEACE: SUSTAINABLE RECONCILIATION IN DIVIDED SOCIETIES (1998).

John Paul Lederach, *Cultivating Peace: A Practitioner's View Of Deadly Conflict And Negotiation*, *in* CONTEMPORARY PEACEMAKING: CONFLICT, VIOLENCE AND PEACE PROCESSES (John Darby & Roger MacGinty eds., 2nd ed. 2008).

JOHN PAUL LEDERACH, THE LITTLE BOOK OF CONFLICT TRANSFORMATION (2003).

Joel Lee, *Culture and Its Importance in Mediation*, 16 PEPP. DISP. RES. L.J. 317 (2016).

Leslie, Levin, et al., *The Impact of International Lawyer Organizations on Lawyer Regulation*. 42 FORDHAM INT'L L.J. 407–440 (2018).

Roy J. Lewicki & R.J Robinson, *Ethical and Unethical Bargaining Tactics: An Empirical Study*. 17 JOURNAL OF BUSINESS ETHICS 665–82 (1998).

Ji Li & Carrie Menkel-Meadow, *Dispute Process Choices Among Chinese Companies in the United States: Some Preliminary Data and Analysis*, 27 HARV. NEGOT. L. REV. 295–335 (2022).

I, DANIEL BLAKE (BC Films 2016).

Niccolò Machiavelli, The Prince (Harvey Mansfield, trans., 2nd ed. University of Chicago Press 1998) (1532).

Avishai Margalit, On Compromises and Rotten Compromises (2010).

Janet K. Martinez, *Designing Online Dispute Resolution.* J. Disp. Resol. 135–136 (2020).

Janet K. Martinez & M. Watanabe, *ODR System Design: An Analytical Framework with Examples.* 10 International Journal on Online Dispute Resolution 55–59 (2023).

Makau Matua, *What is TWAIL?*, Proceedings of the American Society of International Law at its Annual Meeting 94 (2000).

Francis E. McGovern, *Dispute System Design: The United Nations Compensation Commission*, 14 Harv. Negot. L. Rev. 171 (2009).

Paul Meerts, Diplomatic Negotiations: Essence and Evolution (2019).

Carrie Menkel-Meadow, *Alternative Dispute Resolution, in* Max Planck Encyclopedia of International Law (2018).

Carrie Menkel-Meadow, *Are Cross-Cultural Ethics Standards Possible or Desirable in International Arbitration?, in* Mélanges en l'honneur de Pierre Tercier (Peter Gauch, Franz Werro, & Pascal Pichonnaz eds., 2008).

Carrie Menkel-Meadow, *Are There Systemic Ethics Issues in Dispute System Design—And What We Should [Not] Do About It: Lessons from International and Domestic Fronts.* 14 Harv. Negot. L. Rev. 195–221 (2009).

Carrie Menkel-Meadow, *Compromise, Negotiation, and Morality*, 26 Negotiation J. 483–497 (2010).

Carrie Menkel-Meadow, *Conflict Theory, in* Encyclopedia of Community: From the Village to the Virtual World (Kareen Christensen & David Levinson eds., 2003).

Carrie Menkel-Meadow, *Correspondences and Contradictions in International and Domestic Conflict Resolution*, J. Disp. Resol. 319 (2003).

Carrie Menkel-Meadow, *Cross-cultural disputes and mediator strategies, in* Routledge Handbook Of Intercultural Mediation (Dominic Busch ed., 2022).

Carrie Menkel-Meadow, *Deconstructing Henry: Negotiation Lessons From Kissinger's Career*, 35 Negotiation J. 348–358 (2019).

Carrie Menkel-Meadow, *Ethical Ordering in Transnational Legal Practice? A Review of Catherine A. Rogers's Ethics in International Arbitration*, 29 Geo. J. Legal Ethics 209–238 (2016).

Carrie Menkel-Meadow, *Hybrid And Mixed Dispute Resolution Processes: Integrities Of Process Pluralism, in* Comparative Dispute Resolution Research Handbook (Maria Moscati, Michael Palmer & Marion Roberts eds., 2020).

Carrie Menkel-Meadow, *In the Land of Blood and Honey: What's Fair or Just in Love and War Crimes? Lessons for Transitional Justice, in* Framing Law and Crime: An

INTERDISCIPLINARY ANTHOLOGY (Caroline Joan S. Picart, Michael Hviid Jacobsen, & Cecil Greek eds., 2016).

Carrie Menkel-Meadow, *International Dispute Resolution*, *in* COMPLEX DISPUTE RESOLUTION, VOL. III (2012).

Carrie Menkel-Meadow, *Is ODR ADR?: Reflections Of An ADR Founder At 15th ODR Conference At The Hague*. 3 INTERNATIONAL JOURNAL OF ONLINE DISPUTE RESOLUTION 4–6 (2016).

Carrie Menkel-Meadow, *Mediation 3.0: Merging the Old and the New*. ASIAN JOURNAL ON MEDIATION 1–20 (2018).

Carrie Menkel-Meadow, *Negotiating the American Constitution (1787–89): Coalitions, Process Rules and Compromises*, *in* LANDMARK NEGOTIATIONS FROM AROUND THE WORLD: LESSONS FOR MODERN DIPLOMACY (Emmanuel Vivet ed., 2019).

Carrie Menkel-Meadow, *Peace and Justice: Notes on the Evolution and Purposes of Plural Legal Processes*, 94 GEO. L.J. 553–579 (2006).

Carrie Menkel-Meadow, *Process Pluralism In Transitional/Restorative Justice: Lessons From Dispute Resolution For Cultural Variations In Goals Beyond Rule Of Law And Democracy Development In Argentina And Chile*, INTERNATIONAL JOURNAL OF CONFLICT ENGAGEMENT & RESOLUTION 3–32 (2015).

Carrie Menkel-Meadow, *Regulation of Dispute Resolution in the United States of America: From the Formal to the Informal to the Semi-Formal*, *in* REGULATION OF DISPUTE RESOLUTION—ADR AND ACCESS TO JUSTICE AT THE CROSSROADS (Felix Steffek, Hannes Unberath, Reinhardt Greger, Hazel Genn, & Carrie Menkel-Meadow eds., 2013).

Carrie Menkel-Meadow, *Remembrance of Things Past? The Relationship of Past to Future in Pursuing Justice in Mediation*, 5 CARDOZO J. CONFLICT RESOL. 97–105 (2004).

Carrie Menkel-Meadow, *Restorative Justice: What Is It and Does it Work?*, 3 Ann. Rev. L. & Soc. Sci. 161–87 (2007).

Carrie Menkel-Meadow, *Roots and Inspirations: A Brief History of the Foundations of Dispute Resolution*, *in* THE HANDBOOK OF DISPUTE RESOLUTION (Michael Moffit & Robert Bordone eds., 2005).

Carrie Menkel-Meadow, *Taking the Mass Out of Mass Torts: Reflections of a Dalkon Shield Arbitrator on Alternative Dispute Resolution, Judging Neutrality, Gender and Process*. 31 LOY. L.A. L. REV. 513–550 (1998).

Carrie Menkel-Meadow, *Unsettling the Lawyers: Other Forms of Justice in Indigenous Claims of Expropriation, Abuse, and Injustice*, 64 U. TORONTO L.J. 620 (2014).

Carrie Menkel-Meadow, *Variations in the Uptake and Resistance to Mediation Outside of the United States*, *in* CONTEMPORARY ISSUES IN INTERNATIONAL MEDIATION AND ARBITRATION: THE FORDHAM PAPERS 1914 (Arthur Rovine ed., 2015).

CARRIE MENKEL-MEADOW, VERY SHORT INTRODUCTION TO NEGOTIATION (2022).

CARRIE MENKEL-MEADOW, *Whose Culture? Whose Laws? Mediation Ethics Comments on Case 12. 2*, *in* MEDIATION ETHICS: CASES AND COMMENTARIES (Ellen Waldman ed., 2011).

Carrie Menkel-Meadow, *Why and How to Study Transnational Law*, 1 U.C. IRVINE L. REV. 97–129 (2011).

Carrie Menkel-Meadow, *Why Hasn't the World Gotten to Yes?* 22 NEGOTIATION J. (2006).

Carrie Menkel-Meadow, *Why We Can't "Just all Get Along": Dysfunction in the Polity and Conflict Resolution and What We Might Do About It*, J. DISP. RES. (2018).

CARRIE MENKEL-MEADOW, ET AL., DISPUTE RESOLUTION: BEYOND THE ADVERSARY MODEL (3rd ed., 2018).

COMPLEX DISPUTE RESOLUTION: INTERNATIONAL DISPUTE RESOLUTION (Carrie Menkel-Meadow ed., 2011).

COMPLEX DISPUTE RESOLUTION: MULTI-PARTY DISPUTE RESOLUTION, DEMOCRACY AND DECISION-MAKING (Carrie Menkel-Meadow ed., 2012).

CARRIE MENKEL-MEADOW, ET AL., MEDIATION: PRACTICE POLICY AND ETHICS (3rd ed. 2020).

CARRIE MENKEL-MEADOW, ET AL., NEGOTIATION: PROCESSES FOR PROBLEM SOLVING (3rd ed. 2020).

Carrie Menkel-Meadow & Irena Nutenko, *The Next Generation: Creating a New Peace Process in the Middle East*, 24 NEG. J. 567–584 (2009).

CARRIE MENKEL-MEADOW & MICHAEL WHEELER, WHAT'S FAIR? ETHICS FOR NEGOTIATORS. (2004).

Avital Mentovich, et al., *Legitimacy and Online Proceedings: Procedural Justice and the Role of Income*, 57 L. & SOC'Y REV. 129 (2023).

J.G. MERRILLS, INTERNATIONAL DISPUTE SETTLEMENT (5th ed. 2011).

J.G. MERRILLS, INTERNATIONAL DISPUTE SETTLEMENT (6th ed. 2017).

John Henry Merryman, *Thinking About the Elgin Marbles*, 83 MICH. L. REV. 1881 (1984–85).

John Henry Merryman, *Two Ways of Thinking About Cultural Property*, 80 AM. J. OF INT'L L. 831–53 (1986).

BENJAMIN MILLER, WHEN OPPONENTS COOPERATE: GREAT POWER CONFLICT AND COLLABORATION IN WORLD POLITICS (2002).

MARTHA MINOW, BETWEEN VENGEANCE AND FORGIVING: FACING HISTORY AFTER GENOCIDE AND MASS VIOLENCE (1998).

Martha Minow, *Do Alternative Justice Mechanisms Deserve Recognition in International Criminal Law? Truth Commissions, Amnesties and Complementarity at the International Criminal Court*, 60 HARVARD INT'L L. J. 1–45 (2019).

George Mitchell, Making Peace (1999).

Robert Mnookin, Bargaining with the Devil: When to Negotiate, When to Fight (2010).

Robert Mnookin, *When Not to Negotiate: A Negotiation Imperialist Reflects on Appropriate Limits*, 74 U. Colo. L. Rev. 1077–1108 (2003).

Robert Mnookin, et al., *Barriers to Progress at the Negotiation Table: Internal Conflicts Among Israelis and Among Palestinians*, 6 Nev. L. J. 299 (2006).

Mayo Moran, *Cardinal Sins: How The Catholic Church Sexual Abuse Crisis Changed Private Law*, 21 Geo. J. Gender & L. 95 (2019).

Comparative Dispute Resolution Handbook (Maria Moscati, Michael Palmer, & Marion Roberts eds., 2021).

Research Handbook on Comparative Dispute Resolution (Maria Moscati, Michael Palmer, & Marion Roberts eds., 2020).

Vidya Nadkarni, *Bipolarism and Its End: From the Cold War to the Post-Cold Wat World*, *in* The International Studies Encyclopedia (Robert A. Denemark and Renée Marlin-Bennett eds., 2010).

Third World Approaches to International Law: On Praxis and the Intellectual (Usha Natarajan, John Reynolds, Amar Bhatia, & Sujith Xavier eds., 2018).

Gary Noesner, Stalling for Time: My Life as an FBI Hostage Negotiator (2018).

Jacqueline Nolan-Haley, et al., Global Issues in Mediation (2019).

Luke Nottage, *The Vicissitudes of Transnational Commercial Arbitration and the Lex Mercatoria: A View from the Periphery*, 16 Arbitration International 53 (2000).

Sarah M. H. Nouwen, *Exporting Peace: The E.U.'s Mediator's Normative Backpack*, 1 European Law Open 26–59 (2022).

Sarah M. H. Nouwen, *Peacemaking*, *in* Cambridge History of International Law, Vol. XII (Eyal Benvenisti and Dino Kritsiotis eds., 2024).

International Law Stories (Noyes, John, Laura Dickinson & Mark Janis eds., 2007).

Lester Nurick & Stephen J. Schnably, *The First ICSID Conciliation: Tesoro Petroleum Corporation v. Trinidad and Tobago*. 1 ICSID Review—Foreign Investment Law Journal 340–347 (1986).

Nick O'Brian, *Administrative Justice in the Wake of I Daniel Blake*, 89 The Political Quarterly. 82–91 (2018).

Susan Moller Okin, et al., Is Multiculturalism Bad for Women? (1999).

Angel E. Oquendo, Through Thick and Thin: From Human Rights Principles to Politics Across the Americas and Beyond (2022).

Jan Paulsson, The Idea of Arbitration (2014).

NOMOS: COMPROMISE IN ETHICS LAW AND POLITICS (Roland Pennock & John Chapman eds., 1979).

STEPHEN PINKER, THE BETTER ANGELS OF OUR NATURE: WHY VIOLENCE HAS DECLINED (2011).

FERNANDA PIRIE, THE ANTHROPOLOGY OF LAW (2013).

SUSAN PODZIBA, CIVIC FUSION: MEDIATING POLARIZED PUBLIC POLICY DISPUTES (2013).

KARL POPPER, OBJECTIVE KNOWLEDGE: AN EVOLUTIONARY APPROACH (Rev. ed. 1972).

Sharon Press & Ellen Deason, *Mediation: Embedded Assumptions of Whiteness?*, 22 CARDOZO J. CONFLICT RESOL. 453–498 (2021).

PUBLIC INTERNATIONAL LAW & POLICY GROUP, THE INTERNATIONAL NEGOTIATIONS HANDBOOK: SUCCESS THROUGH PREPARATION, STRATEGY AND PLANNING (2007).

PUBLIC INTERNATIONAL LAW AND POLICY GROUP, ANALYSIS OF THE LEGAL OPTIONS FOR ESTABLISHING A TRIBUNAL FOR THE CRIME OF AGGRESSION UNDER THE AUSPICES OF THE COUNCIL OF EUROPE AND EUROPEAN UNION (2023).

ITAMAR RABINOVICH, MIDDLE EASTERN MAZE (2023).

Orna Rabinovich-Einy, *Process Pluralism in the Post-COVID Dispute Resolution Landscape*, 10 TEXAS A&M LAW REVIEW 55–73 (2022).

Orna Rabinovich-Einy & Ethan Katsh, *Artificial Intelligence and the Future of Dispute Resolution*, *in* ONLINE DISPUTE RESOLUTION-THEORY AND PRACTICE (D. Rainey, E. Katsh, & M. Abdel Wahab eds., 2021).

Orna Rabinovich-Einy & Ethan Katsh, *Technology and the Future of Dispute Systems Design*, 17 HARV. NEGOT. L. REV. 151–165 (2012).

Daniel Rainey, *Third Party Ethics in the Age of the Fourth Party*, 1 INTERNATIONAL JOURNAL OF ONLINE DISPUTE RESOLUTION 37–56 (2014).

ONLINE DISPUTE RESOLUTION—THEORY AND PRACTICE: A TREATISE ON TECHNOLOGY AND DISPUTE RESOLUTION (Daniel Rainey, Ethan Katsh, and Mohamed S. Abdel Wahab eds., 2nd ed. 2021).

JOHN RAWLS, A THEORY OF JUSTICE (1971).

STEVEN R. RATNER, ET AL., ACCOUNTABILITY FOR HUMAN RIGHTS ATROCITIES IN INTERNATIONAL LAW: BEYOND THE NUREMBERG LEGACY (3rd ed. 2009).

ALISON DUNDAS RENTELN, THE CULTURAL DEFENSE (2005).

WILLIAM HERNANDEZ REQUEJO & JOHN L. GRAHAM, GLOBAL NEGOTIATIONS: THE NEW RULES (2008).

DAVID REYNOLDS, SUMMITS: SIX MEETINGS THAT SHAPED THE TWENTIETH CENTURY (2007).

OLIVER RICHMOND, VERY SHORT INTRODUCTION TO PEACE (2014).

Robert Ricigliano, Making Peace Last (2012).

Elsa Walsh Rios, *The Negotiator*, The New Yorker (1996).

Horst W. J. Ritell & Melvin B. Webber. *Dilemmas in a General Theory of Planning*, 4 Policy Sciences 155–69 (1973).

Cheryl Rivers, *Lying, Cheating Foreigners!! Negotiation Ethics Across Cultures*, 12 International Negotiation 1 (2007).

Catherine Rogers, Ethics in International Arbitration (2014).

Nancy Rogers, et al., Designing Systems and Processes for Managing Disputes (2nd ed. 2019).

Dennis Ross, The Missing Peace: The Inside Story of the Fight for Middle East Peace (2004).

Robert I. Rotberg, Israeli and Palestinian Narratives of Conflict: History's Double Helix (2006).

Truth vs. Justice: The Morality of Truth Commissions (Robert Rotberg & Dennis Thompson eds., 2000).

Contemporary Issues in International Arbitration and Mediation—The Fordham Papers (Arthur Rovine ed., 2014).

Rowe, Mary, *The Ombudsman as Part of a Dispute Resolution System*, 7 Negotiation J. 353–62 (1991).

Jeffrey Z. Ruben & Frank E.A. Sanders, *Culture, Negotiation, and the Eye Of The Beholder*, 7 Negotiation J. 249 (1991).

Craig Rubenstein & Robert Zelizer, Building Peace: Reflections from the Field (2009).

Jeswald Salacuse, *Is There a Better Way? Alternative Methods of Treaty-Based, Investor-State Dispute Resolution*, 31 Fordham Int'l L.J. 128 (2007).

Jeswald Salacuse, *The Emerging Global Regime for Investment*, 51 Harv. Int'l L.J. 428–51 (2010).

Jeswald Salacuse, The Global Negotiator: Making, Managing and Mending Deals Around the World in the Twenty-First Century (1998).

Frank E.A. Sander & Stephen B. Goldberg, *Fitting the Forum to the Fuss: A User-Friendly Guide to Selecting an ADR Process*, 10 Negotiation J. 49–68 (1994).

Phillipe Sands, The Last Colony—A Tale of Exile, Justice amid Britain's Colonial Legacy (2023).

Amy J Schmitz, *Evolution and Emerging Issues in Consumer Online Dispute Resolution (ODR)*, *in* The Cambridge Handbook on Emerging Issues at the Intersection of Commercial Law and Technology (Nancy Kim ed., 2022).

Andrea Kupfer Schneider, *Bargaining in the Shadow of (International) Law: What the Normalization of Adjudication In International Governance Means for Dispute Resolution*, 41 N.Y.U. J. Int'l L. & Pol.Politics 789 (2009).

Andrea Kupfer Schneider, *Carrie Menkel-Meadow: Dispute Resolution in a Feminist Voice*, 10 Texas A & M L. Rev. 151 (2022).

Andrea Kupfer Schneider, *Getting Along: The Evolution of Dispute Resolution Regimes in International Trade Organizations*, 20 Mich. J. Int'l L. 700–763 (1999).

Andrea Kupfer Schneider, *Public and Private International Dispute Resolution*, *in* The Handbook of Dispute Resolution (Michael Moffitt & Robert Bordone eds., 2005).

Andrea Kupfer Schneider, *The Day After Tomorrow: What Happens Once a Middle East Peace Treaty is Signed?*, 6 Nev. L. J. 401 (2006).

Andrea Kupfer Schneider, *The Intersection of Dispute System Design and Transitional Justice*, 14 Harvard Neg. L. Rev. 289 (2009).

Andrea Kupfer Schneider, *The Next Wave of Effective Dispute Resolution: Developing Emotional and Social Intelligence*, Asian Journal of Mediation (2023).

Andrea Kupfer Schneider & Natalie C. Fleury, *There's No Place Like Home: Applying Dispute System Design Theory to Create a Foreclosure Mediation System*, 11 Nevada L.J. 368–96 (2011).

Andrea Kupfer Schneider & Nancy Welsh, *The Thoughtful Integration of Mediation into Bi-lateral Investment Treaty Arbitration*, 29 Harvard Neg. L. Rev. 71–144 (2013).

Simon A.B. Schropp & David Palmeter, *Commentary on the Appellate Body Report in EC-Bananas III (Article 21.5): Waiver-thin, or Lock, Stock, and Metric Ton?*, 9 World Trade Rev. 7–57 (2010).

Thomas Schultz & Thomas Grant, Very Short Introduction to Arbitration (2021).

M. Schwartz, *The Nature of the Relationship Between Corporate Codes of Ethics and Behavior* 32 J. of Business Ethics 247–262 (2001).

James K. Sebenius, *Caveats For Cross-Border Negotiations*. 18 Negotiation J. 121–128 (2002).

James K. Sebenius, *Dealing with Blocking Coalitions and Related Barriers to Agreement: Lessons from Negotiations on the Oceans, the Ozone, and the Climate*, *in* Barriers to Conflict Resolution (Kenneth Arrow, Robert H. Mnookin, Lee Ross, Amos Tversky, & Robert Wilson eds., 1995).

James K. Sebenius, *Mapping Backward: Negotiating in the Right Sequence*, 7 Negotiation (2004).

James K. Sebenius, Negotiating the Law of the Sea (1984).

Amartya Sen, The Idea of Justice (2009).

GREGORY SHAFFER, EMERGING POWERS AND THE WORLD TRADING SYSTEM: THE PAST AND FUTURE OF INTERNATIONAL ECONOMIC LAW (2021).

Gregory Shaffer & Wayne Sandholtz, *The Rule of Law Under Challenge: The Enmeshment of National and International Trends*, SSRN (2023).

YUVAL SHANY, ASSESSING THE EFFECTIVENESS OF INTERNATIONAL COURTS (2014).

Daniel L. Shapiro, *Reconciliation Systems Design: A Systemic Approach to Collective Healing in Post-Conflict Societies*, 26 HARVARD NEG. L. REV. 193 (2021).

PROMISES (Promises Film Project 2001).

Kenneth Sharpe, *Learning the Wisdom to Seize the Moment: How Negotiators Encourage the Learning of Practical Wisdom for Themselves and Others*, 36 NEG. J. 169 (2020).

Susan Sturm & Howard Gadlin, *Conflict Resolution and Systemic Change*, J. DISP. RESOL. (2007).

DINAH L. SHELTON, ADVANCED INTRODUCTION TO INTERNATIONAL HUMAN RIGHTS LAW (2014).

KATHRYN SIKKINK, THE JUSTICE CASCADE: HOW HUMAN RIGHTS PROSECUTIONS ARE CHANGING WORLD POLITICS (2011).

JOSEPH SIRACUSA, VERY SHORT INTRODUCTION TO DIPLOMACY (2010).

ANNE-MARIE SLAUGHTER, A NEW WORLD ORDER (2004).

Stephanie Smith & Janet Martinez, *An Analytic Framework for Dispute System Design*, 14 HARV. NEG. L. REV. 123 (2009).

M Sornarajah, *On Fighting for Global Justice: The Role of the International Lawyer in Third World Approaches to International Law*, *in* THIRD WORLD APPROACHES TO INTERNATIONAL LAW: ON PRAXIS AND THE INTELLECTUAL (Usha Natarajan, John Reynolds, Amar Bhatia, & Sujith Xavier eds., 2018).

FREDERICK STANTON, GREAT NEGOTIATORS: AGREEMENTS THAT CHANGED THE MODERN WORLD (2010).

FELIX STEFFEK, ET AL., REGULATING DISPUTE RESOLUTION: ADR AND ACCESS TO JUSTICE AT THE CROSSROADS (2013).

Jean Sternlight, *Is Alternative Dispute Resolution Consistent with the Rule of Law?*, 56 DEPAUL L. REV. 569 (2007).

Jean R Sternlight, *Pouring a Little Psychological Cold Water on Online Dispute Resolution*, J. DISP. RESOL. 1 (2020).

ALEC STONE SWEET & FLORIAN GRISEL, THE EVOLUTION OF INTERNATIONAL ARBITRATION: JUDICIALIZATION, GOVERNANCE, LEGITIMACY (2017).

Alec Stone Sweet, *Arbitral Lawmaking and State Power: An Empirical Analysis of Investor-State Arbitration*, 8 J. INT'L DISP. SETTLEMENT 587–609 (2017).

ACCOUNTABILITY FOR ATROCITIES: NATIONAL AND INTERNATIONAL RESPONSES (Jane Stromseth ed., 2003).

JANE STROMSETH, ET AL., CAN MIGHT MAKE RIGHTS: BUILDING THE RULE OF LAW AFTER MILITARY INTERVENTIONS (2006).

THE CONSENSUS BUILDING HANDBOOK: A COMPREHENSIVE GUIDE TO REACHING AGREEMENT (Susskind, Lawrence, Sarah McKearnan, and Jennifer Thomas Larmer eds., 1999).

TOSHIFUMI TANAKA, THE PEACEFUL SETTLEMENT OF INTERNATIONAL DISPUTES (2018).

Ramesh Thakur, *A Dispute of Many Colours: France, New Zealand, and the Rainbow Warrior Affair*, THE WORLD TODAY 209–214 (1986).

LEIGH L. THOMPSON, THE MIND AND HEART OF THE NEGOTIATOR (5th ed. 2012).

COLIN THUBRON, THE SHADOW OF THE SILK ROAD (2007).

C TITI, THE PARTHENON MARBLES AND INTERNATIONAL LAW (2023).

Robert Toscano, *The Ethics of Modern Diplomacy*, *in* ETHICS AND INTERNATIONAL AFFAIRS: EXTENT AND LIMITS (Jean Marc Coicaud and Daniel Warner eds., 2001).

DESMOND TUTU, NO FUTURE WITHOUT FORGIVENESS (1999).

United Nations, *Guidance for Effective Mediation* (2012).

WILLIAM URY, ET AL., GETTING DISPUTES RESOLVED: DESIGNING SYSTEMS TO CUT THE COSTS OF CONFLICT (1988).

Rory Van Loo, *The Corporation as Courthouse*, 33 YALE J. ON REGUL. 547–602 (2016).

EMMANUEL VIVET, LANDMARK NEGOTIATIONS FROM AROUND THE WORLD: LESSONS FOR MODERN DIPLOMACY (2019).

MEDIATION ETHICS: CASES AND COMMENTARIES (Ellen Waldman ed., 2011).

Elsa Walsh, *The Negotiator*, THE NEW YORKER (1996).

SHARON WAXMAN, LOOT: THE BATTLE OVER THE STOLEN TREASURES OF THE ANCIENT WORLD (2009).

Nancy Welsh & Andrea Kupfer Schneider, *Becoming 'Investor-State Mediation'*, 1 PENN ST. J.L. & INT'L AFFS. 86 (2012).

Nancy Welsh, et al., *Negotiation Theories Engage Hybrid Warfare*, 24 CARDOZO J. CONFLICT RESOL. 543 (2023).

Jodi Wexler, *The Rainbow Warrior Affair: State and Agent Responsibility for Authorized Violations of International Law*, 5 B.U. INT'L L.J. 389–412 (1987).

White & Case & Queen Mary School of Commercial Arbitration, *2021 International Arbitration Survey: Adapting Arbitration to a Changing World* (2021).

Christopher Whytock, *Some Cautionary Notes on the 'Chevronization' of Transnational Litigation*, 1 STAN. J. COMPLEX LITIG. 467 (2013).

WILDE, OSCAR: A LIFE IN QUOTES (Barry Day ed., 2000).

Leah Wing, *Ethical Principles For Online Dispute Resolution: A GPS Device For The Field.* 3 INTERNATIONAL JOURNAL ON ONLINE DISPUTE RESOLUTION 12–29 (2016).

Leah Wing, et al., *Designing Ethical Online Dispute Resolution Systems: The Rise of the Fourth Party*, 37 NEGOTIATION J. 49–64 (2021).

A. Zarkada-Fraser & C. Fraser, *Moral Decision-making in International Sales Negotiations*, 16 J. OF BUSINESS AND INTERNATIONAL MARKETING 274–293 (2001).

William Zartman, *The Timing of Peace Initiatives: Hurting Stalemates and Ripe Moments, in* CONTEMPORARY PEACEMAKING: CONFLICT, VIOLENCE AND PEACE PROCESSES (John Darby & Roger McGinty eds., 2003).

I. WILLIAM ZARTMAN & MAUREEN R. BERMAN, THE PRACTICAL NEGOTIATOR (1984).

I. WILLIAM ZARTMAN & SINISA VUKOVIC, RETHINKING CONFLICT RESOLUTION AND MANAGEMENT (2023).

BUILDING PEACE: REFLECTIONS FROM THE FIELD (Craig Zelizer & Robert Rubenstein eds., 2009).

Cases, Statutes & Treaties

African Charter on Human and Peoples' Rights (1981).

Advisory Opinion on the Legal Consequences of the Separation of the Chagos Archipelago from Mauritius, International Court of Justice, February 25, 2019.

Alabama Claims Arbitration (*U.S. v. Great Britain*, 1872).

Case Concerning Military and Paramilitary Activities in and against Nicaragua (Nicaragua v. United States of America), 1986 I.C.J. 14 (June 27).

Chromalloy Aeroservices v. Arab Republic of Egypt, 115 I.L.M. 140 (1996).

Convention on the Recognition and Enforcement of Foreign Arbitral Awards (New York Convention), art. V, June 10, 1958, 330 U.N.T.S. 38.

Convention on the Rights of the Child, (1989), 1577 U.N.T.S. 3.

Convention on the Settlement of Investment Disputes between States and Nationals of Other States (ICSID Convention, 1965), 17 U.S.T. 1270.

Convention on the Settlement of Investment Disputes Between States and Nationals of Other States (Washington Convention, 1965), 17 U.S.T. 1270.

Cour de Cassation de Belgique, S.04.0129.F/1 (Dec. 21, 2009).

Cour de Cassation, Chambre Sociale, No. 09-41.030 (Sept. 29, 2010).

Energy Charter Treaty (1994), 2080 U.N.T.S. 95.

European Convention for the Protection of Human Rights and Fundamental Freedoms, 312 U.N. T. S.221 1950.

European Regulation on Online Consumer Dispute Resolution, Reg. EU No. 524/2013 amending Regulation (EC) No. 2006/2004 and Directive 2009/22/EC (Regulation on consumer ODR)

Hague Convention on the Civil Aspects of International Child Abduction, (1980), T.I.A.S. No. 11,670.

International Bar Association Guidelines on Conflicts of Interest in International Arbitration (2014).

International Chamber of Commerce, ICC Arbitration Rules (2021).

Laminoirs-Trefileries-Cableries de Lens, S. v. Southwire Company, 484 F. Supp. 1063 (N.D. Ga. 1980).

London Amendment to the Montreal Protocol on Substances that Deplete the Ozone Layer, June 29, 1990, UNEP/OzL.Pro. 2/3 Annex II.

Montreal Protocol on Substances that Deplete the Ozone Layer (1987), 1522 U.N.T.S. 3.

New York Convention on the Recognition and Enforcement of Foreign Arbitral Awards, 21 U.S. T. 2517, 330 U.N.T.S. 38 (1958).

North American Free Trade Agreement (NAFTA, 1994), 32 I.L.M. 289 and 605 (1993).

OECD Regulation 22

Protocol Relating to the Status of Refugees, (1967), 606 U.N.T.S. 267.

Pulp Mills on the River Uruguay (*Argentina v. Uruguay*), 2010 I.C.J. (Apr. 20), https://www.icj-cij.org/case/135.

Rainbow Warrior Case: *New Zealand v. France* (1990), 82 I.L.R. 500.

Regulation (EU) No. 524/2013 on Online Dispute Resolution for Consumer Disputes, O.J. (L 165) 1 (2013).

Rome Statute of the International Criminal Court (Treaty of Rome, 1998), 2187 U.N.T.S. 90.

Ruling Pertaining to Differences Between France and New Zealand Arising From Rainbow Warrior Affair, 19 U.N. Rep. Int'l Arb. Awards (1986).

S.A.S. v. France, App. No. 43835/11, Eur. Ct. H.R. (2014), http://hudoc.echr.coe.int/eng?i=001-145466.

Soering v. the United Kingdom, 161 Eur. Ct. H.R. (ser. A) (1989).

South Pacific Nuclear Free Zone Treaty (1985).

Statute of the International Court of Justice, June 26, 1945, 59 Stat. 1055, T.S. No. 933.

The Loewen Group, Inc. and Raymond L. Loewen v. United States of America, ICSID Case No. ARB(AF)/98/3, 42 I.L.M. 811 (2003).

United Nations Charter 59 Stat. 1031, T.S. No 993 1945.

United Nations Convention on International Settlement Agreements Resulting from Mediation, U.N. Doc. A/RES/73/199 (2018).

United Nations Framework Convention on Climate Change—Paris 2015.

United Nations Convention on the Law of the Sea, Dec. 10, 1982, 1833 U.N.T.S. 3.

Velasquez v. Rodriquez v. Honduras, Inter-American Ct. of Human Rights 1988. Ser 6, No. 2.

Index